INTERNATIONAL LAW
AND
THE HAGUE'S 750TH ANNIVERSARY

International Law and The Hague's 750th Anniversary

edited by

Wybo P. Heere

T.M.C. Asser Press

ISBN 90-6704-109-2

T.M.C. Asser Instituut - Institute for Private and Public International Law, International Commercial Arbitration and European Law
Institute Address: R.J. Schimmelpenninckiaan 20-22, The Hague, The Netherlands; Mailing Address: P.O. Box 30461, 2500 GL The Hague, The Netherlands; Tel.: (31-70)3420300; Fax: (31-70)3420359; Internet: www.asser.nl.
Over thirty years, the T.M.C. Asser Institute has developed into a leading scientific research institute in the field of international law. It covers private international law, public international law, including international humanitarian law, the law of the European Union, the law of international commercial arbitration and increasingly, also, international economic law and the law of international commerce. Conducting scientific research, either fundamental or applied, in the aforementioned domains, is the main activity of the Institute. In addition, the Institute organizes congresses and postgraduate courses, undertakes contract-research and operates its own publishing house.
Because of its inter-university background, the Institute often cooperates with Dutch law faculties as well as with various national and foreign institutions. The Institute organizes *Asser College Europe*, a project in cooperation with East and Central European countries whereby research and educational projects are organized and implemented.

PREFACE

According to historical sources, the City of The Hague was justified to celebrate its 750th anniversary in 1998. Almost from the beginning, the City of The Hague has been linked to the *trias politica* and later to diplomacy, when it became clear that the Dutch 'Staten-Generaal' were firmly established in The Hague. With the Dutch governmental circles concentrated in the city, diplomacy entered the scene and The Hague became the diplomatic city of the Netherlands. As a natural result, various international gatherings, debates, congresses and treaty negotiations were brought to The Hague.

In fact, The Hague has become the prominent venue for international legal institutions and events and the home for peaceful settlement of international disputes. As the future location for the International Criminal Court, The Hague's name has become attached to the development of international humanitarian law. It was, therefore, entirely appropriate also to focus, in 1998, on The Hague's unmistakeable importance to the international legal community. Thus, within the framework of the year's commemorative celebrations, the T.M.C. ASSER Instituut, in cooperation with the 'Stichting 750 jaar Den Haag', organized *The Hague's 750th Anniversary International Law Conference*.

For the T.M.C. ASSER Instituut it was an important event that sparked intellectual and academic discussion. Once again, it brought many international scholars and diplomats to The Hague to participate in topical debates on the wide-ranging issues of international law. The proceedings of the Conference, which are contained in the present publication, contribute to the development of international law and, at the same time, mark the anniversary celebration and clearly demonstrate the continuing interest that the international academic and professional legal community attach to The Hague as 'the City of International Law'.

The editor of this book, Wybo P. Heere, has produced yet another professionally edited volume. He was assisted by Robert van de Rijt of Leiden University, who worked with great enthusiasm and dedication on this project under the guidance of Marjolijn Bastiaans, publisher of T.M.C. ASSER Press. Their joint effort made it possible to realize this publication within a reasonable time-limit.

The Hague, March 1999

Gerard J. Tanja
General Director,
T.M.C. Asser Instituut

TABLE OF CONTENTS

PRIVATE INTERNATIONAL LAW

INTERNATIONAL COMMERCIAL ARBITRATION

CLOSING SESSION

The International Court of Justice and the Proliferation of International Judicial Organs
Chair: H. Corell

INTRODUCTION

In 1998, the City of The Hague commemorated its 750th anniversary.

To celebrate this historical event, a Foundation, 'Stichting 750 jaar Den Haag', had been established, in order to coordinate the large number of activities that would be organised during this year.

In order to emphasize the fact that The Hague has been an international judicial centre of activities during the past decades, the T.M.C. Asser Instituut, in cooperation with the 'Stichting 750 jaar Den Haag', had the pleasure to undertake the organization of a special International Law Conference to which lawyers from all over the world were invited.

Besides members of the T.M.C. Asser Instituut and the 'Stichting 750 jaar Den Haag', the Conference's Programme Committee was composed of representatives of the following relevant Hague organisations, institutions, etc.: International Court of Justice, Carnegie Foundation, Permanent Court of International Arbitration, Hague Conference on Private International Law, International Criminal Tribunal for the Former Yugoslavia, Institute of Social Studies, Hague Bar Asociation, Netherlands Ministry of Justice and Council of State.

The Programme Committee decided to concentrate The Hague's 750th Anniversary International Law Conference on the following main themes:

- international criminal law;
- interstate dispute settlement;
- international commercial arbitration;
- international humanitarian law;
- private international law;
- the regulation of international trade.

Within this framework, a number of panels was especially devoted to aspects of 'The Hague, Legal Capital of the World', i.e., concerning the International Court of Justice, the (future) International Criminal Court and the Iran-US Claims Tribunal. Besides, representatives of the Netherlands Ministry of Foreign Affairs, Europol, the International Court of Justice, the International Criminal Tribunal for the Former Yugoslavia, the Hague Conference on Private International Law, the Organization for the Prohibition of Chemical Weapons, the Iran-US Claims Tribunal and the Permanent Court of Arbitration, were panel chairmen or panel members at the Conference.

This publication contains the papers on a broad range of subjects of international law that were submitted by speakers during The Hague's 750th Anniversary International Law Conference.

Dr Robert C.R. Siekmann
Head of Research, T.M.C. Asser Institute
Chairman of the Programme Committee

OPENING ADDRESS BY W.J. DEETMAN, BURGOMASTER OF THE MUNICIPALITY OF THE HAGUE

THE SYNERGY BETWEEN THE CITY OF THE HAGUE AND INTERNATIONAL LAW

Excellencies, ladies and gentlemen,

It is a pleasure to welcome so many renowned specialists in the field of international law, many of them associates of the Asser Institute, at the occasion of The Hague's 750th Anniversary International Law Conference.

The Hague, Legal Capital of the World – as former Secretary General Boutros Ghali has once labeled our city – is the inspiring title of the theme of this conference. And, of course, being called the judicial or legal capital of the world fills us with pride and honour. I am convinced, and the city council shares this conviction with me, that The Hague is the natural environment for large law conferences such as this.

Our city has a long and strong traditional bond with international law. The Hague, seat of the Dutch government since the sixteenth century, has been a city of diplomacy for centuries. Because The Hague was 'easily accessible and not so far from London, Berlin, Paris or even St.Petersburg', it was chosen to be the venue of the First Peace Conference at the turn of the century, 99 years ago.

Henceforth The Hague would gradually and regularly prove itself an exemplary host to international organisations, some of them perpetuating the traditions that were established at the 1899 Conference. These organisations include the Permanent Court of Arbitration, the International Court of Justice, the International Tribunal for the former Yugoslavia and the Organisation for the Prohibition of Chemical Weapons. Recently the United Nations Diplomatic Conference decided that if the intended International Criminal Court will actually be established, it will be accomodated in The Hague. There is no need to say that this decision, which we consider as another acknowledgment of the judicial importance of The Hague, filled us with pleasure and delight.

The Netherlands has a strongly entrenched parliamentary tradition which even precedes its formal recognition as an independent and sovereign nation by the European Great Powers of that time at the Peace of Westphalia in 1648. Since those early days of political independence The Hague, the country's seat of government and of the legislature, has been a home for diplomats. And of course The Netherlands sent its own envoys all over the world.

Setting a tradition to be associated with the Netherlands for centuries to come, Hugo Grotius' *De Jure Belli ac Pacis*, which he wrote in 1625, is considered the

W.P. Heere (Ed.), International Law and The Hague's 750th Anniversary

first modern treatise on the waging of war and the laws and regulations governing warfare.

This tradition is reflected in the 1899 and 1907 Peace Conferences and in the international courts and tribunals which now have their seats in The Hague.

Apart from the main international judicial institutions, The Hague is presently home to a number of international organisations. Besides the Organisation for the Prohibition of Chemical Weapons that I already mentioned, these organisations include the Permanent Bureau of the Hague Conference for Private International Law and the Iran-US Claims Tribunal.

Enshrined in the long legislative history of The Netherlands – once a Republic ruled by representatives of highly independent provinces and since the end of the Napoleonic area a constitutional monarchy – solidarity and open debate are the hallmarks of public life in the Netherlands, with international political issues often in the spotlight.

The constitutional mandate on the maintenance of international relations obliges the government to 'promote the development of the international rule of law.'

THE HAGUE, JUDICIAL CAPITAL

The Hague's traditional role in the settlement of international judicial disputes originated with the 1899 Hague Convention for the Pacific Settlement of International Disputes, which established the Permanent Court of Arbitration. Eight years later, the 1907 Hague Convention augmented the previous one and still forms the foundation of the activities of the Permanent Court of Arbitration which is seated in the Peace Palace, that was inaugurated in August 1913. Unfortunately a year later the First World War broke out.

The Hague was also the seat of the League of Nations' Permanent Court of International Justice. Its successor, the International Court of Justice, the principal judicial organ of the United Nations (that succeeded the League of Nations after the Second World War) is likewise based at the Peace Palace. And, talking about the Peace Palace, of course the impressive world famous Peace Palace Library may not go unmentioned.

Apart from the presence in our city of United Nations related institutions, the synergy between The Hague and international law is also strongly emphasised by the presence of a large number of other institutions that deal with international law such as the Asser Institute, to mention only one.

Ladies and gentlemen,

The concept of individual responsibility for crimes under international law has its foundations in the Hague Conventions respecting the Laws and Customs of War on Land. The international trials of war criminals at the end of the Second World War were based on those Conventions as are the present-day mandates of the International Tribunals for the former Yugoslavia and for Rwanda.

It is more than fifty years ago that the most serious war criminals of the Second World War were tried before the international tribunals of Nuremberg and Tokyo. Also fifty years ago the United Nations adopted the Genocide Convention and this year we commemorate the fiftieth anniversary of the Universal Declaration of Human Rights.

Within two weeks from now, the United Nations Diplomatic Conference in Rome will decide whether an International Criminal Court will be established. Of course, the outcome of this Conference depends on a large quantity of political debates and discussions. But we have good hope and little doubt that the Conference will come to a successful conclusion and that the International Criminal Court will indeed be established in our city. To us it will once again confirm the synergy between The City of The Hague and international law.

Thank you for your attention.

INTERNATIONAL CRIMINAL LAW

Judicial Co-operation in Criminal Matters

Chair: C. Fijnaut

JUDICIAL COOPERATION AND ORGANIZED CRIME IN THE EUROPEAN UNION

Cyrille Fijnaut*

1. INTRODUCTION

The subject to be addressed by this panel is complex, but one that is of great interest. In recent years the European Council, the European Commission and the European Parliament have continued to stress the importance of intensive police and judicial cooperation between the Member States to ensure that organized crime in the European Union is combatted effectively. The Commission and the Parliament have repeatedly taken the position that intergovernmental cooperation is, in fact, no longer sufficient to control organized crime and that the time has come to set up a European Prosecutor's Office and transform the UCLAF (the Unit on Coordination of Fraud Prevention at the European Commission) into a communitarian bureau of investigation. The activities of such a bureau would no longer be restricted to combatting European Community (EC) fraud, but would encompass organized crime in general.

In this debate on intergovernmental cooperation in the fight against organized crime versus a more communitarized approach, it is not easy for an academic researcher to choose a position. There are several reasons for this. Firstly, because there is a serious lack of empirical research on the topics being discussed here, i.e. organized crime, and police and judicial cooperation. Secondly, we should realize that the very ideological issues that are involved here are closely bound up with the constitutional future of the European Union. Thirdly, we should not lose sight of the fact that the debate about the effectiveness or otherwise of police and judicial cooperation is also prompted by institutional conflicts within the European Union between – roughly speaking – the European Commission and the European Parliament on the one hand, and the European Council and the Member States on the other.

Nevertheless, to get the discussion off the ground, I would like to make a few general comments about the development of judicial cooperation in the European Union against the background of the problem of organized crime in this part of the world.

* Professor of Criminology and Criminal Law, KU Leuven; Professor of Law, New York University School of Law

W.P. Heere (Ed.), International Law and The Hague's 750th Anniversary

2. THE PROBLEM OF ORGANIZED CRIME

In recent years it has generally been argued in official documents that organized crime poses a major threat to the European Union and its Member States. Personally I have a problem with this idea. Not only because it completely overlooks the fact that the nature and scale of organized crime differ widely in the various Member States, but also because it takes no account of the fact that in virtually all the Member States organized crime has not gained control of any legitimate sectors of the economy or of any crucial sectors within government. For this reason it is better, in my view, to argue that organized crime currently poses not so much a threat as a challenge to the European Union and its Member States.

At this point I should point out straight away that what goes for organized crime in general, also applies to the part played by organized crime in EC fraud. One of the latest annual reports on fraud prevention published by the European Commission states that a total of 50 criminal networks have been found to be engaged in this type of fraud in the European Union. Not a large number by any stretch of the imagination, certainly not compared with the 841 investigations into organized crime that were started in Germany in 1997, and the 162 investigations conducted in Belgium in 1996. Purely on the basis of these figures, one is justified in asking whether in fact there are empirical arguments for organizing a supranational criminal justice system in the European Union with a view to combatting this type of crime.

There is another good reason for asking this question. In the official debate about combatting organized crime it is invariably assumed that, where organized crime is an international phenomenon, a large degree of international or supranational criminal cooperation is needed to stamp out the problem. This view should not be taken at face value, however. After all, organized crime is only an international problem insofar as it involves the transport of illegal goods and services. When it comes to production and distribution, this is mainly a local problem, in the same way as corruption and 'protection' are always confined to one particular place. This means that international or supranational cooperation must be regarded as complementing the repressive and preventive measures that are implemented by local and national authorities in each individual country. Besides, if the battle against organized crime is not well organized at national level, inter-state cooperation in this field will not yield much in the way of results.

3. THE DEVELOPMENT OF JUDICIAL COOPERATION

There is a long history of judicial cooperation in Europe. Within the context of this discussion, however, it is appropriate to make a distinction between its development up to the signing of the Treaty of Amsterdam (in conjunction with the Action Plan to combat organized crime, which was adopted by the European Council in April 1997) and the development that is inherent in this Treaty. In my view, the Treaty of Amsterdam can therefore be regarded as an important milestone in the history of judicial cooperation in Europe.

3.1. **A difficult patch in recent years**

After the Second World War it was the Council of Europe that – with treaties like the Convention on extradition (1957) and the Convention on mutual assistance in criminal matters (1959) – brought structure to the organization of international mutual assistance between the signatory countries. These treaties are fairly complex owing to the stringent conditions they impose, the many grounds for refusing mutual assistance and the generous scope for reservations. Do they, therefore, no longer satisfy the requirements of our modern-day society? The lack of empirical research in this area makes it difficult to come to any conclusion. My impression is that the forms in which mutual assistance can be provided under the terms of these treaties are still very much relevant to this day and age, but that the limited human and other resources invested by the parties concerned to provide national support for this mutual assistance are the root of a great many problems when it comes to implementation: misunderstandings between authorities, lengthy procedures, and so on. Nevertheless, back in the 1980s the Council of Europe was convinced that the treaties in question should be integrated and modernized with a view to intercepting international communication and conducting cross-border surveillance, amongst other reasons. The efforts it made in this respect came to nothing, however. This failure was a serious setback for the Council of Europe because it seriously undermined its key role in this area.

Around the same time, however, the European Community had to put up with the fact that the Member States were not really willing to adapt the existing organization of European mutual assistance. Towards the end of the 1970s the then French President Giscard d'Estaing called for the creation of an 'espace judiciaire Européen' [European judicial area]. The only thing to emerge from this was a draft Convention on mutual assistance in 1980. And to date only a few countries have ratified the five supplementary conventions that were signed between 1987 and 1991, such as the Convention on the transfer of sentenced persons and the Convention on the simplification and modernization of methods of transmitting extradition requests. Compared with this failure, the Schengen Agreement (1985) and the Convention applying the Schengen Agreement (1990) represent a major success. Not only because the latter is gradually being ratified by more and more Member States, but also because it currently plays an important part in the day-to-day business of police cooperation between the signatory countries.

The Maastricht Treaty has undoubtedly given new impetus to efforts to modernize international mutual assistance in criminal matters. Within the context of the (intergovernmental) Third Pillar, judicial cooperation – along with police cooperation and customs cooperation – has been defined as a subject of mutual importance for the Member States. In the area of judicial cooperation, the 1993 and 1996 working programmes stipulated that attention would be focused on new supplementary conventions on extradition and mutual assistance on the one hand, and on the development of a network of liaison and contact magistrates on the other. In the mid-1990s – in the run-up to the Intergovernmental Conference to review the Maastricht Treaty – some rather disparaging comments were written, especially by officials at the European Commission and the European Council, about what had been achieved within the Third Pillar. In my view, however, this censure was rather misplaced. Not only did the results achieved correspond to a large extent with the – perhaps rather unambitious – intentions in the working programmes, in themselves they were really quite remarkable. The Europol Convention, which is also of great importance for judicial cooperation, can be characterized as a 'bloodless revolution' in the history of international police cooperation in Europe, while the Convention on extradition is described by experts in the field as a 'quantum leap' in the way international mutual assistance is organized. Yet the development of a Convention on mutual assistance has suffered unnecessary delays; the draft version is shortly due to be completed, however. The Maastricht Treaty has therefore borne fruit in this area.

The European Commission has always had trouble accepting the fact that the Member States were not and still are not prepared to hand over part of their sovereignty to 'Brussels' in the field of criminal law enforcement of the communitarian legal order, not even where it involves combatting fraud concerning the financial resources of the Community. In 1994 the Commission therefore proposed entering into an agreement that would substantially increase the scope for the Member States to work together and with the Commission to combat this kind of fraud. In the convention that was eventually signed in July 1995, this scope is extensively curtailed to ensure that the Member States retain the freedom to decide for themselves on a case-by-case basis what form mutual cooperation in this area should take. The Commission was not willing to take this defeat lying down, however. This can be inferred from the Regulation of 11 November 1996 concerning the powers of the UCLAF to carry out on-the-spot checks and inspections on the Member States' territory. This Regulation sets out a number of options whereby the results of specific actions can be used in criminal investigations conducted in the Member States. It is also evident from the second protocol of 19 July 1997 to the aforementioned convention, which addresses a number of issues that were left out of the negotiations on this convention, such as the exchange of information between the Member States and the European Commission.

Following on from this, it should be pointed out that the European Commission, with the backing of the European Parliament, has not given up its efforts to communitarize the fight against organized crime to some extent. This is demonstrated by the Corpus Iuris project, which develops proposals for European criminal law and criminal procedure in the area of communitarian fraud and fraud prevention, and advocates that a European Prosecutor's Office should be set up. It might also be concluded from the reform of the UCLAF into a communitarian bureau of investigation, which would be in a position to lend support to the Member States with criminal investigations into organized crime. One could therefore say that the European Commission advocates both direct and indirect communitarization of the fight against organized crime.

3.2. The possible impact of the Treaty of Amsterdam

The Treaty of Amsterdam is a document that should be read in conjunction with the Action Plan to combat organized crime, which was mentioned earlier. This is because in some respects the Plan is the elaboration of a number of provisions that are included in the new Chapter VI of the Treaty.

Although the Treaty gives the European Commission slightly more scope to take initiatives with a view to combatting economic and financial organized crime, on the whole it does not embody its efforts to organize the fight within a communitarian framework. Clearly, the basic principle is that intergovernmental cooperation in this area must be stepped up. This is demonstrated by the fact that the Member States have agreed to do their utmost to ratify the aforementioned conventions on judicial cooperation before the end of 1998. The intention to actively organize the network of contact and liaison magistrates – with a view to improving this cooperation in practice – is another, cogent demonstration of this basic principle.

One of the main aspects that needs to be addressed in this respect is the question of the relationship between this magistrates' network and Europol. And certainly now that the Treaty of Amsterdam stipulates that Europol should be more involved in criminal investigations in the Member States, albeit in a supporting role, it is important that this issue be resolved satisfactorily.

4. CONCLUSION

In view of the relative seriousness of the problem of organized crime in the European Union, the intergovernmental framework of institutions and forms of cooperation that is now being built up within the Union must be sufficient over the next few years to support the efforts that each of the individual Member States is presently making in order to bring this type of crime more under control.

The Member States will only have to invest the necessary resources in order to take advantage – in the right way and on a large scale – of the opportunities that present themselves. Otherwise the idea that a communitarian approach to organized crime is more appropriate will once again take hold.

At the moment the intergovernmental approach is not only appropriate on the basis of the above empirical argument. As long as the European Union does not continue any further down the road to federalism, this is also, from a normative point of view, the only possible approach. This is demonstrated all too clearly by the difficult history of intergovernmental cooperation in the past few decades: as long as the Member States retain their independence in a number of crucial areas, they are not prepared to relinquish the hard core of their monopoly on violence, which is exactly what police and judicial cooperation is all about.

One of the consequences of this conclusion is that the European Commission would do better to defer its quest for its own communitarian criminal procedure for the time being. Moreover, since the UCLAF is directing more and more of its resources at combatting organized crime in general, it would be better to incorporate certainly the operational aspects of this unit within regular police cooperation ventures between the Member States of the European Union, in other words within Europol, which will itself become a more operational police organ in the near future.

Selected Literature

Action plan to combat organized crime, *OJ*, 15 August1997, C 251/1-18.

Bundeskriminalamt, *Lagebild Organisierte Kriminalität Bundesrepublik Deutschland,* (Wiesbaden 1997).

European Commission, *Anti-fraud stategy of the Commission and fight against major crime harmful to Community interests* (Brussels, 6 April 1998).

European Parliament, *Final report on judicial cooperation in criminal matters in the European Union,* 11 February1998, A4-0058/98 (rapporteur: R. Bontempi).

Fijnaut, C., 'De criminele politiek in de Europese Gemeenschap', *Panopticon* (1992) pp. 572-589.

Fijnaut, C., 'Naar een "Gemeenschappelijke" regeling van de politiële en justitiële rechtshulp', in C. Fijnaut, J. Stuyck and P. Wytinck, eds., *Schengen: proeftuin voor de Europese Gemeenschap?* (Antwerpen, Kluwer 1992) pp. 89-117.

Fijnaut, C., 'Georganiseerde misdaad: echt een bedreiging voor de Europese Unie', in B. Raymaekers and A. van de Putte, eds., *Lessen voor de eenentwintigste eeuw* (Leuven, Universitaire Pers Leuven, 1998) pp. 165-185.

Knudsen, B., 'La fraude au détriment du budget de la Communauté', *Revue de Science Criminelle et de Droit Penal Comparé* (1995) pp. 65-74.

Vervaele, J., 'Rechtshandhaving van het gemeenschapsrecht: een boedelscheiding tussen de eerste en de derde pijler', *Nederlands Juristenblad* (1995) pp. 1298-1305.

Vogel, J., *Combatting international organized crime by international cooperation: the German view* (German national report for section IV of the XVIth international congress of penal law in Budapest, 5 to 11 September 1999).

NATIONAL SOVEREIGNTY AND INTERNATIONAL CRIME

Ernst M.H. Hirsch Ballin*

INTRODUCTION

In an interdependent world with fast connections and present-day communication techniques, state borders are no longer an obstacle for international crime. Anybody – the tourist, the salesman, the investor, the employee, the criminal – can easily travel across borders or take advantage of modern communication devices, including the World Wide Web. It is only the police and public prosecutors who remain stationary where others easily progress. In 1993, in my address at the Celebration of the Centenary of the Hague Conference on private international law, I raised the same points, and pleaded for 'a more open approach to one another's criminal justice systems'. My conclusion was (and still is): 'Our first concern should no longer be to decide *where* crime is punished but to ensure *that* it is punished.'[1]

But even now, many lawyers and politicians continue to consider judicial affairs a domain of essentially national sovereignty.[2] If they understood these sovereign powers as a duty and responsibility to act and to cooperate, I could still support this view. In practice, however, the claim for sovereignty in judicial affairs appears to function in many cases as an obstacle for other states that might have an interest in trying perpetrators of a cross-border crime. Traditional concepts such as the territorial principle underline the pretended sovereign claim on other states to refrain from efforts to investigate or punish acts committed on another's territory.[3]

* Senator and Professor of International Law (Tilburg University); former Minister of Justice of the Netherlands.

[1] Célébration du Centenaire de la Conférence de La Haye de droit international privé 19 mai 1993 / Celebration of the Centenary of the Hague Conference on private international law 19 May 1993, The Hague (Permanent Bureau of the Conference) 1993, p. 19. Cf., also my guest lecture at Twente University on September 13, 1993, 'Internationale criminaliteitsbestrijding', in *In Ernst, Oriëntaties voor beleid, Gebundelde toespraken van minister E.M.H. Hirsch Ballin* ('s-Gravenhage, Sdu 1994) and in Publikatie nr. 58 van de Stichting ABC Advies (Berlicum 1994).

[2] Justly critical about the role this concept continues to play in international law is Louis Henkin, *International Law: Politics and Values*, (Dordrecht/Boston/London, Martinus Nijhoff 1995) pp. 8 ff.

[3] Cf., Henkin, op.cit. n. 2, at p. 235: 'That the territorial state may exercise jurisdiction is indeed self-evident. That its jurisdiction ought to be exclusive is less clear.'

W.P. Heere (Ed.), International Law and The Hague's 750th Anniversary

In theory, every problem can be solved within the existing framework of treaties for judicial cooperation and extradition. In practice, however, many difficulties arise. In organized crime, it is almost impossible to try criminal activities in one country separately from those in other countries. Often, the authorities 'in charge' according to the territorial principle do not act on behalf of the state that has the biggest stake in the case. The state of the *locus delicti,* though acting within its exclusive sphere of competence, may have neither the tools nor information nor the will to act effectively.

INTERNATIONAL INTERTWINEMENT IN CRIMINAL MATTERS

What is this all about? A random collection of examples drawn from recent news reports may shed some light on our topic.[4] In November last year, an international conference in Oslo considered the extent of child labor, according to Unicef inflicted upon 250 million children between 5 and 14 years of age, who have to toil under often extremely harsh conditions.[5] In the same month, the 29 member countries of the OECD reached an agreement on a Convention against corruption, which was signed on December 17, 1997.[6] In December last year, The Hague police officers arrested in cooperation with the police of the Netherlands Antilles on Curaçao (Netherlands Antilles), one of the most wanted Colombian cartel leaders, Quiceno Botero. Botero was charged with trafficking cocaine to the Netherlands.[7] Also in December, the US Department of State posted an advertisement in several international newspapers. The US authorities offered a reward of up to $4 million for information leading to the arrest of two Libyan nationals, indicted for the bombing of a Pan Am airplane in 1988, causing the death of 270 people aboard and on the ground at Lockerbie, Scotland.[8]

In February of this year, the *Washington Post* reported that Colombian drug circles had subcontracted their Caribbean smuggling to Puerto Rico-based trafficking gangs because of the open access from this island to the US mainland.[9] The gang leaders themselves are from the Dominican Republic, and they ship the cocaine and heroin via islands throughout the Caribbean to Puerto Rico. Some efforts in law enforcement seem to have only a limited effect: in March there were news reports on how Mafia leaders managed to influence

[4] See also the numerous books on the internationalization of crime, e.g. Stephen Handelman, *Comrade Criminal, The Theft of the Second Russian Revolution* (London, Michael Joseph 1994); Jean Ziegler, *Les seigneurs du crime: Les nouvelles mafias contre la démocratie*, (Paris, Le Seuil 1998).

[5] *Süddeutsche Zeitung*, October 28, 1997.

[6] *http://www.oecd.org/daf/cmis/bribery/20nov1e.htm*

[7] ANP, 26 December 1997.

[8] *International Herald Tribune*, 20-21 December 1997.

[9] *International Herald Tribune*, 17 February 1998.

Colombian politics from within prison.[10] Criminal organizations are in a position to move their operations according to the situation in the countries concerned, effectively evading law enforcement. Transnational organized crime thus poses a serious threat to governability in several countries. According to William J. Olson, a 'direct threat comes from the ability of major criminal gangs to challenge governments, either through violence, intimidation or corruption.'[11]

These examples were drawn from the global playground. In Europe, specific forms of cross-border crime have emerged. In January, customs officials in Northern Germany reported a threefold increase in the seizure of cocaine five years after opening the border with the Netherlands in conformity with the Schengen agreement.[12] Also in January, five Dutch cities joined forces in an attempt to improve the recovery of parking fines from German and Belgian citizens. In March of this year, news reports on fraud with documents of origin for meat export to Russia induced political upheaval in the Netherlands. British beef, not admitted because of the presence of BSE in Britain, had allegedly been sold as Dutch beef to Russia.[13] And finally, according to a recent report by the European Commission, the black market economy in Western Europe is estimated being 16 percent of GDP, compared with 5 percent in the 1970s. This sector benefits from the open borders within Europe, shoulder to shoulder with the legal part of the economy.[14]

THREE APPROACHES

Most of us will recognize the need for a different approach to law enforcement in cross-border criminal matters. As usual, only a combination of different approaches can bring about the progress we need. I shall discuss three different possible approaches: (1) the recognition of (some) powers for law enforcement across borders, (2) internationalization of law enforcement for certain types of crime, and (3) redefining the significance of state borders in law enforcement.

THE RECOGNITION OF (SOME) POWERS FOR LAW ENFORCEMENT ACROSS BORDERS

As long as we have borders between states, cross-border developments should be consistent. The problem with the present situation is that the public sphere

[10] *Die Welt*, 6 March 1998.

[11] William J. Olson, 'International Organized Crime; The Silent Threat to Sovereignty', in *The Fletcher Forum of World Affairs*, Vol. 21:2 (Summer/Fall 1997) p. 65, at p.75.

[12] *Die Welt*, 15 January 1998.

[13] *Brabants Dagblad*, 13 March 1998.

[14] *International Herald Tribune*, 10 June 1998.

continues to be separated by state borderlines, where social and economic life – including its dark sides – has become integrated.[15] The introduction of the single currency – the Euro – aggravates this situation. There is clearly more pressure and support for observing the time schedules in the European Monetary Union than for the rather loose promises for progress at Europol. Here, in the city of The Hague, Europol could have opened its gates in January 1994. But on the legal side Europol is now, 4 years later, still under construction, although it has achieved some remarkable results. The Europol Convention will come into effect in October – but a number of protocols still have to be ratified in some Member States.

Since the beginning of this decade the Netherlands and its neighbouring countries have begun to explore direct forms of cooperation between police officials and public prosecutors. Year after year, the European Councils urge a swift development in Europol and the Third Pillar of the European Union in general, but then the ministers of Justice and Home Affairs quarrel about ten or twenty new positions at Europol headquarters and the debate on the treaties often drags on. Once a treaty has been signed, the debate is resumed with the respective parliaments. I do not doubt the need for careful consideration and effective judicial control, but it is also true to say here that justice delayed is justice denied. In the long run, the European Union cannot do without some executive powers in the field of law enforcement. My conclusion is that open borders require a joint cross-border law enforcement.

INTERNATIONALIZATION OF LAW ENFORCEMENT FOR CERTAIN TYPES OF CRIME

The second approach I want to distinguish will be discussed in depth in a special section. The International Criminal Court shall not only deal with genocide and violations of international humanitarian law, but also with certain other exceptionally serious crimes of international concern. Gradually, an internationalization of law enforcement takes effect. It is part of a trend towards internationalization of criminal law in general. We can observe a gradual extension of international requirements to punish certain crimes in the national context. The recent OECD Anti-Bribery Convention is one of the latest examples.

[15] Cf., Vincenzo Vasile, 'La "Maastricht" della mafia e la frontiera dell'Est', in Giovanni Fiandaca and Salvatore Costantiono, eds., *La mafia, le mafie, Tra vecchi e nuovi paradigmi* (Roma/Bari, Laterza 1994) pp. 349-360.

REDEFINING THE SIGNIFICANCE OF STATE BORDERS IN LAW ENFORCEMENT

The last part of the three possibilities is the most unusual, and in the eyes of some people perhaps the most unorthodox approach. Principles of sovereignty and long-standing traditions of international law have confirmed it repeatedly: the place where a crime has been committed must be the normal and exclusive basis of jurisdiction in criminal affairs.[16] But let's go back to the reasons for this scheme. One reason is that the jurisdiction must be suitable for mutual recognition. Otherwise, jurisdiction would become a source of endless conflicts between states. The other reason is that a public power implies a public duty. If the authorities of a sovereign state are in charge of their territory, it is up to them to deal with law and order within their borders.

These two reasons were both valid and convincing as long as real life could be separated according to the same territorial borderlines. Nowadays this presumption is no longer true. In private international law, the territorial approach has been put into perspective for similar reasons. It is, in many cases, the social characteristics rather than the place (or places!) where a contract has been signed that decide the law to be applied.

In search for an approach to law enforcement appropriate to the border-crossing nature of many criminal activities, there are reasons to authorize any state experiencing the consequences of a criminal act, to take action. That is why terrorism and drug-trafficking are subject to different jurisdiction schemes – the universality principle and the protective principle, laid down in specific international legal instruments.[17] Numerous other bilateral and multilateral treaties seek to counterbalance the effects of the territorial principle through extradition and other forms of legal cooperation, mostly based on the territorial principle as point of reference.[18]

But this will not be sufficient. Especially under the conditions of globalization and economic integration, territorial approaches will continue to block or delay effective law enforcement. Although a general recognition of the protective principle will help, the intertwinement between acts committed on different territories will require that law enforcement should be regarded as a joint responsibility. That is why in 1987 the *Third Restatement of Foreign Relations Law of the United States* adopted a more flexible approach with the 'principle of reasonableness'.[19]

[16] Peter Malanczuk, *Akehurst's Modern Introduction to International Law*, 7th revised edn. (London/New York, Routledge 1997) pp. 110 ff..

[17] Henkin, op.cit. n. 2, at pp. 246 ff.; Lyal Sunga, *The Emerging System of International Criminal Law, Developments in Codification and Implementation* (The Hague/London/Boston, Kluwer 1997).

[18] Christine van den Wyngaert and Guy Stessens, eds., *International Criminal Law, a Collection of Internnational and European Instruments*, (The Hague/London/Boston, Kluwer 1996).

[19] See Henkin, op.cit. n. 2, at p. 245.

At the 9th Interamerican Congress of Public Ministries, on November 24, 1996, the US Attorney-General Janet Reno said: 'we must not allow ourselves to be distracted into thinking extradition is a question of sovereignty. It is not. It is a question of justice.' I endorse this approach, not only with regard to extradition but also for legal cooperation in criminal affairs in general. Police and prosecution officers should be obliged to help the authorities in other states. Of course this will require a standardization of some elements in penal law and criminal procedure, in conformity with human rights and all other principles of fair trial.[20] But there is also a strong need for a more flexible attribution of the competence to act. Federal states with a multiple system of criminal law offer a good example for what we need in an interdependent world in general: a priority system rather than a system of exclusive competence. The authorities of a state in the position to act, *should* act; that is what I elsewhere called the responsibility principle[21]. The territory – the place where criminal acts have physically been committed – can play a role in a system of priority, not as an excluding but as an enabling reason. In many cases, the question of where a criminal organization has its 'seat' or where its victims live, will be more important – or perhaps the question of where a criminal activity has been entangled with the economy. According to the territorial principle, a state may have priority in law enforcement, but if its authorities fail to do so, another state may assume responsibility, perhaps because its nationals are the perpetrators – or the victims. The authorities in the other state should then be willing to cooperate with them.

My final conclusion is that we need a magnanimous acceptance of criminal jurisdiction by any state with substantive interest. A magnanimous acceptance under three conditions:

- a system of priority rules;
- an obligation to cooperate in investigation and trial;
- mutual acceptance of the relevant principles concerning fair trail.

Of course, such a new approach to international legal cooperation in criminal affairs needs careful elaboration. The G8 at their Birmingham Summit supported a proposal to negotiate a UN Convention against transnational organized crime.[22] Together with the TMC Asser Institute, we will start a research project at Tilburg University this year. In my opinion, the time is ripe to overcome the prejudice that we must live up to a territorially separated world of law enforcement.

In the international law of our times, sovereignty cannot serve as a pretext for arbitrary rule and injustice. This has been recognized with respect to human rights violations and more recently with respect to weapons of mass destruction. It should also be recognized with respect to international crime.

[20] Cf., J.M. Silva Sánchez, *Fundamentos de un sistema Europeo del derecho penal, Libro-Homenaje a Claus Roxin,* J.M. Bosch, Barcelona (1995).

[21] Ernst M.H. Hirsch Ballin, 'Beyond the Limits of The Territoriality Principle', in Erik Denters and Nico Schrijver, eds., *Reflections on International Law from the Low Countries in Honour of Paul de Waart* (The Hague/Boston/London, Martinus Nijhoff 1998) pp. 278-287.

[22] *http://www.library.utoronto.ca/www/g7/birmingham/finalcom.htm*

JUDICIAL CO-OPERATION IN THE FIELDS OF DRUG-TRAFFICKING, MONEY LAUNDERING AND FRAUD

W. Bruggeman*

1. INTRODUCTION

Police authorities lay the groundwork for the activities of the judicial authorities. Therefore, the roles that these two authorities fulfil are inextricably linked. Co-operation between police authorities should prepare the way for and support effective enforcement of the law (in the prosecution phase). At the same time, such co-operation should take place within a framework of legal and authorised gathering of evidence.

The need for improved co-operation also results from one of the fundamental transformations affecting both the national and the international scene, being the focus of the criminal justice system. Whereas the system used to be geared towards crime suppression by means of the prosecution and punishment of individual offenders (with custodial sanctions and fines as the major repressive tools), (part of) the system has moved in another direction. The main purpose is not limited any longer to punish the individual but, also aims to dismantle the criminal organisation, to which he/she belongs and to get hold of the profits he/she made through his criminal activities. [1]

Among the major transformations in the field of substantive law, a tendency exists to 'dilute' individual responsibility within organisations and to penalise behaviour of external supporters of organised crime (lawyers, doctors, interior decorators) and to punish mere participation in certain organisations.

The transformations in the field of procedural law are even more visible than those in the field of substantive law. Regarding crime investigations, there is a radical shift from reactive to pro-active policing. New techniques that were in the past only used by security services, are presently available to law enforcement officers.Quite frequently, preambles to domestic legislation or international instruments dealing with organised crime depict this phenomenon as an emergency situation that justifies departures from traditional rules and principles.

Protecting the rights of the individual is becoming one of the principal tasks of law enforcement. Thus, police authorities should aim, from the very start, to ensure the effectiveness of law enforcement, using an approach that takes account of the interests of offenders as well as of victims.

* Assistant Co-ordinator Europol Drugs Unit.

[1] Follow-up of The Hague political declaration on global action plan against organised crime, UN General Assembly, Res 52/58 of 12 December 1997, Annex III.

The functions that law enforcement authorities fulfil can be divided into separate phases. The relationship between law enforcement bodies and the public prosecution department should be studied further (meaning phase by phase) both at national and at international levels. It should also be examined in the light of their respective and differing responsibilities and the interdependence between them in each of the phases, phases that differ in the respective EU Member States.

The focus in this contribution is primarily on the international aspects, and especially on the application of the Schengen Agreement and the Maastricht/ Amsterdam Treaty on European Union. Nonetheless, we should endeavour to place this approach within a broader framework – a framework that includes other forms of co-operation.

2. JUDICIAL FUNCTION OF THE POLICE

2.1. General

The distinction between the administrative and judicial functions of the police is important, given that the public prosecution department fulfils a limited role with regard to its administrative tasks. Criminal records are, however, often used for administrative purposes. Also proactive policing makes differentiation more difficult, and different legal and ethical rules concerning pro-active policing may cause tensions when police officers of different countries engage in common international co-operation schemes. Asymmetry that seems to exist regarding the principle of proportionality and subsidiarity, may cause clashes when it comes to international co-operation (principle of judiciarity). [2]

The judicial function of the police should be examined within the framework of criminal proceedings, which proceedings begin with the very first step in an investigation and end when a convicted offender, having served his sentence, regains his freedom. These proceedings can be divided into four classical categories, namely the investigation, the prosecution, the trial and the enforcement of the sentence.

The first two proceedings in particular require fine-tuning. Both of these proceedings can be divided into different phases. The investigation consists of two phases, namely the investigation *sensu lato*, or the task of establishing that an offence has been committed and the evidence gathering to prove culpability of the suspected persons; and the investigation *sensu stricto,* the process of investigating an individual offence. The prosecution also consists of two phases, namely the judicial investigation and the enforcement of the sentence.During the

[2] Chr. van den Wyngaert, 'The transformation of international criminal law as a response to the challenge of organised crime, *International Review of Penal Law*' (1998 to be published).

judicial investigation phase, the impact of the prosecuting authorities on police investigations is direct, although organised differently in most countries.

Most criminal trials have their origin within law enforcement agencies or within one of the many other bodies vested with investigative powers. The criteria on the basis which police authorities have to act are formally regulated and vary from country to country. Moreover, once a crime has come to the attention of the police, they are required – sooner or later – to involve the public prosecution department. Usually, dismissals by the police (either with or without an official police report) are not legally recognised. In most of the EU countries, judicial authorities are formally in charge of criminal investigations.

The responsibilities of the public prosecution department (and in some countries those of the examining magistrate as well) include:

– establishing guidelines for the police and granting permission to carry out certain (special) measures, which tasks comprise exercising authority over law enforcement. In most countries, the constitution or laws lay down whether or not criminal proceedings are to be governed by the principle of expediency, which enables the public prosecution department to waive those proceedings;

– exercising authority/control over police activities and providing admissible evidence;

– (contributing to) policy development.

Whereas international police co-operation used to operate informally, without treaty basis, a number of treaties have now been made that regulate police co-operation in great detail. The first of such treaties was the 1990 Schengen Convention, followed by the 1995 Europol convention and by the 1997 Convention on Customs Co-operation. Of these, only the Schengen Convention has entered into force as yet. However, the Drugs Unit of Europol (EDU) has been operating since 1995 on the basis of a Joint Action of the EU. [3]

The distinction between police co-operation on the one hand and co-operation between judicial authorities on the other hand has been clearly defined in the Schengen Convention (Art. 39): police authorities shall assist each other for the purposes of preventing and detecting criminal activities, insofar as national law does not stipulate that the request is to be made to legal authorities and provided that the request or the implementation thereof does not involve the application of coercive measures.

This provision begs the question as to what the meaning of coercive measures is: does the term refer to physical coercion, or do infringements of general human rights, especially of the right of privacy (e.g. telephone taps, covert surveillance with sophisticated technical equipment) also qualify as coercive measures? The

[3] Joint Action of 10 March 1995 and 16 December 1996 extending the mandate of EDU.

answer to this question may vary from one state to another [4] and still needs to be further discussed at the international level.

Police co-operation, even now that it has been formalised in international conventions, is still much easier than co-operation between judicial authorities, where more conditions and obstacles apply. Nevertheless the power and/or control of the public prosecution department – particularly in the area of international co-operation – has been increasingly expanded at the structural level. This is especially true now that law enforcement authorities have acquired certain investigative and executive powers on the basis of treaties. The remaining question concerns the role, which can be played by the public prosecution department in the newly developed international policing frameworks.

The principle that operational policing and information or evidence gathering ought to be properly supervised and directed by prosecuting or investigating authorities also holds for international co-operation. Therefore, after having analysed specific police functions, the relationship between the police and judicial authorities will be further studied (see chapter 3).

2.2. **Specific**

2.2.1. *Information exchange between law enforcement authorities*

As already mentioned, international (police) co-operation in general and information exchange in particular, take place within one of the following two frameworks, namely collaboration between police authorities (which is based on informal/formal agreements between law enforcement agencies), or collaboration between governments (which is on the basis of treaties/conventions and becoming ever more important).

Cross-border information exchange is one area in particular where co-operation has taken place on an informal basis (grey circuit). Currently, however, this form of co-operation is becoming increasingly more formal with the implementation of treaties and agreements. This is an important development and respecting certain foreign rules and forms seems essential, for it would be unacceptable to 'launder' information or evidence which has been illegally or irregularly obtained abroad.[5] Much depends on the nature of the information (i.e. whether it is personal/non-personal, hard or soft etc.) as well as its ultimate

[4] C.M. Bevers and J.A.C. Joubert, *Schengen investigated. A comparative interpretation of the Schengen provisions on international police co-operation in the light of the European Convention on human rights* (Kluwer 1996) p. 592.

[5] Game and Mackarel, 'The admissibility of evidence obtained abroad into criminal proceedings – The Interpretation of mutual legal assistance treaties and use of evidence irregularly obtained', *European Journal of Crime, Criminal Law and Criminal Justice* (1996) pp. 99-119.

destination (the police or judicial authorities). Another factor of ever-increasing influence is the issue of protecting the privacy of the individual.

The international resources vary (UN Conventions, Council of Europe regulations, the Nordic Agreement, the Benelux Agreement, Schengen, Amsterdam, Naples II, UCLAF and Europol). For this reason, police autonomy, and thus the role of the public prosecution department, are governed by very different regulations.

A number of bilateral treaties regulating information exchange concerning minor cross-border traffic usually empower law enforcement authorities to engage in direct cross-border information exchange. The control exercised by the public prosecution department becomes indirect as none of these regulations make provisions for interaction with the police.

In order to improve the exchange of information, modern instruments increasingly use 'central authorities' or central bodies, responsible in each contracting state for international co-operation, and liaison officers. This evolution is now paralleled by comparable transformations in the field of judicial co-operation.

The Benelux Treaty (Brussels, 27 June 1962) applies primarily to *commissions rogatoires* (Art. 23) and the transfer of official reports (Art. 42); support in the investigation and establishing the perpetration of criminal acts (Art. 26); and border crossing (Art. 27). Remarkably, neither the treaty nor the 29 April 1969 agreement include any specific provisions for information exchange between law enforcement authorities.

The posting of liaison officers abroad facilitates information exchange between law enforcement agencies (regardless of whether the officer concerned is posted on the basis of Article 47 of the Schengen Implementing Convention of 19 June 1990 or the 1988 United Nations Drugs Convention). Often, the post falls also under the authority of the public prosecution department of the country sending the officer. Under the Nordic Agreement and Article 47 of the Schengen Implementing Convention, it is now possible to post a liaison officer on a collaborative basis to serve the interests of several countries. However, such action would hinder the judiciary in exercising its authority and control, due to the fact that no specific monitoring tasks are foreseen.

The Maastricht Treaty on European Union (7 February 1992) made it possible not only to exchange information (Europol Liaison Officers at Europol) and to create the Europol information(Art. 7) and analysis system (Art. 10), but also to create databases (European Information System, Customs Information System, and Europol). The liaison officers operating in the Europol Drugs Unit have been entrusted with a specific task within the framework of bilateral co-operation, also confined by the Europol Convention (Art. 5). This kind of co-operation differs from the general co-operation at Europol, which is a form of multilateral co-operation, primarily focusing on the intelligence (not always to be considered as evidence) function. Therefore, the information system and more particularly the analyst's system (Art. 10), are offering a unique framework including hard *and* soft data, in relation to differing categories of persons, (suspects, contacts and associates, informants, victims, witnesses). The co-operation that takes place in this context falls most frequently beyond the scope of the official influence of the public prosecution department, unless otherwise determined by the national legislation of the respective Europol National Units and their Europol Liaison Officers.

The fact that Europol organs, their members and Europol employees benefit from immunities and moreover, that they may not give evidence in an outside court or make statements without the approval of the director of Europol is at the basis of a lot of criticism. Nevertheless, this system is indispensable in order to create trust, a basic condition for most of the law enforcement agencies to forward sensitive intelligence to their organisation.

The EU Treaty of Amsterdam (Brussels, 1997) confirms the necessity (Art. 29) for closer co-operation between police forces, custom authorities and other competent authorities in the Member States, both directly and through Europol, and also for closer co-operation between judicial and other competent authorities of the Member States. More directly Article. 30 states that common action in the field of police co-operation shall include:

– operational co-operation between the competent authorities including the police, customs and other specialised law enforcement services in the Member States;
– . . . exchange of relevant information, in particular through Europol;
– co-operation and joint initiatives in . . ., exchange of liaison officers, . . .

The Council shall also provide co-operation through Europol and shall within a period of five years after the date of entry into force of the Treaty of Amsterdam (Art. 30):

– enable Europol to facilitate and support the preparation, and to encourage the co-ordination and carrying out, of specific investigative actions by the competent authorities of the Member States, including operational actions of joint teams comprising representatives of Europol via support capacity;
– adopt measures allowing Europol to ask the competent authorities of the Member States to conduct and co-ordinate their investigations in specific cases and to develop specific expertise which may be put at the disposal of Member States to assist them in investigating cases of organised crime;
– promote liaison arrangements between prosecuting/ investigating officials specialised in the fight against organised crime in close co-operation with Europol.

Common action (Art. 31) on judicial co-operation in criminal matters shall include:

– facilitating and accelerating co-operation between competent ministries and judicial or equivalent authorities of Member States in relation to proceedings and the enforcement of decisions;

– ensuring compatibility in rules applicable in the Member States in relation to proceedings and the enforcement of decisions;
– ensuring compatibility in rules applicable in the Member States, as may be necessary to improve such co-operation;
– preventing conflicts of jurisdiction between Member States;
– progressively adopting measures establishing minimum rules relating to the constituent elements of criminal acts and to penalties in the field of organised crime.

So it is clear that the Treaty of Amsterdam is offering and will guarantee an ambitious framework for police and judicial co-operation.

In my opinion the more operative powers foreseen in Article 30 encourage the debate about immunities, which are *no* more justified when participating into investigations within the Member States, (thus after ratification of the Treaty of Amsterdam). Also the role of UCLAF is worthwhile to be mentioned (1st pillar), being inherent to the responsibility of the Commission combating community fraud and by protecting the community financial interests, based on Article 280 of the Treaty of Amsterdam. This organisation is staffed not only by customs and police officers but also by prosecutors and lawyers, all integrated in one agency. They have the right to participate and to initiate controls within the EU Member States.

But following criticisms concerning the undemocratic way in which some EU-instruments are developed and the lack of judicial control, the role of the European Parliament and of the European Court of Justice[6], however remaining very limited, have been reinforced.

There is a major concern about the far-reaching power of Europol, that is not (except control at national level in the European National Units) counterbalanced by any specific form of judicial control. The co-operation that takes place via Interpol is based on Interpol's statute and is reinforced by a number of treaties (e.g. the United Nations). Interpol is a law enforcement organisation and does not – *per se* – directly affect the position of the public prosecution department and its influence on the police. Nevertheless, several Interpol functionalities (e.g. rogatory letters, warrants of arrests…) are directly monitored by judicial authorities. Nevertheless, Interpol is not based on a real intergovernmental approach.

2.2.2. *Special Police Techniques*

The Benelux Treaty makes no explicit provisions for cross-border surveillance operations (though such provisions are implicit in Art. 26). Cross-border surveillance is done on the basis of the Schengen Implementing Convention (Art.

[6] In a number of additional protocols to existing EU conventions and in the future for non-EU conventions that will be incorporated in the EU such as the Schengen Convention.

40) or an international request for legal assistance (European Convention on Assistance in Legal Matters, Strasbourg 1959, in which case the involvement of the public prosecutor is mandatory). The Schengen Implementing Convention is most clear, but also makes provisions for proactive measures. Co-operation takes place by the use of such instruments as *commissions rogatoires* or expedited procedures. The Naples II Convention (not yet ratified) further develops these functionalities for customs services.

Cross-border pursuit is regulated by the Benelux Treaty (Art. 27) and the Schengen Implementing Convention (Art. 41). The use of controlled deliveries is regulated by Article 11 of the UN Convention against Illicit Traffic in Narcotic Drugs and Psychotropic Substances (1988), art. 73 of the Schengen (Implementing) Convention (14 June 1985 and the Agreement of 19 June 1990) and the Naples II Convention.

The respective roles of the police and public prosecution department in dealing with these special techniques are not regulated at international level. The foundations laid down by international agreements for the use of special police techniques should serve to intensify the role of the public prosecution department. Experience, however, has shown that the interpretation of this role varies from country to country and is exclusively a variable of national rules and regulations.

2.2.3. *Main changes*

All these developments lead to basic changes, especially within the European Union framework. This evolution can be marked and characterised by the following changes:

unofficial	→	official
interpolice	→	intergovernmental
simple	→	complicated
non integrated	→	integrated approach

The changes within the police co-operation framework are now at the origin of more developed judicial co-operation, although the intensity and flexibility of judicial co-operation is still far beyond the level of police co-operation.

3. CO-OPERATION WITH THE JUDICIARY SUBSEQUENT TO POLICE CO-OPERATION

Given the judicial powers vested in law enforcement authorities and the provisions for international co-operation that are used between police agencies, the position of judicial authorities in general, and – on a more specific level – that of the public prosecution department require further examination.

Judicial co-operation was established long before police co-operation became crystallised and structured by the Schengen Convention(s) and the Maastricht/ Amsterdam Treaty on European Union. Nowadays the growth, intensification and diversification in the field of police co-operation is by no means matched by a comparable development in the field of co-operation between judicial authorities.[7] In Europe, the most important conventions in this field are still the 1957 Convention on Extradition and the 1959 Convention on Mutual Assistance in Criminal Matters and their additional protocols, all elaborated during the 1950s, within the Council of Europe. Unlike in the field of extradition and mutual assistance in criminal matters, the Council of Europe convention on transfer of criminal proceedings and of executions of criminal judgements has hardly been a success, judging from the number of ratifications of both instruments received. Except for some minor improvements, the chapter on mutual assistance in the Schengen Convention has not brought any spectacular innovations or transformations. In addition the EU has drafted a convention on extradition and is currently preparing a Convention on Mutual Assistance in Criminal Matters.

Rogatory commissions (Art. 38 of the Benelux Treaty) remain the basis and enable public prosecutors to contact each other directly with requests for mutual legal assistance. The European Treaty on Mutual Assistance in Criminal Matters (20 April 1959) only provides for direct transfer of information in urgent cases. Moreover, it increasingly happens that the treaty is found to be outdated and it has been known to cause delays. The use of simplified procedures (*kleine rechtshulp*), which are more frequently needed, has been facilitated by the Schengen Implementing Convention.

In most countries, the involvement of public prosecutors (the public prosecution department, the examining magistrate) is a *conditio sine qua non* for carrying out a request for mutual legal assistance. The police should make every effort to act in conformity with the law and judicial authorities both during the preliminary phase and when carrying out *commissions rogatoires*.

In practice, the police often have to work in a vacuum, especially during the pre-judicial phase – unless granted specific and autonomous powers. Those powers, however, have to be carried out under the authority and/or supervision of the judicial authorities from the outset. Although this is the case in many countries, there are countries – such as Great Britain – where this does not apply. The more intensely the public prosecution department co-operates with police authorities (such as in Scandinavian countries), the closer the bond between the two and the less frequent the occurrence of action taken in conflict with or beyond the scope of the law. Closer co-operation also means fewer opportunities for the police to withdraw from authority and control.

[7] Chr. van den Wijngaert, 'The transformation of international criminal law as response to the challenge of organised crime', *International Review of Penal Law* (1998 to be published).

We should note here that the police usually refrain from involving the judicial authorities where such involvement is not mandatory. This tendency not only applies to the exchange of information intended for use in criminal proceedings, but also to the use of special police techniques. Insofar as information is concerned, this authority/control may be exercised both directly and indirectly (at a general or specific level).

This gives rise to a number of problems. To begin with, law enforcement authorities have no official procedures or guidelines to determine which country is best suited for taking action. Moreover, the need to establish a consistent approach at the international level to obtain evidence by legal means often receives too little attention. There are also various gaps in policies (concerning such areas as priorities, deployment of resources, decisions to prosecute, etc.). As a result, the different speeds with which police and judicial authorities operate present the danger that policy diverges in two different directions, which in turn, may lead to problems (such as that of inadmissible evidence).

4. ESTABLISHING A JUDICIARY WITHIN AN INTERNATIONAL FRAMEWORK

Due to the current efforts to create a structure for co-operation between police authorities, we are now facing the question of how to set in motion a parallel process of establishing an international public prosecution department or process and developing regulations to govern their roles. At present, a number of initiatives have been taken to facilitate this process. Certain countries (including Belgium and the Netherlands) have succeeded in introducing a national public prosecutor without undermining the fundamental and traditional authority of the public prosecution department.

The national public prosecutor (*nationaal magistraat*) in Belgium is entrusted with three tasks: 1) co-ordination; 2) centralisation and 3) advice. The first task consists of co-ordinating operations and investigations of the kind of criminal offences that can take on national or international proportions due to their magnitude or repercussions. The second task consists of centralising operations and investigations after submitting proposals and recommendations to public prosecutors working at the local level for the public prosecution department. This task is performed, among other things, through intervention in conflicts arising from cases that fall under the authority of several government bodies. The national public prosecutor also has (some) central authority in relation to the management of information on special international (cross-border) operations (such as controlled deliveries). He is authorised to take all urgently needed decisions in such matters, and where possible, to do so in consultation with local public prosecutors.

The national public prosecutor was established, first in an official circular letter and then by law, as the only Belgian official authorised to act as a contact person in relations with foreign authorities concerning all matters requiring the intervention of the judicial authorities, without prejudice to the authorities of the public prosecutors responsible for cross-border crime involving neighbouring countries. His authority also extends to information assistance as provided for in the Schengen Implementing Convention (Art. 39) and cross-border surveillance operations and pursuit (Arts. 40 and 41), for which permission may or may not be granted in Belgium to foreign police authorities (or vice versa). The same applies to activities performed via the Schengen-Sirene Bureau.

The national public prosecutor fulfils a key role as a central contact person in every respect, an intermediary and where necessary, a steering body for the police. For this reason, the functions and responsibilities connected to this post should be laid down in and regulated by national and international laws and structures. The national public prosecutor's tasks also include a bi-annual control of Belgian liaison officers posted abroad. In addition, he serves as the contact person for new cases, cases to which no criminal justice agency in Belgium has been actively assigned.

Naturally, we are still left facing the question of whether it is possible to establish similar regulations within the framework of the European Convention on Assistance in Legal Matters (1959). We also have to examine the role of the national public prosecutor in non-urgent requests for legal assistance and the significance of that role for co-operation in the framework of Europol.

It should also be pointed out here that a good number of EU Member States have entrusted their respective public prosecution departments with (some of) the authority over and/or supervision of the national co-ordination of international information exchange and co-operative measures (National Central Bureau Interpol, Europol National Unit, Schengen SIRENE Bureau).

In relation to the Amsterdam Treaty, it has also to be mentioned that a step by step integration of the Schengen acquis, within the EU will have to be achieved within a period of five years.

In my opinion, however, this approach is too inadequate and fragmented a response to the actual problems facing law enforcement authorities. Every effort should be devoted to create an international forum for consultation concerning pre-judicial and judicial measures. At a more general level, that forum should also offer EU Member States the opportunity to establish their position concerning such aspects of prosecution as options legality and humanness. In other words, the forum should be a structure of triangular consultation at the European level. An international structure of this kind should also have the legal potential to safeguard conformity of police activities to the law. The purpose of developing this forum is not to create a substitute authority. Efforts in this direction should aim, rather, at establishing a general instrument by which to test legitimacy (use of admissible evidence) in combination with specific relationships of authority where legally established (e.g. rogatory commissions, special police measures). Moreover, a structured framework of co-operation between law enforcement authorities and the public prosecution department would help to support policy (e.g. Europol) at the intergovernmental level.

Within this framework the principle of trust is of extreme importance. This has to be based on a good knowledge about competencies available in the different Member States, and additionally the criteria (priorities) fixed by public prosecutor department and law enforcement agencies, in agreement or not. Important is whether and under which condition information can be made available. It is also important to clarify the dispatching mechanisms for distribution and allocation of competencies.

Nowadays the co-operation between judicial authorities has become an important item within the EU third pillar decision making process. Several initiatives were initiated recently, albeit that the EU has no power to enact directly applicable legislation (regulations and directives) in the field of criminal law, except when such legislation aims at administrative control of criminal behaviour.[8]

Framework for the Exchange of Liaison Magistrates to Improve Judicial Cooperation Between the Member States of the European Union (JHA/96/227)

The guidelines laid down in this Joint Action (22 April 1996) will serve as a reference when Member States decide to send *Liaison Magistrates* to another Member State or to exchange Liaison Magistrates, on the basis of bilateral or multilateral arrangements (Art. 1). By establishing direct links with the competent authorities of the Host State, *Liaison Magistrates* shall encourage and accelerate all forms of *judicial co-operation* in criminal and, when appropriate, in civil matters. Depending on the arrangements between the home and the host Member States, *Liaison Magistrates tasks* may include any activity connected with handling exchange of information and statistics (Art. 2).

Article 2 of the joint action describes the tasks of liaison public prosecutors as follows:

– Generally, the tasks of liaison public prosecutors include all activities aimed at supporting and expediting all forms of co-operation between judicial authorities

[8] Van den Wijngaert, 'The transformation of international criminal law as a response to the challenge of organised crime', *International Review of penal law* (1998 to be published).

in criminal and civil proceedings – especially by establishing direct contacts with the judicial authorities of the Receiving State.
– Based on the agreements between the sending and receiving countries, the tasks of the liaison public prosecutor can also include all activities relating to the exchange of information and statistics which are aimed at: a) increasing the knowledge that the countries have of each other's systems and of the legal databases of participating Member States and b) improving relations between the different legal professions in each Member State.

According to Article 3, each Member State shall inform the others of initiatives already under way and those taken to implement this Joint Action. Moreover, the Member States shall *inform* on their exchanges of Liaison Magistrates to the General Secretariat of *the Council* annually.

Some EU countries (the first was France) have posted a liaison public prosecutor in other countries.

JOINT ACTION ESTABLISHING A MECHANISM FOR EVALUATING THE APPLICATION AND IMPLEMENTATION AT NATIONAL LEVEL OF INTERNATIONAL UNDERTAKINGS IN THE FIGHT AGAINST ORGANIZED CRIME (Crimorg 5 – 8 September 1997)

The objective is to create a mechanism for evaluation of the application and implementation at national level of international undertakings in the fight against organised crime. Experts designated by the Member States, according to Article 3 shall carry the evaluation. Each Member State shall designate one to three experts among the fields of police, customs or *judicial nature* (Art. 3). The troika will choose three experts who will constitute the evaluation team (Art. 4).

A JOINT ACTION TO CREATE A EUROPEAN JUDICIAL NETWORK (Crimorg 1 rev 1, 14 October 1997)

Article 1 affirms that a network of judicial contact points shall be set up between the Member States of the EU in order to strengthen judicial co-operation between Member States in the fight against organised crime, by establishing direct contact between authorities responsible for judicial co-operation and judicial action against forms of serious crime. According to Article 2, the *European Judicial Network* shall be made up within the context of international co-operation (organised crime). The same Article, point 5, talks about *liaison magistrates* and their competencies. Article 4 explains the functions of contact points, which, on the base of Article 8, shall be linked by a telecommunications network. Article 13 says that the Council shall assess the role of the Networks in relation with Europol.

The European Judicial Network (in creation) will partly solve all the urgent non-local and special responsibilities of authority. In addition a consultation framework (for some or other prosecutors) should be established, into which the public prosecution department's general structures of co-operation can be incorporated.

Note: it is not yet decided whether this relation will be of a pure technical or of a more operational nature.

NOTE ABOUT THE COMMISSION[9] MULTIANNUAL FINANCIAL SUPPORT PROGRAMMES:

Within the EU strategy the European Commission sets up an organisational framework to deal with co-operation.

Sherlock provides for training and exchanges in the area of migration, particularly the trade in forged documents. *Grotius* deals with training and exchanges in the judicial area. *Stop* provides training and exchanges for judges, prosecutors, frontier officials and others who in the course of their duties come into contact with people exposed to trafficking for purposes of exploitation. *Oisin* concerns increased co-operation between police forces. *Daphne* is aimed at voluntary organisations working with children and women exposed to violence and sexual exploitation. The purpose of *Odysseus* is to reinforce practical co-operation between people working on forged documents, border controls and questions relating to asylum and migration. The objective of the *Falcone* programme is to promote closer co-operation between people (magistrates, prosecutors, law enforcement agencies, customs, etc.) working in the field of law enforcement in the Member States.

JOINT ACTION ON GOOD PRACTICE IN MUTUAL LEGAL ASSISTANCE IN CRIMINAL MATTERS (Crimorg 33, 10 December 1997)

Recommendation 16 (Action Plan – High Level Group) refers to the need to 'accelerate procedures for judicial co-operation in matters relating to organised crime and reduce delays in transmission and responses to requests'. Thus, the Joint Action proposes in Article 2 that Member States provide a statement of good practice in executing requests for legal assistance in criminal matters and,

[9] Also to be mentioned for information: the legal co-operation programmes of the Council of Europe such as DEMO, DROIT, THEMIS and CODE are focused on legal assistance to the CEECS in all fields of law.

once a year, a monitoring report. Both these documents should be available to all Member States through the European Judicial Network.

JOINT ACTION (...) EXCHANGE OF INFORMATION IN RESPECT OF PAYMENT CARD CRIME
(Enfopol 9, 3 December 1997)

This Joint Action wants to promote and facilitate the exchange of information concerning payment card crime by establishing a network of contact points in Member States. Accordingly, each Member State shall establish a national contact point located, where possible, with the central national contact point of Rec. 19 (Art. 2.1). The national law shall govern relationships between the national contact points and national law enforcement agencies, judicial and other relevant authorities.

Article 3 is dedicated to the nature of information to be changed, while Article 4 concerns confidentiality.

PRE-ACCESSION PACT ON ORGANIZED CRIME
(Crimorg 31, 2 March 1998, agreed /JHA on 28-29 May 1998)

Principle 3 expresses the intent to co-operate fully in the development and effective operation of central law enforcement and judicial bodies responsible for the fight of organised crime. These bodies are central national bodies (REC. 1), central national contact points (REC. 19), national multidisciplinary teams (REC. 20) and European Judicial Network (REC. 21). In order to achieve common strategies and actions, assistance by Europol is contemplated as appropriate. Principle 4 says that the CCEEs and Cyprus will consider establishing among themselves a judicial network that will facilitate the gradual incorporation of such a Network into the Network of the European Union. Principle 6 concerns the mutual practical support for investigations and operations that includes, for instance, mutual exchange of police officers and public prosecutors for traineeships.With reference to rogatory letters and other judicial requests principle 9), the CCEEs and Cyprus make a statement of good practices in accordance with the Joint Action on best practices in mutual assistance in criminal matters. Training is the subject of principle 11, that mentions different programs such as PHARE and MEDA and, in the Third Pillar such as OISIN, GROTIUS and FALCONE, as interesting initiatives for law enforcement agencies or judicial authorities. In order to improve the existing co-operation between Member States, Principle 14 states the desirability of extending the current liaison officers network, including magistrates.

Asset Tracing and Seizure. Joint Action Concerning the Arrangements for Co-operation Between Member States (Crimorg 32, 3 March 1998)

Article 1 says that each Member State shall provide a user-friendly guide, including contact points, which will be available to Europol and the European Judicial Network. Article 3 states that Member States shall encourage direct contact between investigators, investigating Magistrates and prosecutors. Article 4 concerns judicial region in which the investigation occurs. According to Article 5 Member States shall inform their judiciary with the best practice in international co-operation, and ensure the appropriate training to all investigators, investigating Magistrates and prosecutors. The Presidency and, as appropriate, in co-operation with Europol and the European Judicial Network, shall as necessary arrange seminars to promote and develop best practice and to maximise the compatibility of procedures.

Draft Convention on Mutual Assistance in Criminal Matters

The Council is making substantive progress on a draft convention on mutual legal assistance in criminal matters with a view to reaching global agreement in the near future. The purpose of this convention is to provide for a more efficient and faster judicial co-operation in criminal matters, taking account of new investigation methods such as hearing by videoconferences or interceptions of (satellite) telecommunications, given the main international legal instrument in this area (the Council of Europe Mutual Assistance Convention dates from 1959). This convention has to be established in conformity with national law and relevant international instruments protecting the rights of accused persons, including the 1950 European Convention on Human Rights.

According to agreement reached, Member States will have the possibility to declare at any time following ratification of this new Convention that they will not apply this newly agreed provision ('opting-out'). Another main provision of the draft Convention concerns interception of telecommunications where it is important that tapping possibilities match with new technology. A further problem relates to rules on the compliance with the formalities and procedures indicated by the requesting Member State when executing rogatory letters and, more particularly, to the possibility of setting deadlines for examining requests for assistance.

Agreement is already reached on a number of provisions such as the restitution of articles obtained by criminal means, the controlled deliveries, the sending and service of procedural documents, the possibility of a temporary transfer of persons held in custody for purposes of investigation, the spontaneous exchange of information, the requests for mutual assistance (whether to send a request directly to the competent judicial authority, via the central authority, Interpol or other, including the EU bodies).[10] and the investigations by officers acting under cover of false identity. It is obvious that the future acceptance of this convention will intensify the role of prosecuting authorities with the European Union, although it is regrettable that not all new police methods (such as deals with criminals) are included.

After having studied recent EU joint actions and conventions, some of them still being in discussion, the question arises again how to ensure a better co-ordination between police and justice co-operation dealing with international co-operation, and how to enhance judicial control.

In general the Schengen Convention describes the link between both, to be exercised at national level. The other frameworks are not that clear and further clarification and additional measures are necessary.

First prejudicial deliberations on arising questions could better guarantee harmonisation of police and judicial action as an early stage of decision making. Then, structuring the operational (European) police actions would suppose that several preliminary questions are put:

- in which countries sufficient police capacity can be guaranteed;
- in which countries prosecution is possible;
- which countries are willing to start prosecution;
- which countries are willing to enforce a sanction;
- in which country prosecution has already been started;
- in which country the suspect is undergoing or about to undergo a sanction involving deprivation of liberty;
- in which country sufficient items of evidence can be gathered;
- to which countries proceedings could be transferred;
- to which countries enforcement could be transferred;
- which countries are willing to accept proceedings being transferred to them;
- which countries are willing to accept enforcement being transferred to them;
- of which country the suspect is a national or which is his state of origin;
- in which country the suspect is ordinarily resident;
- in which country the victim is ordinarily resident;
- in which country the penalties then can be improved are deemed sufficiently high;
- which countries would benefit financially under enforcement of e.g. confiscation.

A prejudicial deliberation about these questions would offer quite some advantages, both in the domain of criminal justice maintenance and legal protec-

[10] In my opinion, such as UCLAF and EUROPOL (liaison network).

tion. Police and justice actions should really be harmonised in an early and therefore timely stage.

Theoretically, one could distinguish seven models for future developments at the international level (in addition to national initiatives):
– *status quo* (not to be considered as a new development);
– restructuring and qualitative improvement of the existing judicial framework, taking into account specific needs in order to facilitate an integrated and interactive police/prosecution department approach;
– liaison magistrates;
– national or contact magistrates, active within a European Union network;
– a formal European Union (Third Pillar) structure for improved co-operation between leading prosecution authorities in the Member States;
– integration of judicial authorities within the EU frameworks (UCLAF, Europol);
– the creation of an EU prosecution department, as proposed by Mr. De Angelis of the European Commission, making additional use of a network of specialised prosecution authorities in the Member States (Community fraud);
– a genuine European Union prosecution department.

The first five proposals appear particularly interesting and include *ad hoc* participation of the magistrate into international (e.g. at Europol) initiatives for improved case related co-ordination of investigations. The creation of any real European structures is premature at this stage, although in 1996-1997, a number of experts convened by the European Commission.[11] has elaborated a proposal for a more effective system to fight EU fraud, that would also safeguard the human rights of suspects. The proposal leaves the national court systems intact, but introduces a European Public Prosecution where jurisdiction would extend to the whole territory of the Union.

The actual concrete plans are less ambitious, especially within the framework of the third pillar. Awaiting further clarification of the role of the European judicial network with Europol, first one should also support the idea that all of the principles and implementing measures for international co-operation in criminal matters should undergo fundamental reconsideration.[12] Shorter and more direct lines of communication, including those leading from the public prosecution department via the national and liaison public prosecutors should be more firmly established in international agreements that determine whether and where pursuit is permitted and by which authorities. Agreements containing well-defined conditions could serve to simplify a good number of the complex procedures resulting from such police actions (transfer, extradition, etc.). However, a real European public prosecution department could not be effective or even necessary until a legal system, and possibly a law enforcement agency with

[11] The initiative came from DG CC (the Directorate General for financial control) and UCLAF.
[12] *Algemeen Politieblad*, 1993, No. 142, pp. 10-11.

executive powers, is put into operation at the European level and European criminal law and criminal procedures are accepted.

Concerning the place and the role of judicial authorities in their relation with Europol, in step with the widening of its mandate and in view of its operative powers to work together with national authorities. As was already mentioned (Art. 31, Treaty of Amsterdam) the Council of the EU would – within a period of five years after the date of entry into force of the revised Treaty – establish a 'liaison arrangement between prosecuting/investigating officials, specialising in the fight against organised crime in close co-operation with Europol.' Also the relation between judicial network in establishment and Europol has to be clarified within a period of three years. The question here remains open whether the relation is technical and/or operational. In this respect it should be recalled that the High Level Group suggested that, if the experience of a network would prove to be positive, it could in the future be examined whether in the long run the network should be transformed into a more permanent structure which could become an important interlocutor of Europol.[13]

A centralised network, consisting of liaison magistrates or officials, posted in The Hague, with a view to closely co-operating with Europol, is to be rejected.[14] A better solution is to maintain the decentralised network, and to represent their interests within the ENUs. This is more compatible within the global Europol concept, although this might change after ratification of the Treaty of Amsterdam, creating a possible need for improved co-operation with judicial authorities also at EU level. This should not rule out that the network will make use of the Europol secured network for the channelling of especially to be secured information.

A similar exercise on the possible involvement (not only technical) with UCLAF merits a separate study, taking into account that UCLAF is part of the 1st pillar.

5. CONCLUSION

Do we need an actual European Public Prosecution Service? The answer is NO. However, efforts should be made to compensate for the absence of such a service by introducing measures to increase opportunities for co-operation between and with judicial authorities. We do, however, need to remain realistic.

The discussion concerning a margin of independence and autonomous police powers is in full progress in numerous EU Member States. The steps being taken

13 See Recommendation 21, Council of the European Union, 7421/97 JAI 14, 21 April 1997, p. 35.

14 G. Vermeulen, 'A European Judicial Network linked to Europol?', in Search for a model for structuring transnational criminal investigations in the EU, *Journal of European comparative Law* (Maastricht, 1997) p. 347.

in that direction as a result of those discussions differ in individual Member States due to their different judicial systems.

Nowadays, public prosecution departments no longer limit their activities to a purely reactive approach (restricted to the *ad hoc* and passive gathering of evidence), this approach being based only on preliminary law enforcement activities at the international level. A network of public prosecutors (national, liaison or border public prosecutors) is needed in order to improve and expedite co-operation between law enforcement officials without making fundamental changes to the structure of their authorities. A similar formula for bilateral co-operation or co-operation within the framework of Schengen or Europol would seem the strategy best suited to ensure the integration necessary in the European Union. New initiatives at the European level are only needed once a European policy concerning criminal law, prosecution and law enforcement is implemented as a consequence of legislation at the European level. In the meantime, we should welcome any initiatives that have the potential to improve the co-operation between prosecution authorities, both with regard to strategy (or policies) and to operations.

Is this sufficient in itself? My answer is, again: no. I believe that we can benefit from the Nordic example. Moreover, as I pointed out in a previous publication[15], there is a need for a general framework for judicial co-operation. This is especially true in cases where these authorities assume authority from police agencies in the interests of the end phase of the judicial process (extradition, transfer of proceedings, etc.). I therefore think that some concrete steps can be taken in the short term to improve the coherence of intergovernmental co-operation:

– the continuous assessment of international co-operation particularly in the pre-judicial stage. A clear distinction needs to be made here between assessment and direction of police activities. Direction by prosecution authorities is only needed and possible in the case of a criminal procedure.

– the formulation of coherent internal rules within the criminal justice system concerning the place (i.e. country) in which legal action is to be taken. This problem arises in the early intelligence stage of international police co-operation. The general principles could be imposed by treaty on all partners concerned and should include: the interest of the victim, the interest of the offender, the guarantee of prosecution, the statutory provision for imposing penalties and enforcing sentences, and additional criteria relevant to particular types of crime.

– the vertically and horizontally integrated direction of international legal action, at both national and EU levels.

[15] Willy Bruggeman, 'Policing in Europe: A New Wave', in Monica den Boer, ed., *The Implementation of Schengen: First the Widening, Now the Deepening* (Maastricht, EIPA 1997) pp. 111-128.

Such a framework is essential in order to increase the integration between co-operating law enforcement and judicial authorities. This should be seen in combination with the official establishment and reinforcement of the already mentioned networks of national, liaison and contact magistrates. In my opinion, this is more realistic, at this stage, than trying to create a full-blown European Union prosecution department. Further integration of the prosecuting authorities into, e.g., the Europol framework should then only be evaluated again, in line with the post 'Amsterdam' developments.

INTERSTATE DISPUTE SETTLEMENT

The International Court of Justice
Chair: C.G. Weeramantry

The Position of the ICJ in the UN Constitutional System
Chair: E. Suy

FACT-FINDING BEFORE THE INTERNATIONAL COURT OF JUSTICE

Shabtai Rosenne*

Da mihi factum, dabo tibi jus.

Every jurist understands that before he or she can give a worthwhile legal opinion, he or she must know the facts. This applies when the lawyer is giving advice, and it applies equally when he or she is rendering a decision. International law, and with it international lawyers and international litigation, are no exception. The Statute of the International Court of Justice makes adequate provision for clarification of two aspects of the facts. One is the orderly presentation in contentious cases of facts by the parties in their pleadings, written and oral. The second is the ability of the Court in both contentious and in advisory cases to make its own enquiry into facts – so far rarely used.

Article 49 of the Rules of Court requires the Memorial to contain a statement of the relevant facts, and the Counter-memorial to contain an admission or denial of the facts and additional facts, if any. Although relevancy in that context is a subjective assessment, that provision assures the presentation and the airing of the facts and of any arguments on them throughout the written proceedings in every contentious case. If by Article 38 of the Rules a unilateral application instituting proceedings must contain a succinct statement of the facts and grounds on which a claim is based, the later pleadings require the formal and systematic development of the statement of facts by each party.[1] The generic name for this adversarial presentation of facts is 'evidence'.[2] Article 48 of the Statute empowers the Court to make all arrangements connected with the taking of evidence. The wording of that provision is general. It is not limited, as a rapid reading of it might suggest, only to the oral proceedings. Article 50 empowers the Court at any time to arrange for the carrying out of an enquiry or giving an expert opinion – a provision used only twice, each time in the same case, in the merits and the compensation phases of the *Corfu Channel* case.[3]

* Member of the Institute of International Law; Honorary member of the American Society of International Law. This article is based on address at the Asser Colloquium on the International Court of Justice on 2 July 1998.

[1] The Court has given an explanation of the word 'succinct' in its judgment in the *Land and Maritime Boundary between Cameroon and Nigeria* (Preliminary Objections) case, Judgment of 11 June 1998, paras. 98-101.

[2] The word 'evidence' appears in Arts. 44, 48 and 52 of the Statute and in Arts. 57, 58, 62, 63, 66 and 79 of the Rules.

[3] *ICJ Rep.* (1949) pp. 4, 237.

W.P. Heere (Ed.), International Law and The Hague's 750th Anniversary

The second faculty open to the Court is its ability to make its own investigation into the facts if it is not able to reach satisfactory conclusions on the basis of the facts as the parties have presented them.[4] There has been no instance of this yet, but isolated discussion of this aspect suggests that in a contentious case the Court would not assume a task of this nature without the agreement of the parties.[5] (This is something distinguished from the research that an individual judge may undertake.) Articles 95 and 107 of the Rules of Court are at the apex of this emphasis on facts. Those provisions require a judgment and an advisory opinion to include a statement of the facts. The Court is free to determine what facts are relevant for any judgment or advisory opinion, and there have been cases, both in the Permanent Court and in the present Court, in which a judgment or an advisory opinion went straight *in medias res* without any statement of facts.[6] This paper concentrates on the Court and modern scientific and technological facts.

Before doing that, however, we must note the special problem of fact-finding that the Court faces when one of the parties does not appear or fails to defend its case, for that is part of the Court's case-law on evidence. In those circumstances, Article 53 of the Statute of the Court requires the Court to satisfy itself that the claim is well founded in fact and law. The Court's experience of facts in this type of case is mixed. In the *Corfu Channel* (Compensation) case, the Court appointed a Committee of Experts to examine the figures and estimates submitted by the United Kingdom. The Experts placed a higher figure on the damages than was claimed, so the Court awarded the amount claimed on the basis of the *ne ultra petita* rule.[7] In the provisional measures phase of the *Anglo-Iranian Oil Company* case, the Court relied only on the facts as presented in the Memorial. However, provisional measures phases alone are not really indicative for the treatment of the merits. In the two *Fisheries Jurisdiction* cases against Iceland, the Court again relied only on the facts as stated by the applicants in their written and oral pleadings. There was no attempt to challenge or verify those facts. In the *Nuclear Tests* cases, the Court disposed of the cases on preliminary grounds without

[4] This follows Art. 50 of the Statute.

[5] The principal discussion of this aspect took place in the *Military and Paramilitary Activities in and against Nicaragua* (Merits) case, *ICJ Rep.* (1986) at p. 25 , paras. 30-31, p. 38, para. 57 and p. 40, para. 61. This is one of the more questionable features of that judgment, which has excited widespread controversy.

[6] In the Permanent Court, see the *Phosphates in Morocco* case, *PCIJ, Ser. A/B*, No. 74 (1938); and in the present Court, the *Rights of U.S. Nationals in Morocco* case, *ICJ Rep.* (1951) at p.109; and in an Advisory Opinion, *Legality of the Threat or Use of Nuclear Weapons*, *ICJ Rep.* (1996) at p. 226. The Court is always aware, from the documentation submitted to it by the Secretary-General or the equivalent officer of a specialized agency requesting an opinion, what prompted the organ concerned to request the opinion. The requirement of the Rules is technically met by a reference in the judgment or advisory opinion to the instrument instituting the proceedings and the subsequent proceedings.

[7] *ICJ Rep.* (1949) pp. 237, 241.

having to consider the merits. In the *U.S. Diplomatic and Consular Staff in Tehran* case, the facts on which the merits of the case depended were – in the Court's own words – matters of common knowledge which had received extensive coverage in the world press and in radio and television broadcasts from Iran and other countries.[8] In the *Military and Paramilitary Activities in and against Nicaragua* (Merits) case, one of the witnesses called by the applicant was closely questioned by the member of the Bench with the nationality of the absent respondent party, and in fact he retracted large parts of his evidence-in-chief. Nevertheless, the Court preferred that evidence, partly on the ground that a state that does not take part in the proceedings waives its right to cross-examine the witnesses.[9]

There is no question that modern international relations, and hence modern diplomacy and modern international litigation, is daily becoming increasingly concerned with scientific and technological facts. The law too, all law including international law, has to face this. For governments, this interdisciplinary work does not present any insurmountable problem. Faced with any matter of this kind, most governments can call upon appropriate expertise, whether in the country itself – from its academic, scientific, military and technological communities – or from the outside. The development of government positions in the Third United Nations Conference on the Law of the Sea, which posed innumerable questions relating to almost every branch of human knowledge, activity and science, provides an excellent example for this. A small illustration is seen in the evolution of the so-called *Bay of Bengal* clause, Article 7, paragraph 2, of the United Nations Convention on the Law of the Sea. That was originally drafted with the Ganges/Brahmaputra River delta particularly in mind. However, it raised problems for any country with or near a river delta. That provision went through a series of drafts, indicating prolonged and widespread governmental study of the problem of deltas.[10]

For the International Court of Justice, for all courts and tribunals in fact, the position is quite different. Courts, even with the widest powers for obtaining

[8] *ICJ Rep.* (1980) at p. 6, para. 12. Nevertheless, reliance on the media, especially in cases of non-appearance, must be treated with care. Cf., the retraction by CNN of an important story broadcast by a Pulitzer Prize journalist, in the *International Herald Tribune*, Tel-Aviv edition, 4-5 July 1998 at p. 5.

[9] *ICJ Rep.* (1986) at p. 25, para. 30. Facts that have come to light since suggest that the Court erred in its findings of fact in this case. See Sh. Rosenne, *The World Court: What it is and how it works*, 5th edn. (1995) p. 152.

[10] For that Convention, see United Nations, Division for Ocean Affairs and the Law of the Sea, *The Law of the Sea: United Nations Convention on the Law of the Sea; Agreement relating to the Implementation of Part XI of the United Nations Convention on the Law of the Sea,* Sales No. E.97.V.10 (1997). On that legislative history, see University of Virginia, Center for Oceans Law and Policy: S. Nandan and Sh. Rosenne, eds., *The United Nations Convention on the Law of the Sea: A Commentary*, Vol. II (1993) at p. 95. No doubt many geographers, geologists and other experts on river deltas were consulted world-wide before that text was finally settled.

'evidence', do not have this unlimited ability to place a telephone call or send a fax or today an e-mail to whomsoever they wish for an expert practice-oriented opinion as a matter of applied science. They are all largely dependent on the evidence placed before them. In practice they will have recourse to outside experts only when their participation in the proceedings has been agreed between the parties and the Court. Nevertheless, as Sir Robert Jennings has written, the International Court has not infrequently employed cartographers, hydrographers, geographers, linguists and even very specialized legal experts to assist in the understanding of the issues in a case before it.[11] That is a significant observation. It highlights the tension that inevitably exists between the legal conception of 'fact' and of evidence, and the conception which other disciplines, especially the exact and applied sciences, hold about facts and evidence. This calls for a closer examination in so far as it concerns litigation in the International Court of Justice. In addition, thanks to new provisions inserted into the Statute when it was redrafted in 1945, the Court now has the power to request of 'public international organizations' what is termed 'information relevant to cases before it'.[12] This is not limited to the specialized agencies which, however, by virtue of the relationship agreements concluded between them and the United Nations are obliged to render appropriate assistance to the International Court. The Statute does not state how this information is to be given, and there is no reason why the experts of the appropriate public international organization should not supply it in person, and be subject to questioning by the parties and from the Bench.

The existence of this tension appeared in the first contentious case to come before the present Court – the *Corfu Channel* case.[13] The issue concerned the facts of offensive and defensive naval operations in mine-infested waters in a situation of post-war international tension and uncertainties. One sentence in the judgment on the merits in that case illustrates the point. 'Being anxious to obtain any technical information that might guide it in its search for the truth, the Court submitted the following question to the Experts appointed by it' (p. 20). The Experts were three senior neutral naval officers with wartime experience, and the questions were formulated after the parties had been given the opportunity to make suggestions to the Court.[14] In producing their reports, the Experts acted as professional naval officers reporting on a naval incident to their authorities.

[11] R. Jennings, 'International Lawyers and the Progressive Development of International Law', in J. Makarczyk, ed., *Theory of International Law at the Threshold of the 21st Century: Essays in honour of Krzystof Skubiszewski* (1996) p. 416. This may be unknown to the parties. I understand that such outside persons are temporarily attached as members of the Registry staff, and have to make the solemn declaration set out in Art. 25 of the Rules.

[12] Statute, Art. 34, para. 2. On the application of this, see Sh. Rosenne, *The Law and Practice of the International Court 1920-1996*, Vol. II (1997) p. 638.

[13] *ICJ Rep.* (1949) p. 4.

[14] *Corfu Channel* case, Pleadings, Vol. V, at pp. 230, 240, 243, 246, Docs. 249, 266, 275, 279. The parties did not avail themselves of that invitation and left the matter in the hands of the Court.

Those reports did not decide the case. They supplied the Court with 'correct and impartial information' (p. 21) on which the Court could base its findings of fact as the foundation for its decision. The use of the word 'information' has its interest. 'Information' is distinguished from 'evidence'.

That was the first occasion on which the International Court, as opposed to governments, had enlisted impartial and professional assistance to supply it with information necessary for it to reach a tenable conclusion. That was the first occasion on which the International Court, and probably any international tribunal, accepted that legal criteria and experience alone could not always be adequate for the tasks that the Court had to perform. Nevertheless, the Court has so far refrained from pursuing a similar course when faced with carefully prepared technical and professional contentions in both advisory and contentious cases. It has always attempted to resolve these issues solely through the application of the Court's legal techniques. Three examples illustrate this, one from the advisory jurisdiction and two from the contentious jurisdiction.

In the advisory jurisdiction, the most striking instance is found in the Advisory Opinion on *Legality of the Threat or Use of Nuclear Weapons.*[15] The only piece of impartial scientific information officially before the Court, and then not in that case but in the parallel case of *Legality of the Use by a State of Nuclear Weapons in Armed Conflict*,[16] was a report by the Director-General of the World Health Organization entitled *Health and Environmental Effects of Nuclear Weapons.*[17] In the Advisory Opinion under consideration, the Court stated quite clearly that it found it unnecessary 'to study various types of nuclear weapons and to evaluate highly complex and controversial technological, strategic and scientific information' (p. 237, para. 15). In another place the Court referred to the 'material before the Court' regarding the causes of damage in nuclear weapons, but without any indication of what that material was or its provenance (p. 243, para. 35). That indeed was in the introductory paragraph to the main part of its opinion. In one of the operative clauses of that Advisory Opinion the Court went so far as to refer to the 'elements of fact at its disposal' (p. 266, para. 105 (2) E). This did not prevent a remarkable Dissenting Opinion by Judge (now Vice-President) Weeramantry largely devoted to the nature and effects of nuclear weapons.[18] In that Dissenting Opinion Judge Weeramantry found it necessary to examine the specific facts, 'at least in outline' (p. 451), because 'bland and disembodied language should not be permitted to conceal the

[15] *ICJ Rep.* (1996) p. 226.

[16] *Idem*, p. 66

[17] WHO Doc. A46/30, 26 April 1993.

[18] See *supra* n. 15, at p. 429. Judge Weeramantry in effect was continuing his Dissenting Opinion in the parallel case, ibid., at p. 97. These opinions themselves follow on his earlier opinion in the *Request for an Examination of the Situation in accordance with Paragraph 63 of the Court's Judgment of 20 December 1974* in the *Nuclear Tests* (*New Zealand* v. *France*) case, where he concentrated on the environmental impact of submarine nuclear tests. *ICJ Rep.* (1995) p. 317.

basic contradictions between the nuclear weapon and the fundamentals of international law' (p. 452). The purpose of that observation here is to illustrate the Court's handling of difficult scientific questions exclusively within the confines of a legal concept of 'facts'.[19]

The second illustration, and in some respect the more serious, is the Judgment in the *Continental Shelf* case between Tunisia and Libya.[20] Certainly, the core issue in that case was the legal meaning of the fundamental concept of the continental shelf as the natural prolongation of the land domain (p. 43, para. 36). Each side produced a large quantity of technical evidence on the geological and geomorphologic history of the formation of the relevant part of the sea-bed. Clarification of that issue would have gone a long way towards disposing of the case as a whole. Much of that judgment examines the contentions of the parties regarding the character of the seabed. That had been the subject of 'very abundant examination by the Parties, and of detailed scientific studies by their experts [necessarily partisan – Sh. R.] during the written and oral proceedings' (p. 41, para. 32). That was to require the Court to appreciate a Libyan argument based on a 'comparatively recently developed theory known as plate tectonics' (p. 59, para. 52). However, the Court concluded this lengthy if simplified account of geological theories with the following:

> '[I]t is not possible to define the areas of continental shelf appertaining to Tunisia and to Libya by reference solely or mainly to geological considerations. The function of the Court is to make use of geology only so far as required for the application of international law. It [the Court] is of the view that what must be taken into account in the delimitation of shelf areas are the physical circumstances as they are today; that just as it is the geographical configuration of the present-day coasts, so also it is the present-day sea-bed, which must be considered. It is the outcome, not the evolution in the long-distant past, which is of importance' (p. 53, para. 61).

To say that the issue thus examined was close to the core of the case is not a satisfactory answer to the question of principle that is being examined here. That question addresses the correctness and even the appropriateness of a procedure that allows and even requires the parties to go to the lengths that they did in this case, and to incur the heavy expenditure that they did incur, only to be told that in legal terms what is relevant is the sea-bed as it exists today, and not how it was formed over millions of years and its evolution in the long-distant past. On the other hand, if the geological history had been found to be relevant, the question could have arisen whether the Court alone should even attempt to assess that

[19] My views on these cases themselves are set out in an article entitled 'The Nuclear Weapons Advisory Opinions of 8 July 1996', *Israel Yearbook on Human Rights* (1997) p. 263.

[20] *ICJ Rep.* (1984) p. 18. Actually, if this material was irrelevant for the decision, some method should have been found to apprise the parties of this earlier in the proceedings, if only to save them unnecessary expenditure.

technical evidence as submitted to it. If, as in this case, the Court is to find that there is no relevance in certain scientific evidence and the issues to which that evidence is directed, procedures need to be put into place to permit the matter to be dealt with as early as possible. The written proceedings should in most cases present a sufficient basis, with perhaps a short hearing directed exclusively to that issue. This would simplify the proceedings on the merits and clarify the final decision of the Court. That aspect of this case has been brought in here to illustrate how modern science comes into modern international relations and hence into modern international litigation, and the need for the Court to adapt its procedures to this.

The Court seems to have reached a similar position in the *Gabčíkovo-Nagymaros Project* case between Hungary and Slovakia.[21] A major factual issue in this case related to the contention of Slovakia's responsibility for a grave and immediate peril to the environment to Hungary's detriment. On this, the judgment states that the verification of the existence of the grave and imminent peril invoked by Hungary and of the absence of any means to respond to it other than the measures actually taken by Hungary to suspend the work, 'are all complex processes'. The judgment continues:

> 'Both parties have placed on record an amount of scientific material aimed at reinforcing their respective arguments. The Court has given most careful consideration to this material, in which both Parties have developed their opposing views as to the ecological consequences of the Project. It concludes, however, that, as will be shown below, it is not necessary, in order to respond to the question put to it in the Special Agreement, for it to determine which of those points of view is scientifically better founded' (para. 54).

Nevertheless, later in that judgment the Court made pronouncements regarding the environmental impact of the Project and the duties of the parties in regard to the protection of the environment, which was a key issue for their future relations: 'The numerous scientific reports which have been presented to the Court by the Parties – even if their conclusions are contradictory – provide abundant evidence that this impact and these implications are considerable' (para. 139 ff.). Would it not have been better for the Court to have sought impartial technical information and thus rendered a judgment more specific on these scientific matters?

This brings me to the crux, and here let me recall at the start that the International Court is not the only superior court to have to face this problem. There is, however, one major difference between the International Court and other superior courts. The International Court is a court of first instance and a court of last

[21] Judgment of 27 September 1997, not yet published in the Court's usual bilingual format, and is cited here from the mimeographed text made available by the Registry. That judgment is also available on the Court's website, http://www.icj-cij.org, and on the United Nations website.

resort, for its judgments are final and without appeal. It is this provision of Article 59 of the Statute that is likely to pose special difficulties for the Court when confronted with this kind of question.

The Supreme Court of the United States has frequently had to face this problem, and the Federal Rules of Evidence make appropriate provision for it. The Court reviewed the issue of scientific evidence at the end of 1997, in a tort case involving medical injuries.[22] Justice Breyer delivered an important concurring opinion regarding the duties of a trial judge to ensure that any and all scientific testimony or evidence admitted is not only relevant, but also reliable.

> 'This requirement will sometimes ask judges to make subtle and sophisticated determinations about scientific methodology and its relation to the conclusions an expert witness seeks to offer, particularly when a case arises in an area where the science itself is tentative or uncertain'.

The learned Justice continued:

> 'I want specially to note that, as cases presenting significant science-related issues have increased in number...judges have increasingly found...ways to help them overcome the inherent difficulty of making determinations about complicated scientific or otherwise technical evidence. Among these techniques are an increased use of...pretrial conference authority to narrow the scientific issues in dispute, pretrial hearings where potential experts are subject to examination by the court, and the appointment of special masters and specially trained law clerks.'

Justice Breyer referred here to an *amicus curiae* brief filed by the *New England Journal of Medicine*. The brief suggested that reputable experts could be recommended to courts by established scientific organizations, such as the National Academy of Sciences or the American Association for the Advancement of Science. He then quoted a provision in the Rules of Evidence to the effect that the court may, of its own motion or on the motion of any party, appoint an expert on behalf of the court. The parties may agree on this expert, or the Court may make the choice. He concluded:

> 'Given this kind of offer of cooperative effort, from the scientific to the legal community, and given the various Rules-authorized methods for facilitating the court's task, it seems to me that [the Court's] gatekeeping requirement will not prove inordinately difficult to implement; and that it will help to secure the basic objectives

[22] *General Electric Company et al Petitioners* v. *Joiner et ux* (1997) Nos. 96-188, 118 S. Ct., 512; LEXIS 7503 at *3. *Certiorari.* This was a toxic tort case, and the action in the Supreme Court related to the lower court's handling of expert evidence. Copy of the opinion of the Supreme Court received through the courtesy of Mr Peter Bekker, of McDermott, Will & Emery of New York.

of the Federal Rules of Evidence; which are, to repeat, the ascertainment of truth and the just determination of proceedings.'[23]

The *amicus curiae* brief filed by the *New England Journal of Medicine* deserves closer scrutiny.[24] Discussing the nature of scientific evidence, the brief made the following remark:

> 'Perhaps the most important hall mark of science is its complete reliance on objectively verifiable evidence. That usually means that something must be counted or measured. The reliance on concrete evidence distinguishes science from all other human endeavors' (p. 5).

Dealing with medical evidence, the brief explains the scientific method. First the scientist needs to formulate the question he wants to answer and design a study that is capable of answering it. After the study is designed, researchers must collect data. 'This is the concept that many nonscientists are least comfortable with, because it "reduces everything to numbers"'. The brief points out (p. 10) that 'everything' cannot be reduced to numbers, but some things can and must be; and it continues:

> 'To reach a conclusion about the physical world, we need numbers because they are often the only way that evidence can be expressed. What is enumerated depends on the study design. When the data are assembled, they must be analyzed appropriately. Often the analysis consists of comparing one set of data with another set to lead to a logical conclusion' (p. 10).

The brief turns to the final step in a research study, drawing the proper conclusions. 'Interpreting a study is perilous because of the strong temptation to reach conclusions that are more encompassing than the evidence will support' (p. 11). And it goes on: 'Mistakes in drawing conclusions are particularly likely when researchers have strong preconceptions about the question they are studying. The conclusions of research study must be limited to those – and only those – that follow logically and necessarily from the data' (p. 11).

The brief looks at what it terms 'Peer review and Publication'.

> 'In science, the requirement for verifiable evidence must be met, no matter what the researchers are or what their credentials. Not even Nobel laureates are permitted to base a scientific conclusion on educated speculation. (They can, of course, speculate or hypothesize, but that speculation will not be accepted as evidence unless it is put to the test.) One of the most important protections against unwarranted conclusions is the system of peer review and publication...Researchers are expected to write up their

[23] LEXIS ibid., at *8.

[24] Brief received through the courtesy of Mr Donald Schnabel of New York, and the *New England Journal of Medicine*, Boston, Massachusetts.

study in a standardized way, with sections dealing with the methods, results, and conclusions, and submit the paper to a scientific journal. The editors of the journal then send the paper for evaluation by other scientists working in the same field. This process of peer review is the cornerstone of scientific research. (Note that scientists performing peer review evaluate the researchers' study design, technical methods, analysis and interpretation, not their principles, theories or hypotheses.)

The reason peer review is so important is that even the most honest researchers cannot be expected to judge their own work dispassionately. They are likely to be enthusiastic about their ideas and, almost by definition, not aware of flaws in the design of their study or the interpretation of their data. The process of interpretation is seldom clear-cut, and it is easy to be unaware that the data are inadequate to support the conclusions. Without the discipline of organizing and presenting their evidence, and without the criticism and revisions stimulated by the peer-review process, researchers may unconsciously misrepresent their work or exaggerate its importance' (pp. 11-12).

Next the brief examines scientific uncertainty. In addition to the reliance on objective evidence collected in properly designed studies, science is also characterized by its tentativeness. 'This may seem counterintuitive to nonscientists who may think science is "cut-and-dried". But, in fact, good scientists rarely reach absolute conclusions' (p. 13). After some further interim discussion, the brief addresses the major question of defining evidence in science and in law.

'The most important feature of scientific research is its dependence on objective evidence. No scientific conclusion can be accepted without evidence. This is perhaps the only feature of science that is absolute. The law also depends on evidence, but the term has a different meaning in a courtroom. The opinion of a properly qualified expert witness is considered to be "evidence". Expert witnesses need not, however, produce objectively verifiable data to buttress their opinions, let alone point to a consistent body of research published in peer-reviewed scientific journals. In a sense, this is the reverse of the scientific method. In science, objective evidence leads to an opinion; in the courtroom, the opinion of an expert becomes evidence. A court's emphasis on the qualifications of expert witnesses is very different from the standards of science, in which *ad hominem* considerations are minimized. Scientists are trained to look at the strength of the data, not the credentials of the researcher.

Associated with the law's emphasis on the credentials of expert-witnesses is a highly individualistic view of science. In the courtroom, the testimony of expert-witnesses may be based on their own research, published or unpublished' (p. 17).

Against that background the brief approaches the cardinal issue of how to bring science and the law together. It is this passage that particularly attracted Justice Breyer's attention. It makes the constructive suggestion that reputable experts could be recommended to courts by established scientific organizations. 'These experts, representing neither side, could evaluate the expert testimony and generally interpret for the judge the current scientific knowledge about the matter at hand. In essence, the scientific community, by relying on its usual methods of research, peer review and publication, would be helping the judge to fulfill his or her required ... role of screening testimony for reliability and relevance' (pp. 18-19). And the conclusion:

> 'A scientific question can be answered only through rigorous scientific research. There should not be one standard for scientists and another for the courtroom' (p. 19).

This idea of combining the rigour of the scientific community with the requirements of the courtroom is worthy of further consideration in the international context. In a sense, that is what the Court did in the merits phase of the *Corfu Channel* case when it requested experienced neutral naval officers to assist it in establishing, or perhaps in better understanding, conflicting or inconclusive testimony about the facts. The Court was careful in that case not to allow the experts to decide the case. 'The Court cannot fail to give great weight to the opinion of the Experts who examined the locality in a manner giving every guarantee of correct and impartial information' (p. 21). From all the facts and observations which it mentioned, the Court drew its own conclusions (p. 22), and those conclusions formed the basis for the conclusions in law on which the Court decided the case.

The concept of enlisting duly qualified scientific bodies in a binding decision-making process has been introduced into modern international law in the United Nations Convention on the Law of the Sea of 1982 (see supra n. 10). Article 289 provides that in any dispute involving scientific or technical matters, a court or tribunal exercising jurisdiction under the Convention may, at the request of a party or *proprio motu*, select in consultation with the parties no fewer than two scientific or technical experts chosen preferably from the relevant list prepared in accordance with Annex VIII of the Convention, to sit with the court or tribunal but without the right to vote. The International Court can (under Article 287 of the Convention) exercise jurisdiction under this Convention, so that Article 289 could be applicable to it provided that the Court is satisfied that it is not incompatible with any provision in the Statute. Annex VIII of the Convention is based on the same conception. It deals with what is there termed 'Special arbitration', that is arbitration by a panel not necessarily composed of lawyers. Four types of special arbitration are envisaged there, relating to: (1) fisheries, (2) protection of the marine environment, (3) marine scientific research and (4) navigation, including pollution from vessels and by dumping. For this purpose, lists of experts are to be drawn up by the Food and Agriculture Organization, the United Nations Environment Programme, the Intergovernmental Oceanographic Commission and the International Maritime Organization. While the parties to a special arbitration do have a certain freedom as to whether the panel shall be composed exclusively of persons on the appropriate list, the International Tribunal for the Law of the Sea, established by Article 287 and Annex VI of that

Convention, will be bound to apply Article 289. In Article 15 of its Rules of Tribunal it has established a regular procedure for the application of Article 289.[25]

The International Court of Justice is the principal judicial organ of the United Nations,[26] and there is a widespread view that this makes it the principal judicial organ of the whole United Nations system. That system includes not only the specialized agencies, two of which (FAO and IMO) only are mentioned in Article 289 of the Law of the Sea Convention, but also a vast and perhaps amorphous conglomeration of miscellaneous organs (many of which would defy formal description within the terms of Article 7 of the United Nations Charter[27]), embracing virtually every branch of human activity. Alongside the inter-governmental bodies, there are an even larger number of non-governmental organizations, including many scientific bodies meeting the requirements that the *New England Journal of Medicine* has enumerated.

Justice Breyer was speaking as a member of the highest court in the land, in a case that had already gone through appropriate proceedings in the lower courts. He mentioned three ways to help judges overcome the inherent difficulty of making determinations about complicated scientific or otherwise technical evidence: pre-trial conference, pre-trial hearings, and the appointment of special masters and specially trained law clerks.

All these machineries exist, at least potentially, in the Statute and Rules of the International Court.

The concept of pre-trial conference was introduced formally (it has always existed in fact) in Article 40, paragraph 1, of the amended Rules of 1972 (previously Article 37 of the 1946 Rules). It is now retained, in a slightly revised form, as Article 31 of the Rules of 1978. As formulated, and as applied in practice in effect from the establishment of the Permanent Court in 1922, these conferences have been limited to participation of the representatives of the parties and the President (including the Acting President) alone, apart from the all-important Registrar. They are 'off the record' in the sense that whatever notes participants may make of them, no formal record is published. No other member of the Court is present. Much of what is discussed at these conferences is not controversial, or not seriously so, such as the fixing of time limits and other aspects of procedure.

[25] Doc. ITLOS/8, 28 October 1997. In fact the idea is older, and is found in Art. 9 of the Convention on Fishing and Conservation of the Living Resources of the High Seas of 1958. That envisaged compulsory dispute settlement by a commission consisting of persons 'specializing in legal, administrative or scientific questions relating to fisheries, depending on the nature of the dispute to be settled'. 559 UNTS 285. No dispute was settled through the application of that provision.

[26] UN Charter, Art. 7.

[27] Cf., D. Sarooshi, 'The Legal Framework Governing United Nations Subsidiary Organs', 67 *The British Year Book of International Law* (1996) p. 413.

The time has come for reconsideration of the function and nature of these consultations and of participation in them. For non-controversial matters, there is no need for any change. But in complicated matters, the question may be asked whether there is not room for developing the whole concept of 'consultation' into some form of pre-trial conference at which issues in dispute could be narrowed down. Could not other Members of the Court be added to the participants? The Vice-President and perhaps the next senior judge? Judges of the nationality of the parties, whether Members of the Court or *ad hoc*? Or perhaps the Chamber of Summary Procedure could be converted into a kind of Steering Committee at which pre-trial controversial aspects could be examined and narrowed down? The President and Vice-President are *ex officio* members of that Chamber and there are provisions for the participation of national or *ad hoc* judges. There are other possibilities, but this is not the place to detail them. The essential point is that under the current Statute and Rules of Court the possibility of a more developed pre-trial conference than has been encountered hitherto certainly exists, and that consideration should be given to expanding its role in appropriate cases. For instance, should the parties in the *Tunisia/Libya* case have been obliged to pursue expensive pleadings about plate tectonic theories if the Court was to find them irrelevant? Could not some procedure have been devised for that issue of relevance in those proceedings to be ironed out earlier? Should Hungary and Slovakia have been put to the huge expense of experts' reports and pleadings, only to be told that the scientific data was irreconcilable, leaving the Court to making some general statements about their duties in regard to the protection of the environment and its reconciliation with economic requirements – problems which in their generality are well known?

The possibility of pre-trial hearings where potential experts are subject to examination by the Court is something that needs to be explored. The Statute would certainly permit the introduction of this procedure, through Article 48. What little experience there is of the examination of party-called experts by the Court in formal hearings – in the *South West Africa* (Merits) cases, for instance – leaves the reader with a deep feeling of unease. By temperament, by training, and by experience, very few of the Members of the International Court of Justice are really qualified to assess the credibility of a witness or the reliability of an expert. The diplomatic or academic background of many of them militates against their finding that a witness was not telling the truth, or that an expert was not being objective or even that the person was not qualified, or holding that a document filed was for any reason not authentic or accurate and for that reason inadmissible. In the *Corfu Channel* (Merits) case the Court simply said what it said '[w]ithout deciding as to the personal sincerity of the witness...or the truth of what he said'.[28] In the *South West Africa* (Merits) case the Court's unease at the

[28] See *supra* n. 13, at p. 16. Re-reading that witness's evidence after the passage of nearly 50 years, one is impressed at the diplomatic manner in which the Court then disposed of the issue of his credibility. It is doubtful if a domestic court would have been so refined.

hearing of a long series of witness-experts and its unhappiness when their expertise was challenged on the *voir-dire* comes through virtually every page of their long testimony.[29] If the authenticity or accuracy of a document is challenged, usually a discreet way is found to dispose of the issue, but occasionally contentions relying on that document have been withdrawn, not requiring any reaction from the Court. [30]

Finally we come to the idea of special masters. In the Anglo-American legal system, the term Master is applied to court officials with quasi-judicial powers, usually subject to control of a judge or an appeal to a judge. A special master is an officer of the court appointed, after consultation with the parties, to assist the court, for instance by hearing about the facts and reporting to the court before the case comes to trial. This leaves the decision to the court. There is nothing to prevent the International Court from adopting such a procedure when it is faced with complicated facts, and especially with technical facts. Here again, Article 48 of the Statute at least, and together with it Articles 49 and 50, supply a statutory basis for the introduction of this type of proceeding.

At the same time, a word of caution is required. It would be essential that all these procedures, if they become applicable in the International Court and in international litigation generally, should be narrowly focused on an immediately relevant issue, whether of fact or of law, or of both, on which the parties and the Court have agreed. If that is not done, there is always a risk that they would degenerate into what is sometimes called a 'fishing expedition'. In domestic litigation processes such as 'discovery' are sometimes used for this purpose, under the control of the court or tribunal seised of the case, and there is no reason why similar practices should not be introduced into the Court's procedure.[31] But that is essentially a procedure between the parties. The three procedures suggested in the US Supreme Court which are seen to be appropriate and applicable in the International Court are not purely procedures *inter partes*, but require the active participation of the Court or its delegated representatives in all phases.

* * *

[29] Cf., on this, K. Highet, 'Evidence, the Chamber and the ELSI case', in R.B. Lillich, ed., *Fact-finding before International Tribunals*, Eleventh Sokol Colloquium (1992) at p. 54, n. 58. See also D.V. Sandifer, *Evidence before International Tribunals*, revised edn. (1975) p. 340.

[30] An incident of this character occurred in the *Arbitral Award of the King of Spain* case, *ICJ Rep.* (1960) p. 192. It is not mentioned in the judgment, but see Pleadings, Vol. II, at pp.168, 169. In the *Maritime Delimitation and Territorial Questions between Qatar and Bahrain* case, one party has challenged the authenticity of a large number of documents filed by the other party. After consultations with the President and after deliberation the Court in its Order of 30 March 1998 adopted a special procedure for dealing with the matter at the stage of the written proceedings, which are pending at this writing, the further proceedings being reserved.

[31] For my earlier suggestions in this regard, see 'Lessons of the Past and Needs of the Future', in C. Peck and R. Lee, eds., *Increasing the Effectiveness of the International Court of Justice* (1997) pp. 466, 489.

The Permanent Court of International Justice adopted the first Rules of Court in 1922. These were amended slightly in 1926, 1927 and 1931. They were thoroughly revised in 1936. The records of the Permanent Court's discussions on those Rules of Court have been published. Experience has shown those records to be essential for a proper understanding of the Rules. The International Court of Justice adopted those Rules, with minor modifications, in 1946. They were amended in 1972 and thoroughly revised in 1978. No records of those discussions have been published. Yet on closer inspection one can see that basically, the Rules as they exist today do not differ in their fundamentals from those first adopted in 1922, notwithstanding the thick crust of judicial experience deposited on them. The original Rules were in the nature of things heavily influenced by international arbitration practice as it had developed throughout the nineteenth century. The 1978 Rules incorporate modifications and additions for the most part based on accretive judicial experience. Yet in fact the Rules have only been seriously re-examined twice since their initial promulgation, in the revisions of 1936 and of 1978. Neither of those revisions disturbed the fundamental structure or elements of the Rules of Court as first set out by the Permanent Court.

It is becoming increasingly realized that international law – all law in fact – is growing daily more interdisciplinary and even multi-interdisciplinary. This interdisciplinary character has two aspects. In one sense, it is becoming more and more difficult to break the law down into independent or semi-independent branches or categories. The classification of a rule of law is a matter of great difficulty, both philosophically and pragmatically. In international law and relations this finds expression in the virtual impossibility of separating substantive and adjectival law – the black-letter rules of the law themselves and the rules of procedure for their application. The second sense of this interdisciplinary character serves to indicate that the law cannot be successfully developed, understood, or applied, in a world of itself. It is interfused with other disciplines, with other branches of human activity, of human interest and of human science. The brief quotations from the *Nuclear Weapons* Advisory Opinion give an inkling of what is in mind.

With these developments rapidly unfolding before our eyes, we have to ask ourselves repeatedly whether the machinery for the application of the law is adequate for twenty-first century life and tasks. Can the principal judicial organ of the United Nations continue to be governed and to govern itself and its activities on the basis of rules now over 75 years old? One can go further. In intellectual and academic circles the question is being asked with growing frequency, whether the settlement of disputes through courts composed exclusively of lawyers is the most appropriate form of a dispute settlement organ. That is the challenge. That is where the Court's procedures for handling evidence and scientific information are urgently in need of *aggiornamento*, of bringing up to date. We have to be grateful to the *New England Journal of Medicine* and to Justice Breyer for their showing us some of the ideas that have to have their place in a modern judicial system.

THE INTERNATIONAL COURT OF JUSTICE AND EQUITABLE MARITIME BOUNDARY DELIMITATION

Barbara Kwiatkowska*

The theme of this Conference – 'The Hague, Legal Capital of the World' – is owed in the decisive measure to The Hague providing the permanent seat of the ICJ as the principal judicial organ of the United Nations. As President Stephen M. Schwebel pointed out in his Statement to the 52nd General Assembly, the United Nations Secretary-General Kofi Annan, in visiting The Hague in March 1997, 'visited what is increasingly seen as the judicial capital of the world'.[1]

When President Schwebel remarked on the occasion of the Court's 50th Anniversary: 'That the Court has made significant contributions to the development of international law – the law of the sea and the law of the United Nations in particular – is unquestioned',[2] he likely had in mind the magnificent jurisprudence initiated by the *Anglo-Norwegian Fisheries* and the *North Sea Continental Shelf* Judgments which laid the foundation for the Court's doctrine of application of equitable principles to maritime boundary delimitation.[3] This

* Professor of International Law of the Sea and Deputy Director of the Netherlands Institute for the Law of the Sea (NILOS), Faculty of Law, Utrecht University.

[1] Statement of the President of the International Court of Justice, Judge Stephen M. Schwebel, to the 52nd United Nations General Assembly, UN Doc. A/52/PV.36, 27 October 1997, pp. 1-5, at p. 1. On the visit of the Secretary-General Kofi Annan to the Court, see *ICJ Communiqué* No.97/5 (24 February 1997); *Report of the International Court of Justice 1 August 1996-31 July 1997,* p. 44, para.145, UN Doc. A/52/4, 1997.

[2] Stephen M. Schwebel, 'Fifty Years of the World Court: A Critical Appraisal', in *Are International Institutions Doing Their Job?, Proceedings of the 90th ASIL Annual Meeting, Washington D.C., 27-30 March 1996*, pp. 339 and 345 (1997); and Plenary Address by President Stephen M. Schwebel on The Contribution of the International Court of Justice to the Development of International Law, elsewhere in the present publication. See also Sir Robert Y. Jennings, 'The International Court of Justice After Fifty Years', 89 *American Journal of International Law* (1995) p. 493; Barbara Kwiatkowska, 'The International Court of Justice and the Law of the Sea – Some Reflections', 11 *International Journal of Marine and Coastal Law* (1996) pp. 491, 499-504, 528-532.

[3] For the origin of the modern exposition of equity, see the 1937 *Diversion of Water from the Meuse* Dissenting Opinion of Judge Hudson, *PCIJ Series A/B*, No.70, pp. 25, 76-77, stating that 'under Article 38 of the Statute, if not independently of that article, the Court has some freedom to consider principles of equity as part of the international law which it must apply.' Cf., Manley O. Hudson, *The Permanent Court of International Justice 1920-1942 – A Treatise* (1943) p. 618.

The Precedential Opinion of Judge Hudson was invoked in the *North Sea* Pleadings Vol.II (Counsel Shigeru Oda) 5 November 1968, p. 200, and subsequently, in the *Fisheries Jurisdiction* Pleadings (UK) (Counsel Silkin, 25 March 1974) p. 473; the *Tunisia/Libya* Pleadings, Vol.I (Memorial of Tunisia) pp. 166 and 167, Vol.IV (16 September 1981, Counsel Jennings) p. 417; the *Tunisia/*

W.P. Heere (Ed.), International Law and The Hague's 750th Anniversary

doctrine has thereafter been restated and further crystallized in all the next decisions involving maritime delimitation,[4] through which the Court and its Chambers contributed importantly to the development of the modern law of the sea as part of the global system of peace and security and as part of general international law. All these Judgments were subsequently implemented through bilateral treaty practice of the respective parties to the disputes concerned.

At the same time the increasing consistency of the Court's doctrine of equitable principles *infra legem* reached a significant stage in the 1993 *Denmark* v. *Norway* (*Jan Mayen*) Judgment which marked notable progress in the accomodation of the operation of equity with by then crystallized principles and rules of the new law of the sea. This progress, apart from the jurisprudence of the Court itself, is also being reinforced by third-party settlements of other courts and tribunals.[5] In a follow-up to the landmark *Denmark* v. *Norway* Judgment, equitable maritime delimitation – in combination with territorial and land boundary questions – is presently involved in three cases. Two of them, namely the

Libya (Merits) Dissenting Opinion of Judge *ad hoc* Evensen, *ICJ Rep.* (1982) pp. 290-291; the *Nicaragua* v. *USA (Provisional Measures)* and *(Merits)* Dissenting Opinions of Judge Schwebel, *ICJ Rep.* (1984) pp.198-9, (1986) pp. 392- 393; the *Denmark* v. *Norway* (Jan Mayen) Separate Opinion of Judge Weeramantry, *ICJ Rep.* (1993) pp. 234-236, and p. 255, n.1; the *Gabčíkovo-Nagymaros Project* Separate Opinion of Judge Koroma, *ICJ Rep.* (1997 in press) and Dissenting Opinion of Judge *ad hoc* Skubiszewski, idem, para.17.

[4] See *Tunisia/Libya Continental Shelf (Merits)* Judgment, *ICJ Rep.* (1982) p. 18 and *Tunisia* v. *Libya (Application for Revision and Interpretation)* Judgment, *ICJ Rep.* (1985) p. 192; *Canada/ United States Delimitation of the Maritime Boundary in the Gulf of Maine Area* Judgment (Chamber), *ICJ Rep.* (1984) p. 246; *Libya/Malta Continental Shelf (Merits)* Judgment, *ICJ Rep.* (1985) p. 13; *El Salvador/Honduras: Nicaragua Intervening Land, Island and Maritime Frontier Dispute* Judgment (Chamber), *ICJ Rep.* (1992) p. 351; *Denmark* v. *Norway Maritime Delimitation in the Area Between Greenland and Jan Mayen* Judgment, *ICJ Rep.* (1993) p. 38.

In the *Greece* v. *Turkey Aegean Sea Continental Shelf (Jurisdiction)* Judgment, *ICJ Rep.* (1978) p. 3, the Court found that it had no jurisdiction to entertain Greece's Application. The *Portugal* v. *Australia East Timor* Judgment, *ICJ Rep.* (1995) p. 90, involved the 1989 Indonesia/Australia Treaty on the Zone of Cooperation in an Area Between the Indonesian Province of East Timor and Northern Australia. In a follow-up to the *Guinea-Bissau* v. *Senegal Arbitral Award of 31 July 1989* Judgment, *ICJ Rep.* (1991) p. 53, and the bilateral delimitation/joint development agreement reached by the parties, the *Guinea-Bissau* v. *Senegal Maritime Delimitation* case was discontiued by means of the Court's Order, *ICJ Rep.* (1995) p. 423.

[5] See the 1977 and 1978 *Anglo/French Delimitation of the Continental Shelf* Decisions of the Court of Arbitration, 18 *RIAA*, pp. 3, 271, and 18 *ILM* (1979) pp. 397, 463 ; 1977 *Argentina/Chile Beagle Channel* Award of the Court of Arbitration and related instruments, 21 *RIAA* (1997) pp. 55-264; 1981 *Iceland/Norway Continental Shelf Area Between Iceland and Jan Mayen* Recommendations of the Conciliation Commission, 20 *ILM* (1981) p. 797; 1981 *Dubai/Sharjah Maritime and Land Boundaries* Award of the Court of Arbitration, 91 *ILR* (1993) p. 543; 1985 *Guinea/Guinea-Bissau Delimitation of the Maritime Boundary* Award of the Arbitration Tribunal, 25 *ILM* (1986) p. 251, and 77 *ILR* (1988) p. 636; 1988 *Egypt/Israel Taba Area* Award of the Arbitration Tribunal, 27 *ILM* (1988), p. 1421, 28 *ILM* (1989) p. 611 and 80 *ILR*, p. 226; 1989 *Guinea-Bissau/Senegal Maritime Frontier* Award of the Arbitral Tribunal, 83 *ILR*, p. 1; 1992 *Canada/France Delimitation of Maritime Areas* Award of the Court of Arbitration, 21 *RIAA* (1997) p. 267 and 31 *ILM* (1992) p. 1165.

Qatar v. *Bahrain* (Merits) and the *Cameroon* v. *Nigeria* (Merits) cases are pending before the Court,[6] whereas the *Eritrea/Yemen* case is pending before the Arbitral Tribunal, which is presided over by Sir Robert Jennings and also comprises two present Members of the Court, Judge Rosalyn Higgins and the current President, Judge Schwebel.[7]

In the light of the jurisprudence of the Court and arbitral decisions, the doctrine of equitable principles is the fundamental norm of customary international law that provides for effecting maritime delimitation by agreement, in accordance with equitable principles, taking account of all relevant circumstances, so as to arrive at an equitable result. Equity operates in this case strictly within the law, and there is consequently no question of any decision *ex aequo et bono*. Moreover, equity has in this case no function of mitigating or modifying the rigidity of legal rule(s), but aims at seeking an equitable result *ab initio*. This is clearly reflected by the requirement of respect for all circumstances that may be relevant in a particular case for the purpose of achieving an equitable result, and by the fact that the use of no single delimitation method, including the Queen method of equidistance, is in all circumstances obligatory. These requirements of customary law governing the Court's doctrine are codified in Articles 74/83 of the 1982 United Nations Law of the Sea Convention[8] which provide for effecting the delimitation of the continental shelf and the exclusive economic zones (EEZs) by agreement, in accordance with international law as referred to in Article 38 of the ICJ Statute, and in order to achieve an equitable solution.[9]

As far as the conceptual framework of applying by the Court of equity *infra legem* to maritime boundary delimitation is concerned, I assume we all agree that the most remarkable exposition of such framework is contained in a Separate Opinion appended by Vice-President Christopher G. Weeramantry to the *Denmark* v. *Norway* Judgment. This is because while reflecting throughout 68 pages

[6] The decisions delivered so far by the Court in these cases include: two *Qatar* v. *Bahrain Maritime Delimitation and Territorial Questions Between Qatar and Bahrain (Jurisdiction and Admissibility)* Judgments, *ICJ Rep.* (1994) p. 112 and (1995) p. 6; *Cameroon* v. *Nigeria Land and Maritime Boundary Between Cameroon and Nigeria (Provisional Measures)* Order, *ICJ Rep.* (1996) p. 13 and *Cameroon* v. *Nigeria (Preliminary Objections)* Judgment of 11 June 1998, *ICJ Rep.* (1998 in press).

[7] See *Report of the Secretary-General on the Work of the Organization*, UN Doc. A/51/1, August 1996, p. 108, para.766. Cf., two essays by Daniel J. Dzurek, *Eritrea/Yemen* Dispute Over the Hanish Islands, 4 *IBRU Boundary and Security Bulletin* (1996/1) pp. 70-77 and Commentary on the Hanish Islands Dispute, 1 *Eritrean Studies Review* (1996) pp. 133-152.

[8] For the text of the 1982 Convention which entered into force on 16 November 1994, see 21 *ILM* (1982) p. 1245. For the text of the 1994 Agreement Relating to the Implementation of Part XI of the Convention which entered into force on 28 July 1996, see 33 *ILM* (1994) p. 1309. See also 34 *ILM* (1995) p. 1393. For the status of the Convention and the Part XI Agreement, as at 16 November 1997, see no. 35 *UN Law of the Sea Bulletin* (1997) p. 19.

[9] See the main text accompanying *infra* nn. 40-42. Cf., Plenary Address of President Schwebel, *supra* n. 2.

of his excellent analysis on the jurisprudential content and practical application of the doctrine of equity in the field of maritime delimitation, Judge Weeramantry does not loose sight of what he calls 'the broader equitable landscape lying beyond', which is indeed indispensable for a proper appreciation of all far-reaching legal questions raised by an equitable jurisprudence.[10]

An advantage of the conceptual framework drawn by Judge Weeramantry also lies in its perfect timing. Until the *Denmark* v. *Norway* Judgment, the uncertainties of equity – which the Vice-President rightly finds as being intrinsic to its operation and as amounting to one of its strenghts[11] – were compounded by the fact that the law of the sea has been undergoing a process of spectacular change.[12] Consequently, as he observes, it was no cause for surprise that 'flexible principles superimposed upon so fluid a subject should have failed to produce a greater predictability of legal result'.[13] The *Denmark* v. *Norway* Judgment crowned the equitable jurisprudence at the time when the principles and rules of the modern oceans regime reached the stage of significant crystallization. The most valuable doctrinal surveys also have already been written by that time. Such surveys, which are all taken into account in Judge Weeramantry's Opinion, include in particular an outstanding essay by Ambassador Shabtai Rosenne on 'The Position of the International Court of Justice on the Foundations of the Principle of Equity in International Law'[14] and several works written by the Members of the Court.

In fact, for the past three triennia the Court has been presided over by the Judges who all contributed prominently to the theory and practice of equitable maritime boundary delimitation. Former President Sir Robert Jennings (1991/94), who was involved in the famous *Anglo/French* arbitration and all delimitation decisions of the Court in the years 1982/1995, elaborated closer on his approach in two brilliant essays published prior to the *Denmark* v. *Norway* Judgment.[15] While Sir Robert did not participate in the *Gulf of Maine* Chamber, he borrowed

[10] *Denmark* v. *Norway (Jan Mayen)* Separate Opinion of Judge Weeramantry, *ICJ Rep.* (1993) pp. 211-279.

[11] *Idem.*, p. 254, para.156, and p. 255, para.159.

[12] *Idem.*, pp. 256-257, para.161.

[13] *Idem.*, p. 257, para.162.

[14] Shabtai Rosenne, *An International Law Miscellany*, chapter 7: The Position of the International Court of Justice on the Foundations of the Principle of Equity in International Law (1993) pp. 201-230; reprinted from *Forty Years of the International Court of Justice: Jurisdiction, Equity and Equality* (1988) pp. 85-108, as relied upon in *Denmark* v. *Norway (Jan Mayen)* Separate Opinion of Judge Weeramantry.

[15] Sir Robert Jennings, 'Equity and Equitable Principles', 42 *Annuaire Suisse de Droit International* (1986) pp. 27-38, and 'The Principles Governing Marine Boundaries', in *Staat und Völkerrechtsordung, Festschrift für Karl Doehring* (1989) pp. 398-408, as both relied upon in *Denmark* v. *Norway (Jan Mayen)* Separate Opinion of Judge Weeramantry. Cf., Barbara Kwiatkowska, 'Equitable Maritime Delimitation, as Exemplified in the Work of the International Court of Justice During the Presidency of Sir Robert Yewdall Jennings and Beyond', 28 *Ocean Development and International Law* (1997) pp. 91, 92.

from Judge André Gros the analogy of the early days of the English Court of Chancery when the result of suit was said by the cynics to depend upon the size of the Chancellor's foot.[16] In his attempt to move away from this concept towards a more predictable system of equitable procedures, Sir Robert has hoped in 1989 for 'the wheel coming full circle'. Since the legal entitlement to the EEZ and the continental shelf up to 200 miles became based on the principle of distance to the exclusion of natural prolongation, the circle could be closed by the necessary resort in maritime delimitation to equidistance as normally implied by the principle of distance.[17]

The chance seemed increased when President Jennings was joined by another outstanding advocate of the concept of equity as modifying the rigidity of a legal rule, Judge Shigeru Oda, as his Vice-President.[18] But the almost unanimous *Denmark* v. *Norway* (*Jan Mayen*) Judgment – in which the then President Jennings and Vice-President Oda and Judge Weeramantry, as well as both next Presidents, Judges Mohammed Bedjaoui and Stephen M. Schwebel, all concurred – made it clear that the wheel did not come full circle. The Judgment did, however, confirm the *Gulf of Maine* and the *Libya/Malta (Merits)* finding as to the use of equidistance in the first stage of provisional delimitation between opposite states.[19] Whether the wheel will yet come or not full circle in the pending *Eritrea/Yemen* arbitration presided over by Sir Robert or in any other case remains to be seen, but such prospect does not seem likely.

Sir Robert's immediate successor as President, Judge Mohammed Bedjaoui (1994/97), has been a supporter of an autonomous role of equity as a 'lead rule' and marked his prominence in the equitable jurisprudence by serving as an Arbitrator in the *Guinea/Guinea-Bissau* and *Guinea-Bissau/Senegal* Tribunals and by participating in all the respective decisions of the Court since 1982.[20] Whereas Judge Bedjaoui was not a Member of the *Gulf of Maine* and the *Gulf of Fonseca* Chambers, he presided over the *Burkina Faso/Mali* Chamber, which

[16] Jennings, Equity, loc. cit. n. 15, at p. 31, quoting the *Gulf of Maine* Dissenting Opinion of Judge Gros, *ICJ Rep.* (1984) p. 386, para.41. Cf., views of Judge Jennings quoted in *Denmark* v. *Norway (Jan Mayen)* Separate Opinion of Judge Weeramantry, *ICJ Rep.* (1993) pp. 226-227, para.54.

[17] Jennings, The Principles, loc. cit. n. 15, at p. 408.

[18] See Barbara Kwiatkowska, 'Judge Shigeru Oda's Opinions in Law-of-the-Sea Cases: Equitable Maritime Boundary Delimitation', 36 *German Yearbook of International Law*(1993) pp. 225, 288-294 .

[19] *Denmark* v. *Norway (Jan Mayen)* Judgment, *ICJ Rep.* (1993) pp. 59-62, paras. 49-53.

[20] See especially the *Libya/Malta (Merits)* Joint Separate Opinion co-authored by Judge Bedjaoui with two other advocates of the autonomous role of equity, Judges Ruda and Jiménez de Aréchaga, *ICJ Rep.* (1985) pp. 76-92, as cited in *Denmark* v. *Norway (Jan Mayen)* Separate Opinion of Judge Weeramantry, *ICJ Rep.* (1993) p. 223, para.37 and p. 256, para.159. But note support of equidistance as the most equitable delimitation line in the 1989 *Guinea-Bissau/Senegal* Dissenting Opinion of Arbitrator Bedjaoui, paras. 147-149. Cf., Barbara Kwiatkowska, 'The Law of the Sea Related Cases in the International Court of Justice During the Presidency of Judge Mohammed Bedjaoui (1994/1997)', in *Liber Amicorum – Mohammed Bedjaoui* (1998 in press).

considered resort to equity *infra legem* in the context of land boundary delimitation.[21] This experience resulted in Judge Bedjaoui's admirable survey on 'L "Énigme" des "principes équitables" dans le droit des délimitations maritimes', where he describes equity as 'a riddle wrapped in a mystery inside an enigma', although he admits the increasing consistency of the doctrine of equitable principles.[22]

An overall importance of the Court's role in this respect also found reflection in a Statement made in 1994 by then President Bedjaoui to the 49th General Assembly where he pointed out: 'The Court itself, incidentally, has on several occasions explained that the fact of its deciding in law by no means rules out – quite to the contrary – due regard for equity *infra legem* or, in other words, "that form of equity which constitutes a method of interpretation of the law in force, and is one of its attributes".'[23] This approach corresponds to the view of Ambassador Rosenne relied upon in the *Denmark* v. *Norway* Separate Opinion of Vice-President Weeramantry as summarizing well the operation of equity *infra legem* in the general jurisprudence of the Court as follows: 'It [the Court] has permitted the first steps to be taken towards creating a conception of international equity, not *contra legem* in the sense that it is sometimes said that a decision *ex aequo et bono* may be a decision *contra legem*; but *intra legem*, it being the substantive law, and not the agreement of the parties, that calls for its application.'[24] And in another part of his Opinion, Judge Weeramantry agrees with Rosenne that: 'The International Court has been very careful – and in this respect it may be possible to speak of a "position" since fundamental questions of judicial policy are involved – to formulate its resort to "equity" not in terms of "opposition" to "law", but in terms of fulfilling the law and if necessary supplementing it.'[25]

[21] *Burkina Faso/Mali Frontier Dispute* Judgment, *ICJ Rep.* (1986) pp. 554, 567-568, paras. 27-28, and p. 633, paras. 149-150; and Separate Opinion of Judge *ad hoc* Abi-Saab, idem, pp. 662-663, paras. 16-17. Cf., Rosenne, *An International Law Miscellany*, op. cit. n. 14, at pp. 208, 214 and 218.

[22] Mohammed Bedjaoui, 'L'Énigme' des 'principes équitables' dans le droit des délimitations maritimes', XLII *Revista Española de Derecho Internacional* (1990) pp. 367, 387, as cited in *Denmark* v. *Norway (Jan Mayen)* Separate Opinion of Judge Weeramantry, *ICJ Rep.* (1993) p. 217, paras. 14 and 18.

[23] Statement of the President of the International Court of Justice, Judge Mohammed Bedjaoui, to the 49th United Nations General Assembly, UN Doc. A/49/PV.29, 13 October 1994, p. 1, at p. 4, reprinted in the *ICJ Yearbook 1994-1995* (No.49) pp. 207, 211-212. Cf., M. Bedjaoui, 'La place de la Cour internationale de justice dans le système général de maintien de la paix institué par la Charte des Nations Unies', 8 *African Journal of International and Comparative Law* (1996) pp. 541, 545.

[24] *Denmark* v. *Norway (Jan Mayen)* Separate Opinion of Judge Weeramantry, *ICJ Rep.* (1993) p. 233, para.70 and pp. 238-9, para.89, n.1, quoting Shabtai Rosenne, *The Law and Practice of the International Court*, 2nd edn. (1965/1985) p. 605. This view is retained in Shabtai Rosenne, *The Law and Practice of the International Court, 1920-1996*, 3rd edn. (1997) pp. 1595-1596 .

[25] *Denmark* v. *Norway (Jan Mayen)* Separate Opinion of Judge Weeramantry, *ICJ Rep.* (1993) p. 231, para.64, p. 234, para.73, and pp. 241-242, paras. 99-101, quoting Rosenne, The Position, op. cit. n. 14, at pp. 88-89; reprinted in Rosenne, *An International Law Miscellany*, op. cit. n. 14, at pp. 204, 230.

The current President, Judge Stephen M. Schwebel (1997/2000), has been involved in all maritime delimitation decisions of the Court since 1981, was a Member of the precedential *Gulf of Maine* Chamber[26] and serves at present as an Arbitrator in the *Eritrea/Yemen* Tribunal.[27] He was not a Member of the *Gulf of Fonseca* Chamber, but through his *Tunisia/Libya* and *Libya/Malta* Opinions on third state intervention,[28] Judge Schwebel – along with Judges José Sette-Camara, Shigeru Oda and Sir Robert Jennings, who all also filed Opinions in the two negative Libyan decisions and who later formed part of the *Gulf of Fonseca* Chamber – importantly contributed to a more liberal approach to such intervention in maritime delimitation. In culmination of this process, the *Gulf of Fonseca* Chamber, in its unanimous Judgment of 1990, for the first time in the history of the World Court, granted a state permission to intervene as a non-party under Article 62 of the ICJ Statute.[29]

The essence of the doctrine of equitable principles was adequately seized in Judge Schwebel's *Gulf of Maine* Separate Opinion when he remarked that 'on a question such as this, the law is more plastic than formed, and elements of judgment, of appreciation of competing legal and equitable considerations, are *dominant*.'[30] In a similar vein, he observes in his Plenary Address delivered at this Conference that: 'Whether the salience of equitable considerations in maritime delimitation is sound in law is a matter of controversy. But what is beyond controversy is the influential role played the Court.'[31]

While concurring in the *Gulf of Maine* Judgment, Judge Schwebel voiced his disagreement with the Chamber's treatment of the inclusion of the Bay of Fundy into the Gulf of Maine for purposes of calculations of proportionality. In the *Libya/Malta (Merits)* case, Judge Schwebel found the process which the Court followed with respect to reliance on the notional intercontinental (Africa-Libya/Europe-Italy) equidistance, treatment of the proportionality tests and other issues

[26] See S.M. Schwebel, *Justice in International Law – Selected Writings of Judge Stephen M. Schwebel*, chapter 6: Chambers of the International Court of Justice Formed for Particular Cases (1994) pp. 93-124.

[27] See *supra* n. 7.

[28] *Tunisia/Libya (Application by Malta for Permission to Intervene)* Separate Opinion of Judge Schwebel, *ICJ Rep.* (1981) pp. 35-40; *Libya/Malta (Application by Italy for Permission to Intervene)* Dissenting Opinion of Judge Schwebel, *ICJ Rep.* (1984) pp. 131-147 and *Libya/Malta (Merits)* Dissenting Opinion of Judge Schwebel, *ICJ Rep.* (1985) pp. 172, 172-178.

[29] *El Salvador/Honduras Land, Island and Maritime Frontier Dispute (Application by Nicaragua for Permission to Intervene)* Judgment, *ICJ Rep.* (1990) p. 92. Cf., Jennings, loc. cit.n. 2, at pp. 499-500; Kwiatkowska, loc.cit. n. 15, at pp. 96-99.

[30] *Gulf of Maine* Separate Opinion of Judge Schwebel, *ICJ Rep.* (1984) pp. 353, 357 (emphasis added). Cf., idem, pp. 357-358, as reaffirmed in the *Libya/Malta (Merits)* Dissenting Opinion of Judge Schwebel, *ICJ Rep.* (1985) p. 187. See also the *Tunisia/Libya (Merits)* and *Tunisia* v. *Libya (Application for Revision and Interpretation of the Judgment)* Separate Opinions of Judge Schwebel, *ICJ Rep.* (1982) p. 99, and (1985) p. 246; and his *Denmark* v. *Norway (Jan Mayen)* Separate Opinion quoted in the main text accompanying *infra* nn. 45-46.

[31] Plenary Address of President Schwebel, *supra* n. 2.

to be so far from that followed in the *Gulf of Maine* case and other adjudications that he dissented from the 1985 Judgment.[32] He reiterated his criticism in the 1993 *Denmark* v. *Norway* Separate Opinion remarking that: 'The obscure measure of adjustment of the median line between Libya and Malta appears to have had the benefit of inspiration, if divine, then from Roman gods, for the line selected just happened essentially to coincide with the limit of the claims of a third State, Italy, whose claims the Court paradoxically earlier had declined to pass upon.'[33]

President Schwebel was no less critical of the boundary arrived at in the *Denmark* v. *Norway* Judgment observing that: 'In the current case, the measure of adjustment seems to have followed, if not from the inspiration of Norse gods, then from considerations of symmetry, once the decision was made to furnish 'equitable access' to the southern sector in which capelin may be fished.'[34] He added that: 'In Selden's seventeenth-century days, equity was described as the Chancellor's conscience, variable indeed; it was as if the standard of measurement called a foot were to be the length of the Chancellor's foot, "an uncertain measure". (Polllock, ed., *Table Talk of John Selden,* 1927, p.43.) Nowadays, equity is to be impressionistically measured by the length of opposite coastlines.'[35] Notwithstanding his apparent discomfort, Judge Schwebel concurred in the *Denmark* v. Norway Judgment believing that on the whole: 'Based on large and loose approaches such as its gross impression of the effects of differing lengths of coasts, its desire to afford equitable access to fishing resources, and the attraction of the symmetrical conjoinder of indicated lines of delimitation, the Court comes up with a line which, given the criteria employed, may be as reasonable as another.'[36]

In the ending sentence of his Separate Opinion, Judge Schwebel remarked that: 'Where this leaves the law of maritime delimitation, to the extent that such a law subsists, is perplexing.'[37] However, a number of other authorities would agree that the elegantly drafted *Denmark* v. *Norway* Judgment, through confirmation of the two-stage decision-making process of the Court and through its masterly findings regarding the issues of substance, fulfilled Sir Robert's anticipation as to the degree of predictability and judicial consistency required

[32] *Libya/Malta (Merits)* Dissenting Opinion of Judge Schwebel, *ICJ Rep.* (1985), p. 172, raising his criticism with the limited scope of operation of the 1985 Judgment which resulted from rejection of Italy's Application in the 1984 *Libya/Malta (Intervention)* Judgment, idem, pp. 172-178; and with inadequate justification of the Court's boundary line by the applicable principles of law and equity, idem, pp 178-187.

[33] *Denmark* v. *Norway (Jan Mayen)* Separate Opinion of Judge Schwebel, *ICJ Rep.* (1993) pp. 118, 125.

[34] *Idem*, pp. 125-126.

[35] *Idem*, p. 126.

[36] *Idem*, pp. 128-129.

[37] *Idem*, p 129.

from equity operating *infra legem*.[38] This results from the Court's pronouncements on the uniformity of the effects of treaty and customary law governing equitable maritime boundary delimitation, as well as on the single boundary line, proportionality, resource factors and other substantive issues.[39]

The 1977 *Anglo/French* Decision, which was the first to address the North Sea-introduced distinction between conventional and customary rules, was significant in its finding that the equidistance/special circumstances rule of the 1958 United Nations Continental Shelf Convention (Article 6) should be regarded as giving expression to the customary norm of equitable principles enunciated in the *North Sea* Judgment.[40] It is, therefore, equally significant that the *Denmark* v. *Norway* Judgment now determined that the equidistance/special circumstances rule of the 1958 Convention (Article 6) – which the Court had the very first occasion to apply in the *Denmark* v. *Norway* case[41] – 'produces much the same result' as an equitable principles/relevant circumstances rule of customary law, and that likewise the requirements of the 1982 Law of the Sea Convention (Articles 74/83) correspond to those of customary law.[42] This uniformity will significantly facilitate the equitable delimitation settlements between parties and nonparties to the respective treaties.

At the second stage of its decision-making process in the *Denmark* v. *Norway* (Jan Mayen) case, the Court adjusted its provisional boundary line so as to attribute a larger area of maritime space to Denmark than would the equidistant (median) line, and for the purpose of defining the final line, it divided the area of overlapping claims into Zones 1, 2 and 3.[43] Ultimately, the factor of the marked disparity in coastal lengths of Greenland and Jan Mayen was decisive in determining the course of the boundary in Zones 2 and 3 of the area of overlapping claims which were not subject to an equal division, whereas the fisheries factor influenced the division of Zone 1 into two parts of equal area so as to ensure an equitable access to the migratory stock of capelin in this zone for the vulnerable fishing communities concerned. With respect to the division of Zone 1, the *Denmark* v. *Norway* Judgment entails therefore a precedential reliance on exception of 'catastrophic repercussions' established by the *Gulf of*

[38] See Jennings, Equity, loc. cit. n.15, at p. 38, quoted by Eduardo Jiménez de Aréchaga, Counsel of Denmark, ICJ *Denmark* v. *Norway* Verbatim Record of Pleadings, CR 93/2. at p. 60.

[39] Cf., Kwiatkowska, loc. cit. n. 15, at pp. 101-107, including remarks, *idem*, p. 107, on implementation of the Court's Judgment by means of the 1995 Denmark/Norway Agreement.

[40] 1977 *Anglo/French Delimitation of the Continental Shelf* Decision, para.70, as quoted in the *Denmark* v. *Norway (Jan Mayen)* Judgment, *ICJ Rep.* (1993) p. 58, para.46.

[41] *Denmark* v. *Norway (Jan Mayen)* Judgment, *ICJ Rep.* (1993) p. 58, para.45.

[42] *Denmark* v. *Norway (Jan Mayen)* Judgment, *ICJ Rep.* (1993) pp. 58-59, paras. 46-48, and Separate Opinion of Judge Weeramantry, idem, pp. 234-235, paras. 75-77, and pp. 259-261, paras. 172-179; *supra* n. 9 and *infra* n. 53. By analogy, the same applies to Art. 15 of the 1982 Law of the Sea Convention.

[43] *Denmark* v. *Norway (Jan Mayen)* Judgment, *ICJ Rep.* (1993) p. 77, para.87, and pp. 79-81, paras. 91-94, including sketch map No.2, at p. 80.

Maine Judgment with a view of taking account of economic factors in drawing an equitable boundary line.[44] President Schwebel considers this *Denmark* v. *Norway* finding questionable[45] and cautions that:

> 'the Court by this holding of distributive justice has departed from the accepted law of the matter, as fashioned pre-eminently by it. It is not suggested that this departure from principle and precedent is legally fatal. If what is lawful in maritime delimitation by the Court is what is equitable, and if what is equitable is as variable as the weather of The Hague, then this innovation may be seen as, and it may be, as defensible and desirable as another. It may be more defensible and desirable than that concerning the length of coastlines.'[46]

I assume not many of us would challenge that 'what is equitable is as variable as the weather of The Hague', but perhaps some of us may wonder whether by its reliance on the fisheries factor, the *Denmark* v. *Norway* Judgment has indeed departed 'from the accepted law of the matter, as fashioned pre-eminently' by the Court? While endorsing the Court's finding, Vice-President Weeramantry states in his Separate Opinion that:

> 'Access to fishery resources is a matter to which the Court has rightly devoted particular attention and I am in agreement with this approach and with its resultant effect upon the overall delimitation.'[47]

It is true that the Court and other tribunals, basing themselves on the premise that equity does not operate in maritime boundary delimitation as *justitia distributiva*, have tended to exclude the relevance of economic (and likewise environmental) factors to such delimitation with a view to ensuring the application of equity *infra legem* and in a manner as objective as possible. But as I have hoped elsewhere, this restrictive position could be subject to evolution towards more liberal approach, under which economic considerations were to be included into circumstances relevant to maritime delimitation.[48] The reason of my hope, as now fulfilled by the *Denmark* v. *Norway* Judgment, was the fact that the Court has never restricted relevant circumstances to those which are pertinent to legal

[44] *Idem*, pp. 71-72, paras. 75-76, quoting the *Gulf of Maine* Judgment, *ICJ Rep.* (1984) p. 342, para.237.

[45] *Denmark* v. *Norway (Jan Mayen)* Separate Opinion of Judge Schwebel, *ICJ Rep.* (1993) pp. 118-120.

[46] *Idem*, p. 120.

[47] *Denmark* v. *Norway (Jan Mayen)* Separate Opinion of Judge Weeramantry, *ICJ Rep.* (1993) p. 268, para.212. Cf., idem, pp. 245-247, paras. 110-121, and p. 277, para.241. Note also strong emphasis on applicability of economic factors in the 1989 *Guinea-Bissau/Senegal* Dissenting Opinion of Arbitrator Bedjaoui.

[48] See Barbara Kwiatkowska, 'Economic and Environmental Considerations in Maritime Boundary Delimitations', in Jonathan I. Charney and L.M. Alexander eds, *International Maritime Boundaries* (ASIL 1993) pp. 75, 103-113.

entitlement to the delimited areas, but held instead that equity requires the taking into account of all those considerations that are pertinent to 'the institutions' of the continental shelf and 200-mile zones as they have developed within the law, and to the application of equitable principles to their delimitation.[49]

Moreover, as Judge Weeramantry noted, however restricted was the *Gulf of Maine* exception of 'catastrophic repercussions', it amounted to a recognition that fisheries factors 'can play a part in the overall result',[50] and the Court has already partly acknowledged that also other economic circumstances may be relevant to maritime boundary delimitation.[51] Due to the essential relevance of those circumstances to maritime delimitation, the subjectivity inherent in their consideration would not seem to be a decisive factor, especially that even such objective factors as the geography necessarily require arbitrary or, as President Schwebel put it, 'impressionistic'[52] assessments. Nor would the changeableness of resource factors, due to depletion over time, justify the rejection of those factors by the Court. This more liberal approach is also supported by the open-endedness of Articles 74/83 of the Law of the Sea Convention which leaves it to states themselves, or to the Court and other tribunals, by which methods should a goal of an equitable solution based on international law be achieved.[53] Were an appreciable role aligned by the *Denmark* v. *Norway* Judgment to fisheries factors prove to be exceptional, there still exists an additional, unstated alternative that, in spite of a formal rejection of the relevance of economic factors, the Court and other tribunals do and will continue – within their judicial discretion perceived by Judge Weeramantry as a necessary part of the judicial process[54] – to take such factors into account in the delimitation process.[55]

Whether in form of expressly articulated principle or that of unstated alternative, the fisheries and other resource related considerations do, moreover, conform with global traditions of equity aligned by Vice-President Weeramantry to the concepts of a higher trust of earth resources and their conservation for the

[49] Cf., *Libya/Malta (Merits)* Judgment, *ICJ Rep.* (1985) p. 40, para.48; as cited in *Denmark* v. *Norway (Jan Mayen)* Separate Opinion of Judge Weeramantry, *ICJ Rep.* (1993) p. 261, para.181.

[50] *Denmark* v. *Norway (Jan Mayen)* Separate Opinion of Judge Weeramantry, *ICJ Rep.* (1993) pp. 269-270, para.219. Cf., Prosper Weil, *The Law of Maritime Delimitation – Reflections* (1989) p.261, noting that: 'One cannot help asking oneself, however, whether, although it defends itself against the charge, the Chamber did not in fact treat socio-economic factors as a consideration which could not be ignored'.

[51] Cf., Kwiatkowska, loc. cit n. 48, at p. 108.

[52] See *supra* n. 35.

[53] See *Libya/Malta (Merits)* Judgment, *ICJ Rep.* (1985) pp. 30-31, para.28; and *supra* n. 42.

[54] *Denmark* v. *Norway (Jan Mayen)* Separate Opinion of Judge Weeramantry, *ICJ Rep.* (1993) pp. 251-252, paras. 140-142, quoting (idem, p. 252, n.1) Christopher G. Weeramantry, 'The Importance of Philosophical Perspectives in the Judicial Process', 6 *Connecticut Journal of International Law* (1991) p. 599. Cf., Rosenne, *An International Law Miscellany*, op. cit. n. 14, at pp. 211-212.

[55] Cf., Kwiatkowska, loc. cit. n. 44, at p.107 and p. 110.

benefit of future generations.[56] A particular obligation – stressed by the Vice-President – of the multicultural Court to search in all these traditions of equity[57] has been recently fulfilled through contributions made by the 1997 *Hungary/Slovakia Gabčíkovo-Nagymaros Project* Judgment and an excellent Separate Opinion appended to it by Vice-President Weeramantry to the development of environmental law.[58] These contributions include recognition of the modern concept of the environmental protection for present and future generations, reaffirmation of the *sic utere tuo ut alienum non laedas* principle, definition of the critical concept of sustainable development, and other pronouncements to be further addressed by former Counsel of Hungary, Professor Alexander Ch. Kiss.[59]

In conclusion, we may feel inclined to share the view of President Stephen M. Schwebel that the equitable jurisprudence provides an outstanding instance exemplifying an 'intrinsic' authority of the Court's decisions and the coherence of its case-law in terms of fundamental factors which enable the Court to contribute to the development of international law.[60]

[56] *Denmark* v. *Norway (Jan Mayen)* Separate Opinion of Judge Weeramantry, *ICJ Rep.* (1993) pp. 273-279, paras. 233-248.

[57] *Idem*, p. 273, para.234. Cf., Christopher G. Weeramantry, 'Some Practical Problems of International Adjudication', 17 *Australian Yearbook of International Law* (1996) pp. 1, 11-15.

[58] *ICJ Rep.* (1997 in press). On significance of the *Gabčíkovo-Nagymaros Project* Judgment, see Statement of President Schwebel, *supra* n. 1, and his Plenary Address, *supra* n. 2.

[59] Alexander Ch. Kiss, 'The International Court of Justice and the Protection of the Environment', elsewhere in the present publication. Cf., Barbara Kwiatkowska, 'The 19th United Nations General Assembly Special Session to Review Implementation of Agenda 21 and the *Hungary/Slovakia Gabčíkovo-Nagymaros Project* Judgment', A paper presented at the SEAPOL International Conference on Ocean Governance and System Compliance in the Asia-Pacific Context, Rayong, Thailand, 9-11 December 1997.

[60] See Plenary Address of President Schwebel, *supra* n. 2.

THE INTERNATIONAL COURT OF JUSTICE AND THE PROTECTION OF THE ENVIRONMENT

Alexandre Kiss*

One of the most fascinating problems in law is the response of a legal system to challenges created by the emergence of new problems. The need to protect human rights by international legal rules and institutions, the necessity to elaborate legal regimes for the outer space and for the deep seabed and, more recently, the awareness of the deterioration of the biosphere as a consequence of human activities were such challenges.

The UN Charter which established the International Court of Justice gives the Court the power to decide legal disputes concerning environmental matters which are submitted to it by the parties to the dispute. Agenda 21 drafted by the UN Conference on Environment and Development, encourages the recourse of states to the ICJ in this field (Chapter 39.10). Even long before this exhortation, a large number of international environmental treaties and conventions including provisions concerning environmental protection provided for the submission of disputes arising from their interpretation or application to the ICJ. Today most of the major treaties concerning environmental protection include such provisions.

In a statement at the UN Conference on Environment and Development held in Rio de Janeiro in June 1992, sir Robert Jennings, then President of the Court, declared that the Court was ready to accept such matters and to participate in the development of general international law and of environmental law in particular. Another expression of the Court's willingness to address the environmental aspects of international legal problems was its decision to establish a seven-member chamber for environmental matters. So far the Chamber has not been used.

During the past decade, the International Court of Justice has had submitted to it five matters concerning environmental protection. Three of the matters address the impact of nuclear weapons or weapons testing on the environment. Two cases more generally arose from environmental harm. Although one of the latter cases has been settled by negotiation between the parties[1] the Court used the opportunity to discuss the other questions which were submitted to it to develop environmental concepts and norms.

* President, European Council on Environmental Law.

[1] Case of Certain Phosphate *Lands in Nauru* (*Nauru* v. *Australia*).

W.P. Heere (Ed.), International Law and The Hague's 750th Anniversary

BASIC ENVIRONMENTAL CONCEPTS AND PRINCIPLES

The Court recognized several times the fundamental importance of environmental protection. In a contentious case filed by Australia and New Zealand against France challenging the legality of nuclear testing in the South Pacific, the Court held that the prior proceedings had closed and no new basis for jurisdiction existed, but noted that its conclusion was 'without prejudice to the obligations of States to respect and protect the natural environment.'[2] In the Advisory Opinion on the Legality of the Threat or Use of Nuclear Weapons (hereafter 'Advisory Opinion')[3] it stated that the environment is under daily threat and the use of nuclear weapons could constitute a catastrophe for the environment. In his separate opinion Judge Weeramantry stressed this point, making reference to the statement of the World Commission on Environment and Development. He also evoked the threat of a nuclear winter[4] which would also endanger the world's food production,[5] contaminate and destroy the food chain, imperil the ecosystem and produce lethal levels of heat and blast.[6] In his Declaration commenting on the Advisory Opinion, Judge Bedjaoui, President of the Court, affirmed that the existence of nuclear weapons is a challenge to the very existence of humanitarian law, 'not to mention their long-term effects or damage to the human environment, in respect to which the right to life can be exercised.'[7]

In two different statements, the Court declared that the environment is not an abstraction but represents the living space, the quality of life and the very health of human beings: in the Advisory Opinion and[8] in the *Gabčíkovo-Nagymaros Project* case.[9] As a consequence, the Court found that states have the obligation to respect and protect the natural environment.[10]

It is important to note that the Court places such obligations in the time dimension which is inherent in environmental protection:

> 'Throughout the ages, mankind has, for economic and other reasons, constantly interfered with nature. In the past, this was often done without consideration of the

[2] See Request for an Examination of the Situation in Accordance with Paragraph 63 of the Court's Judgment of 20 December 1974 in the *Nuclear Tests* case (*New Zealand* v. *France*), Order of 22 September 1995, *ICJ Rep.* (1995).

[3] Legality of the Threat or Use of Nuclear Weapons, Advisory Opinion of July 8, U.N. Document, reprinted in 35 *ILM* (1996) pp. 809, 1343.

[4] Dissenting opinion, pp. 16-19.

[5] *Idem*, p. 27.

[6] *Idem*, p. 29.

[7] Declaration, para. 20.

[8] *Idem*, para. 29.

[9] *Gabčíkovo-Nagymaros Project* (*Hungary* v. *Slovakia*), Judgment of 28 September 1997, General List No.92, para. 112.

[10] Order of 22 September 1995 in the Request for an Examination of the Situation in Accordance with Paragraph 63 of the Court's Judgment of 20 December 1974 in the *Nuclear Tests* case, *ICJ Rep.* (1995) p. 306, para. 64.

effects upon the environment. Owing to new scientific awareness and a growing awareness of the risks for mankind – for present and future generations – of pursuit of such interventions at an unconsidered and unabated pace, new norms and standards have been developed, set forth in a great number of instruments during the last two decades. Such new norms have to be taken into consideration, and such new standards given proper weight, not only when States contemplated new activities but also when continuing with activities in the past.'[11]

This statement combines the guiding principle concerning past and present activities: they all should be directed by present international legal norms.[12] In his dissenting opinion, Judge Herczegh emphasizes this point, expressing his regret that the Court did not apply present international environmental rules in the declaratory part of the Judgment.[13]

The position of the Court in the Advisory Opinion and in the *Gabčíkovo* case also opens another perspective, that of future generations, already mentioned in the Advisory Opinion in its reference to 'human beings, including generations unborn.'[14] Judge Weeramantry reminds readers in his separate opinion that the rights of future generations have woven themselves into international law through major treaties, through juristic opinions and through general principles of law recognized by civilized nations.[15]

The Court also makes it clear that the concern of a State for its natural environment constitutes an 'essential interest' of that State.[16] The Court recognized in the *Gabčíkovo* case that the Project's impact upon, and implications for the environment are of necessity a key issue.[17] However, as Judge Herczegh points out in his dissenting opinion, the Court did not consider ecological concerns superior to financial ones. According to him, the Court should have given priority to the environment, applying the principle *in dubio pro natura.* [18]

Another important statement of the Court provides a definition of sustainable development: it is found in the reconciliation of economic development and the protection of the environment.[19] In his separate opinion, Judge Weeramantry, at the time Vice-President of the Court, develops the relationship between the two principles of environmental protection and sustainable development and con-

[11] *Gabčikovo* case, para. 140.

[12] See also Vice-President Weeramantry's statement on the inter-temporal aspect of all treaties dealing with projects impacting on the environment, separate opinion, p.22.

[13] Dissenting opinion, pp. 2-3.

[14] *Gabčikovo* case, para. 29.

[15] Dissenting opinion, p. 17.

[16] *Gabčikovo* case, para. 53.

[17] *Idem*, para. 140.

[18] Dissenting opinion, pp. 9-10.

[19] *Gabčikovo* case, para. 140.

cludes that in its correct formulation the right to development does not exist in the absolute sense, but is relative always to its tolerance by the environment. [20]

SPECIFIC RULES

On these bases, the *dicta* of the Court also pronounce international law rules and legal solutions to concrete problems. In particular, the Court recognizes a fundamental rule stemming from the Stockholm and Rio Declarations, although it formulates it in a different way. It announces:

'The existence of the general obligation of States to ensure that activities within their jurisdiction and control respect the environment of other States or of areas beyond national control is now part of the corpus of international law relating to the environment.' [21]

Discussing the Advisory Opinion, Judge Weeramantry stresses that customary international law prohibits environmental damage.[22]

In the *Gabčíkovo* case the Court added that the Parties together should look afresh at the effects on the environment of the operation of the power plant.[23] The Court expressed a general understanding that awareness of the vulnerability of the environment and the recognition that environmental risks have to be assessed have become much stronger since the 1977 Treaty's conclusion.[24] The separate opinion by Vice-President Weeramantry develops in this regard the principle of continuing environmental impact assessment which must assess the effect of the project throughout its period of active operation.[25] Such approach corresponds to the important general statement in the judgment that:

> 'The Court is mindful that in the field of environmental protection, vigilance and prevention are required on account of the often irreversible character of damage to the environment and of the limitations inherent in the very type of reparation of this type of damage.'[26]

The judgment also mentioned that Hungary and Slovakia agree on the need to take environmental concerns seriously and to take the required precautionary measures.[27] Similarly, in discussing the Advisory Opinion, Judge Weeramantry expressed the view that the Request enabled the Court to recognize and, in reach-

[20] *Gabčíkovo* case, separate opinion of Vice-President Weeramantry, p. 4.
[21] Advisory Opinion, para. 29.
[22] Dissenting opinion., pp. 49-52.
[23] *Idem.*
[24] *Gabčíkovo* case, para. 112.
[25] Separate opinion, p. 20.
[26] *Gabčíkovo* case, para. 140.
[27] *Idem*, para. 113.

ing its conclusions, apply the precautionary principle which is a part of customary law.[28]

The Court also recognized, however, that international legal rules tending to protect the environment have limits. In the first place, the Court stated in the *Gabčíkovo* case that neither of the Parties contended that new peremptory norms of environmental law had emerged since the conclusion of the 1977 Treaty.[29] In his separate opinion, Vice-President Weeramantry asks the question whether the Court, in the discharge of its traditional duty of deciding between the parties, has done justice to rights and obligations of an *erga omnes* character when the case involves environmental damage of a far-reaching and irreversible nature.[30] In the Advisory Opinion, the Court considered that environmental treaties could not have intended to deprive a State of the exercise of its right of self-defence under international law because of its obligations to protect the environment, but it added:

> 'Nonetheless, states must take environmental considerations into account when assessing what is necessary and proportionate in the pursuit of legitimate military objectives. Respect for the environment is one of the elements that go to assessing whether an action is in conformity with the principle of necessity and proportionality.'

This approach is supported, indeed, by the terms of Principle 24 of the Rio Declaration which provides that

> 'Warfare is inherently destructive of sustainable development. States shall therefore respect international law providing protection for the environment in times of armed conflict and cooperate in its further development, as necessary.'[31]

The Court concluded that while existing international law relating to the protection and safeguarding of the environment does not specifically prohibit the use of nuclear weapons – a position which is criticized by Judge Koroma in his dissenting opinion[32] – it indicated important environmental factors that are properly to be taken into account in the context of the implementation of the principles and rules of the law applicable in armed conflict.[33]

[28] Dissenting opinion, pp. 50-52.
[29] *Gabčíkovo* case, para. 112.
[30] Separate opinion, pp. 25-26.
[31] Advisory Opinion, para. 30.
[32] Dissenting opinion., p. 16.
[33] Advisory Opinion, para. 33.

SOURCES OF INTERNATIONAL ENVIRONMENTAL LAW

The preceding considerations throw a light on the sources of international environmental law relied on by the Court.

It is normal that the high jurisdiction placed importance on international treaty provisions, such as Article 35, paragraph 3 of the Additional Protocol of 1977 to the Geneva Convention of 1949 and the Convention of 18 May 1977 on the Prohibition of Military or Any Other Hostile Use of Environmental Modification Techniques.[34] It also insisted on the principle that for the interpretation of existing treaties new developments of international environmental law are relevant.[35] This conforms to the approach of the Court that takes into account the time dimension,[36] and is of fundamental importance for the development of international environmental law.

The jurisprudence of the Court also recognizes the development of an international customary law rule first formulated by Principle 21 of the Stockholm Declaration and confirmed in Principle 3 of the Rio Declaration.[37] Quoting Principle 24 of the Rio Declaration in the Advisory Opinion in order to support the Court's approach is also significant.[38] The Advisory Opinion additionally refers to General Assembly Resolution 47/37 of 25 November 1992 on the Protection of the Environment in Times of Armed Conflicts, as being 'also of interest' in the context of the question submitted to the Court. All this shows an openness to new forms of creation of international norms.[39] This is particularly important in a field as new as international environmental law.

CONCLUSION

Albeit states could have more frequently availed themselves of the opportunities which they have created to submit environmental disputes to the International Court of Justice, it can be concluded that the Court has applied the terms of the

[34] *Idem*, para. 27.

[35] *Gabčíkovo* case, paras. 104 and 112.

[36] See also Vice-President Weeramantry's statement in his separate opinion in the *Gabčíkovo* case, p. 20: 'Environmental law in its current state of development would read into treaties which may reasonably be considered to have a significant impact upon the environment, a duty of environmental impact assessment and this means also, whether the treaty expressly so provides or not, a duty of monitoring the environmental impacts of any substantial project during the operation of the scheme.'

[37] Advisory Opinion, para. 29; *Gabčíkovo* case, para. 53.

[38] *Idem*, para. 30.

[39] Vice-President Weeramantry expresses the conviction in his separate opinion (p.19) that when a duty such as the duty to protect the environment is so well accepted that all citizens act upon it, that duty is part of the legal system in question and can be accepted as one of the general principles of law recognized by civilized nations.

declaration made by its President at the Conference of Rio de Janeiro by contributing, as often as it had has been given the possibility, to the development of international environmental law. In his report to the UN General Assembly, Judge Stephen Schwebel, the present President of the Court commented on the *Gabčíkovo-Nagymaros* case, which will be considered as a leading case in this matter as follows:

> '*The importance of that Judgment not only for Hungary and Slovakia, but also for the interpretation, application and development of international law, is considerable. It is a Judgment of significance for the law of treaties, of State responsibility, of international watercourses, of the environment and of State succession.*'[40]

[40] UN General Assembly, 52nd Session, A/52/PV.36. 27 October 1997.

THE IMPACT OF DECISIONS AND RESOLUTIONS OF THE SECURITY COUNCIL ON THE INTERNATIONAL COURT OF JUSTICE

Christopher Greenwood*

Twenty years ago, it would have been most unlikely that a panel on the International Court of Justice would have discussed the impact of Security Council resolutions and decisions on the work of the Court. Until the 1990s, criticism of the Security Council tended to concern its failure to act in particular cases, rather than the comparatively few resolutions and decisions which it did adopt. The impact of the Security Council on the work of the International Court has become an important topic today precisely because the Security Council is now able to act in respect of its primary responsibility for the maintenance of international peace and security. In considering the problems to which this can give rise, it is important to bear in mind that the increased activity and effectiveness of the Security Council in addressing threats to international peace and security is one of the most positive developments to have occurred in international law.

1. THE INSTITUTIONAL RELATIONSHIP OF THE COURT AND THE COUNCIL

The Security Council and the International Court of Justice are both principal organs of the United Nations. It is, therefore, necessarily the case that there is a close institutional relationship between them which is reflected in the provisions of the Charter and of the Court Statute. Even if one leaves aside the provisions on the role of the Council in such matters as the election of judges[1] or the admission

* Professor of International Law, London School of Economics and Political Science; Barrister. The subject matter of this panel obviously touches upon the proceedings between Libya and the United Kingdom in the *Case Concerning the Interpretation and Application of the Montreal Convention (Aerial Incident at Lockerbie)* of which the International Court is currently seised. The author appeared as counsel for the United Kingdom in the two phases of this case which have already been before the Court. The present paper is given in a personal capacity and must not be taken as in any way representing the view of the Government of the United Kingdom or as indicating the arguments which that government has submitted, or may in the future submit, in the course of these proceedings. As the *Lockerbie* case is still before the Court, it would obviously be inappropriate for this paper to discuss that case as such.

[1] Statute of the Court, Arts. 7-15.

W.P. Heere (Ed.), International Law and The Hague's 750th Anniversary

of a state which is not a member of the United Nations to participation in the Statute of the Court,[2] the Charter and the Statute clearly envisage a role for the Security Council in relation to the work of the Court:

– *Article 36(3) of the Charter* envisages that the Security Council may make recommendations to states that a legal dispute should be referred to the Court. This provision has been invoked only once (in the *Corfu Channel* case).[3] A recommendation of the Council under this provision is, of course, only a recommendation and does not of itself confer jurisdiction upon the Court.

– *Article 96 of the Charter* provides that the Security Council can request an advisory opinion from the Court. Here, the resolution of the Council is what gives the Court the right to exercise its advisory jurisdiction. The Council has, however, made such a request on only one occasion (the *Namibia* case of 1971).[4]

– *Article 94 of the Charter* provides that the Security Council may take measures to enforce a decision of the International Court of Justice in contentious proceedings, in circumstances where one of the parties to those proceedings has failed to perform the obligations incumbent upon it under a judgment rendered by the Court. The Council has never made use of this power as such[5] but it has taken action to facilitate the implementation of decisions of the Court, in particular in the recent *Chad/Libya* case.[6]

– *Article 41 of the Statute* provides that the Court should report the indication of provisional measures to the Security Council with the implication that the Security Council may then take those measures into account in its own actions. Conversely, the International Court may take into account Security Council action when deciding upon the indication of provisional measures of protection.[7]

The Charter is, however, silent on the relationship between the Council and the Court in cases where the same set of facts has given rise to issues being raised before both bodies. It is also silent on the substantive relationship between decisions or resolutions of the Council and the decisions of the Court. It is clear that the Charter does not create a hierarchical relationship between the Court and the Council. It is also plain from the practice of both organs that there is no rule, comparable to the provisions of Article 12 on the relationship between the Council and the General Assembly, which debars the Court from dealing with a matter simply because the same set of circumstances have come before the

[2] UN Charter, Art. 93; Statute, Art. 4.

[3] Security Council Resolution 22 (1947); *ICJ Rep.* (1948) p. 3.

[4] Security Council Resolution 284 (1970); *ICJ Rep.* (1971) p. 3.

[5] Although the United Kingdom unsuccessfully attempted to obtain measures to enforce the decision of the Court in the *Corfu Channel* case.

[6] *ICJ Rep.* (1994) p.6. By Resolutions 910 and 915, the Council provided for the establishment of an observer group to monitor Libyan withdrawal from the disputed area in accordance with an agreement by the parties on the implementation of the Court's decision; 100 *ILR*, pp. 101-114.

[7] See, e.g., the Provisional Measures decision in the *Cameroon* v. *Nigeria* case, *ICJ Rep.* (1996) p. 23, in which the Court referred to letters written by the President of the Security Council to the two states calling for an end to the use of force, UN Doc. S/1996/150.

Security Council.[8] Conversely, there is no reason why the Security Council cannot exercise its responsibility for the preservation of international peace and security, simply because a case has been brought before the International Court of Justice which relates to the same circumstances. There is, however, an obvious need for caution by both organs in such circumstances and for a degree of co-operation rather than confrontation between them.

2. THE SUBSTANTIVE RELATIONSHIP

It is clear that Security Council resolutions and decisions can have an important effect on the substantive questions which come before the Court. This is true in the case of resolutions which are not binding under the Charter. Such resolutions may have *legal effects* even if they are not *legally binding*. In addition, they may form an important part of the factual matrix before the Court. For example, resolutions calling upon states not to recognise a particular state of affairs, such as the establishment of the 'Turkish Republic of Northern Cyprus,'[9] or the claims to change the status of Jerusalem[10] or the Golan Heights[11] are an important indication of the position taken by the international community as a whole. Similarly, in the recent Advisory Opinion on *Nuclear Weapons*[12] the Court took note of Resolution 984 (1995) in which the Security Council expressly welcomed the security assurances given by the nuclear-weapon states. In addition, a non-binding resolution of the Security Council may have an effect on interpretation of binding Security Council decisions.

The main importance, however, is where the Security Council resolution contains a decision of the Council which is binding under Chapter VII of the Charter.[13] Consideration of such decisions has sometimes involved a degree of confusion regarding their relationship with the general body of international law. On that subject, a number of points require clarification.

First, the Security Council is not a legislature in the municipal sense (indeed, analogies between the organs of the United Nations and the organs of government in a nation-state should not be taken too far, as they can often serve to mislead rather than clarify). It does not lay down new rules of law of general application. In establishing the International Criminal Tribunal for the Former

[8] See, e.g., the decisions of the Court the *Aegean Sea Continental Shelf* case, *ICJ Rep.* (1976) p. 13 and the *Diplomatic and Consular Staff in Tehran* case, *ICJ Rep.* (1979) p. 7.

[9] Security Council Resolutions 541 (1983) and 550 (1984).

[10] Security Council Resolution 478 (1980).

[11] Security Council Resolution 497 (1981).

[12] *ICJ Rep.* (1996) p. 225.

[13] This is not the place to enter into the debate about whether Security Council resolutions may be binding under other provisions of the Charter, on which see the *Advisory Opinion on Namibia*, *ICJ Rep.* (1971) p. 3 at pp. 52-53.

Yugoslavia, for example, the Security Council was careful not to attempt to alter the substantive law which that Tribunal would have to apply.[14]

Secondly, the Security Council is not a judicial organ making determinations that would normally be made by a court. Again, in adopting Resolution 827 establishing the International Criminal Tribunal, the Security Council, contrary to what has been suggested by some commentators, did not venture an answer to the question of whether the conflict in Bosnia-Herzegovina was of an internal or international character. That matter was left to be determined by the Tribunal.[15]

Thirdly, the Council is, however, empowered to take decisions under Chapter VII which may require a state to act in a particular way, even though under other rules of international law - whether derived from treaty or custom - it may have had the right, or even the duty to act differently. In other words, the Security Council is not bound to act only within the framework of the law as it exists outside the Charter. Without the power to depart from that law, the whole system of Chapter VII (which is the lynchpin of the Charter, dealing as it does with the all important priority of maintaining international peace) would become unworkable. For example, Article 41 of the Charter gives the Security Council power to decide on measures for 'complete or partial interruption of rail, sea, air ... communications'. It would be impossible for the Security Council to take such action unless its decision could require states to depart from the provisions of, for example, air services agreements and the Chicago Convention. Similarly, in imposing sanctions on the Federal Republic of Yugoslavia, the Security Council had to take action which was incompatible with the legal regime for navigation on the River Danube.[16]

It is obvious, therefore, that a decision of the Council can have a considerable impact on the work of the International Court of Justice. Suppose that the Federal Republic of Yugoslavia brought an action against another Danube state for non-compliance with the Danube legal regime, the alleged non-compliance consisting solely of the measures taken by that state in the implementation of the Security Council decision on sanctions. Under Article 103 of the Charter, the obligation of that state to comply with the decision imposing sanctions (an obligation derived from Arts. 2(5) and 25 of the Charter) prevailed over its obligations under the Danube Treaty. In the hypothetical court case, the respondent state could not, therefore, be held responsible for violating obligations under the Danube Convention *vis-à-vis* the Federal Republic of Yugoslavia, when all that it had done was to implement the sanctions decision. That is not because the Security

[14] Security Council Resolution 827 (1993). See also the Report of the Secretary General, United Nations Doc. S/25704, para. 29.

[15] See *Prosecutor* v. *Tadić*, decision of the Appeals Chamber of the International Criminal Tribunal for the Former Yugoslavia of 2 October 1995, 105 *ILR*, p. 419 at pp. 489-95, paras. 71-78.

[16] Security Council Resolutions 757 (1992), 787 (1992) paras. 9 and 13, 820 (1993) paras. 15-17 and 925 (1995). See also the Final Report of the Security Council Sanctions Committee, United Nations Doc. S/1996/946 at paras. 33-40.

Council decision is treated as a higher form of law than the Danube Convention, but because the Charter itself imposes upon all Member States an obligation to comply with decisions of the Security Council and, by virtue of Article 103, that Charter obligation to comply with the decision prevails over obligations under the other treaty.

In passing, it should be added that although Article 103 refers only to obligations under the Charter prevailing over *obligations* under other treaties, the same principle must also apply to *rights* arising under other treaties. If a state cannot rely upon its obligation to act in a particular way as an excuse for non-compliance with its obligations under the Charter, then, *a fortiori*, it cannot rely upon a right under that other treaty.[17]

3. CONCLUSION

The impact of Security Council resolutions and decisions has led a number of commentators to suggest that the Court should assert a power of judicial review over such Security Council actions. Space does not permit a full discussion of this question. I can only mention a few considerations which need to be borne in mind in considering that question.

1. There is no hint of such a power in each the Charter or the Statute of the Court.
2. Proposals to give the Court such a power or to provide for other means of judicial review of decisions of the Council were made at the San Francisco Conference and rejected there, in part because it was considered that they would seriously impair the effectiveness of the Council.
3. The Court itself has denied that it has such a power of judicial review in the Advisory Opinions on *Certain Expenses*[18] and *Namibia*.[19] The fact that the Court has taken that position in advisory proceedings, where a resolution could be directly in issue, suggests that, *a fortiori*, there are no grounds for asserting such a power of review in contentious proceedings.
4. The assertion of a generalised power of judicial review of Security Council resolutions and decisions could have a destabilising effect on the workings of

[17] There is an interesting analogy with Article 234 of the EEC Treaty, which permits a state to depart from its obligations under the EEC Treaty, in certain circumstances, in order to comply with an obligation arising under a treaty with a non-member state concluded before the member country became party to the EEC Treaty. In *Commission* v. *United Kingdom (Case C-146/89) (Territorial Sea)*, [1991] ECR I-3533, the European Court of Justice held that the United Kingdom could not rely upon this provision of the Treaty to give effect to rights arising under the pre-existing treaty, in that particular case the right to extend its territorial waters by drawing its baselines by reference to a new method.

[18] *ICJ Rep.* (1962) p. 151 at p. 168.

[19] *International Court of Justice Reports* (1971) p. 16 at p. 45.

> Chapter VII of the Charter, if a decision taken by the Security Council, for example, to impose economic sanctions, could be challenged, perhaps many years after it was taken. That would induce an element of uncertainty which could hang like a sword of Damocles over every sanctions regime on which the Council might decide. It is not that the Court is not capable of acting quickly, the recent proceedings in *Breard*[20] are a reminder that this is so. The problem is rather that, in a legal system which has no statute of limitations or fixed periods for proceedings of any kind, the Court may not be confronted with a question about the validity or effect of a Security Council resolution until many years after that resolution was adopted. It is noticeable that many other systems which permit judicial review of various kinds of governmental acts impose very strict time-limits.

The Security Council is not above the law but that proposition should not be confused with the quite separate question of whether its decisions and resolutions are subject to some form of judicial review. The revitalisation of the Security Council is probably the greatest achievement of the last ten years. It is important that the rediscovered effectiveness of the Council should not now be undermined.

[20] *Case Concerning the Vienna Convention on Consular Relations* (*Paraguay* v. *United States of America*), 37 *ILM* (1998) p. 810. In that case, the application was filed on 3 April 1998, the Court held oral hearings on the question of provisional measures of protection on 7 April and gave its decision on 9 April.

RECONSIDERING THE RELATIONSHIP BETWEEN THE ICJ AND THE SECURITY COUNCIL

Peter Malanczuk*

1. INTRODUCTION

In the decades from 1945, the year of the establishment of the UN, until the end of the Cold War the relationship between the International Court and the Security Council remained of secondary importance in practice (although not in theory) for two main reasons. First, the Security Council was largely paralysed in its capability to act by the East-West conflict and the excessive use of the veto of the permanent members in favour of themselves and their own constituencies. Second, the Court, for various reasons, remained very much under-used and had a rather small case load.

The situation has changed in both aforementioned respects. Since 1990, the Security Council has engaged in taking action in a broad variety of matters on an unprecedented scale.[1] Not only its composition, powers and the veto have politically come into question again, but also the legal limits of its authority are subject of continuing debate among scholars and judges. The workload of the Court, on the other hand, has increased considerably, with cases brought from many parts of the world. These include the recent applications submitted by Libya against the United States and the UK in connection with the Lockerbie incident and the case filed by Bosnia and Herzegovina against Yugoslavia (Serbia and Montenegro) which have raised central issues concerning the relationship between the Court and the Security Council and the power of the Court to review decisions of the Council.[2] In a broader context, the topic is part of the general

* Professor of International Law. Director of the Institute of Globalization, International Economic Law and Dispute Settlement (*GLODIS*) and Head of the Department of International Law of the Law Faculty, Erasmus University Rotterdam. Honorary Guest-Professor at Nankai University, Tianjin, and at the China University of Political Science and Law, Beijing. Counsel of Lalive & Partners, Geneva.

[1] See P. Malanczuk, *Akehurst's Modern Introduction to International Law*, 7th edn. (1997) pp. 385 et seq.

[2] See for example, T.M. Franck, 'The "Powers of Appreciation": Who Is the Ultimate Guardian of UN Legality?', 86 *American Journal of International Law* (*AJIL*) (1992) pp. 519-523; E. McWhinney, 'The International Court as a Constitutional Court and the Blurring of the Arbitral/Judicial Processes', 6 *Leiden Journal of International Law* (*LJIL*) (1993) pp. 279-7; G.R. Watson, 'Constitutionalism, Judicial Review, and the World Court', 34 *Harvard International Law Journal* (1993) pp. 1-45; E. McWhinney, 'The Inaugural Manfred Lachs Memorial Lecture – Manfred Lachs

W.P. Heere (Ed.), International Law and The Hague's 750th Anniversary

debate on the 'constitutional crisis' of the United Nations and on the direction into which the international legal order is to develop in the next century.

The main question in this connection which has been brought to the forefront in particular by Libya's challenge to resolutions of the Security Council, in the words of Judge Shahabuddeen:

> 'is whether a decision of the Security Council may override the legal rights of states, and if so, whether there are any limitations on the power of the Council to characterize a situation as one justifying the making of a decision entailing such consequences. Are there any limits to the Council's powers of appreciation? In the equilibrium of forces underpinning the structure of the United Nations within the evolving international order, is there any conceivable point beyond which a legal issue may properly arise as to the competence of the Security Council to produce such overriding results? If there are any limits, what are those limits and what body, if other than the Security Council, is competent to say what those limits are?'[3]

2. THE BASIC RELATIONSHIP BETWEEN THE COURT AND THE SECURITY COUNCIL

As far as the wording of the UN Charter and the Statute of the ICJ is concerned, Professor Greenwood has already given an overview of the relevant legal provisions concerning the interaction between the International Court of Justice (ICJ) and the Security Council. The basic relationship between the two bodies, however, is not explicitly defined in the Charter. The general view in the literature is that there is no hierarchy among the Court and the Council; they operate independently on a co-ordinate and equal level, each body within its own sphere of competence and determining its own competence itself.

In particular, it is clear from the negotiating history of the Charter, that the Court was not conceptualized as a 'constitutional' court in the sense that it should enjoy the generalized power to review the legality of Security Council action (or of other UN organs) and be able to determine that certain acts or decisions are

and the International Court of Justice as Emerging Constitutional Court of the United Nations', 8 *LJIL* (1995) pp. 41-52; M. Bedjaoui, *The New World Order and the Security Council – Testing the Legality of Its Acts* (1995); T.D. Gill, 'Some Legal and Political Limitations on the Power of the UN Security Council to Exercise Its Enforcement Powers under Chapter VII of the Charter', 26 *Netherlands Yearbook of International Law* (1995) pp. 33-138; K. Roberts, 'Second-Guessing the Security Council: The International Court of Justice and Its Powers of Judicial Review', 7 *Pace International Law Review* (1995) pp. 281-327; J.G. Gardam, 'Legal Restraints on Security Council Military Enforcement Action', 17 *Michigan Journal of International Law* (1996) pp. 285-322; M. Koskenniemi, 'The Place of Law in Collective Security', 17 *Michigan Journal of International Law* (1996) pp. 455-90; J.E. Alvarez, 'Judging the Security Council', 90 *AJIL* (1996) pp. 1-39. See further the literature cited below.

[3] *Questions of Interpretation of the 1971 Montreal Convention arising from the Aerial Incident at Lockerbie* (*Libya* v. *UK*; *Libya* v. *USA*), Provisional Measures, Order of 14 April 1992, *ICJ Rep.* (1992) p.3 et seq. Separate opinion of Judge Shahabudeen, p. 33.

null and void. It seems that the prevailing view is still that each organ of the United Nations has the autonomy to determine the scope of its own competence under the Charter.[4] Neither the Charter nor the Statute thus provides for any specific review procedure of this kind. The Court also took note of this fact in the *Expenses* case[5] and in the *Namibia* case.[6] In fact, as noted by Judge Skubiszewski in a recent thorough analysis, to date no mechanism of judicial review in the proper sense of the term (as applicable, for example to the relevant procedures before the US Supreme Court, the German *Bundesverfassungsgericht* or the European Court of Justice) has been established and 'in nocase did the Court assume the role of an appeal or reviewing instance in the strict sense of judicial control of constitutionality.'[7]

3. PARALLEL ACTIVITIES OF THE COURT AND THE COUNCIL AND EXCLUSIVE POWERS OF THE COUNCIL

A different question is whether and to which extent the Court may be limited in the exercise of its functions by the Security Council. This issue has arisen most prominently with regard to parallel activities of the Security Council and the Court in the same matter in cases involving a threat to international peace and security.[8] As noted above, Article 24 of the Charter confers 'primary responsibility for the maintenance of international peace and security' on the Security Council. Does this imply *vis-à-vis* the Court that the Council enjoys *exclusive* powers to deal with a particular dispute affecting international peace and security and to take decisions to resolve it barring the Court's jurisdiction in the same matter?

As a starting point, it is important to note that there is no provision in the Charter (or in the Statute of the Court) concerning the relationship between the Council and the Court that corresponds to Article 12 ensuring the primacy of the Council *vis-à-vis* the Assembly. The general view has therefore come to prevail in the literature that both the Council and the Court may be concerned with the

[4] See Gill, loc. cit. n.2, at p. 116 et seq.; M. Herdegen, 'The "Constitutionalization" of the UN Security System', 27 *Vanderbilt Journal of Transnational Law* (1994) pp. 135-159.

[5] *Certain Expenses of the United Nations* (Art. 17, para. 2 of the Charter), *ICJ Rep.* (1962) p. 161 at p. 168.

[6] *ICJ Rep.* (1971) p. 16 at p. 45.

[7] K. Skubiszewski, 'The International Court of Justice and the Security Council', in V. Lowe and M. Fitzmaurice,eds., *Fifty Years of the International Court of Justice. Essays in honour of Sir Robert Jennings* (1996) p. 606 at p. 627.

[8] See E. Klein, 'Paralleles Tätigwerden von Sicherheitsrat und internationalem Gerichtshof bei friedensbedrohenden Streitigkeiten – Zu Fragen der Zuständigkeit und Organtreue', in R. Bernhardt, et al., eds, *Völkerrecht als Rechtsordnung – Internationale Gerichtsbarkeit – Menschenrechte, Festschrift für Hermann Mosler* (1983) pp. 467-491.

same dispute at the same time.[9] The *Tehran Hostages* case[10] and the *Nicaragua* case[11] are the main precedents for rejecting the objection that a dispute falls within the competence of the Security Council and was therefore not admissible to judicial proceedings, as well as the objection that the Court could not hear a case concerning a dispute actually pending before the Council or in which the Council had already made a recommendation or taken a decision.[12]

In the literature there is ample support of the view that the Security Council, as the organ charged with primary responsibility for the maintenance of peace, 'does not enjoy priority of any kind over the ICJ.'[13] The Court and the political organs of the UN are seen as each having their own range of functions. In the settlement of disputes the Council and the Court exercise their functions within their respective competences independently of each other.[14] The Security Council may act in accordance with Chapters VI or VII of the Charter, while the Court may have jurisdiction over a contentious legal case in accordance with its Statute, or give an advisory opinion on a legal issue at the request of a competent international organ or body. The Court and the Council may deal with the same matter simultaneously, or the procedures may overlap in time or follow one another.

It is further argued that the differences of the procedures of the Security Council and the ICJ prevent that any objection of *lis pendens* or *res judicata* may be raised against the ICJ acting simultaneously, or prior to or after the Security Council, in a case pending before the Council. This is deduced from the different nature of the procedures of the Council and the Court and from general principles of law. Further support is found in the circumstance that no restrictions on the freedom of the ICJ to act are to be found in the wording of either the Charter or the ICJ Statute. The consequence of this view is that the relationship between the ICJ and the Security Council is limited to the obligation to 'pay due respect to each other' in the sense that they have to 'take each other's decisions into consideration'[15] when exercising their respective functions.

[9] See Klein, loc. cit. n. 8; Gowlland-Debbas, 'The Relationship between the International Court of Justice and the Security Council in the Light of the *Lockerbie* case', 88 *AJIL* (1994) pp. 643 et seq.; E. Klein, 'Die Internationalen Organisationen als Völkerrechtssubjekte', in Wolfgang Graf Vitzthum, ed., *Völkerrecht* (1997) p. 354.

[10] *United States Diplomatic and Consular Staff in Tehran*, Judgement, *ICJ Rep.* (1980) pp. 3 et seq. See Klein, loc. cit. n. 8 , at pp. 471-474, also with a discussion of the *Corfu Channel* case and the *Aegean Sea Continental Shelf* case,pp. 469-471.

[11] *Nicaragua* case, *ICJ Rep.* (1984) pp. 433-434, referring to the *Tehran Hostages* case, *ICJ Rep.* (1980) p. 21.

[12] See H. Mosler, 'Article 92', in B. Simma, ed., *The Charter of the United Nations. A Commentary* (1995) p. 990.

[13] J. Delbrück, 'Article 24', in B. Simma, ed., *The Charter of the United Nations. A Commentary* (1995) p. 402, with reference to Klein, loc. cit. n. 8, at p. 474 and R. Escher, *Friedliche Erledigung von Streitigkeiten nach dem System der Vereinten Nationen* (1985) p. 10 et seq.

[14] Mosler, loc. cit. n.12, at p. 990.

[15] Delbrück, loc. cit. n. 13, at p. 403; See also Mosler, loc. cit. n. 12, at p. 991.

Dogmatically, this view may perhaps be based upon the principle of what German doctrine calls *Organtreue*. In a more general sense this principle is considered to be an essential principle of any (national, international or supranational) organization. It stipulates the mutual obligation of loyalty towards the organization as a whole that exists not only between the organization as such and its constituent elements (*Gemeinschaftstreue*, *Bundestreue*), but also between the organs of the organization.[16] This principle means that organs of an organization are required to exercise their powers in mutual respect of each other and by being guided by the purpose and structure of the organization.[17] As applied to the relationship between the Security Council and the ICJ this would mean that the Court may legally qualify a certain state act or even an act of the Security Council itself in a different way than the Security Council does. Vice versa, it also implies that the Security Council is at liberty in the maintenance of international peace and security to assume that a decision of the Court has failed to have a pacifying effect in a particular conflict.[18]

The question arises whether there are nevertheless exclusive competences of the Security Council, which prevent the Court from considering a matter and/or render an application to the Court inadmissible.[19] However, the practice of the two organs does not point into such a direction. As noted above, the absence of a provision corresponding to Art. 12 in the UN Charter in relation to the Court does not *per se* exclude jurisdiction of the Court in matters falling under Chapter VII of the Charter. In the *Nicaragua* case the Court rejected the argument that it would not have any authority concerning matters falling under Chapters VI and VII of the Charter.[20] Additional support for this position of the Court can be found in the Order of 8 April 1993 in the *Case Concerning Application of the Genocide Convention (Request for Indication of Provisional Measures)* filed by Bosnia and Herzegovina v. Yugoslavia (Serbia and Montenegro).[21]

The question remains whether there are nevertheless types of disputes which are so highly political and not suitable for adjudication that, in spite of the legal aspects they include, these aspects should not be considered by the Court, with the result the settlement of the dispute must be left entirely to the Council.[22] As noted by Judge Oda in his Dissenting Opinion in the *Nicaragua* case, the 'overwhelmingly political nature' of the conflict notwithstanding its legal aspects may be considered as an argument to deny that the Court may become involved in the matter.[23] This would appear to be in line with the 'political question'

[16] See Klein, 'Die Internationalen', loc. cit. n. 9, at p. 354; Klein, loc. cit. n. 8 , at p. 482.

[17] Ibid., at p. 354.

[18] For further discussion see Skubisczewski, loc. cit. n. 7, at pp. 606 et seq.

[19] Skubiszewski, loc. cit. n. 7., at p. 619.

[20] *Nicaragua* case, *ICJ Rep.* (1984) pp. 434-435, para. 95.

[21] *ICJ Rep.* (1993) p. 3 at pp.18-19, para. 33.

[22] See Skubiszewski, loc. cit. n. 7, at pp. 621-622.

[23] *ICJ Rep.* (1986) p. 212 at p. 238, para, 55, and p. 239, para. 57.

doctrine or equivalent forms of 'judicial self-restraint' used in different guises by national constitutional courts in limiting their own power to intervene. However, so far there is no practice of the ICJ in this direction.[24]

4. THE NEW CHALLENGES ARISING FROM THE *LOCKERBIE* CASES

The *Lockerbie* cases currently pending before the Court have raised more serious problems of the parallel exercise of powers between the Security Council and the ICJ regarding the same matter. Similar problems seemed also to arise from the above-mentioned case filed by Bosnia Herzegovina concerning the application of the Genocide Convention against Yugoslavia (Serbia and Montenegro). The application was to a certain extent motivated by the wish to have the legality of the mandatory arms embargo imposed by the Security Council on former Yugoslavia and also against Bosnia reviewed by the Court. In its original application, Bosnia had, *inter alia*, requested the Court to decide that the arms embargo was impairing its right to self-defence and that

> 'Security Council resolution 713 (1991) and all subsequent Security Council resolutions referring thereto or reaffirming thereof must not be construed to impose an arms embargo upon Bosnia and Herzegovina, as required by Articles 24(1) and 51 of the United Nations Charter and in accordance with the customary doctrine of *ultra vires*.'[25]

Apart from some opinions of judges attached to the Order of the Court of 13 September 1993, however, no relevance was given to this point and, subsequently, Bosnia and Herzegovina no longer argued it. The following will therefore be limited to the *Lockerbie* case.

Briefly stated, the background to the *Lockerbie* case is as follows. In 1992, the Security Council, acting under Chapter VI of the Charter, decided at the request of the UK and USA in Resolution 731 (1992), *inter alia*, that Libya should surrender to the United Kingdom and the United States for prosecution two Libyan nationals who were charged with the terrorist action of placing a bomb in a PanAm flight over Lockerbie (Scotland). Libya then filed a request before the Court to indicate provisional measures against the UK and USA based upon the principle *aut dedere aut iudicare* laid down in the 1971 Montreal Convention for the Suppression of Unlawful Acts against the Safety of Civil Aviation. Three days after the hearing on this request for provisional measures was closed and while the Court was clearly seized with the matter and in deliberations, on 31

[24] Noted by Skubiszewski, loc. cit. n. 7., at p. 622, also showing the irrelevance of the *Lockerbie* case in this context: the Court was practically left with no other choice than not to act because the Council had in fact excluded the ability of the Court to indicate provisional measures.

[25] Order of 13 September 1993, p. 7.

March 1992, the Security Council adopted Resolution 748 (1992) under Chapter VII which decided that Libya had to comply with the requirement of Resolution 731 to 'provide a full and effective response' to the requests from France, the UK and the US and to take certain measures concerning international terrorism. The Council also ordered that certain sanctions were to be applied against Libya if it failed to comply. The Court, confronted with this new *fait accompli* directly affecting the legal question of extradition before it, invited the parties on 4 April 1992 to submit by 7 April any comments they had on the implications of Resolution 748 for the proceedings before the Court. In its Order of 14 April 1992,[26] by eleven votes to five, the Court finally held that under the circumstances of the case it was not necessary to indicate provisional measures.

The Court noted that in issuing the Order it did not 'make definite findings either of fact or law on the issues relating to the merits' and stressed that 'the right of the Parties to contest such issues at the stage of the merits must remain unaffected by the Court's decision.'[27] However, it decided that the parties as members of the UN 'are obliged to carry out the decisions of the Security Council in accordance with Article 25 of the Charter' and that at the stage of deciding on provisional measures the Court 'considers that *prima facie* this obligation extends to the decision contained in Resolution 748 (1992).'[28] It further held that 'in accordance with Article 103 of the Charter, the obligations of the Parties in that respect prevail over their obligations under any other international agreement, including the Montreal Convention.'[29] The Order also reserved the Court's power to reconsider the legal relevance of Resolution 748 at a later stage of the proceedings. At the same time the Court clarified that it had not pronounced on any of the other questions raised in the proceedings, including the question of whether the Court had jurisdiction.[30]

In fact, what has happened is that under the new circumstances the Security Council had created by adopting Resolution 748 while the case was *sub judice*, the Court was left with no other choice than to deny the request for provisional measures in order to avoid a direct conflict with the Security Council. This is reflected in quite a number of the opinions of judges attached to the Order.[31]

[26] See *supra* n. 25; See T. Stein, 'Das Attentat von Lockerbie vor dem Sicherheitsrat der Vereinten Nationen und dem Internationalen Gerichtshof', 31 *Archiv des Völkerrechts* (1993) pp. 206 et seq.; B. Graefrath, 'Leave to the Court What Belongs to the Court – The Libyan Case', 4 *European Journal of International law* (1993) pp. 184, 205; M. Mohr, 'Der Lockerbie-Fall vor dem UN-Sicherheitsrat und Internationalem Gerichtshof', *Demokratie und Recht* (1992) pp. 305 et seq.; Gowlland-Debbas, loc. cit. n. 9; Martenczuk, *Rechtsbindung und Rechtskontrolle des Weltsicherheitsrates. Die Überprüfung nichtmilitärischer Zwangsmassnahmen durch den Internationalen Gerichtshof* (1996) pp. 73 et seq.

[27] See *supra* n. 25., at p. 15, para. 38.

[28] Ibid., at p.16, para. 39.

[29] Idem.

[30] Ibid., para. 42.

[31] For a survey and analysis see Skubiszewski, loc. cit. n. 7, at pp. 616-619.

There were also several dissenting opinions of judges arguing that the Court may have indicated provisional measures to prevent an aggravation and extension of the dispute.[32] But any kind of provisional measures adopted by the Court would have questioned the authority of the Security Council under Chapter VII and, at this stage, without sufficient investigation, briefing, argument and deliberation in the appropriate legal procedure, the Court was simply not in a position to take a stand on that matter. It therefore had to bend to the Council, at least in this phase and be it by recognizing the validity of the Council's action and its consequences for the protection of the rights of the respondents only *prima facie*.[33]

At a minimum, one can say that at this preliminary stage of the proceedings, the problems raised by parallel competences of both bodies remained unresolved.[34] However, while proceedings in The Hague were continuing, the Security Council took a further step by adopting Resolution 883 on 11 November 1993. This resolution extended the scope of the sanctions against Libya for reasons of non-compliance with Resolution 748 and is still in force, being reviewed by the Security Council every 120 days.

The current phase of the 'reconsideration of the relationship between the Council and the Court' is marked by the Judgement of the Court in the *Lockerbie* case of 27 February 1998[35] in which the Court decided that it has jurisdiction and that the Libyan Application was admissible, enabling it to proceed to the merits of the case. Without entering into too many details, the main issues of the decision will be highlighted, as far as relevant for the topic under consideration in this paper. The issues concerning only the interpretation of the Montreal Convention itself will therefore not be considered. Moreover, as the arguments of the respondents and the judgment are largely the same in both the cases against the USA and the UK, it suffices in the following to select the case against the UK.

The UK raised objections to the jurisdiction of the Court and to the admissibility of the application and considered both to be of 'an essentially preliminary character.' One of the arguments put forward by the UK was that even if Libya enjoyed the rights it claimed under the Montreal Convention, they were superseded by Resolutions 748 and 883. Under Articles 25 and 103 of the Charter these resolutions would have priority over all rights and obligations arising from the Montreal Convention. The UK further argued that due to these Resolutions, the only dispute that existed was now between Libya and the Security Council, which the Court could not entertain.[36]

The Court rejected this objection on the formalistic ground that Resolutions 748 and 883 were in fact adopted later than the Application was filed (3 March

[32] Ibid., at pp. 114 et seq.

[33] See also Skubiszewski, loc. cit. n. 7, at pp. 517-619

[34] Mosler, loc. cit. n.12, at p. 991.

[35] Judgement of 27 February 1998 (Libya v. UK).

[36] As summarized in the Judgement of 27 February 1998 (Libya v. UK) para. 37.

1992). Referring to its earlier jurisprudence in the *Nottebohm* case and the *Right of Passage* case the ICJ determined that 'if the Court had jurisdiction on that date, it continues to do so; the subsequent coming into existence of the above-mentioned Resolutions cannot affect its jurisdiction once established.'[37]

The UK objection as to admissibility centered on the argument that the issue or issues in dispute are 'now regulated by decisions of the Security Council, taken under Chapter VII of the Charter', binding on both Parties and that these resolutions, in case of any conflict with other rights or obligations, have overriding effect under Article 103 of the Charter. In the view of the UK:

> 'resolutions 748 and 883 are legally binding and they create legal obligations for Libya and the United Kingdom which are determinative of any dispute over which the Court might have jurisdiction.'[38]

The Court, however, upheld the Libyan counter-argument that the only relevant date for determining admissibility of the Application is the date of its filing. As Resolutions 748 and 883 were adopted at a later date, the Court found that it could not take them into consideration. With regard to the earlier Resolution 731, the Court decided that 'it could not form a legal impediment' to the admissibility of the Application 'because it was a mere recommendation without binding effect, as was recognized moreover by the United Kingdom itself.'[39]

A further request advanced by the UK concerning admissibility was that the court should rule that the intervening Security Council resolutions 'have rendered the Libyan claims without object.'[40] The Court interpreted this objection as requesting the Court not to proceed on the merits which must be examined in the light of the framework of its earlier jurisprudence that events subsequent to the filing of an application may 'render an application without object' and in the light of Article 79 of the Rules of Court ('Rules'), dealing with preliminary objections. The reasoning in this respect is rather technical and the argument is presented in a complicated manner.[41] The case rested on Article 79 (7) of the Rules and the issue was whether the UK objection was of an 'exclusively' or 'non-exclusively' preliminary nature. The Court held that Libya's rights on the merits would not only be affected by a decision to sustain the UK objection at this stage of the proceedings, but 'would constitute, in many respects, the very subject-matter of that decision.' The objection would do much more than 'touch[ing] upon subjects belonging to the merits of the case'; it was seen as being 'inextricably interwoven' with the merits. The Court also stated that the UK itself had in its previous communications with the Court 'implicitly acknowledged that the

[37] Ibid., para. 38.
[38] Ibid., para. 41.
[39] Ibid., para. 44.
[40] Ibid., para. 46.
[41] Ibid., paras. 47-50.

objection raised and the merits of the case were "closely interconnected".' The Court therefore found that the UK objection did not have 'an exclusively preliminary character' and decided to consider it when it reaches the merits of the case.[42]

In accepting jurisdiction on the basis of such technical and rather narrow argument, the Court has again skilfully avoided a direct confrontation with the Security Council in matters of substance. At the same time it has *pro forma* upheld its right to exercise its judicial function parallel to the Security Council at least in procedural terms, even if, in the end, it may have to accept the authority of the relevant Security Council resolutions in the merits. The Security Council can live with this as long as there is no clear indication in a decision by the Court to the effect that the legality of the resolutions at issue is being questioned in substance. The Court has been careful to avoid this impression in the wording of its decision to accept jurisdiction. Its message seems to be that the Court, as a judicial body, cannot really decide on the legal effect of the resolutions and their relevance to the case until it has gone through full judicial proceedings. The real conflict has thus again been merely postponed and the question of the substance of the parallel functions of the Court and the Council in case of irreconcilable decisions is still in abeyance. Equally in abeyance is the related question of whether the Court could assume the power of some form of incidental judicial review of Security Council resolutions – as distinct from their mere interpretation – in contentious cases.

5. CONCLUSIONS

It is generally accepted that the Security Council enjoys wide discretion in deciding when to apply collective measures under Chapter VII of the UN Charter to preserve peace and security. In other words, a threat to the peace in the sense of Article 39 seems to be whatever the Security Council says is a threat to the peace, which is a political decision and, as a matter of principle, not easily subject to legal evaluation.[43] However, especially with regard to the use of force under Chapter VII, this does not necessarily mean that the authority of the Security Council is unlimited and open to its complete political discretion. The Security Council is also bound by the Charter and has to act within the law. Under Article 25 the members of the UN have agreed to carry out decisions of the Council 'in accordance with the present Charter.' Under Article 24 (2), in discharging its duties, the Council 'shall act in accordance with the Purposes and Principles of the United Nations.' These purposes and principles are laid down in Article 1(1)

42 Ibid., paras. 50-51.

43 See Malanczuk, op. cit. n. 1 , pp. 425-430; I. Österdahl, *Threat to the Peace. The Interpretation by the Security Council of Article 39 of the UN Charter* (1998).

of the Charter. Indeed, individual opinions of judges have referred to these substantive limitations.[44] In agreeing to the Charter the members have therefore not given a *carte blanche* to the Council to do whatever it pleases and to act as if it were an absolute sovereign.

The practice of the Security Council since 1990 clearly shows that there has been considerable extension of the notion what constitutes a threat to the peace within the meaning of Article 39. However, even if one would take the view that this practice has gone beyond the original framework envisaged by the drafters of the Charter and the broad discretionary powers accorded to the Council, this does not necessarily mean that this practice is illegal *per se* or constitutes action *ultra vires* of the powers of the Council. It can be argued that subsequent practice under the Charter is an important method in interpreting the Charter, even if it may in fact amount to an informal amendment of the wording of the Charter, as long as it can be shown that the 'established practice' is within the scope of the organization's activity (rather than only within the wording of its constituent document).[45] Without being able to enter into the details of this discussion concerning *ultra vires* acts of international organizations in general and the scope of the specific powers and the so-called general powers of the Security Council in particular, all that is intended to be pointed out here is that members of the UN may condone by acquiescence the extension of the powers of the Security Council under the principle *qui tacet consentire videtur*. Another point to be taken into consideration is that there is no institutionalized procedure in the United Nations by which the validity of the exercise of the discretionary powers of the Security Council can be reviewed. This implies, given the decentralized nature of the international legal system, that insurmountable difficulties may arise in practice if one would like to attach the legal effect of being considered null and void *ab initio* to certain acts of the Council alleged to be *ultra vires*. Cases that need to be considered in this connection are, for example, if only the addressee of a measure adopted by the Security Council claims that it is illegal, or if the membership of the UN is divided on that matter. Only an institutionalized procedure in an organization such as the UN could avoid serious disruptive effects of such a situation and provide for the required legal certainty.[46]

In the absence of an established institutionalized procedure – apart from the limited possibilities offered by the advisory opinion procedure – to judicially control Security Council decisions, especially such taken under Chapter VII, can or should the Court assume such a power as the US Supreme Court did in 1803 in *Marbury* v. *Madison*?[47] First, it must be said that an analogy to the consti-

[44] See Judge Weeramantry in the *Lockerbie* case and Judge *ad hoc* Lauterpacht in *the Bosnia Genocide* case.

[45] See K. Zemanek, 'Is the Security Council the Sole Judge of its Own Legality?', manuscript by courtesy of the author for *Liber Americorum Judge Mohammed Bedjaoui* [forthcoming].

[46] See the argument by Zemanek, loc. cit. n. 45, manus. 22.

[47] *Marbury* v. *Madison*, 1 Cranch 137 (1803).

tutional situation underlying *Marbury* v. *Madison* is misleading because there is no comparable separation of powers on the international level. Also there are different kinds of so-called judicial review in other national legal systems which equally cannot be transplanted 'lock, stock and barrel' to the position of the ICJ within the UN system.

Nevertheless, there may be scope for controlling Security Council decisions through the Court also in contentious cases, assuming that it has jurisdiction, which is not likely to be often the case in practice. While it is difficult to conceive that a determination of the Council under Article 39 that there is a threat to international peace is as such reviewable – because it would mean that the Court would have to substitute the Council's political judgement by a political judgement of its own for which it is not qualified – a review of the legality of specific measures adopted by the Council under Chapter VII, in my view, is not entirely impossible in exceptional cases.

The Council has to respect certain fundamental principles of international law, even if it may otherwise derogate from international law when acting under Chapter VII. Reference can be made in this connection to norms of *ius cogens*, to international humanitarian law or basic human rights, to self-determination or the principles protecting the very existence of states, or to manifest procedural defects in the decision-making of the Council. Moreover, it can be argued that the Security Council is manifestly exceeding its powers under Chapter VII if it adopts general law-making functions, as in the case of the establishment of the UN Compensation Commission for Claims against Iraq.[48] As we know from the *Tadić Appeals Chamber* case[49] similar questions have arisen with regard to the judicial functions assigned to other subsidiary bodies created by the Council, such as the Tribunals for the former Yugoslavia and for Rwanda. At least from the Court's point of view, for example, the Council cannot manifestly disregard the principle of proportionality, or dispose of elementary principles of justice and due process which are inherent in the very concept of law and part of the judicial function to protect.

Such extreme cases may be unlikely in practice, but they are not entirely hypothetical. The more active a powerful body becomes, the more likely is the abuse of its powers, whether intentionally or not. The Court must seek a complementary role with the Council to achieve the purposes of the Charter, but at the same time it is necessary to remember that it also is not the creature of the

[48] See P. Malanczuk, International Business and New Rules of State Responsibility? - The Law Applied by the United Nations (Security Council) Compensation Commission for Claims against Iraq, in: K.-H. Böckstiegel, ed., *Perspectives of Air Law, Space Law and International Business Law for the Next Century, Proceedings of an International Colloquium, Cologne, June 7-9, 1995 to celebrate 70 Years Institute of Air and Space Law and 20 Years Chair for International Business Law of the University of Cologne* (1996) pp. 117-145.

[49] The International Criminal Tribunal for the former Yugoslavia, Appeals Chamber Decision on the Tadić Jurisdictional Motion (2 October 1995) Case no. IT-94-1-AR72.

Security Council. The Court must have an inherent power to control the most extreme forms of such abuse. Where necessary, it must have the residual power, wisely and exercised in a restrained manner, to make up its own mind to declare whether or not a measure of the Security Council remains within the bounds of the law. This is part of its judicial function and the Court may have to develop this aspect on a case-by-case basis in the future, even if the particular applications filed by Libya in the *Lockerbie* case may fail for one reason or another. The Security Council is not above the law and the Court remains the 'ultimate guardian' (to borrow from Thomas Franck) of the law of the Charter.

PRIVATE INTERNATIONAL LAW

Cross-Border Injunctions in Civil Procedure

Chair: J.H.A. van Loon

Embassy Employees and State Immunity

Chair: P.J.I.M. de Waart

Interpretation of Private International Law Treaties

Chair: A.V.M. Struycken

Regulation of the Internet

Chair: K. Boele-Woelki

Judicial and Administrative Co-operation in Family Law Matters
Chair: M. Sardenberg

CROSS-BORDER INJUNCTIONS: A BLESSING OR A CURSE?

Jan J. Brinkhof*

1. PROBLEM

Twenty-five years ago, anyone in Europe who wished to protect his invention by means of a patent had to apply for it in each and every country. This application had to meet all the local requirements. At that time, there were not insignificant differences between national patent laws, both in substantive and in procedural law. In some countries, for example, applications were thoroughly examined to meet the substantive requirements for the granting of the patent, while in other countries, no or less thorough investigations were combined with some kind of a registration system. This inevitably made it necessary to call in local technical and legal experts. Furthermore, translations were often required. And, of course, in each country one had to pay for the obtaining and maintenance of patents.

This was an extremely unsatisfactory situation, not only for inventors in Europe, but also for those outside Europe, who desired protection in Europe. And this was by no means an ideal situation for the Member States of the European Economic Community. They had to maintain their own national bodies for the granting of patents that partly repeated the work of foreign patent offices. The patent system of that time was complicated, expensive and not very efficient.

2. SOLUTION

Clearly, something needed to be done to ameliorate this situation. Steps were taken, the most important being the entry into force of the Convention on the Grant of European Patents (EPC) in 1977. The EPC created a common procedure for the grant of patents. A European Patent Office (EPO) was set up with the task to examine the applications according to the rules of patent law, as laid down in the Convention. The EPO more or less grants a patent on behalf of the contracting states. A European patent is commonly seen as a bundle of national patents. After the grant of the patent, national patents out of this European bundle patent are submitted to the same regulations as those granted according to national procedures. The differences between national patent laws have dimin-

* Vice-President, Court of Appeal, The Hague; Professor of Industrial Property Law, Utrecht University.

W.P. Heere (Ed.), International Law and The Hague's 750th Anniversary

ished. National patent laws were harmonised by the European Convention on the Unification of Certain Points of Substantive Law of Patents for Invention (signed in Strasbourg in 1963, entered into force in 1980) and the EPC. The EPC has proven to be a great success. The number of applications and patents granted is impressive and continues to grow, whilst the number of contracting states has steadily increased.

Summarising, substantive patent law is at present harmonised on essential issues. As a result of the EPC, centralised granting of patents is a possibility. With a single application and one single procedure, a bundle of national patents can be obtained. Major progress has clearly been made.

3. REMAINING PROBLEM: LITIGATION

But still, the construction is not finished. Patents can be the cause of disputes. How and by whom should these disputes be decided? Besides the limited possibility of opposing the grant of a European patent at the EPO, legal proceedings on infringements and nullification of national patents originating from the European bundle patent should be litigated before national courts. That causes some problems.

Let's assume that a company has been granted a European patent for a certain medicine that is valid in all contracting states of the EPC. Let's also assume that a competitor markets a product that, according to the patentee, infringes the patent rights, in all those same contracting states. Will the patentee have to start infringement proceedings in every single state? And will each national judge have to judge the defense that the patent is invalid?

Having to take legal action is in general a necessary evil: it takes time, it costs money and energy that cannot be used for normal work, it disturbs relations and often creates large and long lasting uncertainties. Having to take legal action against the same alleged violator in different countries about the same infringement and the same question of nullity is plainly disastrous. Judges in different contracting states find the situation rather unattractive. They have to redo the work of their foreign colleagues.

A greater objection might be that the decisions of the various judges could differ. Seen strictly theoretically, this should be excluded by the partly harmonised and partly unified laws that ought to form the basis of the judges' decisions. The possibility of varying outcomes, however, is considerable. The outcomes are, among other things, decided by opinions on the meaning of the patent system, the expertise of the judges, the possibilities for a trial, the costs and the existence of prejudices against, e.g., large and/or foreign companies. These circumstances vary from country to country. Diverging decisions are therefore absolutely not imaginary. The uncertainty of law that results from this, creates a heavy burden for patentees and their competitors. Is it wise to continue certain activities and investments? Within the European Union, this situation is downright unacceptable.

Until recently, people generally assumed that national judges could only pass judgement on infringements and validity of patents that were valid within their country. In the UK, it has been judged that disputes about foreign patents were not 'justiciable'. For the patentee, that leaves no choice other than to start legal proceedings in all countries where infringements have been ascertained. After the granting procedure, nothing is left of the unity of the European patent.

4. CROSS-BORDER INJUNCTIONS

After a judgment of the Dutch Supreme Court in 1989[1] in a trade mark case, that a Dutch judge could prohibit defendants from infringing foreign rights, patentees have often requested the Dutch judges to not only prohibit infringements of Dutch patents, but also of foreign patents. Dutch judges have decided in favour of the patentees in several cases. This has caused various reactions. According to an American lawyer, the Netherlands deserves its place on the map by these cross-border injunctions in cases of infringements of patents. An Italian commentator once pointed out the interest of the Dutch and American multinationals in 'terrorist' and 'cross-border' decisions and suggested that Dutch judges let themselves being used by large companies. An English judge would consider cross-border injunctions as a threat to the European patent system, while patentees in Germany are sometimes advised by their patent agents and lawyers to take their assets away from the Netherlands in order to avoid a Dutch judge declaring that the case is within the jurisdiction of the court. One can deduct that cross-border injunctions have caused some commotion. Dutch lawyers and judges, sometimes designated as 'Rambo-lawyers' and 'Cowboy-judges' respectively, have got something to explain to the other countries.

I cannot go into all aspects of the problems concerning cross-border injunctions, but I will illustrate some using an example. A Belgian patentee has got a European patent that is valid in the Netherlands, Germany, France and the

[1] HR 24 November 1989, *NJ* (1992) p. 404 (*Interlas/Lincoln*). In its decision the Dutch Supreme Court expressed the following view:

> 'Unless the law, the nature of the obligation or a juridical act produces a different result, the person who is obliged to give, to do or not to do something *vis-à-vis* another is ordered to do so by the judge upon the demand of the person to whom the obligation is owed. In general there is no reason to assume that such an order cannot be given when the case is about an obligation – possibly an obligation under the law of a foreign country – which has to be fulfilled outside the Netherlands. A more restrictive vision ... finds no support in law and would have, at a time of increasing international contacts, the undesirable effect on legal practice that in the case of torts with an international character – like infringement of intellectual property rights and unfair competition in several countries, or environmental pollution crossing borders – the Dutch injured party would be compelled to go to court in every country concerned.'

UK. According to the patentee, his patent rights are being infringed in all countries, by different companies. These companies are part of a concern of which the headquarters is located in France. The patentee issues a summons on the French parent company, and the Dutch, German and English subsidiaries to appear before the Dutch judge, and asks the judge to find the defendant to have infringed his European patent in France, the Netherlands, Germany and the UK.

5. INTERNATIONAL JURISDICTION

The first question for a Dutch judge in a case like this is whether he has international jurisdiction. In this case, this question needs to be answered according to the Brussels Convention on Jurisdiction and the Enforcement of Judgments. The principal rule is laid down in article 2, which contains a fundamental principle of the Convention: a defendant domiciled in a contracting state is to be sued in the courts of his domicile: *actor sequitur forum rei.*[2] On the basis of this provision, read together with Article 53, the Dutch judge has jurisdiction to try the action against the Dutch defendant. Until recently, the Dutch judge assumed that his jurisdiction to try the claims against the other defendants was based on Article 6(1) of the Brussels Convention, which provides:

> 'A person domiciled in a contracting state may also be sued: (1) where he is one of a number of defendants, in the courts for the place where any one of them is domiciled.'

This interpretation of Article 6(1) of the Brussels Convention, seems to give the patentee considerable space to find a suitable court. A court is deemed suitable when the infringement injunction can be obtained quickly, well, effectively and cheaply, in those countries where infringements have been ascertained. By this interpretation, the patent judge in The Hague became indeed attractive to patentees who were confronted with infringements of several national patents out of the European bundle patent. What made it even more attractive was the existence of the *kort geding proceedings.* For a relatively low price, the patentee could obtain an effective pan-European injunction.

6. ARTICLE 6(1) BRUSSELS CONVENTION

Was this the solution? As I pointed out before, opinions were mixed. There is some friction. Firstly, this interpretation of Article 6(1) conflicts with the

[2] A. Dashwood, R. Hacon and R. White, *A Guide to the Civil Jurisdiction and Judgments Convention* (Deventer 1987) p. 21.

principal rule of Article 2. In Case 189/87[3] *Kalfelis* v. *Schröder*, the European Court pointed out that the jurisdiction provided for in Article 6(1) is an exception to the principle that jurisdiction is vested in the courts of the state of the defendant's domicile. The exception must be treated in such a manner that there is no possibility of the very existence of that principle being called into question. According to the Court, that possibility might arise if the plaintiff were at liberty to make a claim against a number of defendants with the sole object of ousting the jurisdiction of the courts of the State where one of the defendants is domiciled. In order that such a possibility may be excluded, there must be a connection between the claims made against each of the defendants. The European Court ruled:

> 'For Article 6(1) of the Convention to apply there must exist between the various actions brought by the same plaintiff against different defendants a connection of such a kind that it is expedient to determine the actions together in order to avoid the risk of irreconcilable judgments resulting from separate proceedings.'[4]

Furthermore, neither forum-shopping nor uncertainty about the question which court has international jurisdiction, is something that the Brussels Convention tried to stimulate.

In the UK, a party that had been sued in the Netherlands tried to move the English judge to issue an injunction for the plaintiffs in the Netherlands to continue the suit there (anti-suit order). Neither the High Court nor the Court of Appeal has given such an order although both were of the opinion that the Dutch judge had no jurisdiction.[5] The Court of Appeal referred questions about this to the European Court of Justice.

[3] [1988] ECR 5565.

[4] Compare Jenard who observed in his Report (OJC59 5.3.79):

In order for this rule to be applicable there must be a connection between the claims made against each of the defendants, as for example in the case of joint debtors. It follows that an action cannot be brought solely with the object of ousting the jurisdiction of the courts of the State in which the defendant is domiciled.

[5] The Court of Appeal considered:

'We have every confidence that the Dutch Court will, when deciding what to do, take into account that this Court will be referring to the European Court of Justice questions to elucidate how articles 6, 16(4), 19 and 24 should be applied to the dispute. It will give proper weight to our conclusion that it would be wrong for this Court to anticipate the decision of the European Court. It will, we believe, also consider carefully the other views expressed in this judgement and, of course, the submissions of the parties and the facts.'

7. COURT OF APPEAL THE HAGUE ON ARTICLE 6(1) BRUSSELS CONVENTION

Very recently, the Court of Appeal in The Hague has expounded how it interprets Article 6(1) of the Brussels Convention.[6] According to the judgment of the Court, this article can no longer form a basis for jurisdiction in suits against foreign defendants allegedly infringing foreign patents. However, if the defendants cooperate, one can judge that that would be a case of a joint action. In that case, all defendants can be sued before a single court. Not before the judge of the place of residence of one of the defendants, to the choice of the plaintiff, but just for the judge of the place of residence of the defendant who is in charge of the common acting. In that case, according to the court, not only has justice been done to the principal rule of Article 2 and the exceptional character of Article 6(1), but also the decision matches the decision of the European Court in the case *Shevill* v. *Presse Alliance*[7] with regard to article 5(3).

Jurisdiction over injunctions of infringements of foreign patents seems a sensitive subject. An explanation could be that the granting of patents was traditionally a task for each separate state that was among others being led by considerations of economical politics, A foreign judge who prohibits an economic activity in another state will find resistance.[8] Sovereignty is at stake.

[6] Case *Expandable Grafts et al.* v. *Boston Scientific B.V. et al.*, 23 April 1998.

[7] Case 68/93 [1995] ECR 415. The substance of the case concerned an international libel which had been written in the press. The Court held:

> '(31) In accordance with the requirement of the sound administration of justice, the basis of the rule of special jurisdiction in Article 5(3), the courts of each contracting state in which the defamatory publication was distributed and in which the victim claims to have suffered injury to his reputation are territorially the best place to assess the libel committed in that State and to determine the extent of the corresponding damage.
>
> (32) Although there are admittedly disadvantages to having different courts ruling on various aspects of the same dispute, the plaintiff always has the option of bringing his entire claim before the courts either of the defendant's domicile or of the place where the publisher of the defamatory publication is established.'

[8] Compare High Court of Justice (Mr. Justice Aldous) in the case of Plastus Kreativ AB v. Minnesota Mining and Manufacturing Company, 8 and 9 December 1995, [1995] R.P.C., p. 447:

> 'For myself I would not welcome the task of having to decide whether a person had infringed a foreign patent. Although patent actions appear on their face to be disputes between two parties, in reality they also concern the public. A finding on infringement is a finding that a monopoly granted by the state is to be enforced. The result is invariably that the public has to pay higher prices than if the monopoly did not exist. If that be the proper result, then that result should, I believe, come about from a decision of a court situated in the state where the public have to pay the higher prices. One only has to imagine a decision of this court that the German public should pay to a British company substantial sums of money to realise the difficulties that might arise. I believe that, if the local courts are responsible for enforcing and deciding questions of validity and infringement, the conclusions reached are likely to command the respect of the public. Also a conclusion that a patent is infringed or not infringed involves in this country a decision on validity as in this country no man can infringe an invalid patent. In the present case the plaintiffs

8. ARTICLE 16(4) BRUSSELS CONVENTION

Assuming that the obstacle of Article 6(1) can be overcome, another problem remains, caused by Article 16(4), relating to exclusive jurisdiction. This Article states:

> 'The following courts shall have exclusive jurisdiction, regardless of domicile:
> (...)
> (4) in proceedings concerned with the registration or validity of patents...the courts of the Contracting State in which the deposit or registration has been applied for, has taken place or is under the terms of an international convention deemed to have taken place.'

Only a judge in the country where the patent has been registered can nullify patents. The annulment of a foreign patent is therefore never within the jurisdiction of a Dutch judge. What has to happen if a defendant who has been accused of the infringement of a patent, claims that the patent is invalid? This is not in the least an academic problem. In many infringement cases, we see the defense that the patent is invalid. English judges are of the opinion that the judge

admit the validity of the patent and therefore, there is no dispute upon the matter. However, it will be implicit in the judgement of this court that there has been infringement, and that, between the parties, the patent is valid. Thus, I believe it is at least convenient that infringement, like validity, is decided in the state in which it arises.

I also believe that it would not normally be right for the courts of this country to decide a dispute on infringement of a foreign patent in respect of acts done outside this country provided there is an adequate remedy in the relevant country. The local court is able to look at the particular acts in the context in which they are carried out. If it happened that there was not an adequate remedy in the other state, then it might be appropriate that action be taken in a state in which there was an appropriate remedy.'

Compare High Court of Justice (Mr. Justice Aldous) in the cases of *Chiron Corporation* v. *Murex Diagnostics* and of *Chiron Corporation* v. *Organon* (29 November 1994), F.S.R. 1995, 338:

'I have already referred to the fact that the Dutch Court granted an injunction restraining infringement of the equivalent Dutch patent in Holland and also granted injunctions in relation to corresponding patents in other European countries. I understand that the Dutch Court concluded that the law of infringement and validity was the same in Holland as in those other countries and therefore its conclusion should be applied to those countries as well as in Holland.

At one time I wondered whether it would be right for this court to do the same as the Dutch Court, but have concluded that it would not be right for this court to grant an injunction which had an effect outside the United Kingdom. Further I believe that the Dutch Court was correct not to grant an injunction preventing trade in the United Kingdom. Even though the basic law as to validity and infringement of patents is the same in Holland as it is in this country, the factual matrix is unlikely to be the same as the procedure for ascertaining the facts and scientific evidence are different. Further this case shows that there are many considerations which have to be taken into account by a United Kingdom judge before deciding that injunctive relief is appropriate, which do not appear to be relevant in a Dutch Court. Thus it would be unlikely that a Dutch Court could be sure that an injunction would be appropriate in the United Kingdom upon an application in Holland for interlocutory, preliminary or final relief.'

in this case has no longer jurisdiction on the basis of Article 19 Brussels Convention. In the above-mentioned decision of the court in The Hague it was judged that the jurisdiction over the infringement claim does not disappear because of the defense that the patent is invalid. But the judge will have to stay the infringement proceedings until the foreign judge has decided upon the invalidity of the patent.

If the judge has jurisdiction to handle cases of infringement of foreign patents, he needs to answer another question, namely which laws are applicable. Unfortunately, limitations of time prevent me from examining this question.

9. CONCLUSIONS

What conclusions can be drawn? Firstly, it should be clear that the possibilities offered by the Brussels Convention to have infringements of patents in several countries judged by a single judge, are few, as a result of the limitations of Article 6(1) and Article 16(4). The drafters of the Brussels Convention seem to have forgotten the infringement of parallel rights of intellectual property.

Secondly, the need for a solution to the problem is growing. It is to be hoped that at the review conference of the Brussels Convention, this problem will attract the attention it deserves.In my view the actual situation as regards litigation does not meet the economic and commercial reality in Europe. Big disputes should be decided by a real European court.

EMBASSY EMPLOYEES AND STATE IMMUNITY: THE 1982 ILA DRAFT

Paul J.I.M. de Waart*

One might have expected that the post-Berlin Wall victory of the global market over the age-old sovereignty of states would have taken the sting out of the *jure imperii - jure gestionis* controversy. After all, the present wave of privatization urged states all over the world to stand back. Civil servants enjoy no longer a special status in labour law. Their employment contracts are, so to say, commercialized. One might also have expected that the market would also have substantially changed the role of embassies through its offer of telecommunication services, such as fax, internet and email. However, all the historic and modern positions so far had no impact on state immunity and embassy employees.

On the contrary, the stepping aside of states in favour of the civil society appears to have given a fresh impetus to the classic ideas of the economist Adam Smith, the ideologist or prophet of the free market, in respect of the wealth of nations and the role of the state: 'The system of natural liberty leaves the sovereign only three duties: (1) the defence of the country; (2) the administration of justice; and (3) the maintenance of certain public works.'[1] The maintenance of diplomatic and consular relations were not included, so much prevailed the market in his treatise. This omission may be explained by his concept of the role of a statesman:

> '[T]he statesman, who should attempt to direct private people in what manner they ought to employ their capitals, would not only load himself with a most unnecessary attention, but assume an authority which could be safely trusted, not only to no single person, but to no council or senate whatever, and which would nowhere be so dangerous as in the hands of a man who had folly and presumption enough to fancy himself fit to exercise it.'[2]

Smith' contemporary, the international lawyer Emery de Vattel dealt not so much with diplomatic relations as with consular relations, and that from the angle of commerce. He did not discuss the role of ambassadors or embassies, but the one of consuls and consulates as one of the most modern and useful institutions in his

* Prof. em. of International Law, Vrije Universiteit, Amsterdam.
[1] Adam Smith, *The Wealth of Nations* (1776) the Cannan edn. (1937) p. 651.
[2] Ibid, at p. 423.

W.P. Heere (Ed.), International Law and The Hague's 750th Anniversary

days, to take care of the protection of de rights and privileges of their nation in international commerce.[3]

1. ILC DRAFT: EMBASSY EMPLOYMENT CONTRACTS

The United States delegate in the Sixth (legal) Committee of the 52nd UN General Assembly, Mrs. Linda Jacobson, explicitly mentioned the controversies concerning Article 11 of the ILC Draft, dealing with contracts of employment of embassy employees. In her view, the provisions of this Article became less adequate with time because the current major labour- employment issues facing diplomatic missions were not addressed.[4] These issues related to law suits against foreign states for action in respect of downsizing, reorganization and closing of diplomatic facilities and the withdrawal of diplomatic missions from participating in bankrupt social security systems for their locally hired personnel. On behalf of the USA she argued that first and foremost the gap must be bridged between the current scope of Article 11 of the ILC Draft and state practice. This Article reads:

> '1. Unless otherwise agreed between the States concerned, a State cannot invoke immunity from jurisdiction before a court of another State which is otherwise competent in a proceeding which relates to a contract of employment between the State and an individual for work performed or to be performed, in whole or in part, in the territory of that other State.
> 2. Paragraph 1 does not apply if:
> (a) the employee has been recruited to perform functions closely related to the exercise of governmental authority;
> (b) the subject of the proceeding is the recruitment, renewal of employment or reinstatement of an individual;
> (c) the employee was neither a national nor a habitual resident of the State of the forum at the time when the proceeding is instituted; or
> (c) the employer State and the employee have otherwise agreed in writing, subject to any consideration of public policy conferring upon the courts of the State of the forum exclusive jurisdiction by reason of the subject-matter of the proceeding.'[5]

Comments and observations of governments and international organizations on the first ILC Draft of 1986 did not result in substantial amendments apart from the deletion of the final part of paragraph one of Article 11 which read: 'if the employee has been recruited in that other state and is covered by the social security provisions which may be in force in that other state.'

[3] Emery de Vattel, *Le droit des gens ou principes de la loi naturelle, appliqués à la conduite & aux affaires des nations & des souverains* (1758) p. 120.

[4] Press Release GA/L/3059 of 11 November 1997.

[5] *ILM* (1991) pp. 1565-1575.

2. ILA DRAFT: RESTRICTION OF SOVEREIGN IMMUNITY

The ILC Draft does not differ essentially from the 1982 ILA Draft Articles for a Convention on State Immunity. The latter Draft intended to harmonize the differences between the European codification of the restrictive theory of sovereign immunity as reflected in the 1972 European Convention on State Immunity and the American codification as set forth in the Foreign Sovereign Immunities Act of 1976. The restrictive approach also underlay the 1978 State Immunity Act of the United Kingdom, the Pakistan Act of 1981, the South-African Foreign States Immunities Act of 1981 and the Canadian Act of 1982. The Committee member from the then USSR Professor Bogdanov considered the ILA Draft for that very reason as a too one-sided document because it minimized the impact of less restrictive legislation of other countries.[6]

Article III of the ILA Draft, dealt with employment contract under the heading of 'Exceptions to Immunity from Adjudication' as follows:

> 'A foreign State shall not be immune from the jurisdiction of the forum State in the following instances inter alia
> (...)
> C. Where the foreign State enters into a contract for employment in the forum State, or where work under such a contract is to be performed wholly or partly in the forum State and the proceedings relate to the contract. This provision shall not apply if:
> 1. At the time the proceedings are brought for the employee is a national of the foreign State; or
> 2. At the time of the contract for employment was made the employee was neither a national nor a permanent resident of the forum State; or
> 3. The employer and the employee have otherwise agreed in writing.
> This provision shall not confer on tribunals in the forum State competence in respect of employees appointed under the public (administrative) law of the foreign State.'[7]

The ILA Report stated that Article III.C closely followed the language of Article 5 of the European Convention on State Immunity and was quite similar to section 4 of the 1978 UK State Immunity Act.

It should be noted that the ILA Draft Convention – Article IX A – is without prejudice to other applicable international agreements as well as the rules of international law relating to diplomatic and consular privileges and immunities, to immunities of foreign public ships and to the immunities of international organizations. According to the second saving clause – Article IX B – nothing in the Convention shall be interpreted as conferring on tribunals in the forum state any additional competence with respect to the subject matter (*ratione materiae*).

6 The International Law Association, *Report of the Sixtieth Conference, Montreal 1982* (1983), pp. 325-326, 337, 338 and 340.

7 Ibid, at p. 8.

This saving clause particularly referred to Article III C, i.e. contracts of employment between an individual and a government.

The Draft Convention owes to the Committee member Professor Seyerstedt from Norway that the above mentioned specific reservation was included in the final text of Article III.C: 'This provision shall not confer on tribunals in the forum State competence in respect of employees appointed under the public (administrative) law of the foreign State.' Seyerstedt had argued, originally in vain, that most users of the Convention will not immediately combine the provision of Article III.C with Article IX.B.[8] He had also stated that practice is not so consistent in respect of state organs that performed merely *acta jure gestionis*, such as trade delegations and state railways. The discussion on what is decisive in distinguishing *acta jure imperii* from *acta jure gestionis*: the nature or the motive continues in the Sixth Committee on the ILC Draft to this very day.

3. NATURE V. PURPOSE OF COMMERCIAL CONTRACTS

Mrs. Jacobson saw in the Sixth (legal) Committee of the 52nd UN General Assembly little chance of reconciling the important issue of criteria for determining commercial activity and measures of constraint According to her, consensus must await the further development of state practice and customary international law. Her Chinese colleague, Mr. Duan Jilon, reiterated China's position on the topic. He argued that in judging whether or not a transaction was commercial, its nature and purpose had to be taken into account.

China, former socialist countries like the Russian Federation, third world countries like India, but also France, are strongly in favour of the purpose-approach. The position of France may explain that the European Convention does not deal with the issue. Nevertheless it is not yet a party to the Convention.

Article I(C) of the ILA Draft reflects the prevailing western view on defining commercial activities:

> 'The term "commercial activity" refers either to a regular course of commercial conduct or a particular commercial transaction or act. It shall include any activity or transaction into which a foreign State enters or in which it engages otherwise than in the exercise of sovereign authority and in particular:
> 1. Any arrangement for the supply of goods or services;
> 2. Any financial transaction involving lending or borrowing or guaranteeing financial obligations.
> In applying this definition, the commercial character of a particular act shall be determined by reference to the nature of the act, rather than by reference to its purpose.'[9]

[8] Ibid, at pp. 331-332.
[9] Ibid, at p. 6.

The ILC Draft is more careful. Its Article 2 (1c) defines a commercial transaction as

> '(i) any commercial contract or transaction for the sale of goods or supply of services;
> (ii) any contract for a loan or other transaction of a financial nature, including any obligation of guarantee or of indemnity in respect of any such loan or transaction;
> (iii) any other contract or transaction of a commercial, industrial, trading or professional nature, but not including a contract of employment of persons.'

However, according to Article 2 (2) 'I[n] determining whether a contract or transaction is a "commercial transaction" under paragraph 1(c) reference should be made primarily to the nature of the contract or transaction, but its purpose should also be taken into account if, in the practice of the state which is a party to it, that purpose is relevant to determining the non-commercial character of the contract or transaction'. Moreover, this provision is without prejudice to the use of the term or to the meanings it may be given to in other international instruments or in the internal law of any state. The (op)position of the above-mentioned states as regards the nature-purpose debate makes it improbable that the convening of a diplomatic conference, as was decided by the General Assembly in 1994, might overcome the existing controversies on short notice.

4. SMALL SIGN OF HOPE

The current diplomatic conference in Rome on the establishment of a criminal court gave states a welcome pretext to postpone the proposed diplomatic conference on the 1991 ILC Draft on immunities of states and their property to 1999 or thereafter. Western states like to avoid a failure. Even when the diplomatic conference might result in the adoption of the text of the ILC Draft, the problem will not be solved unless the proponents of the purpose standard will switch over and ratify the intended convention on jurisdictional immunities of states and their property. However, there is one small sign of hope. The French delegate, Mr. François Alabrune, stated in the Sixth Committee that different rules on immunities of states, resulting from national legislation or from the determination by courts on that topic ran the risk of having disparities of laws becoming greater. In his opinion the ILC Draft would eliminate disparity by giving states the same rights and the same duties. This compliment sounds encouraging from a representative of a state which is a confirmed defender of the motive approach of *jure gestionis*.

From a worldwide perspective the statement of the Dutch Supreme Court of 28 May 1993 in the case between the Russian Federation and the Pied-Rich BV at Amsterdam that the nature of the act is decisive and not the purpose is somewhat too firm. However, developing international law neither excludes that the Supreme Court ruled as it did in the context of the law of the forum state.

The Dutch position will now be dealt with more in detail and depth by the panel members Mrs. Schrevelius and Mr. Gloor. The latter will discuss the relationship between state immunity and the dismissal of embassy employees, the former the attitude of Dutch courts and state practice towards contracts of embassy employees. Let us now enjoy their opinions which may turn the balance in favour of the ILC Draft, expressed as they will be in the legal capital of the world.

EMPLOYER STATES AND SOVEREIGN IMMUNITY: THE GENEVA LABOUR COURT PRACTICE

Werner Gloor*

1. INTRODUCTION

Persons entitled to international immunities do not only act in the diplomatic forum, they also participate, *more privatorum*, to the normal social life of the guest state, by concluding contracts over sale, lease and services. They must respect the laws of the receiving state, if no specific exemption exists[1]; their position of immunity not only means that they are not subject to the local law, but can, *eventualiter*, mean that they are not subject to the local *jurisdiction*.

Whether an international person is eligible for immunity, and if so, to what extent, depends on the nature of that person and the nature of the dispute at hand. State immunity is not identical to the immunity of an international organisation;[2] and the immunity of a diplomat[3] is not the same as the immunity granted to a consul[4] or an international civil servant.[5] Employment disputes with locally hired staff are much more likely to interfere with the diplomatic functions than disputes related to sale or lease contracts.

The civil courts of Geneva have had to deal with immunity-related cases since the time of the League of Nations.[6] However, the local Labour Court (TPH) was

* Attorney-at-law, member of the Geneva Bar. The author is also a clerk at the Geneva Labour Court, where he is in charge of drafting decisions for the Court. Earlier versions of this article have been published, in *German*: 'Arbeitgeberstaaten in der Praxis des Genfer Arbeitsgerichts', *ArbR* (Bern, Stämpfli, 1996) pp. 49 - 72; in *French*: 'Etats employeurs dans la pratique du Tribunal des Prud'hommes de Genève', 9 *International Geneva Yearbook*, (1997) pp. 49 - 63.

[1] For example Art. 12 al. 3 Age Insurance Law (LAVS) and Art. 33 OLAVS; Cf., Arrêts du Tribunal Fédéral Suisse (ATF) 120 V 405, *M.* v. *Ivory Coast.*

[2] Cf., ATF 118 Ib 562, *Fougerolle* v. *CERN* = Semaine Judiciaire, Geneva (SJ) (1993) p. 278 = 102 *ILR* p. 209; Tribunal des Prud'hommes (TPH) 17 November 1993, *Malek* v. *Ligue des Etats Arabes*, affirmed by Chambre d'appel des Prud'hommes (CAPH) 16 October 1995.

[3] CAPH, 24 March. 1998, *Lorenzo* v. *Van Meeuwen*; TPH, 24 March 1993, *Marbella* v. *Iacovou,* affirmed by CAPH, 3 November 1993; TPH, 1 March 1989, *El Hanzouli* v. *Al Baiz*, Jahrbuch für Schweizerisches Arbeitsrecht (*JAR*) (1989) p. 439.

[4] TPH, 29 June 1988, *Desta* v . *Pinto*, *JAR* (1989) p. 304; Cour de Justice (CJ) 6 December 1966, *Barakat* v. *Toletti*, *SJ* (1968) p. 264.

[5] Tribunal administratif, Genève, 15 June 1977, *X* v. *Genève*, *SJIR* (Schweizerisches Jahrbuch für Internationales Recht) (1978) p. 145; TPH, 16 March 1993, *Senanayake* v. *Yammin*.

[6] Cf., G. Perrenoud, *Régime des privilèges et immunités des Missions diplomatiques étrangères et des Organisations internationales en Suisse* (Lausanne 1949) p. 165 ss.

W.P. Heere (Ed.), International Law and The Hague's 750th Anniversary

not concerned about immunity problems for many years.[7] That is not to say that disputes between employers who held positions of immunity and their local staff did not arise. Rather these disputes were considered not to be *triable* by courts, for reasons of public international law and the then prevailing rules of labour litigation procedure.[8] In exchange, the Swiss government usually assisted parties to find an amicable settlement.[9] The situation changed after the decision of the Swiss Federal Supreme Court of 22 March 1984 re *Calopristi* v. *India.*[10] The claimant was an Italian clerical aid of the Indian embassy in Bern. The Federal Court, qualifying the contract as private law transaction, rejected India's plea of sovereign immunity. This decision created an avalanche of similar proceedings in Geneva against employers in positions of immunity;[11] plaintiffs were suing not only states, but also diplomats, consuls, international organisations and international civil servants.[12]

This present report tries to outline the principle and extent of jurisdictional immunity of employer states in the light of the Geneva Labour Court's practice. Its case law is widely based. on foreign and international legal sources.[13] The matter at hand concerns not only public international law, but also private international law. However, questions of territorial and material competence, as well as procedural issues are not examined here.

2. STATE IMMUNITY

Under customary international law, no state may exercise its jurisdiction over another state without its consent: *par in parem non habet iurisdictionem.* The absolute immunity rule is based on the principle of sovereign equality of states. However, as states started to extend commercial activities after 1918, the rule lost

[7] The first suits were filed against *Permanent Missions*, TPH, 30. January 1965, *Romios* v. *Délégation du Nigéria*, driver; TPH, 16 December 1971, *Tsakos* v. *USA* = 75 *International Law Reports (ILR)* p. 78.

[8] According to Art. 1 al. 1 lit. d of the *Loi sur la juridiction des Prud'hommes (LJP)*, enacted on 30 March 1963, the Labour Court had no competence (jurisdiction) over 'contestations entre personnes physiques et morales jouissant de l'immunité de juridiction et leur personnel'.

[9] Sometimes there was some need of pressure. Strong *suggestions* were also addressed to the courts, not to accept the cases.

[10] ATF 110 II 255 = 82 *ILR*, p. 14, with critical annotation by Monnier, *SJIR* (1985) p. 235 and Vischer, *SJIR* (1986) p. 242.

[11] Since 1985, almost 100 similar suits have been filed with the Geneva Labour Court; astonishingly no other suit against an employer state has been filed in Bern since *Calopristi* v. *India.*

[12] For an overview in French: cf,. W. Gloor. 'Employeurs titulaires de l'immunité de juridiction', in *Le Juriste suisse face au droit et aux jugements étrangers* (Fribourg, 1988) p. 262; *idem*,'Contrat de travail et immunité de juridiction', *SJ* (1995) p. 649 ss.

[13] In contrast to private international law, public international law is *international* not only as to its objects, but also as to its *legal sources*.

its strength, first in Belgium, Italy and in Switzerland,[14] and after 1945 also in France, Germany, Spain, Great Britain and the United States. Today the *restrictive* rule of state immunity is generally accepted; this is confirmed by the existence of treaties[15] and draft conventions,[16] national legislation,[17] governmental declarations,[18] the case law of municipal courts [19]and legal teaching.[20]

[14] Cf., ATF 44 I 49. For the Swiss Federal Supreme Court practice since then: J.-F. Egli, 'L'immunité de juridiction et d'exécution de Etats étrangers et de leur agents dans la jurisprudence du Tribunalfédéral', in Festschrift 100 Jahr SchKG (Zurich 1986) p. 201; Forni, 'Die Gerichts- und Vollstreckungsimmunität fremder Staaten in der bundesgerichtlichen Rechtsprechung', *SJIR* (1986) p. 15 ss.; Simonius, 'Privatrechtliche Forderung und Staatenimmunität, in Festgabe zum Schweizerischen Juristentag 1985 (Basel 1985) p. 335; W. Habscheid, 'Die Staatenimmunität im Erkenntnis- und Vollstreckungsverfahren', in Festschrift Giger (Zurich 1989) p. 213 ss.; Ch. Dominicé, 'Gerichts- und Vollstreckungsimmunität fremder Staaten und Staatsoberhäupter', *Schweizerische Juristische Kartothek* (*SJK*) No. 634, 1 July 1992.

[15] See, e.g., the European Convention on State Immunity, signed in Basel, on 16 May 1972 (ECSI, RS 0. 273.1); Message of the Federal Council, 27 May 1981, FF 1981 II 937; Ch.-M. Krafft, 'La Convention européenne sur l'immunité des Etats du 16 mai 1972', *SJIR* (1975) p. 11; Ch. Karczewski, 'Das Europäische Uebereinkommen über Staatenimmunität vom 16. 5. 1972', 54 *Rabels Zeitschrift* (1990) p. 533; up to date, the ECSI has been ratified by Belgium, Luxemburg, the Netherlands, Austria, Switzerland, Great Britain, Cyprus and Germany. The Italian Corte di cassazione applies the convention as an expression of customary international law, cf., Cass., 13 February 1992, *Guerrero* v. *Stato di Francia*, *Rivista di diritto internazionale privato e processuale* (*RDIPP*) (1994) p. 398.

[16] E.g., the International Law Commission's (definitive) Draft, 'Convention on Jurisdictional Immunities of States and their Property', *ILC Yearbook*, Vol. II, Part Two (1991) p. 12 ss.

[17] USA: *Foreign Sovereign Immunities Act*, 1976; GB: *State Immunity Act*, 1978; Singapore: *State Immunity Act*, 1979; Pakistan, *State Immunity Ordinance*, 1981; South Africa: *Foreign States Immunities Act*, 1981; Canada: *State Immunity Act*, 1982; all texts in: G.-M. Badre, *State Immunity* (The Hague, 1984). Add: Australia, Foreign States Immunities Act, 1985, *ILM* (1986) p. 716 and Argentina, Ley No. 24.488 sobre Inmunidad Jurisdiccional de los Estados Extranjeros, *Boletín Oficial*, 28 June 1995.

[18] In particular in response to a questionary submitted to the ILC; e.g., Swiss response to the ILC Draft, *ILC Yearbook*, Vol. II, Part One (1988) p. 163 = *SJIR* (1988) p. 212.

[19] *Leading cases*: Austria, Supreme Court, 6 August 1958, Neustein, 65 *ILR*, p. 3; Germany, federal Constitutional Court, 30 April 1963, *Empire of Iran*, 45 *ILR*, p. 57; USA, Court of Appeal, 2nd Circ., 9 August 1964, *Victory Transport*, 35 *ILR*, p. 110; Canada, Supreme Court, 31 May 1971, *Venne* v. *Congo*, 64 *ILR*, p. 24; France, Court of Cassation, 17 January 1973, *SA Hôtel George V*, 64 *ILR*, p. 61; GB, Court of Appeal, 13 January 1977, *Trendtex*, 64 *ILR*, p. 111; Italy, Court of Cassation, 21 October 197, *Jazbez*, 77 *ILR*, p. 602; Pakistan, Supreme Court, 8 July 1981, *Quereshi* v. *USSR*, 64 *ILR*, p. 585; Brazil, Supreme Court, 14 April 1982, *Syria* v. *Egypt*, 91 *ILR*, p. 288; India, Supreme Court, 5 November 1986, *Dhalla*, 92 *ILR*, p. 530; Spain, Supreme Court, 1 December 1986, *Diana* v. *RSA*, 86 *ILR*, p. 512; Netherlands, Supreme Court, 22 December 1989, *Van der Hulst* v. *USA*, 94 *ILR*, p. 374; Australia, Supreme Court of Victoria, 17 February 1992, *Ried* v. *Nauru*, 101 *ILR*, p. 193.

[20] Fundamental: G.-M. Badre, *State Immunity* (The Hague, 1984) p. 240; H. Damian, *Staatenimmunität und Gerichtszwang* (Berlin, 1985) p. 261; J.W. Dellapenna, *Suing Foreign Governments and Their Corporations* (Washington, 1988) p. 481; R. Esser, *Klagen gegen ausländische Staaten* (Frankfurt a. M., 1990) p. 336; G. Martino, *L'immunità giurisdizionale degli stati stranieri tra regionalismo ed universalismo* (Salerno, 1990) p. 314; I. Pingel, *Les immunités des Etats en droit international* (Bruxelles, 1998) p. 542.; Ch. Schreuer., *State immunity; Some recent developments* (Cambridge, 1988) p. 199; Cosnard, *La soumission des Etats aux tribunaux internes* (Paris, 1996) p. 320.

According to the restrictive rule of state immunity, foreign states are only entitled to (jurisdictional) immunity with respect to acts performed with sovereign power (*acta iure imperii),* but not when they engage in private law transactions, similar to those of private persons (*acta iure gestionis*). The main problem is to *qualify* the particular act or activity of the state. Qualification is effected *lege fori.*[21] Generally, courts rely more on the *nature* than on the *purpose* of the act.[22]

3. EMPLOYMENT CONTRACTS

3.1. General observations

Employment contracts present the particularity that they, in opposition to commercial contracts, imply the (permanent) subordination of the employee to the employer, and its integration into the employer's business. The state, when acting as an employer, underlines this fact by recruiting its *fonctionnaires* by an unilateral, administrative decision (nomination). However, beyond its territory, the state's *imperium* ceases; it is then obliged to resort to techniques and forms of *private law.*[23] Therefore, the conclusion by a foreign state of an employment contract in the forum state is deemed *a priori* to be a *commercial act*, i.e., accomplished *iure gestionis.*[24]

3.2. Locally recruited embassy staff

The employment contracts with locally hired, subordinate personnel of diplomatic, permanent or consular representations present some difficulties.[25] These employees perform work in an environment of core governmental activity; if the receiving state accepts that its tribunals deal with complaints of such employees,

[21] *BVerfGE* 46, 342 = *Neue Juristische Wochenschrift* (*NJW*) (1978) p. 485; G. Walter, *Internationales Zivilprozessrecht der Schweiz* (Bern, 1995) p. 60.

[22] Cf., Art. 2 al. 2 ILC Draft 1991, *ILC Yearbook*, Vol. II, Part Two (1991) p. 13; D.W. Greig, 'Forum State Jurisdiction and Sovereign Immunity Under the International Law Commission's Draft Articles', 38 *ICLQ* (1989) p. 256 ss.; ATF 120 II 400, p. 406.

[23] Badr, op. cit. n. 21, at p. 94; A. Grisel, *Traité de droit administratif*, Vol. I (Neuchâtel, 1984) p. 477; ATF 110 II 255, cons. 4 d; 113 Ia 371 cons. 2.

[24] Cf., Art. 5 al. 1 ECSI: 'A Contracting State cannot claim immunity from the jurisdiction of another Contracting State if the proceedings relate to a contract of employment between the State and an individual where the work has to be performed on the territory of the State of the forum.'

[25] These employment contracts are specially dealt with in Art. 11 of ILC Draft 1991:

> '1. Unless otherwise agreed between the States concerned, a State cannot invoke immunity from jurisdiction before a court of another State which is otherwise competent in a proceeding which relates to a contract of employment between the State and an individual for work performed or to be performed, in whole or in part, in the territory of that other State.

it risks violating a principle of diplomatic law, confirmed by custom and treaty: *ne impediatur legatio.*[26]

In these cases it is not the nature of the *legal transaction* or the *denomination* of functions transferred, but only the nature of the activity really performed by the local employee[27] which is central to the existence and extent of the defendant employer state's[28] jurisdictional immunity. In cases where the plaintiff performed only subordinate, ancillary functions at the mission, the employer state can not invoke its sovereign immunity.[29] Should the claimant, however, be in charge of governmental functions or otherwise closely involved in the decision-making process at the mission, the plea of sovereign immunity would be admitted.[30]

2. Paragraph 1 does not apply if:
a) the employee has been recruited to perform functions closely related to the exercise of government authority;
b) the subject of the proceedings is the recruitment, renewal of employment or reinstatement of an individual;
c) the employee was neither a national nor a habitual resident of the State of the forum at the time when the contract of employment was concluded;
d) the employee is a national of the employer State at the time when the proceeding is instituted;
e) the employer State and the employee have otherwise agreed in writing, subject to any considerations of public policy conferring on the courts of the State of the forum exclusive jurisdiction by reason of the subject-matter of the proceeding.'

[26] Cf., Vienna Convention on Diplomatic Relations of 18 April 1961 (VCD, RS 0.191.01, preamble; Vienna Convention on Consular Relations of 24 April 1963 (VCR, RS 0.191.01), as well as the headquarters agreements between Switzerland with the international organisations established at Geneva, Bern and Basel (see RS. 192.120.1 ss.); *Département fédéral des affaires étrangères, Direction de droit international public* (*DFAE/DDIP*), Legal Opinion, 23 March 1983, *SJIR* (1984) p. 140 ss.).

[27] Some Arab representations in Geneva are used to hire low ranking diplomats among the Arab students at the local university; they are recruited through private *law employment contract.*

[28] The employer is the sending state, not its diplomatic mission. Diplomatic and consular representations have no legal personality. See Cour de Justice, Geneva, 7 December 1984, *Champel, SJ* (1985) p. 169 = 102 *ILR*, p. 181; ATF, 31 July 1990, Bankruptcy Chamber, *Hacco;* Tribunal of Rome, 23 Oktober 1967, 71 *ILR*, p. 238; Cass. civ., 7 January 1992, *RecueilDalloz Sirey* (1992) I. R p. 43; L. Dembinsk, *The Modern Law of Diplomacy. External Missions of States and International Organisations* (Dordrecht, UNITAR, 1988) p. 28.

[29] TPH, 17 December 1971, *Tsakos* v. *USA,* translator at a cultural manifestation = 75 *ILR*, p.78; TPH, 16 April 1987, *Landano* v. *USA,* telephone operator = *JAR* (1988) p. 424; TPH, 24 June 1987, *Epoux Leyson* v. *Saudi Arabia*, private servants of the Saudi Ambassador; TPH, 1 December 1993, *Moudrik* v. *Iraq*, secretary, affirmed by CAPH, 1 September 1994; 16 September 1992, *Cuarto* v. *Qatar*, warden = *JAR* (1993) p. 111; 27 April 1994, *Nicoud* v. *USA*, driver = JAR 1995 79; 16 February 1995, *Kuchen* v. *USA*, assistant to the visa department of the general consulate = *JAR* (1996) p. 327; TPH, 8 Oktober 1997, *Baron* v. *France*, gardener at the general consulate.

[30] TPH, 12 December 1990, *Solaiman* v. *Iran*, announced as 'cook' to the host state, but in reality was a political secretary, Nr. 2 at the Iranian general consulate, and directly reporting to the information minister., affirmed by CAPH 12 December 1991; TPH, 11 December 1991, *Nour* v. *Egypt*, chief of press; TPH, 24 June 1993, *Razid* v. *Iraq*, official interpreter, affirmed by CAPH, 14 Februari 1994, but on further appeal reversed by Federal Tribunal, ATF 120 II 408 = *Schweizerische Zeitschrift für Internationales und Europäisches Recht* (*SZIER*) (1995) p. 605, with critical annotation by Gloor, *SJ* (1995) p. 649.

The Geneva Labour Court's decisions are in accordance with the dominant court practice[31] and literature[32] of most of OECD Member States; these developments have also influenced the work of the International Law Commission, which, coincidentally, holds its meetings in *Geneva*. Only Canada,[33] Portugal,[34]

[31] *Leading cases*: Switzerland, Federal Tribunal, 22 May 1984, *Calopristi* v. *India*, in: ATF 110 II 255 = 82 *ILR*, p. 14; Italy, Cass., 15 May 1989, *Toglia* v. *GB*, secretary, *RDIPP* (1989) p. 691; Austria, Oberster Gerichtshof (OGH), 21 November 1990, *Walishauser* v. *USA*, photographer, *Oesterreichische Juristen-Zeitung* (*ÖJZ*) (1992) p. 661; OGH, 8 July 1992, *M. Y.* v. *USA*, secretary, *Praxis des Internationalen privat- und Verfahrensrechts* (*IPRax*) (1993) p. 185, with critical comment Seidl-Hohenveldern, p. 190, and OGH, 14 June 1989, *X* v. *France*, assistant to visa department, *Zeitschrift für Rechtsvergleichung* (*ZfRvgl*) (1990) with comment Seidl-Hohenveldern = 86 *ILR*, p. 583; Spain, Supreme Court, 1 December 1986, *Diana* v. *South Africa*, secretary, 86 *ILR*, p. 512; Germany, Bundesarbeitsgericht (BAG), 3 July 1996, *X* v. *Argentine*, *Der Betrieb* (1997) p. 1087 = *Arbeitsrechtliche Praxis* (*AP*) Nr. 1 ad § 20 GVG; Belgium, Cour du travail de Bruxelles, 22 Oktober 1992, *Q. M. A.* V. *Portugal*, teacher, *Pasicrisie Belge* (1992) Ii, p. 104; Netherlands, Supreme Court, 22 December 1989, *Van der Hulst* v. *USA*, secretary = 94 *ILR*, p. 37; France, Cour de Cassation, 2 April 1996, *Coco* v. *Argentina*, clerical worker at embassy's press office, Recueil Dalloz Sirey (1996) I.R. p. 117; and Cour de Cassation, 11 January 1997, *Saignie* v. *Japan*, 86 *Revue critique de droit international privé* (*RCDIP*) (1997), p. 322, comment Muir-Watt; Brazil, Supreme Court, *Veuve X* v. *GDR*, in: Revue internationale du travail (*ILO*) (1992) p. 336; Argentine, Supreme Court, 22 December 1994, *Manauta* v. Russian Federation, *La Ley* (1995) - D - p. 208, clerical worker at embassy's press office, = *Clunet* (1996) p. 413; Greece, Areiopagos, 1398/86, *X* v. State Y., *Revue hellénique de droit international* (1989-1990) p. 389; USA, Court of Appeals, 7th Circ., 8 December 1987, *Segni* v. *Spain*, sales representative at the consulate, 98 *ILR*, p. 55; Japan, Tokio District Court, 31 May 1982, *Tomoko Uozumi* v. *EEC Delegation*, *Japanese Annual of International Law* (1992) p. 127; New Zealand, Court of Appeal, *Sutton* v. *Governor of Pitcairn*, secretary, 1 *NZLR* (1995) p. 426 = 104 *ILR*, p. 508.

[32] G. Cataldi, 'I recenti sviluppi della giurisprudenza italiana in materia di controversie di lavoro con Stati stranieri', *RDIPP* (1991) p. 690 ss.; L. Sbolci, *Controversie di lavoro con stati stranieri et diritto internazionale* (Milano, 1987) p. 310.; B. Pérez., *Régimen juridico de empleados de misiones diplomáticas* (La Plata, 1980) p. 247; D.W. Greig, op. cit. n. 23; Chueca and Diez-Hochleitner, 'La admisión de la tesis restrictiva de las inmunidades del Estado extranjero en la reciente practica española', *Rivista di diritto internazionale* (*RDI*) (1988) p. 8 ss.; H. Fox,'Employment contracts as an exception to State Immunity: is all Public Service immune ?', 66 *BYIL* (1995) p. 97 ss.; R. Garnett, 'State immunity in employment matters', 46 *ICLQ* (1997) p. 81 ss.; S. Sucharitkul, 'Fifth Report on Jurisdictional Immunities of State and their property', *ILC-Yearbook*, Vol. II, Part One (1983) p. 27 ss.; L. Barnhoorn, 'Staatsimmuniteit en ontslag for security reasons', *Nederlands Juristenblad* (1990) p. 1345 ss.; I. Seidl-Hohenveldern., 'Staatsimmunität gegenüber Dienstnehmerklagen von Botschaftspersonal', *IPRax* (1990) p. 1990; F. Vischer, Arbeitsverhältnis eines Botschaftsangestellten, Immunität des ausländischen Staates', *SJIR* (1986) p. 243 ss.; Prof. *R. Higgins*, as claimant's counsel, arguments in re *Sengupta* v . *Republic of India*, England, Employment Appeal Tribunal, 17 November 1982, 64 *ILR*, p. 352; Russomano, 'La inmunidad de jurisdicción laboral en el derecho brasileño', *Derecho Laboral* (Montevideo) (1975) p. 652 ss.

[33] Supreme Court, 21 May 1992, *The Public Service Alliance* v. *USA*, 94 *ILR* pp. 264 and *283*.

[34] Supreme Court, 11 May 1984, X. (Portuguese clerical worker at foreign embassy) v. *State Y*, *Boletim do Ministério da Justiça* (*BJM*) Nr. 337, p. 305 ss., cf., also Correia, 'Portugals Stellung zur Frage der Staatenimmunität', 34 *Archiv des Völkerrechts* (1996) p. 120 ss.

Finland[35] and Ireland,[36] whose tribunals seem to look to the *purpose* rather than the *nature* of the activity, and Great Britain for statutory reasons,[37] grant the sending state immunity in labour disputes with locally engaged staff.

Examining the case of the official *interpreter/ translator* of the Iraqi Mission, the Geneva Labour Court, followed by its *Chambre d'appel*, considered that his activity of interpretation was *closely related* to the exercise of government authority, and thus the claim to sovereign immunity had to be accepted. Thereafter, the plaintiff brought the case to the Federal Supreme Court. Surprisingly, the federal judges, by a 3 : 2 majority decision, overruled the lower court's decision, stating that an interpreter/ translator performs a mere mechanical activity, since he does not participate in any decisions. The Federal Supreme Court, however, agreed that this was a borderline case.[38]

The question of whether immunity should be granted when claimants are nationals of the defendant employer state is largely unresolved. Referring to Article 5 al. 2 ECSI 1972,[39] and to Article 11 al. 2 lit. d of the ILC Draft Convention, as well as to the practice of foreign courts,[40] the Geneva Labour Court considered that jurisdictional immunity must be maintained,[41] unless the claimant shows evidence that in his own country he would not have access to

[35] See Supreme Court, Supreme Court Rep. 1993, Case No. 120, *X* (local Embassy clerk)v. *Turkey*, *Clunet* (1998) p. 154.

[36] Ireland, Supreme Court, 12 March 1992, *Burke* v. *Canada*, Chauffeur, 12 *International Labour Law Reports* (1992) p. 304 = 95 *ILR*, p. 467.

[37] London, Employment Appeal Tribunal (EAT), 17 November 1982, *Sengupta* v. *Republic of India*, office aid, Industrial Court Reports (*ICR*) (1983), p. 221 = 64 *ILR* (1983) p. 352; EAT, 8 Oktober 1993, *Ahmed* v. *Saudi Arabia*, affirmed *ICR* (1996) p. 25 (CA) = 2 *All ER* (1996) p. 248.; EAT, 14 December 1994, *Jayetilleke* v. *Bahamas*, accountant, 107 *ILR*, p. 622; EAT, 10 July 1995, *Abdelghafar* v. *United Arab Emirates*, 107 *ILR*, p. 625; Art. 16 al. 1 lit. a StIA maintains immunity in respect of all employment's contracts at foreign embassies and consulates regardless of the nationality of the employee or the position held (see Garnett, op. cit. n. 33, p. 87).

[38] Swiss Federal Tribunal, 13 December 1994, *Razid* v. *Iraq* , ATF 120 II 408 = *SZIER* (1995) p. 605, and *SZIER* (1996) p. 392, with critical comment from Schwander, at p. 395 and Gloor, *SJ* (1995) p. 649.

[39] According to Art. 5 al. 2 ECSI, the non-immunity rule 'shall not apply were the individual is a national of the employing state at the time when the proceedings are brought'. That provision has for the first time been applied with respect to Cyprus, THP, 25 October 1993, *Stephanidou* v. *Cyprus*, locally recruited, Cypriot secretary.

[40] Bruxelles, Tribunal du travail, 28 May 1991, *Queiroz Magalhaes Abrantes* v. *Etat du Portugal*, *Revue belge de droit international* (1992) p. 610 [reversed on appeal, see *Pasicrisie belge* (1992) II, 104]; Amsterdam, Local Court, 5 April 1979, *J. A. P. d. S.*v. *Portugal*, *Netherlands Yearbook of International Law* (1980) p. 290; Paris, Cour d'appel, 30 November 1930, *Sakharoff* v. *Russian Trade Delegation*, 7 *ILR* (1933-1934) p.170.

[41] See TPH, 11 December 1991, *Nour* v. *Egypt*, Egyptian chief of press section; TPH, 19 February 1992, *De Angelis* v. *Italy*, Italian cleaner, affirmed by CAPH, 3 September 1992; TPH, 2 February 1993, *Mostafa* v. *Egypt*, Egyptian driver, affirmed by CAPH, 9 November 1993; TPH, 15 February 1994, *Gentile* v. *Italy*, Italian driver;TPH 15 June1994, *Dos Santos* v. *Brazil*, Brazilian housekeeper at ambassador's residence; TPH, 6 December 1994, *Andara* v. *Venezuela*, Venezuelan housekeeper at ambassador's residence.

courts, or must fear for his life and security.[42] The Court stated that if sending states engage *nationals* as members of their administrative, technical or service staff, normally they do so for reasons of enhanced trust.[43]

The Labour Court found that the exception to the non-immunity rule in the Basle Convention and the ILC Draft reflects *customary international law*; that the erosion of sovereign immunity has not yet reached such a stage. Foreign case law shows that employer states give their nationals access to their own courts, especially to their administrative jurisdictions.[44]

The Swiss Federal Supreme Court, however, did not share this opinion and, ruling on an appeal filed by an Egyptian driver of the Egyptian Mission, overruled and remanded the case to the Labour Court, in spite of the strong diplomatic protest on the part of the Egyptian government.[45]

In a more recent decision, the Swiss Federal Supreme Court stated that neither the *nationality* nor the *place of recruitment* are determining factors in the decision on the immunity issue. Thus, it rejected the plea of sovereign immunity of an employer state, sued by a member of its Mission service staff, who was its national and had been hired, on a private law basis, in its capital [46].

It appears that the federal judges of Lausanne were not prepared to accept that in the age of non-discrimination, access to courts[47] at the place of work[48] should depend on purely accidental elements as plaintiff's nationality. Nevertheless, it

[42] TPH, 3 April 1991, *Shah* v. *Pakistan,* Pakistani. driver, death threats confirmed by Swiss embassy in Islamabad; TPH, Gr. 12 January 1994, *Castro* v. *Argentine*, Argentine. butler; unconfirmed reprisals.

[43] E.g., ATF, 23 September 1983, 'Auflösung des Beamtenverhältnisses mit einer Botschaftssekretärin aus Sicherheitsgründen', in: P. Hänni, *Rechte und Plfichten im öffentlichen Dienst* (Freiburg 1993) Case Nr. 182.

[44] See ATF 117 Ib 353, *Swiss member of Swiss embassy* v. *Swiss Government*; France, Conseil d'Eat, 7 January 1987, *Félicien,* French secretary at the French Embassy in Mexico, *RCDIP* (1998) p. 687, with comment Rodière; Spain, Tribunal Supremo, 15 March 1991, *S.*, *Revista española de derecho internacional* (1992) p. 246.

[45] See Federal Tribunal, 16 November 1994, *Mostafa* v. *Egypt*, 120 II 400 = *SZIER* (1995) p. 600 and *SZIER* (1996) p. 386, with critical comment Schwander. Thereafter, having been convinced by the Swiss Government that court proceedings will be fair, the Egyptian Mission decided to come to court and to defend on the merits. Similar decisions: Austria, OGH, 14 June 1989, *French Consular Employee* v. *France,* 31 *ZfRVgl* (1990) p. 300, with critical comment Seidl-Hohenveldern = 86 *ILR*, p. 583; Belgium, Cour du travail de Bruxelles, 22 September 1992, *Queiroz Magalhaes Abrantes* v. *Portugal*, Port. teacher, 179 *Pasicrisie belge* (1992) II, p.104; Netherlands, District Court of Amsterdam, 25 Oktober 1990, *Bruno V.* v. *Italy*, Ital. employee at Ital. Cultural Institute (annexe to embassy) *NYIL* (1992) p. 447.

[46] ATF, 22 May 1997, *Andara* v. *Venezuela*, unreported.

[47] The Plaintiff explicitly invoked Art. 6 al. 1 European Convention on Human Rights (ECHR) and was said to be ready to bring the case, if necessary, to the Strasbourg Court. In reality, as he got formal *access to court*, he wanted a decision *as to the merits*.

[48] Cf., Art. 115 Swiss Private International Law Statute (PIL) and Art. 343 al. 1 Swiss Code of Obligations (CO).

must be recalled that even in the view of the Strasbourg organs, ECHR law is superseded by the immunity rules of public international law.[49]

4. CONCLUSION

It may be easy to obtain a decision against an employer state, but it is much more difficult to have it enforced. There are not many states which are prepared to abide by judgments delivered in these litigations.[50] For rather evident reasons, the Swiss Foreign Ministry shows little enthusiasm to assist a plaintiff in enforcing its money judgment. Besides, international law forbids attachment of embassy bank accounts[51] or embassy cars. Such enforcement measures may only be directed against the defendant state's *commercial assets* in the forum state. In addition, Third World countries usually do not have commercial assets located in Switzerland[52] and, consequently, plaintiffs finally obtain nothing.

As a remedy, it is conceivable to suggest that the host state should indemnify holders of non-enforceable judgments against employer states. It may be said that the forum state incurs an administrative liability for that impossibility towards frustrated claimants. Local embassy staff whose legal titles against foreign states are sacrificed on the altar of forum state's superior interests should be indemnified according to the provisions of the Federal State Liability Act.[53]

[49] *ECHR, Series B.*, No. 16, *Golder* case, p. 52; European Commission of Human Rights, 4. December 1995, *N.* v. *Italy, RDI* (1996) p. 142; European Commission of Human Rights, 12 December 1988, *Spaans* v. *Netherlands,* 107 *ILR*, p. 1; cf., Golsong/ Karl/Miehsler/Vogler/Wildhaber, *Internationaler Kommentar zur Europäischen Menschenrechtskonvention* (Köln, 1992) n. 104 ad Art. 6 EMRK; Velu and Ergec, *La Convention européenne des Droits de l'Homme* (Bruxelles, 1990) § 465, p. 408; W. Pahr, 'Die Staatenimmunität und Artikel 6 Absatz 1 der Europäischen Menschenrechtskonvention', in: *Mélanges Modinos* (Paris, 1968) p. 222 ss.

[50] Up to this day, only 1 out of 90 claimants has succeeded to enforce a money judgment against his employer state (attachment of US-assets at the Swiss National Bank at Berne, in re: *Landano* v. *USA*, cf., *Tribune de Genève*, 17 October 1990). Some States, tired of this judicial guerrilla, gave hand to a compomise with the claimant and paid part of the amount of the money judgment.

[51] Cf., Geneva, Cour de Justice, Autorité de Surveillance, 8 May 1998, *Rochdi* v. *Qatar*; Berne, Appellations-hof, 5 January 1998, *Kuchen* v. *USA*.

[52] However, Heads of State and other members of governmental élites may hold *private accounts* in Switzerland, fuelled with embezzled public moneys.

[53] RS 170.32; cf., Knapp, *Précis de droit administratif*, 4th edn. (Genève 1991) Nos. 2164: 'De l'indemnisation pour actes licites de l'Etat.'

EMBASSY EMPLOYEES AND STATE IMMUNITY: THE ATTITUDE OF DUTCH COURTS

Y.M. Schrevelius*

1. INTRODUCTION

I am a lawyer in Rotterdam. In my legal practice I have dealt with several labour disputes between embassies/consulates and their employees. In the majority of these cases an out-of-court settlement was reached. This is to be preferred to proceedings in court. Apart from the risk that the foreign State successfully invokes immunity, there is the problem of enforcement of the judgment. The case law demonstrates that in the context of employment matters the main area of contention is that of the immunity of jurisdiction and not the immunity from enforcement. I will focus on the issue of immunity of jurisdiction. Since the beginning of the 1980s, 10 judgments of the Subdistrict Court of The Hague have been published. Of the 10 published cases, 3 cases have subsequently been submitted to the District Court of The Hague. In one case the Supreme Court gave a judgment. At this moment one case is pending in the Supreme Court.

2. *VAN HECKE* V. *UNITED STATES OF AMERICA*

In the late 1970s, it was the Subdistrict Court of Rotterdam[1] that allowed a claim of a consular services assistant of the American consulate-general in Rotterdam by default. Mr Van Hecke was dismissed with immediate effect, so he claimed payment of his salary until the lawful termination of his contract.

3. *GOOTJES* V. *THE KINGDOM OF BELGIUM*

Some months later a Dutch woman, who had been employed in the administrative service of the Belgian consulate-general in Rotterdam, summoned Belgium to appear before the local court with a claim similar to that of Mr Van Hecke. She was, however, less successful. Belgium was represented in court and

* Beker c.s. Advocaten in Rotterdam, the Netherlands.

[1] *Van Hecke* v. *United States of America*, Subdistrict Court of Rotterdam, 15 November 1977 (unpublished)

W.P. Heere (Ed.), International Law and The Hague's 750th Anniversary

the defendant's plea of immunity was accepted. The judge considered that the Kingdom of Belgium was acting in a public capacity and was not acting 'like any other private person', even if the plaintiff was an administrative employee who was not entitled to the same privileges as were granted to consular officers. According to the judge,[2] the court could not interfere with the dismissal policy of a foreign state. The approach of absolute immunity based on the place or location of employment was not repeated afterwards.

4. *KRIJGSMAN* V. *REPUBLIC OF TURKEY*

Six years later in August 1985, the Subdistrict Court of The Hague[3] deemed itself competent to take cognizance of an employment dispute between Mrs Krijgsman, a Dutch national who worked as a secretary at the embassy of the Republic of Turkey. In its decision the court stated that questions of immunity had to be resolved by determining whether the act in question was 'sovereign' or 'commercial'. In applying this test, the court did not focus on the place of employment but instead placed emphasis on the status and position of the employee. As the employee had no civil service or diplomatic status and was not in a position of responsibility, the court concluded that the contract involved the foreign state 'acting on the same footing as a private individual'. Principles of territorial connection were also relied upon by the court in rejecting the plea of immunity. In this case the employee was Dutch and had been recruited in the Netherlands.

5. *'T HOOFT* V. *REPUBLIC OF FRANCE*

In 1985 in the case of *Mr Van 't Hooft* v. *the Republic of France*, the Subdistrict Court[4] deemed itself competent to take cognizance of an employment dispute between Mr Van 't Hooft, who had Dutch nationality and worked at the French Embassy in The Hague, and in the Republic of France. The defendant's plea of immunity was rejected with reference to the position held by the employee.

[2] *Gootjes* v. *The Kingdom of Belgium*, Subdistrict Court of Rotterdam, 13 April 1978, *NYIL* (*Netherlands Yearbook of International Law*) (1979) p.442.

[3] *Krijgsman* v. *Republic of Turkey*, Subdistrict Court of The Hague, 1 August 1985, *NYIL* (1988) p. 435.

[4] *'t Hooft* v. *the Republic of France*, Subdistrict Court of The Hague, 10 January 1985, *NIPR* (*Nederlands International Privaatrecht*)(1988) No. 125.

6. *DAS DORES AMORIN* V. *COMMONWEALTH OF AUSTRALIA*

In 1986 two cases were brought before the Subdistrict Court of The Hague.[5] In the first case of Mr Das Dores Amorin v. the Australian embassy, the Hague Subdistrict Court also rejected a claim by the embassy to immunity in respect of a dispute between a Portugese butler who had no diplomatic or civil service status (see Judgment of 3 March 1986). This default Judgment, in which the butler's dismissal was held to be unlawful, was subsequently quashed when it turned out that the butler had been employed as a butler not by the embassy, but by the ambassador personally.

7. *VAN DER HULST* V. *UNITED STATES OF AMERICA*

7.1. **Subdistrict Court of The Hague**

The Subdistrict Court of The Hague (see Judgment of 18 March 1986) also declared itself competent in the case of Mrs Van der Hulst, a Dutch woman, who had been employed as a secretary at the Foreign Commercial Service Department of the United States embassy since 1 July 1984. Her employment was evidenced by a letter of 26 June 1984. In addition she received a 'notification of personal action', which stated that the appointment was dependent on the satisfactory result of a security check. On 29 August 1984 she was dismissed 'for security reasons'.

Thereupon, Mrs Van der Hulst applied to the Subdistrict Court of The Hague for the dismissal to be declared null and void, and for the United States to be ordered to pay her salary from the date of dismissal. The United States entered an appearance and filed an interim claim that the Subdistrict Court should declare itself to have no jurisdiction on the ground of the immunity from jurisdiction enjoyed by the United States, since governmental acts connected with state security were involved in whether or not staff were appointed at the embassy. Mrs Van der Hulst disputed this by arguing that since the United States had entered into a transaction under Dutch law as a private person by employing her, there was no question of an act *jure imperii* in this case. Moreover, she was not part of the diplomatic personnel and did not have access to information which could present a security risk. The defendant referred to the Vienna Convention on Diplomatic Relations of 18 April 1961.

The Subdistrict Court took the view that the contract of employment had been concluded by the United States through the Foreign Commercial Service, as an act *jure gestionis*, and held that it was competent to take cognizance of the

[5] *Das Dores Amorin* v. *Commonwealth of Australia*, Subdistrict Court of The Hague, 3 March 1986, *NIPR* (1987) No. 137.

dispute with reference to Article 13, paragraph 1 of the draft Convention of the International Law Commission, Article 5 of the European Convention, the Foreign Sovereign Immunities Act of the United States (FSIA) and a 1980 Judgment of the Court of Appeal of the District of Columbia.

Furthermore, the Judgment held that the contract had not been entered into in the context of the ambassador's security function. In the balancing of interests involved, the interest of the forum in protecting its own labour force (the Judgment held that personnel recruited locally should not be obliged to start proceedings in a remote court of the foreign state) weighed more heavily than the interest of the foreign state. The Judgment of the Subdistrict Court shows an approach in which the immunity issue is resolved by reference to the nature of the function of the employee, the nationality of the employee and the recruitment in the forum state.

7.2. District Court of The Hague

The United States appealed against this Judgment to the District Court of The Hague. The District Court concentrated on the security check and took the view that the institution and conduct of such a check had to be classified as a typical governmental act. As regards the question whether the United States had been right in terminating the legal relationship for security reasons, the Dutch courts did not therefore have jurisdiction. The District Court quashed the Judgment of the Subdistrict Court in its Judgment of 21 December 1987 and declared it not competent to take cognizance of the claim.

7.3. Supreme Court

Mrs Van der Hulst appealed in cassation against this Judgment to the Supreme Court. The Supreme Court[6] dismissed the appeal.

The Supreme Court held that, generally speaking, a state entering into a private contract may not appeal to immunity of jurisdiction. However, there are exceptions to this general rule. In the present case, the receiving state should allow the employing state the competence to conclude or continue – in the exercise of its diplomatic mission and consular services – an employment contract subject to the condition of a satisfactory security investigation. The judgment on the results of such an investigation should be left to the discretion of the sending state, with the exclusion of the judgments of either the employee or the receiving State. According to the Supreme Court, it may not be assumed that

[6] *Van der Hulst* v. *United States of America*, Supreme Court, 22 December 1989, *NYIL* (1991) p. 379.

a receiving state which concludes an employment contract, forfeits its right to invoke immunity, even if that contract has a private law character.

In this case, it was not so much the place of employment or the status of the employee, as the nature of the claim and the purpose of the act that was taken into account, this act being not so much the bilateral employment agreement as the unilateral 'Notification of Personnel' (the sovereign element). Allowing the claim to proceed would have involved the court in investigating matters of state security. The nationality of the employee was totally ignored.

The decision has come under attack from a number of scholars, who have argued that if a contract existed, closer investigation of the function of Mrs Van der Hulst and of the significance of the notification of personnel action would have been needed. The universal view is that when a (local) employee has a subordinate function (no immunities or privileges), there is no reason to exempt a labour dispute from access to a local court. Courts should not be quick to presume that their jurisdiction in such disputes would unduly interfere with the performance of the functions of the embassy.

The judgment of the Supreme Court is unsatisfactory as it grants an immunity of jurisdiction that is wider than the European Convention's provision on employment contracts.

Furthermore, the Judgment gives no support to the legal practice of protecting private persons when they enter into employment contracts with foreign states. The interest in comity towards the Unites States has been favoured at the expense of the interest of Mrs. Van der Hulst in obtaining redress.

8. *FASIL* v. *KUWAIT*; *ALAO* v. *KENIA*; *OZORIO* v. *CUBA*

In the late 1980s and the beginning of the 1990s, the Subdistrict Court of The Hague declared itself competent in five cases. In the following three cases the employee did not have Dutch nationality:

– a person of Ethiopian nationality employed as a chauffeur by the embassy of Kuwait (Judgment of 31 August 1988);[7]

– person of Portuguese nationality employed as a housekeeper by the embassy of Cuba (Judgment of 24 January 1990);[8]

– person of Italian and Argentine nationality employed as a translator by the embassy of Cuba (Judgment of 15 April 1992).[9]

These cases show that nationality was ignored with regard to the immunity question. In three of the eleven cases I have mentioned it was not even clear what nationality the employee had.

7 *Fasil* v. *Kuwait*, Subdistrict Court of The Hague, 31 August 1988, *NIPR* (1989) No. 446.

8 *Alao* v. *Kenia*, Subdistrict Court of The Hague, 4 April 1989, *NIPR* (1989) No. 308.

9 *Ozoria* v. *Cuba*, Subdistrict Court of The Hague, 24 Januar 1990, *NIPR* (1990) No. 315.

9. *ARIAS* V. *VENEZUELA*

9.1. Subdistrict Court of The Hague

In a recent case a woman, Mrs Arias, who had dual nationality (Argentine and Dutch since 1987) and who had been employed in the administrative service of the embassy of Venezuela, was unlucky in her dispute with Venezuela. At the time (1980) when the contract was entered into, she was neither a national of the Netherlands nor habitually resident in the Netherlands (Mrs Arias had lived in the Netherlands for some months).

With reference to the connection of nationality or habitual residence to the forum State as provided for in the special article devoted to employment contracts in the European Convention on State Immunity and the draft version of ILA and ILC, the Subdistrict Court held that it was not competent to take cognizance of the dispute. Mrs Arias was advised to start proceedings in Venezuela.

9.2. District Court of The Hague

Mrs Arias appealed against this Judgment to the District Court of The Hague.[10] The Judgment was upheld on appeal, so Mrs Arias appealed in cassation. The Supreme Court has not yet given a Judgment.

In this case, emphasis is placed on the nationality of the employee at the time when the contract of employment is concluded. That the employee was a Dutch national at the time when the proceedings were instituted was not relevant. To ward off immunity she should have been a habitual resident or have had the nationality of the foreign state at the time the contract was concluded. In using only this territorial criterion, a form of absolute immunity is created with regard to actions by employees who do not have habitual residence nor the nationality of the forum state at the time when the contract of employment is concluded. Third-country nationals and nationals of the foreign state irrespective of their position, will not have access to the local courts. Only nationals and residents are protected. All employees, regardless of their nationality, should be entitled to access to the local courts.

This is granted under European law in Article 48 (2) of the EC Treaty, which provides the right to free movement and includes the right to non- discrimination on the basis of nationality in working conditions. National legislation that attaches different terms to the conditions of employment of national and alien employees is prohibited.

[10] *Arias* v. *Venezuela*, District Court of The Hague, 4 Februar 1998, *JAR* (1998/67).

Furthermore, Article 6 of the European Convention on Human Rights of 1950 states that 'everyone is entitled to a fair and public hearing by a tribunal in the determination of his civil rights', which has been interpreted to include a right of access to a State's court. A similar provision in international law is Article 26 of the International Convenant on Civil and Political Rights 1966.

If the Supreme Court will not set aside the Judgment in the case of Mrs Arias, the majority of the personnel employed by foreign embassies or consulates will not be afforded adequate protection by the courts.

10. CONCLUSION

The decisions show different approaches in Dutch judicial practice. In applying the sovereign/commercial act test, emphasis is placed on the status of the employee. Looking at the status, a line can be drawn between officials and subordinates and that is, generally speaking, a reasonable distinction. The nature of the claim is decisive when investigating matters of state security. Focusing on the nature of the claim, it draws a distinction between the economic and non-economic aspects of an employment dispute. This distinction should not be given too much weight. The territorial nexus between the forum and the employee and the employment contract has been applied as a method to resolve the immunity question, but this criterion is discriminatory.

Although the Netherlands has embraced the relative immunity doctrine to a certain extent, state immunity still exists in the employment context. In order to properly implement a doctrine of restrictive immunity, an approach is required that gives appropriate weight to the interest of the employee.

INTERPRETATION OF PRIVATE INTERNATIONAL LAW TREATIES: INTRODUCTORY REMARKS

A.V.M. Struycken*

Private International Law Treaties include, I would think, at least for the purpose of our discussion today, the uniform substantive law treaties. Private International Law deals with the problems stemming from the multiplicity and diversity of systems of private law. One of the possible solutions is to make uniform the rules of substantive law. Private International Law (PIL), as a legal science, should extend its scope to this possible solution for its main problem. This does not exclude the fact that the expertise of those who concentrate on uniform substantive law, is to be recognised with great respect.

No discussion is needed about the question of the objective of PIL Treaties. As F.C. von Savigny,[1] P.S. Mancini,[2] T.M.C. Asser and others pointed out, it is to bring about uniformity of rules and, as a consequence, harmony on both sides of the border.

This object and purpose have to be kept in mind when treaty rules have to be interpreted (Art. 31 Vienna Treaty on the law of treaties). Signature and ratification is one thing; enhancing uniform interpretation is something else. Courts should resist the temptation to interpret treaty provisions in the context of the system of their national law; they have to keep in mind the 'autonomy' of treaty rules in relation to national law. They have to onderstand treaty rules in the same way as an existing, or an imaginary, supra-national court, in charge of giving an authoritative opinion for the community of contracting states, may be supposed to do. Particularly, where such a court does not exist, national courts should keep in mind the case law of other contracting states. If such case law is not decisive, it is at least a weighty factor.

There is a problem for states which adhere to a dualistic approach in their constitutional order. The public international law side of the international convention is a concern for the government, whereas courts and other practitioners have to stick to the statutory enactment by which the treaty provisions have been made the law of the land. Courts should be empowered, it is submitted, to look beyond the statutory provisions in order to make sure that their decisions are in line with the purpose of the convention.

* Professor of Private International Law, University of Nijmegen.

[1] F.C. von Savigny, *System des heutigen Römischen Rechts*, Volume 8 (1849) pp. 30-32.

[2] See the famous article by P.S. Mancini, (Clunet 1873) pp. 221 ss., 285 ss.

W.P. Heere (Ed.), International Law and The Hague's 750th Anniversary

Drafters of conventions should be aware of the problems that courts may encounter in the future. The text of the conventions should be drafted with utmost care. It may be tempting to agree on a text that is susceptible of different interpretations, when in fact there is no consensus among the negotiators and consensus appears to be hardly possible to attain. If problems remain unsolved, it should be clearly said so, and such an unsolved problem is not within the scope of the convention. To the extent that their law permits to do so, courts will be free to find a solution that is in harmony with the convention rules.

A more or less official explanatory report may be most helpful. The Hague Conference on Private International Law has been providing such reports for all conventions it has brought about since 1951. It is a part of the *Actes et documents* of the Hague Conventions. Already since 1893, the Conference has put out such *Actes et documents*. In the European Union, everybody is aware of the great weight that has been attributed to the Reports by P.Jenard and P. Schlosser. The EC Court has never failed to refer to those reports. The Report by M.Giuliano and P.Lagarde on the EC Convention of Rome 1980 on the law applicable to contractual relationships appears not to have less authority.

In the absence of a supra-national court, there is a real risk of diversity in the interpretation of international conventions, the more so when time goes by and convention texts are no longer entirely appropriate in new situations. Supreme Courts of contracting states may disagree, and then a conflict of laws reappears on the basis of one single convention text. I may refer to the well known *Hocke* judgment by the *Cour de cassation* of 4 March 1963 concerning the Geneva Convention on bills of exchange. The Hague Rules are another example; national enactments differ and so does case law. Parties to a bill of lading may choose, or be deemed to choose, one national enactment rather than another. I may refer to the famous *Alnati* case of 1966. That case was a Hague Rules case, not more, although the *Hoge Raad*, the Dutch Supreme Court, availed itself of the opportunity to render a decision that went far beyond the problem to be solved. The problem was that the Belgian enactment of the Hague Rules differed from the Dutch version inspired by the Rules though enacted before the Dutch ratification. A choice of either version by the parties to the contract of carriage of goods by sea under a bill of lading should not have made any difference, but it did.

Case law reveals that some problems are specific for some convention, whereas other problems turn out to be of more general importance. I may draw your attention to two such questions.

Imagine that in a convention containing choice of law rules a provision is lacking that says that, in case the application of such a rule would lead to a result that is manifestly contrary to the public policy of the state concerned, the application of the rule may be refused. Is it correct to state that, save express provisions to the contrary, nevertheless the public policy may be invoked as if the convention would contain an express provision to that effect? The *Cour de cassation* gave an affirmative answer to this question.[3] In the *Elisabeth Boll* case, in which the International Court of Justice rendered its judgment in 1958, the Netherlands and Sweden had a fierce debate on this point. Unexpectedly, the Court found that this point was not relevant for the final decision. That does not mean that the answer on the question raised was clear beyond any doubt.

In private law systems there is a borderline between the area where, to a large extent, parties to a legal relationship are free to strike a deal and the area where they have to respect a framework of mandatory rules protecting superior social interests. In the former, arbitration is possible, in the latter it is not. The borderline is not very clear. It is more or less between patrimonial law affairs and family law affairs. It is submitted that the line is not different from the one that separates the domain of the 'juridiction contentieuse' from the domain of the 'juridiction gracieuse'.

Some private international law treaties deal with patrimonial interests, such as maintenance after divorce. The question may be asked whether, as a general rule, it is correct to state that whatever the law applicable according to the choice of law rule of such a convention, litigating parties are always free to agree that the court will apply the lex fori and, in spite of the convention rule, the court shall decide accordingly.

The French *Cour de cassation* made the following statement in its judgment of 6 May 1997 (*Hannover International* v. *Baranger*) concerning a sales contract: *Mais attendu que pour les droits dont elles ont la libre disposition, les parties peuvent s'accorder sur l'application de la loi française du for malgré l'existence d'une convention internationale* [...] (considering however that for rights which parties are free to dispose of, they may agree on the application of the French *lex fori* in spite of the existence of an international convention [...]).[4] Such a general statement is not to be found in a judgment by the *Hoge Raad* of 21 February 1997.[5] It is a case about maintenance after divorce. According to the rule of the Hague 1973 Convention, Iranian law should apply. In a laborious reasoning specifically geared to the Convention, the *Hoge Raad* arrived at the conclusion that parties could validly agree on the applicability of the (Dutch) *lex fori*.

Indeed, there is something to be said about the interpretation of Private International Law Treaties.

[3] *Cour de cassation*, 6 July 1988, Revue critique de d.i.p. (1989) p.72, note Y. Lequette.

[4] See Revue critique de d.i.p.(1997) p. 514, note B. Fauvarque-Cosson; (Clunet 1997) p.804, note D. Bureau; Bertrand Ancel and Yves Lequette, *Grands arrêts de la jurisprudence française de droit international privé*, 3rd edition (1998).

[5] Comment by P. Vlas, *Ars Aequi*, No. 11 (1997) p. 820; comment by Mathilde Sumampouw, *Netherlands International Law Review* (1998) p. 115; comment by Th. M. de Boer, *Nederlandse Jurisprudentie*, No. 416 (1998).

RULES OF INTERPRETATION APPLICABLE TO PRIVATE INTERNATIONAL LAW TREATIES: AN OVERVIEW

Christophe Bernasconi*

1. INTRODUCTION

When asked to present a methodical catalogue of so-called 'rules of interpretation', a lawyer's first reaction tends to be rather cautious. Instead of the malleable aids required, such rules of interpretation may indeed become unwieldy instruments. Many of the 'rules' or 'principles' offered are general, if not equivocal or even contradictory. Furthermore, as with statutory interpretation, the choice of a 'rule', for example of 'restrictive interpretation', may in a given case involve a *preliminary choice of meaning rather than a guide to interpretation.*[1] In other words, sometimes rules of interpretation only serve as a means to justify or explain a desired result, rather than to ascertain the proper meaning of a legal text. Keeping the pitfalls of this truism in mind, I will nevertheless try to identify and describe some of the rules of interpretation applicable to Private International Law (PIL) Treaties.

Rules of interpretation applicable to Conventions have to be determined on the grounds of the basic nature or aim of the Convention. Whether it be one establishing uniform international law such as the Vienna Convention of 1980 on International Sale of Goods or a traditional conflict of laws Convention like most of the Hague Conventions – a Convention performs a *specific function*, which is to *unify certain rules*. Obviously, this goal can only be realised if, once the Convention has entered into force, there is also uniformity in its interpretation by the courts of the States Party to it. Divergent interpretations of a Convention throughout the various states, at least in the long-run, can be extremely harmful to a Convention, preventing other countries from adhering to it, and eventually ruining all efforts made to adopt it.[2]

The need for uniform interpretation has been expressly embodied in the text of various Conventions, such as in Article 16 of the Hague Convention of 1986 on

* Secretary at the Permanent Bureau of the Hague Conference on Private International Law

[1] Ian Brownlie, *Principles of Public International Law*, 4th edn., p. 626.

[2] This can be illustrated by the Hague Convention of 1961 on the Protection of Minors and the divergent interpretations that were adopted with regard to its Art. 3. These divergent interpretations, among other things, drove the Hague Conference to negotiate a new instrument, the 1996 Convention on the Protection of Children, see Adair Dyer, *Report on the Revision of the 1961 Hague Convention on Protection of Minors* (April 1994) pp. 6 ff.

W.P. Heere (Ed.), International Law and The Hague's 750th Anniversary

the Law Applicable to Contracts for the International Sale of Goods, where it is stated:

> 'In the interpretation of the Convention, regard is to be had to its international character and to the need to promote uniformity in its application.'[3]
> Uniform interpretation and application being so closely linked to the basic aim and purpose of a Convention, this principle is valid in general and applies even if a Convention does not expressly refer to it. Hence, in interpreting the Convention, strict attention has to be paid to two closely related principles: the Convention's *international character* and the need to promote *uniformity in its application*. How to give life to these principles is a different problem – one, however, which deserves very close attention.

2. METHODS OF INTERPRETATION

I shall start my analysis of various methods of interpretation by referring to the Vienna Convention on the Law of Treaties of 1969. In its Articles 31 to 33, the Vienna Convention codifies the comparatively few general principles, which appear to constitute *general rules* for the interpretation of treaties.[4]

2.1. **The starting point: the textual or objective approach**

The first of the principles mentioned in Article 31 of the Vienna Convention states that

> 'a treaty shall be interpreted in good faith in accordance with the ordinary meaning to be given to the terms of the treaty in their context and in the light of its object and purpose.'

Hence, the starting point of interpretation is the *elucidation of the meaning of the text, not an investigation ab initio into the intentions of the parties*. In other words, the Vienna Convention embodies the so-called *objective* approach, not the *subjective* approach, according to which the primary aim and goal of treaty interpretation is to ascertain the intention of the parties. Hence, under the Vienna Convention, there exists a presumption that the intentions of the parties are reflected in the text of the treaty which they have drawn up.

[3] Similar provisions can be found, for example, in Art. 7(1) of the already mentioned Vienna Convention on International Sale of Goods, and in Art. 18 of the Rome Convention on the Law Applicable to Contractual Obligations.

[4] In my opinion, these rules also apply to Private International Law Conventions as a whole and should not be restricted to provisions which usually are characterised as public international law, such as the *final clauses* or the *preamble* of a Treaty.

Not only does the objective or textual approach provide a clear starting point for the process of interpretation, it also sets the necessary limits to this process. The *textual interpretation* made it possible, for example, to refute the early attempts made by some German scholars to limit the scope of The Hague Convention of 1961 on the Protection of Minors solely to the *nationals* of the States Party to it.[5] In Article 13, this Convention indeed clearly states that it 'shall apply to all minors who have their habitual residence in one of the contracting States.' There is hardly anything in the wording of this Convention that pleads in favour of limiting its personal scope solely to the nationals of states party to it.

2.2. The teleological approach (*purposive construction*)

Of course, the *textual or objective approach* does not mean that there is no latitude in interpretation at all. A well-known example in this context is the *Fothergill* v. *Monarch Airlines* case, decided in 1980 by the House of Lords.[6] It involved the Act of Parliament implementing the Warsaw Convention of 1929 on the Liability of Air Carriers as amended here at The Hague in 1955. According to this Convention, 'damage' of baggage must be declared within seven days; does this obligation also apply to the 'loss' of part of the baggage contents? The Court of Appeal held that as a matter of ordinary English the term 'damage' referred only to *physical injury* to baggage and did not extend to partial loss of contents. The House of Lords reversed the decision. Their Lordships held that although on a literal interpretation in an English legal context 'loss' was to be differentiated from 'damage', that was not an appropriate method of interpretation of an international convention. They ruled that a *purposive construction* was to be adopted.[7] The purpose of the required notice (Art. 26 of the Warsaw Convention) was to ensure that the airline received prompt information so as to enable it to take the necessary steps including, if possible, recovery of objects lost. Hence, on its true construction, Article 26 applied both to *damage* to baggage as well as to *loss* of contents. The plaintiff was therefore required to lodge a complaint for the lost articles within seven days of receiving his baggage. However, as the only complaint he had made did not refer to the loss of any articles but only to the damage to his suitcase, his claim (amounting to L 16.50) failed.

[5] See for example Jacobs, *NJW* (1967) p. 1066.

[6] [1981] *AC* 251, [1980] 2 *All ER* 696, [1980] 3 *WLR* 209.

[7] See the second part of the first principle mentioned in Art. 31 of the Vienna Convention on the Law of Treaties ('in the light of its object and purpose').

[8] 87 *NIPR* (1997), No. 70.

[9] For the following, see Peter Mankowski, 'Wahl des auf den Scheidungsunterhalt anwendbaren Rechts', *Familie und Recht* (1997) pp. 316-318; M. Sumampouw, 'Article 8 Hague Maintenance Convention 1973 set aside in favour of Party Autonomy: One step too far', *NILR* (1998) pp. 115-128. The major argument of the Court was that Art. 8 had to be interpreted 'in light of the unawareness of the evolution of party autonomy in the field of family law.'

There is no doubt that the *teleological* approach may suit the fact that no Convention operates in a vacuum and has to be kept in line with changes of social reality. On the other hand, it should not be overlooked that the teleological approach also has many pitfalls, one of them being the frontier to be drawn with the textual approach. This may be illustrated by the recent decision of the *Hoge Raad* of the Netherlands, in which the court stated that Article 8 of the Hague Convention of 1973 on the Law Applicable to Maintenance Obligations would not preclude divorced spouses from choosing the law governing their maintenance obligations.[8] This is somewhat surprising since the relevant Article 8 does not refer to party autonomy at all.[9] One might ask, therefore, if the *Hoge Raad* has not over-stretched the possibilities of teleological interpretation and has had recourse to tabooed *creative interpretation* in order to achieve a result, which undoubtedly has arguments in its favour, but clearly has no foundation in the wording of the Convention. Unfortunately, this decision also creates *international disharmony*, since it overlooks the fact that at least one German court reached exactly the opposite conclusion while it was analysing the same problem.[10] However, Article 31, paragraph 3, letter b, of the Vienna Convention expressly states that 'subsequent practice' in the application of the treaty should be taken into account. Hence, a judge interpreting an international treaty should be aware that his decision might well be a small pebble that causes a lot of ripples. This being said, the *Hoge Raad* certainly put its fingers on a very sensitive point: should divorced spouses have the possibility to choose the law applicable to their maintenance obligations? There are a lot of good reasons favouring such a possibility. In my opinion, however, they should be addressed during a possible *revision* of the Convention and not through creative interpretation of the existing text.

2.3. Interpretation of functional concepts: the plain meaning tradition

2.3.1. *General observations*

The importance of the textual approach might be somewhat moderated by the fact that PIL Treaties tend to use – deliberately, one should add – rather broad and general terms, whose wording alone might not always give enough indication of their precise legal meaning. For example, both the 1961 and the 1996 Hague Conventions refer to 'measures directed to the protection of the child.' In order to determine the precise meaning of this broad and *functional* (i.e. *non-specific* terminology), which as a term of art is not known within most domestic legislations, one has to have recourse to other principles of interpretation. The 1996

[10] OLG Karlsruhe 24 August 1989, *FamRZ* (1990) pp. 313, 314. See also östOGH 11 October 1995 – 3 Ob 564/95, *ZfRV* 1996/17 LS 1.

Convention provides great assistance by listing, in Article 3, an open catalogue of measures falling within the material scope of the Convention.

While interpreting functional concepts such as 'measures directed to the protection of the child' or even 'rights of custody', one has to resist the tendency to clutch at straws in his or her well-known domestic concepts and to import them into the Convention. Obviously, such a *lex fori-oriented* attitude can cause serious harm to the goal of a uniform application that underlies each PIL treaty. This has been emphasised, for example, by the English Court of Appeal in 1994. The Court had to interpret the meaning of the term 'rights of custody' used in the Hague Child Abduction Convention. It was established that

> 'the Convention is to be construed broadly as an international agreement according to its general tenor and purpose, without attributing to any of its terms a specialist meaning which the word or words in question may have acquired under the domestic law of England.'

And in the *Fothergill* case, the essential feature of this *plain meaning* tradition was stressed by Lord Diplock as follows:

> 'The language of an international convention has not been chosen by an English parliamentary draftsman. It is neither couched in the conventional English legislative idiom nor designed to be construed exclusively by English judges. It is addressed to a much wider and more varied judicial audience than is an Act of Parliament that deals with purely domestic law. It should be interpreted, as Lord Wilberforce put it [...], "unconstrained by technical rules of English law, or by English legal precedent, but on broad principles of general acceptation".'

Hence, to read the words of PIL Treaties, they have to be projected against an *international background.*

2.3.2. *Interpretation of connecting factors*

The principle of uniform interpretation applies of course also to the *connecting factors.* The traditional connecting factor embodied in the Hague Conventions is the concept of *habitual residence.*

The main reasons which incited the Hague Conference to adopt the concept of habitual residence as the main connecting factor for its conventions were the recognised need to retreat from the nationality principle and the difficulties of the concept of domicile, which has different meanings in different countries.

The principal attraction of the concept of habitual residence has always been that it is a simple, non-technical concept that can be applied directly to the facts of cases. Unity of approach in this context does not require a statutory definition of habitual residence – neither positively nor negatively. Both the Hague Conference and most domestic legislators have deliberately refused to provide such a definition; agreement, however, has to be found as to the *method* of determining habitual residence.

The general tendency of courts has been to regard habitual residence as a *factual concept*, which, as I have just mentioned, should not be weighed down by a heavy, artificial definition. It is probably inaccurate to try to develop a series of legal propositions surrounding the meaning of habitual residence, as some national courts in fact did. Eventually, this approach converts the concept into a *technical* legal concept like domicile, and, by the same token, increases the risk of divergent interpretations in different countries.

In my opinion, the House of Lords has taken a more suitable approach in 1990.[11] Lord Brandon of Oakbrook said that the expression 'habitually resident' is

> 'not to be treated as a term of art with some special meaning, but is rather to be understood according to the ordinary and natural meaning of the two words which it contains.'

The term *residence* refers to the place where a person resides, to his or her abode or home. The term *habitual* makes clear that what is meant is not *occasional* or short-term residence.

In his recent comparative study of the subject, Dr Clive from the Scottish Law Commission states that he has not come across any court decision where a person has been found *not* to be habitually resident in a country where he or she has lived for *a year or more*.[12] It seems that after a given period of actually living in a country, the objective time factor outweighs any contention made by a person that she or he never had a firm *intention* to remain in the country concerned. As Lord Ordinary stated in a case in 1993:

> 'It seems to me that, while intention is undoubtedly a very important consideration, there must come a stage when the objective facts point unequivocally to a person's ordinary or habitual residence being in a particular place.'[13]

But even with neutral concepts such as habitual residence, one is by no means sheltered from intricate problems of interpretation. I will just mention two of them.

Let me first mention an English case where the period of residence was *less than one year*.[14] An Israeli couple came to England for a Sabbatical of one year

[11] In re *J. (A Minor) (Abduction: Custody Rights)* [1990] 2 *AC* 562; [1990] 3 *WLR* 492; [1990] 2 *All ER* 961.

[12] Dr E. M. Clive, 'The Concept of Habitual Residence', *The Juridical Review* (1997) Part 3, p. 141.

[13] *Zenel* v. *Haddow*, 1993 SLT 975; 1993 SCLR 872.

[14] In re *S (Minors) (Abduction: Wrongful Detention)* [1994] 1 *ALL ER* 237.

with a possible extension for a second year. During the first year, the couple faced difficulties and the father decided to go back to Israel. Before the end of the one-year period, the mother indicated that she did not intend to return to Israel with the children and applied for a residence order in England. The father applied under the Hague Convention of 1980 on the Civil Aspects of International Child Abduction that the mother had wrongfully retained the children. The court ordered the *return* of the children, finding that they were still habitually resident in Israel. Unfortunately, the judgement does not make clear on what specific grounds this conclusion was reached. Another English court held that a child who was sent from Canada to stay with her father in Minnesota for *a school year* was habitually resident in Minnesota when removed by her mother after some four months.[15] Hence, where the period of residence is less than a year there are court decisions upholding both options.

2.4. The reference to the 'travaux préparatoires'

Let me now come back, once more, to the *Fothergill* case. Another point which was at stake in this *cause célèbre* was the use of the *travaux préparatoires*. It is a well-known fact that the legitimacy of legislative history is not appreciated unanimously in the various legal cultures. In many *civil law* countries, the use of *travaux préparatoires* is deeply rooted and has long been accepted; courts in the United States also easily refer to the legislative history of statutory provisions. In other systems, such as those influenced by the English model, courts have traditionally rejected the use of such materials. In the *Fothergill* case, however, four of the five opinions concluded that consideration should be given not only to *travaux préparatoires*, but also to foreign case law and scholarly writing interpreting the Convention. Their conclusion was partially based on the Vienna Convention on the law of treaties. Article 32 states that when the textual approach either leaves the meaning ambiguous or obscure, or leads to a result which is manifestly absurd or unreasonable, recourse may be had to what the Vienna Convention calls 'supplementary means of interpretation', including the preparatory work of the treaty. One should not, however, emphasise the apparent hierarchy of sources that seems to characterise Articles 31 and 32. In its commentary to the Final Draft of what eventually became the Vienna Convention, the International Law Commission pointed out that the various elements enumerated in these Articles should operate in conjunction and would not have the effect of drawing a rigid line between 'supplementary' and other means of interpretation. This is why recourse to so-called supplementary means of interpretation may also be had to verify or confirm a meaning that emerges as a result of the textual approach. This being said, the *Fothergill* decision – a

[15] *Findlay* v. *Findlay* (No. 2), 1955 SLT 492.

landmark decision on the subject of treaty interpretation – also illustrates the caution that, at least sometimes, may be appropriate in this context. At the Conference on air carrier liability held in The Hague, two delegates proposed an amendment that would have removed the ambiguity that led to the litigation. They eventually withdrew their proposal, stating that this was on the understanding that the existing text had the meaning expressed in their amendment. In his opinion, Lord Diplock considered this legislative background for what it was worth but noted that, based on his experience in such international conferences, he did 'not attach any great significance' to this statement. He then added: 'Machiavellianism is not extinct at international conferences.'

The *travaux préparatoires* of Hague Conventions are published in the *Proceedings* (*Actes et documents*) of the Sessions. In this context, I would like to make a special reference to the *Explanatory Reports*. These Reports are generally written by one expert chosen from among the delegates and very often contain a wealth of useful background material.

3. CONCLUSIONS

Much more could be said about the interpretation of PIL Treaties: how, for example, should an *ordre public* clause or a *reservation* clause be interpreted? What about Conventions done in more than one language?[16] As far as The Hague Conventions are concerned, I would only like to mention that the 1961 Convention on the *protection of minors* was the last to be in French exclusively. The Conventions of 1961 relating to the form of testamentary dispositions and the one abolishing the requirement of legalisation for foreign public documents were also drafted in English, but the French text prevails in case of divergence between the two texts. It is only since the *Adoption* Convention of 1965, that both texts are regarded *equally authentic*.

Let me conclude by stating that The Hague Conference is very much aware of the importance of a uniform interpretation of its Conventions. This is, for example, why the Permanent Bureau systematically *collects judgements* issued in application of various Hague Conventions. It has, by way of illustration, a collection of more than 700 judgements relating to the Child Abduction Convention and it tries to make this information accessible to the courts and authorities of other states. It organises, on a more or less regular basis, meetings on the operation of various Conventions, where problems are discussed and possible solutions analysed.

The issue of uniform interpretation is also a very important and sensitive topic for the Hague Conference's current project, i.e., a Convention on international jurisdiction and the effects of foreign judgements in civil and commercial

[16] See Art. 33 of the Vienna Convention on the Law of Treaties.

matters. The Permanent Bureau has proposed a system of *expert panels* in order to ensure uniform interpretation, but the issue still has to be discussed. It seems to me that an adequate and effective solution to the tricky problem of uniform interpretation might well influence the success of this project.

CONFLICTS BETWEEN PRIVATE INTERNATIONAL LAW TREATIES

Paul Volken*

(1) The present contribution will deal with the often discussed but, in its legal form, little known problem of conflicting international treaties by: (I) looking at the underlying facts that cause such conflicts, (II) examining the legal nature of the phenomenon, (III) analyzing some principal elements of the solution, and (IV) discussing some recent case law. In doing so, this article will not address the entire field of international treaties, but rather limit itself to the so-called law-making conventions, leaving aside international instruments of a more political, technical or economic nature.[1]

1. THE UNDERLYING FACTS

a. National rules for international activities

(2) One of the characteristic phenomena of our century lies in the internationalization of almost all elements of life. On the one hand, we have to admit that the legal rules, under which such international activities are adjudicated, are in their essence still of a strictly national character. This situation is due to the established social order in the world, according to which the bulk of our legislative, rule-imposing power still lies with the sovereign national states, despite the repeated call for globalization. National rules being applied to international activities have become an ever increasing dilemma for today's lawyers. On the other hand, we have to admit that this dilemma is not terribly new for, in substance, it has existed ever since the theory of private international law was established and developed, for the legal profession is and has always been cautious in its reaction and response to new situations. The first approach to adjudicating 'international' factual situations was simply to define the spacious

* Professor of Economic Law and Private International Law, Faculty of Law, Fribourg (Switzerland). I would like to thank my assistant lic. iur. Mattias Johnson for his help in preparing this article. Thanks must also go to Mr. Andrej N. Lushnycky, Director of the American College Program in Fribourg, for his assistance with the English version.

[1] As to the different types of international treaties see, e.g., Ch. Rousseau, *Droit international public*, Vol. I (Paris).

W.P. Heere (Ed.), International Law and The Hague's 750th Anniversary

reach of ones own domestic rules (theory of statutists)[2], whereas a second approach had to wait until Savigny's theory on the seat (i.e. the centre of gravity) of the legal relationship appeared on the scene.[3]

b. The Hague Conference as an answer

(3) An entirely new dimension was introduced into the discussion when, in 1893, Tobias Asser and his academic fellows from all over Europe started the famous Hague Conference on Private International Law.[4] By creating the Conference, Asser was seeking for *un comité central international*, formed by specialists in private international law. The goal was to draft *des règles uniformes [de droit international privé] propres à être adoptées par tous les législateurs des pays membres* of the Conference.

(4) The Asser-group had started its work on the basis of a modest draft consisting of some eight articles[5] with which they intended to cover the whole field of private law and civil procedure: personal capacity, family law, succession, property, contracts, torts, jurisdiction, enforcement and judicial assistance. However, after the first fifteen days of negotiations, the original eight rules had already been transformed into a series of seven or eight isolated topics[6], each of which was destined to become (and progressively did become) a separate international convention. In other words, at the very first session of the Hague Conference, the original Asser-idea of aiming at one single and comprehensive document which would cover the entire private international law-field was jeopardized and the whole subject-matter cut into pieces. Despite these changes, the new philosophy proved to be successful. In 1905, after only twelve years of activities, there were already seven International Hague Conventions. Twenty years later, in 1925, there were eleven. In 1996, the number of International Hague Conventions had increased to 33.[7] Thus, demonstrating the impressive progress for Asser's unification idea!

[2] As to the theories developed by the statutists see M. Gutzwiller, *Geschichte des Internationalprivatrechts. Von den Anfängen bis zu den grossen Kodifikationen* (Basel, 1977) p. 7 ss., spec. p. 16 n. 25, p. 17 n. 26, p. 29 ss.

[3] Ch. von Bar, *Internationales Privatrecht*, Vol. I (München, 1987) pp. 401-405.

[4] Actes de la Conférence de La Haye de droit international privé, 1ère session du 12 au 27 septembre 1893, 2ème partie, La Haye 1893, pp. 9, 4 and pp. 27, 28.

[5] See *supra* n. 4, at pp. 29, 30.

[6] Ibid, at p. 85 ss.

[7] Hague Conference, Collection of Conventions, The Hague 1996, pp. 407 ff.

c. The proliferation of treaties

(5) The Hague Conference was, however, not the only international agency whose mission was dedicated to the international unification and/or harmonization of law through elaboration of multilateral conventions. In 1883, before the establishment of the Hague Conference, the Union of Paris had already begun to internationally harmonize the law for the protection of industrial property and the Union of Berne had undertaken the same activities with respect to the international protection of literary and artistic works. And, shortly after that, new international organizations became active to achieve similar goals in the different fields of international transportation (waterway, railway, road and air). Most important for the further development of the international unification of private and commercial law was the creation of UNIDROIT in 1940, the Council of Europe in 1949, the European Union in 1957 and the UNCITRAL in 1966.[8]

(6) In the last fifty years, the number of international associations and organizations working in the field of unifying international law has substantially increased. The vast majority of those agencies attempted to achieve their tasks of harmonizing or unifying law by promoting multilateral treaties. As a consequence, the number of international law-unifying conventions ready to be ratified by Member States has dramatically augmented and the risk of having conflicting rules coming from different international conventions has increased accordingly.

(7) Recently, a Swiss court had to deal with a maintenance-claim brought by a minor living in Switzerland against his father who happened to live in France.[9] The first question relating to Swiss jurisdiction was favourably answered based on Article 5 number 2 of the Lugano-Convention, a treaty prepared by a joint undertaking of EU and EFTA-countries. The second question as to which law should be applied received a clear answer in favor of Article 276 of the Swiss Civil Code; the answer had its basis in Article 4 of the Hague Convention of 2 October 1973 on the Law Applicable to Maintenance Obligations. As to the third question – i.e. the enforcement of a possible Swiss decision in France – after a short hesitation between Article 31 ss. of the Lugano-Convention and Article 4 ss. of the Hague Convention of 2 October 1973 on the Recognition and Enforcement of Decisions Relating to Maintenance Obligations, precedence was (correctly) given to the latter text. But, at the same time the question was raised whether the New York Convention of 20 July 1956 on the Collecting of Maintenance Obligation Abroad also had a role to play in the present case.

(8) The positive answer with respect to the application of each of the conventions mentioned may lead to different reactions: On the one hand, law professors may express enthusiastic praise for such impressive results which have

[8] P. Volken, *Konventionskonflikte im internationalen Privatrecht* (Zürich, 1977) S. 1, 2, n. 1, 2.

[9] Unpublished decision; liquidated by agreement after information on the pertinent conventions applicable.

been rendered possible by the excellent work of the international unification of law. On the other hand, the average practitioner might react with displeasure and worry over the fact that he or she should have studied not less than five different conventions in order to solve a modest maintenance case between Villette (CH) et Gaillard (F).

2. THE LEGAL NATURE OF THE PHENOMENON

(9) Technically speaking, conflicts between international treaties are not conflicts between the treaties themselves, but rather the problem of irreconcilable treaty-made legal rules. A conflict between treaties occurs when two or more legal rules, each of which is taken from a different convention, should, for the sake of solving a case, come to simultaneous or concomitant application but where such application leads to irreconcilable contradictory results. For instance, according to the rule taken from convention A, the substantial rules of the law of State A should be applicable, whereas the rule taken from convention B refers to the law of State B.

In this sense, the problem of conflicting treaties can be related to the phenomenon of conflicting or contradictory legal rules in general.[10] Accordingly, conflicting legal rules as such are not limited to law-making treaties but rather such conflicts can be found on all levels both of the national and the international legal order.

(10) According to Wilfried Jenks[11], this kind of conflict is, to some extent, inherent to the modern form of international unification of law. And whereas René David[12] asked for more internationally harmonized law and characterized the unification movement as 'one of the fundamental tasks of this century's lawyers', as they had to look for 'the reconstitution of a ius commune in international legal relations', Jenks reminded that the international unification process also has its drawbacks. Therefore, he asked for prudence in the international legislative process and for guidance, to enable the international practice to resolve the problems of conflicting treaty-rules in a rational way.[13]

3. POSSIBLE SOLUTIONS

(11) As the problem of conflicts between international treaties belongs to the vaster field of contradictory legal rules in general, possible solutions should also be looked for from this broader angle. The problem of conflicting rules can be

[10] P. Volken, op. cit. n. 4, at p. 45.

[11] W. Jenks, 'The Conflict of Law-making Treaties', *BYIL* (1953) p. 401.

[12] R. David, 'The Methods of Unification', *AJCL* (1968) p. 22.

[13] W. Jenks, loc. cit. n. 11, at pp. 427, 453.

evaluated from a political, a more factual or a simple remedial point of view.

(12) The political aspect focuses upon the interdependence between the coherence of a legislative process and the frequency of real conflicts. As to international treaties, one can say that, if the international framers of legal texts were more careful in their drafting, the practitioners would have fewer problems with possible conflicts. In particular, things would not be so difficult if each international organization would limit its activities to a particular subject-matter. However, the situation changes substantially when the European Union in Brussels starts to prepare conventions for subject-matters in which the Hague Conference or the Council of Europe have already done the work and vice versa.[14]

(13) The factual point of view relates to the substantive nature of the texts or treaties in conflict. The risk of conflict diminishes to the degree of substantial differences between the subject matter of two treaties. Thus, it seems unlikely to have a conflict between the Hague Conventions of 1 June 1970 on the Recognition of Divorces[15] and of 14 March 1978 on the Celebration of Marriages[16]. However, the 1970-text refers in its Article 11 to the right to remarry after divorce, and this rule might well enter into conflict with Article 3 of the 1978-text on the law applicable to marriage.[17] In other terms, factual or latent treaty-conflicts become possible when a convention departs from the substance of its subject-matter and interferes with the subject-matter of another text. Therefore, international treaty-makers should scrupulously stick to their task.

(14) As to possible remedies with respect to cases in which a conflicting situation has occurred, it has often been suggested to have recourse to solutions developed under domestic law and based on principles such as rules of reciprocal consistency or rules of an intertemporal or transitory character.

The famous Article 30 of the Vienna Convention of 23 March 1969 on the Law of Treaties[18] which deals with the problem in question, proposes a solution

[14] Recently information was released according to which the European Union is about to prepare a convention on judicial cooperation in civil matters. Such an undertaking would interfere with the Hague Conventions on Service Abroad (1965), on Evidence Abroad (1970) and on Access to Justice (1980).

[15] See supra n. 7, at p. 128.

[16] Ibid, at p. 243.

[17] Art. 11 of the Divorce Convention reads:

'A State which is obliged to recognise a divorce under this Convention may not preclude either spouse from remarrying on the ground that the law of another State does not recognize that divorce'

And Art. 3 para. 2 of the Marriage-Convention states:

'A marriage shall be celebrated

(1) ...

(2) where each of the future spouses meets the substantive requirements of the internal law designated by the choice of law rules of the State of celebration.'

[18] *AJIL* (1969) pp. 875, 884-885.

that combines all three elements. Thus, we find the consistency-rule, combined with an intertemporal element, in Article 30 paragraph 2:

> '2. When a treaty specifies that it is subject to, or that it is not to be considered as incompatible with, an earlier or later treaty, the provisions of that other treaty prevail.'

In paragraph 3 of Article 30, the intertemporal aspect has been codified:

> '3. When all parties to the earlier treaty are parties also to the later treaty but the earlier treaty is not terminated or suspended (...) the earlier treaty applies only to the extent that its provisions are compatible with those of the later treaty.'

Article 30 paragraph 4 expresses the transitory element:

> '4. When the parties to the later treaty do not include all parties to the earlier one:
> (a) as between states parties to both treaties the same rule applies as in para. 3;
> (b) as between a state party to both treaties and a state party to only one of the treaties, the treaty to which both states are parties governs their mutual rights and obligations.'

(15) Most modern law-codifying treaties provide conflict rules which are based on elements of compatibility, non-interference, *lex prior*, *lex posterior*, *lex specialis* or a combination of such rules.

Within the Hague Conference, it was at its eighth session (1956) when the problem of a possible conflict between different conventions was articulated for the first time. Said session was working on a convention, which later became the Convention of 15 April 1958 on the Law Applicable to Transfer of Title in the International Sale of Goods.[19] One of the crucial points in that convention related to the rights of the unpaid seller in cases where the buyer went bankrupt. Should the seller's reservation of title prevail over the rights of the buyer's creditors to keep the goods staying in the buyer's possession, and if so, according to what law? In this context, a possible conflict with the Nordic Convention of 7 November 1933 on (the universality of) Bankruptcy[20] was advocated, and it was stated that without an adequate reservation, the (new) Hague Convention would be unacceptable for the Scandinavian countries. Thus, the Hague Conference of 1956 had to choose between either a special reservation clause in favour of bankruptcy-proceedings or a rule of compatibility in favour of other possible conventions. The decision was in favour of the latter solution and, for the first

[19] See *supra* n. 7, p. 16.
[20] *League of Nations-Treaty Series*, No 155 (1935) p. 133.

time, a rule of compatibility was introduced into a law-making convention on private international law.[21]

(16) Since the session of 1956, compatibility-clauses, similar to the one in Article 9 of the Convention on the Reservation of Title have become standard in all new Hague Conventions. There were from time to time some variations in combining the different elements mentioned above[22], but the basic policy of preventing possible conflicts with other international law-making conventions remained. Moreover, the need for such clauses was also accepted by other international organizations active in the field of the unification of law[23]. Thus, compared to the situation in the sixties and early seventies, the actual problem of dealing with possible conflicts between treaty-made legal rules is not the lack of compatibility-rules any more but rather lies in the fact that there are too many similar rules of this kind and that too often, and without sufficient reason, recourse to such rules is made.

(17) Real conflicts between international, law-making conventions are very rare in practice. Formally speaking, a conflict between two or more legal rules coming from different international conventions does, and can, only appear where three conditions are cumulatively fulfilled, i.e.: (1) two or more conventions apply to the same factual situation, (2) the pertinent legal rules contained in such conventions provide for contradictory results, and (3), the drafters of the conflicting conventions did not provide for adequate compatibility-rules. Thus, before any complaint about conflicting treaties is justified, each of the three questions mentioned is to be verified, and this verification has to be done with respect to each of the possible treaties in conflict.

The first question relates to the scope of application of the treaties in debate and includes four elements, i.e., the application *ratione personae*, *materiae*, *loci* and *temporis*. Every element must be fulfilled with respect to each treaty in discussion, for if – with respect to one or the other treaty – only one element lacks, the treaty in question would not be applicable to the case and, in so far as said treaty is concerned, no conflict would be possible.

The second question relates to the subject matter of the different treaties. A real conflict occurs only where the substantial solutions differ from and/or contradict each other. If all of three conventions grant jurisdiction in favour of court A, no conflict appears because the solutions are identical. However, as soon as the solution of one of the conventions departs from the two others, the situation changes and we are faced with a latent risk of conflicting treaties.

[21] Art. 9 of the Convention reads as follows:

'The present Convention does not affect conventions concluded or which may be concluded by the contracting States concerning the recognition and the effects of a bankruptcy declared in one of the States party to such a Convention.'

[22] See *supra* § No. 14.

[23] See *supra* § No. 4.

If in such a case even the elements of the third question are fulfilled, i.e., the drafters of the treaties in conflict had failed to provide for adequate rules of compatibility or non-interference, then (and only then) the problem of conflicting treaties becomes real.
(18) As already mentioned, most if not all modern treaties on law-making are nowadays equiped with rules on compatibility, coordination or non-interference with other similar treaties. Despite all such legislative prudence, case law, time and again, confronts us with new problems.

4. RECENT CASE LAW

a. Jan and Marie

(19) Jan from Delft (NL) and Marie from Dijon (F) got married in 1992. In 1993, their daughter Silvia was born in Rotterdam. In 1994, the marriage was dissolved by a Dutch court. One year later, Marie and her daughter came to Fribourg (CH), so the mother could pursue a special diploma in education. At the same time, Jan left for an EU-nomination in Brussels. Once settled in Fribourg, Marie felt the maintenance part of the Dutch divorce decree was too modest whereas the court's rulings as to the father's rights of access to his daughter was too burdensome. Marie therefore asked the Court of Fribourg to modify these two elements of the Dutch divorce decision.[24]
(20) The court in Fribourg had some problems with the law applicable to the amendments requested and the proper steps to follow. As to the maintenance question, the court felt relatively comfortable, as Article 5 number 2 of the Lugano-Convention[25] seems to grant jurisdiction and Article 4 paragraph 2 of the Hague Convention of 1973 on the Law Applicable to Maintenance Obligations[26] also allows the application of Swiss law. However, the modification of the father's access rights proved problematic as it seemed to fall under both the Protection of Minors-Convention of 1961 (Art. 5)[27] and the Child Abduction-

[24] Unpublished.

[25] Art. 5 No 2: 'A person domiciled in a Contracting State may, in another Contracting State, be sued:
1. (...)
2. in matters relating to maintenance, in the courts for the place where the maintenance creditor is domiciled or habitually resident (...).'

[26] Art. 4 para. 2: 'In care of a change in the habitual residence of the creditor, the internal law of the new habitual residence shall apply as from the moment when change occurs.'

[27] Art. 5 para. 1 and 2: '(1) Au cas de déplacement de la résidence habituelle d'un mineur d'un Etat contractant dans un autre, les mesures prises par les autorités de l'Etat de l'ancienne résidence habituelle restent en vigueur tant que les autorités de la nouvelle résidence habituelle ne les ont pas levées ou remplacées. (2) Les mesures prises par les autorités de l'Etat de l'ancienne résidence habituelle ne sont levées ou remplacées qu'après avis préalable aux dites autorités.'

Convention of 1980 (Art. 21)[28]. As to the maintenance aspect, the question was, do the consultation proceedings provided for under Article 5 paragraph 2 of the Minors Convention[29] also have to be observed when the monthly maintenance allocation ought to be changed? In other words, what convention was to be applied to what kind of legal problem?

(21) If the court had started with the compatibility- or incompatibility-rules, the help might not have been important, as Article 19 of the Maintenance Convention states:

> 'This Convention shall not affect any other international instrument containing provisions on matters governed by this Convention to which a contracting State is, or becomes, a Party',

whereas Article 18 of the Convention on the Protection of Minors reads:

> 'Elle [la présente Convention] ne porte pas atteinte aux dispositions d'autres conventions liant au moment de son entrée en vigueur des Etats contractants.'

In other terms, the two clauses accord precedence to one another; they end up in a constant reference back and forth and create a situation similar to *renvoi*.

b. **Van den Boogard**

(22) Antonius van den Boogaard and Paula Laumen[30], both Dutch citizens, were married in Holland in 1957. In 1982, their domicile was transferred to London, where, in 1990, the High Court pronounced their divorce. The financial part of the divorce was settled by granting a lump sum of some £900'000 in favour of Mrs. Laumen. Out of said decision there remained an amount of £350'000 to be paid; Mrs. Laumen asked for enforcement before the Court of Amsterdam.

In the first instance, the Court moved in favour of Mrs. Laumen and, according to her demand, enforcement was granted on the basis of the Hague Convention of 1973 on the Enforcement of Decisions Relating to Maintenance Obligations.

(23) In the second instance, however, the court felt, that as such an important sum was at stake, the enforcement should not be decided on the basis of a simple Hague Convention only, but should rather be examined in the light of Article 31

[28] Art. 21 para. 1: 'An application to make arrangements for organizing or securing the effective exercise of rights of access may be presented to the Central Authorities of the Contracting States in the same way as an application for the return of a child.'

[29] See *supra* n. 27.

[30] EC-Court, decision of 27 February 1997, No. C-220/95; *SZIER/SRIEL* (1998) p. 93

ss. of the Brussels Convention. The question was submitted to the EC-Court which held that the money-decision to be enforced was of a maintenance nature and would therefore fall under the Brussels Convention. As to the possible conflict between the two treaties it was stated that, the Hague Convention, due to its Article 23, does not oppose the application of the Brussel's Convention, irrespective of Article 57 of the latter.

(24) Said decision was manifestly wrong, for the court should have balanced both compatibility rules, i.e., Article 23 of the Hague versus Article 57 of the Brussels text, against each other. By proceeding that way, the court would have realized that Article 57 of the Brussels Convention is the narrower text which grants precedence to the more specialised convention, and the Hague Convention of 1973 is in fact specialised in the enforcement of maintenance decisions.

5. POSSIBLE CONSEQUENCES

(25) From the foregoing reflections two conclusions have to be drawn. First, there are too many law-making treaties with too narrow a topic for each. It is simply unacceptable to have five (or even more) conventions dealing with maintenance questions. Also, it is unacceptable to have four or five different texts on the protection of minors, on succession, on contractual or non-contractual obligations or even on judicial assistance. In this century, the layout of the different topics to be approached has been established. Now, the time has come to bring things together and to proceed to the merger of conventions. The Hague Conference of the future will not have fulfilled its function if there should remain more than three conventions to cover the field of family and succession law. By merging, treaty-made law becomes workable again and the risk of overlapping rule-making decreases.

Second, so far the attempts of coordinating the international activities of law-making have failed. On the one hand, the international organizations, such as UNIDROIT or UNCITRAL, which have a mandate to coordinate international activities did not fulfill their task. On the other hand, expanding organizations, such as the European Union should not try to reinvent everything.

Only if these two aspects are taken seriously, internationally framed law will become workable again and problems with overlapping rules might disappear.

THE DUTCH POLICY DOCUMENT ON THE REGULATION OF THE INFORMATION HIGHWAY

Katharina Boele-Woelki*

Since the Internet is an open network operating across frontiers, it encounters a vast range of the most diverse legal systems, rules and regulations. Is regulation of the Internet feasible or even desirable? If the answer is affirmative the second question of how best to regulate the Internet is a source of considerable controversy. The quest for workable solutions inevitably implies the identification and qualification of what exactly comprises the Internet 'area' and who are the actors involved in it.
Is the time ripe for national or international regulations? Do we know what the Internet will look like within a few years? On 12 June 1998, these questions have been discussed during the annual meeting of the Dutch Law Association. Four different consultative reports on law and the Internet were presented. The rapporteurs dealt with criminal law, private international law and copyright law, and the introductory report described the development of the Internet from a technical system to a social system. The question was raised whether the Internet should be regulated by national statutes. The rapporteur and the members of the Association present at this meeting unanimously pleaded for a very reluctant approach.

It is beyond doubt that the transition to an information society brings many far reaching changes, but does this development necessarily mean a radical break with the past? By analyzing this process, the key question is whether the existing legal instruments are still satisfactory in a digital environment. Would adaptation or amendment of such instruments suffice or are entirely new rules and frameworks required? When a social phenomenon, which has already been regulated by law, appears in electronic form, a simple adaptation of such instruments probably will suffice. On the other hand, new norms and frameworks are needed in case the information highway results in fundamental changes, resulting in intervention on the part of the legislator. Certain issues can become problems when they appear in areas where the law provides no solutions.

In discussing the question of the regulation of the information highway or the Internet, as it is commonly referred to, two approaches can be discerned: a na-

* Professor of Private International Law and Comparative Law, University of Utrecht; the author would like to thank Mrs. Marike Vermeer, research assistent at the Molengraaff Instituut for Private Law, University of Utrecht, for her valuable contribution.

W.P. Heere (Ed.), International Law and The Hague's 750th Anniversary

tional approach and an international approach. Dr. Feldges from Germany will speak about a national legislative approach to an international problem, specifically about the German Act on Information and Communication Services of July 1997. Mr. Smith from England will discuss how we could work together at an international or European level in the field of (a probably neccessary) regulation of the Internet.

Before I shall invite both speakers to give their presentations, I myself would like to give a brief summary of an important and in my mind solid Dutch policy document which recently was published by the Dutch Ministry of Justice, *Legislation for the Information Highway*, which was sent to the Lower House of the Dutch Parliament on 18 February 1998 (*Tweede Kamer* 1997-1998, 25880). In compiling the Policy Document, a systematic study was carried out to determine to what extent existing legislation, usually written for the 'physical world', can be applied to the digital highway. The Policy Document serves as a guide for legislative issues in connection with the information highway. It looks at the information highway; not just the Internet, but also all other forms of telecommunication, digital information carriers, electronic payment systems, etc., are discussed. The Policy Document is limited to those forms of government intervention where legislation is or could be relevant. This does not necessarily imply that legislation will be undertaken. It just should be investigated whether self-regulation is not likely to be a more appropriate means in the given situation. The Policy Document includes in any event the following tasks for the government:

a) the traditional safeguard tasks of the government, such as the protection of civil rights (privacy, freedom of speech, confidentiality of mail, etc.) and
b) supervision of competition.

Three aspects of the current developments are of special interest for the Dutch government's position:

First, the aspect of dematerialisation: know-how, services and information laid down or recorded in intangible form are the engine of the economy. Digitally-stored information is no longer connected to a specific physical carrier or place. Digital information is furthermore inexhaustible since it can be copied endlessly without any loss of quality or destruction;

Second, the aspect of internationalisation: the information society is a totally open society. Information is virtually not connected to any place or state and is able to penetrate even the remotest corners of society. Economical and social developments will find their beginning in sources beyond the reach of national governments.

Third, the aspect of technological turbulence: new information technology and information products are being developed in rapid succession or they converge in new media. The development of technology, the common use thereof and the social and legal problems resulting therefrom, are highly unpredictable and have a high speed of circulation .

The Policy Document discusses the applicability of the three traditional areas of law – private law, administrative law and criminal law – to the information highway. The Policy Document further discusses a few specific areas of law, like the protection of minors and copyright law.

It is important to mention that the Policy Document constitutes a framework of criteria (*toetsingskader*) for the legislator. This framework of criteria is directed towards the actors in the legislation process. This includes the delegates negotiating for the Netherlands on a European or international level with respect to new European and international legislation. The framework should help them to make a consistent balance of interests when drafting new legislation. The framework of criteria is also meant to motivate decisions, especially those which deviate from the general rules as mentioned in the framework. The framework of criteria does not have an imperative character, and, considering the complexity of the issues at stake, should not have one. Furthermore, for certain issues a combination of legal instruments would be appropriate rather than one specific instrument.

The three main features of the informatisation process as mentioned above (dematerialisation, internationalisation and technological turbulence), imply a strong preference for alternatives for formal legislation. On the other hand, however, the uncertain character of the information highway requires legal certainty in some situations. This dilemma is shown in every solution. According to the drafters of the document technology-independent regulations are preferable. With these instruments equality between the 'off-line' world and the 'on-line' world can be established more easily. Such regulations can also better withstand technological turbulence. Self-regulation is preferable in the short term but has also considerable risks. Self-regulation is, for instance, not an appropriate instrument when fundamental principles of a democratic constitutional state (*democratische rechtsstaat*) are at stake. The Policy Document includes certain minimum requirements for self-regulation as an alternative for government regulation. The government safeguards compliance with these requirements. In the long term there can be a need for government regulation when:

1) Technology has reached a level whereby new media displaces traditional media. The government should then create guarantees for accessibility; or
2) When technological development stabilises. In order to stimulate legal certainty the norms that have been achieved by way of self-regulation could then be codified.

It is not possible to give an overview of the whole framework of criteria (*toetsingskader*). I selected the most important – in my view – four criteria.

1) Legislation should preferably take place at the global level, or at least in as many countries as possible. If this is unachievable, regulation at another international level, such as the OECD or the Council of Europe, would be a good alternative. If this level is not to be achieved, the level of the European Union will do. Private law, in particular, is a good area for this purpose. Furthermore,

standardisation and other regulation in the area of economic legislation and other subjects about which there are not many cultural differences, are well suited for legislation.

2) Legislation at the national level can be considered:
– for the protection of fundamental principles;
– when legislation at the international level is not to be achieved, or would take too long
– to strengthen the international competition position of the Netherlands;
– as example for the international legal development.

3) Self-regulation should meet the following requirements:
– the relevant target groups should be sufficiently organised;
– the relevant social interests are being controlled equally;
– there is a sufficient relation between all parties;
– the enforcement of agreements is sufficiently guaranteed.

4) As already mentioned: Government intervention is relevant when fundamental principles of the democratic constitutional state (*Democratische Rechtsstaat*) are at stake. Examples, with respect to the information highway are the protection of civil rights and the prevention and investigation of serious injuries to the legal order and national security.

What is the usefulness of the framework of criteria and how will this guideline be implemented in the legislation process? The Policy Document states that the framework of criteria will take effect at once when preparing and determining regulations, and with the Dutch participation and contribution in international fora. The framework of criteria will be included in the General Directives for legislation. The Policy Document will be implemented in a number of follow-up projects, which will be carried out separately. Monitoring of progress will be coordinated by the Minister of Justice as part of a second national action plan on information highways. The Policy Document will be updated in two years' time.

In conclusion, one could say that the legislative role of the Dutch government remains limited to the traditional regulatory tasks of safeguarding basic norms and values – though in an electronic environment – such as the protection of civil rights, ensuring the enforcement of the law and offering legal certainty. In addition, the government facilitates the use of electronic communications by promoting the transparency and accessibility of the market, fostering the reliability of electronic communications and removing (legal) obstacles. The guiding principle is that the existing norms must also be applicable in the electronic domain. The Policy Document concludes furthermore that this is the case as regards the major elements of the existing legal rules and definitions. The third task of the government is to guarantee an easy access to the fundamental provisions required for the social functioning of individuals and companies. This third task does not yet lead to the use of legal instruments.

Finally, the Policy Document concludes that the existing legal framework is generally – possibly after some adaptation – applicable to the information highway. An observation should be made in this respect: the international character of the information highway does not relate very well with territorially organised governments. Physical borders are irrelevant on the information highway. The Policy Document concludes that for this problem there is no general solution. However, the problem can be diminished by a combination of solutions. Therefore the Policy Document proposes a pragmatic 'multiple-track' solution, whereby the existing national sovereignties are the starting point. For now the proposed measures should create sufficient legal certainty. This depends on the further development of the information highway: whether, in the long run, a more fundamental approach would be necessary, whereby these sovereignties will be affected.

The Dutch Policy Document consists of more than 200 pages. I restricted myself to giving a brief summary of the most important policy aspects which in the Netherlands will be taken into account when the question of regulation of the Internet will be raised, whether on a national or an international level.

CONTENT ON THE INTERNET – LAW, REGULATION, CONVERGENCE AND HUMAN RIGHTS

G.J.H. Smith*

SETTING THE SCENE

The characteristic that distinguishes the Internet from previous forms of electronic communication is that on the Internet, for the first time, everyone is a publisher. This takes us back to the days of pamphlets and little newspapers, when anyone could print a tract and expect to find an audience. Now I can publish a tract not just to my friends and neighbours but to the whole world – without the need to convince an intermediary to print it. For an Internet subscription of £10 a month or less, I can speak to the world. The Internet is a living example of the marketplace in ideas. Judge Dalzell, the first instance judge in the *Communications Decency Act* case in America, described the Internet as 'the most participatory form of mass speech yet developed.'[1] This truth about the Internet is already forcing policy-makers to re-think traditional attitudes to the forms of law or regulation appropriate for electronic mass media.

An equally revolutionary feature of the Internet is that information on the Internet ignores traditional static borders. It ignores geography, it ignores political borders, it ignores legal borders. It also transcends traditional technical borders (for instance between broadcast and telephone networks). Instead of respecting static borders, the Internet creates dynamic substitutes. These new alignments reflect common interests among Internet users. They create on-line communities. These reflect a great variety of cultural, political, linguistic, religious and other interests of widely dispersed users.

THE INTERNET AND NATIONAL LEGAL SYSTEMS

National legal systems are buttressed by the existence of substantial barriers to mobility and global communication. These include economic and social barriers such as time, distance and the cost of re-locating people and assets between jurisdictions. They also include imposed barriers such as political borders with effective customs and immigration controls. The development of private inter-

* Partner, Bird & Bird, Solicitors, London, England.

[1] *ACLU* v. *Reno*, 929 F. Supp. 824 (E.D. Pa 1996)

W.P. Heere (Ed.), International Law and The Hague's 750th Anniversary

national law, and the move towards international co-operation in criminal matters, reflects the existing growth in international trade, communication and mobility in people and assets. But in the realm of information the Internet challenges territorial underpinnings to a degree not previously contemplated.

Time is no longer a barrier: on the Internet content can be delivered instantaneously across geographic and political borders. Distance is irrelevant: not only can messages be transmitted from one part of the globe to another instantaneously, but for the user the location of the content is irrelevant. All that matters is that the content appears on his or her screen. This gives content providers a wide choice of jurisdictions in which to locate the computers holding their Web sites. The Internet also destroys cost barriers. Information can travel from one part of the globe to another almost cost free. A single Web site is available in all jurisdictions with Internet access. To set up a web site means to publish simultaneously to the whole world. The cost to a company of marketing to the whole world is now merely the cost of creating a Web site, compared with the millions of pounds that it used to cost to mount a global marketing and advertising campaign.

These characteristics give the Internet the potential to erode national legal systems based on geographic and political boundaries. While imposed barriers – customs, immigration, tariff and physical – still remain, the Internet challenges their enforceability. Certainly, the police can arrest people and seize their modems. Customs officials and border guards can still control movement of people and physical goods. People responsible for content are vulnerable to enforcement in states in which they live or visit, to which they can be extradited, or in which they have assets. But the information itself is almost immune. In the famous words of John Perry Barlow, 'the Internet routes around censorship'. Once telecommunications links are in place it is extraordinarily difficult for national authorities to prevent information flowing across their borders.

TERRITORY – DRIVERS FOR AN INTERNATIONAL APPROACH

Against this background we can identify a number of drivers creating pressure for an international approach to the challenges raised by the Internet.

Cost of uncertainty

Putting up a Web site exposes the proprietor of the Web site to potential liability in every country of the world from which the site can be accessed. There is a substantial risk attached to the uncertainty of dealing with so many potential jurisdictions. The cost of trying to copy-clear a Web site for all those jurisdictions (assuming that such a goal is even achievable) is immense. Thus the commercial community has a significant interest in reducing the uncertainty and cost of complying with such a plethora of jurisdictions.

Extra-territorial effect

Members of the Internet community, at least, are concerned about the extra-territorial effect of national laws. This occurs when national enforcement spills over beyond the borders of the country. One example of this can be seen in the action of a local German prosecutor against CompuServe over its Internet newsgroups. Quite apart from the controversy stirred up by the prosecution and eventual conviction of CompuServe's local manager, the initial action affected the ability of US CompuServe subscribers to access the full range of Internet newsgroups.

Another example is the action taken by German authorities against the *Radikal* Web site. An edition of this magazine was said to contravene German terrorism laws. The magazine was in fact stored on the computers of an Internet Service Provider ('ISP') in Holland. The action resulted in German ISPs blocking access to all content on the Dutch ISP which hosted the *Radikal* magazine. It also raised the prospect that the proprietor of the ISP in question might be arrested if he visited Germany. Ultimately the magazine removed the offending edition from the Dutch ISP's server. All this in spite of there being no suggestion that the magazine was illegal in Holland. The Internet did in this case also route around censorship – the *Radikal* site was mirrored on about 40 other sites around the world, so as regards the information itself the German authorities' action was ultimately futile.

The Internet community's concept of an international approach to Internet law would probably lean towards insulating content on the Internet from restrictive national laws. It is also arguable that in some respects that would do no more than reflect the reality of the Internet today.

Fear of a foreign flood

Pressure for an international approach may also come from governments with an entirely opposite interest. These governments fear erosion of their own national laws by the flood of uncensored data flowing through the Internet into their countries. Such governments may wish to see an international approach which centres on giving greater effect to national laws by mutual enforcement and increased international co-operation.

The governments of some countries have put in place both technical and legal mechanisms attempting to prevent the full spectrum of Internet content reaching their citizens.

It is very difficult to see how one unified international approach could satisfy both those who wish to see the Internet insulated from restrictive national laws and also those who would like to see their national laws made more effective.

The urge to regulate

I distinguish here between law and regulation. The difference between the two can best be seen by comparing the print press with broadcast media. Print publishers are not licensed. They can publish without prior permission from the State. Print publishers are subject only to general laws, either developed as part of the common law or enacted (in liberal countries) by democratic assemblies – in both cases interpreted and enforced by an independent judiciary. The classic broadcast regulation model is fundamentally different. The legislated content rules are often more restrictive than those for the print media. Broadcasters can function only with a licence. The regulation is discretionary: an official is empowered to write, interpret and enforce codes of practice governing content without recourse to the legislature.

The Internet, because it renders technical boundaries obsolete, poses a challenge to existing national regulatory structures in industries such as broadcast and telecoms. The regulators' first instinct may be to regard the Internet as another form of new media which they should be regulating. The regulators are now debating, both nationally and internationally, what their future role should be in this converged world.

Tidy minds

There is a natural inclination, especially among lawyers, to want to replace chaos with order. But as the Internet is by its very nature a spontaneous order, the result of human action but not of top-down human design, the need for an imposed structure is at the least questionable.

DOES THE INTERNET REQUIRE AN INTERNATIONAL APPROACH?

So does it follow from its international nature that the Internet requires a new international approach? If so, what kind of approach is required? Should it be boundary-oriented – in other words seeking to redefine the applicability of national laws to activity on the Internet, or should it seek to create some kind of new international regime reflecting the international nature of the Internet? If a new regime is required, should it be based on law, on regulation or something else?

Should an international approach be monolithic or pluralistic? Should it seek to impose a single set of rules on content made available through the Internet or should it reflect the dynamically changing borders of the Internet by permitting multiple sets of rules to develop? Should an international approach be Internet-specific, or integrated with terrestrial legal systems? Is it even possible, given convergence and the breakdown of technical barriers, for any approach to be restricted to one type of network such as the Internet? Lastly, what values should an international approach to Internet content laws reflect? Should it reflect the values of the liberal countries with a high degree of regard for freedom of speech, or should it seek to reflect the concerns of the more restrictive regimes? How should provisions such as Article 19 of the Universal Declaration of Human Rights affect an international approach to the Internet?

CURRENT FOCUSES OF DEBATE

The need to find real-world answers to some of these questions is becoming pressing in many areas. The territory question already arises both in policy debates and in the courts. The breakdown of technical barriers has stimulated a debate on the challenge to existing regulatory systems posed by convergence of previous separate content delivery mechanisms. I will look more closely at these territory and convergence questions.

TERRITORY – CRIMINAL

Notwithstanding the high public profile of issues such as pornography on the Internet, the problem of clashing international criminal jurisdiction has first been seriously addressed in the commercial arena: in highly regulated industries such as financial services and pharmaceuticals. These industries are governed by licensing regimes which affect the ability to advertise. Unlicensed activities are punishable as criminal offences. A Web site is available to users in all jurisdictions. The Web site proprietor cannot prevent this. So does a Web site which is available within a particular jurisdiction have, by virtue of its mere availability, to comply with the financial services or pharmaceuticals regulatory regime of the jurisdiction within which it is available; or is more than mere availability required in order to trigger the compliance requirements of that jurisdiction? It is certainly impractical to try to enforce such a national regime across the whole world. This has driven national regulators to develop relatively pragmatic approaches to the enforcement of national legislation. Both the Securities and Exchange Commission in the USA and the Financial Services Authority in the UK have issued detailed guidance addressing when, so far as possible within the constraints of existing legislation, they would be unlikely to take action against overseas Web sites.[2]

What other approaches are possible? One solution often suggested is that if the activity is legal in the country of origin (e.g. where the server is located), that should suffice. However, it is difficult to see the more restrictive regimes in the world accepting that proposition unless the more liberal countries are prepared to harmonise their content laws to restrictive standards. The Treaty of Rome adopts a country of origin and harmonisation approach. But when the European Commission published its Communication on Illegal and Harmful Content on the Internet[3], it recognised the difficulties of achieving uniformity in substantive criminal law. It suggested instead a concept of 'core illegality' – that common minimum standards for illegality could be agreed and enforced only in limited areas such as child pornography, trafficking in human beings, racial hatred, terrorism and fraud.

If increased international co-operation were to result in national laws being extra-territorially enforced, for instance by enhanced extradition proceedings, that would effectively amount to a 'country of receipt' rather than 'country of origin' regime. Under such a regime someone publishing content on the Internet would have to satisfy himself of its lawfulness in all countries of receipt. This is an extremely onerous and effectively impossible task to achieve. If 'country of receipt' were to be reinforced, it would result in a 'most restrictive common denominator' approach to Internet content. That, even if practicable, would surely be resisted by those who see the Internet as having a beneficial effect in increasing the flow of uncensored information around the world. An approach based on increased international co-operation has to address the question 'which laws do we enforce'? Cases such as the *Radikal* incident suggest that even within Europe, in an area of core illegality such as terrorism, agreement may not be easy.

The European Commission Report on Illegal and Harmful Content, whilst advocating increased international co-operation, recognised the human rights aspect of this problem. It stated:

'Some third countries have introduced wide-ranging legislation to block all direct access to Internet via access providers by introducing a requirement for 'proxy servers' similar to those used by large organisations for security reasons, combined with centralised blacklisting of documents, for reasons which go far beyond the limited category of illegal content as defined in this communication.

[2] Securities and Exchange Commission 'Interpretation: Re: Use of Internet Web Sites To Offer Securities, Solicit Securities Transactions, or Advertise Investment Services Offshore' 23 March 1998; Financial Services Authority 'Treatment of material on overseas Internet World Wide Web sites accessible in the UK but not intended for investors in the UK' Guidance 2/98, 28 May 1998.

[3] 'Illegal and harmful content on the Internet – Communication to the European Parliament, the Council, the Economic and Social Committee and the Committee of the Regions' COM(96) 487; www.echo.lu/legal/en/internet/content/communic.html.

Such a restrictive regime is inconceivable for Europe as it would severely interfere with the freedom of the individual and its political traditions.'

A subsequent European Commission Working Party report[4] suggested that information on the Internet should be allowed the same free flow as paper-based information, and that any restrictions should respect fundamental rights such as freedom of expression and the right to privacy. It stated that any international agreement should be in conformity with fundamental rights and European traditions of free expression.

TERRITORY – CIVIL WRONGS

On the Internet we are for the most part considering wrongs done at a distance. It is useful when considering tort jurisdiction on the Internet to create two classes: receipt-oriented and possession-oriented. The first class, receipt-oriented torts, consists of those, such as passing off, trade mark infringement[5], defamation and negligent misstatement, whose essence is the communication of information. In these cases it may be relatively easy for the plaintiff to demonstrate at least the likelihood of damage, such as damage to goodwill or damage to reputation, in the jurisdiction of receipt[6]. After the WIPO Diplomatic Conference[7] decision that 'making available to the public' should be an act infringing copyright, copyright also appears to be gaining some characteristics of a receipt-orientated tort. Many acts of copyright infringement[8] and data protection laws[9] on the other hand are essentially possession- or location-orientated and therefore less likely to give rise

[4] 'Working party on illegal and harmful content on the internet – Report' submitted to the European Commission Telecommunications Council held on 28 November 1996.

[5] Note, however, that in the case of the Community Trade Mark the plaintiff seeking to bring infringement proceedings based on harm within the jurisdiction must satisfy a different test from the 'harmful event' test of the Brussels and Lugano Conventions. Under Art. 93(5) of the Community Trade Mark Regulation (40/94) the plaintiff may bring proceedings in the courts of the Member State in which the act of infringement has been committed or (if permitted under the national law of the Member State) threatened.

[6] However, the damage may not always occur in the country of receipt. See, for instance, *Domicrest Ltd* v. *Swiss Bank Corporation* (*The Times*) 16 July 1998, concerning alleged negligent misstatement. The event giving rise to the damage was held to have taken place in Switzerland (from where the statements were communicated by telephone to the recipients in England). Although the plaintiffs acted on the statements in England by issuing instructions to release goods, the alleged damage itself was held to have occurred in Switzerland and Italy, where the goods were released. The English court therefore did not have jurisdiction under Art. 5(3) of the Lugano Convention over the claim for negligent misstatement.

[7] WIPO Copyright Treaty and WIPO Performances and Phonograms Treaty, both adopted 20 December 1996.

[8] For example, the simple act of copying.

[9] Art. 4 of the Data Protection Directive (95/46/EC 24 October 1995) provides that each Member State shall apply its national law adopted pursuant to the Directive to processing of personal data where (*inter alia*): the processing is carried out in the context of the activities of an establishment of

to actionable harm at a distance from the point at which the offending data is stored.

The consequence of simultaneous world-wide publication on the Internet is that in the case of receipt-oriented torts the plaintiff is likely to have a wide choice of jurisdictions in which to sue. The American courts are already grappling with this. The question of jurisdiction has been actively litigated in a number of Internet-related inter-state jurisdictional disputes. The developing jurisprudence in the USA tends to distinguish between active and passive Web sites in determining whether the Web site proprietor has purposefully availed himself of the jurisdiction in the state of receipt. It is increasingly accepted that mere availability of the Web site is not sufficient to found jurisdiction, even if the plaintiff can establish the possibility of harm within the jurisdiction.

Under the Brussels and Lugano Conventions, once a harmful event within the jurisdiction is established under Article 5(3), the court must assume jurisdiction. It is therefore difficult to see great scope for courts to develop a 'mere availability' doctrine in the case of receipt-oriented torts. Indeed the *Mecklermedia*[10] case, for instance, may point in the opposite direction. In that case Jacob J commented:

> 'To do acts here which lead to damage of goodwill by misleading the public here is plainly passing off. To do those same acts from abroad will not avoid liability.' ...
> '...when an enterprise wants to use a mark or word throughout the world (and that may include an internet address or domain name) it must take into account that in some places, if not others, there may be confusion. Here it is clear DC knew that Mecklermedia used the name 'Internet World' and I do not think it is surprising that it is met with actions in places where confusion is considered likely.'

Whilst *Shevill* v. *Presse Alliance SA*[11], by limiting damages to loss suffered within the jurisdiction, places some practical constraints on the usefulness of Article 5(3), in Internet cases the Article 5(3) exception has the potential to become a vehicle for a receipt-oriented civil liability regime.

The difficulties of arriving at a coherent approach to legal boundaries on the Internet have led to suggestions of alternative international approaches. Thus in the field of domain names and trade marks dispute resolution mechanisms developed in conjunction with WIPO have been suggested.[12] There have been

the data controller on the territory of the Member State; where the data controller is not established on the Member State's territory, but in a place where its national law applies by virtue of international public law; and where the data controller is not established on Community territory and, for the purposes of processsing data makes use of equipment situated on the territory of the Member State, unless such equipment is used only for the purpose of transit through the territory of the Community.

[10] *Mecklermedia Corporation* v. *DC Congress Gesellschaft GmbH* [1998] Ch 40.

[11] [1995] 2 *AC* 18.

[12] See, for example, www.gtld-mou.org/docs/dispute.html.

experiments with on-line arbitration schemes such as the Virtual Magistrate project.[13]

CONVERGENCE

A second area in which cross border issues are currently being considered is in the convergence debate. Convergence is the phenomenon that content no longer respects technical boundaries, so that the Internet can be accessed through television; television and radio programming can be received through computers; computers can be used for telephony and telephones can be used to access Web sites and e-mail. Convergence is usually presented as a three-way coming together of the telecoms, broadcast and IT industries. In fact convergence is four-way. The print press are also a part of the convergence phenomenon, as print content migrates to the Internet and other digital networks. Convergence causes the problem that existing regulatory structures no longer match what is happening in the marketplace.

The international nature of the Internet means that the convergence debate is being carried on at an international as well as a national level, in particular as a result of the European Commission Convergence Green Paper.[14] Earlier we posed the question whether an international approach should be based on law, regulation or something else; and whether it should be Internet-specific or integrated? Those questions form a central theme in the convergence debate and will have to be answered before any new legal or regulatory structures can be devised. The questions are thrown into high relief, because, if the premise of four-way rather than three-way convergence is accepted, we have two highly regulated industries – broadcast and telecoms – colliding with two wholly unregulated industries – IT and the print press.

As with cross-border criminal law and the Internet, a human rights issue arises here: freedom of speech. The print press is, at least in liberal countries, unregulated. It would be unthinkable to license and regulate the print press in the way that has been thought acceptable for broadcast media. The existence of a human rights element has already been demonstrated by the successful challenge to the Communications Decency Act in the USA. The Supreme Court found that the Internet is not a broadcast medium and should be accorded the highest degree of First Amendment protection.[15] In Europe the same principle may not yet be fully accepted. However, there does seem to be some recognition that even if

[13] vmag.cilp.org.

[14] 'Convergence of the Telecommunications, Media and Information Technology Sectors, and the Implications for Regulation. Towards an Information Society Approach' European Commission, 3 December 1997.

[15] *Reno* v. *ACLU* 117 S. Ct. 2329; 138 L. Ed. 2d 874 (1997).

existing regulators did want to regulate content on digital networks and the Internet, the sheer volume of content renders it a futile task.[16]

Nevertheless regulators are concerned about their future roles and may be attracted to new ways in which to exercise a degree of control over content on the Internet. For instance OFTEL, the UK telecommunications regulator, has suggested that there should be an Electronic Communications Standards Authority with power to oversee the classification and rating of Internet content, and that misclassification should be a criminal offence.[17] The European Commission has asked whether convergence will require a reassessment of regulatory responsibilities at a national, Community or international level, and if so in which areas. Its discussion in the Convergence Green Paper appears to envisage that content would fall within the responsibility of a regulator, whether or not the regulator combines that responsibility with other aspects such as service provision and delivery.[18]

Elsewhere in the world there is a wide variety of approaches. The Singapore government is notable for having imposed a broadcast-style licensing regime on the Internet, coupled with technical measures to filter out unacceptable content.

WHAT VALUES SHOULD AN INTERNATIONAL APPROACH REFLECT?

If we are to have an international approach to content on the Internet, it cannot avoid the human rights issues. I have mentioned two areas in which they arise: criminal laws and the convergence debate. There will be others. In fact almost any receipt-oriented tort, such as defamation, is capable of giving rise to these issues in the cross-border context of the Internet.

When we consider the human rights issues, we should have regard to Article 19 of the Universal Declaration of Human Rights. It provides: 'Everyone has the right to freedom of opinion and expression; this right includes freedom to hold opinions without interference and to seek, receive and impart information and ideas through any media and regardless of frontiers.' Had that been written with the Internet in mind, it could not have been better drafted. As mentioned at the start, the big truth about the Internet is that everyone is a publisher. So when we talk about freedom of speech on the Internet, we are not discussing just the rights of press barons or media conglomerates. We are talking here about the rights of individual human beings to make themselves heard. We are fairly and squarely in human rights territory when we consider international approaches to content laws. Therefore the goal of policymakers working towards an international

[16] See, for example, the Report of the UK House of Commons Culture, Media and Sport Committee 'The Multi-media Revolution' 6 May 1998, para. 114.

[17] OFTEL 'Beyond the Telephone, the Television and the PC – III' para. 6.56.

[18] Convergence Green Paper, chapter IV.4

accord on these content issues should be to establish the Internet and other similar networks as media subject only to settled laws protecting free speech and enforced by independent judges. That means no licensing, no regulation and no compromise with regimes that do not respect free speech. The Internet is a force for liberty and we should be jealous to preserve it.

It may be thought unlikely that any international accord conforming to those principles is achievable. But if the policymakers cannot achieve it, then perhaps they had better do nothing. Certainly we are then left with chaos, and a continuing decline in the ability of national legal systems to police their borders. But chaos may not be such a bad thing. District Judge Dalzell said in the Communications Decency Act case:

> 'The absence of governmental regulation of Internet content has unquestionably produced a kind of chaos, but as one of the plaintiffs' experts put it with such resonance at the hearing: "what achieved success was the very chaos that the Internet is. The strength of the Internet is that chaos". Just as the strength of the Internet is chaos, so the strength of our liberty depends upon the chaos and cacophony of the unfettered speech the First Amendment protects.'[19]

In a contest between order which does not respect Article 19 of the Universal Declaration of Human Rights and chaos, chaos has much to be said in its favour.

[19] *ACLU* v. *Reno*, 929 F. Supp. 824 (E.D. Pa 1996).

THE GERMAN ACT ON INFORMATION AND COMMUNICATION SERVICES OF 1997: A NATIONAL LEGISLATIVE APPROACH TO AN INTERNATIONAL PROBLEM

Joachim Feldges*

INTRODUCTION

I am very honoured and pleased with the opportunity to participate in this International Law Conference where judges, professors and attorneys honour this city for its eminent merits in the development of international law.

Our panel, entitled 'Regulation of the Internet', addresses one of the greatest challenges, recently faced by national and international law, which is still far from being controlled. The technical development has allowed the introduction of worldwide communication and new forms of business within a few years. Law and legislation was not prepared for such rapid development. It is only now that international professional organisations in the field of Intellectual Property, as AIPPI, have passed the first resolution on the domain-names in the Internet and their relationship to the law of trademarks and tradenames.[1]

Germany has the privilege to be the first country in the world which has tried to regulate (at least some aspects) of the Internet in the *Act on Information and Communication Services* of 22 July 1997, which came into force on 1 August 1998.[2] Although the need for an international solution to the legal problems which the Internet has raised is undisputed, experiences with national legislation may serve as a valuable basis for the development of an international response to these problems.

In the first part of this presentation, the basic provisions of this Act will be outlined, addressing the definition of tele services and the responsibility of service providers for the content of such services, the protection of personal data in tele services, the system of certification of digital signatures and finally the protection of data bases.

In the second part, I intend to discuss, on the basis of the limited German court practice we have on the Internet, the protection of intellectual property rights including name rights, in view of the registration of protected names or trademarks as domain-names and other uses of such rights on the Internet. Apart

* Pünder, Volhard, Weber & Axster, Munich.

[1] Resolution to Q 143, AIPPI Congress in Rio de Janeiro, 22 – 29 May 1998 (not yet published)

[2] BGBI I (1997) p. 1870 ss.

W.P. Heere (Ed.), International Law and The Hague's 750th Anniversary

from the question of how far the law on name rights and intellectual property rights can be applied to domain-names in the Internet, a major problem in the regulation of the Internet occurs in the field of enforcement of such rights. Apart from the question under which conditions German courts have acknowledged their jurisdiction over services offered on the Internet, many problems remain unsolved as regards the effective enforcement of such judgments in view of the worldwide character of the Internet.

1. THE GERMAN *ACT ON INFORMATION AND COMMUNICATION SERVICES* OF 22 JULY 1997

Prior to the new German *Act on Information and Communication Services* of 22 July 1997, there were no German statutes specifically regulating the Internet or comparable communication networks. The new statute takes its place alongside regulations contained in the *Telecommunications Act* of 25 July 1996,[3] the state treaty on media services between the German states of 18 December 1996 and the general laws which apply to the use of the Internet, in particular the German Copyright Act, the German Trademark Act and German competition law.

1.1. **Purpose and scope of application**

The German *Act on Information and Communication Services* consists of three different Acts and a fourth part amending a number of other Acts such as the Criminal Code and the Copyright Act. The three new Acts are:

- the *Act on the Use of Tele Services*
- the *Act on Data Protection in Tele Services*
- the *Act on Digital Signatures.*

1.2. **Freedom of administrative barriers to the tele services market**

The German legislator has decided in favour of a system keeping the offer of tele services free of administrative hurdles. Therefore, pursuant to Article 1 sec. 4 of the Act, tele services may be run without any authorization or registration by a public authority.

There is, however, an obligation for service providers to disclose their identity. Pursuant to Article 1 Section 6, service providers – this means natural persons or legal persons or associations of persons who provide their own or

[3] BGBl 1 (1996) p. 1120 ss.

foreign tele services for use or provide access for use – when making business offers have to indicate their names and addresses. Associations and groups of persons have to indicate in addition name and address of the persons legally representing them. By imposing that obligation, the German legislator wanted to ensure that an offer can be traced back to its origin.

The right to offer tele services without having obtained an administrative approval might lead to problems in drawing the borderline between tele services on one side and media services such as broadcasting requiring an administrative approval on the other side. A program which had been distributed before by television or broadcasting might then be offered on the Internet. Should this be considered as broadcasting, therefore requiring a licence, or as a free offer of a tele service? Which authorities are competent to control the service on the basis of which law?[4] According to Art. 1 sec. 2 para 4 of the German *Act on Information and Communication Services*, broadcasting, telecommunication services and offers with content in distribution and access services under § 2 of the German Treaty on Media Services are exempted from the application of this Act as far as their editorial arrangement puts the main emphasis on the influence over public opinion. However, it will be difficult to determine in some cases whether the main emphasis lies on the influence over public opinion or whether it has to be seen in individual communication.

1.3. Rules on tele services

Another aspect of major relevance is the service providers' responsibility for the information to which they provide access. A clear regulation of the responsibility of service providers is vital for international business. It is also important, *inter alia*, as regards the infringement of intellectual property rights. This responsibility is now laid down in Article 1 Section 5 of the German *Act on Information and Communication Services*. The basic problem is in the share of responsibility among the various participants in the offer of tele services. The rules provided by sec. 5 can be resumed in the following principles:

1) Service providers are always responsible for their *own content*, i.e., the content which they have contributed to a tele service (sec. 5 para. 1).

2) As regards *third parties' contents*, the following cases have to be distinguished:

2.1) The service provider only provides *access to use*. Access means that the provider only ensures the technical access without making available a particular tele service. A short-time storage and provision of such contents caused by a user's call-up is considered as providing access. In this case, the service provider is not responsible for the content of the tele service (sec. 5 para. 3).

[4] See Roßnagel, *NJW* (1998) pp. 1, 3.

2.2) The service provider makes available a foreign content for use. In this case, the service provider is only responsible if there is positive knowledge of the content on his side and if it was technically feasible and could be reasonably expected that he prevented such use (sec. 5 para. 2).

3) Considerable legal uncertainty has been caused by sec. 5 para. 4. According to this provision, the obligation to bar the use of illegal contents arising from the general law remains unaffected by these provisions if the service provider obtains knowledge of such illegal contents without breach of secrecy under sec. 85 of the German *Act on Telecommunications,* and when barring of access is technically possible and reasonable.

This distribution of responsibilities seems to make sense because a service provider that only ensures the technical access to numerous tele services offered by third parties, cannot control constantly and efficiently the content of all these offers.

How this devision of responsibilities will be realized in court practice, will have to be studied carefully. A recent judgment by the Local Court in Munich in a criminal case demonstrates how far court practice can be from the basic rule adopted by the legislator. The former manager of a major service provider on the Internet was condemned to two years jail as he was held personally responsible for the pornographic content of a tele service to which his company had only provided the technical access. Both, the public prosecutor and the accused appealed the judgment.[5]

1.4. The Act on data protection in tele services

As mentioned above, the German *Act on Information and Communication Services* also comprises a particular Act concerning data protection in tele services. The German legislator recognized the necessity to provide particular rules on the registration and compilation of personal data in connection with the offer of tele services. The provisions on data protection in tele services are in line with the general rules on data protection contained in the Federal *Act on the Protection of Data*. The registration, treatment and compilation of personal data requires that there is either a consent by the concerned person or there is an authorization by law to register and treat such data. As there is not sufficient time to discuss the details, I would like to draw your attention to two particular rules. According to the regulation in sec. 3 para 3, the service provider may not make the provision of tele services dependent on the consent of the user that his data

[5] In a decision of 26 November 1997, the Federal General Prosecutor argued in a similar way as the Local Court. In that case, the access-provider was held responsible to control dangers arising from the nature of tele services. This has been heavily criticised as ignorance of the decision taken by the legislator, see Hoeren *MMR* (1998) p. 97; *NJW-COR* (1998) p. 175.

may be processed or used for other purposes, if access to such tele services is otherwise impossible or cannot be reasonably expected. By this provision, the freedom of the user of tele services to decide without pressure on the use of this personal data, is protected.

Moreover, the legislator has restricted the establishment of user profiles. They are only permissible if pseudonyms are used. In addition, any use of profile covered by a pseudonym may not be combined with data concerning the holder of the pseudonym (sec. 4 para 4 of the *Act concerning Data Protection and Tele Services*).

Although there is indisputably some merit in the attempt of the German legislator to protect personal data in tele services, it is questionable how effective such national law can be with regard to a worldwide communication and business system. It does not seem to be a realistic perspective that those service providers interested in establishing personal user profiles will realise this plan in a country with a severe system of data protection.

1.5. The Act on digital signatures

The third part of the German *Act on Information and Communication Services* deals with the problem of digital signatures. Unusual enough for the German legislative practice, the legislator has decided to define the purpose of this Act expressly. Sec. 1 para 1 reads translated into English:

> 'It is the purpose of the Act to create general conditions for digital signatures allowing them to be reputed as safe and to enable the reliable recognition of fakes of digital signatures and falsifications of signed data.'

Hence, digital signatures are subject to the provisions of this Act in order to enable their use as a reliable mean of authenticity. What is the concept of this Act?

The Act creates a system or certification of digital signatures. Certification agencies require for their activity an authorization by the competent authority which controls their compliance with the law (sec. 4 of the Act on Digital Signatures). Natural and legal persons can request the certification of their digital signatures by such approved certification agencies. The agency is obliged to identify, in a reliable manner, the persons requesting the certification of their digital signatures. The agency has to confirm the reservation of a public signature code to an identified person by a certificate on the signature code. This certificate has to be open for examination at any time for anybody via telecommunication services publicly accessible and, with the consent of the owner of the signature code, has to be available. According to sec. 5 para 3 of the Act, the certification agency is obliged, on the request by the applicant, to use a pseudonym for him in the certificate instead of his name.

Moreover, the certification agencies are obliged to guarantee the secrecy of private signature codes. On the request by the owner of a signature code, the agency is obliged to bar the certificate. If the certificate has been obtained on the basis of wrong indications, or if the agency terminates its activity without being continued by another certification agency.

As far as I can see, such a certification system for digital signatures is unique world-wide. It remains to be seen whether this system will be accepted by the business in the Internet practice.

1.6. **Protection of data bases**

In the context of the *Act on Information and Communication Services*, the German legislator has implemented the European Directive 96/9 of the European Parliament and the European Council of 11 March 1996 on the legal protection of data bases.[6] The German legislator has integrated the protection of data bases into the German *Copyright Act.* The main principles of protection of data bases may be resumed as follows:

A data base is a collection of works, data or other independent elements which are classified systematically or methodically and which are accessible individually by electronic means or in another manner. A computer programme used for the creation of the data base or enabling the access to elements thereof is not considered as part of the data base. This limitation aims to draw the borderline between the protection of computer programmes and the protection of data bases.

Data bases may be protected under two different categories: Either they fulfil the standard of a personal individual creation (sec. 2 para 2 of the German *Copyright Act*) and are protected for this reason as data base works. In this case, they enjoy copyright protection 70 years after the death of the author. A personal individual creation will only be acknowledged if the data base work reveals a particular individual character going far beyond the normal manner to establish a data base. This individual character has to be reflected by the data base itself, maybe in the selection of data, maybe in the way how these data are classified or presented.

Even if this standard is not met, a right *sui generis* may protect the data base if its establishment, control or presentation has required a substantial investment. In this case, the data base may be protected according to sec. 87a ss. of the German *Copyright Act.* The term of protection is much shorter than for normal work being protected by copyright. It extends to 15 years from the 1 January following the first publication of the data base. A substantial modification of the data base may be considered as a new data base in the sense of these provisions (sec. 87a *in fine* of the German *Copyright Act*).

[6] ABl EG Nr. L77, p. 20

Depending on whether the data base is protected by copyright or by the right *sui generis*, different rights are conferred on the proprietor: The permanent or temporary copying, translation, treatment, modification or public distribution of a copyright protected data base is only admissible with the consent of the author. According to sec. 55a of the German *Copyright Act*, the treatment or copying of a data base work is admissible if it is carried out by the proprietor of a copy of a data base work which has been commercialized with the consent of the author or other authorized persons, if and so far as the treatment or copying is necessary for the access to elements of the data base work and for its normal use. If the data base is not protected by copyright, but only by the right *sui generis* on the basis of the investment made in the establishment of the data base, the scope of protection is narrower: It is not allowed to copy a substantial part of a data base. Even such copying of a substantial part of a data base is admissible if it is done for private use or for personal scientific use or for personal use in education at school.

A major problem which will have to be clarified by the courts during the next years will be the definition of what is a substantial part of a data base, as only the copying or publication of such substantial part of a data base is reserved to the proprietor of the data base right. The copying of individual elements which do not represent such substantial part cannot be prohibited by the proprietor of such data base right.

2. PROTECTION OF COPYRIGHT AND INTELLECTUAL PROPERTY IN THE INTERNET IN GERMANY

Having discussed the provisions which the German legislator has enacted in order to address particular problems raised by the Internet, it might be helpful to examine the general law of protection of copyright and intellectual property and to see how these rules are applied to the phenomenon Internet.

2.1. **Acts of exploitation of copyright protected works in the internet**

There are different acts of exploitation of copyright protected works via Internet.

2.1.1. *Digitalization of protected works*

Problems of copyright law start at a very early stage. In order to bring copyright protected works into a form which is suitable for communication via Internet, the works have to be digitalised. The digitalization can be effected, for example, by copying a text via a computer keyboard or by scanning. This first act of digitalizing protected works always brings about storing the obtained data at least for a short time. Hence, this first step could be considered a reproduction of the protected works, pursuant to Section 16 of the German *Copyright Act*.[7] Doubts on this interpretation arise from the fact that reproduction in the sense of Section 16 para. 1 of the German *Copyright Act* requires a certain permanence of the physical specification of the work. Legislative history shows that the notion requires a material setting which makes it possible to perceive the work directly or indirectly by the human senses.[8] More recent statements which are based on the EC Directive on Software Protection and the wording of Section 69 c no. 1 of the German *Copyright Act* find that the first storage of digitalized information is a reproduction in the sense of Section 16 para. 1 of the German *Copyright Act*, at least if the setting is permanent.[9] This opinion can be supported by the argument that, when drafting the German *Copyright Act* in 1962, the German legislator could only have had in mind the then existing possibilities of reproduction. Furthermore, this first act of digitalization can be compared with the copy of a music tape on which the sound is only stored by means of magnetism. Nevertheless, copying a music tape is regarded as reproduction of a protected work.

However, the storage of protected works only for a limited time, i.e., without producing a permanent setting, gives rise to problems. A work stored in the RAM-memory will be destroyed when the computer is switched off. The German Supreme Court holds the view that not each reproduction of a work falls necessarily within the scope of Sec. 16 of the *Copyright Act*.[10] Therefore, some legal experts only want to grant protection if the reproduction leads to intensified use of the work. This would be the case if a work is stored in the RAM-memory because this enables to use the work without having to buy a copy first.[11]

2.1.2. *Browsing of data bases by the internet-surfer*

Far more difficult is the legal assessment of the acts of exploitation of protected works which have once been stored in a virtual library. As far as I can see, the German courts have not yet dealt with the copyright problem of users' online call-ups of protected works stored in electronic data-bases. The problem is that the so-called 'Internet-surfer' will not prepare a copy of the works stored in the data-base but usually 'browses' the virtual library. As the German *Copyright Act* strictly distinguishes the exploitation of works in material form from an ex-

[7] Melichar, 'Virtuelle Bibliotheken und Urheberrecht', *CR* (1995) p. 758; Wenzel, *Urheberrecht für die Praxis*, 3rd edn. (1996) No. 7.14 ff.; Schrey, *Wettbewerbsrechtliche Probleme beim Bildschirmtext*, Diss. (Mannheim, 1989) p. 289.

[8] See M. Schulze, *Materialien*, S. 106. Quite alike BGHZ 17, 266 (269); BGH GRUR (1982) p. 102.

[9] Gerhard Schricker, *Urheberrecht auf dem Weg zur Informationsgesellschaft* (Baden-Baden 1997), p. 110

[10] Schricker, op. cit., p. 111

[11] Schricker, op. cit., p. 112

ploitation in non-material form, it is obvious that browsing a virtual library can only be regarded as a form of non-material exploitation.[12]

Pursuant to Section 15 para. 2 of the German *Copyright Act*, the author has the exclusive right to publicly communicate his work in non-material form, in particular:

No. 1: the right of recitation, performance, representation and presentation (Section 19)
No. 2: the right of broadcasting (Section 20)
No. 3: the right of communicating the work by means of sound or visual records
No. 4: the right of communicating broadcasts (Section 22)

As none of these listed rights complies with the technical functioning of on-line use, it is preferable to speak of a non-listed 'transmission right' which enjoys copyright protection under this Section.[13]

Pursuant to Section 15 para. 3, the communication of a work shall be public if it is intended for a number of persons, unless such persons form a clearly defined group and are inter-connected personally by mutual relations or by a relationship to the organizer. Hence, it has to be assessed whether browsing a virtual library is public communication.

The German courts have held the view that 'public' requires the perception of the protected work by a group of persons *at the same time*. This criterion had been derived from the word 'public' which is defined in Section 15 para. 3. However, the wording of this section does not explicitly require simultaneous perception by a group of persons. In my opinion, the wording of Section 15 allows an interpretation that public communication might well comprise subsequent perception of a protected work by a number of persons.[14] This is due to the fact that the transfer of data via Internet is very quick. Therefore, the sequence of call-ups of a number of online users is not of relevance. The individual user will hardly notice the time difference. Adhering to this literal interpretation of Section 15 of the German *Copyright Act*, it is, therefore, possible to say that disseminating protected works from a data-base via Internet is public communication of a protected work and, therefore, requires a license.

2.1.3. *Adaptation and transformation of digitalised works*

It is one of the most important advantages of digitalized works that they can be easily adapted and transformed in many ways. Section 23 of the German *Copyright Act* provides that adaptations or other transformations of a protected

[12] This view is also held by Melichar, *CR* (1995) pp. 756 (758); Hoeren, *CR* (1996) pp. 517 (518); Schricker, op.cit., p. 130

[13] See Schricker, op. cit., p. 133

[14] See Schricker, op. cit., pp 134 – 136

work may be published or exploited only with the consent of the author of the adapted or transformed work. Hence, it is generally possible to transform a protected work without the consent of the author as long as it is not made accessible to the public or exploited.

However, it has to be noted that, pursuant to Section 23 phrase 2, in the case of cinematographic adaptations of a work, or of the execution of plans and sketches of an artistic work, or of copies of an architectural work, the creation of such adaptation or transformation already requires the author's consent. Thus, producing a multimedia product by combining sound, pictures and movies requires a license if the product is made available to the public or exploited.

2.1.4. *Showing works on display*

To show a protected work on a computer screen is not considered as reproduction of the work under German copyright law.[15]

2.2. **Copyright contract law**

Another factor which is of major importance with regard to the dissemination of copyright protected works on the Internet is the contract on the use of copyright. Frequently, a content provider will already have obtained a license for the exploitation of a protected work. Hence, the question arises whether he is also allowed to exploit the work online under this license. Section 31 para. 1 of the German Copyright Act makes it possible to grant a license to another person to utilize the work in a particular manner or in any manner without limitation. The problem arises from paragraph 4 of this Section, stating that a license purporting to grant rights with respect to unknown means of utilization, and any obligations with respect thereto, shall have no legal effect. Hence, we have to focus on the question of what can be understood as being a known type of use. This is a very problematic issue in German law. Sometimes it creates for content providers an almost insurmountable obstacle to Internet use.

According to the jurisdiction of the German Supreme Court, the moment when a new type of use is perceived by the authors of protected works is decisive. A type of use is known if the authors are adequately informed of the new type of use in its technical and economic dimension or had a reasonable possibility to inform themselves.[16] As regards online-services, it is questionable what has to be seen as a new type of use. The former contracts comprise as a co-matter the broadcasting right which gives the right to provide access to a

[15] See Schricker, op. cit., p. 113

[16] See Schricker, *UrhG*, paras. 31, 32 No. 27; Fromm/Nordemann/Hertin, *UrhG*, paras. 31, 32 No. 10; Ernst, BB 1997, 1057, 1058.

protected work by broadcasting media or equivalent technical devices. Thus, the contracts comprise terrestrial broadcasting and also digital radio and television services. In this context, pay-TV and digital radio are regarded as mere technical novelties but not as an economically independent market.[17]

However, this argumentation cannot be uncritically adopted for the exploitation of works within electronic networks. Here the dissemination occurs irrespective of national borders and of a specific audience. Using an electronic network generally provides access to a protected work for a new audience. Furthermore, in the cases where pictures, text and sound are combined to form a new product, the client does not only get the old information via a new way of transmission but an absolutely new, online specific product. Hence, it is preferable to say that distribution of protected works via Internet is an independent type of use, pursuant to Section 31 para. 4 of the German *Copyright Act.*[18] As the economic and technical possibilities of the Internet were recognized by the public only from the mid-1990s, legal authors in Germany hold the view that only contracts concluded after 1995 comprise, by reference to 'all known types of use', online use of protected works.[19]

I do not need to explain that it is at the moment very difficult for content providers to re-negotiate existing license agreements with respect to online use.

2.3. Internet-related aspects of German trademark law

German trademark law has been the basis for some of the first court decisions on the Internet.

2.3.1. Offers on the internet using trademarks

As regards the offer of goods and services on the Internet by using a specification protected under the German *Trademark Act*, these offers have to be assessed following the same principles which have to be observed when assessing an offer outside of the Internet. Insofar there are no principal differences arising from the nature of the Internet. Problems may, however, arise with regard to the question whether a German court can assume jurisdiction in relation to the infringement of trademarks committed by using a host located outside of Germany. I will return to this later and explain the approach of German courts as regards this matter of jurisdiction.

[17] However, this is not undisputed. Schricker/Katzenberger, UrhG, § 88 (no. 49 with further references)

[18] Ernst, *BB* (1997) pp. 1057 (1058) with further references.

[19] Endter, *NJW* (1996) pp. 975, 976.

2.3.2. Domain-name-grabbing

2.3.2.1. General. A phenomenon which is absolutely Internet-specific is the so-called 'domain-name-grabbing'. Some German courts have dealt with this subject, even if there is no judgment by the Federal Supreme Court up to now.

As the Internet consists of a vast number of individual computers which are interconnected in a non-hierarchical way, the so-called hosts, each of these hosts have to be assigned an address. These addresses consist of a numerical code. However, these numerical addresses can be connected with an alphabetical name. Although this name may consist of any letters whatsoever, for commercial use of the Internet it is very important to chose a name pointing to the users' identity. Hence, the so-called domain-name consists of a top-level domain, e.g., '.de' for Germany, which has no distinguishing capacity and a second-level domain which can easily be remembered. It is clear that company names or trademarks for well-known products or services are of special relevance in this context. The system of registration of domain names is strictly based on priority. The competent body, in Germany called 'Deutsche Network-Information-Center' (DENIC) at Karlsruhe University does not check whether the name applied for is in conflict with existing trademarks or other rights.

2.3.2.2. Approach of German courts. The German courts have dealt with two different types of problems arising from this system of registration. In some cases persons offered services in the Internet under the name of towns like Heidelberg or Kerpen or a legal data service called 'juris'. The corresponding judgments focus on the question of whether or not this use infringed the cities' exclusive right to their names. Various courts were not unanimous in deciding whether the choice of a domain-name had to be considered as the use of a name. The District Court of Cologne denied this in a decision of 17 December 1996[20] arguing that the choice of a domain-name is comparable to the choice of a telephone number or address. The majority of the lower courts decided, however, that the choice of a domain-name has to be considered as the use of a name and can therefore infringe the right of another party to its name.[21]

Whether the choice of a domain-name also constitutes a trademark infringement has been dealt with by the District Court of Düsseldorf in a very recent judgment of 4 April 1997 which is final.[22] This judgment is very instructive because it touches on manifold aspects of law. In this case the defendant had reserved at DENIC the name 'Epson.de' for registration as domain name. The plaintiff, Epson Deutschland GmbH, is the owner of a number of

[20] LG Köln WM (1997) p. 1452.

[21] LG Mannheim GRUR (1997) p. 377 – 'Heidelberg'; LG München I, WM (1997) pp. 1455, 1458; LG Düsseldorf WM (1997) pp. 1444, 1451; LG Lüneburg WM (1997) pp. 1452, 1454.

[22] See *supra* n. 17

trademarks protecting the name 'Epson' in relation to, in particular, computer equipment. The defendant stated before the court that he had made the reservation with the intention to either sell his rights to Epson or license the domain name to another company or person for use on the Internet.

As regards its competence, the court referred to the general principles, governing acts of infringement in mass media. The location where the infringement is committed is not only the location where the media is issued, but also the place where the receiver comes to know the media. The court held that it would mean denying legal protection to the person whose rights were infringed if the location of the server which was used for the infringement would be regarded as the determining factor. The infringer could too easily avoid responsibility by transferring his host computer to a foreign country. Furthermore, the court did not see an obstacle to its jurisdiction in the fact that the potential Internet user himself has to take an individual decision to perceive the provided information by making a call-up.

The court granted a permanent injunction because it found the claim of Epson GmbH well-founded. This judgment was based on the infringement of a trademark, pursuant to Sections 4, 14 para. 1, 2 No. 1, para. 5 of the German *Trademark Act.* Furthermore, the court acknowledged the infringement of a commercial designation, pursuant to Sections 5, 15 of the German *Trademark Act.* In addition, the court saw an infringement of the plaintiff's right to its name, according to Section 12 para. 2 of the German Civil Code and an infringement of Section 1 of the German Act against Unfair Competition under the principles governing obstruction of competitors.

Let me first focus on the infringement of the trademark 'Epson'. Such infringement requires pursuant to Sec. 14 para. 2 of the German *Trademark Act* that use of the trademark was made in the course of business. In this respect the judgment is very interesting. In this case the defendant had stated before the court that he had wanted to sell his rights arising from the reservation to Epson GmbH or license the domain name to a third party. Considering these facts the court held that a cease and desist order against an infringement of a trademark does not require that an infringing act has already occurred. The court regarded it sufficient that there was a clear and present danger of infringement. As use of the domain name by a third party was only possible in the course of business, the court saw a clear and present danger of such use because the defendant had reserved the domains with the intention to license them. However, the wording of the judgment gives the impression that no infringement would have been assumed by the court if the registration of the domain name had been carried out only for purposes of personal communication.

There is another interesting statement in this judgment: assessing the danger of confusion caused by using the trademark the contents of a homepage is not of relevance. The reference point for the assessment of confusion is not the goods or services offered on the homepage but the homepage itself. It does not matter if the goods or services offered by the infringer on his homepage will not easily be confused with the goods or services for which the trademark is registered. In so far, the court refers to a parallel reasoning applied to the title of journals. Regarding these journals it is not of any importance which contents they have as long as the title of both the trademark owner's journal and the infringer's journal might be confused. Furthermore, the court argued that the artificial name 'Epson' has a strong distinguishing capacity so that the persons who perceive this name will most probably think that the homepage with the same name is an official or at least authorized offer of Epson GmbH. Hence, the court stated that a danger of confusion was present. With respect to the defendant's liability for infringing acts committed by a third person – the possible licensee -, the court stated that, as the defendant would have had to be held liable under the principle of causation if a third party had used the name in the Internet, he had to be held equally liable in the case of a clear and present danger of such infringement by third parties.

I have already mentioned that the court acknowledged also infringement of a commercial designation – the protected company name Epson – pursuant to Sections 5, 15 of the German *Trademark Act.* According to Sec. 15 para. 2 of the German *Trademark Act*, it is forbidden to use a commercial designation in the course of business in a manner that brings about the danger of confusion. The court stated that the nature of the infringer's designation is not of any relevance, when assessing the danger of confusion caused by the use of the designation. The only decisive criterion is whether or not the use of the domain-name brings about such danger of confusion. The court argued that the domain-name has the same function as a telephone number, a telegram address or a telex specification, as a special form of designating a company. Even though the domain-name may be a combination of any letters whatsoever, experience teaches that the domain-name is set up in a form which is suitable to point to the firm. Hence, normally a short form of the company's name is used. The judges concluded that a short form of the company's name is used as domain-name in order to make the differentiation of providers in the Internet easier. As this differentiation capacity of the domain-name was endangered by the use of the word Epson by a third party, without authorization of the plaintiff, the court held that Sec. 15 para. 2 of the German *Trademark Act* had been infringed.

Finally, I would like to mention a decision by the Higher Regional Court of Frankfurt a. M.[23] The court had to decide, *inter alia*, whether sec. 8 of the German *Trademark Act* which excludes generic names from registration as a trademark, can also be applied to the choice of domain-names. The court denied that question in accordance with the first instance judgment. Although the court acknowledged the danger that a person choosing a generic name as domain-name achieves, by doing so, a certain monopoly, it argued that one could easily circumvent already existing domain-names by adding other words. With all

[23] OLG Frankfurt a.M, *BB* (1997) p. 545

respect, I doubt whether this argument is really convincing. The possibility to circumvent an existing domain-name is, at least in principle, not broader than to circumvent an identical name or trademark. Moreover, the problem lies in the fact that, by using a generic name, the interest of the public is channeled to the holder of that generic domain-name so that he may achieve a much larger interest for his offer than would have been the case when he had chosen a non-generic domain-name.

Subsequently, the court argued that the examination and surveillance which exists for the registration of trademarks, is missing in the case of domain-names. This argument is correct. In my view, the problem lies in a missing legal basis to exclude generic names from their registration as domain-names. Finally, court tried to decide the question on the basis of unfair competition law and, not surprisingly, failed to use that instrument as an effective barrier to limit any misuse in the choice of generic names as domain-names. The judgment has been rendered by the Higher Regional Court of Frankfurt a. M. in summary proceedings, so that the case could not be referred to the Federal Supreme Court.

CONCLUSIONS

The following conclusions may be drawn from the German approach to regulate at least some aspects of the Internet:

1. The German *Act on Information and Communication Services* of 1997 allows, on a national level, the opportunity to gain some experience on regulations of the Internet, which may be useful when attempting to solve the legal problems caused by the Internet on an international level.
2. The division of responsibilities between service providers and access providers seems to be reasonable. However, practice demonstrates how difficult it is to implement the rule adopted by the legislator into court practice.
3. The attempt to ensure data protection in tele services by a national law will most probably fall short due to the multiple ways to avoid national jurisdiction.
4. The idea to create a system of certified digital signatures merits to be supported. It is too early to evaluate its chances to succeed.
5. The problem of domain-name grabbing seems to be controllable by the courts on the basis of the general laws on protection of names, tradenames and trademarks.

The problem of registration of generic designations as domain-names still waits for a satisfactory solution.

JUDICIAL AND ADMINISTRATIVE COOPERATION IN FAMILY LAW MATTERS: INTRODUCTION

Marília Sardenberg*

At the very outset, let me stress the fact that the decision to include a particular theme relating to children, among so many important subjects of discussion, reflects a rather fresh approach to the child himself or herself and to their special role in society today. In fact children constitute roughly half of the present world's population and they are, perhaps, the group which is mostly affected by the impact of decisions taken at all levels, in all fields, let alone by poverty and social exclusion. Therefore, to focus on children – at the brink of a new millennium – indicates strategic vision and deep concern for human development.

It is a fact that the last two decades of this century have witnessed an ever-increasing and unprecedented worldwide concern for children. It is not necessary to trace back the historical background of this phenomenon and/or to assess its complex implications. It is, however, essential to stress that, throughout the second half of the 20th century, as the needs of children became, gradually and increasingly, the focus of world attention, issues relating to children were upgraded to become a top item in the international political agenda of the present decade. Although rather visible in our contemporary society, this phenomenon is for certain the outcome of a long and multifarious process of evolution in the very concept of human development. Perceptions on the child and on childhood have actually changed over centuries, across cultures and societies.

Maybe one could elaborate that this complex process of evolution was historically summed up in the ten-year drafting exercise of an uniquely consolidated human rights treaty on children – the Convention on the Rights of the Child, adopted by consensus by the United Nations General Assembly, on 20 November 1989. Hence, although hailed as revolutionary and progressive, the Convention on the Rights of the Child actually reflects in its text a strong political compromise between different legal systems and cultural traditions, in respect of universally recognized human rights.

The Convention establishes a comprehensive human rights standard for children both in substantive content and in implementation procedures. The Convention sets up a holistic approach to children's rights, encompassing a full panoply of rights for children including civil, political, economic, social, cultural

* Member of the United Nations Committee on the Rights of the Child; Consul-General of Brazil in Rotterdam.

W.P. Heere (Ed.), International Law and The Hague's 750th Anniversary

and humanitarian rights. Furthermore, it recognizes each and every right as inherent to the human dignity of the child and necessary for his or her full and harmonious development. In this sense, it could be considered as an 'umbrella' Convention.

Most significant is the fact that since its adoption the Convention has been ratified by and is now in force for every country in the world with two exceptions: the United States of America and Somalia (191 States Parties). Its application is – hence – virtually universal: it applies to all children and also to every child under the jurisdiction of the State Party. Thus, States Parties to the Convention clearly undertake a special responsibility and legal commitment before the international community, the national civil society, and before children themselves, to be actively and effectively engaged in the promotion and protection of children's rights. Furthermore, it entails a political commitment to improve the quality of life of children around the world.

By introducing the perspective of rights in all matters relating to children, the Convention inspired new ethics in the light of a democratic perception of the child. From an object of care and protection, the child became a subject of rights. In fact, the child is no longer envisaged simply as a vulnerable human being who needs and should be provided with special protection and assistance, but also as a person with fundamental rights and freedoms who is entitled to participate in the decision making process affecting his or her life. From a passive recipient, the child evolves toward an active and visible citizen who should be prepared for an individual and responsible life in a free society.

Four general principles capture the spirit and philosophy of the treaty as a whole. These principles are non-discrimination (Art. 2), best interests of the child (Art. 3), right to survival and development (Art. 6) and participation (Art. 12).

Although the child emerges as a fully-fledged person in the Convention, the child is nevertheless always envisaged within a family environment, and numerous provisions in the treaty establish its pro-family stance. In fact, from the Preamble and throughout the text, the Convention places great importance on the role of the family.The family is referred to as the 'fundamental group of society' and the treaty further recognizes that 'for the full and harmonious development of his or her personality', a child 'should grow up in a family environment, in an atmosphere of happiness, love and understanding' (Art. 5). In the same provision, the Convention defines 'family' in broad terms, including 'members of the extended family or community as provided for by local custom.'

The Convention addresses many aspects of the parent-child relationship. Article 9 recognizes the rights of the child not to be separated from his/her parents and addresses the cases where parents are living separately and a decision must be made as to the child's place of residence. Furthermore, it also focuses on the child in need of a family. Articles 20 and 21 are provisions which address the question of adoption and other forms of alternative care including intercountry adoption – as 'a measure of last resort' only. Those Articles clearly emphasize that the purpose of adoption should be to meet the needs of the child in the spirit of the principle of the best interests of the child.

On the other hand, specific provisions request that States Parties take the necessary steps designed to prevent and suppress acts of violation of children's rights such as abduction and sale of children, as well as their trafficking (Art. 35). In fact, abduction and sale of, as well as trafficking in children are often linked with the change of elements of the child's identity and pave the way for the illegal adoption of children, including intercountry adoption, for the child's disappearance, for the use of the child in criminal activities, as well as for the inducement or coercion of the child into prostitution and pornography. Although with a prevalent criminal perspective, child's abduction has similar consequences to the ones arising from the illicit transfer of children, mentioned by Article 11 of the Convention, equally contributing to the separation of the child from his or her family.

In view of the transnational nature of these realities, the Convention strongly calls for cooperation. It is fundamental to ensure that agreements are concluded, at the bilateral and multilateral levels, as a means to strengthening cooperation between law enforcement agencies and judicial authorities, ensuring their effective training and sensitization, as well as establishing a system of constant exchange of information, *inter alia*, on suspects involved and perpetrators condemned.

Focusing now on practices and procedures, it should be emphasized that the Convention on the Rights of the Child – as the major international legal reference for the protection of children's rights – has established its own monitoring body, the Committee on the Rights of the Child, which is mandated by Article 43 paragraph 1, to monitor the implementation of the Convention by States Parties and to interpret the meaning of its provisions. The work of the Committee is concentrated, at the national level, on progress achieved and obstacles encountered in the implementation of the Convention, in an on-going process of what is referred to as 'constructive dialogue' with governments of States Parties. During this dialogue, the Committee addresses specific issues such as intercountry adoption and abduction of children, and persistently calls for coherent laws and the observance of the minimum standards as provided in the Convention and other pertinent international instruments such as the Hague Convention on Protection of Children and Cooperation in Respect of Intercountry Adoption, adopted in 1993.

In this regard, it is essential to remark that, in the Committee's views, the Convention on the Rights of the Child and the Conventions emanating from the Hague Conference on Private International Law are compatible, complementary and may reinforce each other in important areas.

It is not possible now to dwell on convergences and divergences. Nevertheless, it is essential to state that the UN Convention and the Hague Conventions on protection of children aim to safeguard children's rights, to prevent abduction and the sale or trafficking in children and to protect them from other forms of exploitation and abuse. There are many examples, throughout the Committee's Concluding Observations which illustrate how the Committee is deeply aware of these serious problems. But it cannot act alone.

On the basis of the mandate accorded by Article 45, the Committee is entitled to relate to other organs and bodies inside and outside the UN system, including NGOs, to foster effective implementation of the Convention and to encourage international cooperation. As I have previously pointed out in this forum, it is my conviction that there is room to explore in depth more concrete possibilities of an operational and innovative exercise of interaction between the UN Convention and the Hague set of Conventions for children, at all levels. In fact this exercise of cooperation between the two systems – both of which accord priority to the role of international cooperation – may develop in a creative model of integration for child law.

As a conclusion, I would like to stress that, due to the ground-breaking significance of its text, the implementation of the Convention on the Rights of the Child is giving impetus, worldwide, and in a catalytic way, to an unprecedented international mobilization for the rights of the child. The outcome of this synergetic awareness raising effort is the realization that children's human rights, today, are part of the fabric of themes which reflect the growing interdependence of modern world, in the social and political arenas. In fact, children's rights are included among the so-called 'global issues', meaning complex issues of a global nature and potential global impact which will require strenghtened international cooperation, at the closing of this century and well into the next.

Maybe a new vision is beginning to emerge, born of a revised understanding of the past, multiple information about the present and different scenarios of what may lie ahead. And through these different scenarios, I would dare to say that children issues – possibly together with environmental questions – will emerge as crucial issues for humankind in the next century.

Today's societies are beginning to demand an evaluation of the environmental impact of each governamental decision – the so-called 'environmental impact analysis'. I do hope that, in the near future, we will be demanding a 'child impact analysis' and national governments will be asked to assess public policies and projects on the basis of how those decisions will affect children...

This is an inspiring vision... It dares us to let go of nostalgic perceptions on childhood and to take up the very present image of the real child of today.

This is a challenge for all of us who work for and with children. This is a challenge for all countries. And it is absolutely true that challenges strain the abilities of national governments to confront them independently. There are no easy answers...

But governments will certainly stand a greater chance of success if they act on a spirit of solidarity and partnership.Common problems require a common global agenda to address them.

In the interdependent world of today, globalization, liberalization, market economy, rapid urbanization, new technologies and media revolution – are not just simple words. Moreover, not only progress is in the air but mostly changes in values and in mentalities.

The fact is that there is an enormous evolutionary change taking place now worldwide. We have to face it and to understand it: we have to accept the new role of the human race – and of children, for that matter... Someone has wisely said: 'To save the planet, we must embrace technology as well as trees.' On the basis of our discussions here today, I would dare to state: 'To save the planet, we must embrace technology, trees and children ...'

ADMINISTRATIVE AND JUDICIAL CO-OPERATION WITH REGARD TO THE INTERNATIONAL PROTECTION OF CHILDREN

William Duncan*

INTRODUCTION

In the modern world children face risks in a variety of cross-frontier situations. Some are caught up in disputes over custody or contact between parents living in different countries. They may be the subjects of parental abduction. Teenagers who runaway abroad face the multiple risks which confront the unaccompanied young person in an alien environment. Some children are the subjects of unregulated intercountry adoption, fostering or other alternative care arrangements. Other forms of cross-border illicit transfer for the purposes of economic or sexual exploitation sometimes occur. Children may be displaced through war, civil disturbance or natural disaster.

The need for international co-operation at all levels, legislative administrative and judicial, in addressing the protection of such children and young persons is becoming well accepted. The UN Convention on the Rights of the Child of 20 November 1989, is replete with reminders of this, through its encouragement of bilateral and multilateral arrangements or agreements in a number of areas,[1] and through more general references.[2] International administrative and judicial co-operation is needed partly for reasons which are well known at the national level. These include the multi-disciplinary nature of child protection work, the requirements of close liaison between the different agencies involved (social work, medical and legal), as well as the vital importance of communicating information concerning children at risk when they move from one area to another. In addition, at the international level, there are linguistic barriers to overcome together with the problems which arise from lack of familiarity with other legal and child protection systems, and the need to accommodate differences, which may have cultural roots, between the systems concerned.

* Professor William Duncan is First Secretary of the Hague Conference on Private International Law.

[1] Art. 11, illicit transfer and non-return of children abroad; Art. 21 (e) intercountry adoption; Art. 22, refugee children; Art. 34, sexual exploitation; Art. 35, sale, trafficking and abduction.

[2] See, e.g., Art. 45.

W.P. Heere (Ed.), International Law and The Hague's 750th Anniversary

EARLY EXAMPLES

One of the first international instruments to recognise the importance of administrative co-operative structures in achieving practical outcomes was the UN Convention of 20 June 1956 on the Recovery Abroad of Maintenance. This Convention, to which there are fifty-seven States Parties, provides for mutual administrative assistance in the processing of intercountry maintenance claims and in the enforcement of maintenance orders, through the channel of designated bodies known as transmitting and receiving agencies. This system is complimentary to, rather than a substitute for, traditional private international law rules which concentrate rather on issues of competence, applicable law and recognition and enforcement of foreign orders. Indeed the various Hague Conventions dealing with maintenance obligations, two of which concern applicable law[3] and two of which concern recognition and enforcement,[4] sit reasonably comfortably alongside the UN Convention. The practical operation of the UN Convention, which has been more successful in certain regions of the world than others,[5] illustrates well one of the most basic requirements for international co-operation, namely that the agencies charged with the responsibilities of co-operation need to be adequately staffed and resourced. They need to be responsive and efficient.

The development by the Hague Conference on Private International Law of administrative and judicial mechanisms for co-operation began, not in the field of child protection, but in relation to international civil procedure, first with the Conventions on Civil Procedure of 1896 and 1905, and then with the Hague Convention of 1 March 1954 on Civil Procedure. Indeed it was the later Hague Convention of 15 November 1965 on the Service Abroad of Judicial and Extrajudicial Documents in Civil or Commercial Matters and the Hague Convention of 18 March 1970 on the Taking of Evidence Abroad in Civil or Commercial Matters, which pioneered the device of the Central Authority as the channel of communication between states. The Hague Convention of 5 October 1961 concerning the Powers of Authorities and the Law Applicable in Respect of the Protection of Minors contained what have been described as 'embryonic' provisions on co-operation, involving for example the exchange of views between authorities taking measures of protection in different states,[6] and the

[3] Hague Convention of 24 October 1956 on the Law Applicable to Maintenance Obligations in Respect of Children and the Hague Convention of 2 October 1973 on the Law Applicable to Maintenance Obligations.

[4] Hague Convention of 15 April 1958 on the Recognition and Enforcement of Decisions Relating to Maintenance Obligations in Respect of Children and Hague Convention of 2 October 1973 on the Recognition and Enforcement of Decisions Relating to Maintenance Obligations.

[5] See note on the operation of the Hague Conventions relating to Maintenance Obligations and of the New York Convention on the Recovery Abroad of Maintenance drawn up by Michel Pelichet, Preliminary Document No 1 of September 1995 for the attention of the Special Commission of November 1995, paragraph Nos. 103-120.

[6] Art. 10.

provision of information about measures taken in one state to certain other states (of the child's nationality). However, the Convention provided no real structure for these communications, and the poor functioning of its co-operation provisions has been regarded as one of its serious flaws.[7]

INTERNATIONAL CHILD ABDUCTION

The Hague Convention of 25 October 1980 on the Civil Aspects of International Child Abduction, to which there are now fifty three States Parties, was the first of the Hague Conventions concerning child protection to make use of the 'Central Authority', and indeed to employ it as an integral part of the procedure for securing the prompt return of children who have been unlawfully removed or retained across international frontiers. The role of the Central Authority is not confined to the communication of information, but extends to active functions in individual cases, which may range from the provision of assistance in discovering the whereabouts of the child to the initiation of judicial or administrative proceedings with a view to obtaining the return of the child.[8] The proper functioning of the Convention, in particular the promptness with which enquiries and return applications are handled, depends as much on the responsiveness and efficiency of the Central Authorities as it does on the legal processes operating in each country. The Special Commissions which are organised by the Hague Conference to review the practical operation of the Convention, and which have occurred up to now at four year intervals, are an important means of promoting co-operation between Central Authorities and of resolving some of the inevitable problems which arise.[9] In fact the Permanent Bureau has a continuing role in this respect, remaining in close contact with Central Authorities, providing contact and other information to them, and helping to maintain good relations between them.

Central Authorities must operate within the constraints of enabling legislation and budgetary controls. This results sometimes in limits on their activities, which may be a source of frustration. For example, Central Authorities have a potentially important role to play in promoting 'the peaceful enjoyment of access rights and the fulfilment of any conditions to which the exercise of those rights may be subject.'[10] Many Central Authorities lack the resources to carry out this

[7] Explanatory Report on the Hague Convention of 19 October 1996 on Jurisdiction, Applicable Law, Recognition, Enforcement and Co-operation in respect of Parental Responsibility and Measures for the Protection of Children by Paul Lagarde, para. 5.

[8] See Art. 7.

[9] See, for the most recent review, the Report of the third Special Commission meeting to review the operation of the Hague Convention of 25 October 1980 on the Civil Aspects of International Child Abduction (17-21 March 1997) drawn up by the Permanent Bureau of the Hague Conference on Private International Law, August 1997.

[10] Art. 21.

role. It is of interest to note that the Council of Europe is currently developing proposals for a new international instrument concerning contact which would require the much more active involvement of Central Authorities in this area.[11] Article 35 (1) of the Hague Convention of 1996 on Jurisdiction, Applicable Law, Recognition, Enforcement and Co-operation in respect of Parental Responsibility and Measures for the Protection of Children also reinforces the role which may be played by Central Authorities in this matter.

It has also been suggested that Central Authorities could play a more active role in helping to secure the situation of the child following his/her return to the habitual residence and pending the outcome of custody proceedings there.[12] In an increasing number of cases the child is returning in the company of an abducting custodial parent, and the establishment of safe temporary living conditions for the child and that parent is essential. Obviously Central Authorities could play a role here, but resource constraints and national limits on their legal powers remain an obstacle.[13]

JUDICIAL CO-OPERATION AND THE 1980 HAGUE CONVENTION

As regards judicial co-operation, the Hague Convention of 1980 does not impose any explicit requirements of communication between the judges in the two countries concerned. However, in an important sense the Convention is founded on a principle of judicial co-operation, in that it requires in effect that the judge in the country to which the child has been abducted should entrust any long term decision concerning custody of, or contact with, the child to the judge in the country of the child's habitual residence. Also the operation of the Convention may involve some division of responsibility between judges in the two countries concerned in that a judge in the country of the child's habitual residence may be asked[14] to rule on the question of whether the removal or retention of the child was wrongful within the meaning of Article 3.

It may well be that the successful operation of the 1980 Convention in certain difficult cases will in future require more direct judicial co-operation between judges in the two countries concerned. This is particularly so where a judge is considering the making of a return order in circumstances where he/she may have

[11] The work is being carried out by the Working Party on Custody and Access which reports to the Committee of Experts on Family Law.

[12] See Working Doc. No. 20 (20 March 1997) submitted by the delegations of Australia, the United Kingdom, Monaco, New Zealand, Norway, Sweden & Switzerland, contained in Annex II of the Report of the third Special Commission meeting to review the operation of the Hague Convention on the Civil Aspects of International Child Abduction (17-21 March 1997). See also Annexes I and III.

[13] Ibid, at para. 60 of the Report.

[14] Art. 15.

legitimate concerns about the safety or living conditions of the child pending the taking of any necessary measures of protection by the authorities of the state to which the child is to be returned. Again, this is especially the case where the child is to be accompanied by the abducting custodial parent, who may herself or himself face accommodation, support, legal assistance and even protection problems on returning to the country of the child's habitual residence. Various legal techniques are being developed to help deal with this problem. The acceptance by the requested judge of 'undertakings' by the applicant in respect of interim arrangements is practised in certain common law jurisdictions.[15] Some doubts have been expressed about the effectiveness of this technique, given the difficulty that may arise in enforcing such undertakings in the country where they are to be carried out. There is the possibility of the applicant seeking, and even being required to seek, in the return country a 'safe harbour' or 'mirror' order which reflects the conditions/undertakings required by the judge dealing with the return application. Finally the judge may wish to be reassured that the authorities of the country to which the child is to be returned are in a position to take any necessary measures of protection, including the determination of custody and contact issues, reasonably promptly.

In a number of these matters, direct or indirect communication between the judges may be very helpful both in speeding the Convention processes and in helping to reinforce the fundamental Convention principle of return. Already there has been some experience of direct judicial communication in the context of abduction proceedings. There is a view that, for reasons of natural justice, such communications should be confined to procedural, and should not extend to substantive, issues. It is of some interest to note that, at a recent Judges' Seminar organised in the Netherlands by the Hague Conference on Private International Law on the subject of the International Protection of Children, judges from thirty countries agreed to raise with their national authorities the potential usefulness of designating one or more members of the judiciary to act as a channel of communication and liaison, inter alia, with judges in other states in respect, at least initially, of issues relevant to the operation of the Hague Convention of 1980.[16]

THE CONVENTION OF 1993 ON INTERCOUNTRY ADOPTION

The Hague Convention of 29 May 1993 on Protection of Children and Co-operation in Respect of Intercountry Adoption, to which there are now twenty six States Parties, places co-operative mechanisms at the centre of a system designed

[15] E.g., United Kingdom jurisdictions, Australia, New Zealand, Ireland.

[16] One of the conclusions of the Judges' Seminar held at 'De Ruwenberg' from 22-25 June 1998.

to regulate an institution which in the past has given rise to too many abuses. One of the most interesting features of the Convention, from the juridical point of view, is that it employs co-operative mechanisms not as a supplement, but as an alternative, to the traditional private international law techniques of establishing uniform rules concerning jurisdiction and applicable law.[17] In relation to jurisdiction, there were two principal reasons for this approach. First it was recognised that the proper regulation of intercountry adoption required both a sharing and a division of responsibilities between the state of the child's origin and the receiving state, and that the designation of their respective functions, in the form of conditions to the making of an adoption under the Convention, was more important than the determination of which country should finally have jurisdiction to make the adoption. Second, there were legitimate differences of opinion as to which country, the state of origin of the child or the receiving state, was the more appropriate to make the adoption. Some states of origin took the view that a child should not be transferred abroad until his/her new status had been firmly established in the state of origin, while some receiving states considered that the child should remain with the prospective adopters for a trial period in the receiving state and that the order should be made there. The outcome was that the Convention remains neutral on the question of jurisdiction, and it is possible for either state to insist on its own position. If the two states concerned cannot agree, then co-operation between them is impossible. In fact, this is less of a problem than might at first appear, because receiving states are generally prepared to accept a situation in which orders are made in the state of origin (subject to their prior agreement under Article 17 (c) that the adoption may proceed). Indeed the anxieties of certain states of origin in this respect are given special recognition in Article 28 of the Convention.

As regards applicable law rules, their absence in relation to matters such as capacity or eligibility to adopt or be adopted are remarkable. For example, while Article 5 a gives the competent authorities of the receiving state the responsibility to determine that the prospective adoptive parents are eligible and suitable to adopt, it does not specify the law applicable to their eligibility. In most cases no doubt the authorities will apply their own laws. Nevertheless, it is possible[18] for authorities of the state of origin to disapprove of the decision taken by the authorities of the receiving state and to insist on the application of their own eligibility requirements.[19] What the Convention provides is a structure which, subject to certain fundamental principles and procedural safeguards, enables co-operation with respect to intercountry adoption, but only in circumstances of which both states approve. At the heart of this co-operative regime based on

[17] However, the rule of 'recognition' by operation of law of adoptions made in accordance with the Convention is, of course, of great importance. See Art. 23.

[18] Ultimately by using a veto through the application of Art. 17 (c).

[19] These might relate, for example, to the age of the prospective adopters relative to the age of the child.

mutual consent lies Article 17 (c) according to which the entrustment of the child with the prospective adopters may only be made if 'the Central Authorities of both states have agreed that the adoption may proceed.' In effect, therefore, the co-operation mechanism of the Convention makes possible the cumulative application of the relevant laws, but only if the state concerned wishes this to be so.[20]

Another important feature of the 1993 Convention regime is the possibility of controlled delegation of Central Authority functions. Some of the general responsibilities of Central Authorities may be delegated to other public authorities or accredited bodies.[21] In addition, many of the functions relating to a specific adoption procedure may be (and in most states will be) carried out by accredited bodies (i.e. usually, adoption agencies complying with specified standards) or public authorities,[22] and more exceptionally (subject to supervision and only with the consent of the states concerned) by other bodies or persons who 'are qualified by their ethical standards and by training or experience to work in the field of intercountry adoption.'[23] This system of delegation is designed to avoid over-centralisation, excessive bureaucracy and cost, as well as to recognise and utilise existing agencies involved and experienced in the work of intercountry adoption. The degree of direct involvement of the Central Authority in particular adoption procedures will differ from one country to another.

Intercountry adoption is appropriate only when alternative family care is not available in the child's country of origin. This generally implies that the country of origin will be one which labours under certain disadvantages. It may have suffered physical disaster or political turmoil. Its economy may be weak, and it may have few resources available to meet the needs of its domestic system of child protection. It is in this context that its Central Authority for the 1993 Convention will be operating. This is rather different from the situation with the Hague Convention of 25 October 1980 on the Civil Aspects of International Child Abduction, which for the most part operates between countries that are relatively well resourced. It also needs to be borne in mind that many of the principal responsibilities of regulation and control fall, under the 1993 Convention, on the shoulders of Central Authorities in the countries of origin.[24] Two consequences flow from this. The first is that the Central Authorities of the countries of origin will need a great deal of support if they are to carry out their functions successfully, in terms, for example, of training and resources. Sec-

[20] See W. Duncan, 'Conflict and Co-operation. The Approach to Conflict of Laws in the 1993 Hague Convention on Intercountry Adoption', in N. Lowe and G. Douglas, eds., *Families Across Frontiers* (M. Nijhoff 1996) p. 577.

[21] See Arts. 8 and 9.

[22] See Art. 22 (1).

[23] See Art. 22 (2).

[24] Preparation of report on the child, supervising consent procedures, preventing undue pressure on biological family, combating corruption, etc.

ondly, a good deal of patience and understanding will need to be shown by other Central Authorities. The Convention is best viewed as a structure which will enable over time the development of improved standards within intercountry adoption (in both receiving countries and countries of origin), rather than as a panacea for the instant remedy of all problems associated with intercountry adoption.

THE HAGUE CONVENTION OF 1996

The Hague Convention of 19 October 1996 on Jurisdiction, Applicable Law, Recognition, Enforcement and Co-operation in respect of Parental Responsibility and Measures for the Protection of Children marks a new phase in the development of co-operation mechanisms within Hague Conventions. In some respects, the Convention adopts the traditional private international law techniques, containing as it does uniform rules on jurisdiction and choice of law in respect of a very wide range of measures for the protection of the person and the property of children, as well as the principle of recognition by operation of law and enforcement of measures taken under the Convention. The Convention also contains rules on co-operation which supplement these private international law rules. What is new about the Convention, in juridical terms, is the way in which the private international law rules themselves, particularly those dealing with jurisdiction, have begun to embody co-operation mechanisms. In particular, Articles 8 and 9 contain procedures whereby jurisdiction may be transferred from one contracting state to another in circumstances where the judge normally exercising jurisdiction (i.e. in the country of the child's habitual residence) considers that the authorities of another contracting state would be better placed in the particular case to assess the best interests of the child. There is also the unusual but significant enabling provision that, 'The authorities concerned may proceed to an exchange of views', envisaging the possibility of direct judicial communication.

Moreover, the co-operation provisions themselves contain certain innovations. The degree of decentralisation is even greater than in the Convention of 1993. Most functions of the Central Authority may be performed either directly or through public authorities or other bodies. This reflects the strong desire of those drafting the Convention to avoid the creation of unnecessary bureaucracy and expense and to make use as far as possible of existing structures.

The co-operation provisions reflect the importance of information exchange in child protection proceedings. The authorities in a contracting state with which the child has a substantial connection will be able to request information concerning the situation of a child from the authorities of the child's habitual residence, and may even prompt consideration by the competent authorities in that state of the need for measures of protection.[25] Equally the authorities of the child's habitual residence, or any other authorities having jurisdiction and contemplating measures of protection, may request information relevant to the protection of the child from the authorities of any other contracting state.[26] In a case where a child is exposed to serious danger and a change in his country or residence occurs, there is an obligation on an authority which has taken, or was contemplating taking, measures of protection to inform the authorities of the child's new country of residence about the danger involved and the protective measures taken or contemplated.[27]

CONCLUSIONS

The value of administrative cooperation between authorities in different states is already well established in areas such as the international enforcement of maintenance obligations and the recovery of children abducted abroad. Such cooperation lies at the heart of the regulatory system for intercountry adoption introduced by the Hague Convention of 1993, which is becoming so rapidly accepted by the international community. In many other areas of international child protection the potential for administrative cooperation has not yet been fully realised, but the Hague Convention of 1996 offers structures which are rich in possibilities, for example, for better facilitating transfrontier parent/child contact, for enhancing our capacity to protect children and young persons who run away abroad, or for regulating the increasingly common cross-border placement of children (other than by adoption). However, the establishment of a Conventional framework for cooperation is not alone enough. As in the domestic, so in the international sphere, the proper resourcing of the responsible authorities is essential. This implies sufficient properly trained personnel, adequately equipped, and with a mandate broad enough to enable clearly-defined goals to be achieved. It implies also the capacity to act speedily, to relate to and utilise the relevant existing child protection services available nationally and internationally, and to operate with the special sensitivities that are required where differences of language and culture are involved. These ambitious conditions for international cooperation are especially difficult for poorer countries to achieve. This calls for understanding, patience and active assistance on the part of the wealthier countries.

Judicial cooperation has always been implicit in traditional private international law approaches, such as the recognition and enforcement of foreign decisions. The idea that judges in different countries may have to perform

[25] Art. 32.
[26] Art. 34 (1).
[27] Art. 36.

complementary functions in respect of the same case has been given limited recognition, for example in Article 15 of the 1980 Convention, and more recently in Article 35 of the 1996 Convention (in the context of transfrontier parent/child contact). The 1996 Convention raises the possibility of an even more radical step, the declining of jurisdiction in favour of a court abroad which is better placed to protect the child. The latest challenge for the judiciary is that of establishing more direct communication with colleagues abroad in certain cases in order to safeguard the child, particularly where a transfer of the child to another jurisdiction in circumstances of risk is being contemplated. There has already been some experience of direct judicial communication, for example between judges in Canada and the United States. The practical, including linguistic, and legal limitations on the development of a more widespread system of direct judicial communication should not be underestimated. There is perhaps future work here for the Hague Conference on Private International Law, in helping to elaborate a structure for judicial communication which has the capacity to overcome the linguistic barriers, which can accommodate the different ways in which courts are organised, and which ensures respect for the requirements of natural justice.

JUDICIAL AND ADMINISTRATIVE CO-OPERATION IN FAMILY LAW MATTERS: CO-OPERATION IN CHILD ABDUCTION AND SIMILAR CASES

Margaret H. Bennett*

For the last 750 years, men have been fighting wars with each other based on their differences: material, ideological, philosophical, cultural and religious. From the Middle Ages particularly, there have been differences between Muslims and non-Muslims. As we approach the year 2000, we now have a divided world whose division is based on these differences. Starting from West Africa, going through the Middle East, across the upper Indian sub-continent into the Far East and out into the Pacific Ocean there is a wide band of Muslim countries with ideologies which are the same or very similar to each other but different from the rest of the world. The people within these Muslim countries are united in one thing. That is their belief in and daily practice of the word of the Prophet Mohammed as written in the Holy Quor'an.

This address is on the subject of judicial and administrative co-operation in Family Law matters particularly co-operation in child abduction and similar cases.

The Quor'an states that in matters relating to children, the principle to be applied in decisions is the question of what is in the best interests of the child. It was my privilege a few days ago to have a meeting with the Grand Kadi from a Sharia Court of Appeal and he read out these words to me.

In all the common law and civil law jurisdictions, the principle of the best interests of the child is also the guiding principle to be applied. This principle is to be found enshrined in the United Nations Convention on the Rights of the Child which has been signed by 191 countries.

The Hague Conference on Private International Law[1] was established to bring together men and women in delegations from the governments of different countries to help find solutions for individual problems that their citizens have with other nationals of different countries and the difficulties which prevent such

* Margeret H. Bennett LLB, Solicitor, Margeret Bennett Solicitors, Carlton House, 5A Bloomsbury Square, London WC1A 2LX; Chairwoman of the Family Law Committee of the International Bar Association, 271 Regent Street, London W1R 7PA. Research for this article was done by Dawn K. Hyun, Syracuse University College of Law

[1] J.H.A. van Loon, The Secretary General, Hague Conference on Private International Law, Permanent Bureau, 6 Scheveningseweg 6, 2517 KT The Hague, Netherlands; tel: +31 (70) 363 3303; Telefax: +31 (70) 360 4867

W.P. Heere (Ed.), International Law and The Hague's 750th Anniversary

individuals in one state achieving solutions to the problems that they have with other individuals in another state. The Hague Conference on Private International Law has been a unique forum to assist these individuals in finding resolutions to their problems in the private law realm. Through the process of creating international conventions, a remarkable achievement has been made in enabling governments of different states to find ways of removing or overcoming their differences in the interests of helping their own citizens in many private law areas.

Although the legal systems, cultural norms and ideological beliefs existing in countries may differ, one thing remains consistent and has enabled delegates from all countries to agree is the belief that the 'best interests of the child' is the overwhelming paramount principle when creating conventions in connection with children and the fundamental principle that all countries agree upon.

A number of Hague Conventions relating to children have been ratified by a significant number of countries. These Conventions have proved to be very successful, providing a system of administrative and legal procedures when dealing with international childrens' issues.

Up to now not one Convention has been ratified by any of the Muslim countries although Muslim countries are members of The Hague Conference. A new age is now however dawning, to coincide with the advent of the new millennium, in that the most recent international Convention relating to children, The Hague Child Protection Convention[2], came into existence on 19 October 1996 and was adopted unanimously by the Member States. This new Convention was signed by Morocco, the first Muslim country to sign a Hague Convention. The expectation is that this Convention will be ratified by Morocco soon. Hopefully, then other Muslim countries will also follow this lead.

The significance of these events can be related to the experience of Member States in applying The Hague Convention on the Civil Aspects of International Child Abduction[3]. The experience has been that it has been very difficult to achieve the return of abducted children either to or from Muslim countries. I say to or from because it is a two-way process and it is as important for the citizens of Muslim countries to have confidence in the judicial systems of non-Muslim countries as it is the other way around, in order to do what is in the best interests of the children of their Muslim citizens.

The implementation of The Hague Child Abduction Convention has had a profound effect on the law as it affects children who move between Convention States. This Convention establishes the method and procedure for the management and administration of a child abduction case. Under the Convention, a

[2] The Hague Convention on Jurisdiction, Applicable Law, Recognition, Enforcement and Co-operation in Respect of Parental Responsibilities and Measures for the Protection of Children dated 19 October 1996.

[3] The Hague Convention on the Civil Aspects of International Child Abduction of 25 October 1980.

Central Authority is set up in each state to facilitate communications between one country and another and to channel individual cases to the courts or other appropriate authorities who will make the decision about returning the child. The decision as to whether or not the child is returned is usually a judicial function and dealt with by judges in court, not in an administrative context. The Hague Child Abduction Convention does not currently require the judges of one country to communicate with the judges of another country. Considering how successful this Convention has been, it is unfortunate that this provision was not included. The new international Hague Child Protection Convention will now require judges in different countries to communicate with each other in child abduction cases. The preamble to the Hague Child Protection Convention states that it came into being following a recognition of the need 'to improve the protection of children in international situations.' There was a desire amongst signatory states to avoid conflicts between their respective legal systems as to jurisdiction, applicable law, recognition and enforcement. The Convention records the importance of international co-operation for the protection of children. The preamble also re-affirms that the best interests of the child are to be a primary consideration.

The underlying principle of The Hague Child Protection Convention is that the competent authorities for dealing with issues relating to a child are those of the state of the child's habitual residence (subject to some exceptions). Accordingly, on the implementation of the Convention between Member States, the conflicts which have in the past arisen where, for example, the state of which the child is a national assumes jurisdiction over a child when the child is habitually resident in another state, will be avoided.

Article 1 sets out the objects of The Hague Child Protection Convention. They are, *inter alia*:

a) to determine the state whose authorities have jurisdiction to take measures directed to the protection of the child;

b) to determine the law which is to be applied;

c) to determine the law applicable to parental responsibility;

d) to provide for the recognition and enforcement of such measures of protection in all contracting states; and

e) to establish such co-operation between the authorities of contracting states as may be necessary to achieve the purposes of the Convention.

Article 7 of The Hague Child Protection Convention deals specifically with the relationship of the Convention to The Hague Child Abduction Convention and provides that in the event of the abduction of a child within the scope of the Child Abduction Convention the provisions of The Hague Child Protection Convention ensure that the state of the child's habitual residence, retains the welfare jurisdiction over the child and restricts the means by which a new state can acquire such jurisdiction. Article 7 of The Hague Child Protection Convention provides that in the case of the wrongful removal or retention of the child, the authorities of the state of the child's habitual residence immediately before the removal or retention, keep their jurisdiction until the child has acquired an habitual residence in another state, and (a) each person, institution or other body having rights of custody has acquiesced in the removal or retention; or (b) the child has resided in the new state for a period of at least one year after the person having rights of custody has or should have had knowledge of the whereabouts of the child and no request for return lodged within that period is still pending and the child has settled in his or her new environment. It should be noted that the 12 month period does not run from the date of the removal or retention as it does in Article 12 of The Hague Child Abduction Convention but from the time when knowledge of the child's whereabouts was received or imputed to the person having custody rights. Article 7(3) further provides that, as long as the authorities in the original state retain their jurisdiction, no steps, other than urgent steps, can be taken by the new state.

I have mentioned above that the objects set out in Article 1 of The Hague Child Protection Convention require the setting up of arrangements to enable co-operation to take place between the authorities of contracting states. Whilst, in some states, for child abduction purposes or intercountry adoption purposes these authorities may be administrative, experience in cases involving child abduction has shown that the authorities involved have usually been judges.

When there is a failure of judicial co-operation between judges from different countries, experience has shown that there have been expensive and time consuming problems. These problems are accentuated in cases involving children. Procedural delays may cause serious damage to the well-being of the child not only because of the ongoing litigious strife between their parents, but also because the children may be subjected to psychological and physical damage due to delay. Any judicial tug of war may hurt a child and will not be in the child's best interests. Contradictory custody orders in different countries create chaos and confusion. There is also the problem of two different legal systems with different philosophies, cultures and religious origins. When courts consider the child's best interests in determining custody, they interpret the concept differently.

Islamic countries, applying the law in accordance with the strict letter of the Quor'an, are often less flexible. In Asian countries, such as Japan, a foreign father is sometimes disadvantaged due to the cultural prejudice against foreigners and strong belief in the mother/child bond. Common law and civil law countries often ignore or give insufficient consideration to cultural and religious issues.

In addition to the above problems, where there is tension or animosity between particular countries, judges may remain biased against foreigners and side with their own nationals in disputes. This should not, however, be permitted to affect individual citizens and particularly the rights of their children.

The reality is that as nations draw closer together, information, capital and goods daily cross international boundaries, people travel regularly from country to country and national boundaries no longer prevent people from meeting or marrying and having children. Sometimes those relationships and marriages end in separation, divorce and custody disputes. The courts in all countries have therefore had to come to terms with becoming part of a global society and dealing with international cases.

The Hague Child Protection Convention provides rules to determine which court in which state should decide the question of what is in the best interests of the child. The Hague Child Abduction Convention requires and mandates the court (to a state to which a child has been abducted) to return that child immediately to the state of the child's habitual residence so that the courts in the child's home state can, with the benefit of all the available information, decide what is in the child's best interests. This will be based upon all the necessary surrounding circumstances including the network of family, friends, cultural or religious community to demonstrate a stable home life and the best educational system for the child.

We already have experience of a statute mandating the co-operation between judges in the United States where there are 50 different jurisdictions. *The Uniform Child Custody Jurisdiction Act* (*UCCJA*)[4] is the uniform law for jurisdiction in child custody cases. The *UCCJA* provides a uniform mechanism to resolve jurisdictional child custody disputes. It has four bases of jurisdiction: (a) home state; (b) significant connection; (c) emergency procedures; and (d) default jurisdiction. The *UCCJA* provides a solution which allows the courts of the best possible place to hear the litigation; a place with the most information about the child and possible custodial arrangements. It not only requires judicial communications as between American States but it also requires judicial communications in international disputes with judges from other countries. The provisions require that the court of one state communicate with a court in another state concerning any proceeding arising under the Act and that communication be authorised whenever the court finds it would be helpful.

Experience of the workings of the *UCCJA* has shown that there are further benefits in judicial co-operation.

An honest assessment of the circumstances and a meaningful non-adversarial conduit for communications facilitating international judicial co-operation needs to be developed. The benefits of such practises are many. Judges can, when conferring with each other, ascertain whether a case can be scheduled earlier in one country than another, prevent procedural delays and discourage continuing and duplicate litigation, ensuring the speedy return of an abducted child.

Judges tend to put more thought and discretion into making the law and make the process less inflexible and harsh. In addition to preventing inter-state competition and conflicts, it also promotes co-operation among states and has the un-

[4] *The Uniform Child Custody Jurisdiction Act,* 9 ULA (1988) p. 115. The *UCCJA* can be found on web site: http://www.hiltonhouse.com as UCCJA.TXT.

expected side effect of expanding the exchange of information which helps judges to openly discuss, negotiate and draft custody and access orders. Judicial co-operation ensures that litigation occurs ordinarily in the state that has more significant connection with the child and family and where more substantial evidence about the child's welfare is available. In this way, vital information and direction on how to handle a problem in a different state can be provided.

The mere fact of co-operation between the authorities of one country and another helps to reduce tension between states and develops familiarity of the workings of different judicial systems.

In the context of child abduction cases, the overriding goal is the prompt return of the child. Judicial co-operation ensures the prompt return of the child and the establishment of procedures to ensure the child's prompt return to the state of his or her habitual residence.

Experience in the handling of child abduction cases by judges demonstrates that there have been difficulties and concerns about returning children into situations that are unknown to the judge. One of the problems has been for judges to ensure that adequate protective measures are in place in the country of the child's habitual residence to which the child is being returned.

The judge in the state to which the child has been abducted has no authority in the state of the child's habitual residence and the child may not be adequately protected against any threats to his or her welfare which made the parent abduct the child in the first place. When The Hague Child Abduction Convention was being drafted, most primary carers of children were mothers and it was envisaged that the abductors would be fathers. The experience of the application of the Convention recently has shown that it is now mostly mothers who abduct their children, often to run away from situations that they find intolerable.

When considering whether to return children to the state of their habitual residence judges sometimes now use undertakings in the form of promises given to the court by the Plaintiff parent that he or she will abide by certain conditions to protect the child on the child's return. For example by providing housing for the child.

Another measure that has been used is that of mirror orders. One of the promises that the judge may request is that both parents will co-operate in applying to the court in the state of the child's habitual residence when the child has been returned to ask that the court of that state should make or register a court order containing the same terms as are set out in the undertakings given to the judge who makes the decision to return the child.

Both of these types of measures have been successfully used and the practice is now growing.

In some international child abduction cases, judges from different countries have already started to communicate and co-operate in building up trust and confidence before the decision is made to return the child. This is the dialogue that is already beginning which is envisaged by The Hague Child Protection

Convention and this is why it is so important that all states representing all ideologies, philosophies, religions and cultures should sign and ratify The Hague Conventions.

Whether it be a common law state, a civil law state, as Islamic state or any other state, we, the international community, as represented at The Hague Conference on Private International Law and the International Bar Association which I represent and the two and a half million lawyers worldwide which the IBA represents, look forward to the future with our Islamic neighbours ratifying the Conventions, with all states experiencing co-operation between judges and all authorities working together in the best interests of children everywhere.

INTERNATIONAL COMMERCIAL ARBITRATION

Alternative Dispute Resolution in Commercial Disputes

Chair: P.A. Wackie Eysten

International Sports Law

Chair: H.T. van Staveren

The Iran-US Claims Tribunal and the UNCITRAL Arbitration Rules

Chair: K. Skubiszewski

The Hague as a Venue for Commercial Arbitration

Chair: J.J. van Haersolte-van Hof

ALTERNATIVE DISPUTE RESOLUTION IN COMMERCIAL DISPUTES: INTRODUCTION

Piet Wackie Eysten*

This panel focuses on alternative dispute resolution (ADR) in the context of international commercial arbitration. This raises a number of questions:
– is ADR a form of arbitration? Artbitration a form of ADR?
(learned debates on 'is arbitration ADR?' in USA: *med-arb.*)
– if so, if ADR is arbitration, what distinguishes it, what is so special about it?
– if not, is it an alternative to arbitration? In what way is ADR an alternative; only in method, or also as regards the actual result?
– if it is a valid alternative, what exactly is the difference?

The origins of ADR are to be found in the USA. In the USA there was dissatisfaction with the so-called 'court calendar congestion' and the disadvantages of court proceedings:
– high costs (pretrial discovery and deposition)
– long duration
– impredictability (jury, punitive damages).

In the UK the situation was hardly any better. Arthur Marriott and Henry Brown (*ADR Principles and Practice*):

> 'There has been an increasing awareness that there is a denial of justice to the vast majority of the population as far as the civil justice system is concerned whose procedures and delays cause unacceptable levels of cost, beyond the reach of all save the wealthiest individuals and companies.'

Commercial arbitration does not provide the solution. Very often selecting and appointing the arbitrators takes considerable time and proceedings, witness hearings, etc., are equally time consuming and costly.

> 'The point has long been reached where conventional arbitration in many industries is blighted by delay, formality and expense, placing arbitration beyond the economic reach of many companies who have entered into arbitration agreements in their contracts without being fully aware of the consequences.'

Therefore, business lawyers looked for alternative ways to settle disputes in a more efficient manner. They found that the influence of a third person, who is

* P. A.Wackie Eysten, De Brauw Blackstone Westbroek.

W.P. Heere (Ed.), International Law and The Hague's 750th Anniversary

neutral to both parties, can be very effective, if merely to facilitate the negotiations between the parties. This resulted in a variety of alternative methods of dispute resolution, collectively referred to as ADR (mediation, minitrial, expert appraisal, neutral evaluation, etc.). The scale ranges from negotiation, through conciliation, mediation, arbitration to adjudication. Prof Frank Sanders (Harvard. 'multi-door courthouse') starts the scale at 'avoidance'.

Here we find the origin of the essential difference between all forms of ADR and all forms of adjudicatory procedure, including arbitration: in ADR the third party does not render a decision, in many cases the mediator does not even give his opinion or advice, but merely facilitates the process. He assists the parties in reaching mutual understanding and helps them settle their dispute themselves. Mediation (ADR in general) is essentially a consensual process.

Experience showed something else too: the result of such negotiations was very often not only a settlement of the actual dispute, but very often the parties found common ground for further agreements and understanding. In the course of the process they discovered common interests, potential possibilities for cooperation, synergy. ADR not only considerably reduced the costs and avoided the long delays of litigation, it also yielded more profitable and positive solutions. Such solutions made it possible to preserve or even enhance personal or business relations which might otherwise have been damaged by the adversarial process.

Besides, the parties experienced that they remained involved in what was after all 'their' dispute. They did not have to hand their file to the lawyer and loose all control. The simple procedure and the informality of the whole process enabled them to take an active part in the proceedings themselves and remain responsible for the ultimate result.

Consequently, ADR developed from merely an alternative way to settle a dispute into a method by which businessmen could reach solutions to their conflicts that turned out to be profitable to both parties. For example: two housewives fight over the last oranges, until they find out that one wants them for the juice, the other for the skins to make marmelade.

Out of many examples in commercial life the dispute between a small American bank and a softwarehouse may be mentioned. The softwarehouse got into financial difficulties, it could not pay off its instalments to the bank, the bank also got into trouble, the parties bombarded each other with claims. They were facing long and costly proceedings which could have lasted for years and would have cost fortunes, and which both companies may not have survived. They decided on mediation. Result: combination of expert know-how of both, resulting eventually in a merger, a niche-bank, specialized in financial services in the software business.

Apart from the fact that

1) ADR is basically a structured form of negotiation, and
2) that a third person (neutral, mediator) facilitates the process,

a third essential feature which distinguishes ADR from court litigation or arbitration is

3) that ADR is non-binding and informal.

Non-binding: either party can opt out at any stage of the proceedings. Once a settlement is reached that settlement is a binding agreement, but before that stage the mediation takes place on a purely voluntary basis. There is no coercion whatever to proceed with mediation. There may be an obligation to enter into mediation by virtue of a mediation clause in a contract. Some contracts provide that mediation or conciliation should be attempted before arbitration or litigation may be initiated.

ADR is characteristically *informal*. The most striking informality is the possibility that the mediator speaks with each of the parties separately: the 'caucus'. This is an enervating concept to seasoned traditional litigants, who unconditionally believe in the gospel of *audite et alteram partem*. And admittedly, it is important that the mediator maintains a perfect balance between the parties. If he talks to the claimant in private, he should also talk with the defendant. The 'caucus' is perhaps the clearest sign that ADR, and mediation in particular, is essentially different from court proceedings.

A typical mediation process consists of four stages:

- Introduction of the mediator and the parties
  Presentation of the case by the parties
  Summary by the mediator
  Calendar for further sessions
- Collecting facts and data
  Experts, witnesses
- Explore and develop alternative solutions
  Analyse options
- Select best solution
  Write down and execute settlement agreement

In common law jurisdictions, ADR has developed very rapidly, both in the field of labour law, family law and commercial disputes. In the USA ADR is offered by various organisations, including the American Arbitration Association (AAA) and the Institute for Dispute Resolution, which was established in 1979 by the Centre for Public Resources (CPR). The Institute has established a registry of some 900 major companies which have undertaken to explore the possibilities of settling disputes through ADR before litigating. Most of the major American law firms have issued a 'pledge' to the same effect.

Some years later the UK followed suit. In 1989 the Centre for Dispute Resolution (CEDR) was incorporated, which has very succesfully launched mediation and other forms of ADR in the United Kingdom. Mr Willis is non-executive director of CEDR.

During the last few years the concept of ADR has obtained a firm footing on the continent as well. Legislation has been introduced in France and Germany.

The Dutch Ministry of Justice is investigating the possibilities of incorporating some form of court-annexed mediation in formal court proceedings.

Very recently the ADR Centre for Industry and Commerce (ACB) was established in The Hague under the auspices of the Confederation of Netherlands Industry and Employers (VNO-NCW). The active involvement of VNO-NCW clearly illustrates the interest businessmen take in this new development. They rightly regard ADR not merely as a way to settle disputes, but as a 'tool of management', which has far greater potential than merely having business disputes decided, settled or solved. During the opening session of ACB, earlier this year, Mr Kees van Lede, CEO of AKZO-NOBEL and Chairman of ACB, pointed to some impressive results in ADR proceedings in which AKZO-NOBEL had been involved in the USA. The total amount 'in dispute' in five ADR-proceedings (four of which were 'court-ordered') amounted to over US$ 300 mln. The solutions reached yielded AKZO-NOBEL some US$ 200 mln and the savings on costs of litigation were estimated at US$ 15 mln. Mr. Van Lede strongly recommended ADR as an alternative to litigation to his colleague-entrepreneurs, mainly for four reasons:

1) it is *your* dispute, it is much better to keep control over it and over its eventual solution yourselves.
2) ADR offers opportunities that court litigation or arbitration cannot give. Very often 'win-win' solutions can be reached.
3) ADR enables you to save and even strengthen personal and business relationships that might be seriously damaged, if not ruined, by protracted court litigation or abitration.
4) Considerable savings in time and costs.

Can we do without courts and without arbitrators henceforth? Of course not. There will always be commercial disputes that cannot be dealt with in a satisfactory way through ADR or where the advantages that can theoretically be achieved are not relevant, for instance where there is no future relationship. Neither does ADR seem to be an appropriate alternative where a principal point of law must be decided. Also an unbalance in the position of the parties may be an obstacle for successful negotiations.

But this does not alter the fact that in many cases ADR can be very beneficial and effective. This can particularly be the case, it seems to me, in international commercial relations, where differences in legal systems and cultures may form an extra handicap in adjudicatory proceedings. In the international context the informality of the process is an extra advantage, it seems to me.

ADR AND ARBITRATION: ADVANTAGES AND DISADVANTAGES IN COMMERCIAL DISPUTES

A. Jan A.J. Eijsbouts*

1. INTRODUCTION

Whilst in the USA ADR is a well-established and generally recognised and accepted mechanism to resolve disputes, in continental Europe still a lot of missionary work has to be done to 'spread the ADR-gospel'.

Associating ADR with the gospel is less far-fetched than it may seem, as is probably best demonstrated by the following quote from John Kendall, litigation partner of Allen and Overy and a former Chairman of the IBA ADR Committee: 'The real worshippers consider ADR as some sort of religion, which therefore does not need rational persuasion and explanation, but merely conversion.'

I must confess that I am certainly not of that school of thought and I can assure you, that in my capacities as Chairman of the Section on Dispute Resolution of the Dutch Association of Company Lawyers and member of the European Advisory Committee of CPR I have learned that this is equally true for the majority of company lawyers in (continental) Europe. Rather than simply becoming converts, we feel that the proof of the pudding is in the eating. So, how does it taste in reality?

Well, from my company's experience with ADR-procedures, mainly in the USA, I can assure you: it is really very tasty! But at the same time I concede that: *de gustibus non est disputandum*. So let me try to convince you of the merits of ADR on the basis of a legal and factual analysis.

2. ADR AS A CONCEPT

Let me first offer you some observations on the concept of ADR. Though from the title of my introduction it is clear that I distinguish between ADR, on the one hand, and (binding) Arbitration, on the other hand, this is not at all undisputed: in the USA ADR stands for all non-court procedures, while the tendency in Europe seems to be to put the primary emphasis on the non-binding nature of ADR. In this light, European lawyers would not consider arbitration a form of ADR. From

* Senior Corporate Counsel at Akzo Nobel N.V.

W.P. Heere (Ed.), International Law and The Hague's 750th Anniversary

a company lawyer's perspective this latter distinction is very important, if not decisive, as I may illustrate later.

So, let me first give you my (European oriented) definition of ADR: it is a collective name for all non-binding dispute resolution procedures, by which the parties in dispute assisted by a neutral person (or persons) endeavour to reach a mutually acceptable solution which is to be laid down in a settlement agreement.

Since this panel session is dealing with commercial disputes, I would like to approach the subject not only from a legal but also from a business point of view. In this context I note that my observations do not necessarily apply to ADR outside the commercial field (such as family, consumer, labour, social security, and administration disputes).

3. LEGAL ANALYSIS

While as lawyers we are of course interested in a legal analysis when it comes to defining advantages and disadvantages of distinct legal procedures, we should at the same time remain realistic and acknowledge that legal argument is not, and should not always be decisive in business as well as in other sectors of society. Sound legal analysis, however, is indispensable for an overall assessment.

There is one *caveat*, however. I shall not address the academic disputes, for instance on the alleged anti-constitutional aspects of ADR, as proclaimed by Owen Fiss in the USA, who fears that the fundamental standards and values embodied in the laws may be disregarded or affected by ADR. Or, in connection with so-called court-annexed ADR, the warnings by Simon Roberts in the UK against the commingling of roles in those instances, where parties are referred to the judge in the capacity of mediator. He submits that 'The beauty of adjudication [...] is that we know unambiguously what we are experiencing: the imposed decision of an authoritative superior. That clarity is lost, once courts begin to involve themselves in the sponsorship of settlement.' There is quite some hesitation, indeed, in Europe to allow the courts to order ADR, as they may in the USA. Although these academic discussions are important, they are beyond the scope of this presentation.

So how do arbitration and ADR compare and differ in a legal sense? The main aspects ADR and Arbitration are claimed to have in common are: flexibility, cost effectiveness, expedition, confidentiality and control by the parties. In this presentation I shall address these claims, and illustrate that not all of these notions are equally valid for both arbitration and ADR.

Let me now turn to a more practical legal analysis of both dispute resolution mechanisms. I would like to concentrate on the following eight aspects.

1) *Consensual aspect of the procedure*
The main aspect ADR and Arbitration have in common is the fact that both procedures are consensual: they are based on agreement between the parties. Of course, one must acknowledge that the development of court-annexed ADR is slightly confusing in this respect, but even in those countries where the court can order ADR, the final result requires the agreement of both parties.

2) *The binding/non-binding nature*
Once the parties have agreed to the dispute resolution mechanism (until which moment both ADR and Arbitration are non-binding), Arbitration is binding and does not require the co-operation of both parties, while ADR requires such co-operation throughout the procedure. Unless and until the settlement agreement is "signed, sealed and delivered" the dispute is not resolved and either party may withdraw at any stage of the procedure. An arbitration procedure will eventually result in an award imposed on and binding for both parties, whether they like it or not.

3) *The role of the neutral(s)*
In line with the comments made under (b) above, the arbitrator has formal authority to decide on the merits of the case, a power that the mediator, as the neutral mentioned in ADR procedures, in principle does not have. He acts merely as facilitator of the process; his only authority is to master the agreed procedure. However, unless he is asked by both parties to give a legal evaluation of the position, which may impact on the final outcome and can be used by the mediator to solve deadlocks, his role is limited to assisting the parties in their endeavours to reach the settlement agreement. While, as a consequence, the arbitrational tribunal should consist of one or more lawyers, the mediator(s) may be expert(s) in other relevant fields, which may accommodate the business needs of the parties.

4) *The procedure*
Though it is often claimed that the arbitration procedure is flexible, this is in reality only true in comparison to court litigation. Of course, parties have some freedom to tailor the arbitration procedure to their needs, particularly in *ad hoc* arbitrations, but once the rules have been established, the agreed procedures have to be followed throughout.

In general, the procedure must comply, of course, with certain basic legal requirements in order to accomplish the result: an award that is compatible with the arbitration rules of the *situs* of the procedure and of the country, where it should be enforced. For instance, the powerful facility for mediators to consult each of the parties separately in a caucus and to obtain confidential information which may assist in the evaluation of possible solutions, is not available to arbitrators at the risk of invalidating the award. It violates one of the primary rules of legal procedure: *audi et alteram partem*, which is held to imply not only that both parties should be heard, but also that they should be heard in each other's presence. Confidential conversation with each party separately, which might enable the mediator in an ADR procedure to better understand such party's positions, motives and interests and to contribute to the solution, is therefore as a rule excluded in arbitration.

Also the rules on taking evidence are rather sacrosanct. Although, particularly in international conflicts between a common law based party and a civil law based party an important feature in arbitration procedures is the possibility to agree on the applicability of the IBA "Supplementary Rules governing the Presentation and Reception of Evidence in International Commercial Arbitration" by which the distinctive differences between the common law and civil law rules on documentary and oral evidence can be bridged.

In contrast, an ADR procedure is completely flexible and parties are free to design jointly with the mediator the procedure as they deem fit for their specific needs. In addition, the mediator has great discretionary powers in applying the rules in accordance with his appreciation of the positions of the parties.

5) *Control by the parties*

One of the acclaimed advantages of arbitration over court litigation is the control which the first affords the parties. This is, however, of limited significance in comparison with the control afforded parties in ADR. Of course, parties may control in advance the arbitration procedure by jointly deciding what procedure to adopt and by varying the rules within certain limits, but once the rules have been established the parties should have no possibilities left to control the actual application of the rules, which is entirely up to the arbitrators.

In contrast, control in ADR means that the parties are really *dominus litis*. They decide to continue or quit and, as mentioned earlier, it is entirely up to them to "sign, seal and deliver". I shall revert to this aspect later in this presentation, since in my opinion it is the basic advantage of ADR for the business community.

6) *The focus*

While the arbitration procedure by its nature focusses on the claim, as it is presented in legal terms by the claimant, and therefore on the legal positions of the parties, the focus in ADR is on the interests of both parties, which may be quite different from their respective legal positions. Particularly the procedural issues which may be displayed by capable counsel with great creativity in legal proceedings, and in fact may render litigations in court or in arbitration cumbersome, costly and time-consuming, are, in principle, of no importance in ADR. If they are not already inclined to do so by themselves, the parties are compelled by the mediator to concentrate on their basic interests and to forget about legal ramifications. In addition, the scope of the ADR procedure may be extended beyond the very issues in the dispute. In fact, other (joint) interests of the parties may be taken into consideration and be included in the settlement.

7) *The result*
While the arbitration award must provide one of the classic legal remedies such as damages, rescission of the contract or of specific performance, the settlement agreement in a successful ADR procedure, as I said earlier, may include a wide variety of solutions, even involving interests of the parties not at all forming part of the initial dispute. The winner, in arbitration and litigation alike, may not at all be a true winner, while in ADR the reaching of agreement implies that there is not even a looser.

8) *Enforcement*
Admission to enforce the award in arbitration can be obtained by a simple procedure in court (*exequatur*), which is not possible for an ADR settlement agreement. If one of the parties decides not to live up to its contractual obligations, the other party must as yet commence legal proceedings to achieve the result sought. In this connection, however, it is interesting to note that the French law on court-annexed mediation, enacted in 1995, enables the judge, if so requested by the parties, to grant homologation of the settlement agreement (to be compared with the possibility of an award on agreed terms in arbitration).

4. BUSINESS ANALYSIS

Though the above legal analysis provides pros and cons for both types of procedures and it may therefore not be possible always to decide on the preferred procedure from a purely legal point of view, I submit that from a business point of view as a rule the advantages of ADR are predominant in cases suitable for ADR. And I would like to add that in most cases ADR is suitable indeed. Only in a limited number of instances a court or arbitration procedure is indicated: for instance in such cases "where delay is beneficial to one of the parties or where there is a large discrepancy in the parties' wealth and resources, and consequently, their bargaining position" or "where it is necessary to create a binding and public precedent" (pp. 74 and 75 of the *Freshfields Guide to Arbitration and ADR*, 1993).

Apart from some manifest advantages, such as cost efficiency (arbitrations are in most cases as costly as court litigation, particularly in international disputes, where both arbitrators and counsel may be quite expensive) , expedition (even complex matters can be resolved in days rather than weeks) and avoidance of the need to cope with complex conflict-of-laws issues, the compelling business advantages are the following:

a) Full control with the parties. Management is not only fully involved throughout the procedure but highly committed and ultimately responsible for the result, which therefore will be more likely to reflect their real business requirements and interests.

b) No restriction to legal remedies.While an arbitration procedure will result in an award imposing such specific legal remedies as damages, specific performance or rescission of contract, the dispute in ADR is not described in legal terms and the parties may extend the playing field beyond the very legal scope of the initial dispute and include other business interests, which they may have in common. The result will therefore invariably better reflect the real business requirements and interests of the parties.

c) Empowerment effect on management. A successful ADR settlement may considerably contribute to the mangement's confidence in their ability to solve their own problems and will increase their understanding of and ability to conduct the negotiation process. Experience shows that it will shift the emphasis from positional bargaining to interest-based bargaining, which will considerably improve the management process in general.

d) Establishment or preservation of business relations. Whilst in arbitration procedures the parties will be inclined to adopt adversarial positions, which may have a disruptive effect on their business relations, it is obvious that a successful settlement in ADR will contribute to creating or enhancing the business relations of the parties.

Therefore, my conclusion, which is shared by my business colleagues who have participated in ADR procedures, is that on balance the positive business analysis should outweigh any possible negative aspects which may result from the legal analysis. In this context I may quote Ted Lightburn (Commercial Director of CEDR), who stated at a Rotterdam University Seminar in 1996:

> 'It struck me as being extremely odd, that we business managers hand over our business disputes to others. They belong to us, they don't belong to the lawyers. Why don't we control them?'

Therefore, let me finish this short presentation with the following submission on the nature of ADR and arbitration. ADR is an additional tool of management in such cases where the parties are not able to resolve their disputes in direct negotiation. It enables the parties to extend the negotiation phase with the help of the mediator and to achieve the business result sought. Whilst ADR is characterised as the "alternative" to court litigation and arbitration, from a business perspective ADR, therefore, should be considered, the natural way of dispute resolution. Arbitration and, even more so, litigation are the alternatives to be considered in case ADR does not lead to the right solution. Really reassuring, however, is that in the overwhelming majority of cases it does and that there is no need to take resort to the real alternatives, arbitration or litigation.

WHY DOES SPORT NEED ITS OWN JURISDICTION?

Heiko T. van Staveren*

Ladies and gentlemen,

Welcome to this Panel of the International Law Conference of The Hague's 750th Anniversary, organised by the T.M.C. Asser Instituut. The subject of our Panel is International Sports Law. In particular, we will discuss the international disputes before national courts and the role of the Court of Arbitration for Sports.

Many sports organisations are reluctant to take their disputes to the national courts. They do not like their members to bring sport disputes to that court, mostly fearing that the original non-serious aspects and rules of the game will be overruled by the law. If so it should be impossible to organize sports events in which the rules of the game allow to accept behaviour which would be illegal outside the game: see the sheet where the boxer is allowed to punch his adversary in the ring, but not on the street. I also mention as an example the correct shoulder push in football, the bodycheck in ice hockey and the stranglehold in judo.

An odd example of the reluctance to the interference of other parties in matters of sport is found in the history of the Royal Dutch Football Association.[1] It happened in January 1927 on the day after New Year's Day when in a football match a defender player was pushing an attacker in the back. Thus the same thing happened to the attacker that regularly happens to any attacker nowadays. The unusual thing about it on that very day was that it was witnessed by a police sergeant who was standing among the public watching the game. That sergeant saw, or at least thought he saw, the defender punching the attacker a number of times and he considered it assault and, therefore, a criminal offence. He grabbed hold of the defender and dragged him off the field, feeling that the offence had to be officially reported. After a report had been made of the offence, the player was allowed to go back on the field, but the match was never finished. The player's club management did not allow its team to continue playing because it felt that normal continuation of the match was impossible. Even though the court could not prove that actual assault had been committed, the Football Association found it necessary to cancel all football matches pending consultations with the Minister

* Professor of Law, Vrije Universiteit, Amsterdam

[1] See A. Wassing, 'De wachtmeester van Zwolle', *Het tuchtrecht van het publiekvoetbal.* (Deventer, Kluwer 1978) pp. 81-84.

W.P. Heere (Ed.), International Law and The Hague's 750th Anniversary

of Justice. After these consultations had taken place, a statement was put out which included the following part of a letter to the Minister:

> 'We are of the opinion that the police's only duty on sports fields is to keep the peace. Maintaining the rules of the game, which do not allow rough play, is the referee's duty.
>
> In participating in the match, the players show their acceptance of this form of supervision. Interference from other parties, especially the police, would make regular practice of the sport impossible. We would respectfully like to ask Your Excellency, therefore, to give clear instructions to the police, to prevent future interference in the events of a game and in the supervision of the match.'

By stating that interference in the game would make regular practice of their sports impossible for players, the letter expressed the aversion to and fear of interference in sports by the government and courts. This was neither a quirk of the time nor a consequence of the amateuristic nature of sports, nor a specific matter of the Royal Dutch Football Association. The international sports disputes in professional cycling which occurred in 1973 and 1990 are relevant examples.

These disputes centred on the condition that at the World Championship Motor-paced Track Cycling, called 'Motorpacing', the pacesetter and the cyclist should have the same nationality. The regulations of the *Union du Cyclisme International* – the International Cyclist Federation – which included this condition since 1973, were first challenged by the Dutch pacesetters Koch and Walrave in that same year, and 17 years later by the Belgian cyclist, Colyn, and his Dutch pacesetter, Zijlaard. They based their challenge on the EC Treaty: they contended that the condition was incompatible with Articles 2, 7, 48, and 59 of that Treaty. As you undoubtedly know from the judgment in the *Bosman* case, those articles, and especially Article 48, include the prohibition on discrimination of employees working in the Member States on the grounds of their nationality. The EC Court of Justice judged that this prohibition also applied to employees in sports, unless a specific regulation or practice was at stake which applied to the sport as such, and which was, therefore, non-economic, such as is the case with the composition of national teams.[2]

Although the judgment could be regarded as favourable to the pacesetters *Koch and Walrave* (which is what the Dutch court did in the case of *Colyn and Zijlaard*[3]), none of the litigating parties ever participated in the World Championships involved as they would have wanted to. Pacesetters Koch and Walrave finally dropped their case. The threat of the International Cyclist Federation to abolish their discipline played an important role in their decision. And in the case

[2] EC Court of Justice, 12 December 1974, *NJ* (1975) p. 148.

[3] President of the District Court of Justice in Rotterdam, 3 January 1990, and the Court of Appeal of The Hague, 3 July 1990, *NJ* (1991) p. 182.

of Colyn and Zijlaard this Dutch/Belgium team was, despite the court's decision, not allowed to start. Thus, the International Cyclist Federation chose to pay the financial penalty.

After the *Koch and Walrave* case, the International Cyclist Federation discussed the desirability of a condition in the regulations which would prohibit pacesetters, cyclists and other parties from taking cycling disputes to civil court. A similar condition already applied in football and was laid down in Article 48 (nowadays Art. 57) and Article 22 of the FIFA regulations and the UEFA regulations, respectively.[4]

This prohibition is the most radical instance of the sport establishment's hostility towards legal proceedings. The prohibition focuses primarily on matters relevant to the sport itself rather than the so-called 'legal side issues', such as renting a playing field, buying a boat, employing a facilities manager or leasing the bar. Due to the developments in high-level sport and professional sport, people have also become increasingly accustomed to the fact that the law cannot and need not be ignored. The prohibition affects, first and foremost, the sport itself, the practice of which would become impossible if it were to be governed by such an everyday thing as the law.[5]

But the rule prohibiting sportsmen from taking legal action in connection with sports disputes is at odds with the basic right of all people to go to an impartial court to settle disputes. This right has been laid down in Article 17 of the Netherlands' Constitution and in Article 6 of the European Convention on Human Rights. That is why, in principle, a judge may ignore this prohibition, for his powers can only be restricted by an appropriate legal condition. An international sports organization's condition does not have that status. Consequently, clashes between a court's decision on sports matters and the views of the sport itself are always possible. So even if a court rules in favour of an individual sportsman or sports club, he/it may lose out after all because he/it may no longer be admitted to the events in that sport.

Fortunately there is a possibility, accepted by the law, to bring disputes up to an arbitration court. Such a court can be installed by the parties in the sport itself. In the Netherlands the Royal Dutch Football Association has already installed in 1956 a standing arbitration court for disputes between its members, the clubs and the players. And there is also in the Netherlands a standing arbitration court for sport sponsoring, which is installed by the Association of sport sponsors and the Federation of all national sport associations of the Netherlands.

It is my opinion that because of their specific knowledge of sport en its rules, the disputing parties have more confidence in the members of these courts and,

[4] The UCI had the same considerations when Joop Zoetemelk went to court in relation to an accusation of using dope during the Tour de France, Cour d'Appel de Paris 26 October 1983. As of last summer, FIFA has considerably softened this prohibition.

[5] See J.L. Janssen van Raay, 'Sport en recht', in Henk Bergman & Hidde van der Ploeg, eds., *Sport en Wetenschap* (Haarlem/Amsterdam, Vriesenborch/Intermediair 1976) pp. 249-250.

therefore, will accept their judgements more readily than those of the regular civil court.

But I am perfectly aware of the fact that my opinion is based on the situation in the Netherlands. So I am very interested in hearing what Mr Reeb, coming from Switzerland, and Mr Nafziger, coming from the United States of America, are going to tell us about, respectively, the international sports disputes for national courts and the role of the court of arbitration for sport.

THE ROLE OF THE COURT OF ARBITRATION FOR SPORT

Matthieu Reeb*

INTRODUCTION

Today sport is obviously influencing ever larger sections of our society as a result of its commercialization, media coverage and internationalization. The considerable financial interests at stake make all the parties concerned by sports activities – be they athletes, sports federations, sponsors or organizers of sports events – highly demanding where law issues are concerned. Potential sources of conflict and reasons for intervention by judges are also constantly increasing. It is clear now that sport can no longer escape the multiplication of legal procedures and disputes which characterize the economic activity and judicial systems of western countries.

For many years, the sports world has developed its own rules and regulations almost completely independently, and today these are regularly in conflict with the laws and jurisdiction of different countries. And, where there is competition, there are sometimes conflicts and new sources of litigation.

The parties involved in a sports-related dispute generally have three possible ways of resolving emerging litigation:

- appeal to the internal authorities created by sports federations, if any; and/or
- take the dispute to the competent state courts; or
- submit the litigation for arbitration.

It is important to point out that the internal tribunals of sports federations cannot validly exclude an appeal by a dissatisfied party to external judicial authorities, namely the state courts or arbitral tribunals. Arbitration allows the achievement of a final decision against which the scope for appeal is very limited (see below). For this reason, arbitration can be an appropriate solution for the settlement of sports-related disputes.

HISTORY

In 1983, the President of the International Olympic Committee (IOC), Juan Antonio Samaranch, and Judge Kéba Mbaye took the initiative of setting up the Court of Arbitration for Sport (CAS). The goal was to provide the international

* Attorney at law, Counsel to the Court of Arbitration for Sport.

W.P. Heere (Ed.), International Law and The Hague's 750th Anniversary

sporting community with an institution able to settle exclusively disputes connected with sport. Another reason for setting up such an arbitral institution was the need to create a specialized authority offering a flexible, quick and inexpensive procedure.

The initial outlines for this concept provided that the IOC should bear all the operating costs of the court. In 1983, the IOC officially ratified the statutes of the CAS, which came into force on 30 June 1984. The Court of Arbitration for Sport became operational as of that date.

At that time, the CAS Statute could be modified only by the IOC Session, at the proposal of the IOC Executive Board.

THE INDEPENDENCE OF CAS

In 1992, a horse rider filed a public law appeal with the Swiss Federal Tribunal (FT) in order to challenge an award pronounced by the CAS. The appellant primarily disputed the validity of the award, which he claimed was that of a court which did not meet the conditions of impartiality and independence necessary for it to be regarded as a proper arbitration court.

In its Judgement of 15 March 1993, the Federal Tribunal recognized the CAS as a true court of arbitration. The supreme court noted that the CAS was not an organ of the International Equestrian Federation (FEI), did not receive instructions from this federation and retained sufficient personal autonomy with regard to it, in that the FEI placed at the disposal of the CAS only three arbitrators out of the maximum of 60 members of which the CAS was composed at this time. However, in its Judgement, the FT also drew attention to the numerous links which existed between the CAS and the IOC: the fact that the CAS was financed almost exclusively by the IOC; the fact that the IOC was competent to modify the CAS Statutes; and the important power given to the IOC and its President to appoint the members of the CAS. In the view of the FT, such links would have been sufficient to call into question the independence of the CAS in the event of the IOC's being a party to proceedings before it. The message of the FT was perfectly clear: the CAS had to be made more independent of the IOC, both organizationally and financially.

This Judgement led to a major reform of the Court of Arbitration for Sport. The major change was the creation of an 'International Council of Arbitration for Sport' (ICAS) to look after the running and financing of the CAS, thereby taking the place of the IOC. The CAS reforms were definitively enshrined in a new 'Code of Sports-related Arbitration', which came into force in November 1994.

In fourteen years of activity, 200 cases have been brought before the CAS. Of these, more than 100 have been filed during the past five years[1].

STRUCTURE

The institution is composed of two entities: the International Council of Arbitration for Sport (ICAS) and the Court of Arbitration for Sport (CAS).

CAS activities are placed under the responsibility of the ICAS, which is composed of 20 members who must be jurists well-acquainted with the issues of arbitration and sports law. These members are appointed in the following manner: the International Federations (IF), the Association of National Olympic Committees (ANOC) and the IOC appoint 4 members each. In turn, these 12 members appoint 4 other members chosen with a view to safeguarding the interests of the athletes. The last four members are appointed by these 16 members and are chosen from among personalities independent of the bodies designating the other ICAS members. The ICAS is composed in such a manner as to ensure a well-balanced representation of the international sports community.

Among other tasks, the ICAS draws up a list of 150 persons who may serve as arbitrators in CAS Panels; it can amend the Code of Sports-related Arbitration; it looks after the financing of the CAS; and appoints the CAS Secretary-General.

The CAS performs its functions through its arbitrators with the assistance of its court office. One of the major new features following the reform of the CAS was the creation of two divisions: an 'Ordinary Arbitration Division', for sole-instance disputes submitted to the CAS, and an 'Appeals Arbitration Division', for disputes resulting from final-instance decisions taken by sports organizations. Each division is headed by a president.

The role of the division presidents is to take charge of the first arbitration operations once the procedure is under way and before the panels of arbitrators are appointed. The presidents are often called upon to issue orders on requests for interim measures or for suspensive effect, and intervene in the process of constituting the panels of arbitrators. The panels of one or three arbitrators subsequently take charge of the procedure until the end.

The 150 CAS arbitrators are appointed by the ICAS for a renewable term of four years. The Code stipulates that the ICAS must call upon 'personalities with a legal training and with recognized competence in sports law'. The appointment of arbitrators follows more-or-less the same pattern as for the ICAS members. The candidates are proposed by the IOC, the IFs and the NOCs; and the ICAS appoints 30 arbitrators from the list of candidates put forward by each of these bodies. Thirty other arbitrators are appointed by the ICAS with a view to

[1] The CAS awards are compiled in the *Digest of CAS Awards 1986-1998*, publication of which is scheduled for August 1998.

safeguarding the interests of the athletes, with the remaining 30 chosen from among independent personalities. Even though some CAS arbitrators are proposed by sports organizations, the fact remains that they must carry out their functions with total objectivity and independence.

The Court Office of the CAS is the secretariat of the Court and of all the panels of arbitrators.

FUNCTIONS OF THE CAS

The CAS fulfils three specific functions. In its first role, the CAS is seized of disputes immediately and directly as an arbitration court of first and sole instance, either by virtue of an arbitration clause contained in a contract or through a submission agreement signed after the dispute has arisen. In this function, the CAS can, for instance, settle disputes arising out of sponsorship contracts, contracts between athletes and managers, contracts granting TV rights in connection with sports events, etc.. These disputes are submitted to the ordinary arbitration procedure.

Secondly, the CAS, through its Appeals Arbitration Division, intervenes as a last instance court of appeal, if a statement of appeal is lodged by any party against a decision by a sports federation, for instance a disciplinary decision. Here, again, the jurisdiction of the CAS must be based on an arbitration agreement or arbitration clause, for example contained in the statutes or regulations of sports federations. These disputes are submitted to the appeals arbitration procedure.

So far, 23 IFs have inserted in their regulations an arbitration clause referring to CAS arbitration.

In its third role, the CAS gives advisory opinions, which may be requested by certain sports bodies (IOC, IFs, NOCs) on any legal issues related to sport. Needless to say, an advisory opinion does not constitute a binding arbitral award.

The working languages of the CAS are French and English. Another language may be chosen by the parties if they agree to do so and if the Panel is also in agreement. The seat of the CAS is in Lausanne, Switzerland. This is also the seat of all arbitration conducted in accordance with the Code of Sports-related Arbitration, even if the hearings are held elsewhere. This means that all CAS arbitration is governed by the Swiss *Federal Act on Private International Law*, insofar as one of the parties is domiciled or has its registered office outside Switzerland. This Act is the *lex arbitrii* and applies to issues such as arbitrability, validity of the arbitration agreement and remedies against awards.

DECENTRALIZATION

1996 was the year of decentralization for the CAS. The ICAS began by creating two permanent decentralized offices, the first in Sydney in Australia, and the second in Denver, in the United States of America. These offices are attached to the CAS court office in Lausanne, and are competent to receive and notify all procedural acts. Creating them made it easier for parties residing in Oceania and North America to have access to the CAS, especially with respect to the time difference between the countries.

Later in 1996, the ICAS created an ad hoc Division with the task of settling finally and within a 24-hour time-limit any disputes arising during the Olympic Games in Atlanta. This ad hoc Division was composed of two co-presidents and 12 arbitrators who were in the Olympic city throughout the Games. To ensure easy access to the ad hoc Division for all participants in the Olympic Games, a special procedure was created for the occasion, which was simple, flexible and free of charge. A total of six cases were submitted to the CAS ad hoc Division in Atlanta.

In 1998, two new special divisions were set up by the ICAS. The first was created for the Olympic Winter Games in Nagano, and the second for the Commonwealth Games in Kuala Lumpur. The success of these ad hoc divisions has played a large part in making the Court of Arbitration for Sport known among athletes, sports organizations and the media all over the world.

ENFORCEMENT OF CAS AWARDS AND LEGAL REMEDIES AGAINST THEM

The awards pronounced by the CAS can be enforced in the countries which have signed the New York Convention on the Recognition and Enforcement of Foreign Arbitral Awards. However, it should be noted that, under the terms of this Convention, enforcement could be refused if the competent authority in the country where the enforcement is sought finds that sports-related disputes are not capable of settlement by arbitration under the law of that country.

Pursuant to the Swiss PIL Act, an award may be challenged before the Swiss Federal Tribunal on only limited grounds, namely, incorrect constitution of the arbitral tribunal, lack of jurisdiction, violation of the principle of equal treatment or incompatibility with public policy. If none of the parties has its domicile or business establishment in Switzerland, they may, by an express statement in the arbitration agreement, exclude all setting aside proceedings, or limit such proceedings to one or several of the grounds mentioned above.

ADVANTAGES OFFERED BY CAS ARBITRATION

These advantages can be listed as follows: confidentiality, specialization of the arbitrators, flexibility and simplicity of the procedure, speed, reduced costs and international effectiveness of the arbitral award.

In terms of confidentiality, the CAS arbitration procedure is private and therefore takes place without the public or the media knowing about it. The hearings are not public. There are, however, cases where the public interest and the right to information are stronger than the obligation of confidentiality. An example of this is where making an award public may have a dissuasive effect, for example, awards pronounced in connection with doping. In such cases, a Panel of the Court of Arbitration for Sport may take the decision to publish the award.

The CAS Rules are designed to avoid formalism and thereby facilitate access to the CAS. Thanks to the great flexibility of the CAS procedure, rapidity is also guaranteed. The appeals arbitration procedure provides for a four-month time limit from the filing of the request for arbitration to the issuing of a final award.

One of the main objectives of the CAS was to establish a low-cost procedure. For example, the appeals procedure is free of charge, which implies that the costs and fees of the arbitrators, plus the administrative costs, are borne by the CAS. There is only a court office fee of SFr. 500.- to be paid by the appellant upon filing the statement of appeal. The situation with respect to the costs is somewhat different in the ordinary arbitration proceedings, which are not free of charge. The parties must pay administrative costs calculated in accordance with the CAS rate (e.g. SFr. 8'250.- for a disputed sum of SFr. 1 million).

Although aged just 15, the CAS already occupies an important place within the international sports community and the world of international arbitration. The growth in its activity shows that this institution answers a real need. At a time when the number of sports-related disputes is growing, the CAS must continue its mission to provide international sport with a dispute-resolution system which fully meets its requirements.

THE COURT OF ARBITRATION FOR SPORT AND THE GENERAL PROCESS OF INTERNATIONAL SPORTS LAW

James A.R. Nafziger*

The Court of Arbitration for Sport (CAS), was formally established by the International Olympic Committee (IOC) in 1984 with its headquarters in Lausanne. The CAS has been moving from aspiration to reality as a central mechanism for resolving sports disputes, especially those related to international competition.[1] Its jurisdiction is broad, extending to 'all activities pertaining to sport and whose settlement is not otherwise provided for in the Olympic Charter.'[2] The CAS does not resolve technical questions, such as the particular rules of the game or scheduling of competition. Instead, it addresses such important issues as the eligibility and suspension of athletes, the adequacy of protections for individual athletes during drug testing, breaches of contract between an athlete and a sports club, the validity of contracts for the sale of sports equipment, and the nationality of athletes for purposes of competition. In a survey of ten recent CAS cases, six involved charges of doping against athletes, two involved non-doping issues of eligibility for competition, one related to an endorsement contract between two private companies, and one concerned violence between two national teams in international competition.[3]

* Thomas B. Stoel Professor of Law, Willamette University College of Law; Vice President, International Association of Sports Law.

[1] The CAS is governed by a Code of Sports-Related Arbitration, Procedural Rules, and Rules for Resolution of Disputes Arising During the Olympic Games. Court of Arbitration for Sport, *Code of Sports-Related Arbitration* (1995). For descriptions of the CAS and its work, see Luigi Fumagalli, 'Il Tribunal Arbitrale dello Sport: Bilancio dell'Attività e Prospettive Future', 47 *Rivista di Diritto Sportivo* (1995) p. 715; James A.R. Nafziger, 'International Sports Law: A Replay of Characteristics and Trends', 86 *AJIL* (1992) pp. 489, 491; Matthieu Reeb, 'The Court of Arbitration for Sport (CAS): An Institution for Settling Sports-Related Disputes by Arbitration', in D. Panagiotopoulos, ed., *Sports & European Community Law* (1998) p. 199; Jean-Philippe Rochat, 'The Court of Arbitration for Sport', 26 *Olympic Review* (Aug.-Sept. 1997) p. 73.

[2] More fully, the CAS resolves:

> 'disputes of a *private* nature arising out of the practice or development of sport, and in a general way, *all* activities pertaining to sport and whose settlement is *not otherwise* provided for in the Olympic Charter. Such disputes may bear on questions of principle relating to sport or on pecuniary or other interests...'.

Art. 4, Statute of the Court of Arbitration for Sport (emphasis added).

[3] Nagano (NAG) 4 & 5 (1998); NAG 2 (1998); Tribunal Arbitral du Sport (TAS) 96/157 (1997); TAS 96/156 (1997); TAS 96/149 (1997); TAS 96/153 (1996); TAS 95/150 (1996); TAS 95/141 (1996); TAS 94/129 (1995); TAS Award of 30 March 1994.

W.P. Heere (Ed.), International Law and The Hague's 750th Anniversary

The CAS arbitrates disputes brought by individual athletes as well as by international and national sports organizations. It also provides summary conciliation between disputing parties and renders advisory opinions. The structure of the CAS includes separate sections for ordinary arbitration and appeals, two decentralized offices in Sydney and Denver, and ad hoc divisions for dispute resolution during and at the site of the Olympic Games, the Commonwealth Games, and other international competition that may invite the CAS to provide on-site services. The advantages of the CAS arbitral procedures have been described as 'confidentiality, specialization of the arbitrators, flexibility and simplicity of the procedure, speed, reduced costs and international effectiveness of the arbitration award.'[4]

As of 1998, the CAS had decided over 200 cases, resulting in more than fifty aribitral awards, ten advisory opinions, and 'many amicable settlements'.[5] The impetus for the rapid growth of the CAS has been agreements between it and international sports federations (IFs) by which the federations have acceded to the compulsory jurisdiction of the CAS.[6] Most international federations have entered into such agreements. In turn, individual athletes submit to CAS jurisdiction within the terms of their membership in federation-affiliated organizations at the national level. In 1993, the International Council of Arbitration for Sport (ICAS) assumed authority to oversee the CAS. This was an important enhancement of the tribunal's independence and prestige because it relieved the CAS of the awkward direct supervision that the IOC had maintained over it.[7] At times that supervision appeared to raise conflicts of interest that are largely avoided in the revised structure.

It is still too early to discern any clear jurisprudential trends among CAS awards. Several interesting rulings nevertheless merit attention. Despite a general rule among IFs of strict liability for doping, a few awards disclose an effort by CAS panels to avoid unnecessarily harsh results.[8] Second, in determining the validity of anti-doping sanctions against athletes, the CAS has consistently relied on the IOC's Medical Code and Drug Formulary Guides, rather than its own interpretations of doping.[9] Third, an important advisory opinion of the CAS

[4] Reeb, loc. cit. n.1, at p. 203.

[5] *Idem*, p. 200; Remarks of Matthieu Reeb, the Hague's 750th Anniversay International Law Conference, 3 July 1998.

[6] See Anthony Polvino, 'Arbitration as Preventative Medicine for Olympic Ailments: The International Olympic Committee's Court of Arbitration for Sport and the Future for the Settlement of International Sporting Disputes', 8 *Emory International Law Review* (1994) p. 372..

[7] *Olympic Review*(July-Aug. 1993) pp. 299, 305-306.

[8] See Aaron N. Wise, 'Sports governing bodies' strict liability drug rule standards', 14 *Sports Law* (Sept.-Oct. 1996) at p. 14; See *Foschi* v. *Fina*, *infra* n. 16.

[9] See, e.g., CAS award in NAG 2 (1998) (deciding *Rebagliati* case at the Nagano Games by reinstating the gold medal of the winner of the snowboarding giant slalom, Canadian Ross Rebagliati, who had tested positive for marijuana). The CAS found, under the Medical Code, that the IOC had no competency to disqualify Rebagliati in the absence of the requisite agreement between the IOC

helped resolve jurisdictional issues in doping cases by establishing the priority of IFs over NOCs.[10] Finally, the CAS has not hesitated to reprimand National Olympic Committees (NOCs), in one case for offending the ideal of fair play by improperly seeking disqualification by the CAS of competing teams.[11]

This brings us to the larger framework for resolving internationally-related sports disputes. Although the CAS is of emerging importance, it is just one of several institutions within the general process of international sports law.

Overall, the development of international sports law has reached a critical point. The general process of international sports law is complex and confusing. Relevant institutions include national governing bodies in sports, international sports federations, the IOC, the CAS, national arbitral tribunals, national courts, and international (largely European) courts and commissions. It is time to consolidate this array of dispute resolution procedures into a more coherent process. A particular need is to reconcile, if not harmonize, rules and procedures of the numerous sanctioning institutions, as well as to clarify jurisdictional boundaries between them. This is not to argue for uniform rules and procedures among those institutions, let alone to expect such uniformity. It is, however, to recognize the merits of coordinating and integrating the regulation of such issues as eligibility for competition, doping, and mobility of athletes between sports bodies. It is, in other words, to argue for a more stable, fairer sanctioning process in the best interests of athletes and international competition.

The international character of major sports competition has shaped the formation of a transnational regime with its own authority and legitimacy. But this regime is obviously complicated. The problem is therefore, how to avoid unnecessary duplication and unfair discrepancies in the overall sanctioning process administered by these institutions. The problem, indeed, is how to promote greater efficiency and collaboration among them. It is a matter of teamwork.

Unfortunately, members of the team of institutions do not play according to the same rules. Nor do they share a single captain. The Olympic Movement and its chosen instrument of formal dispute resolution, the CAS, provide a basic legal framework, but the regime of international sports law remains decentralized. Decision-making is pluralistic. Concurrent jurisdiction to decide who gets to do what to whom, when and with what effect, does, of course, enhance the prob-

and the international skiing federation (FIS) to provide for tests for cannabinoids (marijuana and hashish). The CAS further found that marijuana was not listed as a banned substance in the Drug Formulary Guide that had been published for athletes participating in the Nagano Games.

[10] TAS 94/128 (1995).

[11] See award in NAG 4 & 5 (1998) (reprimanding Czech NOC for contesting eligibility of an United States naturalized hockey player who had played for the Swedish team. Despite its conclusion that the player had been ineligible to compete in matches already concluded in Nagano, the CAS refused to order forfeiture of the disputed matches involving the Swedish team. Forfeiture would have accrued in the standings to the advantage of the Czech team).

ability that *something* will be done to enforce *some* rules. But concurrent jurisdiction also contributes to the confusion of overlapping and sometimes conflicting decisions. This essay is a modest effort to describe a foundation for greater teamwork among sanctioning institutions.

The celebrated case of *Foschi* v. *United States Swimming, Inc.*,[12] ultimately decided by the CAS, highlights the problem of overlapping jurisdictions. A brief summary of this case may be instructive. Jessica Foschi, an amateur swimmer, is subject to the authority of United States Swimming, Inc. (USS), a national governing body for amateur swimming. Following national competition in 1995, Foschi's urine samples tested positive for the anabolic steroid mesterolene. A hearing panel of the USS upheld the evidence but determined that Foschi 'had no knowledge of the manner in which the banned substance entered her body.'[13] After lengthy administrative proceedings, the USS board of directors, acting as a final appeals body, accepted these determinations and imposed several sanctions against Foschi. These included a two-year probation, a rescission of her times in the competition, and a warning that any subsequent determination of doping would result in a lifetime ban on her participation in amateur swimming competition. Subsequently, the USS imposed an outright ban on her eligibility for competition, but reversed itself again by reinstating the original, more modest sanctions. In any event, Foschi was allowed to participate in US trials for the 1996 Olympic Games, where the question of her eligibility for the Games became moot when she failed to qualify for the team.

Under the *Amateur Sports Act* of 1978, which governs internationally-related athletic activity in the United States and of United States athletes, Foschi nevertheless filed a demand for arbitration by the American Arbitration Association (AAA). In her demand she challenged the minimum sanctions that remained against her, especially the threat of a lifetime ban if she should ever be found to have engaged in doping. The USS claimed that Foschi's claim was moot insofar as she was free to compete as long as she remained free of doping. An AAA panel confirmed its competence to hear the matter, however. It then heard extensive testimony and reviewed voluminous documentation. It considered but did not rule on Foschi's claim that she had been denied due process because the rules of the United State Olympic Committee (USOC) do not provide for alternative testing of a controverted urine sample.

The AAA panel decided to rescind all sanctions against Foschi, concluding that they violated fundamental fairness and that they were arbitrary and capricious. In doing so, the panel rejected a strict liability rule of the Fédération Internationale de Natation Amateure (FINA), the international swimming federation whose Doping Control Program and anti-doping rules govern the USS.

[12] In the Matter of Arbitration Between Jessica K. Foschi & United States Swimming, Inc., American Arbitration Association, Case No.77-190-0036-96 (1996).

[13] *Idem.*

The panel noted that the USS had not contested the determination of Foschi's apparent innocence of the circumstances by which the controlled substance entered her body. It ruled that to discount her innocence would be unjust. Ignoring her innocence would only vindicate a questionable purpose of the FINA rules 'to insure that not one guilty party go free, albeit that innocent parties are punished.'[14] That purpose, the panel ruled, 'turns our concept of justice on its head.'[15]

Having rejected FINA's rule of strict liability, the arbitral panel determined that there was a lacuna in the rules of both the USS and FINA. There was simply no authority for the penalty imposed by the USS, however admirable it might have been as a compromise. The AAA therefore sent a strong message that although it would ordinarily be prepared to establish certain presumptions in favor of a governing sports body or its international federation, it could not do so under the circumstances of the case.

This stage of *Foschi* might be viewed simply as yet another national arbitral decision contrary to the rules of an international federation – just the sort of conflict that a decentralized regime engenders. But it is significant that the AAA opinion took account of a FINA decision in a comparable doping case involving an Australian swimmer, Samantha Riley. The AAA opinion therefore gains credibility for its attention to foreign precedent, in other words, for its openness to, if not reliance on, comparative insights – just the sort of approach by a sanction-reviewing institution that should help avoid unnecessary conflicts in the overall sanctioning process.

The AAA's careful decision did not end the matter, however. Instead, FINA reimposed a two-year suspension, retroactive in part to the date of the urine testing. Foschi appealed it to the CAS. On 17 June 1997, the CAS reduced FINA's retroactive suspension to six months and ordered costs against FINA.[16]

Foschi demonstrates both the challenges and the opportunities presented by the fragmented sanctioning process of international sports law. Despite the fragmentation, however, it is possible to define a normative foundation upon which to construct a more stable process. A Canadian judicial decision, *McCaig* v. *Canadian Yachting Ass'n & Canadian Olympic Ass'n*,[17] puts this foundation in sharp relief. Although *McCaig* did not address an issue of sanctions in the strict

[14] *Idem.*

[15] *Idem.*

[16] *Foschi* v. *Fédération Internationale de Natation Amateure (FINA)*, TAS 96/156 (1997). See *N.Y. Times*, 19 June 1997, a t B-16; John Jeansonne, Swim Ban is Overturned, *Newsday*, 18 June 1997, at A61; 73 *World Press Review*, 1 July 1996, at 51; David A. Botwinik & Diane Rapisarda, 'Under the Amateur Sports Act, All Disputes Between American Athletes and the U.S. Olympic Committee Must be Submitted to Arbitration for Resolution', *National Law Journal*, 22 July 1996, at B5, B6.

[17] *McCaig & McCaig* v. *Canadian Yachting Ass'n, Canadian Olympic Ass'n & Bolduc & Alie*, Case No. 96-01-96624 (Q.B. Winnipeg Centre 1996). The author is grateful to Richard Pound for sending him a copy of this opinion.

sense, it did establish principles highly relevant to the current discussion. The applicants for relief, Murray and Amy McCaig, sought a declaration that the respondent, the Canadian Yachting Association (CYA), had ignored an agreement between them that provided for two regattas in order to select the Canadian team for the Mistral class of sailboarding competition in the 1996 Olympic Games. In fact, only one regatta was held because of poor wind conditions that precluded the scheduling of a second regatta. The applicants therefore sought an order directing the CYA to nominate a second regatta to complete the criteria for team selection.

The court concluded that the administrative appeals process had been fully satisfied. It rested its decision on an interpretation of the agreement between the McCaigs and the CYA. In the absence of a provision for an alternative if two regattas could not be held, without fault by either party, the court deferred to what it described as a reasonable construction of the agreement by the CYA. According to the court, '[t]he bodies which heard the appeals were experienced and knowledgeable in the sport of sailing, and fully aware of the selection process. The appeals bodies determined that the selection criteria had been met.'[18] Significantly, the deciding judge wrote as follows: '[a]s persons knowledgeable in the sport and the contractual language, I would be reluctant to substitute my opinion for those who know the sport and knew the nature of the problem.'[19] He expressed 'profound regret that the parties have ended up in court when one realizes that all are genuinely concerned about encouraging our best athletes to achieve their highest level of skills for themselves and for their country.'[20] This observation accords with the reluctance of national legal systems, such as those of the United States and the United Kingdom, to substitute courts for playing fields in sports.

McCaig is typical of modern judicial decisions in several respects. It encourages athletes and sports bodies to enter into carefully drafted agreements. In the event of any ambiguity, claimants therefore carry a heavy burden to obtain relief from reasonable constructions of agreements by sports bodies, even when eligibility for competition may be at issue. *McCaig* thereby discourages recourse to adjudication of disputes related to international sports competition.

It is possible to be more specific, however, about the foundation for applying and reviewing sanctions related to sports competition. There is some order in the chaos. Indeed, it is possible to identify ten normative trends in practice:[21]

[18] *Idem.*

[19] *Idem.*

[20] *Idem.*

[21] This summary draws upon a preliminary outline of normative trends in James A.R. Nafziger, 'International Sports Law as a Process for Resolving Disputes', 45 *ICLQ* (1996) pp. 130, 133.

1) *National sports bodies*

National sports bodies have primary responsibility to avoid and resolve disputes and to apply sanctions, from playing field infractions to eligibility issues. Disagreements between athletes and their respective sports bodies are typically resolved by administrative review within those bodies, by independent arbitration, or by a sequence or other combination of these two institutional methods. National sports bodies are generally subject to the rules of their respective IFs. National law may clarify the relationship between the sports bodies and the IFs or other international authority such as the IOC. In the United States, for example, the *Amateur Sports Act* of 1978 provides that the National Governing Body for each sport shall 'designate individuals and teams to represent the United States in international amateur athletic competition . . . and certify *in accordance with applicable international rules*, the amateur eligibility of such individuals and teams.'[22]

2) *International federations*

IFs may review decisions of constituent national bodies concerning a broad range of issues involving competitions and the status of individual athletes. Rules of the Olympic Charter are supreme, but it remains unclear whether IOC decisions always trump IF decisions. Disagreements between IFs and national sports bodies that transcend national laws are generally resolved by arbitration.[23] Disagreements between IFs and National Olympic Committees are generally resolved by the IOC itself or by the CAS. The results have usually favored the IFs. An example is the advisory opinion of the CAS to subordinate NOC decisions on doping of athletes to the primary jurisdiction of the IFs.[24]

3) *National Olympic Committees*

National Olympic Committees (NOCs) may intervene in disputes involving participation of athletes in sanctioned competition. National laws sometimes accord NOCs exclusive jurisdiction to sanction international competition and to determine the eligibility of athletes to compete. These laws, however, may limit the competence of NOC rulings on such issues to the duration of Olympic training, selection and competition.

[22] *Amateur Sports Act*, 36 USC (1994) para. 393(7) (emphasis added). This rule applies except in the instance of Olympic or Pan-American competition, concerning which the United States Olympic Committee has primary jurisdiction.

[23] International Amateur Athletic Federation (IAAF) rule 20.1, for example, provides that '[a]ll disputes between Members, or between Members and the Council or Congress [of the IAAF], however arising, shall be submitted to the Arbitration Panel [of the IAAF] for determination within three months of the date upon which the disputed decision was made.'

[24] TAS 94/128 (1995).

4) *The International Olympic Committee*

The IOC, on its own initiative or that of an athlete or an IF, may review or deny authority to a broad range of decisions by NOCs. Under the Olympic Charter, the IOC recognizes the 'exclusive powers'[25] of NOCs to represent their countries in sanctioned competition, but it also grants power to the IFs to establish criteria of eligibility and to establish and enforce rules to govern the practice of their respective sports.[26] The IOC nevertheless retains authority as a final arbiter of disputes within the Olympic Movement.

5) *The Court of Arbitration for Sport*

As already noted,[27] the International Council of Arbitration for Sport (ICAS) is an umbrella organization under which many IFs require mandatory arbitration clauses in licensing contracts between athletes and national sports bodies.[28] Athletes enter into these contracts in order to be eligible to participate in IF-sanctioned competition. The arbitration clauses establish a basis for enforcing arbitration awards against individual athletes even when their future livelihood may be at issue. This has become highly significant as the distinction between 'amateur' and 'professional' athletes has faded. Mandatory arbitration of disputes is conducted under the auspices of the ICAS's principal sanction-reviewing institution, the CAS. Its jurisdiction is very broad, encompassing disputes both related and unrelated to the Olympic Games. Since the Atlanta Games in 1996, it has been the principal means of resolving disputes during both the Summer and Winter Games, as well as the Commonwealth Games.

6) *National courts of law*

The widespread adoption of terminal arbitration clauses in licensing contracts, as well as improved methods for more informal resolution of disputes within national sports bodies and the IFs, have not inhibited litigation altogether. Courts of law continue to be important partly because the persistent problem of doping requires heavy sanctions that may raise issues of fairness. Litigation is also important because of a substantial increase in the number of professional or semi-professional athletes. Their financially-related claims may extend beyond the competence of administrative procedures and informal tribunals. Moreover, some claims may not be subject to arbitration clauses, or national law may ensure a right to seek judicial review of arbitral awards. Finally, high-value claims often

[25] *Olympic Charter* (1996) Art. 31(3).

[26] *Olympic Charter* (1996) Art. 30(1), (4).

[27] See *supra* n.. 7.

[28] International Amateur Athletic Federation rule 20.2, for example, provides that '[e]ach Member shall incorporate in its constitution provision that all disputes between that Member and an athlete, or between an athlete and the IAAF, shall be submitted to arbitration. In the case of a dispute between a Member and an athlete and the IAAF, this dispute may, at the option of the Council, be submitted to the IAAF's Arbitration Panel.'

involve issues of fundamental human rights, natural justice, or public order. These issues include a professional athlete's right to work, the right to be heard in administrative proceedings, and the right to be free of bias in those proceedings. We should not exaggerate the impact or volume of litigation, however. For example, by one estimate, only one-tenth of one percent of all decisions of football-governing bodies in Germany went to court.[29] The rate of litigation may, of course, vary according to the litigiousness of a national system.

7) *Relationship between courts and sports bodies and federations*
Ordinarily, courts recognize and enforce rules and decisions of appropriate sports bodies and federations. Courts in the United States, for example, have been reluctant to find either express or implied rights of action in claims by individual athletes against national sports bodies and IFs. They therefore have generally deferred to private processes for resolving disputes.[30] Courts are particularly reluctant to intervene in disciplinary hearings by private bodies. With reference to the notorious judicial exercises in *Reynolds*[31] and *Krabbe*,[32] a leading expert on sports law has observed as follows: 'The threat of claims for damages ... seems to accelerate the efforts to find solutions within the relevant international sports associations and federations.'[33]

8) *Private international law*
Although civil procedures vary from country to country, judicial complaints ordinarily must satisfy several basic requirements of private international law. These requirements may raise 'fiendishly complicated questions of jurisdiction, choice of law, and recognition of judgments.'[34] They include standing to sue, adequate service of process and jurisdiction over defendants, admissibility and justiciability of the complaint, convenience of the forum, and exhaustion of any administrative or other nonjudicial remedies.[35] Parties to a sports contract may

[29] Klaus Vieweg, 'Judicial Review of Sport Related Decisions in Germany', in *International Athletic Foundation, Sport & Law: Supplement to the Official Proceedings of the IAF Symposium on Sport & Law* (1995) pp. 87, 96.

[30] For example, '[t]he courts have been asked on several occasions to rule on Olympic eligibility questions. Generally, the courts have left these matters to the Olympic federations and their own procedures to resolve.' Ray Yasser, et al., *Sports Law: Cases and Materials*, 2nd edn. (1994) p. 93. See, e.g., *Behagen* v. *Amateur Basketball Ass'n of US*, 884 F.2d 524 (10th Cir. 1989).

[31] *Reynolds* v. *International Amateur Athletic Fed.*, 23 F.3d 1110 (6th Cir. 1994) (final dismissal of the case, for lack of personal jurisdiction over the plaintiff, culminating some four years and nine stages of litigation). See Nafziger, loc. cit. n. 21, at p. 134; James A.R. Nafziger, 1 *Pandektis International Sports Law Review* (1993) p. 406.

[32] For a discussion of these cases, See Bernard Hess, 'Hochleistungssportler zwischen internationaler Verbandsmacht und nationaler Gerichtsbarkeit', *ZZPInt* 1 (1996) pp. 371, 383, 405.

[33] Vieweg, loc. cit. n. 29, at p. 96.

[34] Stephen Weatherwill, *Case C-415/93*, 33 *CML Rev.* (1996) pp. 991, 992.

[35] The requirements are expressed here in common law terms, but have civil law cognates.

stipulate an appropriate choice of law to resolve disputes involving sanctions against athletes. If they fail to do so, sports authorities generally choose the proper law in conformity with accepted rules and principles of private and public international law. States ordinarily recognize and enforce foreign arbitral awards or court judgments in accordance with their own positive laws, international agreements, or principles of comity, reciprocity and judicial cooperation.

9) *Regional courts*

Regional courts may hear sports disputes, as in the *Bosman*[36] and earlier cases[37] that have come before the European Court of Justice.

10) *Alternative (more informal) dispute resolution*

The CAS attempts to facilitate conciliation of disputes during ordinary arbitration and has established procedures for mediation.[38] As the regime of international sports law becomes more universal, it is likely that the role of such relatively informal methods for resolving disputes that transcend the authority of national sports bodies and IFs will increase. In East Asia, for example, consultation, mediation and conciliation are essential. Indeed, informal procedures of dispute resolution are often prerequisites to arbitration and adjudication. Even in western industrialized countries, more informal methods of dispute resolution are increasingly important. One constraint to a fuller use of them may be a resistance by sports lawyers who view themselves primarily as litigators. Another constraint on the use of mediation and conciliation to resolve disputes is the intractibility of so many disputes involving doping, other issues of eligibility, and commercial sponsorship. The interests of parties to such disputes are so differentiated and their commitment to those interests – often stated as their 'positions' – is often so hardened that mediation or conciliation is apt to be futile.

Despite these normative trends or practices, the current regime of international sports law is untidy. It is a process in transition, as national sports bodies and IFs gradually assume more responsibility, develop better rules, and thereby gain greater respect in dispute resolution. In this transitional period, the resolution of sports-related disputes is complicated, if not incoherent at times. Gradually, though, national sports bodies and IFs are becoming more skilled and sophisticated in formulating, applying or denying, and reviewing sanctions. As national

[36] *Union Royale Belge des Sociétés de Football Ass'n ASBL* v. *Bosman*, Case C-415/93 [1995] 1CEC 381 (striking down football association rules limiting international transfers and foreign team membership of players, as violations of the Treaty of Rome and European Union law).

[37] *See Walrave* v. *Union Cycliste Internationale*, Case 36/74, *ECR* (1974) p.1405, and *Donà* v. *Mantero*, Case 13/76, *ECR* (1976) p. 1333. For discussion of these issues, see George A. Bermann, et al., *Cases and Materials on European Community Law* (1993) p. 513; Jacques Rogge, 'The Olympic Movement and the European Union', *Olympic Review* (Oct.-Nov. 1995) p. 44.

[38] See Rochat, loc. cit. n. 1.

sports bodies and IFs gain greater insights, their decisions will become more standardized and arbitral tribunals and courts of law will gain greater confidence in deferring to them. Inevitably, experience is a teacher.

National courts can play a useful role in this process. By simply being available to aggrieved parties, they help ensure due process or natural justice. Reliance on litigation to resolve sports-related disputes entails at least three problems, however. First, litigation often is inappropriate or ill-equipped to deal expertly with problems related to sports. *Reynolds* is a prime example of futility in pursuing judicial remedies. Second, as the *Harding* case[39] demonstrates, claimants can abuse the judicial option for purposes of delaying or obfuscating an issue. The flurry of arbitration and litigation that typically marks the eleventh hour before Olympic and other major competitions is often more tactical than justice-seeking. Under time pressures, litigation often serves little more than an *in terrorem* or bullying function.

A third problem in relying too heavily on litigation is that it reinforces the inclination of claimants and their lawyers to pursue adversarial processes of dispute resolution. Instead, greater emphasis should be put on professional collaboration in resolving issues. Sports competition requires a measure of cooperation, after all, and fair play is fundamental to sports activity.

Despite these problems, it has to be recognized that litigation can be instrumental in extraordinary cases. The *Harding* episode, for example, encouraged a settlement of the issues, vindicated the sanctions that the United States Figure Skating Association (USFA) imposed against Tonya Harding and, perhaps most importantly, led to the USFA's reform of its hearing process.

In sum, issues related to sanctions and jurisdiction of dispute-resolution institutions are opposite sides of the same coin. Resolution of these issues would benefit from the development of a more universal set of international legal principles and procedures. Short of that, the transnational regime requires greater reconciliation or harmonization of disparate sanctions and often conflicting procedures for reviewing them. In the absence of clear lines of authority or at least better coordination within the international legal order, sanctions imposed by an institution, often involving considerable commitments of time and resources, may simply be ignored by another institution or require more time and resources on appeal. A salient example is FINA's clumsy refusal in *Foschi* to respect the reasonable decision of arbitration procedure prescribed by national law. Ten normative trends do, however, provide a foundation for improving and streamlining the process by which designated institutions impose and review sanctions.

The Court of Arbitration for Sport will play a central role in establishing appropriate jurisdictional parameters among sanction-applying and sanction-reviewing institutions in sports. Quite likely, however, the institutional structure

[39] See Nafziger, loc. cit. n. 21, at p. 140.

will remain complex. The authority and legitimacy of the international sports regime will therefore continue to rely on evolving principles of paramountcy and cooperation among private and public institutions. It is in everybody's interest to clarify and simplify this process.

THE IRAN-UNITED STATES CLAIMS TRIBUNAL AND THE UNCITRAL ARBITRATION RULES: INTRODUCTION

Krzysztof Skubiszewski*

The discussion on the Iran-United States Claims Tribunal at this conference comes under the heading of 'International Commercial Arbitration'. Let me say at the outset that this is too narrow a category for this particular claims tribunal. While many of its awards can be classified as belonging, in their substance, to the area of commercial arbitration, there are several awards which deal with matters that are not of a commercial nature. The jurisdiction of the Tribunal is much broader than that of an 'ordinary' commercial tribunal, and its awards go beyond what is normally understood by commercial arbitration.

My two colleagues on the panel will deal with the specific question of the application of the UNCITRAL rules by the Tribunal. In my introduction I shall limit myself to some general information on the Tribunal.

The Iran-United States Claims Tribunal was set up by the Governments of Iran and the United States as part of the agreement that resolved the crisis that had arisen in their relations in 1979. On 19 January 1981 the two Governments, through the mediation of Algeria, concluded the so-called Algiers Accords. These consist of two Declarations – the General Declaration (GD) and the Claims Settlement Declaration (CSD) – and five additional instruments aimed at implementing certain provisions of the two Declarations. These Declarations and the related instruments are treaties[1] in the sense of international law, in particular, of the Vienna Convention on the Law of Treaties. The two Declarations are central to understanding the role and functioning of the Tribunal.

The Tribunal consists of nine Members. Each Government appoints three arbitrators. The latter, in turn, select the remaining three by mutual consent. If the party-appointed arbitrators fail to agree, the Appointing Authority designates the third-country arbitrator or arbitrators. The same procedure applies to the ap-

* President, Iran-United States Claims Tribunal.

[1] It does not make any difference whether the Algiers Declarations and the associated instruments are regarded as being one treaty or several treaties within the meaning of Article 2, paragraph 1(a) of the Vienna Convention. In Case No. A/18 the Tribunal said that 'the Algiers Declarations constitute[d] a treaty under international law', 5 *Iran-US CTR*, p. 251 at p. 259. In the *Anaconda* case the Tribunal recalled that it 'ha[d] been instituted by an intergovernmental agreement having the status of an international treaty [...]. This agreement [was] evidenced, *inter alia*, by the two declarations, the General Declaration and the CSD ('Algiers Accords') [...] 13 *Iran-US CTR*, p. 199 at p. 223.

W.P. Heere (Ed.), International Law and The Hague's 750th Anniversary

pointment of the Tribunal's President. The Tribunal conducts its work in three Chambers, and each third-country member is automatically Chairman of a Chamber. One of the third-country arbitrators also acts as President of the Tribunal. The Tribunal held its first session on 1 July 1981.

The Claims Settlement Declaration defines the Tribunal as an 'international arbitral tribunal' (Art. II, para. 1). The Tribunal itself upheld that description by emphasizing that it is 'clearly an international tribunal established by treaty';[2] and 'it is subject to international law'.[3]

In Case No. A27 the Tribunal referred to its competence to decide claims by nationals of one State Party against the Government of the other State Party, and said:

> 'Under contemporary international law, the fact that an individual or a private entity is party to proceedings before a forum created by an international agreement does not deprive that forum and its proceedings of their international legal nature.'[4]

The Tribunal has jurisdiction, first, over private claims, i.e., claims of nationals of the United States against Iran and claims of nationals of Iran against the United States, including certain related counterclaims. To be adjudicated by the Tribunal these claims must have arisen out of 'debts, contracts, expropriations or other measures affecting property rights' before the cut-off date of 19 January 1981. (Art. II, para. 1, CSD) They had to be filed with the Tribunal between 20 October 1981 and 19 January 1982. (Art. III, para. 4, CSD) They were very numerous: 968 so-called 'large cases' and 2892 claims of less than US$ 250,000.00 each.

Certain claims which would otherwise fall under the category of private claims have been excluded from the Tribunal's jurisdiction: claims arising out of events which led to the crisis in the relations between the two States in 1979 (para. 11, GD);[5] and claims arising under binding contracts specifically providing

[2] Case No.A18, 5 *Iran-US CTR*, at p. 261.

[3] *Anaconda* case, 13 *Iran-US CTR*, at p. 223.

[4] *Islamic Republic of Iran* and *United States of America*, Award No. 586-A27-FT, para. 58 (5 June1998).

[5] On 4 November 1979 the compound of the Embassy of the United States in Tehran was overrun by an armed group which occupied the compound and seized as hostages all the diplomats and consular personnel and other persons present. After the release of some of them, 52 hostages were detained. On 5 November 1979 US Consulates in Tabriz and Shiraz were also attacked by militants. The International Court of Justice did not impute the actions of 4 and 5 November 1979 to Iran, but it found that '[t]he approval given to these facts [...] [by the] organs of the Iranian State, and the decision to perpetuate them, translated continuing occupation of the Embassy and detention of hostages into acts of that State', *United States Diplomatic and Consular Staff in Tehran, ICJ Rep.* (1980) p. 3, at p. 35, para. 74. The Court also found that from the very outset Iran failed to protect the Embassy and the Consulates against the attacks on 4 and 5 November 1979 respectively, *ICJ Rep.* (1980) at p. 32, para. 68. Thus Iran has incurred responsibility towards the United States, *ICJ Rep.* (1980) at p. 41, para. 90. Under paragraph 11 of the General Declaration any private and official claims related to these events were excluded from the jurisdiction of the Tribunal. The exclusion

that 'any disputes thereunder shall be within the sole jurisdiction of the competent Iranian courts'(Art. II, para. 1, CSD).

The Tribunal has jurisdiction, second, over 'official claims of the United States and Iran against each other arising out of contractual arrangements between them for the purchase and sale of goods and services'(Art. II, para. 2, CSD). This category is called 'B-Cases.' These claims, too, had to be filed by 19 January 1982. By that date, 77 B-claims had been filed.

Third, the Tribunal is competent to resolve any dispute between the two Governments regarding the interpretation or performance of any provision of the General Declaration (paras. 16 and 17, GD) and any question concerning the interpretation or application of the Claims Settlement Declaration (Art. VI, para. 4, CSD). This category is called 'A-Cases.' Unlike the private claims there is no filing deadline for interpretative disputes. Up till now 30 A-claims cases have been submitted to the Tribunal.

Finally, the 'Undertakings' of the two Governments 'with respect to' the General Declaration[6] give the Tribunal residual jurisdiction over any disputes over bank claims.[7]

The Tribunal decides all cases 'on the basis of respect for law'. It applies 'such choice of law rules and principles of commercial and international law as the Tribunal determines to be applicable, taking into account relevant usages of the trade, contract provisions and changed circumstances' (Art. V, CSD).

All decisions and awards of the Iran-United States Claims Tribunal are 'final and binding'(Art. IV, para. 1, CSD). Normally both municipal and international courts and tribunals do not enforce their decisions. To some extent the Claims Tribunal does. A unique feature of the claims resolution mechanism created by the Algiers Declarations is the Security Account established pursuant to paragraph 7 of the General Declaration as a fund to pay Tribunal awards rendered against Iran in favour of United States Claimants. The original level of the Security Account was US$ 1 billion.[8]

Today's discussion concentrates on the arbitration rules of the United Nations Commission on International Trade Law (UNCITRAL) as applied by the Tribunal. Article III, paragraph 2, of the Claims Settlement Declaration provides that

also comprised any claim related to 'injury to the United States or their property as a result of popular movements in the course of the Islamic Revolution in Iran which were not an act of the Government of Iran.' Paragraph 11 amounted to a waiver of the claims referred to therein.

In response to the above seizure of its staff and property the United States imposed various economic sanctions on Iran. In paragraph 10 of the General Declaration the United States agreed to revoke these sanctions. Claims arising out of them were excluded from the Tribunal's jurisdiction by virtue of paragraph 11 of the General Declaration.

[6] These 'Undertakings'are one of the related instruments of 19 January 1981 referred to above.

[7] G.H. Aldrich, *The Jurisprudence of the Iran-United States Claims Tribunal* (Oxford, Clarendon Press 1996) p. 6.

[8] For the provision on the replenishment of the Account so as to maintain a minimum balance of US$ 500 million, see para. 7, GD.

'the Tribunal shall conduct its business in accordance with [the UNCITRAL rules] except to the extent modified by the Parties [i.e., the two Governments] or by the Tribunal to ensure that this Agreement [i.e., the CSD] can be carried out'. The adaptation of the UNCITRAL rules to the arbitration to be conducted under the Claims Settlement Declaration proved a 'painstaking'[9] task, which, however, was successfully accomplished.

One should remember that the UNCITRAL rules 'have been drafted for use in voluntary *ad hoc* arbitration proceedings.'[10] To serve the purposes of the arbitration under the Algiers Declarations these rules had to be modified and supplemented. In particular, attention may be drawn to the new rule embodied in Article 1, paragraph 3, of the Tribunal Rules of Procedure; this rule replaced the UNCITRAL provision on arbitration agreements between parties to a contract:[11]

> 'The Claims Settlement Declaration constitutes an agreement in writing by Iran and the United States, on their own behalfs and on behalf of their nationals submitting to arbitration within the framework of the Algiers Declarations and in accordance with the Tribunal Rules.'

Thus private parties do not have any influence on the procedure of the Tribunal. This situation contrasts with commercial arbitration, where the parties choose the rules applicable to the arbitration; it points to the Tribunal's different status. In this respect, the Tribunal stands closer to judicial settlement.[12]

Finally, I wish to say that the Tribunal's contribution to the interpretation and development of law cannot be discussed today as it is a different and large subject by itself. However, in view of the topic of this panel, it must be noted that the practice of the Tribunal in applying the UNCITRAL rules constitutes a significant contribution to the understanding and interpretation of those rules. This is because of the Tribunal's large docket and because the Tribunal's awards, decisions and procedural orders are public.

[9] Aldrich, op cit. n. 7, p. 9.

[10] N. Mangård, 'The Hostage Crisis, the Algiers Accords and the Iran-United States Claims Tribunal', in *Festkrift till Lars Hjerner: Studies in International Law* (Stockholm, Norstedts 1990) p. 363, at p. 379. Cf., G. Aksen, The Iran-US Claims Tribunal and the UNCITRAL Arbitration Rules – an early comment, in J.C. Schultsz and A.J. van den Berg, *The Art of Arbitration: Essays on International Arbitration, Liber Amicorum Pieter Sanders 12 September 1912-1982* (Deventer, Kluwer Law and Taxation Publishers 1982) p. 1, e.g., at p. 12.

[11] Mangård, loc. cit. Art. 1, para. 1, of the UNCITRAL Arbitration Rules reads as follows: 'Where parties to a contract have agreed in writing that disputes in relation to that contract shall be referred to arbitration under the UNCITRAL Arbitration Rules, then such disputes shall be settled in accordance with these Rules subject to such modification as the parties may agree in writing.'

[12] In any judicial settlement of disputes parties must act in accordance with the rules of procedure the court has and are in no position to change them. That is the position of private parties in the Claims Tribunal. On the other hand, the Tribunal Rules of Procedure 'may be modified by the Full Tribunal or the two Governments' (Art. 1, para. 1, of those Rules).

THE IMPACT OF THE UNCITRAL ARBITRATION RULES ON DRAFTING THE RULES OF THE IRAN-UNITED STATES CLAIMS TRIBUNAL

Howard M. Holtzmann*

1. INTRODUCTION

I have been asked to comment on what impact the UNCITRAL Arbitration Rules (the 'UNCITRAL Rules') had on the drafting of the Tribunal Rules adopted by the Iran-United States Claims Tribunal (the 'Tribunal') to govern its procedures. The answers are quite simple: the impact was very great, it was largely beneficial, and it demonstrated the usefulness of the UNCITRAL Rules as a flexible framework for effective arbitration in unique circumstances.

The impact of the UNCITRAL Rules derives directly from the Claims Settlement Declaration agreed to by the Governments of Iran and the United States, dated 19 January, 1981.[1] That Declaration was a key element of the so-called Algiers Declarations, a group of inter-related treaties by which the two Governments resolved the political crisis that had arisen following the seizure of the United States Embassy in Teheran and the holding hostage of Embassy personnel.

The Claims Settlement Declaration created a direct link between the new Tribunal and the UNCITRAL Rules by providing that '[t]he Members of the Tribunal shall be appointed and the Tribunal shall conduct its business in accordance with the arbitration rules of the United Nations Commission on International Trade Law (UNCITRAL), except to the extent modified by the parties or the Tribunal to ensure that this Agreement can be carried out'.[2]

When the two Governments agreed that the Tribunal would be formed and its business would be conducted in accordance with the UNCITRAL Rules, they were taking a leap of faith because the UNCITRAL Rules had not been designed by their draftsmen to be used in a situation such as that of the Iran-United States

* International Arbitrator; Member, Iran-United States Claims Tribunal 1981-1994, *ad hoc* Member 1994 – ; Honorary Vice Chairman, International Council for Commercial Arbitration; Honorary Chairman, American Arbitration Association; Member, delegations of the United States to UNCITRAL, 1974 – .

[1]Declaration of the Government of the Democratic and Popular Republic of Algeria Concerning the Settlement of Claims by the Government of the United States of America and the Government of the Islamic Republic of Iran (the 'Claims Settlement Declaration').

[2] *Idem.* Art. III(2).

W.P. Heere (Ed.), International Law and The Hague's 750th Anniversary

Claims Tribunal, and the Rules had never been applied in anything but typical commercial arbitrations.

UNCITRAL, as its name makes clear, is the UN's Commission on International Trade Law and its purpose is to harmonize laws and legal practices related to international trade. As part of its mission to facilitate trade, UNCITRAL in 1976 completed a project to prepare arbitration rules designed for resolving disputes arising in transnational commercial transactions. The objective was to establish procedures that would be acceptable to parties from different legal, economic, social and political systems and that would be workable in tribunals where the arbitrators and parties included persons with different legal backgrounds.

The UNCITRAL Rules were drafted to provide for a tribunal consisting of a sole arbitrator or three arbitrators. As is typical in commercial arbitration, it was expected that the tribunal would be formed for only one case and would have no function or mandate after that case had been concluded.

In contrast, the Claims Settlement Declaration provides for nine arbitrators who would sometimes decide cases as a full Tribunal of nine, and sometimes in panels of three. The Iran-US Claims Tribunal would have not just one case, as the draftsmen of the UNCITRAL Rules had expected, but thousands of cases, and the arbitrators would continue in office not for only one case but until thousands of cases had been decided. Most significantly, the UNCITRAL Rules were designed for commercial cases, while the Tribunal was given jurisdiction not only over disputes of a commercial nature but also disputes between the Governments arising out of the interpretation and performance of treaties, cases that fall within the domain of public international law. Moreover, the draftsmen of the UNCITRAL Rules never anticipated that the Rules would be used in circumstances where the parties included Governments that had no diplomatic relations, where political animosities ran high and in which the atmosphere was often tense.

At the start of the Tribunal in July 1981, its first major task was to adapt the UNCITRAL Rules, using the powers given to it by the two Governments to make the modifications necessary to ensure that the Claims Settlement Declaration could be carried out. The policy of the Tribunal, a policy on which both the Iranian and United States participants agreed, was to make as few modifications to the UNCITRAL Rules as possible. This report describes some of the principal ways in which the UNCITRAL Rules were either amended or interpreted to do that.[3]

[3] For a useful analysis of the application of the Tribunal Rules, see J. S. van Hof, *Commentary on the UNCITRAL Arbitration Rules: The Application by the Iran-United States Claims Tribunal* (1991).

2. THE UNIQUE FORMAT OF THE TRIBUNAL RULES

In drafting the Tribunal Rules the Tribunal adapted a unique format that emphasized the impact of the UNCITRAL Rules by highlighting the relatively few modifications that were made.

Thus, in the Tribunal Rules the numbering of the Articles of the UNCITRAL Rules is followed without change. Each Article of the Tribunal Rules begins with reprinting the corresponding UNCITRAL Article without any changes. This is followed, where applicable, by a section headed 'Modification of the UNCITRAL Rules'. By setting out the modifications separately, the Tribunal Rules make it easy to identify changes and show on their face how close they are to the UNCITRAL Rules and to the provisions of the Algiers Declaration – points that it was useful to emphasize in the sensitive political atmosphere of the times. Many, indeed most, Articles of the Tribunal Rules are identical to the UNCITRAL Rules, and therefore include no section headed 'Modification of UNCITRAL Rules', but rather state following the reprinting of the UNCITRAL text that the particular Article 'is maintained unchanged'.

In the Tribunal Rules, many Articles include a section headed 'Notes'. These Notes are not modifications of the UNCITRAL text, but, rather, are interpretations of the meaning of those Rules or indications as to how the Iran-US Claims Tribunal would apply them. The UNCITRAL Rules purposely provide considerable flexibility for arbitrators. Thus, a central provision of the UNCITRAL Rules states that 'the arbitral tribunal may conduct the arbitration in such manner as it considers appropriate provided the parties are treated with equality . . . .'[4] This provision was maintained unchanged in the Tribunal Rules, and the Notes give the parties guidance as to how this particular Tribunal intended to exercise its broad powers. For example, a Note to Article 15 states that the Tribunal may direct parties to appear for a pre-hearing conference,[5] a procedure as to which the UNCITRAL Rules are silent but which is within the discretion of arbitrators acting under those Rules. Similarly, Notes describe the procedure that will be followed for the examination and cross-examination of witnesses,[6] outline the procedures to govern stenographic transcripts,[7] and set forth the text of the oaths or affirmations to be used by witnesses[8] and experts.[9] The use of such Notes in arbitral rules was an innovation of the Iran-US Claims Tribunal. It permitted the Tribunal to establish procedures on a number of matters without modifying the UNCITRAL text. In practice, the Notes were given as much weight as the Rules themselves.

4 UNCITRAL Rules, Art. 15(1).

5 Tribunal Rules, Art. 15, Note. 4.

6 *Idem*, Art. 25, Note 6(b).

7 *Idem*, Art. 25, Note 4.

8 *Idem*, Art. 25, Note 6.

9 UNCITRAL Rules, Art. 27(2).

3. THE ADDITION OF DEFINITIONS

Another innovation by the draftsmen of the Tribunal Rules was to add a number of definitions which established the meaning that the Tribunal would give to various terms in the UNCITRAL Rules. The inclusion of definitions in the Tribunal Rules was a useful mechanism for adapting the UNCITRAL Rules to the circumstances of the Tribunal.

For example, many Articles of the UNCITRAL Rules use the term 'the arbitral tribunal'. A definition added to the Tribunal Rules clarifies that the phrase 'arbitral tribunal' 'means either the Full Tribunal [of nine] or a chamber [of three], depending on whichever is seized of a particular case or issue'.[10] This definition permitted the UNCITRAL Rules to be used without change in both configurations used by the Iran-US Claims Tribunal.

Another drafting problem that was solved by adding a definition related to the words 'party' and 'parties'. That problem arose from an inconsistency between the UNCITRAL Rules and the Claims Settlement Declaration. The UNCITRAL Rules provide that 'the parties' are the claimant and the respondent, and that those two parties are the ones who have a role in naming the arbitrators and who present their cases at the hearing. Pursuant to the Claims Settlement Declaration the two Governments that participate in naming the arbitrators may, or may not, be the claimant and respondent. In some cases, such as when the claim relates to a sales transaction between them or to a treaty dispute, the two Governments are the claimant and respondent, respectively. But in other cases, such as those involving claims by a private American corporation for alleged breach of contract, the claimant is not one of the two Governments. These complications were resolved by the draftsmen of the Tribunal Rules by making a distinction between situations in which a Government acts as a claimant or respondent and the circumstances in which a Government performs other functions pursuant to the Claims Settlement Declaration. The mechanism for doing this was to add a new definition that described the claimants and respondents in a particular case as the 'arbitrating parties.'[11] To implement this definition a Note was added to each Article of the Tribunal Rules that includes the terms 'party' or 'parties'. The Note states whether the term 'party' in a particular Article means a Government or an 'arbitrating party'. Thus, a Note to the Articles governing the appointment of arbitrators states 'As used [in these Articles] the terms 'party' and 'parties' refer to one or both of the two Governments, as the case may be'.[12] In contrast, the Articles relating to submission of documents and conduct of hearings each includes a Note stating that 'As used [in this Article] the terms 'party' or 'parties'

[10] Tribunal Rules, Definition 3(b).
[11] *Idem*, Definition 3(c).
[12] Tribunal Rules, Notes to Arts 6-8.

means the arbitrating party or parties as the case may be', thereby including private parties in cases in which they were claimants or respondents.[13]

Some situations were a bit more complex because they required different definitions within the same Article. For example, as to one paragraph in the Article relating to the designation of the place of arbitration, the Note clarifies that the term 'parties' means the two Governments, the choice of the place of arbitration being a function relating to the overall operation of the Tribunal in which the arbitrating parties in particular cases had no voice.[14] However, another paragraph in the same Article states that the parties should be given notice of place of any inspection of goods; as to that paragraph, the Note explains that in it the term 'parties' means the arbitrating parties.[15]

Similarly, a Note to an Article governing challenges to arbitrators provides that challenges on 'general grounds' may be made only by a Government, whereas challenges with respect to a particular case may also be made by an arbitrating party in that case.[16]

These examples are illustrative, not exhaustive, and I describe them in some detail to point out the meticulous care and ingenuity that the draftsmen of the Tribunal Rules used in fulfilling their mission to utilize the UNCITRAL Rules in the context of the Claims Settlement Declaration.

4. MODIFICATIONS TO TAKE ACCOUNT OF THE CONTINUING NATURE OF THE TRIBUNAL

Although the UNCITRAL Rules were originally intended for tribunals that each conducted one arbitration and then went out of existence, they were for the most part effective without change for the Iran-United States Claims Tribunal that had thousands of cases and continues for many years. There were, however, two circumstances in which the Tribunal determined that its continuing character required modifications of the UNCITRAL Rules. It made these changes exercising its power under the Claims Settlement Declaration to make modifications 'to ensure' that the purposes of the Declaration 'could be carried out'.[17] The Tribunal interpreted this to mean that it could make modifications necessary to permit it to carry out its work efficiently.

The first such modification related to publication of awards. The UNCITRAL Rules were written in the context of commercial arbitration in which parties expect to resolve their disputes in private, and, accordingly, provide that 'the

[13] E.g., Tribunal Rules, Notes to Art. 15.

[14] Tribunal Rules, Notes to Art. 16.

[15] *Idem.*

[16] *Idem*, Note 1 to Art. 9.

[17] Claims Settlement Declaration, Art. III(2).

award shall be made public only with the consent of both parties'.[18] The Tribunal recognized, however, that as it conducted cases it would develop experience that would facilitate later cases. Tribunal awards in earlier cases would indicate its practices and guide parties in preparing and presenting future cases. With these considerations in mind, the Tribunal amended the UNCITRAL Rules to provide that:

> 'All awards and other decisions shall be made available to the public, except where upon the request of one or more arbitrating parties, the arbitral tribunal may determine that it will ... make available only portions thereof from which the identity of the parties, other identifying facts and trade and military secrets have been deleted.'[19]

I can recall no case in which material has been deleted from a published award in a contested case.[20] While past decisions of the Tribunal are not controlling precedent, and no rule of *stare decisis* applies, the parties and the Tribunal look to past awards for guidance. Thus, it is now rare to see a Tribunal award that does not cite earlier cases. The awards are published in English by the Grotius Press in a series that now numbers 28 volumes, and also appear on a current basis in periodicals of Mealy Publications.

Another modification of the UNCITRAL Rules that was motivated by the continuing character of the Tribunal relates to the tenure of the arbitrators. The Members of the Tribunal have no fixed terms of office. It must be expected that over a long period of years Members of the Tribunal will from time to time resign for personal reasons. The question then arises as to how to handle cases in which a Member has participated but which may not be concluded for some time after his resignation. To promote efficiency, the Tribunal borrowed a procedure from the International Court of Justice, and adopted what has come to be known as the Mosk Rule, named for Richard Mosk, the Member whose resignation prompted adoption of the provision. It states, in principal part, that:

> 'After the effective date of a Member's resignation he shall continue to serve as a Member of the Tribunal with respect to all cases in which he participated in a hearing on the merits . . . .'[21]

This addition is entirely consistent with the Claims Settlement Declaration because it enables the Tribunal to carry out its work more efficiently.

[18] UNCITRAL Rules, Art. 32(5).
[19] Tribunal Rules, Art. 32(5).
[20] In a few awards in agreed terms, parties requested confidentiality on some points.
[21] Tribunal Rules, Art. 13(5).

5. CONCLUSION

Except for the modifications and interpretations described above, and a few adjustments to reflect the administrative arrangements of the Tribunal and the ministerial role of its Secretary-General, the original text of the UNCITRAL Rules has governed the conduct of arbitration by the Tribunal. As one looks at the modifications and interpretations that have been made, it is noteworthy that key UNCITRAL provisions, such as those relating to the appointment of arbitrators and the conduct of arbitral proceedings, have been maintained largely unchanged.

I have described this history of rule-making in some detail because I think that it may be useful to others who consider establishing tribunals in unique circumstances. There are five principal lessons to be learned from this history:

1. The UNCITRAL Rules are acceptable because they are seen as neutral rules – having been recommended by consensus of the UN General Assembly,[22] they are seen as everyone's rules, not the rules of any one party and they give no party a home-court advantage.
2. The UNCITRAL Rules are workable even when the arbitrators and parties come from different legal cultures – at the Tribunal, these include common law, civil law and Islamic law.
3. The UNCITRAL Rules have proven effective for resolving public international law disputes as well as the commercial disputes for which they were originally designed; thus the Tribunal has used the same rules one day in a contract dispute and the next day in a treaty dispute – they work in both.
4. The experience of the Tribunal demonstrates that the UNCITRAL Rules have an inherent flexibility that makes it relatively easy to modify or interpret them to fit the unique circumstances of a continuing tribunal that must conduct a large number of cases.
5. The procedures of the UNCITRAL Rules can operate notwithstanding the existence of intense pressures that may accompany political crises – they have been proven in the cauldron of the Iran-United States Claims Tribunal.

For these reasons, the UNCITRAL Rules have been shown to be an immensely valuable tool for facilitating the use of arbitration in resolving international crises. That, indeed, may be one of the most lasting contributions of the Iran-United States Claims Tribunal.

[22] Resolution 31/98 adopted by the General Assembly of the United Nations on 15 December 1976.

THE APPLICATION OF THE RULES OF THE IRAN-UNITED STATES CLAIMS TRIBUNAL

Koorosh H. Ameli*

INTRODUCTION

I have been asked to comment on the application of the Rules of the Iran-United States Claims Tribunal. The Tribunal's constituent instrument, the Claims Settlement Declaration, provides in Article III, paragraph 2, that 'the Tribunal shall conduct its business in accordance with the arbitration rules of the United Nations Commission on International Trade Law (UNCITRAL) except to the extent modified by the Parties or by the Tribunal to ensure that this Agreement can be carried out.' From its inception on 1 July 1981, the Tribunal began its revision of the UNCITRAL Rules; it issued the Provisionally Adopted Tribunal Rules on 10 March 1982,[1] and issued the Final Tribunal Rules of Procedure on 3 May 1983,[2] without adopting any significant changes as compared with the Provisional Rules.

The Tribunal Rules consist of an Introduction and Definitions, together with 41 articles which are grouped in three sections, namely, Introductory Rules, Composition of the Arbitral Tribunal and Arbitral Proceedings. To these are added Presidential Order No.1 of 19 October 1982, and Internal Guidelines of the Tribunal, adopted on 28 January 1982 and amended on 13 February 1982, 6 December 1983 and 17 January 1984.[3] Presidential Order No.1 concerns the composition of the three chambers, the distribution of the cases among the Full Tribunal and the chambers, the transfer of cases from one chamber to another and the relinquishment of chamber cases to the Full Tribunal, while the Internal Guidelines mainly provide a checklist of topics that might be discussed at preparatory or 'pre-hearing' conferences to be held at the discretion of the Tribunal in each case. Tribunal Rules, Article 15, Note 4.

In the space allotted, I will briefly address the application of the Tribunal Rules in connection with provisions regarding the establishment of time-limits for the submission of written pleadings, pre-hearing conferences, amendment of claims, production of documents and burden of proof.

* Member, Iran-United States Claims Tribunal.

1 Reprinted in 1 *Iran-US CTR*, p. 57.

2 Reprinted in 2 *Iran-US CTR*, p. 405.

3 Presidential Order No.1 and Internal Guidelines, as amended on 13 February 1982, reprinted in 1 *Iran-US CTR*, pp. 95, 98.

W.P. Heere (Ed.), International Law and The Hague's 750th Anniversary

1. TIME-LIMITS FOR SUBMISSION OF WRITTEN PLEADINGS

Article 18, paragraph 1, of the UNCITRAL Rules provides that the period within which the Claimant shall file the Statement of Claim is to be determined by the Tribunal, unless the Statement of Claim has already been included in the Notice of Arbitration. Under Article 23 of the UNCITRAL Rules this period should not exceed forty-five days, unless the tribunal finds its extension justified. The deadline for the filing of claims has been determined by treaty and the Tribunal has recognized that it does not have the power to change or extend it, which for most of the claims is the deadline of 19 January 1982, that is, one year after the entry into force of the Claims Settlement Declaration, as provided under Article III, paragraph 4 of the Declaration.[4] Thus, the provision for the period within which to file the Statement of Claim does not appear in Article 18 of the Tribunal Rules, save for the date 20 October 1981, before which no claims could be filed, as provided in Note 1 to Article 18 of the Tribunal Rules.[5] In practice, the Tribunal has adhered to the treaty deadline of 19 January 1982 for the filing of statements of claim and has refused a number of them, which reached the Tribunal Registry some time after the date 19 January 1982.[6] The treaty had already extended the 45 day period for the filing of claims, provided in Article 23 of the UNCITRAL Rules, to one year which gave the claimants sufficient notice to prepare their statements of claim in time. The Tribunal Rules, Article 3 also provides that '[n]o Notice of Arbitration pursuant to Article 3 of the UNCITRAL Rules is to be given,' that is, prior to and separate from the statement of claim.

The only disputes that may be filed after the date 19 January 1982 are those arising with regard to the interpretation or performance of the Algiers Dec-

[4] Art. III, para. 4 of the Declaration provides: 'No claim may be filed with the Tribunal more than one year after the entry into force of this Agreement or six months after the date the President is appointed, whichever is later. These deadlines do not apply to the procedures contemplated by Paragraphs 16 and 17 of the Declaration of the Government of Algeria of 19 January 1981.' President Lagergren was appointed on 9 June 1981. Tribunal Annual Rpt. 1983, Annex 2. Thus, the later date is 19 January 1982. See also, Tribunal Administrative Directive No.1, para.3, (4 July 1981), reprinted in Iranian Assets Litigation Reporter, p. 3382 (17 July 1981).

[5] This determination was made in Tribunal Administrative Directive No.1, para.2 (4 July 1981), ('the two governments having extended the period for settlement of claims by the parties directly concerned to 19 October 1981, as provided under Article I of the Claims Settlement Declaration.') Tribunal Administrative Directives Nos. 1 to 4 were issued early in the process of modification of the UNCITRAL Rules, and were incorporated with certain modifications in the Final Tribunal Rules, as provided in the Introduction and Definitions, para. 2, of the Tribunal Rules. The Administrative Directives No. 1 (4 July 1981), No. 2 (19 September 1981), No. 3 (24 October 1981) and No. 4 (21 November 1981) have been reprinted in Iranian Assets Litigation Reporter, p. 3382 (17 July 1981), p. 3720 (2 October 1981), p. 3811 (6 November 1981) and p. 3986 (4 December 1981), respectively.

[6] See, e. g., In Re *Cascade Overview Development Enterprises*, – DEC.-Ref. 1-FT (4 May 1982) and In Re *Mohammad Sadegh Jahanger*, – DEC.-Ref. 2-FT (4 May 1982), reprinted in 1 *Iran-US CTR*, pp. 127-128, respectively.

larations by either Iran or the United States against the other as provided in Article III, paragraph 4 of the Claims Settlement Declaration. Because of this treaty provision and its institutional framework, the Tribunal found it unnecessary even for this category of disputes to maintain a provision in Article 18 of its Rules to determine in each case the period within which the Statement of Claim shall be filed. For the same reason, the Notice of Arbitration, referred to in Article 3 of the Rules was also found unnecessary for this category of claims.

As to the Statement of Defence, the UNCITRAL Rules, Article 19, paragraph 1, similar to the provision for the Statement of Claim in its Article 18(1), provides:

> 'Within a period of time to be determined by the arbitral tribunal, the respondent shall communicate his statement of defence in writing to the claimant and to each of the arbitrators.'

However, because of the absence of a treaty deadline for the submission of the Statements of Defence, Article 19, paragraph 1, was modified to read as follows:

> 'Within a period of time to be determined by the arbitral tribunal with respect to each case, which should not exceed 135 days, the respondent shall file his Statement of Defence. However, the arbitral tribunal may extend the time-limits if it concludes that such an extension is justified.'

And Note 1 to Article 19 of the Tribunal Rules provides:

> 'In determining and extending periods of time pursuant to this Article, the arbitral tribunal will take into account
> (i) the complexity of the case,
> (ii) any special circumstances, including demonstrated hardship to a claimant or respondent, and
> (iii) such other circumstances as it considers appropriate.
> In the event that the arbitral tribunal determines that requirement to file a large number of Statements of Defence in any particular period would impose an unfair burden on a respondent to a claim or counter-claim, it will in some cases extend the time periods based on the above-mentioned factors or by lot.'

In a case recently filed with the Tribunal, I had the opportunity to recall the drafting history and practice of the Tribunal under Article 19 of the Tribunal Rules.[7] As I observed there, '[e]arly in its operation, the Tribunal considered the unique situation faced by Iran in having to respond to some 4000 cases filed against it at approximately the same time, as well as Iran's post-Revolution chaos

[7] *Case concerning United States Intervention in Iranian Affairs*, (*Iran* v. *USA*), Case No. A30, filed on 12 August 1996.

and the on-going defense against a ravaging war imposed by Iraq, and consequently agreed to Iranian requests for flexible granting of 3 to 4 extension requests for the filing of principal pleadings by Iran. On the other hand, the United States government and US private claimants, which faced none of these problems, were continuously urging the Tribunal to deny Iranian requests for extension of the filing deadlines, admission of late submissions and evidence, and postponement of the scheduled hearings. Later, however, the United Sates also found it useful to seek similar extensions of filing deadlines in at least some of the 100 cases that had been filed against it at the same time, and the Tribunal found it difficult to refuse such requests in the absence of Iran's objection and also in view of the Tribunal's own backlog resulting from the completion of written pleadings in a growing number of cases that by the time had queued for hearing and decision.'[8]

In the revision of Article 19, the Tribunal was convinced from the outset that the 45 day period for the filing of the statements of defence, referred to in Article 23 of the UNCITRAL Rules, was unreasonable. While unlimited extensions also seemed unreasonable as a means of engaging the Iranian parties into the arbitration process by the filing of their statements of defence, the Iranian parties were also uncertain of the outcome of any future requests for extension necessitated by the sheer volume of the cases against them. Thus, in its earlier modification of Article 19, the Tribunal also added a catch-all provision that stated:

> 'All Statements of Defense shall be filed within a maximum period of six months following the date on which the Statement of Claim is filed. Administrative Directive No.3, para.2(a),(24 October 1981).'

Note 1 to Article 19 of the Tribunal Rules, quoted above, was also adopted by the Tribunal on 16 November 1981 as a response to the situation faced by Iran. Thus, soon after the deadline for the filing of claims had passed, the Tribunal realized that in view of the actual number of claims filed the provision for a maximum period of 6 months for the submission of all statements of defence was simply impractical. Therefore, at its 33rd meeting on 27 January 1982 the Full Tribunal deleted this provision from Article 19, paragraph 1, in view of Iran's situation at the time.[9]

[8] *Idem*, dissenting opinion of Koorosh H. Ameli to the Order of 23 May 1997 (Doc.13), para.18.

[9] As noted in my opinion, *idem*, para. 18, n. 7: 'At the time, Iran faced a considerable number of Statements of Claim filed against it within the three-month period of 19 October 1981-19 January 1982 under the Claims Settlement Declaration, Articles I and III, paragraph 4. Iran's frequent opposition to this six-month limitation and Judge Holtzmann's "strong disapproval" of the Tribunal's decision to delete this provision indicate that the provision was viewed as having considerable impact on the ultimate time limit for the filing of Iran's Statements of Defence. In Judge Holtzmann's view, "the decision had been taken in direct contravention of paragraph 2(a) of Administrative Directive No.3 dated 24 October 1981 and the representations made to claimants thereby" and "that the Tribu-

As to further written statements that under Article 22 the Tribunal may require or allow the parties to present, Article 23 of UNCITRAL Rules provides that:

> 'The periods of time fixed by the arbitral tribunal for the communication of written statements (including the statement of claim and statement of defence) should not exceed forty-five days. However, the arbitral tribunal may extend the time-limits if it concludes that an extension is justified.'

The Tribunal Rules revised Article 23 as follows:

> 'The periods of time fixed by the arbitral tribunal for the communication of written statements (excluding the Statement of Defence) should not exceed 90 days. However, the arbitral tribunal may extend the time-limits if it concludes that an extension is justified.'

Thus, the Tribunal Rules in Article 23 modified the 45-day period to 90 days, while also deleting the references to the time-limits for the filing of the statements of claim and statements of defence, which are treated in Articles 18 and 19 of the Tribunal Rules.

Although not mentioned in the Tribunal Rules, the submission of the reply by the Claimant and the rejoinder by the Respondent usually falls under 'further written statements' and the extension practice of Article 23. As the US claimants began to file hearing memorials and extensive written evidence shortly before the hearings, resulting in the disruption of the proceedings, the Tribunal found it necessary to direct the parties to file evidence and brief in chief and evidence and brief in rebuttal, and stating in the order scheduling the hearing that no new documents shall be filed within the two or three months before the hearing begins in the case.

In practice, the provision of 135 days for the submission of the Statement of Defence in Article 19 or 90 days for the submission of further written statements in Article 23, for the reasons noted above, quickly resulted in four extensions of

nal should, at the very least, issue a new Administrative Directive informing the public of the decision,as one that substantially amended Administrative Directive No. 3." Minutes of the Tribunal's 33rd Meeting, para. 7, 27 January 1982. Iran in its letter of 16 November 1981 had emphasized that the filing of thousands of statements of defense by it to the statements of claim within the short period of maximum six months was simply impossible and in contravention of its right to a fair chance of defense during a civil strife and ravaging war situation, that it regarded as crucial to the arbitration process its right of preparation and submission of counterclaims that should be filed with the statements of defense under Art. 19, para. 3 of the Tribunal Rules, that this problem would become more acute if, as expected, the United States and its nationals were to file more than 3000 claims against Iran within the next two months, that the time periods for Iranian statements of defense must be established on the basis of the complexity of the issues of each case and the workload of the Tribunal, and that the time-limits so established then be extended on the request of Iranian respondents as their requests are evidently justifiable and needless of any further examination of their reasons for the request.'

90 days each for both sides unless one or both parties were prepared to expedite the pleadings. Yet there has been no impediment to the grant of additional extension requests if made by a claimant. The Tribunal has also granted the respondent the same number of extensions for the sake of symmetry with the claimant even in the absence of actual need of the respondent and despite objection of the claimant. Both governments have benefitted from this practice in their claims against each other in such a way that a number of cases are still in the process of written pleadings after 17 years.

The routine grant of four extensions of 90 days each for the consecutive written pleadings, while not provided in the Tribunal Rules, was necessitated by circumstances that were vital to the rights of the Iranian parties and operation of the Tribunal, especially in the earlier years. In the first year, the Tribunal also gradually scheduled submission of the statements of defence in the cases, so that the pressure on the respondents was to some extent distributed time wise. Despite the occasional dissents of some US judges[10] in the first or second year, the Tribunal has been rightly convinced of the necessity of the earlier extensions, hence the Tribunal's productive operation and contribution to the settlement of international disputes and international law in the subsequent years without any actual default proceeding by the Iranian parties. However, there is a question whether such a practice of multiple routine extensions should still continue in the same way after 17 years. The earlier situation and difficulties of the parties have been considerably diminished for some time by the resolution of the bulk of the cases, the end of the war imposed by Iraq and consequent Iranian civil strife. By now, the number of cases remaining in the course of written proceedings is only 16, though some of them are huge. I recognize that it is neither easy to suddenly stop this long practice nor prudent to deny justifiable extension requests; however, the Tribunal should also live up to the expectation that it will resolve the remaining cases with some reasonable date in mind.

2. PRE-HEARING CONFERENCES

Not foreseen in the UNCITRAL Rules, is a provision for holding pre-hearing conferences with the parties. The Tribunal has maintained unchanged the UNCITRAL Rules, Article 15 on General Provisions, dealing with hearings, while it has also added five notes thereto. Note 4 provides:

[10] H.M. Holtzmann, Dissent from Decision Granting Second Extension of Time for Filing Statement of Defence, *PepsiCo, Inc.* and *Zamzam Bottling Co. Azerbaijan, et al.*, Case No. 18, (9 July 1982), reprinted in 1 *Iran-US CTR*, p. 174; R.M. Mosk, Dissent from Order Extending Time for Filing Statement of Defence, *R.J. Reynolds Tobacco Co.* and *Iran, et al.*, Case No. 35 (5 April 1982), reprinted in 1 *Iran-US CTR*, p. 119; see also H.M. Holtzmann, Dissent from Decisions Refusing to Set Times Promptly for Filing Statements of Defence (8 July 1981), reprinted in *1 Iran-US CTR*, p. 178.

> 'The arbitral tribunal may make an order directing the arbitrating parties to appear for a pre-hearing conference. The pre-hearing conference will normally be held only after the Statement of Defence in the case has been received. The order will state the matters to be considered at the pre-hearing conference.'

The Internal Guidelines of the Tribunal, paragraph 2, as adopted on 28 January 1982 (Minutes of 34th Meeting, Ann. III) and remaining unchanged in subsequent revisions, provides a checklist of 11 topics that might be discussed at pre-hearing conferences held pursuant to the Tribunal Rules, Article 15, Note 4. The 'illustrative' list begins with clarification of the issues in the case, identification of the issues to be decided as preliminary questions, status of settlement discussions, desirability of exchange of further written pleadings, documentary evidence, witness lists, type and method of presentation of evidence, appointment of experts, translation of documents, fixing of a schedule for all this and the hearings. The list ends with 'other appropriate matters.' As both the concept of the pre-hearing conference and its list of topics were familiar to the Tribunal members, and the value of such meetings had already been recognized in international arbitration, Note 4 to Article 15 and paragraph 2 of the Internal Guidelines were adopted by the Tribunal without much difficulty. The list was a modest attempt at what 15 years later developed in UNCITRAL Notes on Organizing Arbitral Proceedings, published in June 1996,[11] which has been considered a crucial tool for every arbitration. The roots of Notes 9 to 17 of the UNCITRAL Notes are discernable in the Internal Guidelines of the Tribunal.

In Tribunal practice, however, the pre-hearing conferences were soon found of little use for various reasons, not only because of the sheer number of cases and the limitation of the Tribunal resources, but also due to the unfamiliarity of some of the parties with the factual and legal problems of their case. A pre-hearing conference is useful for planning the proceedings where each party is adequately familiar with his case. However, as the problem became more apparent, the Tribunal limited the holding of pre-hearing conferences to complex cases in the hope of more usefulness, and some time later, the pre-hearing conferences lost their momentum and fell in virtual disuse,[12] although by then the written pleadings indicated that the parties had thoroughly prepared their cases. While the earlier pre-hearing conferences were useful to the parties, especially in the beginning, in getting to know The Hague and the Tribunal, and in opening the way for a number of settlements, other pre-hearing conferences actually had turned into mini-hearings on preliminary questions, which the Tribunal would shortly decide by orders or interim awards following the conference – a practice which raised questions. After many years of disuse, in 1993 the Full Tribunal

[11] Reprinted in 9 *World Trade & Arbitration Materials* (No. 4, July 1997) p. 231.

[12] See Tribunal Annual Report for the period ending 30 June 1994, Annex XI, for the number of pre-hearing and hearings held in each year from the beginning of the Tribunal operation in 1981.

held a pre-hearing conference in an intergovernmental case,[13] aiming at the clarification of certain procedural issues. However, the schedule so established[14] soon fell apart by the Tribunal practice of routine extensions under Article 23 and by other requests not foreseen in the conference. Nevertheless, certainly pre-hearing conferences can be very helpful, even for the present remaining cases of the Tribunal, so long as both parties cooperate in a serious and efficient planning of the rest of the proceedings and maintain the time schedule so established.

3. AMENDMENT OF CLAIMS

Under Article 20 of the UNCITRAL Rules, '[d]uring the course of the arbitral proceedings either party may amend his claim or defence unless the arbitral tribunal considers it inappropriate to allow such amendment having regard to the delay in making it or prejudice to the other party or any other circumstances. However, a claim may not be amended in such a manner that the amended claim falls outside the scope of the arbitration clause or separate arbitration agreement.' The Tribunal revised the last sentence to read: 'However, a claim may not be amended in such a manner that it falls outside the jurisdiction of the arbitral tribunal.'

I am not aware of any problem arising from amendment of a 'defence.' Amendment of a defence has not been at issue in our practice, so far as I can recall. Principally, defence is an argument or evidence against a claim or counterclaim, whose presentation is usually subject to the schedule of the proceedings, although new legal arguments are normally allowed also at the hearing, which may result in inviting the adverse party to submit a post-hearing brief.

The revision made it clear that this Rule must be read in conjunction with the provision in Article III, paragraph 4, of the Claims Settlement Declarations, concerning the treaty deadline of 19 January 1982 for the submission of new claims and other jurisdictional limitations of the treaty. However, the Tribunal has not been able to maintain a uniform practice on this issue, which has been more dependent on the changing attitudes of the chairmen in the definition of the 'amendment' and 'new claim' for each case, than on giving the treaty deadline the precedence due over a Tribunal Rule which itself is expressly subject to the jurisdictional limitations of the treaty. This attitude is discernable in a number of cases, where the facts and circumstances are similar but the Tribunal rulings are different. One does not find even a reference to the treaty deadline of the Claims

[13] Full Tribunal Order of 30 December 1992 (Doc. 187), scheduling the pre-hearing in consolidated Cases Nos. A3, A8, A9, A14 & B61.

[14] Full Tribunal Order of 8 April 1993, in the cases just noted, establishing the schedule of the pleadings after the pre-hearing was held.

Settlement Declaration and its other jurisdictional limitations in *Rockwell*[15] and *Harris*,[16] that are often cited in favor of admission of requested amendments. Even quotation of Article 20 in those cases leaves out its last sentence.

However, in other cases, the Tribunal has adhered to the overriding provisions of its treaty mandate. For example in *Fazeli*, the Tribunal held:

> 'In his Statement of Claim the Claimant raised a claim for expropriation of parcels of land and a savings bank account. No reference was made to any ownership interest in the Fars and Khuzestan National Cement Co. The Request for Amendment thus concerns property different from those mentioned in the Statement of Claim and therefore does not relate to the initial Claim. As such, it cannot be considered an amendment to the Claim within the meaning of Article 20 of the Tribunal Rules, but is tantamount to the filing of a new claim after the jurisdictional deadline prescribed by the Claims Settlement Declaration. Cf., *St. Regis Paper Company* and *The Islamic Republic of Iran*, Award No. 291-10706-1 (29 Jan. 1987), para. 26, reprinted in 14 *Iran-US CTR*, pp. 86, 91 (substitution of Claimant tantamount to filing of a new claim). For this reason the Request for Amendment is denied.'[17]

It should be noted that *St. Regis*, cited in the above quotation, is also based on the same principle elaborated in a Full Tribunal decision in *Raymond International*.[18] In *Westinghouse*, when dealing with a counter-counterclaim presented as amendment to the claim and submitted in the Reply, the Tribunal held:

> 'It is true that Article 20 of the Tribunal Rules allows amendments of claim by a party in the absence of prejudice to the other party. Nevertheless, the Tribunal concludes that to allow an amendment in this instance would be inconsistent with the deadline for filing of claims with the Tribunal contained in Article III, paragraph 4, of the Claims Settlement Declaration.'[19]

While the jurisdictional limitations of the claims under the Claims Settlement Declaration, Article II and their time limitation in Article III, paragraph 4, do not apply to the submission of intergovernmental disputes as to the interpretation and performance of the Algiers Declarations under paragraph 17, I am not sure that for the amendment of the claim in such cases[20] the Tribunal would adopt even the flexibility and judicial economy that it asserted in *Rockwell* and *Harris*, where their application seems questionable in view of the treaty limitations.

[15] *Rockwell International Systems, Inc.* and *Islamic Republic of Iran* (*Ministry of National Defence*), Award No. 438-430-1, para. 71-76, reprinted in 23 *Iran-US CTR*, pp.165-167.

[16] *Harris International Telecommunications, Inc.* and *Islamic Republic of Iran, et al.*, Award No. 323-409-1, paras. 79-87, reprinted in 17 *Iran-US CTR*, pp. 55-57.

[17] Case No. 270, Order of 16 July 1991 (Doc. 90).

[18] Decision DEC 18-Ref 21-FT, p. 3 (8 Dec. 1982), reprinted in 1 *Iran-US CTR*, pp. 394- 395.

[19] *Westinghouse Electric Corporation* and *The Islamic Republic of Iran Air Force*, Award No. 579-389-2 (26 March 1997), para. 320, reprinted in – *Iran-US CTR* –.

[20] See, e.g., Full Tribunal Order of 18 March 1998, paras. 7&10 (Doc. 274) in consolidated Cases Nos. A3, A8, A9, A14 and B61.

4. BURDEN OF PROOF

The Tribunal Rules, Article 24, which does not deviate from the UNCITRAL Rules, provides in paragraph 1 that '[e]ach party shall have the burden of proving the facts relied on to support his claim or defence.' In this connection, it should also be noted that Article 25, paragraph 6 of the Tribunal Rules, maintained unchanged from the UNCITRAL Rules, provides that '[t]he arbitral tribunal shall determine the admissibility, relevance, materiality and weight of the evidence offered.' However, the rules of evidence are generally matters of substantive law, which for most of the issues before the Tribunal is international law and general principles of law, under Article V of the Claims Settlement Declaration, also incorporated in Article 33 of the Tribunal Rules.[21] The provision of Article 25, paragraph 6 of the UNCITRAL Rules is intended to avoid the intervention of the court of the place of arbitration in the course of the proceedings as well as other difficulties by the court of the place of enforcement of the foreign arbitral award. Thus, while evaluation of the evidence may be the province of the arbitrator, the rules by which he does so are subject to the applicable law.

Burden of proof in principle consists of two burdens, one of adducing evidence, satisfactory to the tribunal, of an asserted fact, and the other of persuading the tribunal that the alleged fact is true, that is, the probity or relevance, materiality and weight of the evidence. In this way it becomes important what standard of persuasion the Tribunal applies in accordance with international law or the general principles of law. However, in practice the Tribunal has generally not articulated the standard of persuasion it has required for most important issues. In various cases, the Tribunal has simply concluded from its interpretation of the evidence what in its view should be the fact, without reference to any standard of proof and justifications for it. Thus, an independent examination of the evidence, even as presented in some of the awards, may allow a different conclusion from what the award has reached. The prevailing practice seems to have, in effect, required the proof that the existence of the contested fact is more probable than its nonexistence, that is, the proof by a 'preponderance of evidence' rule of municipal law in civil cases. However, the proof by 'clear and convincing evidence,' requiring persuasive evidence that the truth of the contention is 'highly probable,' has been limited to the defence that the private claimant's evidence of ownership is not credible or authentic, as if it were a charge of fraud in municipal law by a person other than the victim of the fraud. The finding of a *prima facie* case has been made when a party has carried his principal burden of proof on the issue.

[21] Art. 33, para. 1, of the Tribunal Rules, replacing the UNCITRAL provision, provides that '[t]he arbitral tribunal shall decide all cases on the basis of respect for law, applying such choice of law rules and principles of commercial and international law as the arbitral tribunal determines to be applicable, taking into account relevant usages of the trade, contract provisions and changed circumstances.'

In some cases, the Tribunal has accepted a private claimant's statement alone as evidence of the international responsibility of the state,[22] or very easily and without any prior notice, has drawn adverse inference from the lack of presentation of documents assumed to be in the possession of the respondent state or related organs that might prove the claimant's case, usually in the absence of a prior order or even the claimant's request for the production of the document.[23]

In the cases before it, the Tribunal has made various presumptions for shifting the burden of proof to the other side, some of which may seem questionable. A presumption is an assumption of fact that the law allows to be made from another fact established in the action and yet it only shifts the burden of evidence and not also the burden of persuasion of the truth of the asserted fact, which remains upon the party on whom it was originally cast.[24] Inference is also a deduction of fact that may logically and reasonably be drawn only from another fact established in the action, provided that it leaves no room for reasonable doubt or at least the causal connection and essential link have been established between the two facts. A presumption or inference may not be made on the basis of another presumption or inference. It is also unclear where the presumption of non-responsibility of the state in international law and the presumption of legality of conduct – which should apply with even greater force to the acts of a government than those of a private person – have been taken into account by the Tribunal in deciding the private claims. The nature of factual and legal issues of most of these cases is similar to the case in *ELSI*[25] before a chamber of the International Court of Justice, while the treatment of the burden of proof, reasonings and conclusions between them seem quite different.

One area of discomfort has been the US parties allegations of their lack of access to the evidence left in Iran or to the records of the Iranian parties, while the Iranian parties have also complained of their lack of access to their own records left in the United States or to the records of US parties in that country. The Iranian parties have indicated that, as experience has shown, more often US parties have had better access to the favorable and unfavorable evidence and records in Iran than have the Iranian state parties, and that since the revolution did not occur overnight the US parties or their agents in Iran, both before and

[22] See, e.g., *Daley* and *The Islamic Republic of Iran*, Award No. 360-10514-1 (20 April 1988), para. 32, where the Tribunal granted the claim on the basis of the claimant's statement alone, stating that 'the Tribunal is satisfied that there is sufficient evidence to make a judgment on the possession of Mr. Daley's watch. A specific brand, Rolex, is mentioned and the Tribunal finds that it is probable that Mr. Daley, like the majority of business people, would possess and wear a watch in the normal course of events, as he stated in evidence that he was in the habit of doing.' Reprinted in 18 *Iran-US CTR*, pp. 232, 242.

[23] See, e.g., *Birnbaum* and *The Islamic Republic of Iran*, Award No. 549-967-2, paras. 80, 106, 115, 124, 139 (6 July 1993), reprinted in – *Iran-US CTR* –.

[24] See, e.g., US Federal Rules of Evidence, Rule 301.

[25] *Case concerning Elettronica Sicula S.p.A.* (*ELSI*) (*USA* v. *Italy*), Judgment of 20 July 1989, *ICJ Rep.* (1989) p. 15.

after the victory of the revolution, have mostly destroyed or taken out the evidence. In *Buckamier*,[26] the Tribunal attempted to bring a balance to only one aspect of this problem concerning the parties' evidentiary burden by incorporating in it a memorandum of the late Chairman Virally who had earlier presided over the hearing in the case. Thus, Chairman Virally's efforts were left for consideration by other members of the Tribunal. As cited in *Buckamier*,[27] he noted that although a US party who departed from Iran under the revolutionary conditions might be considered to have left behind in Iran some documentation that might have proved his case, the Tribunal must be extremely careful not to expose Iranian parties to claims not properly evidenced. This caution, however prudent, has been frequently overshadowed by other factors.

The claim granted by the Tribunal in *Williams*[28] subsequently turned out to be bogus. As found in a US court proceeding, certain individuals in the United States had used the identity of a dead Mr. Gordon Williams, and by an elaborate scheme, including the innocent participation of a Dutch law firm, had procured the award.[29] The fiasco was uncovered only because the 'award creditors,' having disagreed on the portion of their individual 'reward' and each having asked the Federal Reserve Bank of New York for the whole amount on behalf of Mr. Gordon Williams, the Bank applied to the US court to decide to whom it should pay the amount. The Federal Reserve Bank distributes the awarded sums to US claimants, which it receives from Iran's Security Account in accordance with the instruction of the Tribunal in each case. While the awarded sum has eventually been returned to the Security Account pursuant to the US court order in that proceeding, the Tribunal Award in *Williams* remains a clear proof that the strategy of circumstantial evidence employed by private parties against a government can easily lead to abuse of the Tribunal process, which in this case was discovered only because the beneficiaries were subsequently engaged in a dispute and were unwise enough to approach the Federal Reserve Bank separately for the whole amount of the awarded sum.

In *Ram International*,[30] the Tribunal in 1983 awarded the claim on the basis of a document which was found not authentic in an award rendered in 1991 in another case brought by the same claimants.[31] Both claims had been filed at the

[26] *Buckamier* and *The Islamic Republic of Iran, et al.*, Award No. 528-941-3, para. 67 (6 March 1992), reprinted in 28 *Iran-US CTR*, pp. 53, 74-76.

[27] *Idem.*

[28] *Williams* and *Islamic Republic of Iran, Bank Sepah, and Bank Mellat*, Award No. 342-187-3 (18 December 1987), reprinted in 17 *Iran-US CTR*, p. 269.

[29] *Federal Reserve Bank of New York* v. *Gordon Williams, Husband & Harris, Leonard H. W. van Sandick and Loeff & van der Ploeg* (SDNY 1989), reprinted in Iranian Assets Litigation Reporter, pp. 17185-17201 (28 April 1989).

[30] *Ram International Industries, Inc. et al.* and *The Air Force of the Islamic Republic of Iran*, Award No. 67-148-1 (19 Aug. 1983), *reprinted in*, 3 *Iran-US CTR*, p. 203.

[31] *Ram International Industries, Inc., et al.* and *The Islamic Republic of Iran, et al.*, Award No. 511-147-1, paras. 30-31 (9 May 1991), reprinted in 26 *Iran-US CTR*, pp. 228, 230-240.

same time, but had been given different priorities in the scheduling of the proceedings by the Tribunal and thus the awards in the two cases were rendered at different times and under different compositions of the Tribunal. In both cases, the validity of purchase orders and payments therefor depended on the extension of the stated delivery dates. In both cases, the claimants had presented a letter, dated 15 February 1978 on Iranian Air Force stationary, which extended all delivery dates to 30 June 1980 and was signed on behalf of the Air Force Purchasing Mission in New York. And similarly, in both cases, the respondent had questioned the authenticity of the letter, while in the first one it had been unable to present evidence to substantiate it. As observed in the second case, the Tribunal in the first case 'accepted the extension of the delivery dates until 30 June 1980 and based its conclusions on this fact.'[32] But based on a variety of evidence, including the 'convincing' testimony of the alleged signatory of the letter that it 'is not authentic,' in the second case, the Tribunal found that it 'cannot rely on the letter as a basis for granting the claim.'[33] Consequently, the respondent sought revision of the earlier award. But in a decision on revision the Tribunal – as composed in the earlier case, except for the Iranian judge – found it difficult to acknowledge that the document was a decisive factor in its award.[34] It is clear that in the earlier case the Tribunal had given undue credence to the claimants' proffered evidence without requiring them to present the original letter for examination by the respondent who had questioned the authenticity of the letter, despite the fact that the authentication rule has been generally recognized[35] and is commonplace in most national legal systems. It is also obvious that in the absence of the second case, the lack of authenticity of the basic document would not have been discovered.

However, the Tribunal efforts in the allocation of the burden of proof in two areas, other than the one in *Buckamier* referred to above, are noteworthy. On the proof of US nationality of corporate claimants, the Tribunal in the first year of its operation identified in *Flexi-Van*[36] the type of evidence it required in order to find a *prima facie* case, shifting the burden of rebuttal evidence to the respondent, so that from the totality of such evidence it would draw reasonable inferences and reach conclusions as to the US nationality of the claimant. Despite a well-reas-

[32] *Idem*, para. 30.

[33] *Idem*, para. 31.

[34] *Ram International Industries, Inc. et al.* and *The Air Force of the Islamic Republic of Iran*, Decision No. DEC 118-148-1 (20 Jan. 1994), reprinted in – *Iran-US CTR* –.

[35] The Tribunal has directed production of original documents for inspection, but it has done so under Article 24(3) of the Tribunal Rules concerning production of documents when it has been persuaded of its necessity. The rule of verification of authenticity of evidence obtained out of court has also been adopted in Rule 89(E) of Rules of Procedure and Evidence of the International Tribunal for the Former Yugoslavia.

[36] *Flexi-Van Leasing, Inc.* and *The Islamic Republic of Iran*, Order of 15 Dec. 1982, Case No. 36, Chamber 1, reprinted in 1 *Iran-US CTR*, p. 455.

oned dissenting opinion in that case, which I also shared, the majority opinion at least provided a reasoned guideline as to the type of evidence it required, although it did not elaborate on the burden of persuasion or on the type of rebuttal evidence.

In connection with the allocation of the burden of evidence and persuasion concerning the meaning and scope of Iranian land legislation that allegedly resulted in the expropriation of the claimant's property, the Tribunal in *Hakim*[37] has recently cited an acceptable passage from *Mohtadi*,[38] that

> 'The Tribunal normally would view the responsibility for providing a complete and persuasive explanation of Iranian legislation as falling upon the Respondent. This is because the respondent is surely better positioned than a claimant to explain the meaning and effect of its own laws. Especially where the legislation is confusing and its scope ambiguous, as in the case of the Lands Grant Act, the Respondent may not confine itself to the mere assertion that particular legislation does not apply.
>
> On the other hand, it falls to the Claimant to demonstrate with clarity the facts that bring his property within the scope of the legislation that allegedly expropriated his property. Where, as here, there is no evidence of physical interference attributable to the Respondent ... the Claimant must take particular care to demonstrate that the subject property is, as a factual matter, of the type apparently covered by the Lands Grant Act. In that event the burden would shift to the Respondent to demonstrate that the scope of the Act was in fact narrower than the Claimant suggests.'

It would have been helpful to all concerned if in the course of preparing its Rules of Procedure and Internal Guidelines the Tribunal had also drafted a set of rules or guidelines on evidence in order to give a sense of uniformity and predictability to its practice in various cases. Tribunal's attempt at proof of United States nationality of corporate claimants in *Flexi-Van*[39] was helpful and well received.

5. PRODUCTION OF DOCUMENTS

The Tribunal Rules, Article 24, which has been maintained unchanged from the UNCITRAL Rules, provides in paragraph 3 that '[a]t any time during the arbitral proceedings the arbitral tribunal may require the parties to produce documents, exhibits or other evidence within such a period of time as the tribunal shall determine.'

[37] *Hakim* and *The Government of the Islamic Republic of Iran*, Award No. 587-953-2, para. 82 (2 July 1998), reprinted in – *Iran-US CTR* –.

[38] *Mohtadi, et al.* and *Islamic Republic of Iran*, Award No. 573-271-3, paras. 82-83 (2 Dec. 1996), reprinted in – *Iran-US CTR* –.

[39] *Flexi-Van Leasing*, Inc. and *The Islamic Republic of Iran*, Order of 15 Dec. 1982, Case No. 36, Chamber 1, reprinted in 1 *Iran-US CTR*, p. 455.

In practice, the Tribunal has not found the occasion to apply this provision for the stated authority of its own, perhaps because the parties have frequently taken advantage of this provision to request the Tribunal to direct the other party to produce documents favorable to the requesting party. It is obvious that such a provision does not grant a party the right of discovery. A party request for production of documents may be acceptable under this Rule by the Tribunal in order to strike a balance between the duty of a party to prove the asserted facts and the duty of the other party to cooperate with the Tribunal in resolving the dispute without necessarily carrying the burden of his adversary.

Thus, in practice the Tribunal has required that the request for the production of documents must identify the documents with sufficient specificity and demonstrate the prior due diligence of the applicant to acquire the document independently, or from other sources. More recent practice has also required demonstration of the relevance of the document to the party's case to prove or disprove an assertion in dispute,[40] and that the document does not contain any admission, proposal or statement of a similar nature prepared for or used in settlement negotiations of the case, or that it has not been generated in the preparation of the other party's case.[41] The sanctity and protection of efforts at amicable settlement of disputes do not allow divulgence of matters of negotiation, positions, admissions of facts or terms of settlement, whether communicated in the course of negotiation or prepared for the purpose of negotiation. Similarly, the sanctity of a party's right of defence does not allow a tribunal to require the party to present its own internal studies made in the preparation of its case. This is of course different from the production of surveys made in the performance of a contractual or treaty obligation, especially before the arbitral proceedings are initiated.[42] However, when the survey has promised confidentiality to third parties, the Tribunal has allowed deletion of that part of the document. But if a party's defense rests on its own confidential evidence, which it does not wish to share, the Tribunal has allowed the claim as *prima facie* established.[43]

In many cases the Tribunal has not actually directed a party to produce the requested document, but has stated that the party may consider including the document in its next basic written pleading and evidence or comment on the

[40] Orders of 31 July 1997 and 16 September 1997, para. 2, *Gulf Associates, Inc.* and *Islamic Republic of Iran, et al.*, Case No. 385 (Docs. 274 & 292) Chamber 2; Order of 12 August 1993, para. 1, *Malekzadeh* and *Islamic Republic of Iran*, Case No. 356 (Doc. 103) Chamber 1.

[41] Order of 26 September 1997, para. 3, *Lerner* and *Islamic Republic of Iran*, Case No. 242, Chamber 2. For a rule of customary international law in this domain see *Case concerning Maritime Delimitation and Territorial Questions between Qatar and Bahrain* (*Qatar* v. *Bahrain*) Jurisdiction and Admissibility, Judgment of 1 July 1994, para. 40, *ICJ Rep.* (1994) pp. 125-126.

[42] Full Tribunal Order of 24 May 1994, Case A15 (I:D & I:H), Doc. 1231, para. 4.

[43] *Atomic Energy Organization of Iran* and *United States*, Award No. 132-B7-1 (8 June 1984), reprinted in 6 *Iran-US CTR*, pp. 141, 145.

request. In some cases, the Tribunal has directed a party to produce the document or comment on the request. Rarely has the Tribunal given notice of adverse inference in the order directing production of the requested document. In the absence of a clear indication as to the consequence, it is obvious that misunderstandings can arise for the party expected to produce the document, especially in the first type of orders. In international arbitrations involving parties from different legal cultures and backgrounds, it is helpful for a tribunal to be clearer in its directions. Diplomatic language should not allow misunderstandings or vagueness.

As this Rule entitles the Tribunal '[a]t any time during the arbitral proceedings' to direct a party to produce evidence, it has also been misused by requesting parties for getting in late evidence they already had for some time but for lack of due diligence or foresight did not present in time with their pleadings. If the Tribunal orders the production of such a document the adverse party will either produce it or explain its inability to locate it, which in effect entitles the requesting party itself to present the document as 'only recently found.' In such a situation the Tribunal would naturally not be looking for evidence of the date when the requesting party actually found the document it allegedly did not have before. Sometimes a party might withhold a basic document throughout the course of submission of its written pleadings and evidence, thereby prompting the other party to take certain positions, while before the hearing it presents the basic document by way of a production of document request, as just indicated. While these abusive tactics are played by one party against the other at any stage of the proceedings, they are obviously more prejudicial when the request is made after the written pleadings and evidence are closed, that is, within the 2 or 3 months before the hearing, or when the document is presented by the requesting party at the hearing and characterized as 'recently found.'[44] While it may not be easy for the Tribunal to detect these abuses by private claimants, it has not attempted to do so, even as to the timing of the requests. It is obvious that such requests should principally be limited to the course of the written pleading and evidence of the requesting party, as the requested evidence is supposed to enable it to present its case, including its rebuttal evidence, in that phase and under the schedule of written pleadings established by the Tribunal in advance.

CONCLUSION

The application of the Tribunal Rules should be a rich source of jurisprudence for international arbitration, whether under UNCITRAL Rules or other arbitration rules, despite certain reservations one may have concerning the Tribunal practice.

[44] See, e.g., *Hakim* and *The Islamic Republic of Iran*, Award No. 567-953-2 (2 July 1998), paras. 5-16, reprinted in – *Iran-US CTR* –.

UNCITRAL Rules of 1976, like the International Law Commission's Model Rules on Arbitral Procedure of 1958, could have fallen in abeyance had they not been adopted and developed in the arbitration of the Iran-United States Claims Tribunal. I doubt if many people even knew of the UNCITRAL Rules before 1981, except those who had worked on them in the UNCITRAL Commission, or those who had a glance at them for educational purposes, such as myself. The UNCITRAL Model Law on International Commercial Arbitration of 1985 was drafted with our earlier experience of the UNCITRAL Rules very much in mind. This has similarly been the case not only with the preparation of the UNCITRAL Notes of 1996, but also in the drafting by the Permanent Court of Arbitration of four sets of Optional Rules, in which I was privileged to participate. These Optional Rules have closely followed the UNCITRAL Arbitration Rules. They are: (1) Optional Rules for Arbitrating Disputes between Two States (1992), (2) Optional Rules for Arbitrating Disputes between Two Parties of which only one is a State (1993), (3) Optional Rules for Arbitration Involving International Organizations and States (1996), and (4) Optional Rules for Arbitration between International Organizations and Private Persons.

The fact that the records of our decisions, from the revision of the UNCITRAL Rules to our procedural orders and awards, are public and accessible, even at WESTLAW, makes it possible for users of international arbitration of every kind to share our experience or avoid our shortcomings, some of which I have noted above.

THE HAGUE AS A VENUE FOR COMMERCIAL ARBITRATION – VENUE AND INTERIM MEASURES: A DUTCH PERSPECTIVE

J.L.W. Sillevis Smitt*

INTRODUCTION

The Hague is where the Dutch Government has its seat. The Dutch Parliament (the States-General) is housed in The Hague. The present Queen is living and working in The Hague. However The Hague is not the capital of the Netherlands within the legal meaning of the word. According to our Constitution the King is sworn in and inaugurated in the capital Amsterdam ('de hoofdstad Amsterdam'), as soon as the King has assumed the royal power (See Art. 32 of the Constitution of the Netherlands).

There is a lot of history behind this, on which we can not dwell this afternoon. It is however a clear example, that the law may say one thing, whereas reality is quite a different thing.

The same is true for commercial arbitration. Under Dutch arbitration law the place of arbitration is a determining factor for many legal aspects of the arbitration. It is not required, however, that the arbitration in its actual aspects, such as the hearing, the inspection of certain objects in dispute, the hearing of witnesses or the deliberation of the arbitral tribunal, is carried out at the very place of arbitration.

The law is very flexibile in this respect for all people involved in an arbitration. It requires that each arbitration should have a place and that the arbitral award should make clear, where it was made. It does not require, however, that that is the place, where it all has happened.

THE PLACE OF ARBITRATION IN DUTCH ARBITRATION LAW

Under Dutch law the place of arbitration is determined by the parties and in absence of such determination by the arbitral tribunal (See Art. 1037 Code of Civ. proc.). The law further says, that the place of arbitration also establishes the place where the award shall be made. Furthermore: if the place of arbitration has not been determined, the place mentioned in the award as the place where the

* Advocate of the Supreme Court of the Netherlands; President of the Netherlands Arbitration Institute, Rotterdam.

W.P. Heere (Ed.), International Law and The Hague's 750th Anniversary

award was made shall be deemed to be also the place of arbitration (See Art. 1037, par. 2 Code of Civ. proc.).

The law refers to the place of arbitration in quite a number of provisions, most of which need not to be discussed this afternoon. Two major consequences of the place of arbitration, however, should be mentioned:
1) the place of arbitration determines the applicability of the main provisions of Dutch arbitration law;
2) the identity of the place of arbitration and the place where the award was made, has an overriding importance for the application of the New York Convention on the recognition and enforcement of foreign arbitral awards not in the least for the territorial reservation that many contracting states to the Convention have made as to its applicability (See Art. I of the Conv.).

Ad 1) *Applicability of Dutch Arbitration Law*
Dutch arbitration law does not distinguish between domestic and international arbitrations in the manner as, for instance, the French arbitration law is doing. The distinction Dutch law is making is purely territorial: the main part of the provisions, put together in a separate title (Title I of Book 4 of the Code of Civ. proc.) are applicable to arbitration in the Netherlands; a separate set of provisions are applicable to arbitration outside the Netherlands.

This territorial distinction makes the place of arbitration of overriding importance. The territorial distinction of Dutch arbitration law also entails, that parties, who are not domiciled or actually residing within the Netherlands, may have their arbitration in the Netherlands. In order to obtain that result they have to determine, that the place of arbitration is in the Netherlands, more particularly in a certain city of this country.

Ad 2) *The New York Arbitration Convention 1958*
Very briefly stated, the New York Arbitration Convention is about the enforcement of arbitral awards made in the territory of one contracting state, in the jurisdiction (that is: territory) of another contracting state. In other words, the place of arbitration, more specifically the place where the award was made, determines whether the winning party in an arbitration may be in the position to enforce the award outside the territory of the place of origin.

INTERIM OR PROVISIONAL MEASURES

Many a dispute involves the need of one party to ask for provisional measures in order to prevent further damage or a further breach of its alleged rights.

In civil and commercial disputes the President of a District Court in the Netherlands has jurisdiction to make an order in summary proceedings (*kort geding*). This forum is widely used in the Netherlands for settling all sorts of disputes which, somehow, have an urgent aspect. Whereas most Presidents of a

District Court have not been reluctant to assume jurisdiction in these disputes, it has become common practice in certain fields (such as infringement disputes in the domain of industrial property) to use the summary proceedings in our country as a means of reaching a definite solution without bringing the case before the full tribunal for a judgment on – what may be called – the merits of the case. Even the Dutch Supreme Court has rendered quite a few judgments in summary proceedings, which have become important precedents for the legal practice as a whole.

When Dutch arbitration law was modernised in 1986, the legislator has given ample attention to the need for provisional measures in cases, where the parties have concluded an arbitral agreement. Whereas as a rule a valid arbitral agreement entails that the ordinary courts have no jurisdiction over the dispute, it was considered proper to maintain the jurisdiction of the President of the District Court, if one of the parties is in need of an order for provisional measures with regard to a dispute that has to be submitted to arbitration. The jurisdiction of the President therefore has been maintained, with a proviso however, which constitutes one of the extraordinary and not widely-known features of Dutch arbitration law.

SUMMARY ARBITRAL PROCEEDINGS

The new aspect is that the parties, in their arbitration agreement or in a later agreement, may empower the arbitral tribunal or its chairman to render an award in summary proceedings to the same extent as the jurisdictional power of a President of a District Court. In the event that, notwithstanding such an agreement, the case is brought before the President of the District Court in summary proceedings, the President may declare to have no jurisdiction and refer the case to the summary arbitral proceedings if a party invokes the existence of the said agreement.

In other words: in case the arbitral tribunal or its chairman has the power to render an award in summary proceedings, this in itself does not exclude the jurisdiction of the President of the District Court. He may in his discretion take the case or refer it to the arbitral tribunal. It will all depend on the circumstances of the case (See Art. 1051 Code of Civ.proc.). One of these circumstances may be, that the arbitral tribunal has not yet been appointed, whereas the claimant-party is in urgent need of an order for provisional measures.

The second new aspect is, that an award rendered in summary arbitral proceedings shall be regarded as an arbitral award, to which the provisions of a final arbitral award are applicable.

This implies in fact that on an arbitral award, rendered in summary proceedings, an *exequatur* may be obtained from the ordinary courts, so that it can be enforced in the same manner as a final arbitral award.

Whereas an arbitral award rendered in summary proceeding may be considered as binding within the meaning of the New York Arbitration Convention, such an award may also be enforced outside the Netherlands.

It is a well known problem in international commercial arbitration, that an order of an arbitral tribunal for interim measures can neither be enforced under the applicable domestic arbitration law nor under the New York Convention, because it is not considered to be (finally) binding. By explicitly stating, that an award rendered in arbitral summary proceedings is regarded as a final award, the Dutch *Arbitration Act* of 1986 has solved this problem.

ARBITRAL SUMMARY PROCEEDINGS IN PRACTICE

The largest arbitration institution in the Netherlands (*Raad van Arbitrage voor de Bouwnijverheid*) which administers arbitrations on construction disputes, has forthwith in 1986 adopted the arbitral summary proceedings in its rules.

The Netherlands Arbitration Institute originally did not opt for arbitral summary proceedings in its rules. After a decade the Institute has changed its mind. There were clear indications from the arbitrating parties, that they would like to make formal summary proceedings part of the NAI arbitration process. Consequently the NAI has changed its rules. As from 1 January 1998 arbitral summary proceedings are part of the arbitration rules.

THE NAI ARBITRAL SUMMARY PROCEEDINGS

The NAI Rules provide for summary proceedings in a double manner:

a) even before an arbitration on the merits has been started, a claimant party may apply for summary proceedings. In that case an arbitral tribunal is appointed forthwith by the NAI, consisting of a sole arbitrator. Thus the inevitable loss of time in appointing the arbitral tribunal on the merits is avoided. An arbitral award in summary proceedings may be rendered within the same time or even quicker than an order from the President of a District Court.

b) As from the moment, that the appointment of the arbitral tribunal on the merits has been conveyed to the parties, this tribunal has the power to render an award in summary proceedings. It may do so on a simple written application by one of the parties.

By this twofold jurisdiction the parties to a NAI arbitration may resort to arbitral summary proceedings right from the beginning of the dispute until the final award on the merits has been rendered, with the proviso that the arbitration takes place in the Netherlands. Consequently, the arbitral awards in summary proceedings may be endowed with an *exequatur* in this country and abroad. That is the Dutch perspective.

THE PERMANENT COURT OF ARBITRATION, THE LEGAL CAPITAL OF THE WORLD, AND THE UNCITRAL ARBITRATION RULES

P.J.H. Jonkman*

When I gave the organisers of this conference the title of my intervention, I intended to start by explaining that the Permanent Court of Arbitration came into being as a direct result of the First International Peace Conference, held in The Hague in 1899, and was therefore present at the birth of The Hague as the 'Legal Capital of the World.' But I realise that the time attributed to me this afternoon will not allow me to dwell on this subject in sufficient detail.

Therefore, I shall immediately come to the main subject of our panel: The Hague as a venue for commercial arbitration. In part because of its history as host to the two International Peace Conferences, The Hague has traditionally been perceived primarily as a venue for the resolution of disputes of a *public* international law nature: it was for this purpose that Andrew Carnegie saw fit to endow the 'Palace of Peace' which today houses the Permanent Court of Arbitration (PCA) and the International Court of Justice (ICJ).

The modern-day link between The Hague and international commercial arbitration can be found in the commercial arbitration rules drawn up by the United Nations Commission on International Trade Law (UNCITRAL) in 1976. These rules were developed for the settlement, on an *ad hoc* basis (that is, without the involvement of an arbitral institution) of disputes arising from international commercial transactions. In spite of this, the UNCITRAL Rules have been adapted by a number of arbitral institutions worldwide to serve as institutional rules for arbitration, not only in purely commercial disputes, but also, as in the case of the Iran-United States Claims Tribunal and the Permanent Court of Arbitration, for use in disputes between two states, between a state and a private party, and disputes involving international organizations.

I shall focus today particularly on two aspects of the PCA's contribution to The Hague as a venue for international commercial arbitration: first, the special task of the Secretary-General of the PCA under the UNCITRAL Arbitration Rules and second, the prospect of extending the services of the PCA to the administration of purely commercial arbitrations conducted under the UNCITRAL Rules.

* Secretary-General of the Permanent Court of Arbitration.

W.P. Heere (Ed.), International Law and The Hague's 750th Anniversary

THE SPECIAL TASK OF THE SECRETARY-GENERAL OF THE PCA UNDER THE UNCITRAL ARBITRATION RULES

Because the UNCITRAL Arbitration Rules were developed to provide for non-administered arbitration the drafters of these Rules invented the notion of the 'appointing authority', for the purpose of preventing stagnation in the appointment of arbitrators and putting in place an authority to rule on challenges to arbitrators. They recommended that parties agreeing to apply the UNCITRAL Arbitration Rules, also agree on a person or institution that could act as the 'appointing authority' in the event an arbitrator is not appointed by the party or persons entitled to do so.

For instance, if an arbitral tribunal cannot be constituted because one of the parties refuses to appoint an arbitrator, because the two party-appointed arbitrators are unable to select a third arbitrator, or because there is no agreement between the parties on the choice of an arbitrator, the appointing authority may be requested to make the appointment.

However, it often happens that parties in dispute have not included in their arbitration agreement the name of an appointing authority, either as an oversight, or because they could not agree on this matter. The UNCITRAL Arbitration Rules provide that if there is no appointing authority at the moment that one is needed, either party may request the Secretary-General of the PCA to designate such authority. Since the adoption of the UNCITRAL Rules in 1976, approximately one hundred of these requests have reached the Secretary-General, in a great variety of cases, 75 % of which came after 1992.

The International Bureau of the PCA is often asked how we proceed to deal with requests for the designation of an appointing authority, and whether we have a short list of potential appointing authorities from which to chose. The UNCITRAL Arbitration Rules themselves do not provide any guidelines for the Secretary-General on how to perform his task. This sometimes leads to uncertainty about the Secretary-General's role under the Rules.

In the absence of express guidance from the drafters of the UNCITRAL Rules, there are two main aspects of the designation of appointing authorities for which the International Bureau has had to develop its own practice:

1) how to proceed after having received a request for designation of an appointing authority?
2) how to select the most appropriate appointing authority in each case?

Ad 1) How to proceed after having received a request for the designation of an appointing authority?

We start from the presumption that the Secretary-General of the PCA is in principle obliged to designate an appointing authority, as soon as possible, whenever a request for such designation seems justified. Therefore, the Secretary-General must first determine whether he is *prima facie* competent to act. In order to establish the Secretary-General's competence we examine the following factors:
a) the existence of a written arbitration agreement containing a reference to the UNCITRAL Arbitration Rules;
b) the service of a notice of arbitration by the claimant on the respondent, in accordance with Article 3 of the Rules;
c) evidence of compliance with the procedural requirements of the UNCITRAL Rules, including the prescribed time-limits.

When the result of this enquiry indicates that the Secretary-General is competent to proceed with the designation of an appointing authority, the International Bureau generally first solicits the comments of the other party, to be made within a certain period of time, usually two to four weeks, dependent on the respondent's accessibility. This is not intended to invite any jurisdictional objections or substantive arguments that the other party may wish to make: this is the undisputed realm of the arbitral tribunal under the UNCITRAL Rules. Our experience reveals, however, that a communication from the Secretary-General often has the effect of causing a previously recalcitrant party to cooperate in the appointment process. If a party is willing to make the delinquent appointment within a reasonable period of time, this is preferable to the appointment of the arbitrator by an appointing authority, because it is less costly, and because the tribunal will thus be constituted in a more balanced fashion, in accordance with the spirit of the UNCITRAL Arbitration Rules. In those cases in which the other party raises legitimate objections to the request for designation of an appointing authority, other than those relating to jurisdiction or substantive matters, we discuss the matter with the parties and subsequently decide whether we should proceed with the designation.

There have been several requests submitted to the Secretary-General in which the determination of the existence of a written arbitration agreement containing a reference to the UNCITRAL Arbitration Rules has not been straightforward. When the requesting party relies on a contractual arbitration clause, it is clear that the Secretary-General is not expected to scrutinize the clause with respect to its validity. Article 21(1) of the UNCITRAL Rules makes it abundantly clear that the determination of the jurisdiction of the arbitral tribunal, including a decision on any objections as to the existence or validity of the arbitration agreement, rests with the arbitral tribunal itself.

It is less clear what the scope of scrutiny should be in situations involving subcontracts or related contracts, or when a party asserts that an exchange of correspondence between the parties constitutes an UNCITRAL arbitration agreement. On the one hand, in the absence of a clear, express agreement, the Secretary-General might be justifiably reluctant to proceed with the designation, because the Secretary-General is competent to become involved only if the UNCITRAL Rules apply. On the other hand, one could argue that the very purpose of the Secretary-General's role under the UNCITRAL Rules is to ensure that an arbitral tribunal comes into existence, so that the determination of the existence of the arbitration agreement can be made by the body best-suited to doing so: the arbitral tribunal.

Another case in which the Secretary-General finds it necessary to interpret the UNCITRAL Rules involves a party's attempt to seek an appointing authority even before the arbitration process has actually began, as there is reason to expect that the other party will not cooperate in the appointment of arbitrators, and no appointing authority has been agreed upon.The Secretary-General of the PCA is, in my view, not entitled to grant such a request, because the designation of an appointing authority is meant as an emergency instance.To seek designation of an appointing authority before the commencing of an arbitration would be contrary to the sequence of events provided in the Rules.

Ad 2) How to select the most appropriate appointing authority in each case?

The International Bureau of the PCA does not apply a short list of potential appointing authorities. Over the years we have designated a considerable number (approximately 30) of different appointing authorities. There are some institutions or persons that we have designated more than once, because they seemed to qualify for this task in more than one situation, and have proven they could fulfil this function well. But each case is different and therefore there is no ready-made decision for any of them.

The main objective of the Secretary-General of the PCA is to find for each situation an appointing authority that would reasonably be acceptable to both parties and that is in a position to appoint a qualified arbitrator in the case at hand.

The fact that there is no provision in the UNCITRAL Arbitration Rules which allows parties to refuse to accept or challenge the appointing authority designated by the Secretary-General of the PCA, requires that the selection of this authority be done with utmost care.

There are a number of factors to be taken into consideration in this connection. As a rule the appointing authority should not have the nationality of either party, unless there is a good reason to deviate from this rule. Other important elements for the choice of an appointing authority include: the place of arbitration, the law of the contract, the language in which the arbitration is to be conducted, the subject matter of the dispute, the amount in dispute, the accessibility of the appointing authority to the parties, the immediate availability of the appointing authority to act and the reputation of the appointing authority.

We have examined the question whether there should be two, or even three types of appointing authorities: one whose task it is to appoint a 'second arbitrator' (i.e., the arbitrator that should have been appointed by one of the parties, usually the respondent), another whose task it is to appoint the presiding arbitrator, and yet another who can be called upon to decide on a challenge, pursuant to Article 12 of the Rules. Article 12 makes it clear that the appointing authority, even if it did not in fact make any of the initial appointments, has the power to decide on the challenge. It is less clear whether, for example, the appointing authority designated for the purpose of appointing a second arbitrator is automatically empowered to appoint the presiding arbitrator, in the event the first two arbitrators fail to reach agreement. It could be argued that the appointing authority that is requested to appoint the second arbitrator should be someone who particularly has the confidence of the party that failed to appoint this arbitrator, whereas the appointing authority that is requested to appoint the presiding arbitrator should have the equal confidence of all parties.

We have come to the conclusion that the UNCITRAL Arbitration Rules provide for only one type of appointing authority, impartial to and trusted by all parties. The appointing authority should be qualified to appoint any of the arbitrators and, if necessary, to decide on challenges. In other words, if the Secretary-General of the PCA is requested to designate an appointing authority for the purpose of appointing the second arbitrator, he should take into account that the same appointing authority may also be called upon to appoint the presiding arbitrator or decide on a challenge.

EXTENDING THE SERVICES OF THE PCA TO THE ADMINISTRATION OF PURELY COMMERCIAL ARBITRATIONS CONDUCTED UNDER THE UNCITRAL RULES

I shall now address the prospect of extending the services of the PCA to the administration of purely commercial arbitrations conducted under the UNCITRAL Rules.

Thus far, the PCA has limited itself to dealing with disputes in which at least one state or an intergovernmental organization is involved. This limitation corresponds with the purpose for which the PCA was created: to obviate, as far as possible, recourse to force in relations between states. The decision, in 1935, that the Hague Conventions permitted the PCA to make its staff and facilities available to arbitrations in which one of the parties was not a state, opened the door to the resolution of disputes of a more commercial character, and the PCA adopted specific rules for these types of proceedings in 1962 and again in 1993.

The provision in the UNCITRAL Arbitration Rules for recourse to the Secretary-General of the PCA in obtaining an appointing authority, and the increasing number of such requests, has brought the PCA even further into the sphere of international commercial arbitration. And, for the past ten years, the International Bureau has frequently put its premises and staff in the Peace Palace at the disposal of commercial arbitration tribunals. We usually call these tribunals 'guest tribunals', by which we mean that they do not operate under the auspices and responsibility of the PCA, but just use our facilities. The Bureau helps them to organize their hearings at the Peace Palace. Half a dozen tribunals a year make use of this possibility.

It may prove to be a relatively short step for the International Bureau of the PCA from designating appointing authorities under the UNCITRAL Arbitration Rules (and, in an increasing number of cases, having the Secretary-General asked to serve directly as appointing authority), and from hosting 'guest tribunals' in the Peace Palace, to providing whatever administrative services an UNCITRAL arbitration tribunal may require. There is no real reason why the International Bureau could not do so now, and if a party were to show up at the Peace Palace tomorrow and show us a contractual clause to that effect, it is likely that we would give effect to it. The more serious question is whether the PCA should encourage the use of such services and such clauses, for example, by developing and distributing its own guidelines for administering international commercial arbitration under the UNCITRAL Arbitration Rules.

I am very interested in hearing the views of my colleagues in the panel and of the audience on this question. Madam Chairman, thank you for giving me the opportunity to express some views on the role of the Secretary-General of the PCA under the UNCITRAL Arbitration Rules, and to submit to the members of the panel and the audience the question of whether the PCA should extend its jurisdiction to disputes between private parties.

The PCA is delighted, not only to be the corner stone of The Hague as the Legal Capital of the World, but also to contribute to The Hague becoming a venue for commercial arbitration.

THE REGULATION OF INTERNATIONAL TRADE

DISPUTE RESOLUTION IN THE WTO

James Cameron*

The WTO Agreement ushers in a new era in decision making by the parties and the resolution of disputes. The Dispute Settlement Understanding (DSU) which is Annex 2 of the WTO Agreement creates a Dispute Panel as well as an Appellate Body (AB) to adjudicate on trade disputes between the parties. Under the DSU procedures, if consultations fail to resolve a dispute within 60 days after a complaint has been made, a WTO member may request the establishment of a panel to examine its complaint. The establishment of a panel results in the compulsory transference of jurisdiction to the Dispute Settlement Body (DSB). This is in contrast to disputes made before the International Court of Justice that requires that all parties to the dispute submit to the court's jurisdiction.

Disputes at the WTO are handled expeditiously, with a panel report resolving the dispute issued within a relatively short time of receiving the parties' submissions. Panel procedures are stipulated to conclude a maximum of 6 to 9 months after the commencement of the dispute. Rulings are made within one year from the date of the establishment of the panel. A subsequent appeal of the panel's decision is determined within 2 to 3 months of the issuing of the panel's report. It is anticipated that the overall time frame beginning with the date of establishing a panel to the date of implementing the DSB recommendations and a panel ruling should no exceed 18 months, unless the parties to the dispute agree that there are exceptional circumstances.

No provision in the WTO Agreement explicitly addresses which party has the burden of proof in a dispute settlement proceeding. While past GATT practice offers some guidance on the issue, previous practice may not always be relevant for disputes arising under the WTO Agreement. The burden of proof may vary depending on which covered agreement governs a particular dispute. This is a matter which the AB is dealing with on a case by case basis.

The DSB adopts many characteristics of a domestic court or administrative tribunal. The regularity of providing decisions to an ongoing list of disputes mirrors the court's assizes. The resemblance to administrative tribunals is marked by the expertise panel members have in determining matters with a specific discipline. Trade policy is ultimately developed through their decisions. It is the interpretative function of the panels and appellate bodies that pave the way for

* Director of FIELD, Professor College of Europe, Of Counsel to Baker & McKenzie. Many thanks to Juliana Goldenberg and Kevin Gray for their help in preparing this piece.

W.P. Heere (Ed.), International Law and The Hague's 750th Anniversary

the development of GATT jurisprudence. However, the DSB is not relegated to a judicial function whose purpose is merely clarifying as opposed to making new law. Panel and appellate reports are adopted by the contracting parties and become WTO law. The obligations arising from a decision bind a party in the same manner as the text of the WTO Agreement. As a result, WTO panels and appellate bodies have improved and developed stronger legal analysis in their decisions.

International relations are increasingly determined by economic relations, thus changing the power oriented diplomatic approach of policy formulation to rule-oriented – legal methods and neutral dispute settlement. Dispute panels provide a forum for the airing of disputes regardless of a party's economic power or influence. Developing countries are given an opportunity to challenge the trade measures of countries that would normally predominate international negotiations and multilateral decision-making. Installing a dispute resolution mechanism within the trading regime reinforces the legitimacy of the regime itself and provides a better incentive to comply with international trading requirements.

The advent of the WTO dispute resolution system suggests that the international trade dispute resolution process has become judicialised. Although the move to a more 'juridical' or 'rule-oriented' approach preceded the emergence of the WTO, the DSU erects the legal framework for decision-making that entrenches the dispute resolution bodies as permanent adjudicators. Although the DSB prefers to find a resolution to disputes that is mutually acceptable to the parties, a dispute at the panel stage will inherently require a siding with one party's interpretation of the WTO Agreement over the other party's position. In contrast to the position under the GATT 1947, instead of writing reports that are designed to achieve a consensus among the parties, panels are now 'liberated from the need to satisfy all parties and can concentrate on what the underlying law is, now it should apply to the facts of the case before the panel, and what legal conclusions the panel can permissibly draw from the analysis'[1]. This change is attributable to the negative consensus rule where panel and AB reports are automatically binding subject to negative vote in the Dispute Resolution Body. The procedures under the DSU are thereby able to strengthen the international rule of law.

Since the inception of the WTO in January 1995, there have been 136 disputes brought to the DSB. This poses a marked contrast with the number of disputes under the GATT 1947 under which there were only 36 complaints filed between 1991 and 1994. Most disputes are settled between the parties prior to the appointment of a panel. This may be the result of the binding nature of WTO decisions, the short timeframes, the automaticity of the steps in the process and the strengthened mechanisms for surveillance and enforcement of rulings.

Panels under GATT 1947 were established on an *ad hoc* basis, independent of

[1] P Nichols, 'GATT Doctrine', 36 *Virginia Journal of International Law* (1996) p.379.

any other panels or disputes between contracting parties. There were no specific clauses under the GATT 1947 providing for the establishment of dispute resolution panels, although they were loosely authorised under article XXII and XXIII, which provided for the parties to consult. Moreover, the system was fragmented, with disputes settlement avenues available under the GATT 1947 as well as the Tokyo Round Codes the resulted in forum-shopping, inconsistent rulings and the non-implementation of ruling. Dispute resolution evolved under the GATT as a practical way to administer disputes as opposed to parties engaging in consultations. Panels would be organised to settle the matter but their origin was on an ad hoc basis and usually required the disputant's consent. Since panel reports revolved around the particularity of the matter, they could be easily distanced from other disputes. Any connection between the decisions of the disparate GATT panels was merely coincidental with previous decisions taking on, at best, a persuasive role. The WTO Dispute system adopts a more permanent presence, lending new structure to the DSB.

GATT panels under the GATT 1947 had often been established in response to a particular dispute between the parties that had protracted in an irreconcilable fashion. They would apply the GATT rules and principles where the application would be tailored to a particular dispute. The ruling of other panels would be used merely as a persuasive tool with the ruling primarily based on the facts. WTO panels are under a codified obligation to make their decisions in accordance with international law. This has linked trade law with the world of international law, as decisions were made within the four corners of the dispute and applied to the closed discipline of GATT law general principles of law such as *legitimate expectation* are being used especially by the AB. Customary international law is relied upon for the essential purpose of interpretation. The creation of the AB has led to further sophistication of international trade law. Members respect the institution and, generally, accept the deepening of the rules which govern their behaviour.

Gary Sampson, Director of the Trade/Environment Division of the WTO has often remarked that the WTO is a 'victim of its own success.' His particular perspective is that because of its efficacy the WTO dispute settlement system is attracting cases that it can settle expediently, but may more rightfully be heard in other more specialised fora. The DSB has become so popular that it is overburdened. There are currently over 100 cases in the system. No other international dispute settlement system has ever had to cope with this level of demand. However, the consequences of attracting disputes under a range of agreements, some of them clearly test cases, where the jurisprudence of the GATT 1947 is of limited value have brought severe resource problems to the DSB.

There are a number of practical steps to improve the DSU that might be sensible reforms to the current structure. First, it is evident that there is a tremendous amount of documentation that needs to be managed by a small

Secretariat serving many members and many interests. The evidence submitted to dispute settlement panels needs to be limited in volume. The written presentations may also be limited, perhaps by time limiting the oral representations. Member governments generally insist on their arguments being faithfully recorded in the panel report. This is very time consuming and wasteful of resources. Members should accept the panel's ability to summarise their arguments. Once the report is issued, if a member wishes to declare publicly what it has said, it can make its own documents open to public scrutiny. There is no good reason why confidentiality should continue once a dispute has been settled.

The inevitability of globalisation calls for effective global public policy making. The WTO is already implicated in this process through its existence and through its important function in the resolution of international disputes. Reforms such as accepting *amicus* briefs will help. Establishing an Advocate General or Counsel to the Panel may also assist in developing consistent jurisprudence. Given the rapidly shifting global context in which the WTO now functions, adaptability and flexibility within the DSU will be essential to meet the challenges of this increasingly integrated world.

DISPUTE SETTLEMENT PROCEDURES IN THE WTO – A VIEW FROM THE HAGUE

Ernst-Ulrich Petersmann*

Since the entry into force of the Agreement Establishing the World Trade Organization (WTO) in 1995, the WTO dispute settlement procedures – like the previous GATT dispute settlement system – have become the fastest and most frequently invoked system for the settlement of disputes among governments. Between 1995 and July 1998, 139 dispute settlement proceedings had been initiated on 103 distinct matters involving the majority of the 132 WTO Members; 14 panel, 12 appellate and 3 arbitration reports were adopted, 28 cases were settled bilaterally or were no longer pursued, and a large number of disputes are pending. Why has the WTO dispute settlement system been used, already during its first three years, more frequently than the International Court of Justice (ICJ) during the more than 50 years of its existence? Why were more disputes on environmental protection, or on intellectual property rights, submitted to the WTO than to the ICJ, even though the ICJ was designed as 'the principal judicial organ of the United Nations' (Article 92 UN Charter) and many multilateral environmental agreements and intellectual property conventions negotiated in UN institutions provide for the submission of disputes to the ICJ or to other dispute settlement mechanisms?

There are many reasons why the organizers of this conference should be congratulated for their farsight to stimulate comparative legal analyses of the international courts at The Hague with other dispute settlement procedures and practices in international economic law. More than 200 years ago, in his essay on *Perpetual Peace* (1795), the philosopher *Immanuel Kant* has already explained why the equal protection of individual freedom and of other citizen rights in *domestic* legal systems depends on complementary *international constitutional rules* for the protection of rule of law in *transnational* relations, and why international trade is the most important driving force for the promotion of peaceful cooperation and rule of law among nations. Unfortunately, international lawyers often continue to ignore the increasing 'constitutionalization' of international economic relations through worldwide and regional legal and dispute

* Professor of Law at the University of Geneva and the Geneva Graduate Institute of International Studies. Former legal adviser of GATT and the WTO (1981-1997) as well as of the German Ministry of Economic Affairs (1978-1981).

W.P. Heere (Ed.), International Law and The Hague's 750th Anniversary

settlement systems with compulsory jurisdiction and appellate review, as in WTO and EC law.[1]

Since rules do not enforce themselves, the *rule of law* concept is usually defined in constitutional democracies and in EC law by the availability of compulsory jurisdiction for judicial review of whether governmental measures are in conformity with national and international law.[2] Unfortunately, neither the UN Charter nor the UN Human Rights Covenants are based on such a rule of law concept. Nor can the ICJ, in view of its limited compulsory jurisdiction for less than a third of UN Member States, ensure the international rule of law. Since rule of law and equal protection of individual rights *within countries* often depend on rule of law and judicial protection of freedom and non-discrimination in *international relations*, UN law and also the ICJ require far-reaching reforms in order to realize the democratic ideal of equal protection of freedom and citizen rights under the rule of law.[3] The following contribution draws attention to five structural differences between the UN and WTO legal and dispute settlement systems, which explain the relative success of WTO law and WTO dispute settlement practice and appear important for future reforms of UN law and UN dispute settlement procedures.

1. THE RULE OF LAW REQUIRES COMPULSORY JURISDICTION FOR JUDICIAL REVIEW

The WTO Dispute Settlement Understanding (DSU) is an integral part of WTO law binding on all Members. It provides for compulsory and exclusive jurisdiction of the Dispute Settlement Body (DSB) 'to establish panels, adopt panel and Appellate Body reports, maintain surveillance of implementation of rulings and recommendations, and authorize suspension of concessions and other obligations under the covered agreements' (Art. 2:1). When WTO Members seek redress of a violation of WTO law, 'they shall have recourse to, and abide by, the rules and procedures of this Understanding' without recourse to unilateral determinations of violations or unilateral reprisals (Art. 23). Article 3:2 emphasizes the rule-oriented function of the DSU 'to preserve the rights and obligations of Members under the covered agreements, and to clarify the existing provisions of those agreements in accordance with customary rules of interpretation of public international law' (Art. 3:2). Dispute settlement panels are

[1] See E.-U.Petersmann, 'From the Hobbesian International Law of Coexistence to Modern Integration Law: The WTO Dispute Settlement System', *Journal of International Economic Law* 1 (1998) pp. 175-198.

[2] Cf., E.-U.Petersmann, 'How to Promote the International Rule of Law? Contributions by the WTO Appellate Review System', *Journal of International Economic Law* 1 (1998)pp. 25-48.

[3] See E.-U.Petersmann, 'How to Reform the UN System? Constitutionalism, International Law and International Organizations', *Leiden Journal of International Law* (1997)pp. 421-474.

established automatically at the request of the complaining Member (Art. 6), and panel and Appellate Body reports are adopted automatically within very short time-limits (cf., Art. 20). Article 21 on multilateral surveillance and implementation of dispute settlement rulings also provides for the increasingly used possibility of arbitration awards within 90 days on the 'reasonable period of time' for implementation of dispute settlement rulings. Similarly, and again at the unilateral request of the complaining country, the WTO consistency of implementing measures can be reviewed by the original panel within 90 days.

2. ALTERNATIVE DISPUTE SETTLEMENT METHODS NEED TO BE INTEGRATED

The DSU offers all political and legal methods for the peaceful settlement of disputes set out in Article 33 of the UN Charter, such as bilateral and multilateral consultations (Art. 4), good offices (Arts. 5, 24), conciliation (Arts. 5, 24), mediation (Arts. 5, 24), enquiries (e.g. by 'expert review groups' pursuant to Annex 4 of the DSU), arbitration (Art. 25) and judicial settlement (e.g. Arts. 17-19). But the DSU gives clear priority to the primacy of the *rule of law* by requiring that 'all solutions to matters formally raised under the consultation and dispute settlement provisions of the covered agreements, including arbitration awards, shall be consistent with those agreements and shall not nullify or impair benefits accruing to any Member under those agreements, nor impede the attainment of any objective of those agreements' (Art. 3:5). This legal primacy of the more than 25'000 pages of mostly detailed and precise WTO rules greatly enhances legal security and predictability. It seems largely due to the 'dispute prevention function' of such requirements as the rule of law and as compulsory jurisdiction for judicial review, that more than 20 % of WTO dispute settlement proceedings are settled 'out of court' without a DSB ruling. While the UN Security Council has rarely complied with its obligation to 'take into consideration that legal disputes should as a general rule be referred by the parties to the International Court of Justice' (Art. 36:3 UN Charter), the WTO Appellate Body has effectively become the 'principal judicial organ' of the WTO. Appellate Body reports also refer regularly to general international law principles as applied in the case law of the ICJ; such 'cooperation among international courts' and 'cross-fertilization' of legal systems further enhance the legitimacy, consistency and political acceptability of WTO dispute settlement rulings.

3. THE EFFECTIVENESS OF DISPUTE SETTLEMENT PROCEEDINGS DEPENDS ON CONSENSUS ON THE APPLICABLE SUBSTANTIVE LAW

Most UN Charter provisions relate to general principles of international law, whose interpretation remains politicized and controversial, or to decision-making procedures and institutions. Individual freedom, non-discrimination and other democratic citizen rights are not effectively protected in UN law. Many UN Charter provisions lack democratic legitimacy also because of their power-oriented character (e.g. the provisions discriminating in favour of the permanent members of the Security Council). Like the UN Charter, also the ICJ Statute and Rules of Court are state-centric and no longer consistent with the structural and democratic changes of modern integration law. These and other weaknesses of UN law contribute to the fact that the interpretation of UN law, and the risks of ICJ judgments, are often little predictable.

Most WTO provisions, by contrast, are designed to promote universally recognized principles of individual freedom, market access, non-discriminatory conditions of competition and the rule of law. They derive their legitimacy not only from the today universally recognized economic insight that liberal trade and non-discriminatory competition tend to maximize individual freedom of choice and responsibility (e.g. to adjust to competition and change), real income and consumer welfare, and the efficient allocation of scarce resources in accordance with consumer preferences. The 'ethics of markets' (e.g. regarding the role of undistorted markets as spontaneous information, allocation, co-ordination mechanisms and democratic 'dialogue about values'), and the WTO rules on non-discriminatory market access and competition, are also consistent with *Kant's categorical imperative* that law and governments derive their moral legitimacy from their compliance with universally applicable rules that maximize individual freedom and legal equality of the citizens. Moreover, GATT and WTO rules pursue 'constitutional functions' also vis-à-vis governments by prescribing the use of transparent, non-discriminatory and welfare-increasing policy instruments, by protecting the sovereignty of states to decide on their own policy objectives, and by outlawing power-oriented unilateral reprisals in response to foreign violations of WTO rules.[4]

The WTO treaty, and the ever increasing number of annexed worldwide agreements incorporated into WTO law, promote not only transparency and predictability of the applicable law in WTO dispute settlement proceedings. Member governments also know very well that compliance with GATT and other WTO rules, and also with WTO dispute settlement rulings, hardly ever imposes 'economic sacrifices' on the country concerned. WTO rules and dispute set-

[4] Cf., E.-U.Petersmann, *Constitutional Functions and Constitutional Problems of International Economic Law* (1991) notably chapter VII.

tlement mechanisms rather help governments to protect freedom and equal treatment of their citizens, to implement welfare-increasing policies, and to resist protectionist political interest group pressures and power politics at home and abroad. The participation in GATT and WTO law and dispute settlement procedures not only of states, but also of international organizations (notably the European Communities) and sub-national 'customs territories' (like Hong Kong), and the many WTO provisions on individual access to domestic courts, enhance also the procedural legitimacy of WTO dispute settlement mechanisms.

4. INTEGRATION OF INTERNATIONAL AND NATIONAL RULES AND DISPUTE SETTLEMENT MECHANISMS MAKES THEM MORE EFFECTIVE

Article XVI of the WTO Agreement, and numerous specific WTO rules, require each Member to 'ensure the conformity of its laws, regulations and administrative procedures with its obligations as provided in the annexed Agreements.' The multilateral surveillance and detailed review of the domestic implementing legislation of each WTO Member is one of the major activities of the various WTO Councils and Committees and serves an important 'conflict prevention' function. Nonetheless, many GATT and WTO dispute settlement proceedings were directed against domestic laws rather than individual administrative acts or court decisions.

GATT and WTO disputes are often initiated by private traders and investors which, under their respective domestic laws – such as the 1994 Trade Barriers Regulation of the European Union and Section 301 of the US *Trade Act*, are entitled to request their government to challenge illegal or 'unreasonable' foreign trade measures. In disputes brought by developing countries, the industries involved sometimes also pay the costs for private legal counsel in WTO dispute settlement proceedings, which are increasingly used in addition to the government's lawyers and the legal advice given by the WTO Secretariat to developing countries free of charge (cf., Art. 27 DSU).

Just as the successful conclusion of the 'Uruguay Round' and preceding 'GATT Rounds' was facilitated by the political support from industries and consumer interests in liberal trade, industries are also a major political driving force behind the initiation and implementation of GATT and WTO dispute settlement proceedings.

WTO law includes numerous requirements of granting citizens access to domestic courts and other individual remedies against restrictions or distortions of trade or individual rights. WTO law also increasingly protects substantive private rights, such as intellectual property rights. The availability of such individual rights and decentralized dispute settlement and enforcement mechanisms contributes to the fact that most governments seem to observe most of their GATT and WTO obligations most of the time. Unlike the customary international law requirement of prior exhaustion of local remedies, GATT and WTO law – similar to European Community law – enable access to the GATT and WTO dispute settlement mechanisms even prior to the exhaustion of local remedies.[5] Since GATT and WTO dispute settlement proceedings tend to be much quicker, and to apply stricter legal standards of judicial review, than many domestic court proceedings which often ignore international law, parallel recourse to national and international dispute settlement mechanisms has become a regular feature of GATT and WTO practice. In some disputes, GATT and WTO dispute settlement rulings were explicitly taken into account by domestic courts dealing with similar legal complaints. Unfortunately, there remain many examples of domestic courts disregarding their obligation to construe domestic law in conformity with international law; also the European Court of Justice has so far consistently ignored GATT and WTO dispute settlement case law and the about 25 GATT and WTO dispute settlement findings of inconsistencies between EC law and the GATT or WTO obligations of the EC.

5. NEED FOR DUE PROCESS OF LAW

Justice delayed may amount to justice denied. The ICJ, for instance, has come under increasing criticism for the slowness of the Court in disposing of only two, or at the most three, cases each year. In contentious proceedings, the usually two or three rounds of written pleadings and subsequent oral arguments tend to last several years. The relatively low number of days used each year for formal sittings of the ICJ (e.g. 5 public and 26 private sittings in 1992), the short duration of a 'day in Court' (from 10 a.m. to 1 p.m. with a 20-minutes break for coffee), and the lengthy internal procedures for elaborating a judgment (e.g. with written notes of 40 to100 pages prepared by each of the 15 to17 judges and translated into the other working language) have been criticized as additional causes for the delay of usually several years between the filing of an application and the final ICJ judgments on jurisdiction/admissibility and on the merits.

Most WTO panel and appellate review proceedings have thus far respected the statutory requirement that 'the period from the date of establishment of the panel by the DSB until the date the DSB considers the panel or appellate report for adoption shall as a general rule not exceed nine months where the panel report is not appealed or 12 months where the report is appealed' (Art. 20). The Working Procedures for panels (Appendix 3 of the DSU) allow 2 to 6 weeks for written submissions, 2 to 3 weeks for receipt of written rebuttals, and 1 to 2 weeks for the first and second substantive meeting with the parties as well as with intervening third parties. In Appellate Body proceedings, the appellant has up to

[5] See E.-U.Petersmann, *The GATT/WTO Dispute Settlement System* (1997) pp. 240-244.

10 days for the filing of the written submission; the appellee's submission must be received within 25 days after the date of the filing of the notice of appeal. While the ICJ has only very rarely admitted third countries to intervene, intervention by third WTO Members and 'multiple complaints' are regular features of WTO dispute settlement proceedings. Panel and Appellate Body meetings with or without the parties usually last the whole day. Even though all WTO documents (including panel and appellate reports) have to be translated into three working languages, many oral hearings and almost all other panel and Appellate Body meetings are conducted without translation. While separate or dissenting opinions of ICJ judges are frequent and usually much longer than the majority judgment itself, they continue to be extremely rare and short in GATT and WTO dispute settlement practice.

6. CONCLUSION: LESSONS FROM WTO LAW FOR THE NEEDED REFORMS OF UN LAW AND OF THE ICJ

The page limitations for this publication permit only few comparisons of UN and WTO rules and dispute settlement procedures. Yet, one important insight should no longer be ignored by lawyers and diplomats: The UN Charter and also the ICJ, despite their enormous achievements in promoting sovereign equality and peaceful cooperation of the 187 UN Member States, require far-reaching reforms so as to protect human rights, democratic peace and sustainable development more effectively. Just as the world trading system based on GATT could be reformed in a comprehensive manner only by means of replacing 'GATT 1947' by the 1994 WTO Agreement, the needed 'democratization' and 'constitutionalization' of the UN Charter for the benefit of 'We the peoples of the United Nations' (Preamble UN Charter) cannot be achieved by means of amendments pursuant to Articles 108 or 109 of the Charter.

In order to overcome opposition from non-democracies and the 'prisoners' dilemma' of universal rule-making, states must follow the 'Uruguay Round strategy' and negotiate a *new Charter* that could temporarily coexist with the 1945 Charter (on the model of the transitional coexistence of GATT 1947 and the WTO). Similar to the 1944 Bretton Woods Agreements, the 1945 UN Charter and the 1994 WTO Agreement, such a new 'UN 2000' can succeed in constitutionalizing international law only with leadership from the United States and Europe. The needed 'UN Round' for reforming UN law should follow the 'single agreement approach' and 'incorporation method' of the Uruguay Round by integrating existing UN conventions (e.g. on human rights) into a new UN Charter and by transforming the ICJ into a truly 'principal judicial organ of the United Nations' with worldwide compulsory jurisdiction.[6] The increasingly

[6] See E.-U.Petersmann, 'How to Reform the UN: Lessons from the International Economic Law Revolution', *UCLA Journal of International Law and Foreign Affairs* 2 (1997)pp. 185-223.

universal WTO law and its compulsory dispute settlement system, and also the acceptance by all 40 Member States of the Council of Europe of comprehensive guarantees of rule of law, democracy and compulsory international jurisdiction for the protection of human rights, offer empirical evidence that the needed reforms of the UN must not remain an idealist dream and can promote freedom and rule of law more effectively for the benefit of all citizens.

WTO DISPUTE SETTLEMENT PROCEDURES AND THE EUROPEAN UNION

Bernhard Jansen*

The heavy involvement of the European Communities (EC)[1] in the dispute settlement procedures of the World Trade Organization (WTO) can best be shown in referring to some figures. Of the altogether more than 130 WTO cases initiated since 1995, the year of the inception of the WTO, the EC has been a complaining party in 30 cases, a responding party also in 30 cases and a third party in 28 cases. This figure includes some cases brought against individual EC Member States. Of the 11 cases so far decided by the Appellate Body, the EC has been a complaining party in one case, a responding party in three cases and a third party also in three cases. Thus, the EC was involved in seven out of eleven cases at the appeal stage. Of the 13 cases presently pending at the panel stage, the EC is a complaining party in five cases, a responding party in two cases and a third party in three cases which means that the EC is involved in 10 out of 13 pending cases. These figures show that the EC , together with the United States, is among the most active users of the WTO dispute settlement system.

It is obvious that, if you are among the most active participants in dispute settlement procedures, you do not always prevail with your views. In this context, it is worth mentioning that the cases that are objectively the most difficult ones are those where trade liberalization objectives enter into actual or potential conflict with non-economic objectives, such as environmental concerns, public health considerations, development policy or security interests.

Based on present experience, one can say in general terms that the system works well. But as much as any other human creation, it can of course be further improved. The following observations are therefore not to be understood as a criticism or as the expression of any misgivings with the system, but rather as constructive remarks concerning possible areas of improvement. Following the sequence of the steps that need to be followed in dispute settlement procedures, I would like to focus on those elements that deserve some thought with regard to possible improvements.

Consultations take place behind closed doors, and therefore, little is known about the way in which they are conducted. Experience shows that they are of

* Legal Adviser in the Legal Service of the European Commission. The views expressed in the present contribution are purely personal.

[1] In this contribution, reference will be made to the European Communities as the entity having international legal personality under the Treaty on European Union.

W.P. Heere (Ed.), International Law and The Hague's 750th Anniversary

widely varying quality. Basically, consultations have a double function as a forum for diplomatic exchanges of views with the possibility to arrive at an agreed solution and as an advance warning in a legal dispute on the case held against the respondent. In both contexts, it is also the purpose of consultations to clarify the factual elements of the case. Therefore, consultations are usually prepared by the submission of a number of written questions. Obviously, the quality of the answers depends on the degree of co-operation between the participants. If the answers are of a substantial nature, they may be decisive for the way in which the dispute continues. For this reason, parties should be forthcoming and it would be appropriate to attach some consequences to the lack of co-operation that some WTO Members have unfortunately shown during the consultation phase of the dispute. If a party is under the impression to be in the defensive, it is not infrequent that the answers given during the consultation phase are purely formal and evasive. Presently, there is not much of an incentive to co-operate because no reference can be made at a later stage of the procedure to the attitude taken by a party to the dispute during the consultation phase. A possible solution could be that some negative inferences may be drawn from the lack of responsiveness of a WTO Member during the consultations.

Panel reports have all been appealed (with only one exception, the *Japan film* case which was mainly dealing with factual matters concerning the distribution of photographic films in Japan) and all panel reports have been reversed on certain points by the Appellate Body. This situation is unhealthy for the system and calls for some serious considerations concerning the possibilities for the strengthening of the panel procedure. Any change in the existing panel procedures can only be considered an improvement if it increases the objectivity of these procedures in order to ensure that panel reports will find world-wide legal recognition. Such strengthening of the existing procedures could be achieved mainly in the following manner: the present practice of appointing panellists from countries not involved in the dispute leads to a typical panel composition in which nationals of Switzerland, Hong Kong, New Zealand and a few Latin American countries participate. As a consequence, the panels are not fully representative of all the legal systems of the WTO membership and they are, moreover, composed by panellists from countries with a very specialized trade pattern. In this context, the role of the WTO Secretariat with regard to the composition of panels needs to be made more transparent. The treatment of factual evidence, particularly when having recourse to experts, needs to be further clarified by internal procedural rules of the panels. As yet, panels have adopted divergent standards as regards the timeliness and the sequence in which evidence was accepted. The rules concerning the selection of experts are also presently not sufficiently clear.

In order to ensure coherence and consistency between different panels, which are composed on an ad-hoc basis for each individual case, the WTO Secretariat has been tasked with the legal assistance of the panels (cf. Article 27.1 of the Understanding on Rules and Procedures Governing the Settlements of Disputes).

However, this legal assistance takes place to the exclusion of the parties to the dispute, which means that the parties have no possibility of a dialogue with the lawyers of he WTO Secretariat. Such a possibility should be introduced by allowing the parties to the dispute access to the full file of the panels, including the legal advice received from the WTO Secretariat. Such access would allow the parties to the dispute to comment on the views expressed by the WTO Secretariat which is presently not foreseen. Moreover, panel procedures generally need to become more transparent for the public at large, since justice must not only be done, but must also be seen to be done.

Appeals are subject to overly rigid time-limits which do not allow the Appellate Body to devote a sufficient amount of time to complex trade disputes. A time-limit of 60 to 90 days is clearly insufficient to handle complex issues of law as is frequently the case in the appeals procedures. There is also some lack of transparency in the appeals procedure with regard to the role of the plenary of the Appellate Body which apparently is involved in each individual case, but without the possibility for the parties to the dispute to make any direct representations to the Appellate Body members who are not hearing the case as members of the division dealing with the individual case at hand. It is, therefore, desirable to develop some more precise rules concerning the involvement of the plenary and the possibility of the parties to make representations to all members of the Appellate Body who are involved in the decision-making process. Also in the case of the Appellate Body, justice must not only be done, but must also be seen to be done, which pleads in favour of more transparency for the public at large.

The role of *third parties* could also be reviewed. The present limitations on their participation are difficult to understand and to justify. In fact, third parties have a limited right of participation at the panel stage while they are fully involved in the appeals procedure. These distinctions are incoherent and also seem to be in conflict with the demands of transparency between WTO Members. It also appears desirable to open the panel and appeals procedures in certain situations to more than one respondent in order to mirror the presently existing provisions for the participation of multiple complainants. The need for such an opening exists particularly in cases where the complaint concerns trade measures taken under a preferential agreement, since in such cases all the parties to the preferential agreement usually have an interest to defend the compatibility of the agreement with the WTO rules.

On *implementation* there is presently limited experience. The main question in this regard is what precisely has to happen where a panel or the Appellate Body found a trade measure to be inconsistent with the obligations of a WTO Member under WTO rules. Withdrawal of the offending measure is certainly always an option, but there may also be other options in a particular case. Panels and the Appellate Body usually refrain from making concrete suggestions for the implementation of their recommendations in order to respect the sovereignty of WTO Members. In some instances, this may make the task of a WTO Member that is under an obligation to implement extremely difficult and delicate. It is not yet possible to have the full perspective of all the problems that may arise at the implementation stage. The *bananas* dispute will certainly allow for a better understanding of the functioning of the dispute settlement procedures in this regard. It will be necessary to further observe the developments in this area.

A particular feature of the EC is the participation of its *Member States* in dispute settlement procedures. There are some cases which were brought against individual EC Member States by other WTO Members, more specifically the United States. Since there is no declaration of competence in the context of the WTO, third countries may assume that the EC and its Member States have full rights and obligations under the WTO Agreement. Of course, even without a declaration of competence, there are some obvious differences with regard to existing commitments of the EC and its Member States in the goods sector on the one hand and the services sector on the other hand. In the goods sector, the EC alone has bound a schedule of tariff commitments in the WTO, while Member States have withdrawn their national schedules. In the services sector, commitments have been made on behalf of the EC and its Member States. However, the unity of representation required by the European Court of Justice in its opinion 1/94 has so far always been respected. This means that both in defensive and in offensive cases, the EC has always fully participated in dispute settlement procedures. The need to act jointly may of course slow down the decision-making procedure within the EC with regard to a decision to launch an offensive case *vis-à-vis* another WTO Member in areas of joint competence. In order to remedy this situation, the Amsterdam Treaty contains an additional paragraph to be inserted in Article 113 with a view to enable the Council to decide unanimously to extend EC competence to the areas of services and trade-related aspects of intellectual property rights that are not presently covered by this Article.

HOW TO RECONCILE TRADE AND ENVIRONMENT

J.A. Peters*

INTRODUCTION

I am pleased and honoured to be invited by the Asser Instituut to chair this panel session on trade measures in Multilateral Environmental Agreements (MEAs).The co-operation between the Asser Instituut and the Ministry of the Environment in this field is becoming a strong and durable one, since this is already the third time that we are involved together with the issue of trade and environment.

GLOBALISATION AND ITS EFFECT ON THE TRADE AND ENVIRONMENT DEBATE

In my opinion the developments in the trade and environment debate have to be seen in a much broader context, namely in the context of globalisation. Within the OECD this relationship is studied since a few years now. At the beginning of 1997 this issue was discussed in Vienna at a Workshop on Globalisation and Environment. Some of the elements which have been highlighted there are the following.

Globalisation means the creation of a global information space, growth in global capital markets, the creation of a global market for goods and services and an increased role for international 'rules of the game', in particular those on trade and the environment. Borders between countries will become more vague. The role of the state and national governments will change as well. At the other hand, comparing the present globalisation tendency with the early stage of capitalism one should recognise that in those days, with the rise of the welfare state, the national government played a central role in controlling the consequences of unlimited capitalism and protecting the weak. Nowadays international trade boarders will disappear and the connection with the state will be getting loser. The authority of the state will diminish, but a body where the preconditions can be set under which globalisation can develop further, will still be needed. One of

* Director International Environmental Affairs, Ministry of Housing, Spatial Planning and the Environment of the Netherlands. The article has been written in co-operation with drs. S.M.H. Meijs, Senior Policy-advisor Directorate for International Environmental Affairs, Ministry of the Environment of the Netherlands.

W.P. Heere (Ed.), International Law and The Hague's 750th Anniversary

the key problems will be that globalisation is likely to result in different economic, social and environmental outcomes for different groups within and among countries. This means that differences between countries and groups of countries will not decrease but instead increase. The group of more developed and strong countries will be able to deal with this changing world and will adjust themselves relatively easy. However, most of the developing countries will run the risk of being less able to set the preconditions for the development of their country and to decide on its direction.

Increased international trade is likely to be one key result of globalisation.This will have all kinds of structural, technological and scale effects. The scale effects are often assumed to be negative for the environment. The primary risk for the environment is that the negative scale effects will be larger than the sum of the, presumably positive, technology and structural effects. Also the scale of global foreign direct investment has increased rapidly in recent years, as globalisation has intensified.This may be leading to additional environmental pressures, especially in countries where the environmental policy framework is not adequate, or its implementation is poorly enforced. This means a clear and strong link between trade, investment, environment and development aspects is needed. A transition to sustainable development is a necessary condition for the protection of the ecological foundations of the global economy. Just how dependent we remain for our economic well-being on the productivity of the global ecosystem is often overlooked. What does this mean for the role of governments? From an environmental perspective, for most environmental resources it will never be possible to include all costs in the prices and they will always get a relatively weak interest. An efficient economy and a sustainable environment will therefore continue to require at least two forms of government intervention, one to set the operating rules through which economic development takes place (contribution to sustainable growth); the other to ensure that market failures do not lead to long-term environmental degradation (contribution to sustainable development).

Globalisation also represents increased challenges (and increased opportunities) for regional and global institutions to better integrate environmental and economic objectives. For example, it will be increasingly important to ensure that international financial/economic institutions (e.g. World Bank) and trade organisations (e.g. WTO) take due account of environmental concerns in their work, and that within international environmental organisations (e.g. UNEP) and multilateral environmental agreements due account is taken of competitiveness concerns.

Globalisation implies a need for more efficient forms of international co-operation in all areas of economic activity. In principle, government policies should take place at the level at which environmental problems occur. This means that at least three types of government intervention may be warranted: national policies to internalise the environmental costs, regional co-operation with other governments on common policies, and co-operative arrangements for addressing transboundary and global environmental issues and to establish the global 'rules of the game', such as in the area of trade and environment, investment and multilateral agreements on the environment.

DEVELOPMENTS IN THE WTO AND WITHIN MULTILATERAL ENVIRONMENTAL AGREEMENTS

In my view the interdependency between trade and environment is still growing.

Over the past year we have seen a debate going on in the WTO-Committee on Trade and Environment (CTE) which has been of a more analytical nature. Many countries have given concrete examples of which problems they face in trying to overcome the tendencies between trade goals and environmental goals. The broad and important issue of market access has been discussed. Together with the secretariats of the different multilateral environmental agreements an open debate took place on the relationship between these agreements and the international trade regime. So far from these discussions the following key elements can be drawn:

1. There is a clear desire from the MEA-secretariats for an even more active role and advice from the WTO-secretariat in the negotiating process of the respective MEA. It is obvious that this is also a responsibility of the national governments. Within national governments all relevant expertise on trade issues and trade rules should be brought together whenever an environmental agreement has to be negotiated.
2. The knowledge on MEAs within trade circles as the CTE could and should be improved. The dialogue with the MEA-secretariats should be prolonged and even intensified.
3. The consciousness of MEA-secretariats is growing with respect to the relationship between trade and environment and the possible friction with the trade rules.
4. Lastly, in this respect one can see that the use of particular instruments to implement the objectives of the environmental agreements is carefully considered and analysed.This is very much welcomed. In most cases the proposed solution is a carefully balanced package of trade and non-trade related measures. This is a very positive development which we should support actively in the future.

What can be said in general about the developments in the multilateral environmental agreements, talking about the relation to trade? Within the OECD three of the major environmental agreements have been studied so far, the Montreal Protocol, the Basel Convention and the Convention on International Trade in Endangered Species (CITES). The analysis within the OECD has not yet been completed, but some general conclusions can already be drawn.

First, MEAs are not static but dynamic. There is continuous development and, as I said before, one seems to be more aware of and more sensitive to the implications of the use of trade instruments and of the possible effects on trade.

There is also a growing awareness of how trade (at least sustainable trade) could promote the implementation of the objectives of MEAs.Only in a minor number of MEAs trade-instruments play a role, but at the same time these MEAs belong to the group of most relevant and important ones (CITES, Basel, Montreal, Climate Change Convention, Biodiversity).

The use of trade instruments can not be seen in isolation. Often there is a link with other available instruments, in particular financial and technological support. In most cases there is a package of instruments. The package and mixture of different instruments can differ from country to country. Whenever non trade related instruments (such as financial and technological support) were used, they seem to have promoted the acceptance of trade related instruments, which does not necessarily mean that trade and non trade related instruments should always be combined.

Good data on the effectiveness of the environmental agreements and their instruments are not always available. Often the enforcement of fixed targets is difficult and control mechanisms are weak. The number of contracting parties is also very important. The higher the level of participation, the lesser the risk of a real free-rider problem.

Looking to all the different MEAs there seem to be more cross-cutting issues between them than expected. One could and should learn more of each other's experiences in this respect.

THE FRAMEWORK CONVENTION ON CLIMATE CHANGE

From a trade and environment perspective climate change seems to be the MEA which will have the most interesting developments. Climate change serves to illustrate many of the complex trade-environment issues which are currently under discussion in the WTO. Examples include how to deal within the WTO legal framework with various environmental taxes and, in particular, border tax adjustment for energy, carbon and other taxes on traded goods; the compatibility of eco-labelling and certification schemes with WTO rules; and, how WTO rules will sit along side new, market-based environmental policies like tradeable emission schemes.

The Climate Convention can raise questions about the overall compatibility between legal obligations assumed by governments which are members of the WTO and commitments taken under multilateral environmental agreements, and the measures used to achieve the emission targets, if such targets are agreed to. Will the Climate Convention employ discriminatory trade measures against nonparties to the MEA (the free-riders), which would be in theory against the spirit of basic GATT law covering most-favoured nations and national treatment?

Another problem which could come up relates to the non-flexibility within the WTO in the extraterritorial application of measures relating to production processes in exporting countries. In short, from a WTO perspective the manner in which a foreign product is produced is not a basis on which WTO rights and obligations are established. The underlying thesis is that should any country wish to influence the manner in which products are produced in other countries – however appropriate this may be thought by the importing country – this should not be translated into discriminatory trade measures. The relevance of this for the Climate Change Convention is clear. If a product imported into a country has been produced by a process that emits more greenhouse gas than is thought acceptable according to norms established in the importing country, it cannot be treated differently to a 'like product' (i.e. a product with the same physical characteristics) produced domestically, solely because of the process employed to produce the good, at least according to the present WTO-rules.The example of climate change shows us that many questions are still unanswered and that there is still much potential friction between environmental policies and trade rules.

STATUS QUO OR SUPPORT FOR NEW INITIATIVES AND PROPOSALS?

How should we move further in the near future? So far we have seen no real clashes within the WTO concerning the implementation of an MEA. No GATT or WTO trade dispute has arisen so far over the use of trade measures applied pursuant to an MEA. However, the speed with which the world changes in the direction of more globalisation and the increasing agenda of MEA negotiations, such as the Climate Change Convention, will soon lead to a situation whereby the capacity of the multilateral trading system to respond effectively to sustainable development becomes more and more difficult.Therefore it is of utmost importance that we search for new ideas and initiatives to build more confidence and that we adopt a preventive attitude and provide greater certainty to environment as well as trade negotiators.

One idea is for instance the concept of the *reversal of the burden of proof.*

So far the practice of panels has been to place the burden of proof on the party invoking the exceptions under GATT Article XX. Accordingly, if a measure is found to be inconsistent with other GATT provisions, the defendant has to prove that the measure at issue is justified under at least one of the exceptions listed in GATT Article XX and that the requirements laid down in the headnote to this Article are effectively met. The current practice concerning the burden of proof on GATT Article XX exceptions might be inappropriate when the measure challenged has been adopted pursuant to an MEA. It can reasonably be argued that a measure internationally agreed under an MEA should benefit from a rebuttable presumption that it is justified under GATT Article XX – i.e. that it should be up to the party challenging the measure to prove that it does not fall under any of this Article's exceptions and that the requirements in the chapeau are not satisfied. Within the EU there is growing consensus that it is worthwhile to explore this option further in the near future. The reversal of the burden of proof would undoubtedly represent a positive form of accommodation. Although it will be difficult to reach a consensus on any proposal aimed at enlarging the scope for accommodating trade measures pursuant to MEAs, this approach offers some significant advantages, for instance the fact that no formal changes to substantive WTO provisions have to be secured. In any case the WTO should be supportive of action at the multilateral level for the protection of the environment.

Another idea is the idea of holding a *High Level Meeting* of those with a key interest in the trade and environment discussions. Since the beginning of this year this proposal has gathered increasing support as potentially the best way forward to break the current deadlock and to push new result-oriented discussions (within the CTE as well as in other fora).At the CTE's meeting in March 1998, the European Commission suggested that strengthening the dialogue between top-level trade and environment policy-makers could foster the process by which the CTE debate became relevant to broader WTO decision-making. The main objective of holding a High Level Meeting of those involved in trade and environment would be to help to move the policy debate forward at the political level by contributing to confidence building and highlighting the importance of trade and environment for the WTO's present and future work. At the second WTO Ministerial Meeting which was held in Geneva in May 1998, President Clinton endorsed the proposal of the EU. I hope that the idea will get increasingly support in the near future, in particular from developing countries. Real progress will only be possible when the developed countries are prepared to enter into serious discussions with the developing countries on *all* the WTO agenda issues, including those which are of particular interest to developing countries, such as improvements in the field of market access and issues like agriculture and textiles. Agricultural assistance through output-related policies in many OECD countries has been shown to have imposed high environmental costs on other countries with a comparative advantage in agricultural production and trade. Further reductions of agricultural protection and support present a 'win-win' situation for trade and environment.One of the principal tasks of the WTO is trade liberalisation through the removal of subsidies not justified in terms of WTO rules. One clear way to limit environmental degradation is to reduce subsidies.

The latest initiative which I would like to refer to is the initiative of the WTO-secretariat, in collaboration with the (non-governmental) International Centre for Trade and Sustainable Development to organise *regional seminars on trade and environment in developing countries*. It is to be hoped that through such regional seminars capacity building can be enhanced in developing countries in the area of trade and environment, an integrated approach and transparency can be promoted, the involvement of NG0s from developing countries can be strengthened, and the discussions within the CTE can be pushed further. Lastly, these regional seminars can be used as preparatory meetings for the foreseen High Level Meeting within the WTO at the beginning of 1999. The Netherlands, and in particular the Ministry of the Environment, welcomes therefore this initiative and will support it financially.

CONCLUSIONS

In conclusion I would like to make the following remarks. Talking about the reconciliation of trade and environment from the perspective of multilateral environmental agreements I would like to recommend to following:

1. It is very important to strive for a balanced and general agreed package of measures with room for the use of different sets of instruments for different countries.
2. Clear agreements should be made on how to deal with expected or unexpected negative side-effects of the use of trade related instruments and how in particular developing countries will be supported if they suffer from these effects.
3. It can not be said enough that developed countries should fulfil their obligations and commitments towards the developing countries.
4. Lastly, it is worthwhile to bring environment- and trade negotiators together more often to discuss certain issues which are of concern to both circles. Work is still done in too much isolation in this regard.

We have to get rid of all the cherished suspicion between trade and environment circles which is still alive and focus together on ways to build mutual reinforcement of the environmental and the trade regime. Much is still to be done, but I am confident that in the near future the debate will get a positive turn.

TRADE AND POSITIVE MEASURES IN MULTILATERAL ENVIRONMENTAL AGREEMENTS: EFFECTIVENESS AND SUITABILITY

Winfried Lang*

Concepts usually do not spring from a scholar's mind; they rather come into being as a consequence of a politically motivated process. Such an event also occurred in regard of MEAs; this notion of MEAs emerged during the early years of the 'trade and environment'-debate in the GATT context, especially when during the early nineties the suspicion grew that the Montreal Protocol on substances that deplete the ozone layer could well be incompatible with the rules of free trade as embodied in the GATT; according to this Protocol the trade concerning certain substances could be prohibited. For reasons of dispute-avoidance some arguments in favor of compatibility were sought: 'Multilateral' was one restrictive condition: not each and every environmental agreement should be entitled to interfere with the 'sanctity' of the multilateral trading system; there should be some legal instrument equivalent to GATT, an instrument carrying a high degree of legitimacy; such legitimacy should be based on the gravity of the threat to the environment and on a high number of contracting parties. Thus, neither bilateral nor regional agreements should be qualified as MEAs which would be entitled to compete with global GATT-rules. From the perspective of treaty law MEAs are ruled by the Vienna Convention on the Law of Treaties; neither their *subject* matter nor their number of contracting parties conveys to them any special status (e.g. *ius cogens* or *erga omnes* obligations). According to a GATT-account there exist 185 MEAs.

Beyond treaty law MEAs have several *characteristics* which should be highlighted hereinafter:

– Although any treaty establishes the rights and duties of its contracting parties (states) international environmental law is mainly about economic actors or human activities that have to be framed by the respective states. The conformity of a state's behavior with its obligations under an environmental treaty very much depends on its ability to regulate these activities and to supervise the performance of these actors; this ability requires to a certain degree coercion but also persuasion.

– Not only as far as treaty-making but also as far as treaty-compliance is concerned much depends on the impact of NGOs, public opinion and science. NGOs

* Ambassador of Austria to Belgium, Nato and the WEU.

W.P. Heere (Ed.), International Law and The Hague's 750th Anniversary

are likely to mobilize public opinion and may also act as 'watch dogs' that verify compliance. Science may discover a threat to the environment; it may also provide the means to combat or at least to mitigate that threat and possibly ensuing damage; and science may also be helpful in monitoring compliance with obligations. But the role of science may suffer from one major flaw, namely scientific uncertainty, e.g. disagreement among scientists concerning the seriousness of the danger or the feasibility of an adequate response. This uncertainty is usually exploited by those, who are supposed to bear the costs of the response strategy, namely business. Unless these costs are borne by the community as a whole (tax payers), business tends to postpone its involvement until a certainty of almost 100 % is attained. This reluctance has led to the adoption of the so-called 'precautionary principle' by many governments; this principle requires appropriate action well before and below the 100%-level of scientific certainty.

– The principle of 'reciprocity', once considered as the very basis of international law is not really applicable in the context of environment, a fact that reduces the likelihood of classical countermeasures: in case of a breach of law states must not destroy by way of some kind of 'mutuality' the environment of the wrongdoer; states should also not destroy the 'global commons' on which they all depend in one way or the other.

– Furthermore MEAs have special features in respect of law-making: some make broad use of so-called 'soft law', which may act as a precursor of 'hard law' or as some kind of accompanying regulation with a somewhat lower degree of legally binding force. Some MEAs follow the so-called 'framework-convention cum protocol approach', which means that the first instrument only contains very broad and general obligations, whereas the follow-up instrument (protocol) provides for detailed duties that can be closely monitored and easily verified (see treaties on air pollution in Europe, ozone depletion and climate change).

Effectiveness and *suitability* (better: *adequacy)* are notions that apply in respect of each and every rule, but which have gained increasing prominence in international environmental law. Among the reasons for this situation are the following: the traditional mechanisms of state responsibility (*ex post* remedies) rarely work – some kind of damage can never be repaired or compensated – or have little relevance in an area in which preventive action (*ex ante* remedies) is the only meaningful recipe. Without entering into the broad academic debate on implementation, compliance-control etc. the following should be considered: A rule is '*effective*', if the intended result really is attained; if all participants or players agree that the goal has been achieved or is about to be achieved. A rule is '*adequate*' (suitable), if it includes most or all elements necessary for the achievement of the goal, i.e. all or most measures to overcome existing obstacles have been taken; all or most forces that facilitate a positive outcome have been mobilized.

Trade may have a plurality of impacts on the 'life' of an MEA. Some are mentioned hereinafter:
– *Pollution entitlements* could be traded between states along the lines of joint implementation as mentioned in the Climate Change Convention, i.e. between North and South. It is, however, to be asked whether such trade would correspond to the requirements of equity or fairness; the outcome of pollution-trade could well be that the poorer countries become the 'dumping ground' of the globe.
– *Trade restrictions* could be imposed in order to prohibit trade between parties and non-parties to a treaty (see Montreal Protocol). Such restrictions may, however, collide with obligations under the GATT, especially if trade does not only affect the controlled substances themselves (in bulk) but also downstream products containing or only produced with controlled substances. Especially, if these products have been produced with controlled substances, but no traces of these substances are left in the products concerned; such restrictions would contradict the GATT-rule that so-called 'process and production methods' (PPM) may not be used as trade barriers; therefore (*inter alia*) the contracting parties of the Montreal Protocol have suspended this specific rule.
– *Trade sanctions* could also be imposed, if the competent organs of a MEA conclude that a major case of non-compliance has occurred and that as some kind of punishment the privileges and advantages of membership are taken away from the party at fault (provided that the free exchange of certain substances or products is among the privileges and advantages of membership).
– *Trade measures* constitute also an important feature of the Basel Convention on the transboundary movement of hazardous waste; only by means of a highly sophisticated system of export and imports permits can such waste travel from its state of origin to the state of final disposal. A similar system has been put in place in order to make the Washington Convention on trade in endangered species (CITES) work.
– With *trade* also *interferes* the recent Rotterdam Convention on Prior Informed Consent (PIC), which constitutes the final outcome of many years of regulation-efforts (from soft-law to hard-law) by various agencies dealing with the circulation of hazardous chemicals and pesticides (UNEP, OECD, FAO). A considerable burden is put on the shoulders of exporting countries as regards the compliance of their exporters in respect of procedures prevailing in importing countries. The GATT/WTO conformity of this agreement appears to be assured in the light of Art. XX of GATT and the Uruguay Round Agreement on Sanitary and Phytosanitary measures.

Trade has become an important tool for the operation of several branches of international environmental law. Trade is in some instances even an instrument indispensable to achieve a specific environmental protection goal (see for instance the protection of endangered species). The major question that has still to be settled is the following: May trade restrictions (mainly import bans) only be imposed in order to protect the environment in the importing country, or may such restrictions also be imposed unilaterally in order to protect the environment beyond the national jurisdiction of the importing country (space, high sea, foreign territory)? This problem of extraterritoriality or extrajurisdiction has not been solved in spite of the rulings of two GATT panels (Tuna Case I and Tuna Case II). Questions of sovereignty, questions about the legitimacy of unilateralism versus multilateralism, questions related to the erosion of trade commitments under GATT by reference to environmental objectives, questions of different environmental standards in the North and the South have been raised. The trade community remains concerned that environmental considerations are simply used as a smoke-screen to cover up purely protectionist interests; thus a certain amount of distrust continues to disturb relations between the trade and environment communities.

MEAs appear to be all the more successful as they adopt *positive measures*, among which the following should be mentioned:

– *Exceptions*, or special regimes in favor of certain categories of countries (members of regional integration organizations, economies in transition, developing countries). These exceptions, sometimes criticized as loopholes in the respective treaty system may well encourage third parties to become members of the treaty concerned such as the Montreal Protocol or the Convention on Climate Change; among these advantages may be grace periods (delayed application), lower standards to be abided by, or transfer of technology.

– *Conditional compliance* or 'positive discrimination' means that developing countries may be entitled to make their compliance with treaty obligations dependent on the receipt of certain transfers (finance, technology etc.). Although this 'new conditionality' contradicts traditional concepts such as the 'sovereign equality' of states, it reflects well ideas such as 'equity' or 'fairness', which take into account the various points of departure of countries at different levels of development.

– Most important among these positive measures is the so-called *transfer of technology*, a key component of MEAs, which is supposed to cover countries from the North and the South at the same time. The prevailing philosophy is that of 'capacity-building'; such capacities are frequently missing in the South; thus the North is expected to contribute its fair share. Many MEAs provide for this transfer of technology; they have established special funds for this purpose or request support from the Global Environment Facility (GEF); see the Montreal Protocol and the Convention on Climate Change.

– *Economic incentives* (tax breaks etc.) in the traditional sense are not yet a center piece of most MEAs. Although they may be referred to in 'soft-law'-texts, they are not yet included in many legally-binding texts, because this would probably interfere too much with the internal domain of countries and their respective level of economic development.

In the age of globalization MEAs have become a most important vehicle of international environmental law. As there does exist very little customary law and almost no international jurisprudence, treaty-making and treaty-application are cornerstones of the development of international law in this area. But the weaknesses of the treaty law approach should also not be overlooked; the rigidity or low flexibility of treaty law does not meet the need for a quick adaptation to changes in economic feasibility, scientific/technological progress etc. Furthermore, MEA's do not function in a vacuum; they remain highly dependent on domestic environmental law, on the full transformation of international rules into national law to be applied by courts and law-enforcement officials. Finally, considerable efforts have been spent on complementing the insufficient and modest body of 'real' law by means of so-called 'principles'. Although little consensus exists as to the legal value and exact contents of these principles, they may help to fill loopholes, to facilitate the implementation of obligations and to prepare the making of new rules. International environmental law remains, on the one hand, an area still largely in flux. On the other hand, MEAs appear to have attained a certain level of saturation. Thus, further progress may depend on practical experience and lessons learned during the application of existing MEAs.

Trade and environment have become competing or conflicting issues at a very late stage. This competition or conflict also indicates that the protection of the environment has moved from the margins to the center of the political debate in many, especially developed societies. But trade and environment have also become a focal point in the North-South debate; domestic and transnational interest groups have emerged around this issue area. What remains to be done is 'bridge-building' between the respective 'communities'. Lawyers, who are used to accommodation and compromise may contribute through their practice aimed at clarity and transparency to viable solutions; they may well facilitate such 'bridge-building' and 'confidence-building', from which most parts of our societies are likely to benefit.

THE FRICTION BETWEEN GATT/WTO LAW AND EC LAW: SOME CRITICAL REMARKS ON THE CASE LAW OF THE ECJ

Andrea Ott*

1. INTRODUCTION

While The Hague celebrates its 750th anniversary, the notorious *EC Regulation 404/93* is celebrating its 5th anniversary on the 1st of July.[1] Celebrating may be the wrong expression because nothing has kept the panels, the professors and the politicians so busy in the last five years as the Common Banana Regime of the Community.

Apart from that the Common Banana Regime of the European Community (EC) has become a standing symbol for a policy which is neither economically sound nor consistent with international law,[2] the Banana is also a classic example of the sometimes embarrassing political bargaining which takes place in Brussels and in Luxembourg.

According to the Appellate Body decision of September last year, the EC must bring its Banana Regulation in line with WTO rules by January 1999. It seems quite unrealistic from today‘s perspective that the EC can make it in time, the compromise of June 1998[3] is still inconsistent with the obligations of the GATT and the GATS[4] – even though the Legal Service of the Council and the Commission allege that it is consistent.[5]

In the end the Community will have to pay not only by way of compensations or suspended concessions, but also for the legal damage being done to the constitutional order of the Community.

After about 140 additional Bananas Regulations, two GATT panel reports, two WTO panel decisions, presently about 34 *Bananas* cases of the European

* Dr Andrea Ott, Senior Research Fellow, T.M.C. Asser Institute, The Hague.

[1] *OJ* 1993 L 47/1.

[2] See on the problem of economic effects: Thagesen, Rikke/Matthews, Alan, 'The EU`s Common Banana Regime: An initial evaluation', *Journal of Common Market Studies*, Dec.1997, pp. 615 ff; see on international law: Hahn, Michael J./Schuster, Gunnar, 'Zum Verstoß von gemeinschaftsrechtlichen Sekundärrecht gegen das GATT', *Europarecht* (1993) pp. 261 ff.

[3] *Agence Europe*, No.7251, 27 June 1998, p. 7.

[4] See reaction of the United States and five Latin American countries: *Agence Europe*, Np.7270, 25 July 1998, p. 6.

[5] 'EU biegt ihren Bananen-Markt welthandelskonform zurecht', [http://www.fr.aktuell.de/archiv/fr30t], 1 July 1998.

Court of Justice (ECJ) and some of the national – mainly German – courts, nothing is settled yet and it can be expected that there is still more to come.

2. THE HISTORY OF THE BANANAS REGULATION: POLITICS AND ECONOMICS[6]

In February 1993 the EC introduced a Regulation which intended to unify the import policies of the Member States and establish a single market for the EC as the world's largest importer of bananas since 1988.[7]The previous national regimes were characterized by a great variety and division concerning the imports from different countries of origin and the existing restrictions. France, Greece, Italy, Portugal and the United Kingdom applied quantitative restrictions and licensing requirements. Spain maintained a *de facto* prohibition on imports of bananas, France had special regulations for bananas from its Overseas Departments. On the other hand companies in Belgium, Denmark, Luxembourg, Ireland, Germany and the Netherlands, and after 1995, also in Austria, Sweden and Finland – could import without quantitative restrictions but solely on the basis of tariff measures. Germany enjoyed under the Bananas Protocol, annexed to the Treaty of Rome, a special arrangement of duty-free imports of bananas.[8]

The new Common Bananas Market did not liberalize the Community market but rather extended the restrictions and an import licensing system which discriminated in favour of imports from the Community and the ACP Countries. Since 19 per cent of the consumed bananas were supplied by domestic producers, 16 per cent by ACP countries and about 65 per cent from Latin American producers, this new Regulation led to furious reactions from the producers of so-called Dollar bananas who were losing their markets in Europe.

3. THE GATT/WTO PANELS AND THE BANANAS REGULATION

The disputed Bananas Regulation accompanied the old GATT 1947 when it turned into the WTO with its agreements of GATT 1994, GATS and TRIPS.

1. Even before the enactment of the Bananas Regulation the first GATT panel was initiated by Colombia, Costa Rica, Guatemala, Nicaragua and Venezuela

[6] See history of Regulation f.i.: Banana III: European Communities – Regime for the importation, sale and distribution of bananas, [http://www.ejil.org/journal/vol9/No.1/sr1e-04.html], 19 June 1998, pp. 1 ff.

[7] GATT Panel Report, 34 *ILM* (1995) p. 5; After 1994 it became the second largest importer of bananas after the US: European Communities-Regime for the importation, sale and distribution of bananas, WTO Panel Report, WT/DS27/R/ECU, p.15.

[8] European Communities-Regime for the importation, sale and distribution of bananas, WTO Panel Report, WT/DS27/R/ECU, p.16.

against the national regimes and concluded in May 1993, when these regimes were about to disappear.[9]

2. The next – the second – GATT panel was established in June 1993. In January 1994 it concluded that *Regulation 404/93* was inconsistent with Article I, II and XIII of GATT.[10] Due to the old GATT Dispute Settlement System of consent, the panel report was not adopted, though it led to modifications. They resulted in March 1994 in a Framework Agreement of the EC with Colombia, Costa Rica, Nicaragua and Venezuela.

3. The countries which did not agree with the Framework Agreement – the new WTO members Ecuador and Guatemala, Honduras, Mexico and the US – initiated a WTO panel in May 1996.

This ended with the panel report in April 1997. Again it was stated that the Common Bananas Regime was inconsistent with obligations under the GATT, the Licensing Agreement and the GATS.[11]

In June 1997 the EC submitted an appeal against this report resulting – in the last stage – in the Appellate Body decision of September 1997 which upheld the findings of the panel.[12] Even though the EC has until January 1999 to bring the Bananas Regulation in line with World Trade Law, it will be a more than difficult task to reach a mutual agreement between the Commission, the European Parliament and its 15 Member States in the Council.

Furthermore, it is foreseeable that it will not be very successful – the attained compromise of June 1998 is neither changing the criticised quota nor the license system. After the Germans have given up their resistance for the political reason of not offending the French, only the Dutch objected to the new Common Bananas Regime.[13] This leaves again all the problems to the national courts and the ECJ.

4. IS THE GATT/WTO CASE LAW OF THE ECJ SETTLED?

The case law of the ECJ seems to be a history of repetitive arguments.

The first example is the use of Article 234 EC Treaty (ECT) which addresses the collision of old international agreements of the Member States with the ECT.

[9] See Thagesen, Rikke/Matthews, Alan, 'The EU`s Common Banana Regime: An Initial Evaluation', 35 *Journal of Common Market Studies*, No.4 (December 1997) p. 619; Banana III, [*http://www.ejil.org/journal/Vol9/No1/sr1e-04.html*], 19 June 1998, p. 3.

[10] GATT Panel Report, 34 *ILM* (1995) pp.177 ff.

[11] European Communities – Regime for the Importation, Sale and Distribution of Bananas, Complaint by Guatemala and Honduras, 22 May 1997, WTO panel report, WT/DS27/R/GTM, Complaint by Ecuador, 22 May 1997, WT/DS27/R/ECU.

[12] European Communities – Regime for the importation, sale and distribution of bananas, 9 September 1997, WTO Appellate Body Report, WT/DS27/AB/R.

[13] *Agence Europe*, No.7251, 27 June 1998, p. 6.; 'Massive Drohung', *Der Spiegel* 26/1998, p. 71.

This argument was raised for the first time by the Dutch Government in the *International Fruit Company* decision of 1972 where it was stated that the validity of a measure of the EC must be judged by Article 234 ECT.[14] Twenty years later the German courts seized this legal idea and used it as justification to disobey EC law[15] so that the ECJ had to decide upon it in the *T. Port* case in March this year.[16]

The second example is the question of direct effect of the GATT. Going further than the ECJ, the German courts want to apply international law in the national legal order because it would rank above EC law.[17] This strikes someone as odd because these are the same courts which in difference to the Italian courts in the fifties and sixties denied the GATT, sometimes without any legal reasoning, any effect within the national legal order.[18]

In general, if one looks at the ECJ jurisdiction concerning the GATT and the Bananas Regulation there can be seen a division. Before the Bananas Regulation EC citizens were fighting for a direct application of the GATT concerning other fruits and taxes without success. After the Bananas Regulation Member States got involved and the consequences of the Bananas Regulations and the Framework Agreement were now discussed alongside those of the GATT.

Together with Italian and German courts the ECJ has developed, or better, has cemented a settled case law concerning the old GATT.[19] The ECJ denies the GATT 1947 direct effect because – in its own words – 'it is based on the principle of negotiations undertaken on the basis of reciprocal and mutually advantageous arrangements, is characterized by the great flexibility of its provisions, in particular those conferring the possibility of derogation, the measures to be taken when confronted with exceptional difficulties and the settlement of conflicts between the contracting parties.'

But the Court can review EC law in the light of GATT rules if
a) the Community intended to implement a particular obligation entered into within the framework of GATT, and
b) if the Community act expressly refers to a specific provision of GATT.[20]

[14] *International Fruit Company* (Case 21 to 24/72), [1972] *ECR*, p.1219 at p.1224.

[15] Finanzgericht Hamburg, *EuZW* (1995) pp. 413; Bundesfinanzhof, *EuZW* (1996) p.126 ff.

[16] *T.Port* (Case C-364/95 and C-365/95, ECJ of 10 March 1998, n.y.r.

[17] Bundesfinanzhof, *EuZW* (1996) pp.127-128.

[18] Bundesfinanzhof, 68 *BFHE*, p. 431 at p. 435; Finanzgericht Hamburg, *Entscheidungen der Finanzgerichte* (1970) p.145 at p. 146; Finanzgericht München, *EFG* (1970) p.144 at p. 145; see in comparison the Italian courts: Corte Suprema di Cassazione, *Foro Italiano* (1968) I, pp.2462 ff; Corte Suprema di Cassazione, *Foro Italiano* (1972) I, pp.1963; Corte di Cassazione, *Foro Italiano* (1981) I, pp.1683 ff.

[19] Beginning with *International Fruit Company* (Cases 21-24/72), [1972] *ECR*, pp.1219 ff. over *Germany* v. *Council* (Case C-280/93), [1994] *ECR*, pp. I-4973 ff. to *Chiquita Italia* (Case 469/93), [1995] *ECR*, pp. I-4533 ff.

[20] *Germany* v. *Council* (Case C-280/93), [1994] *ECR*, p. I-5073.

The ECJ could develop this jurisdiction in about 50 GATT/WTO/Bananas judgments over the last thirty years. Apart from these well-known sentences a few cases go even further, demonstrating an obvious form of misinterpretation of GATT and EC law but also of no interpretation at all.

4.1. The approach of the eighties: Misinterpretation of the GATT

a. *Dürbeck case of 1981*

The *Dürbeck* case[21] is quite unique because the ECJ did not even touch upon the topic of direct effect even though the Advocate General focused on it in his opinion. Instead the Court avoided the question by citing, for the first and only time, a GATT panel in its findings. Under the subtitle 'infringement of Article 110 of the Treaty and of the provision of the GATT' the ECJ stated that the GATT panel did not consider the EC measure an infringement of Article I or Article II GATT.[22]

A closer look at the report of the panel of October 1980 leads one to conclude that this finding is a very liberal interpretation of the report, in fact, the report reveals some violations which the ECJ completely ignores.[23]

b. *SIOT case of 1983*

In this decision the Court explains that following Article XXIV (8) GATT the Community must be regarded as a single customs territory because according to Article 9 of the EEC Treaty it is based on the principle of a customs union. From this follows – so the ECJ – that the rules contained in the GATT govern only the Community´s relations with the other contracting parties and cannot be applied within the Community itself.[24]

With this conclusion the Court means that with the forming of a customs union the GATT principles are not applied anymore between the Member States. But for this is not paragraph 8 but paragraph 1 of Article XXIV (24) decisive ('each such customs territory shall, exclusively for the purposes of the territorial application of this Agreement, be treated as though it were a contracting party').

Besides, the Court is misjudging three things.

Firstly, Article XXIV GATT is an exception to the most-favored-nations-clause (Article I GATT) and not to all the other GATT principles.

Secondly, it was never legally solved if the EC is meeting the requirement of Article XXIV GATT which names the necessary requirements for customs unions and free trade areas to comply with GATT. In particular, the legal

[21] *Dürbeck* (Case 112/80), [1981] *ECR*, pp.1095 ff.

[22] *Dürbeck* (Case 112/80), [1981] *ECR*, p. 1120.

[23] EEC Restrictions on imports of Apples from Chile, GATT report of the panel adopted on 10 October 1980, p.12.

[24] *SIOT*(Case 266/81), [1983] *ECR*, p.731 at p. 780.

consistency of the agricultural provisions and the association policy is very doubtful.

Thirdly, the Court has to make a difference between the competence to interpret GATT law and the application of it. After the EC substituted its Member States at the end of the sixties the ECJ is solely competent to judge the implications but nevertheless the EC and its Member States are both bound by the GATT. They still have to apply GATT rules like non-discrimination but within the customs union of the EC, Article 30 ECT (national-treatment) is *lex specialis* to the national-treatment-clause of GATT (Article III).

4.2. Beginning of the nineties: Misinterpretation of EC law

a. *Fediol III (1989), Nakajima, 1991*

In *Fediol III* the Court interpreted for the first time provisions of the GATT – in a rather superficial way.[25]

In both decisions the judges were interpreting EC law which refers to international law, i.e., GATT law. In the *Nakajima* the Court was stressing its obligation to fulfill international law.[26] But this is nothing outstanding but obligatory for the Community. Since the GATT is binding for the Community EC law has to be interpreted in conformity with GATT law. This is confirmed by Article 228 (7) ECT.

b. *Bananas case (Germany v.Council) of 1994*

In the *Bananas* judgment the Court made the still astonishing twist of EC law. According to the Court the Member State, like the individual, can only invoke GATT provisions if they are directly effective.[27] With this the Court was willing to find a special GATT requirement for Article 173 ECT which was never asked before or after this.[28]

4.3. The end of the nineties: No interpretation

a. *Affish case of July 1997*

In *Affish* the Court would have had for the first time the chance to decide upon the effects of WTO Agreements.[29]The Advocate General discussed in length the

[25] *Fediol III* (Case 70/87), [1989] *ECR*, p.1781 at p. 1832.

[26] *Nakajima* (Case C-69/89), [1991] *ECR*, pp. I-2069 ff.

[27] *Germany* v. *Council* (Case C-280/93), [1994] *ECR* , pp. I-4973 ff.

[28] See Bebr, Gerhardt, *Development of Judicial Control of the European Communities* (1981) p. 106.

[29] *Affish* (Case C-183/95), [1997] *ECR*, pp. I-4315 ff.

possible direct effect of the new provisions but in the end he applied the case law of the old GATT to the new GATT – stating that the WTO Agreements are still characterized by great flexibility. Surprisingly, the Advocate General also touched upon the argument of reciprocity, which was used by the Commission for denying direct effect. He opposed this as decisive due to the Community principle of good faith.[30]

The Court avoided addressing the question of direct effect. This was prudent because stressing a still existing flexibility is one of the weakest arguments. In contrast, the WTO Agreements have brought a greater legalization to the International Economic System.[31] Apart from that the Court maybe did not want to be reminded of its settled case law: As it was mentioned above, reciprocity is irrelevant for the interpretation and for the interpretation of a provision, account must be taken of the purpose, the context and the principle of good faith.[32]

b. *T.Port case of March 1998*

The Court was confronted with the German courts' misinterpretation of Article 234 ECT. This Article should justify that the Bananas Regulation as violation of GATT law was not applicable in Germany.

For the first time the ECJ had an easy task because there were many reasons for denying this interpretation. First of all, the established interpretation since *Burgoa* where the Court said that Article 234 ECT confers no rights on the individual.[33] Secondly, Article 234 ECT emphasizes the principle of *pacta sunt servanda* by stating that the application of the Treaty does not affect the commitment by the Member State under an earlier agreement[34] – which is being considered as time limited and an exception.

Consequently, the Court could avoid the question of direct effect – by stating that the GATT or the WTO was not concluded before the EC Treaty and furthermore that Ecuador was not a party of GATT/WTO before 1996.[35]

c. *Hermès case of June 1998*

In this recent case the Court was confronted with the TRIPS Agreement and trade marks.[36] Next to the until now unsolved question of the competence to interpret a

[30] *Affish* (Case C-183/95), [1997] *ECR*, pp. I-4357 ff. in Fn.105; according to this principle every contracting party is responsible for itself in executing fully the responsibilities of an international agreement. The principle of good faith is a rule of customary international law and therefore binding on the Community, See *Opel Austria* case (Case T-115/94), [1997] *ECR*, p. II-39 at p. 70.

[31] See f.i.: E.-U. Petersmann, How to Reform the UN System, 10 *LJIL* (1997) p. 421 at p. 459.

[32] *Kupferberg* (Case 104/81), [1982] *ECR*, p. 3642; *Bresciani* (Case 87/75), [1976] *ECR*, p. 141; *Commission* v.*Germany*, Case C-61/94, I-pp. 3989 ff. at p. 4015.

[33] *Burgoa* (Case 812/79), [1980] *ECR*, p. 2803.

[34] *The Queen, ex parte Centro-Com Srl* v. *HM Treasury and the Bank of England* (Case C-124/95), [1996] *ECR* I, p. 81 at 130.

[35] *T.Port* (Case C-364/95 and C-365/95), ECJ of 10 March 1998, No. 63 to 65, n.y.r.

[36] *Hermès* (Case C-53/96), ECJ of 16 July 1998, n.y.r.

mixed agreement, the Advocate General raised the question of direct effect of the WTO Agreement with completely different arguments than the Advocate General in the *Affish* case. Here he stressed the differences between the old GATT and the new WTO and came to the conclusion that the WTO provisions and the TRIPS provisions could be directly applicable. In the end he concluded that the lack of reciprocity would exclude this direct effect. This was contradictory to the Advocate General in the *Affish* case who thought that reciprocity could not be relevant for the interpretation of an international agreement.

In the end, the Court escaped the confrontation by stating that only an interpretation of national rules in the light of an article of the TRIPS Agreement is necessary, and no ruling on direct effect is required.[37]

However, compared with the above-mentioned *Fediol* jurisdiction[38] it is a step further. If the national court is expected to interpret a TRIPS regulation than it is nothing else than direct effect because finally with this interpretation individuals also rely upon Article 50 TRIPS to acquire their rights.

d. *Silhouette International Schmied of July 1998*

In the *Silhouette International Schmied* the Advocate General delivered his opinion in January 1998 about the question of a principle of international exhaustion for trade marks. Firstly, the Advocate General explains that the exclusion of international exhaustion may be protectionist but the possible lack of reciprocity makes it necessary. Secondly he is underlining his argument with the help of the GATT because the denial of international exhaustion is not contrary to the GATT Agreement and with the view to Article 6 of the TRIPS nothing has changed so far for the new WTO Agreement.[39] In contrast to the opinion of the Advocate General, the Court ruled that national rules providing for exhaustion of trade mark rights are contrary to the Trade Marks Directive without mentioning the GATT/WTO Agreement.[40]

The recent *Italy* v.*Council* case – the Advocate General delivered his opinion in April 1998 – seems to be like a reversed *Bananas* case. In his opinion the Advocate General is analysing a regulation which was adopted to fulfill obligations from GATT. Therefore, the Advocate General sees the requirement[41] or exception fulfilled – namely that the Court can review EC law in the light of GATT law because the Community intended to implement a particular obligation and the Member State can bring forward its claim.[42]

[37] *Hermès* (Case C-53/96), ECJ of 16 July 1998, No. 35, n.y.r.

[38] See 4.2. a. above.

[39] *Silhouette International Schmied* (Case C-355/96), Opinion of Advocate General Jacobs delivered on 29 January 1998, No. 51 and No. 54, n.y.r.

[40] *Silhouette International Schmied* (Case C-355/96), ECJ of 16 July 1998, n.y.r.

[41] See requirement a) chapter 4 above.

[42] *Italy* v. *Council* (Case C-352/96), Opinion of Advocate General Mischo delivered on 28 April 1998, No. 22, n.y.r.

5. CONCLUSION

Two things become obvious after analysing these latest statements and rulings: the Advocate Generals are trying to address the difficult problem of direct effect of the new GATT/WTO but in the end without any consequences for the present case law. Even if one of them sees the possibility of direct effect and going further than other EC bodies, still the doubtful argument of reciprocity prevails. In contrast to that the ECJ just escapes a confrontation or at least pretends that there is no necessity to rule on the question of direct effect.[43]

As a novelty the Advocate General in *Hermès* tries to use the honest argument of reciprocity. However, the reciprocity he mentions, is meant to be political rather than legal which gives the EC the possibility to respond in its commercial policy flexibly to the trade measures of the US and other trading partners.

This political reciprocity could guide the judgments of the Court in the future: because the past legal arguments of flexibility and reciprocity of the GATT are not convincing, the silence about the GATT is even less. Moreover, both approaches are contradicting the case law of the Court concerning international law. Therefore it would be wise if the Court would bring the argument of political reciprocity forward instead of hiding behind a wall of well-known and repetitive sentences. Nevertheless it remains only the second-best solution for the monistic system of the EC which derives from international law.[44] It would be at least worth a try to solve the contradiction that WTO law is part of EC law and is ranking above secondary EC law but has only an incomplete effect (see *Fediol III* and the recent case *Italy* v.*Council*) within its legal order.[45]On a broader scale the contradiction is not resolved that the EC legal order is an open system[46] which is generally friendly towards international agreements, giving it primacy over secondary law and national law and even direct effect whereas GATT gets a special dualistic treatment.[47] In addition, the Court is surrendering the con-

[43] See also for the discussion of the recent opinion and decisions: Mavroidis, Petros i.a., panel discussion at the 6th Geneva Global Arbitration Forum on 3./4.12.1997, Vol. 32, *JWTL* April 1998, p. 147 at p. 155.

[44] *Van Gend en Loos* (Case 26/62), [1963] *ECR*, p. 1 at p. 12.

[45] Pescatore sees a contradiction to the standard of good faith commanded by international law: Pierre Pescatore, Free Trade and the European Union – The Reconciliation of interests and the revision of dispute resolution procedures in the framework of the WTO, Academy of European Law Trier in cooperation with the Legal Service of the European Commission, 11./12.6.1998 in Brussels, p. 19 ff.

[46] As the Dutch Government called it in the *SIOT* case: *SIOT* (Case 266/81), [1983] *ECR*, p. 741.

[47] See *Haegeman II* (Case 181/73), [1974] *ECR*, p. 449 ff. about the integration of international agreements and *Sevince* (Case C-192/89), [1990] *ECR*, p. I-3500 about the integration of secondary international law. See for the direct effect of international agreements: *Pabst & Richarz* (Case 17/81), [1982] *ECR*, p.1331 ff.; *Kupferberg* (Case 104/81), [1982] *ECR*, p. 3641 ff; *Anastasiou* (Case C-432/92), [1994] *ECR*, p. I-3127.

stitutional legal order to a Bananas policy which is an outraging example of a breach of GATT law.[48]

So not confronting the problem at all is no solution at all and is only enhancing the danger that German courts judge the Regulations on the Common Bananas Regime as *'ausbrechende Rechtsakte'* in the sense of the *Maastricht* judgment of the German *Bundesverfassungsgericht*.[49] This means nothing else than sacrificing the EC constitutional principle of the primacy of European Law over national law for the Common EU Banana.

[48] Whether the German courts are doing any better – is quite doubtful. Their jurisdiction is also characterized by misinterpretation and denial. What the *Finanzgericht* is calling in-conformity-with-Article-234 ECT the ECJ names 'the GATT has binding effect in the Community', and the BFH stated explicitly that it is not decisive if the GATT principles are directly applicable.: BFH, *EuZW* (1996) p. 128 ('Wäre von einem Anwendungsvorrang des Völkerrechts auszugehen, so könnte es geboten sein, dem Vorrang auch einer nicht berufungsfähigen Völkerrechtsnorm von Amts wegen Geltung zu verschaffen').

[49] BVerfG Entscheidungen, Band 89, p. 155 at p. 188.

THE BEEF HORMONE DISPUTE: DOES WTO LAW PRECLUDE PRECAUTIONARY HEALTH STANDARDS?

Wybe Th. Douma*

1. INTRODUCTION

Is it harmful to human health to consume beef from cows treated with growth hormones? According to the USA and Canada, it is perfectly safe to eat such beef. According to the EC, the negative effects for human health might show only after a long period of time. Therefore, the use of growth hormones was banned as a precautionary measure in the EC. Moreover, the importation of beef from cows raised using these hormones was prohibited, much to the distress of the USA and Canada. Both countries initiated WTO proceedings against the EC. Both the Panels and the Appellate Body (AB) held the EC ban incompatible with the present WTO rules and more specifically the Agreement on the Application of Sanitary and Phytosanitary Measures (SPS agreement).[1] Oddly enough, both sides claimed to have won. The EC Commission even stated that the ruling presented 'a victory for European consumers'.[2] In itself, this already makes the beef hormones dispute an interesting case to examine.

Another interesting aspect of this case is formed by the role attributed to the precautionary principle. This principle was defined in the (non-binding) Rio Declaration of 1992 as follows: 'Where there are threats of serious or irreversible damage, lack of full scientific certainty shall not be used as a reason for postponing cost-effective measures to prevent environmental degradation.' More or less in line with this concept, Article 5.7 of the SPS Agreement allows for precautionary protection measures in cases where relevant scientific evidence is insufficient. Oddly enough, the EC explicitly stated that it was *not* invoking that provision. Instead, the EC tried to rely on the precautionary principle as a binding rule of international customary law – a submission which is still open to a considerable amount of debate, because many still regard the principle as merely a non-binding political piece of 'soft law'. Examining this aspect of the case is all the more important if one realises, that the next dispute between the USA and the EC on precautionary EC measures with regard to antibiotics in animal feed is already on its way.

* Senior Research Fellow, T.M.C. Asser Instituut, The Hague.

1 WT/DS26/AB/R and WT/DS48/AB/R, 16 January 1998.

2 Press release, Brussels, 16 January 1998.

W.P. Heere (Ed.), International Law and The Hague's 750th Anniversary

Finally, the beef hormone dispute can be placed in the light of the broader discussions on the national sovereignty to take protective measures (including deciding how high the protection level is set) and the modernisation of the international trade regime. These topics were touched upon at the WTO/GATT 50th anniversary conference that took place in May 1998. At that occasion, president Clinton noted that the WTO Agreement in its preamble 'explicitly adopts sustainable development as an objective of open trade, including a commitment to preserve the environment and to increase the capacity of doing so'. He stressed the importance of ensuring that economic competition among nations does not become a race to the bottom in environmental protections, consumer protections and labour standards. The starting point should be levelling up, not levelling down. Furthermore, Clinton expressed that the operationalisation of the concept of sustainable development implies that 'international trade rules must permit sovereign nations to exercise their right to set protective standards for health, safety and the environment and biodiversity'. He even went so far to express that '[n]ations have a right to pursue those protections – even when they are stronger than international norms'.[3] The EC ban on hormones beef forms an example of protection stronger than international norms. Still, it does not seem likely that the president of the USA was referring to the *Beef hormone* dispute. Rather, his remarks seem to be a reaction to yet another environmental case lost. After all, just before Clinton's speech, the USA had lost the *Shrimp/turtle* dispute.[4] Before that, the *Gasoline* dispute had been lost.[5] Under the old GATT system, the two Tuna dolphin disputes[6] were also decided against the liking of the USA. Back then, the adoption of panel reports could be vetoed by any GATT Member, including parties to a dispute. Consequently, the USA prevented the formal adoption of the two Tuna dolphin panel reports. Since the new rules on dispute settlement came into force, it is virtually impossible to prevent adoption of reports. Thus, if the outcome of the disputes is felt to be undesirable because they stand in the way of operationalising sustainable development, the rules of the game need to be changed.

The main question that will be dealt with in this paper is whether WTO law as it stands today, and especially the SPS Agreement (applicable in the *Beef*

[3] Address by President W.J. Clinton, Monday 18 May 1998, [http://www.wto.org/wto/anniv/clinton.htm].

[4] The Panel report (WT/DS58/R) was circulated to the WTO Members on 15 May 1998. The Panel found that the import ban on shrimp and shrimp products as applied by the USA is inconsistent with Art. XI:1 GATT and cannot be justified under Art. XX GATT. For a discussion of the Panel report and the subsequent AB report (WT/DS58/AB/R), see *Jurisprudentie milieurecht* 1998/166, with note by W.Th. Douma.

[5] United States – Standards for Reformulated and Conventional Gasoline (WT/DS2/R and WT/DS2/AB/R). The Panel report, as modified by the AB report, was adopted by the DSB on 20 May 1996. The USA announced implementation of the recommendations of the DSB as of 19 August 1997.

[6] BISD 39S/155-205 and DS29/R.

hormone dispute), is obstructing the possibility to adopt precautionary measures. This could be the case if the international standards, in combination with WTO provisions referring to these standards, bring about a levelling down effect. A comparison with the EC system will be made, where a special mechanism (laid down in Article 100A para. 4 EC Treaty) provides EC Member States with the opportunity to apply national standards that are stricter than EC harmonization measures. After having examined this topic, attention will turn to the way in which higher protection levels are dealt with in the WTO. Then, the *Beef hormone* dispute itself will be turned to. The paper ends with concluding remarks, in which among other things the implementation of the DSB recommendations by the EC is discussed.

2. HIGHER PROTECTION LEVELS IN THE EC SYSTEM

Over the years, the EC has established a balanced system which aims at sustainable development, or sustainable growth respecting the environment as it is called in Article 2 of the EC Treaty. Contrary to the WTO, the EC itself sets out to harmonize legislation of its Members where this is necessary to ensure free trade and the establishing and functioning of the free market (Art. 100A). Although the latter Article demands of the Commission that it takes as a base a high level of protection in its proposals where health, safety, environmental protection and consumer protection are concerned, this does not mean that the final result always ensures a level which is as high as the level of protection in all Member States of the EC. When at the occasion of the Single European Act the veto power over the adoption of internal market measures was lost, states aiming at high protection levels (like Germany, Denmark and the Netherlands) were afraid they would have to level down their national laws and regulations. That is why Article 100A para. 4 EC Treaty was created. That provision enables states to apply their stricter standards instead of levelling down to the level of standards agreed upon in the EC measure. In order for them to be allowed to do so, they have to notify the Commission. That institution is to confirm the provisions involved after having verified that they are not a means of arbitrary discrimination or a disguised restriction on trade between Member States.[7]

At the two occasions that the Commission verified claims by Germany[8] and

[7] See P.J.G. Kapteyn and P. VerLoren van Themaat / L.W.Gormley, eds., *Introduction to the law of the European Communities,* 3d edn. (Kluwer Law International, London/The Hague/Boston, 1998) pp. 679-681.

[8] Commission decision of 2 December 1992 (*OJ* (1992) C 334, p. 8). That decision was annulled on procedural grounds by the ECJ for lack of mentioning a reason (Case C-41/93, *French Republic* v. *Commission,* [1994] ECR, p. I-1829). A second decision (Commission decision 94/783 of 14 September 1994, *OJ* (1994) L 316, p. 43) again allowed Germany to upkeep its PCP ban and was extensively motivated.

Denmark[9] to uphold a complete ban on a hazardous substance called PCP in spite of a directive allowing for certain use of PCP, the Commission submitted in its decisions that there existed scientific uncertainty about the harmful effects of PCP in countries where there already was so much other pollution. The benefit of the doubt was thus given to the protection of human health and the environment. Oddly enough, the Commission in its extensive motivation never mentioned the precautionary principle. This principle was codified in Article 130R(2) of the EC Treaty via the Treaty on European Union that entered into force on 1 November 1993, i.e., at least before Denmark made its request. At any rate, the Commission showed its willingness to interpret Article 100A para. 4 in a precautionary way.

If the Treaty of Amsterdam enters into force, the option to hold on to stricter national measures in spite of harmonizing directives or regulations will be dealt with more extensively in the EC Treaty itself, solving many problems surrounding the present Article 100A(4). Unfortunately, new problems will also arise, especially where precautionary measures are concerned.[10]

3. HIGHER PROTECTION LEVELS IN THE WTO SYSTEM

As noted above, the WTO also subscribes to the concept of sustainable development. It does not set out to harmonize the laws of its Members in the way the EC does. Nevertheless, it is realised that it is for the better of international trade when WTO Members would apply the same standards. Thus, the SPS Agreement – applicable in the *Beef hormone* dispute – contains provisions which are aimed at stimulating the use of such standards. But does it allow for stricter national standards like the EC does?

The Agreement elaborates rules for the application of the provisions of GATT 1994 which relate to the use of sanitary or phytosanitary measures, in particular the provisions of Article XX(b) and the introductory clause (the *chapeau*) to that provision. Under the SPS Agreement, national governments are still allowed to take measures necessary to protect human, animal or plant life or health.[11] However, a number of specific, detailed requirements have to be met. According to Article 2(4) SPS Agreement, measures which conform to the relevant provisions of the SPS Agreement are 'presumed to be in accordance with the obligations of the Members under the provisions of GATT 1994 which relate to

[9] Commission decision 96/211 of 26 February 1996 (*OJ* (1996) L 68, p. 32).

[10] See W.Th. Douma, 'Het Verdrag van Amsterdam en het milieu: twee stappen vooruit, een stap terug?', *Tijdschrift voor Milieu en Recht*, No. 9 (1997) pp. 179-184.

[11] More specifically, the SPS Agreement applies to measures to protect human or animal life from risks arising from additives, contaminants, toxins or disease-causing organisms in their food, to protect human life from plant- or animal-carried diseases, to protect animal or plant life from pests, diseases, or disease-causing organisms, or to prevent or limit damage to a country from the entry, establishment or spread of pests (Annex A, point 1).

the use of sanitary or phytosanitary measures, in particular the provisions of Article XX(b)'.

Which requirements need to be fulfilled? First of all, the measures are to be 'applied only to the extent necessary to protect human, animal or plant life or health', 'based on scientific principles'[12] and 'not maintained without sufficient scientific evidence' (Art. 2(2) SPS Agreement).[13] Moreover, the measures may not 'arbitrarily or unjustifiably discriminate between Members where identical or similar conditions prevail, including between their own territory and that of other Members' nor shall they be 'applied in a manner which would constitute a disguised restriction on international trade' (Art. 2(3) SPS Agreement).

The Agreement differentiates between national measures based on international standards, guidelines and recommendations and other, stricter national measures. The first type of measures is favoured, as shows from Article 3(3) SPS Agreement which demands that WTO Members 'shall base their sanitary or phytosanitary measures on international standards, guidelines or recommendations where they exist, as otherwise provided for in this Agreement, and in particular in paragraph 3.' According to Article 3(2), such measures shall be deemed to be necessary to protect human, animal or plant life or health, and presumed to be consistent with the relevant provisions of this Agreement and of GATT 1994.

Things become more complicated when states want to go further.[14] Article 3(3) explains that measures stricter than international standards, guidelines or recommendations are only allowed if there exists a scientific justification for them (situation 1) or if they are established in accordance with the provisions of Article 5 (situation 2, described extensively below). Both for situations 1 and 2, it is stipulated that the stricter measures have to be in conformity with the other SPS Agreement provisions.

In a footnote to the text of the SPS Agreement, it is explained that for the purposes of this specific provision on situation 1, there is a scientific justification if, on the basis of an examination and evaluation of available scientific information in conformity with the relevant provisions of the Agreement, a Member determines that the relevant international standards, guidelines or

[12] It could very well be defended, that the precautionary principle by now forms an accepted scientific principle, but this does not seem to be what the drafters of this provision intended, as follows from the next condition on sufficient scientific evidence (although again, it is defendable that precautionary measures are based on sufficient scientific evidence) and the separate provision on precautionary measures.

[13] With the exception of precautionary measures adopted under the strict conditions described in Art. 5(7) SPS Agreement, discussed extensively below.

[14] Because some international standards, guidelines or recommendations tend to opt for the least common denominator of protection, it can easily happen that a WTO Member would want to opt for stricter measures. Moreover, it should not be forgotten that new scientific information might take quite a while before leading to alterations to international standards which are only established after lengthy procedures.

recommendations are not sufficient to achieve its appropriate level of sanitary or phytosanitary protection.

As for the second situation, compliance with the provisions of Article 5 of the SPS Agreement is made obligatory. This Article deals with risk assessment and determination of appropriate levels of protection. Among other things, it contains a specific provision on precautionary measures. Attention will now focus on the individual paragraphs of this Article.

'Article 5, Assessment of Risk and Determination of the Appropriate Level of Sanitary or Phytosanitary Protection

> '1.Members shall ensure that their sanitary or phytosanitary measures are based on an assessment as appropriate to the circumstances, of the risks to human, animal or plant life or health, taking into account risk assessment techniques developed by the relevant international organizations.
> 2. In the assessment of risks, Members shall take into account available scientific evidence; relevant processes and production methods; relevant inspection, sampling and testing methods; prevalence of specific diseases or pests; existence of pest- or disease-free areas; relevant ecological and environmental conditions; and quarantine or other treatment.'

In itself, these first two paragraphs might be interpreted in a precautionary way in the sense that not only risks for which full scientific evidence exists but also risks for which strong indications exist could be justified. However, since there is a special paragraph 7 which deals with situations where relevant scientific evidence is insufficient, this does not seem to be what the drafters of these paragraphs intended.[15]

The following paragraph discusses several specific economic factors which are to be taken into account when assessing risks.

> '3. In assessing the risk to animal or plant life or health and determining the measure to be applied for achieving the appropriate level of sanitary or phytosanitary protection from such risk, Members shall take into account as relevant economic factors the potential damage in terms of loss of production or sales in the event of the entry, establishment or spread of a pest or disease, the cost of control or eradication in the territory of the importing Member, and the relative cost-effectiveness of alternative approaches to limiting risks.'

[15] In the booklet issued by the WTO Secretariat in May 1996, entitled *Understanding the World Trade Organization Agreement on Sanitary and Phytosanitary Measures*, it is explained that the process of risk assessment and determination of acceptable levels of risks in itself 'already implies the routine use of safety margins to ensure adequate precautions are taken to protect health' (p. 9). Such safety margins are in line with the precautionary principle. However, that principle focuses on situations where measures are taken for which no full scientific certainty exists, whereas safety margins are applied in situations where the heart of the matter is based on full scientific certainty.

The next paragraph shows some remarkable aspects, first of all because of its choice of words and secondly because it seems to contravene the sovereignty of WTO Members to decide for themselves which level of protection they see as suitable. It deals with the proportionality of measures taken by Members:

> '4. Members should, when determining the appropriate level of sanitary or phytosanitary protection, take into account the objective of minimizing negative trade effects.'

What seems to be required here is that the benefits of the measure are not out of proportion to the negative trade effects. The problem with the wording in which this provision is put is the fact that especially measures aiming at the protection of the life and health of humans can hardly be called 'less appropriate' just because they have a large negative impact on trade. One can compare this with the similar decisions that have to be made when infrastructural works are planned. If a roundabout at a certain place costs 200,000 euro and will statistically cause an average of two victims of car accidents per year and traffic lights at the same spot cost only 20,000 euro and will cause an average of six victims per year, opting for the last solution might very well be the more appropriate choice to make. However, it is definitively not a choice for a more appropriate level of protection.

It may also be objected that Article 5(4) SPS Agreement might hinder WTO Members to set their own high, strict levels of protection. If a state wants to ban a substance which statistically speaking causes harm to a small group of persons, say one in ten thousand persons each year, in my opinion this is for the state to decide. If the state holds this to be an appropriate level of protection, the fact that a ban has negative trade effects should not stand in the way of adopting such a measure. The objective of the protection of human life and health (as well as of animals and plants), is not to be made subordinate to the objective of minimizing negative trade effects.

As this test is not phrased in very strict terms (Members are merely asked to take this kind of proportionality into account) in practice it does not seem likely that measures will be held in violation of this provision and therefore annulled.

A different kind of proportionality test is formulated in stricter terms in the sixth paragraph of Article 5.

> '6. Without prejudice to paragraph 2 of Article 3, when establishing or maintaining sanitary or phytosanitary measures to achieve the appropriate level of sanitary or phytosanitary protection, Members shall ensure that such measures are not more trade-restrictive than required to achieve their appropriate level of sanitary or phytosanitary protection, taking into account technical and economic feasibility.'

In yet another footnote, the SPS Agreement explains that for purposes of this paragraph, a measure is not more trade-restrictive than required unless there is another measure, 'reasonably available taking into account technical and economic feasibility, that achieves the appropriate level of sanitary or phytosanitary protection and is significantly less restrictive to trade.' For once, the Agreement thus makes life not particularly hard for governments faced with the claim that their measures are disproportionate. It might not be easy to come up with alternative measures which fulfil all of these requirements.

The following seventh paragraph of Article 5 incorporates the precautionary principle, although in a restricted form when compared with the usual interpretation given to it. When no full scientific certainty exists, the SPS Agreement envisages the possibility of taking provisional precautionary measures which are to be reviewed as soon as possible.

> '7. In cases where relevant scientific evidence is insufficient, a Member may provisionally adopt sanitary or phytosanitary measures on the basis of available pertinent information, including that from the relevant international organizations as well as from sanitary or phytosanitary measures applied by other Members. In such circumstances, Members shall seek to obtain the additional information necessary for a more objective assessment of risk and review the sanitary or phytosanitary measure accordingly within a reasonable period of time.'

The precautionary principle appears in a growing number of international treaties. The definitions and conditions for application of the principle presented there are not all the same, but similarities do prevail. The SPS Agreement differs from these treaties when it asks that precautionary measures may be adopted only 'provisionally'.[16] By demanding that additional information is to be obtained and used to review the precautionary measures, it is assured that they will be based on the best available information. However, what is a Member to do when the additional information which becomes available is still insufficient? Some claim, that if after a reasonable period of time no scientific evidence of a risk can be found, the measure cannot be maintained.[17] Such an interpretation is not altogether convincing. The text of Article 5.7 does not demand that precautionary measures are revoked under these circumstances. It merely says that they are to be reviewed within a reasonable period of time on the basis of obtained additional information. As long as extra information does not lead to another conclusion, the precautionary measures can be maintained.

One textual flaw of this provision is the fact that it implies that measures taken in a situation where scientific evidence is insufficient are necessarily not based on

[16] This condition seems to have played a decisive but criticisable role in the position taken by the EC not to invoke Art. 5.7, as will be discussed below.

[17] J.J. Barceló III, 'Product standards to protect the local environment – the GATT and the Uruguay Round Sanitary and Phytosanitary Agreement', 27 *Cornell International Law Journal* (1994) pp. 755-776 at p. 764. The author adds, that in such a case, 'one could hardly understand how the measure could be a genuine health or environmental measure in the first place'. He does follow a more precautionary line of reasoning when assuming that it would be appropriate in these kinds of cases to let the burden of proof rest with the country challenging another Member's standards.

an objective assessment of risk. Of course, measures should always be based on the best information available, or, in the words of the SPS Agreement, on the 'available pertinent information'. In those cases where not all the information is available yet, taking measures when enough indications are gathered which show that damages might occur is in line with the precautionary principle. It seems awkward, to say the least, to refer to such precautionary measures as measures which are based on a less objective assessment of risk.[18]

As was shown in this section, the SPS Agreement in many respects is elaborate enough, but – even in spite of the use of footnotes – it is not always clear how provisions are to be interpreted. By turning to the *Beef hormone* dispute now, it will be investigated how the Panel and the Appellate Body interpreted the provisions discussed above.

4. THE BEEF HORMONE DISPUTE

The subject of this dispute was the safety for the consumer of beef of cows treated with growth hormones. These hormones are administered to the cattle in the USA as well as in Canada in order for the animals to grow faster, which gives the farmers a competitive advantage. The Canadian as well as the USA governments claim that eating the meat of animals treated with hormones does not cause any health effects on humans. The EC is not convinced of this. According to the EC, there does exist a risk that human health might be endangered from eating hormone treated meat and meat products. In addition, it claims that the European consumer, just recovering from the BSE crisis, is just not willing to accept such meat. Therefore, the EC banned the use of the hormones in question as a means of speeding up growth.[19]

Because the majority of beef from the USA and Canada is from farms where hormones are used for growth promotion, the EC legislation forms an import ban on USA and Canadian beef. After fruitless consultations between the two countries and the EC, both countries requested a panel to be established to examine the matter. The two panels consisted of the same three persons[20] and came to the principal conclusion that the EC ban was not based on a risk assessment, that it was not based on existing international standards and not justified, that it amounted to discrimination or a disguised restriction in international trade and that the ban was thus inconsistent with the requirements of the

[18] Compare Art. 2(2) SPS Agreement, where it is more accurately stated that measures are not to be 'maintained without sufficient scientific evidence', except as provided for in Art. 5(7).

[19] Council Directive 96/22/EC prohibiting the use in livestock farming of certain substances having a hormonal action and related measures, *OJ* (1996) L 125, p. 3.

[20] Namely Thomas Cottier (Switzerland), Peter Palecka (Czech Republic) and Jun Yokata (Japan).

SPS Agreement. From this panel decision, it was concluded that a comprehensive precautionary risk policy under WTO law is no longer possible.[21] By examining the panel decisions as well as the decision of the Appallate Body, which also concluded that the EC measures violated WTO law, it will be investigated whether this negative conclusion is justified.

The EC prohibited six hormones for growth promotion purposes, three of which are also naturally occurring hormones produced by humans and animals (oestradiol-17ß, progesterone and testerone) and the other three artificially produced ones (trenbolone, zeranol and melengestrol acetate or MGA). For five of the hormones at issue the Codex Alimentarius Commission[22] had set up standards allowing for their use, or concluded that it was not necessary to set such standards.

According to the EC, the prohibitions were necessary and justifiable from the point of view of the protection of human health. Although no full scientific certainty exists on the risks of eating beef of cows treated with these hormones, the EC is of the opinion that there are enough indications that such a risk is present. In conformity with the precautionary principle the EC thus finds itself justified to take measures. According to the EC, the fact that the USA does not agree with the measures is due to 'the greater attachment of the European Communities to the precautionary principle'. The USA claims that the EC misunderstood the principle, as it calls for taking action based on preliminary or inconclusive scientific information where it might be important to act in the absence of conclusive scientific information. Interestingly enough, the USA comes up with global climate change as an example of the correct application of the precautionary principle.[23] The USA also claimed, that Article 5.7 reflected the precautionary approach. However, the European Communities had admitted that its ban was not pursuant to Article 5.7.[24] Instead, the EC came up with the argument that the precautionary principle is already a rule of international customary law or at least a general principle of law and should be used to interpret the other provisions of the SPS Agreement. The alleged legal status of the precautionary principle is denied by the other parties to the dispute. The USA

[21] Hilf and B. Eggers, 'Der WTO-Panelbericht im EG/USA-Hormonstreit. Anstoß zum grenzenlosen Weltbinnenmarkt für Lebensmittel oder Eigentor der WTO?', *EuZW*, No. 18 (1997) pp. 559-566.

[22] The Codex Alimentarius is an organisation established jointly by the FAO and WHO in 1962. Its purpose is to guide and promote the elaboration and establishment of definitions and requirements for food, to assist in their harmonisation and thus in facilitating international trade. The Codex is in the process of reviewing its procedures of standard setting, among others to fulfill its role attributed by the WTO in an improved way.

[23] According to the USA, which had objected to a need to act in the field of climate change for a long time because of a lack of evidence, preliminary scientific information had indicated a need to act as a precaution even though a full scientific understanding had not yet been achieved (WT/DS26/R/USA, para. 207).

[24] WT/DS26/R/USA, para. 207.

claims that the precautionary principle is no 'principle of customary international law' but rather an 'approach', the content of which differs from case to case. Canada agrees that the precautionary principle should be labelled as 'precautionary approach' because it is not yet a part of international public law. It is recognized however, that the 'precautionary approach or concept' can be seen as an emerging principle of international law' which in the future could crystallize into a 'general legal principle as referred to in Article 38(1) Statute ICJ.'

Why did the EC not invoke the precautionary provision provided for by the SPS Agreement itself? Did one presume that the EC measures would not fulfil the conditions laid down in Article 5.7, notably the one that demands that measures are to be adopted provisionally? In the Panel report, the EC is quoted stating that its measures were not provisional but definitive.[25] In my view, another approach could have been followed. Several arguments could support such a line of action. After all, the SPS provision does not state that only provisional measures can be adopted. It only says that Members may provisionally adopt measures. After obtaining additional information, the measure is to be reviewed. Such a measure could be a regular one. Moreover, the measures were 'maintained as a precautionary measure' as long as the 'harmless or harmful effects' of the use of the growth hormones oestradiol 17/ß, progesterone, testosterone, trenbolone and zeranol (i.e., five out of the six hormones under discussion in the dispute) awaited to be examined in detail. The EC itself had stated this explicitly in the preamble of the 1981 directive on growth hormones.[26] Thus, the decision not to invoke Article 5.7 is open for debate. After all, precaution means that in case of doubt, one is to err on the side of caution.

The Appellate Body upheld the Panel's finding that the EC import prohibition was inconsistent with Articles 3.3 and 5.1 of the SPS Agreement. It did reverse several of the Panel's findings. Upon examining the text of the AB decision, it becomes evident that there is some reason for the EC to be relieved about the modifications the Appellate Body introduced. It interpreted the provisions of the SPS Agreement in a way that does leave the EC much more leeway to adopt a new decision that also prohibits hormones in beef, as long as it is accompanied by a better motivation.[27]

For instance, the AB found that when a Member's measure is not based on international standards in accordance with Article 3.1 SPS, it is not up to that Member to show that its SPS measure is consistent with Article 3.3 SPS, as the Panel had said. In other words, Article 3.3 does not form an exception to a general rule. In order to uphold a measure consistent with Article 3.3 SPS, such a

[25] *Idem*, para. 239.

[26] Council Directive 81/602/EEC of 31 July 1981, *OJ* (1981) L 222, p. 32. Directive 81/602 was repealed by Council Directive 96/22/EC of 29 April 1996, *OJ* (1996) L 125 , p. 3.

[27] The available options are discussed in the last section of this paper.

measure, *inter alia*, has to meet the requirements of Article 5. Furthermore, the AB agreed with the EC that risk assessment was not only quantitative and that risk evaluation involved not only laboratory conditions but also real world potential adverse effects to human health. It also made clear that when a panel is charged with determining whether sufficient scientific evidence exists to warrant the maintenance by a WTO Member of a particular SPS measure, it 'may, of course, and should, bear in mind that responsible, representative governments commonly act from perspectives of prudence and precaution where risks of irreversible, e.g. life-terminating, damage to human health are concerned.' However, the AB does not hold it possible that the precautionary principle overrides the provisions of Article 5.1 and 5.2 SPS Agreement.

Unfortunately, the Appellate Body refrained from taking a position as to the legal status of the precautionary principle. It even went so far as stating that it was 'unnecessary, and probably imprudent' to take a position on this 'important, but abstract, question'. It was noted that this question 'continues to be the subject of debate among academics, law practitioners, regulators and judges' and that according to some it has crystallized into what the Appellate Body describes as a 'general principle of customary international *environmental* law' with the emphasis added by the Appellate Body, which thus seems to indicate that this might be something different than a general principle of customary international law.

5. CONCLUDING REMARKS

Does international trade law as it stands today bring about a levelling down of precautionary protection standards? This was the main question investigated in this paper. After having shown that within the EC, harmonization measures based on Article 100A EC Treaty do not preclude national precautionary measures if the provision of Article 100A(4) EC Treaty is invoked, WTO law was turned to. Studying the SPS Agreement, it became clear that a mechanism exists allowing for precautionary measures in cases where relevant scientific evidence is insufficient (namely Art. 5.7). That provision can only be invoked to provisionally adopted measures. As was explained in the section on the *Beef hormone* dispute, that condition seems to have been the major reason why the EC did not invoke Article 5.7 SPS Agreement.

The EC ban on hormone beef was held incompatible with the SPS Agreement. This was due to the fact that the ban was stricter than existing international standards on the use of growth hormones and the EC did not meet the conditions applicable in such cases. However, the AB made clear that the SPS Agreement does make it possible to uphold standards stricter than the ones agreed upon at the international level. The explanation given to the conditions set out in the SPS Agreement does not seem to preclude precautionary measures like the ones of the

EC on hormones altogether, as long as it is based on a risk assessment as to the specific risks brought about by growth hormones for human health. Still, clarifications remain necessary as to situations in which the specific provision on precautionary measures (Art. 5.7 SPS Agreement) will need to be used instead of the regular provisions (such as Arts. 5.1 and 5.2 SPS Agreement). In other words, the question that remains to be answered is whether the EC can invoke the latter provisions after having performed a risk assessment which still leaves some doubts, or whether in that case it can only provisionally adopt precautionary measures under Article 5.7 SPS Agreement.

The Dispute Settlement Body (DSB) adopted the AB and Panel reports on 13 February 1998. The period for implementation was set by arbitration at 15 months from the date of the adoption of the reports.[28] This means that the period expires on 13 May 1999. The EC has undertaken to comply with the recommendations of the DSB within the implementation period. In a press announcement, it was explained that the EC had three options to choose from. The first option would be to open the borders to hormone meat, but the Commission believes that this is not acceptable from a consumer health point of view. The second option would be to accept the WTO ruling, maintain the existing EC legislation banning hormone meat and then negotiate a compensation to the US and Canada on the basis of the WTO rules. The third and final option would be to have experts conduct a formal risk assessment, focusing specifically on the potential health risks from hormone residues in meat and meat products, and then adapt EC legislation on the basis of this risk assessment where necessary. This would imply that a group of eminent experts would be asked to examine the health risks associated with the consumption of hormone meat, it was stated. By mid December 1998, eight expert groups were assembled to carry out this task and the independent Scientific Committee on Veterinary Measures related to Public Health (SCVPH) was asked to evaluate the scientific knowledge and evidence, but results were not yet available.[29] Adapting EC legislation in time thus might turn out to be as hard for the EC as it is for EC Member States to implement EC directives in time.

[28] WT/DS26/15 and WT/DS48/13 of 29 May 1998. The Commission had pleaded for a much longer implementation period (namely 39 months: two years for a risk assessment and 15 months for any necessary legislative action thereafter), because 15 months would be insufficient to complete a risk assessment and to implement possible legislative measures.

[29] Second bi-annual BSE follow-up report, Commission Communication of 18 November 1998, COM(98)598 final, point 6.2.

INTERNATIONAL HUMANITARIAN LAW

Humanitarian Crises

Chair: H.-P. Gasser

Regulation of Warfare

Chair: E.P.J. Myjer

LAW IN HUMANITARIAN CRISES: INTRODUCTORY STATEMENT

Hans-Peter Gasser*

The world is beset by many types of 'humanitarian crises', i.e., crises that have devastating effects on human beings: hunger, the wholesale destruction of the natural environment, the squandering of natural resources indispensable for mankind's survival, unequal access to health care, etc. For the purpose of this discussion, I would like to limit the scope of my remarks to humanitarian crises of a particular kind: those that arise in or are caused by armed conflict.

What do we mean by 'humanitarian crisis', especially when the term is used in conjunction with 'law' - by implication, international humanitarian law? We understand international humanitarian law as comprising those rights and obligations of an international character relating to all types of humanitarian issues that arise in situations of armed conflict. Originally, humanitarian law was mainly concerned with the plight of wounded soldiers on the battlefield and prisoners of war. Gradually, however, the focus shifted to protecting the civilian population from the effects of warfare. On the one hand, civilians had to be shielded from the direct effects of hostilities: this was done by strengthening the principle of immunity for civilians from acts of war. On the other hand, it was also necessary to protect civilians who found themselves temporarily in the hands of the enemy, whether as prisoners or as inhabitants of occupied territories: human rights law adapted to the conditions of armed conflict.

It may be pointed out that it was in The Hague that governments first agreed on international rules of warfare; indeed, the Hague Regulations respecting the laws and customs of war on land (1899 and 1907) are at the origin of the city's claim to be the 'legal capital of the world'. Subsequently, The Hague did not manifest any active interest in the law of war, and the substantive matters dealt with in the 1907 Hague Regulations are now covered by the 1949 Geneva Conventions and their 1977 Additional Protocols. But the lull was only temporary. Both the Organization for the Prohibition of Chemical Weapons and the International Criminal Tribunal for the former Yugoslavia are in The Hague. Moreover, the Dutch government has just extended an invitation to the United Nations to set up the International Criminal Court in The Hague. These decisions bear witness not only to the city's hospitality but also to its determination to contribute to efforts aimed at making international humanitarian law credible.

* Editor-in-Chief, International Review of the Red Cross; International Committee for the Red Cross, Geneva.

W.P. Heere (Ed.), International Law and The Hague's 750th Anniversary

On a completely different level, but a very important one indeed for the understanding of the law and its teaching, it is worth mentioning that a Yearbook of International Humanitarian Law is about to be launched in The Hague.

But the purpose of our discussion is not so much to celebrate the past as to examine the problems we are facing today and those that lie ahead. Our topic, as we have just defined it, is law as it applies to humanitarian crises arising in conflict situations. At the outset of our short analysis, we should perhaps point out that these and other crises cannot be solved through humanitarian policy or action alone. I say this not merely out of modesty and because our time is limited. The fact is that there is no such thing as a vague 'humanitarianism' which has, or could fairly be expected to have, answers to all the ills in the world. To put it differently, humanitarian law, policy or action are no substitute for tough decisions that must be taken by those who are in power.

Armed conflict and other forms of violence seldom break out without a motive. They are the result of unsolved problems of a political nature, of tensions for which no acceptable remedy has been found, of a lack of procedures to settle such issues. From a humanitarian standpoint, we can only appeal to all those who are in a position to take action to defuse such situations before they degenerate into open conflict. Repeated failure of the organized international community to find peaceful solutions to emerging conflicts is the real tragedy of our times.

At the risk of being misunderstood, I believe that a second preliminary remark is in order. While terrible human tragedies have been caused by armed conflict in the recent past, it would be wrong to assume that they are peculiar to the post Cold-War period, with the breakdown, in 1989/1990, of a supposedly stable world order, and that such tragedies have never occurred before. This is of course not true. Has genocide in Rwanda caused more or less suffering than the slave trade in the 18th and 19th centuries? Was the war in Yugoslavia more or a less 'humane' than the German aggression against Eastern Europe during the Second World War - or than the Japanese occupation of part of China in the late thirties? Is it possible to compare the crimes committed in Lebanon in the seventies and eighties with the horror stories of crusaders wading knee-deep in blood in the streets of Jerusalem? These are futile questions, and to look for answers makes no sense. We are not called on to compare degrees of human suffering but to make every effort to ensure that such suffering does not recur - either now or in the future.

If we are to do so, we must first attempt to understand the nature of modern conflicts.

1. Most conflicts today take place within the territory of a single state. They tear apart what should be an organized and structured nation but all too often is not. They are frequently the result of misguided attempts at nation-building or an inability to adapt structures to the real needs of the population or the various populations. Weak governments cling to claims of sovereignty instead of solving their countries' problems. The personal interests of the governing class, or

family, prevail over all other considerations. The result is permanent tensions and even civil war, often fought with the utmost cruelty.

2. Weapons, particularly light weapons, are cheap and easily available. This foments violence. In the hands of 'combatants' without any formal training, often youngsters, such weapons, even the most ordinary ones, cause untold death and destruction because the principle of distinction between military targets and the - protected - civilian population no longer has any meaning.

3. The omnipresence of the media influences the course of hostilities, and not always in a favourable way. However, since information on conflicts and their effects on human beings is both easily and instantly available, no one today can plead ignorance and thereby justify his inaction.

4. The international community is much better equipped to respond to the strictly humanitarian problems caused by conflicts than it was only twenty years ago. In particular, humanitarian assistance can be organized at short notice and shipped anywhere in the world. The international community certainly has a much more impressive record on this count than it has in the area of conflict settlement.

5. Non-governmental organizations play a very important role in conflict situations today, not only by providing assistance to people in need but also by denouncing unacceptable violations of human rights.

Given the nature of modern conflicts, what can be done to minimize the risk that they will result in humanitarian crises?

First of all, as I have said, underlying political problems and tensions must be identified and their existence acknowledged. Satisfactory solutions must then be found in time, that is to say, before conflict erupts. Only governments can find such solutions; international humanitarian organizations are powerless in this respect. However, various measures can and must be taken to prevent human tragedies from occurring when conflict does break out.

1. Norms must be established and accepted which guarantee a modicum of humanity, even in situations of violence. These norms already exist: the 1949 Geneva Conventions, supplemented by a number of other treaties and by rules of customary law. While the law is not perfect, it is a satisfactory tool for limiting suffering and destruction. There is no need to embark on another lengthy and costly codification process.

2. Everyone, including government troops and irregular or rebel forces, must agree to respect a code of conduct comprising a set of fundamental rules, such as 'respect the wounded', 'don't use violence against unarmed people, especially women and children' and 'don't evict civilians from their homes'. Everyone must know these rules and behave accordingly, even in the most chaotic situations.

3. When serious crimes are committed during a conflict, the culprits must be prosecuted and punished. It is mainly up to domestic courts to judge such crimes. As for international criminal tribunals, their first and foremost purpose is to demonstrate the international community's concern to see that States fulfil their

international obligation to uphold justice, in particular by prosecuting war criminals who fall within their jurisdiction.

To conclude, international humanitarian law expresses the international community's determination to ensure that everyone is treated with a modicum of humanity, even in a situation of extreme violence which is armed conflict. While the primary responsibility of governments and international organizations is the peaceful settlement of disputes, political discourse must, as a matter of urgent priority, give greater consideration to humanitarian concerns.

ACCESS TO VICTIMS: RECONCEIVING THE RIGHT TO 'INTERVENE'

Marc Weller*

1. THE PROBLEM

The classical international law doctrines which have dominated the discipline up to about 1990 would have perceived an obvious and inherent tension between the notion of humanitarian intervention and the fundamental concept of sovereignty on which the entire state system is purportedly predicated. For, sovereignty is traditionally defined as the supreme power over all objects and subjects within a given territory to the exclusion of the exercise of any other public power.

Intervention, of course, denotes the exercise of public authority by one state or public authority in the territory of another state, or in relation to it, without the consent of the latter state. Some would add that such an unauthorized exercise of authority must be of a coercive kind, in order to cross the threshold from interference, which may be politically undesirable but is not necessary unlawful, to intervention, which is unlawful by definition.

Humanitarian 'intervention' refers to forcible action by one state, a group of states or an intergovernmental organization in the territory of another state without the consent of the latter, undertaken on humanitarian grounds or in order to restore constitutional governance. As distinguished in classical doctrine from the 'rescue of nationals abroad', action is not taken by a state on behalf of its own nationals faced with threats abroad, but the intended beneficiary of the 'intervention' is the population of the target state itself, or a significant segment thereof.

The presumption that humanitarian action constitutes intervention and is therefore, *prima facie*, unlawful was reflected in international standards, state practice and scholarship. Although the United Nations Charter does not expressly prohibit intervention by states, article 2 (7), which rules out United Nations intervention in matters essentially within the domestic jurisdiction of states, has been widely invoked to extend in its application beyond action of the organization itself. Forcible intervention would, at any rate, be precluded by the prohibition of the threat or use of force enshrined in Article 2 (4). General Assembly standards on non-intervention confirm this view. Indeed, the famous Declaration on the Inadmissibility of Intervention 2131 (XX) of 1965 proscribes

* Deputy Director, Centre of International Studies, University of Cambridge.

W.P. Heere (Ed.), International Law and The Hague's 750th Anniversary

intervention 'for any reason whatever', and Resolution 36/103 of 1981 rules out armed or subversive action "under any pretext whatsoever". The Declaration on the Enhancement of the Effectiveness of the Principle of Refraining from the Threat or Use of Force in International Relations annexed to Resolution 42/22 of 1987 confirms that "no consideration of whatever nature may be invoked to warrant resorting to the threat or use of force in violation of the Charter."

The International Court of Justice expressed itself in a similar way in the *Nicaragua* Judgment, when it held that an exception to the prohibition of intervention would "involve a fundamental modification of the customary law principle of non-intervention" for which it could find no support in state practice (1986 ICJ 13, 116, 205, 209). Indeed, it has been frequently noted by scholars that the pre-1990 cases which could have been justified with reference to the doctrine of humanitarian 'intervention' are marked by the failure of the intervening state to invoke that doctrine. The overwhelming humanitarian emergencies in Uganda and Cambodia were not formally invoked as a legal justification for the armed actions undertaken by Tanzania and Vietnam respectively. Instead, both states chose to rely on a rather extensive view of self-defence. India's action in relation to Bangladesh is slightly more ambiguous, inasmuch as humanitarian considerations were initially invoked, before India, too, relied on self-defence. Even that action triggered, of course, considerable condemnation in the United Nations General Assembly and elsewhere.

The United States similarly chose to rely on purported authorizations from regional organizations or arrangements when attempting to justify so-called pro-democratic interventions in the Dominican Republic, in Grenada and in Panama. In addition, in the latter two cases, self-defence was formally invoked as the principal legal justification. It is interesting to note that in these two cases, and especially in the instance of Panama, the United States government argued at a political level that the action was also one which vindicated the will of the local population. However, even the United States government was, at that stage, unwilling to create a precedent in favor of forcible action designed to establish democratic governance in accordance with the will of the people, made manifest in elections. Hence, it chose not to advance this argument at the legal level, for example when justifying the operation in the United Nations Security Council.

The prohibition of humanitarian 'intervention' before 1990 is also strangely confirmed by the attempts to enshrine such a right in international standards in the context of humanitarian law. The drafting history of Article 18 (2) of Protocol II to the Geneva Conventions of 1977 is particularly instructive. A legal obligation to tolerate even non-forcible humanitarian action was rejected and instead it was confirmed that even activities 'essential for the survival' of a civilian population 'shall be undertaken subject to the consent of the High Contracting Party concerned'. Similarly, the more recent attempts by the United Nations General Assembly to establish a New Humanitarian Order remain subject to the requirement of consent of the target state of humanitarian actions.

The non-governmental, scholarly Institut de Droit International has held that offers of assistance in cases where the life or health of the population is threatened cannot be considered unlawful intervention. "However, such offers of assistance shall not, particularly by virtue of the means used to implement them, take a form suggestive of a threat of armed intervention or any other measure of intimidation", the Institut added after a difficult and divisive debate. While it is true that within the Institut and outside of it, some scholars have consistently advocated a right of forcible humanitarian action, it must also be admitted that their views were very much the position of the outsider, reflected neither in international standards, nor in state practice or even broadly based scholarly opinion, at least until 1990 that is.

Since 1990, of course, a fundamental shift appears to have taken place. The advocacy of a right to humanitarian 'intervention' is now, if not the majority view, at least a very respectable position. More importantly, there have occurred some 15 instances of humanitarian actions. Many have been based on the exercise of United Nations Chapter VII authority. But others have been based on purported authorizations from regional organizations or arrangements, which were lacking in previous authorization under Chapter VIII of the Charter, and only some of which attracted subsequent support from the Security Council. In addition, in some instances, states have acted by way of informal coalitions, or through collective agencies which do not claim Chapter VII status, on the basis of a right of humanitarian intervention which is now alleged to exist in customary international law. Most famously, the United Kingdom argued in parliamentary testimony relating to Iraq, the first case of this new practice, somewhat incongruously and rather boldly that "the practice of states does show over a long period that it is generally accepted that in extreme circumstances a state can intervene in another state for humanitarian reasons."

Even if this astonishing assertion had come at the conclusion of the episodes of 'intervention' which have occurred since then, it would be difficult to support within the traditional strands of legal discourse. For, if, as was clearly established, humanitarian 'intervention' was unlawful before 1990, then it is hardly possible to establish in accordance with international law 'sources' doctrine that a change to the *jus cogens* prohibition of the threat or use of force could have come about over the past decade.

2. THE INADEQUACY OF THE PROPOSED EXPLANATIONS OF RECENT PRACTICE

A number of views have been proposed, reflecting this difficulty. Alas, neither of them is fully persuasive:

1. Some scholars argue that humanitarian 'intervention' remains unlawful. However, this view appears to be inconsistent with the fact that there have now been a number of rather significant cases which were formally justified by the states taking action, and others supporting them, as humanitarian 'intervention'. None of these actions has triggered significant condemnations from other states. The slightly more sophisticated version of this view would argue that humanitarian 'intervention' remains unlawful, but that the intervening states can be assured that their action will not be internationally condemned. However, given the nature of the prohibition of the use of force as an undisputed *jus cogens* rule, and given the fact that its violation constitutes an international crime of state which requires a response by all other states, such juridical pragmatism must remain unpersuasive. In addition, the fact that the claim of intervening states to have acted as a matter of right has not been opposed remains unaddressed.

2. Another, rather cautious view, accepts that humanitarian actions have recently proliferated. However, they are justified in terms of United Nations Charter law, rather than international custom. That is to say, there has occurred a procedural shift in the interpretation of Articles 2 (7) and 39 of the Charter. That shift permits a wider interpretation of the notion of 'threats to the peace' which permit Chapter VII action. The ultra cautious variant of this view would hold that the Security Council can now authorize the use of force where a humanitarian emergency results in external ramifications which threaten regional peace and stability. References to the destabilizing nature of the flow of refugees into neighbouring states, or to the danger of the spread of hostilities, in some Security Council resolutions, are invoked in this context. The slightly more daring variant recognizes that the Security Council has, in fact, found in several instances expressly that the suffering of a population itself can constitute a threat to the peace, even if there are no significant external consequences. Ultimately, however, both these views remain unsatisfactory, inasmuch as they can only explain the episodes where there actually existed a formal Chapter VII mandate authorizing forcible action. The unopposed claims to a right based in general custom are either unpersuasively argued away, or they are ignored.

3. Some, mainly United States-based scholars argue that humanitarian 'intervention' was never prohibited by Article 2(4) of the United Nations Charter, inasmuch as it would not be an action "inconsistent with the purposes of the United Nations", or because it would not actually affect the "political independence or territorial integrity" of the target state. This proposition is plainly not in accordance with the drafting history of the Charter, or its consistent interpretation in state practice since 1945. It is not possible to overturn the fact

that humanitarian 'intervention' was regarded as unlawful under Article 2 (4) the United Nations Charter before 1990, simply by declaring that it was, in fact, lawful.

4. The now dominant view justifying humanitarian action asserts that there has occurred a change in custom, as is evidenced in the pattern of post 1990 practice. Humanitarian action, it is asserted, is now permissible in cases of grave and persistent violations of human rights. Appealing though it is, this argument, too, is doomed to failure. First of all, the United Nations Commission on Human Rights routinely identifies a whole series of situations of the gravest and most persistent violations of human rights. However, there is no suggestion that all the states concerned have opened themselves to the humanitarian 'intervention' treatment. Perhaps even more fundamentally, in most of the individual cases, states participating in, or supporting the practice in the Security Council, have stated that the circumstances of the particular instance were exceptional and unique. Hence, they actively declared that there exists no opinio juris which would transform the individual episode into a precedent indicating a change in custom. Of course, one can argue that this precaution loses its credibility if states claim in a whole series of similar cases that each of them is, in fact, exceptional and unique. However, this argument does not help overcome the fact that the prohibition of the use of force is a *jus cogens* rule, which can only be changed if there is clear and express *opinio juris* of a very special kind. The existence of such legislative intent cannot simply be imputed and is impossible to demonstrate in relation to humanitarian 'intervention'.

5. Another theory which has great appeal was pioneered by Professor Teson and, in a slightly different version, by Professor Reisman. This view, which comes close to the one which will be proposed below, is based on the right to political representation and self-determination. However, in the incarnation proposed by Professor Teson which holds that only governments which are truly representative can rely on the protection of the doctrine of non-intervention, and the view that international law permits the making of "war" in the defence of human rights, appears to be too open ended to find support in the practice of states as it stands at present. Professor Reisman's argument, developed in relation to the Grenada intervention, on the other hand, provides a starting point for the justification of so-called 'pro-democratic' intervention, but is too limited to explain other types of humanitarian action.

Considerations of self-determination and of the ultimate nature of the state are, however, of primary relevance when seeking to explain the phenomenon of humanitarian action, as these two authors would hold. After all, so-called intervention is alleged to be unlawful, inasmuch as it constitutes a fundamental interference with the rights of the state. These rights are derived from a definition of sovereignty to which, it was hitherto alleged, certain inherent rights attach, including the right of non-intervention.

Of course, it is by now clear that the state is not a real person, endowed with real rights from birth. Instead, the state is a social construct. Its rights are based, on the one hand, in the grant of constitutional authority by its constituents made manifest in its constitution. In that sense, the state enjoys authority only to the extent that competence has been transferred to it by the population which constitutes its corporate personality *inter alia* through the state. I say *inter alia* because competence is of course not uniquely or exclusively or supremely located in the state. Instead it is assigned to various different layers of authority, including local and regional government, supranational organs such as those of the European Union, the United Nations Council, etc. Secondly, even the public powers which have been assigned to these differing layers of authority are circumscribed by international law. No local, regional, 'national' or supranational authority can, for example, lawfully engage in torture or genocide.

The fact that the authority of the state is limited and based on the will of the governed is undisputedly accepted by all governments. Of course, the majority of state governments which have exercised power since 1945 were not really based on the actual will of those they effectively controlled. The myth of the exercise of state powers on the basis of the will of the governed could be maintained through a semantic conversion of the doctrine of internal self-determination. In fact, the doctrine of representation and internal self-determination has been bastardized to an extent that it now serves to disenfranchise the very populations it purports to enfranchise.

This result has been achieved through a simple trick. While international law and political philosophy uniformly espoused by governments of all ideological persuasions establish a criterion of legitimacy, the notion of representativeness and internal self-determination has been turned on its head. Hence, international legal standards, created by governments, do indeed confirm that the authority to govern must be based on the will of the governed. For example Resolution 36/103 which was already mentioned above solemnly reiterates 'the sovereign and inalienable right of states freely to determine its own political, economic, cultural and social system ... in accordance with the will of the people.' Note that, while expressly referring to the will of the people, this right of internal self-determination appertains not directly to them, but to 'the state'. And it is simply presumed that whatever political, economic or social system exists within a state must necessarily exist as a result of the exercise of the will of the people. Hence, effectiveness of control by state authorities is simply equated to legitimate governance.

The doctrine of non-intervention, which theoretically aims to protect the free transmission of the will of the people through the constitutional structure from external adulteration, is then converted into a static principle which protects the 'stability' of the state and 'any of its institutions' and the 'political order'. In this way, the content of the right to internal self-determination is semantically and contextually reduced to be literally coextensive with the doctrine of non-intervention. And the doctrine of non-intervention protects whatever political system happens to exist, whether or not it is in any way representative of the popular will.

The Orwellian conversion of representativeness as the object of protection of the international legal order into effectiveness that was achieved over the past decades was, however, not complete. There are a number of instances where the presumption that effective authority equals a right to represent exclusively those who are under the effective control of a particular government is reversed. These cases where effective control does not attract a right to represent a population internationally can be described as instances of fundamental dissociation; they are manifestations of the underlying principle that the authority to govern must be based on the will of the people. While this may appear to be a bold contention at first sight, these cases are, in some respects, so well established in international practice that they are hardly noticed. It is the contention of this paper that the phenomenon of humanitarian action merely reflects an extension of this well established practice, however hesitantly.

The question of the justification of humanitarian actions is, therefore, not one of the creation of a new exception to the prohibition of the use of force. Instead, the question is: What are the circumstances where the presumption of the exclusive power of effective authorities to represent a population or a constitutionally relevant segment thereof is overcome? And to what extent can states act directly in accordance with the expressed or implied desires of a population which is manifestly not represented by the purported government or authority? And finally, what is the international constitutional process for the administration of this process?

3. FUNDAMENTAL DISSOCIATION

It is possible to distinguish a number of types of cases of fundamental dissociation. The first category of cases an obvious one: that of inherent dissociation.

3.1. **Inherent dissociation**

A colonial territory enjoys legal personality separate from the metropolitian state, even if the latter exercises absolutely effective authority. The colonial state is legally required to relinquish governmental authority and must permit an act of self-determination to take place. If it fails to actualize the rights of the colonial people to decide free upon their political status and, if they so desire, to establish their own state and a governmental system, the colonized people are positively entitled to mount a campaign of resistance against the effective authorities. In response to repression by the colonial state, the self-determination entity is entitled to use force and to receive international assistance in support of its struggle.

Obviously, in this instance, the claim of the colonial authorities to be legally entitled to represent the population that is being effectively controlled is tainted. Unless and until such an exercise of authority is terminated, or vindicated through an exercise of the will of the colonial people, it constitutes an inherently internationally unlawful act. In fact, the presumption that effectiveness equals a right to represent is reversed and representation is instead provisionally vested in one or more national liberation movements, which need not be in control of territory. In cases of the repression of an indigenous campaign of self-determination, international actions, including the very activities which in other circumstances would constitute intervention, are permissible in accordance with the wishes of the legitimate, and not the effective, representatives of the nascent sovereign, i.e., the colonial population.

Similarly, in cases of secondary colonialism, the claim to represent on the basis of effectiveness is not internationally accepted. Hence, despite the continuous and uninterrupted display of state authority by Morocco and Indonesia in relation to the Western Sahara and Eastern Timor respectively, the right to represent is still subject to confirmation or express rejection through a referendum. The same phenomenon is evidenced in cases of internal colonialism (formerly Southern Rhodesia and South Africa), where an alien people exercised political control over the indigenous majority, which remained unrepresented.

Finally, it is undisputed that the right to represent is obviously unavailable in relation to populations which were incorporated through the international use of force. Hence, the United Nations Security Council expressly indicated that Iraq could not claim to act for Kuwait, however effectively it controlled that territory in the aftermath of the invasion of August 1990. Instead, the government of Kuwait, which had lost all effectiveness and had been displaced to Saudi Arabia, continued to be able to articulate the will of the sovereign, i.e., to engage in international legal acts on behalf of the population of Kuwait. This included the right to request foreign armed assistance by virtue of the right to self-defence.

3.2. Active dissociation: Secession outside of the colonial context

An inherent dissociation occurs at the moment of the violation of fundamental legal principles (self-determination, apartheid, non-use of force), automatically disrupting the presumption of representation based on effectiveness from that point onwards. In the case of active dissociation, an entity within an existing state contrives to remove itself from the constitutional structure of that state and to establish a new state. Classical international law has frowned upon claims to unilateral, opposed secession, and has sought to restrict such claims to instances of colonial self-determination entities seeking independence. However, recently there appears to have emerged a rather limited trend to recognize a right of a population to remove itself from the control of the present effective authorities outside of the colonial context.

This new, limited right was presaged in the campaigns of the Baltic republics for a revival of their independence. Although that instance was an ambiguous one, inasmuch as a significant number of states had never accepted, *de jure*, the incorporation of the republics into the USSR, it pointed the way towards subsequent developments in relation to the Socialist Federal Republic of Yugoslavia (SFRY). For, the USSR constitution actually guaranteed a right to secession for the constituent republics. The dispute about who would exercise control over the actualization of this right remained unresolved, as the USSR as a whole dissolved before a definitive view could be taken.

The unilateral declarations of independence of Croatia and Slovenia in summer of 1991 could also find a basis in constitutional law. According to the 1974 SFRY constitution, sovereignty was principally located in the individual federal units, which enjoyed an express right to self-determination and secession. The Belgrade government argued that such a right, if indeed it existed, could only be exercised according to procedures established by the central authorities, and with the consent of all other federal units. It proceeded to take forcible action against the two republics, by way of a purported internal 'police action'.

The response of the international community, led by the European Union and its Member States, was interesting and novel. Long before recognition of the two republics as states, as early as August 1991, it was confirmed that Slovenia and Croatia enjoyed separate legal personality in international law, that they were entitled to the protection of their territorial integrity and unity, and that the Belgrade government could no longer use repressive measures against them. Force not being available, this meant that the central authorities no longer had a means of opposing secession.

Ultimately, it was found that the entire SFRY had dissolved. Hence, it would not have been possible to exhaust good faith negotiations with a view to achieving independence through constitutional procedures, rather than unilateral actions. Instead, all of the republics that wished it could obtain independence unilaterally, provided such a decision was backed by a manifestation of popular will through a referendum.

The Yugoslav precedent indicates that international law does take account of the constitutional status of an entity and will legally privilege active dissociation where a federal-type constitution locates sovereignty within the individual federal unit. However, as the case of Kosovo demonstrated, the presumption of representation is removed through active dissociation only under very restrictive conditions. Thus far, that entity, which also enjoyed federal status under the SFRY constitution but was not formally a republic, has not been accorded separate legal personality. Although forcible international action has now been taken in relation to it, such action has thus far been focussed on the suppression of abuses of the population, and is not as yet directed towards the facilitation of independence for Kosovo. However, this may change over time.

Similarly, the initial response to the secession of Chechnya sought to deny it the status of a constitutionally-based self-determination entity. With the dissolution of the USSR and the independence of Russia, Chechnya had in fact been promoted to the status of a Federal Republic within the newly formed Russian Federation. However, the Russian Federal constitution determined that ultimately, sovereignty was located in the centre, and not in the individual republics. The centre had then transferred the right to exercise some sovereign powers to the level of the Republics, but such authority did not originate in them. Hence, as opposed to the Yugoslav Republics which could claim original sovereignty and which could actualize it through secession, Chechnya was not a genuine constitutional self-determination entity. Rather than confirming a separate legal status for it, the European Union, for instance, confirmed the continued territorial integrity of the Russian Federation, and merely demanded that the central authorities cease violating human rights when re-establishing effective control.

As subsequent events relating to Chechnya have demonstrated, the eventual success of unilateral opposed secession is of course not precluded, even for entities which are neither colonial nor constitutional self-determination entities. The difference relates to the fact that international law assigns a separate legal status to those entities which are either inherently or actively dissociated from the central authorities. Their struggle for independence is legally privileged to the same extent that the authority to represent of the central authorities is challenged. Other entities will only enjoy the benefit of the protection of human rights and the law of internal conflict while mounting the campaign for independence.

While active dissociation has thus far only been applied in the very narrow context of constitutional self-determination entities, the case of Chechnya after the 1997 transitory agreement with the Russian Federation may point towards one other category of cases which may be legally privileged. Chechnya's status has changed as a result of the signing of the agreement. While, formally, the agreement does not resolve the issue of Chechnya's purported independence, it does appear to grant a status similar to constitutional self-determination to it. If the Russian Federation were now to use force against it, the international response might well differ from the tacit acceptance of Russia's claim to territorial integrity and unity that was previously displayed in relation to it.

The same would probably apply where stable *de facto* entities are concerned. These are entities which have over a considerable period of time administered themselves in the manner of an independent state, without having claimed that status, or in the abence of widespread acceptance of such a claim. If, for example Taiwan were to be invaded by Chinese armed forces, this would manifestly violate the separate legal personality which has emerged over nearly half a century of active self-administration. The nominal claim of China to be entitled to represent Taiwan, which is nearly universally accepted, would thus be strongly resisted if ever it were to be translated into the re-establishement of effective control against the will of the population. In fact, the United States claims a legal right to use force in accordance with the express or implied desire of the population under those circumstances.

It must be noted, however, that *de facto* entities which have been created in violation of *jus cogens* rules will not stabilize in a way which would attract the protection of the international legal order. Hence, the effectiveness that is being exercised by the authorities in the Turkish occupied part of Cyprus cannot ever translate itself into a claim to independent statehood, as it was brought about through the unlawful use of force. Similarly, in the case of Southern Rhodesia after the unilateral declaration of independence, the exercise of control by the white minority regime could not ever serve to meet the criterion of effective government for the determination of independent statehood. And considerable international effort was expended to achieve a resolution of the Bosnia conflict which would avoid accepting that armed intervention and genocide and ethnic cleansing can result in statehood for the so-called Srpska Republic.

3.3. Express dissociation through elections or anti-constitutional coups

Express dissociation relates to two principal types of cases where a population has been given the opportunity to declare directly that it is not represented by the effective authorities. This will occur either where an existing government has permitted the holding of elections, where such elections have been lost and where the existing authorities then fail to transfer power to the winners of the elections. Or, express dissociation occurs where a constitutional consensus has been restored, for example where a popular referendum has endorsed a new constitutional settlement at the conclusion of a civil war, and where that freshly manifested constitutional consensus is overturned by way of a coup.

In relation to Burma, the United Nations General Assembly has consistently demanded that the military regime must transfer power to the elected members of parliament under the leadership of Aung San Suu Kyi, whatever the effectiveness of control it exercises. The United Nations Security Council spectacularly authorized the use of force to vindicate the will of the people of Haiti when a military regime overthrew the freshly elected government of President Aristide. The Council also adopted sanctions against UNITA when it failed to respect the will of the people which had been made manifest in internationally monitored elections in Angola. The reversal of the constitutional consensus that had been achieved in Burundi through a military coup triggered the formal adoption of sanctions by a sub-regional coalition of states. The Economic Community of West African States (ECOWAS) intervened forcibly in Liberia, arguing, *inter alia*, that this action was necessary in order to reestablish a structure of authority in that state based on the will of the people. ECOWAS also mounted a military operation which ultimately reversed the military coup that had taken place in Sierra Leone. Finally, South African and some Botswanan troops have intervened in Lesotho in order to protect constitutional governance, again based on a purported mandate from a sub-regional integration organization.

Of course, this practice does not indicate that it is permissible to take international action on behalf of all populations which do not enjoy the benefit of truly representative government (whatever that may be). Instead, practice thus far only indicates that no government or authority can claim to exclusively represent the very population which has just expressly declared that that government or authority, or the political system it embodies, is not representative. In those circumstances, it is simply impossible to uphold the presumption that effectiveness equals representation, and international action can be taken directly in accordance with the express or implied desire of the population that has been manifestly disenfranchised by the effective authorities.

3.4. **Effective dissociation: Collapse of authority or civil war**

Effective dissociation occurs where the constitutional structure of a state has been fundamentally disrupted through conflict. Such a disruption may take the form of a collapse of state authority in its entirety, as was the case in Somalia. When establishing UNOSOM II, the United Nations Security Council expressly authorized forcible international action with a view to restoring a constitutional system of governance. As was already noted, similar considerations informed the ECOWAS action in Liberia, and, in rather an indirect way, the Italian-led coalition operation that was launched when civil society collapsed in Albania. In all of these circumstances, agents of the international community took forcible action which was aimed at re-establishing legitimate governance in the face of a breakdown of authority. The fact that there were factions exercising effective authority on the ground was deemed irrelevant. Instead, action was taken directly in accordance with the implied or express wishes of the population.

Frequently, this aim can of course be achieved with the cooperation of factions which have engaged in a violent contest about the exercise of effective control. The termination of the Cold War has brought about a whole spate of settlements to protracted civil conflicts of this kind. In all of these instances (Angola, Cambodia, the Central American states, Mozambique, Namibia, etc), the right to exercise authority and to represent a population was not based on the extent of effective control that had been achieved through violent strife. Instead, there was restored with international involvement a constitutional consensus, often formally endorsed through a referendum. There would then inevitably follow internationally monitored or even internationally managed elections, to ensure that, at least at that initial point, the exercise of governmental power would indeed be based on the will of the people.

The loss of power to represent on the part of governments or authorities engaged in civil conflict through effective dissociation is also evidenced in another, now quite consistent pattern of international practice. Scholarly opinion has long debated whether a government which is faced with civil conflict may receive international military assistance in its campaign to retain or restore effective authority over all parts of the state territory. However, in state practice up to 1990, the right of established governments to receive support was not subject to serious question. But since 1990, the picture has changed dramatically. The United Nations Security Council now routinely imposes arms embargoes against all sides in a civil conflict, including the government. The essential claim of the established government to be legally entitled to act in accordance with one of the principal prerogatives of states, to import the equipment for national defence, is thus rejected where active internal confrontation of a certain intensity has cast doubt on the right of that government to continue to represent the population.

3.5. Implied dissociation: Active or passive extermination

Finally, implied dissociation relates to the circumstances which are generally referred to when discussing so-called humanitarian intervention. Where a government actively exterminates a population, or a constitutionally significant segment thereof, it cannot conceivably claim the exclusive right to represent internationally that very population. Similarly, a government which denies to a population that which is urgently necessary for its survival cannot rely on the doctrine of non-intervention and sovereignty, which is, after all, nothing but the legal reflection of the corporate personality of the constituents whose survival is at issue. Hence, international action, whether authorized by the UN Security Council, whether carried out by regional organizations or arrangements or by *ad hoc* coalitions of states or even individual states, is legally permissible. Such action does not constitute intervention because, as in all the instances to which reference has been made above, it has been taken in accordance with the expressed or implied desire of the ultimate sovereign, the population, which is manifestly not represented by the effective autorities. This simple and obvious fact has now been evidenced in a consistent pattern of practice, relating to Iraq, Liberia, Somalia, Bosnia and Herzegovina, Rwanda, Zaire-Rwanda, the Central African Republic and Kosovo.

Hence, humanitarian action does not involve a new exception to the prohibition of the use of force, but a reversal of the presumption that effectiveness equals a right to represent under certain narrowly defined circumstances. Such a reversal of this presumption is of course temporary and often limited to certain aspects of the exercise of public powers. Given the limited space available here, it is only possible to hint at the international administration of such direct action on behalf of populations or constitutionally relevant segments thereof.

4. PROCESS

The doctrine of humanitarian intervention has often been objected to on the ground that it is open to abuse, especially by powerful global or regional powers. It is clear, however, that the doctrine of fundamental dissociation has been internationally administered in one way or another for several decades, without significant abuse having occurred. The recent broadening of its application has been conducted within an emerging international constitutional framework which is capable of constraining the international action that is undertaken directly on behalf of populations under the narrowly defined circumstances that have been identified above.

4.1. Defininition of the threat to IPS / Threshold of international interest

In virtually all of the 15 or so instances of post 1990 forcible humanitarian action, an objective international agency will have authoritatively identified that a particular situation is no longer an exclusively internal affair of the state concerned and instead a matter of direct international interest. The additional determination that there exists a case of dissociation has also often been made by international agencies. Ideally, this will be achieved through a formal finding by the United Nations Security Council, acting under Article 39 of the Charter. However, Regional arrangements or agencies and other international bodies and at times even individuals (the UN Special Rapporteur for human rights in Iraq, for example) have performed a similar function. Of course, the credibility of such findings is not necessarily as high as an Article 39 determination by the Security Council might be. But the involvement of an authoritative third party in confirming the existence of a situation of fundamental dissociation does minimize the risk of abuse of this doctrine considerably.

4.2. Authoritative determination of the required minimum action

Often, the body which makes a finding as to the existence of a circumstance of fundamental dissociation will also identify what minimum international action can be taken directly on behalf of a particular population. This may relate merely to the monitoring of the situation on the ground (Iraq, Bosnia, Kosovo), to the creation of humanitarian access (Somalia, Bosnia, Iraq, Zaire-Rwanda, Albania,

Kosovo), the active protection of threatened populations (Rwanda, Bosnia 'safe areas'), the restoration of 'order' and finally the holding of elections or even the restoration of a constitutional consensus (Albania, Somalia, Liberia, Haiti, Sierra Leone, Central African Republic, Lesotho, Kosovo).

4.3. **Authorization of action**

Forcible humanitarian action does not involve a *prima facie* violation of the prohibition of the threat or use of force, as it is undertaken in accordance with the expressed or anticipated consent of the sovereign. Hence, there is no requirement for formal authorization in order to render such an operation lawful. Nevertheless, it is of course preferable that action is taken on the basis of a Chapter VII mandate, which serves to clarify unambiguously the extent of action that may be lawfully taken to meet the situation. The status of mandates granted by regional organizations or arrangements, or other intergovernmental organziations is somewhat complex, given the different constitutional authority that may or may not have been granted to the organization by its members (e.g., the OECS or ECOWAS). Difficult problems might also be perceived to arise in relation to action mandated by such organizations or arrangements, in relation to non-members (e.g. NATO), especially inasmuch as these will generally not have the backing of prior Security Council authorization. However, as humanitarian action is based in the doctrine of fundamental dissociation and does not involve Article 2 (4), the actual lawfulness in terms of general international law of the respective operation is not necessarily affected, whatever the constitutional implications for the respective organization or arrangement.

4.4. **Identification of privileged agent**

The practice of humanitarian action since 1990 shows a very broad spectrum of different types of actors which have undertaken operations on behalf of populations or constitutionally significant segments thereof. In the context of Somali, the United Nations itself formally and unambiguously dispatched its own force (although of course made up of national contingents assigned to it) directly under Chapter VII. In several other instances, UN forces have operated in a mixed setting of Chapter VI and Chapter VII authority, depending the particular function in which they were engaged, and depending on the point in time in the evolution of a particular episode.

Regional organizations or arrangements, and also collective self-defence organizations which are not covered by Chapter VIII, have also involved themselves in humanitarian action. At times this has occurred at the request or with the prior approval of the United Nations Security Council (NATO in Bosnia and Herzegovina). In other instances action was taken and only retroactively acknowledged by the Council (ECOWAS in relation to Liberia, and very hesitantly in relation to the removal of the military regime in ECOWAS, and NATO in relation to Kosovo). The United Nations has also launched a joint UN/regional force in Liberia – a case where the credibility of the regional force had been lost on the ground.

Finally, there are operations of self-selected coalitions. In several instances, the 'leader' state of such a coalition has proposed an international action to the Security Council, which then encouraged the action. The coalition leader would then be free to assemble a group of the able and willing (US in UNITAF, US in Haiti, France in Rwanda, Canada in Rwanda/Zaire, Italy in Albania). In some of these instances it must be noted, however, that the forces contributed by other states amounted to little more than a token presence intended to dilute the impression that the coalition leader was 'intervening' perhaps to further its own agenda. Similarly, in relation to action taken outside of a Security Council mandate, states have tended to form coalitions, rather than acting unilaterally (Iraq and Lesotho).

4.5. **Quality control and the termination of authority**

The international monitoring or supervision of humanitarian action is of course mostly performed within the framework of the United Nations Security Council. If the action is taken under a Council mandate, the first means of quality control will tend to be the mandate itself, perhaps supported by an explanatory report of the United Nations Secretary-General, establishing the aims and modalities of the operation. These aims and modalities are at times drafted with the specific intent to ensure that a particular mission does not stray from its humanitarian aims, as was the case when the Council authorized the French-led operation in Rwanda.

The United Nations' own operations are of course subject to direction from the United Nations Secretariat and to control through the Council itself. However, it has to be admitted that this very intrusive involvement of the organization and its membership has failed to ensure effectiveness and accountability of United Nations actions in several very important episodes, which include Bosnia and Herzegovina and Somalia.

Perhaps in reflection of this practice, command and control is now more often than not exercised by coalition leaders of collective defence structures (NATO, SFOR/IFOR). These kinds of operation will tend to attract a significant and regular reporting requirement, enabling the Security Council to follow the activities of the states or organizations concerned and to establish or re-establish control over the operation where necessary. Thus far, these reports have tended to be comprehensive, giving a reasonably realistic picture of the situation on the ground and of the activities of the 'intervention' force. In fact, one might say that some such reports have exceeded in their quality those of the United Nations Secretary-General in relation to United Nations managed operations.

In some circumstances, the Security Council has deployed a small United Nations monitoring mission along with the 'intervening' force, to generate a direct source of information and perhaps to influence the conduct of the operation indirectly through this presence.

Where action was taken by regional organizations or other arrangements without prior Security Council notification, these bodies have nevertheless tended to send the texts of their decisions 'authorizing' the action to the Security Council, essentially inviting endorsement by the Council. There have also been occasional reports submitted to the Council under those circumstances. Such discipline has not always been in evidence in relation to the latter phases of the coalition operation concerning northern and southern Iraq, however, and there has been some evidence of the undue stretching of humanitarian action in that instance. In the initial phase, due to the close relationship of this action with the deployment of a small UN guards contingent and the UN-led distribution of humanitarian aid, coalition activity was, however, indirectly reported to the Council through the Secretary-General.

5. AN EMERGING INTERNATIONAL CONSTITUTIONAL SYSTEM FOR HUMANITARIAN ACTION?

This presentation has attempted to provide an explanation of the quite startling and ever proliferating international practice of humanitarian action since 1990. Instead of considering this issue in terms of the prohibition of the use of force, a theory of fundamental dissociation has been proposed. This doctrine is inherent in the modern concept of the state and does not need to be established by way of a new rule of customary law. Instead, it is based on the observation that the doctrine of representation which underpins the very definition of the state and of its role in the international system, is being increasingly acted upon by agents of the international community. This is not a new phenomenon, but one which has existed for some time, at least in relation to cases of inherent dissociation.

The scope of application of this doctrine remains restrictive. There is no pretense that violations of human rights in general, or a failure to adopt a fully democratic structure of governance, results in an instance of fundamental dissociation. Instead, the doctrine applies in circumstances where it is simply inconceivable to argue that an effective authority can fully represent the population it controls, or where there is no effective authority.

The doctrine of fundamental dissociation is ultimately based in political theory, but it is not an exercise in theory. Instead, it is based on empirical observation and provides a unifying framework which helps explain both well established types of international action, and apparently novel phenomena in state practice. This explanation can address all recent instances of humanitarian action, but its credibility does not depend on such action being taken in relation to every single instance of dissociation. While the doctrine permits action in all cases of fundamental dissociation, a failure of the organs of the international community to take action in some of them does not affect its explanatory force.

In addition, an attempt has been made to link the application of this doctrine to an international constitutional mechanism for its administration. This mechanism is in some respects well established and effective. However, quality control and accountability need to be improved over time, both in relation to United Nations-managed operations and others.

MEANS AND METHODS OF WARFARE AND THE COINCIDENCE OF NORMS BETWEEN THE HUMANITARIAN LAW OF ARMED CONFLICT AND THE LAW OF ARMS CONTROL

Eric P.J. Myjer*

Writing about 'the maintenance of peace and a possible reduction of armaments' as the ideal to which the endeavours of all governments should be directed the following observation was made:

> '[..]The ever increasing financial charges strike and paralyse public prosperity at its source; the intellectual and physical strength of the nations, their labour and capital, are for the most part diverted from their natural application and unproductively consumed; hundreds of millions are spent in acquiring terrible engines of destruction, which though to-day regarded as the last world of science are destined to-morrow to lose all value in consequence of some fresh discovery in the same field. National culture, economic progress and the production of wealth are either paralysed or perverted in their development.[..]'[1]

These are not the words of the leader of one of the major powers at the dawn of a new era after the fall of the wall (the new world order), nor those of the Secretary General of the United Nations, voicing alarm about a great many states in the developing world where a large part of the population lives in great poverty and where at the same time huge sums are spent on armaments. No, these words were written exactly hundred years ago on 12 August 1898 by the Russian Count Mouravieff on behalf of the Russian Tsar when inviting states to the first Peace Conference, which was to take place in The Hague in 1899. This will be celebrated in 1999. But it is part of the glow of The Hague on this birthday party about it being a global centre for international law, of which, with an eye on the

* Associate Professor of Public International Law, Europa Institute, Faculty of Law, Utrecht University. The author likes to thank Ige Dekker for his comments.

[1] 'The maintenance of general peace and a possible reduction of the excessive armaments which weigh upon all nations present themselves, in the existing conditions of the whole world, as the ideal towards which the endeavour of all Governments should be directed.

The humanitarian and magnanimous views of His Majesty the Emperor, my august master, are in perfect accord with this sentiment...', Russian circular note dated 12 August 1898 proposing the First Peace Conference handed (on behalf of the Russian Tsar) to the diplomatic representatives August 12/24, 1898 by Count Mouravieff the Russian Minister for Foreign Affairs during the weekly reception in the Foreign Office, Petrograd., diplomatic correspondence, in James Brown Scott, ed., *The Hague Conventions and declarations of 1899 and 1907*, at XV.

W.P. Heere (Ed.), International Law and The Hague's 750th Anniversary

subject area of this panel, *The Law of The Hague*[2] certainly cannot be missed out on.

This First Hague Peace Conference and especially the following Second Hague Peace Conference led to some important developments, not only with regard to arms control, but also with regard to 'the laws and customs of war',[3] as central subjects of these conferences. It led to a few conventions and declarations of which especially the ones in the area of the law of armed conflict are well known. In the Hague Convention of 1899 Respecting the Laws and Customs of War on Land we find expression of the central principle underpinning the law of armed conflict, namely that '*the right of belligerents to adopt means of injuring the enemy is not unlimited.*'[4]

With regard to weapons during the last decade we have witnessed a few remarkable developments both in the area of arms control and in that of the humanitarian law of armed conflict. Most notably are the conclusion of the Chemical Weapons Convention (CWC),[5] the Comprehensive Test Ban Treaty[6] (which bans testing of nuclear devices and thereby puts an essential restriction on

[2] 'The law of The Hague, or the law of warfare, determines the rights and duties of belligerents in the conduct of operations and limits the choice of warfare methods', Jean Pictet, International humanitarian law: definition, in Henry Dunant Institute, *International Dimensions of Humanitarian Law* (1988), at xx. Apart from The Law of The Hague there is the Law of Geneva referred to by Pictet as, humanitarian law that 'tends to safeguard military personnel placed *hors de combat* and persons not taking part in hostilities.' Pictet, ibid., at xix. These two areas, which comprise the Laws of War, or the Law of Armed Conflict (Compare Detter de Lupis, *The Law of War*, at xx, or Roberts and Guelff, *Documents on the Laws of War* (1989), at 1ff., have become 'so closely interrelated that they are considered to have gradually formed one single complex system, known today as *international humanitarian law*. The provisions of the additional Protocols of 1977 give expression and attest to the unity and complexity of that law.' International Court of Justice (ICJ): Advisory Opinion on the Legality of the threat or use of nuclear weapons (8 July 1996), 35 *ILM* (1996) p. 809, at p. 827 under 75, emphasis added. In the following, I will opt, however, for a half-way house and will refer to the complex of rules interchangeable as the humanitarian law of armed conflict [compare H.H.G. Post, 'Some curiosities in the sources of the law of armed conflict conceived in a general international legal perspective', in L.A.N.M. Barnhoorn and K.C. Wellens, *Diversity in Secondary Rules and the Unity of International Law* (1995) pp. 83 ff.], or the law of armed conflict.

[3] Mouravieff, diplomatic correspondence, at xviii.

[4] Art. 22 of the Regulations Respecting the Laws and Customs of War on Land in the Annex to the Convention. This obligation was repeated in the corresponding article of the Annex to the 1907 Hague Convention Respecting the Laws and Customs of War on Land. Earlier this principle was contained in the Declaration of 1874, which followed the Petersburg Declaration of 1868, 'which was primarily designed to avoid unnecessary suffering', Detter de Lupis, *The Law of War*, at p. 177. F. Kalshoven (*Constraints on the waging of war*, 1987), stresses the importance of this principle in Art. 22 by referring to it as 'The most basic rule with respect to the employment of means of warfare.'

[5] Convention on the Prohibition of the Development, Production, Stockpiling and the Use of Chemical Weapons and on their Destruction, 32 *ILM* (1993) pp. 800-873.

[6] Comprehensive Test Ban Treaty (1996),35 *ILM* (1996) pp. 1439-1478.

the proliferation of nuclear weapons), the Ottawa Convention,[7] the Protocol on Blinding Laser Weapons (Protocol IV)[8] and the revised Protocol II (1996) to the Convention on Certain Conventional Weapons (CCW).[9] Furthermore the International Court of Justice rendered its important advisory opinion on the question of the legality of the threat or use of nuclear weapons, thereby touching on some important issues relating both to the international law of arms control and the international (humanitarian) law of armed conflict.[10]

When one approaches the theme of this panel – regulation of warfare – from a traditional viewpoint, there appears to be a dichotomy between means and methods of warfare, in the sense of the humanitarian law of armed conflict on the one hand, and the issues of a complete ban on chemical weapons in case of the CWC and the Ottawa ban on anti-personnel mines under the law of arms control on the other. For with regard to weapons the (humanitarian) law of armed conflict is primarily about restrictions on the means and methods of warfare to prevent 'superfluous injury or unnecessary suffering' in case of war, whereas the law of arms control is about (numerical) restrictions, or even a complete ban of certain categories of weapons also in peacetime, as is the case with these two conventions. On closer inspection, however, there is a far less sharp distinction, for not only can the arrangements mentioned be justified in terms of both areas; both branches of international law also overlap (interact). In the former case, one of *ius in bello*, the primary consideration is humanitarian, although we may assume that the conclusion of agreements finds its limitation in considerations of security. The driving force for arrangements under the law of arms control, the latter case, however, are considerations for improved security, whereas broadly speaking these may also have an impact on the humanitarian level.

Logically speaking therefore the distinction appears to be more in the point of departure than in the result, for both under the humanitarian law of armed conflict regarding means and methods of warfare and under the law of arms control the final agreements are about *restrictions* on weapons. And on closer inspection looking at the purposes (and principles) of these arrangements also there we find a coincidence. It is important to realize this, for it shows us exactly where these areas of international law hang together.

[7] Convention on the Prohibition of the Use, Stockpiling, Production and Transfer of Anti-Personnel Mines and on their Destruction, 36 *ILM* (1997) pp. 1507-1519.

[8] This Protocol, which prohibits the use of lasers designed to cause permanent blindness to enhanced vision (also the sale is prohibited), was adopted at the Review Conference (1996) of the Convention on Prohibitions or Restrictions on Use of Certain Conventional Weapons Which May Be Deemed To Be Excessively Injurious or To Have Indiscriminate Effects (April 1981) (In short: Convention on Certain Conventional Weapons (CCW). See also *The Arms Control Reporter* (1995) at 860-3.2-3 and (1996) 860.3-16-18.

[9] Convention on Prohibitions or Restrictions on the Use of Certain Conventional Weapons which may be Deemed to be Excessively Injurious or to Have Indiscriminate Effects (1981), in A. Roberts and R. Guelff, op. cit. n. 2, pp. 473 ff.

[10] Ibid., n. 2.

Let us take for instance the *Chemical Weapons Convention*. This Convention encompasses both a measure of humanitarian law and a measure of arms control, for it is both about a ban on the use of chemical weapons, and on having them (the availability, production, etc). The ban on the use of chemical weapons repeats the ban under the Geneva Protocol,[11] which turned into a customary rule.[12] This rule answers to the principle of distinction, referred to by the International Court of Justice as one of the cardinal principles 'constituting the fabric of humanitarian law

> '...The first is aimed at the protection of the civilian population and civilian objects and establishes the distinction between combatants and non-combatants; States must never make civilians the object of attack and must consequently never use weapons that are incapable of distinguishing between civilian and military targets.'[13]

The related obligation of not *having* these weapons is essential to prevent the actual – under any circumstances – occurrence of any use as well as the proliferation of these weapons.[14] This innovative[15] element (including its actual

[11] 'Determined for the sake of all mankind, to exclude *completely* the possibility of the use of chemical weapons, through the implementation of the provisions of this Convention, thereby *complementing the obligations assumed under the Geneva Protocol of 1925*'. (preambular, emphasis added).

[12] This issue, however, is controversial given reservations of the kind made by Parties to the Protocol like the UK ('The protocol is only binding on the United Kingdom as regards the powers which have Signed and ratified or who have acceded to it and it ceases to bind the United Kingdom towards any Power whose armed forces or the armed forces of whose allies fail to respect the prohibitions', *Manual of Military Law* (1958) at p. 216. In other words, use in second strike would remain possible. Similar ones were made by countries like Canada, Belgium, France, the Netherlands or the USSR. The Protocol was 'regarded by such states as containing not an absolute prohibition on the use of such weapons, but only as an agreement not to use such weapons first', Roberts and Guelff, op. cit. n. 2, at p. 138. In their opinion, however, the majority view is, that 'the prohibitions in the protocol should be viewed as having become part of customary international law.' The ban on use under the CWC, however, is absolute, since reservations to the Convention are excluded (Art. XXII).

[13] See ICJ *supra* n. 7, at p. 78.

[14] See, e.g., the following preambular paragraph of the Convention: 'Convinced that the complete and effective prohibition of the development, production, acquisition, stockpiling, retention, transfer and use of chemical weapons, and their destruction, represent a necessary step to the achievement of these common objectives' (like 'Determined to act with a view to achieving effective progress towards general and complete disarmament under strict and effective international control, including the prohibition and elimination of all types of weapons of mass destruction'. See also *supra* n. 11)

[15] 'Innovative' refers to the comprehensive nature of the obligations under the CWC. This is lacking in the case of the Biological Weapons Convention (BWC) (*Arms Control and Disarmament Agreements*, texts and histories of the negotiation, US Arms Control and Disarmament Agency (ACDA)(1996) pp. 98-100). Like in the case of the CWC the use of biological weapons is forbidden under the 1925 Geneva Protocol. Unlike the case with the CWC, the controversy regarding the reservations was not solved in the BWC, which does not contain a ban on its use, but is about non-possession and production. Notwithstanding the fact that there are 131 States Parties to the 1925 Con-

verification process) was agreed upon in the Conference on Disarmament in Geneva.

The *Ottawa Convention* contains a total ban on a certain category of weapons, i.e., anti-personnel mines, not only on the use but also on the possession, and consequently the destruction of all existing ones,[16] and therefore appears to be an arms control treaty, i.e., a disarmament treaty. It is, however, striking that there is only an almost 'hesitant' reference to the dimension of arms control by referring to the confidence building nature of these measures.[17] Without any hesitation its preambular paragraphs, however, professes it to be of an essential humanitarian law of armed conflict character. This is not surprising since it was especially the humanitarian movement, of which the 'Lady Diana' aspect was a very important element, that formed the push behind the conclusion of this treaty.

> 'Basing themselves on the principle of international humanitarian law that the right of the parties to an armed conflict to choose methods of warfare is not unlimited, on the principle that prohibits the employment in armed conflicts of weapons, projectiles and materials and methods of warfare of a nature to cause superfluous injury or unnecessary suffering and on the principle that a distinction must be made between civilians and combatants' (preambular para).[18]

vention (at 1 July 1988 according to the US Department of State (and 114 according to depositary)(Roberts and Guelff, op. cit. n. 2, at p. 21 and p. 144), whereas there are 91 States Parties to the BWC (ACDA (1996) at 104) there appears to be less controversy about a ban on its use, either conventionally, or customary. According to F. Kalshoven (Arms, Armaments and International Law, *Recueil des Cours*, 1985-II, at p. 267) '(T)hese restrictions on application of the prohibition, and in particular the condition of reciprocity, have largely lost their significance with the entry of the prohibition into the body of customary international law' Compare also L. C. Green, *The Contemporary Law of Armed Conflict* (1993) at p. 131. or B.V.A. Röling in SIPRI, *The Law of war and Dubious Weapons* (1976), at p. 7. See also The Final Declaration of the Conference of States Parties to the 1925 Geneva Protocol and Other Interested States on the on the Prohibition of Chemical Weapons, of 11 January 1989, 28 *ILM* (1989) pp. 1020-1022 as well as UN Doc. SIRES (1991) p. 1687, preambular. Effective verification of the ban on possession of biological (bacteriological) weapons under the Biological Weapons Convention, however, is lacking.

[16] '1. Each State Party undertakes never under any circumstances: a) To use anti-personnel mines; b) To develop, produce, otherwise acquire, stockpile, retain or transfer to anyone, directly or indirectly, anti-personnel mines; c) To assist, encourage or induce, in any way, anyone to engage in any activity prohibited to a State party under this Convention. 2. Each State Party undertakes to destroy or ensure the destruction of all anti-personnel mines in accordance with the provisions of this Convention.'

[17] 'Recognizing that a total ban of anti-personnel mines would also be an important confidence-building measure' (preambular, Ottawa), see *supra* n. 7, at p. 1509.

[18] Compare also 'Stressing the role of public conscience in furthering the principles of humanity...'(also preambular). Convention on the Prohibition of the use, stockpiling, production and transfer of anti-personnel mines and on their destruction (Ottawa Convention), 36 *ILM* (1997) pp. 1509-1519.

With even more force we find this emphasis on the humanitarian law character in the case of the revised protocol on mines (Protocol II)[19] to the 1981 Convention on Certain Conventional Weapons and in that of the Protocol on Blinding Laser Weapons (Protocol IV).[20] Another case embedded in both the law of arms control and the (humanitarian) law of armed conflict is that of the Biological Weapons Convention,[21] where at present an Ad Hoc Group is considering ways to strengthen the Convention, preferably via verification measures like those under the CWC.[22] This dual character is not surprising for this Convention like the Chemical Weapons Convention originated in the 1925 Geneva Protocol. Reference to both aspects can be found in the Convention and recently in the Final Document of the Fourth Review Conference.[23]

This distinction between so-called issues of humanitarian law of armed conflict and of the law of arms control is also apparent from the way these agreements are being negotiated in the 'traditional fora'. Arms control and disarmament issues are, and have been, predominantly negotiated in the Conference on Disarmament (CD), or its predecessors. Given the *security dimension* there always has to be consensus. That way the Chemical Weapons Convention was negotiated in the CD. The same was the case with the negotiations for the Comprehensive Test Ban Treaty. This, however, is a special case for when India did prevent a consensus being reached, Australia lifted the draft out of the CD and presented it to the UN for endorsement and signature by as many states possible.[24]

[19] Protocol on Prohibitions or restrictions on the Use of Mines, Booby-Traps and other devices.

[20] Blinding means *permanent* blindness: '..an irreversible and uncorrectable loss of vision which is seriously disabling with no prospect of recovery' (Art. IV). By referring to this element of permanence laser weapons are being tested against the principle of necessity.

[21] The Convention on the Prohibition of the Development, Production and Stockpiling of Bacteriological (Biological) and Toxin Weapons and on their Destruction (1972)

[22] The mandate of the group was 'to consider appropriate measures, including possible verification measures, and draft proposals to strengthen the Convention' (Final Document Fourth Review Conference (BWC/CONF.IV/9). It was decided that the Ad Hoc Group 'intensify its work with a view to completing it as soon as possible before the commencement of the Fifth Review Conference', scheduled for 2001. Ibid. Also *The Arms Control Reporter* (1997) at 701.A2.

[23] Arms control: '..to act with a view to achieving effective progress towards general and complete disarmament' and 'will facilitate the achievement of general and complete disarmament under strict and effective international control' (Preambular, Convention). This is again repeated in the Final Document (BWC/CONF.IV/9) at p. 14. The humanitarian law of armed conflict aspect can in a broad sense be seen to be reflected in the reference to 'the realization of the purposes and principles of the Charter of the United Nations.' and the reference that 'such use (of these agents, E.M.) would be repugnant to the conscience of mankind and that no effort should be spared to minimize this risk' (both Preambular, Convention). The Final Document again repeats this.

[24] By not joining the consensus, India let, in other words, its own security considerations prevail. Since this was to be the very reason to adopt the consensus-rule in the operating procedures of the CD in the first place, India's attitude seems to be legitimate and not *contra legem*. For this very reason the case of the CTBT is a special one. The lifting of the negotiated draft out of the CD and the presenting of it by one of the CD-members (Australia) to the General Assembly of the United Na-

That certain countries regarded a ban on anti-personnel mines as an issue having security implications, can be seen from the fact that for instance the United States were of the opinion that this matter should be dealt with in the CD.[25] In spite of the fact that within the CD a special coordinator was appointed, the Members of the CD could not agree on a mandate. In the following negotiations at the global Conference in Oslo the focus was completely on the humanitarian aspect. It was this Conference, in which also the United States took an active part, that led to the Ottawa Convention.

Treaties of a predominantly humanitarian law character will, as the general reference indicates – the law of Geneva[26] – be negotiated in the Geneva context of the International Committee of the Red Cross (ICRC) via special conferences of the ICRC. But the development of the humanitarian law aspect of the law of armed conflict is not the exclusive prerogative of the 'Red Cross', as the Oslo Conference has demonstrated. All of these conferences are open to a much wider participation, including the active participation of NGOs, than is the case with the exclusive CD.[27] Another forum for discussion of the substantive matter of both arms control and humanitarian law issues is of course a Review Conference of a Treaty or Convention. This is where the negotiations on the amended Protocol (II) on mines to the CCW, as well as the added Protocol (IV) took place namely in the context of the Review Conference of this Convention. Given the character of this particular Convention, also there the humanitarian considerations prevailed.

But if these areas are so closely intermingled, are we then in fact not talking about semantics? Is there, in other words, any point in clinging to a distinction between humanitarian law of armed conflict and law of arms control and should not one devise another name which points to the interconnection between these branches? This, in my opinion would be a mistake, for although there is a lot of identity between these two branches, they are not identical. With regard to the two branches under discussion today – the law of arms control and the (humanitarian) law of armed conflict – some of the following distinctions can be mentioned:

– The area of humanitarian law of armed conflict in general is much wider, than that it merely encompasses arrangements regarding means and methods of warfare, for it also deals with such wide ranging issues as the rights and duties of neutrals or the treatment of prisoners of war, the wounded and sick, shipwrecked,

tions to be recommended for endorsement appears to be a breach of good faith with regard to the operating procedures of the CD. This raises questions about procedural fairness and thereby of legitimacy in future cases, as discussed by Franck, ibid., at p. 7 ff. See my intervention at p. 108 in the *Proceedings of the Fourth Hague Joint Conference*.

[25] CD/PV.770.33. See also statement US Permanent Representative on 15 May 1997, ibid.

[26] 'The law of Geneva or, by its correct name, humanitarian law tends to safeguard military personnel placed *hors de combat* and persons not taking part in hostilities.', Pictet, loc. cit. n.2, at xix.

[27] In 1996 it was decided to expand the membership of the CD with 23 members to 61 members.

the protection of civilians. Compare for the latter the respective Geneva Conventions;[28]

– Breach of the rules of the humanitarian law of armed conflict may also entail individual responsibility;[29] that of rules of arms control will lead to state responsibility;[30]

– In spite of the mix of humanitarian and security concerns when concluding either an arms control agreement or a humanitarian law one, as indicated above, the principal considerations remain security, respectively humanitarian, for the aim of arms control is principally increased security; that for restrictions in the area of the law of armed conflict is the protection of people (soldiers and civilians) and thereby humanitarian. And to make things more complicated much will depend on the security concept [31] entertained by a state as well as its threat perception, for instance in the case of numerical arms control;

– The norms of the humanitarian law of armed conflict – be they conventional or customary – apply to any employment of weapons, irrespective of the level to (in) which they are controlled. The reverse, however, cannot be held, although the ICJ in its crucial consideration with regard to nuclear weapons made clear that considerations of self-defence, which can be held to be the 'bottom-line'

[28] 1949 Geneva Convention I for the Amelioration of the Condition of the Wounded and Sick in Armed Forces in the Field ; 1949 Geneva Convention II for the Amelioration of the Condition of Wounded, Sick and Shipwrecked Members of Armed Forces at Sea; 1949 Geneva Convention III Relative to the Treatment of Prisoners of War; 1949 Geneva Convention IV Relative to the Protection of Civilian Persons in Time of War.

[29] On the Basis of the Nuremberg Tribunal's decision this responsibility is imputed to leaders that violate humanitarian law; under the Yugoslav Tribunal's jurisdiction the prospect is raised 'of a major advance for the authority of international organizations to enforce the new law against war by making leaders – and even some followers- personally accountable.' Thomas M. Franck, *Fairness in international law and institutions* (1995) at p. 279. See Principle I of the Nuremberg Principle I: '(a) person who commits an act which constitutes a crime under international law is responsible therefore and liable to punishment'. Compare also Art. 1 of the Yugoslav tribunal ('..shall have the power to prosecute *persons responsible for* serious violations of International humanitarian law..'(emphasis added) and Art. 7 (individual criminal responsibility). See also Opinion and Judgment of the International Criminal Tribunal for the Former Yugoslavia in *Prosecutor* v. *Dusko Tadić* (7 May 1997) in 36 *ILM (1997)* pp. 936 ff. and pp.947 ff. respectively under pp. 621 ff. and pp. 661 ff. Compare also the jurisdiction *ratione materiae*: Grave breaches of the Geneva Conventions of 1949 (Art. 2); violations of the laws or customs of war (Art. 3), as adopted by S/RES/827 (1993) of 25 May 1993 and the report of the Secretary-General S/25704 of 3 May 1993, both in 32 *ILM* (1993) pp. 1163 ff. This is of course notwithstanding the fact that states are the primary objects of humanitarian law. 'They have the first responsibility for ensuring that their military and civilian personnel comport themselves in accordance with customary and treaty based standards, whether in transnational or civil conflict', Franck, ibid., at p. 280.

[30] Compare the ILC *Draft Articles on State Responsibility viz.* Art. 1, 16 in 37 *ILM* (1998) pp. 440-467.

[31] *Viz* Military security or economic security. See E.P.J.Myjer, 'The law of disarmament and arms control: implications for the law of the sea', in R.B. Byers, ed., *The denuclearisation of the Oceans* (1986) at p. 105.

principle of any security concept, and thereby central to the law of arms control, might take precedence over the principles and rules of humanitarian law.[32]

Distinctions like these point to the validity of the very differentiation in separate branches of international law, but only awareness of the points of interaction between these branches may lead to a more automatic test of arrangements under consideration, e.g., a draft treaty, for conformity with some of the principles of the other branch. In this respect for the sake of completeness a third branch of international law that interacts with each of these branches and in which there is a coincidence of norms should be mentioned, namely that of *(the law of) collective security*, where it concerns the use of military force in general, which is of relevance in the realm of arms and security. The very issue of self-defence as mentioned above is for instance a core principle of this area of international law. These overlaps suggest a wider area (branch) of international law, with certain common characteristics. This is the area, which can be referred to as *the international law of military security*. Within it all three branches of general public international law -the law of arms control, the humanitarian law of armed conflict and the law of collective security- interact [33], where they deal with restrictions on weaponry with regard to its possession and use. In all cases furthermore the developments within the field were also stimulated by humanitarian concerns. Each branch, however remains to have its own distinctive characteristics.

The core[34] principle with regard to the 'means and methods of warfare', namely that the right of parties to a conflict to choose methods or means of

[32] '..that the threat or use of nuclear weapons would generally be contrary to the rules of international law applicable in armed conflict, and in principle the rules and principles of humanitarian law; However, the Court cannot conclude definitively whether the threat or use of nuclear weapons would be lawful or unlawful in an extreme circumstance of self-defence, in which the very survival of a State would be at stake'; see ICJ *supra* n. 2, 105 under E.

[33] Interesting is that both Greenwood and Blix in their respective contributions to the Centennial of the Hague Peace Conference point to the closeness and mutual influence of these respective areas. Greenwood refers both to 'the boundary between the laws of war and disarmament' (sub-para 19) and to the effect of the laws of war and laws against war (E.M.: read: the law of collective security) (sub-paras. 23 ff.). With regard to the latter aspect he concludes that there is a need for further study of the relationship between the Law of the United Nations Charter (E.M.: read also the law of collective security) and the laws of war (sub-para. 191). Christopher Greenwood, *International humanitarian law and the laws of war*. Blix points at the limitations in the means and methods of warfare, on humanitarian/ rationalistic grounds (sub-paras. 9-21). Hans Blix, *Development of international law relating to disarmament and arms control since the First International Peace Conference of 1899*. Both are preliminary reports for the Centennial Commemoration of the First Hague Peace Conference 1899. See also *supra* n. 4.

[34] Best refers to it as the core principle of the law of armed conflict (law of wars; humanitarian law of armed conflict). For given that restraint in the conduct of armed conflict is the purpose of 'laws and customs of war, wherever and whenever they are found, it follows as surely as night follows day that their basic principle must be the banning of methods and means which, if used, would negate that aim.' Geoffrey Best, *War and Law since 1945* (1997) at p. 253.

warfare is not unlimited, shows us where the *humanitarian law of armed conflict* and the *law of arms control* are tied together. For each approach will lead to restrictions on (the use of) weapons. Each approach thereby contributes to the control of the level and intensity in which a conflict might turn into an armed conflict.

This brings me back to the overall theme of this panel, the 'regulation of warfare', the restrictions states involved in an international armed conflict have in the application of military hardware in order to achieve their military objective, for instance in pushing back an aggressor state. For even in the case of a legitimate self-defence states are not absolutely free in the employment of weapons. In conclusion, it therefore seems worthwhile to refer to what development the general principle regarding means and methods of warfare has led, which standards should be applied in the area of arms control.

As indicated already the 1899 and the 1907 Hague Conventions made clear that belligerents were not free to adopt any means of injuring the enemy.[35] Also Additional protocol I repeats this basic rule in Article 35(1).[36] This general principle led to the development within the law of armed conflict of the following general principles ruling the application of military force:

– *the principle of distinction*:[37]in war targets can only be of a military character, that need to be distinguished from civilian targets;

– *the principle of necessity*: military force only in so far as necessary to overcome the enemy;

– *the principle of proportionality*: use of force should be proportional to the attack, at least the force anticipated;

The essence of these principles, that is also of a customary law character,[38]

[35] 'The right of belligerents to adopt means of injuring the enemy is not unlimited' (Art. 22 Regulations Respecting the Laws and Customs of War on Land in the Annex to the Convention)(see *supra* n. 4).

[36] 'In any armed conflict, the right of the Parties to the conflict to choose methods or means of warfare is not unlimited' (35(1) 1977 Geneva Protocol I).

[37] Hans Blix, 'The principle of distinction is the premise of several important rules regarding means and methods of warfare', in Henry Dunant Institute, *International Dimensions of Humanitarian Law* (1988) Means and methods of combat, at p. 142: Best underlines that this principle precedes the principle that the right of belligerents to adopt means of injuring the enemy is not unlimited: 'The statement of that fundamental principle concerning what violence could be done to "the enemy" came long, long after the achievement of a preliminary fundamental limitation: a consensus agreement among civilized States to restrict combat to combatants and to distinguish them, whom we still call combatants, from non-combatants, whom we now call civilians.' G. Best, *War and Law since 1945* (1994) at p. 254.

[38] 'A large number of customary rules have been developed by the practice of States[..]The "laws and customs of war" – as they were traditionally called – were the subject of efforts at codification undertaken in The Hague (including the Conventions of 1899 and 1907), and were based partly upon the St Petersburg Declaration, as well as the results of the Brussels Conference of 1874. This 'Hague Law' and more particularly, the Regulations Respecting the Laws and Customs of war on Land, fixed the rights and duties of belligerents in their conduct of operations *and limited the*

finds application in numerous specific rules.[39] In its important Advisory Opinion on *the legality of the threat or use of nuclear weapons* the Court refers to 'the cardinal principles contained in the texts constituting the fabric of humanitarian law':

> 'The first is aimed at the protection of the civilian population and civilian objects and establishes the distinction between combatants and non-combatants; States must never make civilians the object of attack and must consequently never use weapons that are incapable of distinguishing between civilian and military targets'[40] (this refers to my (EM) earlier principle of distinction).
>
> 'According to the second principle, it is prohibited to cause unnecessary suffering to combatants: it is accordingly prohibited to use weapons causing them such harm or uselessly aggravating their suffering. In application of that second principle, States do not have unlimited freedom of choice of means in the weapons they use' (this refers to my principle of necessity).[41]

Next to these principles the Martens Clause[42] as introduced at the First Hague Peace Conference is also important as far as 'means and methods' of warfare are concerned. Reference to the Martens Clause can be found in the four Geneva

choice of methods and means of injuring the enemy in an international armed conflict. ' (ICJ, Advisory Opinion, p. 827 under 75, see *supra* n. 2) See also p. 827 under 79: 'Further these fundamental rules are to be observed by all States whether or not they have ratified the conventions that contain them, *because they constitute intransgressible principles of international customary law*'. Also the ICJ refers to the report of the Secretary General on the Statute of the Yugoslav Tribunal as unanimously approved by the Security Council, which indicated the rules of humanitarian law that had to be regarded beyond any doubt as customary law (see p. 838 under 81).

[39] Compare Art. 23 of the 1907 Hague Convention which states that it is forbidden 'to employ arms, projectiles, or material calculated to cause unnecessary suffering', and which is repeated in the second basic rule regarding 'methods and means of warfare' of the 1977 first Geneva Protocol, these basic rules being: '1.In any armed conflict, the right of the parties to the conflict to choose methods or means of warfare is not unlimited. 2. It is prohibited to employ weapons, projectiles and material and methods of warfare of a nature to cause *superfluous injury or unnecessary suffering*. 3. It is prohibited to employ methods or means of warfare which are intended, or may be expected, to cause widespread, long-term and severe damage to the natural environment.'(Art. 35).

[40] See ICJ *supra* n. 2, at p. 78. In its Advisory Opinion the ICJ, however, omits, to give a thorough analysis of the law of armed conflict. On the laws and customs of war see Georg Schwarzenberger, *International Law as applied by International Courts and Tribunals, Vol.II, The Law of Armed Conflicts* (1968) p. 15 ff.

[41] See ICJ *supra* n. 2, at p. 78.

[42] 'Until a more complete code of the laws of war is issued, the High Contracting Parties think it right to declare that in cases not included in the regulations adopted by them, populations and belligerents remain under the protection and empire of the principles of international law, as they result from the usages established between civilized nations, from the laws of humanity and the requirements of the public conscience.'(Preamble to the 1899 Hague Convention respecting The Laws and customs of war on land (II), and repeated in the 1907(IV) Hague Convention respecting The laws and customs of war on land). See Scott *supra* n. 1, at p. 102.

Conventions.[43] This clause, as stressed again by the ICJ, is to be regarded a fundamental rule of customary law.[44] It is repeated again in Article 1 (2) of Additional Protocol I of 1977:

> 'In cases not covered by this Protocol or by other international agreements, civilians and combatants remain under the protection and authority of the principles of international law derived from established custom, from the principles of humanity and from the dictates of public conscience.'

Perhaps it can even be held that this very Martens Clause offers the most pertinent standard in the area of overlap between the humanitarian law of armed conflict and that of the law of arms control.[45]

The cases discussed today represent novel developments with regard to concrete means of warfare. Both the Chemical Weapons Convention (1993) and the Ottawa Convention show us developments of a comprehensive nature both in the area of the humanitarian law of armed conflict and in that of arms control, for they not only ban its *use* (means and methods), but also its *possession*. Their aim is to remove some means altogether. Of these the CWC appears the most remarkable (notable) given the detailed verification system, which is lacking in the case of the Ottawa Convention. This in fact underlines my thesis that the existence of chemical weapons is a security concern, whereas that of land-mines is less so.[46]

In introducing our panel's topic these are some observations of an academic involved in both the law of arms control and the (humanitarian) law of armed conflict. Of great interest to international lawyers is the perspective of the practitioner, be they diplomat or international civil servant, for their views most certainly will offer new insights. That is why we are fortunate to have Mr Paul van den IJssel, who as a diplomat took part in the negotiations of the Ottawa Convention. He as the diplomat-negotiator can draw the picture of the way in

[43] In Art. 63 Geneva Convention I, Art 62 Geneva Convention II, Art. 142 Geneva Convention III, and Art. 158 Geneva Convention IV, all in Roberts and Guelff, op. cit. n. 2. See also Rupert Ticehurst, 'The Martens Clause and the Laws of Armed Conflict', *International Review of the Red Cross*, no 317, March-April 1997, pp. 125-134.

[44] See ICJ Advisory Opinion *supra* n. 2, para. 78, para. 84.

[45] Compare the ICJ, ibid., in para. 87: 'Finally, the Court points to the Martens Clause, whose continuing existence and applicability is not to be doubted, as an affirmation that the principles and rules of humanitarian law apply to nuclear weapons'. On the Martens Clause and this Advisory Opinion of the ICJ see Rupert Ticehurst, 'The Martens Clause and the Laws of Armed Conflict', *International Review of the Red Cross*, No. 317, March-April 1997, pp.125 134.

[46] However, within the United States the Pentagon still appears to attach some weight to anti-personnel landmines. Although the United States did not join the Ottawa Convention, the Clinton Administration issued a moratorium on the use of landmines. It now, however, appears to be under pressure from the Pentagon to repeal this moratorium for 'the Pentagon contends that it needs to continue using 'mixed' mines – anti-tank mines that are salted with anti-personnel mines to keep enemy soldiers from taking them apart quickly.' New York Times editorial in *IHT*, 12 May 1998.

which the Ottawa process gained speed and how the Convention has to be understood. Mr Jean-Louis Rolland, as an international civil-servant responsible for the verification process of the Chemical Weapons Convention, is involved with the actual compliance under this Convention. He may point us to certain lacunae in this Convention, for how such conventions are applied in practice may be another matter.

LANDMINES AND THE OTTAWA PROCESS

Paul van den IJssel*

INTRODUCTION

There is an old saying that goes:

> *Diplomacy is to do and say*
> *The nastiest things in the nicest way*

I hope that by the end of my presentation you will not entirely agree with this piece of ancient wisdom.

It is a privilege to have been invited to address this seminar today. Unlike many of the speakers at this Conference I am not a legal scholar. I have been working on the landmine problem at the Netherlands Ministry of Foreign Affairs since January 1995. This morning I speak in a private capacity. My comments do not necessarily reflect the views of the Dutch Government.

The subject I have been asked to discuss is landmines and the Ottawa Process, a very broad topic indeed. I should like to take the following five questions as the basis of my presentation.
1) why have landmines and anti-personnel mines in particular become the focus of such intensive political, diplomatic and public debate?
2) why was traditional diplomacy unable to respond satisfactorily to the problem of landmines?
3) what are the key elements of the Ottawa Convention?
4) what remains to be done now that the Ottawa Convention has been concluded?
5) is the Ottawa Process merely an incident, or can it serve as a model in dealing with other international problems?

1. WHY LANDMINES?

The 20th century has seen a sharp increase, in both absolute and relative terms, in the number of civilian lives claimed by war. Perfectly legitimate weapons such as bombs, grenades and so on were largely responsible. No one is considering

* Senior Policy Adviser Ministry of Foreign Affairs, the Netherlands.

abolishing them, yet there is an almost universal consensus that, sooner or later, we should ban anti-personnel mines. What makes this category of weapons so different?

The differences are, I think, twofold. Inherent to a landmine is its inability to discriminate between combatants and civilians. Every footstep, every touch of the tripwire is considered hostile, and will explode the mine. What is more, mines are not smart. When the purpose for which they were laid has long lost its relevance, they will remain active, and will lay in wait – sometimes for decades – to claim a victim. The use of landmines conflicts with the generally accepted principles of the International Law of Armed Conflict that:

- the right of belligerents to adopt means of warfare is not unlimited, and
- the use of weapons calculated to cause unnecessary suffering is prohibited.

In an attempt to reconcile the use of anti-personnel mines with these two principles, Protocol II to the Conventional Weapons Convention on mines, booby traps and other devices, was adopted in 1980. This was the first international instrument to deal specifically with landmines. But Protocol II only bans the use of mines against civilians, not against military objectives. This approach has turned out to be ineffective. I shall return to this point later.

So far, I have only looked at the interest International Law has shown in landmines. The amazing thing about them, however, is not so much the attention that has been devoted to them in legal and diplomatic circles as the political and public interest they have generated – an interest that first emerged in the early 1990s. The post-Cold War years witnessed the end of a great number of regional and internal conflicts which had, till then, seemed insoluble. UN peacekeeping missions were sent to every corner of the globe. But the termination of hostilities did not bring an end to war casualties. Indeed, the reverse was true, especially among civilians. Able once again to travel freely in their countries, people were falling victim to landmines. Suffering in faraway places became a western reality when the mines began to claim victims among the peacekeepers. And it was at this point that the world began to understand the sheer magnitude of the problem. There were millions of landmines, scattered over countries far and wide. And every year they were killing or maiming 25,000 people, most of whom were civilians.

The first political response came in 1993 when President Mitterand – having just visited mine-infested Cambodia – proposed amending Protocol II to tighten the provisions on the use of landmines. By this time too, non-governmental organisations were urging a complete ban on anti-personnel mines as the only effective solution to the problem. But in 1993, most states wanted to keep them in their arsenals. There was a widely held belief among governments that the problem was caused by abuse, and was not inherent to the weapon itself. It would suffice to tighten up the rules. At this point, I should like to say a few words about the distinction between landmines, anti-personnel mines and anti-tank mines. When we use the term mines, more often than not we are talking about anti-personnel mines. These small, inexpensive weapons are lurking in the ground by the million, and they are the main source of the humanitarian problem. Though anti-tank mines kill people as well, and can block lifelines, the human suffering they cause is negligible when compared with the scourge of anti-personnel mines. It is for this reason that international efforts focus on banning these weapons. Protocol II deals with all mines, but the strictest provisions only apply to anti-personnel mines. And the Ottawa Convention is devoted exclusively to them.

Let us return to the attempts to tighten up Protocol II. The Review and Amending Conference got under way in 1995, after four preparatory meetings. But it soon became clear that the outcome would fall short of the expectations of many governments, and of all the non-governmental organisations. The debate took little, if any, account of the humanitarian nature of the problem. Many states were unwilling – for military or economic reasons – to accept far-reaching restrictions on the use and transfer of anti-personnel mines. Due to the consensus nature of the Conference, these states were able to block all the more ambitious proposals. The results were disappointing, and this led to growing support for a total ban. The main question now was how further progress could be made.

It is humanitarian concern, and not security problems, that has fuelled the debate on landmines. Security for all and greater stability – the key objectives of disarmament and arms reduction – do not apply to the landmine problem. For landmines are purely defensive weapons. Nonetheless, elements of the disarmament approach play an important role in the landmine debate. I refer here to matters such as universality and verification, in particular. But I shall return to these points later.

2. WHY THE OTTAWA PROCESS?

In April 1996, a small group of people met in the Quakers' office in Geneva. The meeting took place in the margins of the third session of the Conventional Weapons Convention Review Conference. But the group did not focus on the disappointing turn events were taking at the Conference. Instead, the members of this group – representatives of 10 nations as well as a number of non-governmental organisations – discussed ways of achieving a total international ban on anti-personnel mines. This meeting marked the start of what came to be known as the Ottawa Process. The nations and organisations represented in that room had come to the conclusion that the Review Conference would at best achieve a few improvements, but would certainly not come up with a convincing response to the problem. What was needed was a total ban on anti-personnel mines. I am sure that despite the general optimism displayed at the meeting, no one could have imagined that only a year and a half later more than 120 states would have reached the same conclusion. But this is exactly what happened in Ottawa. Under mounting public pressure, driven by an impressive international campaign coordinated by the International Campaign to Ban Landmines and its coordinator Ms Jody Williams, more and more governments publicly announced their support for a total ban. Some introduced unilateral bans on use, production and transfer.

But views differed among the supporters. Some regarded a total ban as an ultimate objective, to be achieved step-by-step. These nations were in favour of putting the issue on the agenda of the Conference on Disarmament in Geneva, the traditional disarmament forum. But this would have seriously slowed the process. The Conference on Disarmament works on the basis of consensus, and its membership includes some well-known opponents of a total ban. Its negotiating processes lack transparency, making it difficult to mobilise public opinion. But for some, this was precisely the reason for wishing to pursue this course. In the spring of 1997, various attempts were made to get the Conference on Disarmament to negotiate a ban on anti-personnel mines. The more it became evident these attempts were doomed to fail, the greater the support for the Ottawa Process. By this stage, it had become abundantly clear that a completely different approach would have to be adopted if a ban was to be achieved in the not-too-distant future. For the record, those people who had met in that room in Geneva in April 1996 had no blueprint to work from. Instead, they played things by ear.

But what exactly were the elements that set the Ottawa Process apart from other, more conventional approaches? From the start, there were a few countries that formed a core group. Interestingly, they included both western and non-aligned states – a highly unusual combination, especially when it comes to arms-related issues. This core group, with Canada as its informal leader, was the powerhouse of the process. There was, at the early stages, another group of countries – the opposition, as it were – that favoured negotiations in the Conference on Disarmament. But due to the poor progress made there, this group lost its momentum and some of its members joined the Ottawa core group. Throughout the process, this core group of governments cooperated very closely with non-governmental organisations. And this was unique, certainly in the disarmament world. Not only were the NGOs permitted to attend meetings, they were also invited to voice their opinions and table proposals. As a result, the NGOs became aware of the difficulties, and of the countries that needed extra targeting. This turned out to be very useful at the later stages of the Ottawa Process.

There was a clear-cut objective. The goal was nothing more or less than the total elimination of anti-personnel mines. Added to this, procedures were transparent. Every round of consultation and negotiation was open-ended, and the draft treaty text, drawn up by Austria, was available to all interested countries and organisations. The Ottawa Process did not work on a consensus basis. It was instead a coalition of the willing, with countries deciding for themselves whether they wanted to join or keep out.

But probably the main element that set the Ottawa Process apart was the immense public and political interest it generated. The active involvement of Diana, Princess of Wales and the Nobel Peace Prize for the International Campaign to Ban Landmines, and its leader, Jody Williams, gave it an enormous boost.

To illustrate its success, I should like to give you some figures. In April 1996, representatives of 10 nations met in Geneva. By October of the same year, 50 nations were involved. The Oslo Conference in September 1997 was attended by delegates from 90 nations, and more than 120 states signed the Convention in December 1997. This was unprecedented.

3. WHAT ARE THE KEY ELEMENTS OF THE CONVENTION?

At the heart of the agreement is the ban on the use, production, stockpiling and transfer of anti-personnel mines. States Parties also undertake to destroy all anti-personnel mines under their jurisdiction or control. These are the core obligations, which are worked out in more detail in the articles of the Convention. The obligation to destroy mines also applies to those that have been laid. What we are talking about here is, in fact, demining. These mines are to be destroyed within 10 years of the entry into force of the Convention in the country in question. This period may be extended. In order to meet their demining obligations States Parties may ask each other for assistance.

The agreement also enforces compliance. In the event of an alleged violation, the depositary, the Secretary-General of the United Nations, may, under certain conditions, send a fact-finding mission to investigate. This provision is far more intrusive that the relevant provisions of Protocol II, but it cannot be compared to the elaborate verification regimes set out in the Chemical Weapons Convention, the Comprehensive Test Ban Treaty or the Treaty on Conventional Forces in Europe. The argument in favour of adopting a less intrusive regime is that anti-personnel mines are defensive weapons. Violations endanger neither the security of other countries nor the stability of a region. Landmines constitute no threat to international security. They are a humanitarian problem. The agreement does not provide for a permanent, independent secretariat. It is up to the depositary and the annual meeting of States Parties to organise the necessary activities.

4. FURTHER WORK

The Ottawa Process has been more successful than anyone could have imagined. But it is not yet over. For its goal is not the conclusion of an agreement banning anti-personnel mines, but their elimination. The Convention is the main tool, but it is not the only one.

What remains to be done? Firstly, the Convention must become universal. We must continue to put pressure on states that are major stockpilers and users of landmines to adhere to its provisions. The United States recently announced that it will accede by 2006, if by that date alternatives have been found to anti-personnel mines. It has abandoned its attempt to exempt mixed munitions, a sophisticated mixture of anti-personnel and anti-tank mines, from the ban.

Some argue that the Ottawa Convention can have little effect if the main producers and stockpilers refuse to come aboard. If this were a typical disarmament issue, I would be inclined to agree. But landmines are a humanitarian problem. The major military powers play an important role – but this role is not crucial. In the short term, the states that matter most are those that are afflicted by the scourge of landmines. And most of them have signed the Convention.

One question that has now arisen is whether the Conference on Disarmament should open negotiations on a transfer ban on anti-personnel mines. Those in favour argue that such a ban would be the first step in a process that would ultimately lead to the major producers and stockpilers signing the Convention. But it is far more likely that the negotiations will be used by some states to divert attention from the Ottawa Convention, and to relegitimise anti-personnel mines. It is ominous that these states suddenly seemed willing to negotiate a complete ban on transfers, when only two years ago they fiercely resisted adding meaningful transfer restrictions to Protocol II.

It is important to ensure rapid entry into force. The Ottawa Convention will enter into force six months after the fortieth ratification. The score is now 21. Some optimists have predicted that the fortieth ratification will be deposited before the beginning of Autumn. Though it will cost me a bottle of *Burgundy Grand Cru*, I certainly hope they are right.

Demining is an essential element. The Ottawa Convention is an attempt to stop the production and use of new mines. But it also provides for the removal of existing ones. Less developed, mine-infested states will not be able to deal with the problem on their own. More international assistance will be needed. This is a major element in the discussions on the implementation of the Convention, and many signatories have agreed to step up their efforts. An interesting question is whether Ottawa signatories should only provide assistance to other Ottawa signatories. In that case, countries that refuse to ban anti-personnel mines would be excluded. I am in favour of such an approach, except, of course, in the event of acute humanitarian emergencies.

5. THE OTTAWA PROCESS: AN INCIDENT OR A MODEL FOR THE FUTURE?

The last point I would like to discuss is whether the Ottawa Process can serve as a model in dealing with other humanitarian problems, for instance small arms. Or will it remain unique?

Let us go back to the key elements of the process, and assess whether they may be applicable in the future. Firstly, a core group of states: this important element of the Ottawa Process can certainly be applied to other issues. Groups of countries are increasingly joining forces on an *ad hoc* basis to further a given cause. The recent Swedish/Irish initiative on nuclear disarmament is a good illustration. A close relationship with non-governmental organisations was another major factor that contributed to the success of the Ottawa Process, and this will be more difficult to achieve in other cases. For here, the core group of governments and the NGOs agreed on all the key substantive and procedural elements. There are few other issues where the views of the two parties converge so closely. There was, in addition, a clear-cut objective, and this again will make the Ottawa Process a difficult act to follow. The problem of small arms is, for example, far more complicated.

But transparency is certainly something that can apply in other cases too, though this may be more difficult when it comes to typical disarmament issues. It also holds true for the formation of a coalition of the willing. In the case of typical disarmament or arms reduction issues, such a coalition is relatively pointless, unless the major stockpiler states are part of it. Nonetheless, it is an approach that could be adopted in many other cases. The last, key element to the success of the Ottawa Process was the immense political and public interest it generated. And this will be the most difficult element to repeat. Though non-governmental organisations in particular were responsible for generating this interest, quite a bit of luck was involved. We all know that public and political interest can fade very rapidly if more interesting events occur. Luck always plays a role. And the Ottawa Process was very lucky.

Though all these elements may be in evidence, they have to be applicable at the same time. And it is unlikely that such a situation will arise again in the near future. Nonetheless, I do not feel that the Ottawa Process is an incident. Factors that played a role such as NGO involvement, and *ad hoc* core groups, will be more prominent in the future too. But the Ottawa Process is a tailor-made formula. Though the same material may be used again, a different pattern will have to be found.

The Ottawa Process is a success. Although we have not yet eliminated anti-personnel mines, the Ottawa Convention has given the world an excellent tool with which it can achieve this objective. We need now to universalise the agreement, and set to work demining. When the Convention enters into force, we will have to ensure that it is implemented properly. The Ottawa Process has not yet reached its conclusion. But it has shown how a coalition of medium-sized powers and non-governmental organisations can make a difference.

I should like to end on a personal note. I have been involved in the Ottawa Process from the moment of its conception. It was my privilege to represent the Netherlands from that first meeting in Geneva, through the successive core group meetings, up to the signing ceremony in Ottawa. It was a very special experience, one that I shall never forget. I have already said that the Ottawa Process was very lucky. So was I.

CHEMICAL WEAPONS CONVENTION AND THE VERIFICATION PROCESS

Jean-Louis Rolland*

It is a special pleasure for me, representative of the Organisation on the Prohibition of Chemical Weapons (OPCW), to speak at this International Law Conference commemorating the 750th anniversary of the city of The Hague. On behalf of the Director-General of the Organisation I would like to congratulate all participants with this anniversary and to wish successful completion of this important conference.

The Hague has a special meaning for the OPCW. Not only because its Headquarters are located here, but also because the efforts of the international community aimed at banning the use of chemical weapons and achieving its complete elimination have also started here almost exactly a century ago. It took mankind over 22 centuries since the first reports of the use of arsenic smoke in the Peloponesian War to agree on a set of measures to control chemical weapons. Restrictions on the development of such weapons were agreed at the First International Peace Conference held in The Hague in 1899, at which the signatory states pledged to 'abstain' from using projectiles that could spread 'asphyxiating or deleterious gases'.

Unfortunately, this agreement did not prevent the use of chemical weapons during World War I. The first large scale poison gas attack took place not so far away from The Hague, at Ypres on 22 April 1915 when 6,000 cylinders containing 168 tonnes of chlorine gas were used against both soldiers and civilians. By the end of the war, an estimated 124,200 tonnes of chemical agents had been used. The chemical weapons used during World War I caused one million casualties, more than 90,000 of which were fatal. Between 13 and 20 million rounds of chemical munitions which failed to function were scattered across the battlefield, many of them even now remaining a live reminder of human folly and cruelty.

Immediately after World War I a number of attempts were made to ban the use of chemical weapons. The Versailles Treaty of 1919 included a special article reaffirming the previous agreements regarding chemical weapons, and also prohibited the production of such weapons by Germany. Public outrage at the effects of chemical weapons led in 1925 to the signing in Geneva of the Protocol for the Prohibition of the Use of Asphyxiating, Poisonous or Other Gases, and

* Director of Verification, Organisation for the Prohibition of Chemical Weapons.

W.P. Heere (Ed.), International Law and The Hague's 750th Anniversary

Bacteriological Methods of Warfare. The Protocol which was accepted by the League of Nations at the conclusion of the Geneva conference on the arms trade, reaffirmed the prohibition of chemical weapons as a general principle of law, and extended it to include a ban on the use of bacteriological weapons. However, the scope of the Geneva Protocol was limited in that it prohibited the use of chemical weapons in war, but not their development, production or stockpiling. Moreover, many states that ratified or acceded to the Protocol added their own reservations that diminished its effectiveness. The development, production and stockpiling of chemical weapons thus continued. The first open breach of the Geneva Protocol occurred in 1935-1936 when chemical weapons were used during the war in Abyssinia. Research work conducted before and during World War II led to the discovery of the first nerve agents – tabun, sarin and soman – and during 1950s and 1960s to the development and production of their new generation – the so-called V-agents. The growing threat to humanity posed by these developments, as well as by the emergence of binary chemical weapons, the use of herbicides and tear gas during the Viet Nam War and the chemical attacks during the Iran-Iraq War, all this reinforced the international community's desire to conclude a total ban on chemical weapons.

A resolution of the United Nations General Assembly in 1961 established a body for disarmament known as the Eighteen Nations Disarmament Committee. The membership of this body was enlarged several times, and its name has consequently changed, initially to the Conference of the Committee on Disarmament, then to the Committee on Disarmament and, finally, to the Conference on Disarmament. The work of this Geneva based body first resulted in the Convention on the Prohibition of the Development, Production and Stockpiling of Bacteriological and Toxic Weapons and on their Destruction which entered into force on 26 March 1975. The Biological Weapons Convention, although lacking a verification regime, can be seen as the first step towards establishing a comprehensive ban on chemical weapons, since Article IX of that Convention urged its states parties to continue negotiations to reach an agreement on the prohibition of chemical weapons. The development of the chemical industry and the increase in the number of potential possessors of chemical weapons stimulated a more intense debate on chemical weapons disarmament.

It took another 11 years of intensive negotiation – which included four different national drafts of the future treaty submitted by its participants, two international conferences in Paris and Canberra and two bilateral agreements between the United States and the Soviet Union – to arrive on 3 September 1992 at the acceptance by the Conference on Disarmament of the text of the Convention on the Prohibition of the Development, Production, Stockpiling and Use of Chemical Weapons and on their Destruction, thus concluding two decades of negotiating.

The United Nations General Assembly adopted the text by consensus, and on 13 January 1993 the Chemical Weapons Convention was opened for signature in Paris. It was immediately signed by 126 states. It took another four years of intensive negotiation of detailed implementing and administrative procedures within a Preparatory Commission and the requisite ratification by 65 states for the Convention to enter into force and for the Organisation for the Prohibition of Chemical Weapons (OPCW) to be born, on 29 April 1997. The First Conference of the States Parties in May 1997 elected 41 members of the Executive Council of the OPCW and appointed Mr Jose M. Bustani as the first Director-General.

* * *

The one hundred years it took to achieve the results described above (see also the annex) have a special significance, not only in time but also in geography. The process which was triggered at The Hague by the 1899 First International Peace Conference completed its century-long historical loop also at The Hague with the establishment of the OPCW. The building, which now houses its Headquarters, was formally inaugurated by Her Majesty Queen Beatrix of the Netherlands on 20 May 1998.

The arrival at The Hague of an international organisation responsible for the supervision of a general and complete ban on chemical weapons was therefore hardly incidental. On the other hand, the addition of the OPCW to the family of important international bodies promoting the rule of law and peace has undoubtedly contributed to the image of The Hague as the 'legal capital of the world'.

On behalf of the Director-General I would like to extend our best wishes to the authorities and citizens of The Hague and to express the hope that this city continues to provide a comfortable environment for pursuing the noble causes of the international organisations located here.

Annex

Chemical Weapons Convention (CWC)

Entry into force : 29 April
Membership : 110 (2 contracting states, 56 signatories)
including : – all P-5 members of UN Security Council
– four CW possessors
– eight possessors of former CWPFs
– eight O/ACW possessors

(compare: NPT – 65 Member States at EIF+1, including a number of significant absentees)

OPCW Structure

(Chart 1, p. 398)

Secretariat Structure

(Chart 2, p. 399)

CWC Main Objectives

– DISARMAMENT
(destroy within 10-year period all chemical weapons and related facilities and activities)

– NON-PROLIFERATION
(monitor chemicals and related industries that deal with scheduled chemicals)

CWC Prohibitions

– using CW
– engaging in any military preparations to use CW
– developing, producing, otherwise acquiring, stockpiling or retaining CW, or transferring directly or indirectly CW to anyone
– assisting, encouraging or inducing, an [in] any way, anyone in any activity prohibited to a State Party under the Convention

CWC Undertakings

– destroy CW (OCW)
– destroy abandoned CW
– destroy CW production facilities
– do not use riot control agents as a method of warfare

CWC AT A GLANCE

UNPRECENDENTED MECHANISM OF UNIVERSAL AND UNDISCRIMINATED ABOLITION OF A WHOLE CLASS OF WMD AND NON-PROLIFERATION WITHOUT PREJUDICE TO FREE TRADE

– disarmament and prevention of re-emergence and proliferation
– careful balance of intrusive verification and protection of unrelated confidential information
– arms control and economic development

Implementation

– Articles III, IV, V, VI, X, and Verification Annex – detailed reporting and on-site verification procedures
– Article IX – clarifications and challenge inspections
– Article X – assistance and protection against chemical weapons
– Article XI – economic and technological development
– Article XII – ensuring compliance, sanctions
– Article VII – strong legal mechanism to ensure effective and uniform implementation

Declarations and Information

(CWC provisions)

– Initial declarations of CW and related facilities as well as RCAs (Article III) and chemical industry facilities (Article VI)
– Information on protective programs (Article X)
– Annual declarations of past and future activities regarding chemical industry, transfers of scheduled chemicals
– General, detailed and annual plans/declarations of destruction of CW and CWPFs [Chemical Weapons Production Facilities]

(status of implementation)

Declared Facilities (as of 20 May 1998)

Types of facilities	*Number of facilities*	*Number of countries*
CWPFs	58	8
CWSPs	33	4
CWDFs	7	1
Old and Abandoned CWs	42	8
Schedule 1 chemicals	24	19

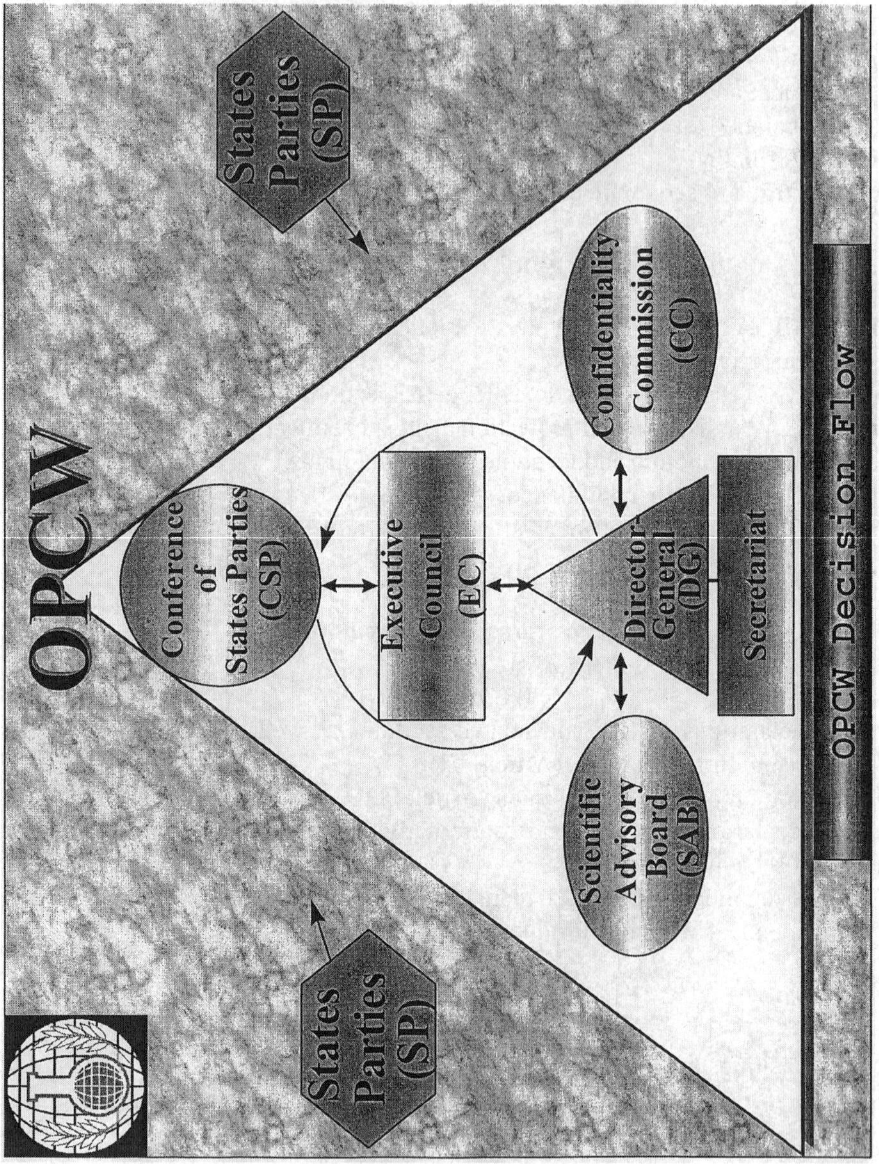

Chart 1. OPCW General Structure

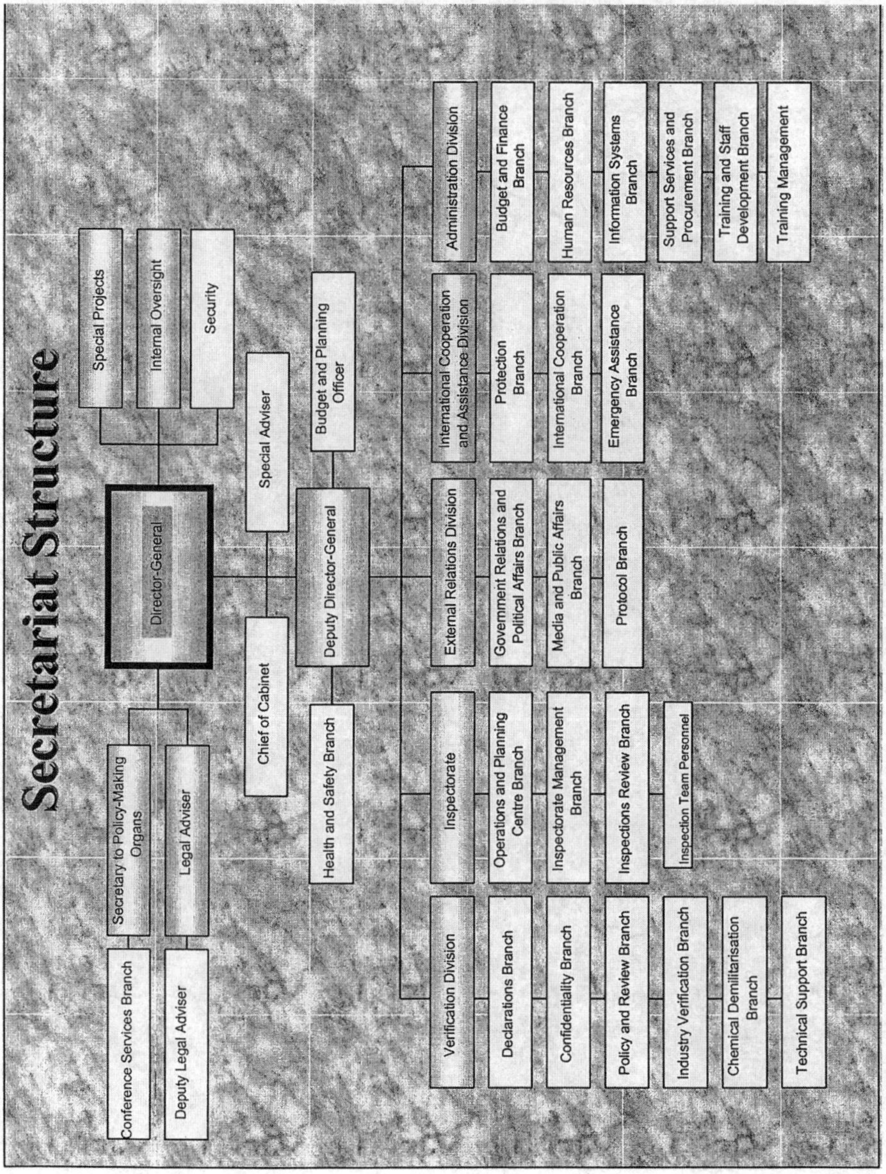

Chart 2. OPCW Secretariat Structure

Type of facilties	*Declared/(Inspectable)*
Schedule 2 chemicals	274/(109)
Schedule 3 chemicals	403/(338)
DOCs	3612/(3503)

Inspections

(CWC provisions)

– CWSFs	– Schedule 1
– CWPFs	– Schedule 2
– CWDFs	– Schedule 3
– O&ACW	

– Challenge Inspections and Investigations of Alleged Use of CW

(status of implementation)

by beginning of June 1998

222 inspections in 25 Member States
– 56 (25%) industry inspections (Schedule 1 and 2)
– 166 (75%) CW-related inspections

90% of inspector days spent at CW-related sites

no challenge inspections or investigations of alleged use of CW

Confidentiality

(CWC provisions)

– Safeguards against disclosure of unrelated national security, business or other proprietary information built into the inspection procedures in the text of the Convention, including its Verification Annex (ex. managed access)
– Annex on the Protection of Confidential Information
– OPCW Policy on Confidentiality
– Manual on Confidentiality Procedures (internal Secretariat document)

(status of implementation)

82% of declaration-related material classified
– 63% – OPCW Highly Protected
– 10% – OPCW Protected
– 9% – OPCW Restricted
– 18% – unclassified

79% of final inspection reports classified
– 42% – OPCW Highly Protected
– 37% – OPCW Protected
– 17% – OPCW Restricted
– 4% – unclassified
– 'need to know'
– strict access procedures for staff
– building configuration
– notification of staff having access
– documentation of audit trail
– regular confidentiality audits (up to 100%)
– Electronic Data Management System (VIS-EDMS)
  – installed March-April 1997
  – three audits (June 1997, January 1998 and May 1998)
  – full (and hopefully final) audit (October 1998)

National Implementation Measures

(CWC provisions)

Each State Party in accordance with constitutional processes shall:
– '*prohibit natural and legal persons* anywhere on its territory or in any other place under its jurisdiction ... *from undertaking any activity prohibited to a State Party* ..., including enacting penal legislation with respect to such activity';
– 'not permit in any other place under its control any activity prohibited to a State Party'; and
– 'extend its penal legislation ... to any activity prohibited to a State Party ... undertaken any where by natural persons, possessing its nationality, in conformity with international law'.
– '*cooperate* with other States Parties and afford appropriate form of *legal assistance* to facilitate the implementation of [its] obligations'.

Cooperation and legal assistance could be needed in connection with:
– institution of procedures
– prosecution of alleged offenders
– investigations
– extradition

(Role of the OPCW)

Responsibility to achieve the object and purpose of the Convention and to provide a forum for consultation and cooperation among States Parties

OPCW: Lean and Efficient

– annual assessed budget:
  – 1997 (8 months) : NLG 88.8 million
  – 1998 : NLG 122.4 million
– 500-strong Secretariat, including 206 inspectors (126 until 1 July 1998)
– 3:2 ratio of VER and INS staff to other support staff
– 112 days on site per inspector in the 7 [8] months of 1997
– costs of inspections in 1997 NLG 2.8 million out of which NLG 1.8 million for CW-related inspections (does not include costs of in-kind services provided by inspected States Parties and salaries of inspectors)

CLOSING SESSION

The International Court of Justice and the Proliferation of International Judicial Organs
Chair: H. Corell

THE CONTRIBUTION OF THE INTERNATIONAL COURT OF JUSTICE TO THE DEVELOPMENT OF INTERNATIONAL LAW

Stephen M. Schwebel*

The International Court of Justice is the 'principal judicial organ of the United Nations'. All States Members of the United Nations are by that fact parties to the Court's Statute; non-members (such as Switzerland and Nauru) may and have become parties. The Court's contentious jurisdiction in principle encompasses any kind of international legal dispute. This is reflected in its case-law, which covers a wide spectrum of legal issues, ranging from questions of boundaries to fisheries to the use of force to international humanitarian law to arbitral awards to diplomatic immunities to investment disputes.

One does not have to look further than this town, however, to realize that the International Court of Justice is not the only international judicial body: In 1981, the Iran-US Claims Tribunal was established in The Hague, in 1993 the International Criminal Tribunal for the Former Yugoslavia. In fact, the last decades have seen a proliferation of judicial bodies: human rights courts, courts of regional economic organisations, *ad hoc* claims tribunals, an array of international administrative tribunals, trade dispute settlement mechanisms and investment dispute settlement bodies, and the International Tribunal of the Law of the Sea, have all been established. An International Criminal Court currently is under negotiation.

There is more than one reason for the proliferation of international judicial bodies. Since the establishment of the World Court in 1922, international law has changed and expanded drastically. Whereas the Statute of the Court reflects the classical view of international law that states are its only subjects, international law has witnessed the gradual appearance of other actors. Hand-in-hand with this development, the range of disputes has changed; judicial bodies were needed in which individuals or corporations could bring claims directly against states, or in which individuals could be tried for having committed international crimes.

Moreover, the body of international norms has grown remarkably. Subsystems of international law, such as international trade law and human rights law, have evolved. This development has coincided with the establishment of specialised, and regional and universal, judicial bodies whose jurisdiction is confined to matters within a defined subject area. These tribunals were required to deal with the increased workload – in some cases, thousands of claims – and to

* President, International Court of Justice.

W.P. Heere (Ed.), International Law and The Hague's 750th Anniversary

specialise in the handling of certain types of disputes. They too have also contributed to the development of international law within their spheres.

With judicial proliferation, a certain overlap of jurisdiction is unavoidable. Take for example the question whether acts of genocide were committed during the conflict in the former Yugoslavia. The Security Council set up an *ad hoc* Tribunal, the International Criminal Tribunal for the Prosecution of War Crimes in the Former Yugoslavia, to try individuals charged with crimes committed in the former Yugoslavia since 1991. The Tribunal may determine the guilt or innocence of individuals accused of the commission of war crimes and acts of genocide. At the same time, the case concerning the *Application of the Convention on the Prevention and Punishment of the Crime of Genocide* is before the International Court of Justice. Bosnia-Herzegovina and the Federal Republic of Yugoslavia accuse each other of having violated the Genocide Convention by promoting acts of genocide in Bosnian territory. The Tribunal has to pass upon the criminal responsibility of individuals, while the Court is asked to determine the international responsibility of states. But both judicial bodies will or may have to determine the same basic question: do the acts charged or committed amount to genocide?

Other areas of overlap in the jurisdiction of international judicial bodies are likely. The World Court has dealt with the law of the sea for seventy-five years. The International Tribunal for the Law of the Sea (ITLOS) will deal not only with the interpretation of the Third United Nations Convention on the Law of the Sea, and not only with claims of individuals, corporations and public authorities in that immense sphere, but with the law of the sea – essentially the inter-state law of the sea – as the World Court has contributed to shaping it. Inevitably it will also deal with subjects such as interpretation of treaties, another area of law much influenced by the judgments and opinions of the Court. Over time, there surely will be interplay and interaction between ITLOS and the Court.

Differing outcomes or even the same outcome with differing reasoning may affect the uniformity, even the coherence, of international law. Or the law may be enriched by the interplay of distinctive perspectives. A proper respect by one body for the jurisprudence of others will be required.

Within this system of specialisation, the role of the International Court of Justice as the 'principal judicial organ' of the world community attains a still fuller significance. Unlike specialised judicial bodies, it enjoys a general and comprehensive substantive jurisdiction. Unlike bilateral or regional judicial bodies, it is available to all states of the international community. It uniquely is the principal judicial organ of the United Nations. Its decisions thus may carry an importance in and beyond the areas of international law which it may examine in a particular case or advisory proceeding, in and beyond the geographical regions of the states parties to the case, and in respect of and beyond the particulars of the dispute. The Court for some seventy-five years has been in a position to contribute significantly to the formation and development of international law, and it has exploited that position. That history was analyzed and expounded through the 1950s by Sir Hersch Lauterpacht in his magisterial work, '*The Development of International Law by the International Court.*'

Of course, Article 59 of the Statute of the Court provides that '[t]he decision of the Court has no binding force except between the parties and in respect of that particular case.' Nevertheless, it is undeniable that the decisions and opinions of the Court may have an influence extending beyond the particular case. Decisions may influence the legal and practical interests of states that are not parties to the dispute. States tend to regard them as authoritative pronouncements on the current state of international law and to apply them to their own concerns. The content of customary international law, or the governing interpretation of a treaty, may be influenced or even determined by a judgment of the Court. The Court's decisions thus enjoy, as Lauterpacht has put it, an 'intrinsic' authority within the international community.[1]

The Court itself has characteristically followed its own reasoning, although it is not bound by precedent. It has good reasons for doing so: its decisions are a repository of legal analysis and experience to which it is natural to adhere. They embody what the Court has considered or determined to be the law. Respect for decisions given in the past makes for legal certainty and continuity, for a measure of predictability; it enhances stability. The coherence and consistency of its decisions has strengthened the Court's legitimacy, thereby promoting respect for its jurisprudence.

This 'intrinsic' authority of the Court's decisions and the coherence of its case-law are fundamental factors which enable it to contribute to the development of international law. The Court's contributions have in fact been considerable. As a judicial organ, however, its contributions to the development of international law are inherently different from the process of codification and progressive development of international law by such bodies as the International Law Commission or by international conventions.

The Statute obliges the Court to decide in accordance with international law . This means that the Court cannot create new law where there is none. Instead, it has to find and apply existing law. The Court has held that its 'duty is to apply the law as it finds it, not to make it'.[2] Whether it follows that, under its Statute, the Court is empowered to find that there is no law in point, that there is a *non liquet*, is controversial. For decades that question was a matter of doctrinal controversy. With its Advisory Opinion – one might say, Opinions – on *The Legality of the Threat or Use of Nuclear Weapons*, that doctrinal controversy sprang to life.

[1] Sir Hersch Lauterpacht, *The Development of International Law by the International Court*, revised edn. (Cambridge 1982) p. 22.

[2] *South West Africa* cases, Second Phase, Judgment, *ICJ Rep.* (1966) p. 48.

In any event, the Court does not develop international law in the abstract. Its contribution to the development of international law takes place in the determination of a particular dispute or in giving a requested advisory opinion. The Court develops international law through the application of international norms to particular circumstances, by elaborating the content of a norm, by expanding upon it in certain situations. If the Court finds, for instance, that a practice of states has consolidated a nascent rule, the Court contributes to the development of the law. The Court may do so when it identifies a principle of international law, elaborates on its meaning, and applies it to a specific situation.

The Court has been sensitive to the dynamic development and the 'continuous evolution of international law'.[3] This is particularly evident in the areas of the law of the sea, international humanitarian law and international environmental law.

The Court has made significant contributions to the development of international law in these areas, and others such as the law of treaties, the law of international organizations, self-determination, state succession and international arbitration. It would be beyond the limits of these remarks to go into its contributions in all those areas. Let me refer to a few areas of international law which are prominent in current legal debate. I shall deal with the Court's contribution to the development of the legal concept of rights and obligations *erga omnes*, and to the concept of equity in the allocation of scarce natural resources. I will then refer to some salient examples from the Court's jurisprudence in the areas of international humanitarian law and international environmental law.

1. RIGHTS AND OBLIGATIONS *ERGA OMNES*

A notable contribution is the Court's holdings about rights and obligations *erga omnes*. The first time the Court had the opportunity to address such common interests was in the 1951 *Reservations to the Genocide Convention* case in which it held that:

> 'In such a convention the contracting States do not have any interests of their own; they merely have, one and all, a common interest, namely the accomplishment of those high purposes which are the *raison d'être* of the convention.'[4]

This holding laid the basis for the Court's *obiter dictum* in the *Barcelona Traction* case, in which the Court made its first explicit reference to obligations which were not owed only to a particular state, but *erga omnes*, towards the

[3] *Barcelona Traction, Light and Power Company, Limited* (*Belgium* v. *Spain*), Second Phase, Judgment, *ICJ Rep.* (1970) p. 33.

[4] *Reservations to the Convention on the Prevention and Punishment of the Crime of Genocide*, *ICJ Rep.* (1951) p. 23.

international community as a whole. Referring to the obligations of a state concerning the treatment of foreign nationals in its territory, the Court held that:

> 'an essential distinction should be drawn between the obligations of a State towards the international community as a whole, and those arising vis-à-vis another State in the field of diplomatic protection. By their very nature the former are the concern of all States. In view of the importance of the rights involved, all States can be held to have a legal interest in their protection; they are obligations *erga omnes*.'[5]

As examples of such obligations, the Court cited the outlawing of acts of aggression and of genocide, and basic human rights, such as the protection from slavery and racial discrimination.

In *Barcelona Traction*, the Court thus recognized a legal interest in every state in the performance of *erga omnes* obligations. This meant that they were *erga omnes* not only in the sense that they were owed to the international community of states but that every state was entitled to invoke the responsibility of the state violating an *erga omnes* obligation.

The concept of *erga omnes* obligations aroused attention and approval in the legal literature. The concept was strengthened by the appearance of *jus cogens* obligations which by definition are owed to all states. Due to its dynamic character, the concept of rights and obligations *erga omnes* has been subject to further development and serves a central conceptual purpose in areas such as international humanitarian and environmental law.

The International Law Commission has included *erga omnes* obligations in its draft articles on state responsibility. The draft endeavours to regulate claims arising from the breach of certain *erga omnes* obligations. Furthermore, the concepts of *erga omnes* and *jus cogens* underlie the much disputed notion of 'international crimes of states' as a special category of international delicts. Intensive discussions, both in and outside the International Law Commission, on the practical consequences of the enforcement of *erga omnes* obligations, show that the development of this legal concept is still in train. Some might say, with regard to state crimes, under strain.

2. EQUITY

Another contribution of the International Court of Justice to the development of international law is the role it has attributed to the concept of equity. Over the years, the Court and its predecessor have refined concepts of an equitable

[5] *Barcelona Traction, Light and Power Company, Limited* (*Belgium* v. *Spain*), *Second Phase,* Judgment, *ICJ Rep.* (1970) p. 32.

character, such as good faith, acquiescence and estoppel. In the *Gulf of Maine* case, the Chamber characterised equity as

> 'a fundamental norm whose existence in the legal convictions not only of the Parties to the present dispute, but of all States, is apparent from an examination of the realities of international legal relations.'[6]

Equity has played an important part in the Court's jurisprudence concerning maritime boundaries. The Court thus may be said to have introduced a fairness-discourse into the positivist international legal structure.

The starting point for this development is the 1969 *North Sea Continental Shelf* cases. In these cases, the Court first considered the applicability of the equidistance principle, which it then rejected, because, *inter alia*, under the given factual circumstances, its application in its view would have produced 'unnatural and unreasonable' results. Instead, it directed the parties to delimit their maritime boundaries in accordance with 'equitable principles'.

The Court's ruling had a significant bearing on the negotiations of provisions relating to maritime delimitation at the Third United Nations Conference on the Law of the Sea, influencing the decision to give equity an explicit role. The Conference went further than the Court: it produced a formula for maritime delimitation in which an 'equitable solution' became the predominant designated standard.

The new Convention gave no legal guidance on what constitutes an 'equitable solution'. The Court remained free to interpret and further develop its content. In its subsequent four maritime delimitation cases, the Court referred to 'equitable principles', such as proportionality. The application of these 'equitable principles' had to lead to an 'equitable result', as provided in the Convention. The Court gave priority to the equity of the result, when it held that

> '[i]t is however the goal – the equitable result – and not the means used to achieve it, that must be the primary element in this duality of characterization.'[7]

The role the Court had attributed to equity may have influenced the attribution of other resources: the 1997 Convention on the Non-Navigational Use of Watercourses includes provision for the 'equitable use' of river water. It directs watercourse states to utilize watercourses in their respective territories 'in an equitable and reasonable manner'. The Convention articulates a series of principles relevant to an equitable apportionment of river water.

[6] *Delimitation of the Maritime Boundary in the Gulf of Maine Area*, Judgment, *ICJ Rep.* (1984) p. 299.

[7] *Continental Shelf (Libyan Arab Jamahiriya/Malta)*, Judgment, *ICJ Rep.* (1985) pp. 38-39.

Whether the salience of equitable considerations in maritime delimitation is sound in law is a matter of controversy. But what is beyond controversy is the influential role played by the Court.

4. INTERNATIONAL HUMANITARIAN LAW

The very first Judgment of the International Court of Justice, *The Corfu Channel* Case, bears directly upon questions of international humanitarian law. In its Judgment, the Court held that the applicability of the 1907 Hague Conventions to times of war did not mean that elementary humanitarian law was only applicable in international armed conflict. On the contrary, there were 'certain general and well-established principles' such as 'elementary considerations of humanity', which, were 'even more exacting in peace than in war'.[8]

In 1951, the International Court of Justice issued a landmark opinion on the question of *Reservations to the Genocide Convention*, to which I referred earlier. The Court pointed out that the General Assembly, together with the states which adopted the Convention, intended to obtain the widest possible participation of states in the Convention without sacrificing its object. Therefore, the object and the purely humanitarian and civilizing purpose of the Convention 'limit both the freedom of making reservations and that of objecting to them'.[9]

The Court furthermore held that the crime of genocide shocked the conscience of mankind and was contrary to moral law and to the spirits and aims of the United Nations. It found that 'the principles underlying the Convention are principles which are recognized by civilized nations as binding on states, even without any conventional obligation' and that the condemnation of genocide, and the co-operation required to prevent any acts of genocide, had a universal character.[10]

The Judgment made two important contributions to humanitarian law: first, it limited the possibility of making reservations to international conventions with humanitarian and civilizing objects. Second, it declared that the obligation not to commit genocide was binding on all states as customary law. The Court's references to the 'universality' of the obligation and its 'inderogability' were the ingredients for the conceptualization of *jus cogens*, of which the prohibition to commit genocide is a prime example, indeed, one of the few accepted examples.

It need not be added that the Court's Opinion on *Reservations to the Genocide Convention* critically influenced provisions of the Vienna Convention on the Law of Treaties in respect of reservations.

[8] *Corfu Channel (United Kingdom* v. *Albania)*, Merits, Judgment, *ICJ Rep.* (1949) p. 10.

[9] *Reservations to the Convention on the Prevention and Punishment of the Crime of Genocide*, Advisory Opinion, *ICJ Rep.* (1951) p. 24.

[10] Ibid., at p. 23

Another major contribution to international humanitarian law was the Court's 1986 Judgment on the merits in the case concerning *Military and Paramilitary Activities in and against Nicaragua*. The Court classified the activities of the contra rebels against the Sandinista Government as an armed conflict not of an international character. The acts of the contras against that Government were therefore governed by the law applicable to non-international conflicts. However, the actions of the United States in and against Nicaragua fell under the legal rules relating to international conflicts.

A multilateral treaty reservation of the United States appeared to preclude the Court from applying the Geneva Conventions to the case. However, the Court held that the conduct of the United States could be judged according to the fundamental general principles of humanitarian law. What is more, it found certain provisions of the Geneva Conventions to be customary law, holding that 'the Geneva Conventions are in some respects a development, and in other respects no more than the expression' of fundamental principles of humanitarian law.[11] The Court accordingly held that:

> 'there is an obligation on the United States Government, in the terms of Article I of the Geneva Conventions, to 'respect' the Conventions and even 'to ensure respect' for them 'in all circumstances', since such an obligation does not derive only from the Conventions themselves, but from the general principles of humanitarian law to which the Conventions merely give specific expression.'[12]

The Court also held that common Article 3 of the Geneva Conventions defining certain rules to be applied in armed conflicts of non-international character contained rules which 'constitute a minimum yardstick' reflecting 'elementary considerations of humanity'. It thus concluded that certain norms governing non-international conflicts were substantially the same as those applicable to international armed conflicts.

The Judgment of the Court in this case met with a mixed reaction on a number of counts. On this count, some critics reproached the Court for the bareness of the evidence and reasoning supporting its conclusions. The Court failed to survey, assemble and evaluate the evidence of the international practice in order to demonstrate the existence of the international customary norms that it asserted.

Nevertheless, the positive contributions of the *Nicaragua* case to the development of international humanitarian law are considerable. As the Nuremberg Tribunal declared the Hague Conventions to reflect customary international law, so has the Court declared the Geneva Conventions to reflect customary international law. Its conclusion that certain basic humanitarian principles should be applicable in all situations involving violence of high in-

[11] *Military and Paramilitary Activities in and against Nicaragua (Nicaragua* v. *United States of America),* Merits, Judgment, *ICJ Rep.* (1986) p. 113.

[12] Ibid., at p. 114, para. 220.

tensity are significant. The protection of the individuals concerned by international law accordingly does not depend on the will of their governments to be legally bound by the provisions of humanitarian conventions. The entrenchment of international humanitarian law in the corpus of customary law thus has promoted, or has been meant to promote, the protection of those most affected by armed conflict: its victims.

International humanitarian law was again a subject before the Court, in the 1996 Advisory Opinion on the *Legality of the Threat or Use of Nuclear Weapons*. It held that the threat or use of nuclear weapons would generally be contrary to the principles and rules of humanitarian law; at the same time, the Opinion equivocated on the legality of resort to nuclear weapons in self-defence.

In the case concerning the *Application of the Convention on the Prevention and Punishment of the Crime of Genocide*, currently before the Court, the parties each allege the other to have violated the Genocide Convention during the conflict in the former Yugoslavia. This is the first time that an international court is asked to adjudicate upon the responsibility of a state for genocide.

5. INTERNATIONAL ENVIRONMENTAL LAW

The Court's contributions to the development of international environmental law have also been significant. The Court's contributions to that area of law are not just recent. The first decision was taken as early as 1929, by the Permanent Court of International Justice.

In its Judgment on the *Territorial Jurisdiction of the International Commission of the River Oder*, the Permanent Court held that:

> '(The) community of interests in a navigable river becomes the basis of a common legal right, the essential features of which are the perfect equality of all riparian States in the user of the whole course of the river and the exclusion of any preferential privilege of any one riparian State in relation to the others.'[13]

From this principle it follows that water resources such as rivers, lakes or groundwater may not be used by states in such a manner as to prevent or otherwise limit other 'riparian' states from making use of their right of access to that shared resource. In the wake of this decision, a series of international agreements on the prohibition of pollution of watercourses have been drawn up. The principle further underlies the 1997 Convention on the Non-Navigational Use of International Watercourses.

Another principle of international environmental law – as well as a principle

[13] *Territorial Jurisdiction of the International Commission of the River Oder*, *PCIJ Series A*, No. 23 p.27.

of law of wider reach – has its origins in the *Corfu Channel* decision, in which the Court determined

> 'every state's obligation not to allow knowingly its territory to be used for acts contrary to the rights of other states.'[14]

The responsibility not to cause damage to the environment of other states or of areas beyond national jurisdiction has been accepted as an obligation by virtually all states. It was included as Principle 21 in the Stockholm Declaration and as Principle 2 in the Rio Declaration (neither of which however are binding instruments); it has been reflected in a series of international conventions; it represents the cornerstone of international environmental law.

In the *Fisheries Jurisdiction* case (*United Kingdom* v. *Iceland*), the Court set standards for the conservation of living resources of the sea:

> 'It is one of the advances in maritime international law, resulting from the intensification of fishing, that the former *laissez faire* treatment of the living resources of the sea in the high seas has been replaced by a recognition of a duty to have due regard to the rights of other states and the needs of conservation for the benefits of all. Consequently, both parties have the obligation to keep under review the fishery resources in the disputed waters and to examine together, in the light of the scientific and other available information, the measures required for the conservation and development, and equitable exploitation, of those resources ....'[15]

This dictum recognized the duty of states to have 'due regard' to the 'needs of conservation for the benefits of all' – a duty that extends to the high seas. It has provided a basis for the establishment of further limitations on the rights of states, in respect both to fisheries and other shared natural resources. The UN Convention on the Law of the Sea accordingly provides that, in the Exclusive Economic Zone, the coastal state must ensure through conservation and management measures that living resources are not endangered by over-exploitation, taking into account the best scientific evidence available to it.

Two recent cases bear on international environmental law. In its Advisory Opinion on the *Legality of the Threat or Use of Nuclear Weapons*, the Court emphasized that environmental considerations are an important element to be taken into account in armed conflicts:

> 'States must take environmental considerations into account when assessing what is necessary and proportionate in the pursuit of legitimate military objectives. Respect for

[14] *Corfu Channel (United Kingdom* v. *Albania)*, Merits, Judgment, *ICJ Rep.* (1949) p. 22.

[15] *Fisheries Jurisdiction (United Kingdom* v. *Iceland), Merits,* Judgment, *ICJ Rep.* (1974) p. 31; *(Federal Republic of Germany* v. *Iceland)*, Merits, Judgment, *ICJ Rep.* (1974) p. 199.

> the environment is one of the elements that go to assessing whether an action is in conformity with the principles of necessity and proportionality.'[16]

Respect for the environment in international armed conflicts has been considered in several international instruments and in Principle 24 of the Rio Declaration. In its Advisory Opinion, the Court left no doubt that this obligation applies to all states and does not depend on adherence to the relevant international instruments.

Finally, in the *Gabčíkovo-Nagymaros* case, the Court referred to the corpus of new environmental norms and standards that has been developed in the last two decades:

> 'Such new norms have to be taken into consideration, and such new standards given proper weight, not only when States contemplate new activities but also when continuing with activities begun in the past. This need to reconcile economic development with protection of the environment is aptly expressed in the concept of sustainable development.'[17]

This dictum acknowledged not only the duty of states to take into account newly evolving environmental norms when concluding an international convention or undertaking a new activity. Environmental principles such as sustainable development are also relevant to the application of existing instruments, obligations and activities.

These are some salient examples of how the Court has contributed to the development of international law. The Court will continue to play this role in the future. International law has been developing at an ever faster pace; and the growing number of specialized international judicial bodies have made their contributions to this development. What is more, the international law-making process has gained an impressive and often underestimated momentum. At the same time, the world remains beset with actions, even with political programmes, that are *contra legem*. The Court thus finds itself in a legal and practical position that is rather different from the times in which its 'intrinsic' authority seemed unchallenged. It is important that the Court is sensitive to these considerations and that it endeavours to maintain its position at the forefront of modern legal development. At the same time, the Court must nurture the confidence of states in its fidelity to its jurisdictional limits and to the existing governing principles and provisions of international law.

The Court will have ample opportunity to do so: since the early eighties there has been an exponential increase in recourse to the Court. The ten cases currently pending raise significant questions of international law in a variety of legal areas. There is reason to suppose that this positive trend is likely to endure and expand,

[16] *Legality of the Threat or Use of Nuclear Weapons*, Advisory Opinion, *ICJ Rep.* (1996) p. 242.

[17] Case concerning the *Gabčíkovo-Nagymaros Project (Hungary* v. *Slovakia)*, Judgment, para. 140.

at any rate if international tensions do not mount to the heights of the thirties or of the Cold War. If so, this will give the Court the opportunity to make further contributions to the development of international law.

THE FUTURE OF THE LAW OF THE SEA TRIBUNAL IN HAMBURG

Barbara Kwiatkowska*

It is the greatest honour and pleasure for me to participate in this Plenary Session with two most important personalities in international law – the President of the principal judicial organ of the United Nations, Judge Stephen M. Schwebel and the United Nations Under-Secretary-General for Legal Affairs, Dr. Hans Corell. At the same time, since the law of the sea forms the most important branch of general international law, I am pleased to open my presentation by conveying to you warmest greetings from the President of the International Tribunal for the Law of the Sea (ITLOS), Judge Thomas A. Mensah, whose trip to Ghana prevented him from addressing you here today.

The ITLOS is formally not a United Nations organ, which has an advantage of bringing it, in principle, beyond the fallout of the financial crisis of the United Nations.[1] However, the ITLOS is a treaty organ in the United Nations context. It was established under the United Nations Convention on the Law of the Sea (LOS Convention)[2] with an invaluable support of the New York Office of Dr. Corell, who also honoured by his presence a special Inaugural Session of the Tribunal held at its seat in the Free and Hanseatic City of Hamburg on 18 October 1996, when the 21 newly elected Judges of the ITLOS were sworn.[3]

The ITLOS Statute, which forms a part of the LOS Convention, is moreover closely modelled on the Statute of the International Court of Justice (ICJ), and so are the ITLOS Rules and Resolution on Internal Judicial Practice modelled on the respective instruments of the ICJ. The interest of the 15 Members of the Court and the 21 Members of the ITLOS in their respective judicial activities is, therefore, mutually reinforcing.

The pioneering Presidency of the Tribunal by Judge Mensah coincides with the current triennium of the Court covering the years 1997-2000, with Judge

* Professor of International Law of the Sea and Deputy Director of the Netherlands Institute for the Law of the Sea (NILOS), Faculty of Law, University of Utrecht.

[1] But note that the issue of non-payment by certain states of their assessed contributions equally applies to the ITLOS budget. See main text accompanying *infra* n. 10.

[2] For the status of the 1982 LOS Convention and the 1994 Part XI Agreement as at 16 November 1997, see *UN Law of the Sea Bulletin*, No 35 (1997) pp.19-28.

[3] *ITLOS Press Release*, No.2, 18 October 1996. For the composition of the ITLOS, see Annex to this paper below. The constituent instruments of ITLOS, its decisions and *Press Releases* are available on the United Nations website [http://www.un.org/Depts/los/_.htm].

W.P. Heere (Ed.), International Law and The Hague's 750th Anniversary

Mensah having been elected as the first ITLOS President[4] four months prior to election of Judge Schwebel as the ICJ President on 6 February 1997.[5] A sister-relationship between these two standing courts – operating under constituent instruments and deciding pursuant to international law – was also reflected by the fact that ceremonies of presentation of a monumental work by Ambassador Shabtai Rosenne on *The Law and Practice of the International Court* were hosted last year by Dr. Corell in his Office of Legal Affairs in New York (30 October), by President Schwebel at the Court in The Hague (11 November) and by President Mensah at the ITLOS in Hamburg (12 November).[6]

I shall not, Mr. Chairman, engage into detailed analysis of the law and up-to-date practice of ITLOS which was so ably presented in its first Report for the Period 1996-1997 submitted to the Meeting of States Parties to the Law of the Sea Convention held last month in New York.[7] An excellent analysis of this law and inaugural practice may be found in recent writings of Ambassador Rosenne, President Mensah, Judges Nelson, Treves, Laing and Anderson and other Members of the Tribunal.[8]

Well, Rome wasn't built in a day, but if a good start makes fifty percent of success, the ITLOS may be considered as already having been successful. This applies both to the Tribunal's organization and to its inaugural jurisprudence, which I shall now briefly address with a view of showing that they do provide a sound ground for a positive view as to the Tribunal's future.

As it follows from its first Report to States Parties, the Tribunal emerged from its initial organization with the establishment of a standing Chamber of Summary Procedure, a Sea-Bed Disputes Chamber, a Chamber for Marine Environment

[4] Election of the President and the Vice-President of the International Tribunal for the Law of the Sea, *ITLOS Press Release,* No.1, 5 October 1996. For Biographical Data of President Thomas A. Mensah and Vice-President Rüdiger Wolfrum, see UN Doc. SPLOS/11, 25 June 1996, at p. 85 and p.157.

[5] Judge Stephen M. Schwebel Elected President of the International Court of Justice, Judge Christopher G. Weeramantry Elected Vice-President, *ICJ Communiqué*, No.97/2 (including Biographical Data), 6 February 1997 [http://www.icj-cij.org].

[6] S. Rosenne on *The Law and Practice of the International Court 1920-1996*, Vols I-IV, 3rd edn. (1997).

[7] Report of the International Tribunal for the Law of the Sea for the Period 1996-1997 – Prepared by the Tribunal, UN Doc. SPLOS/27, 23 April 1998; and Report of the Eighth Meeting of States Parties, New York, 18-22 May 1998 – Prepared by the Secretariat, UN Doc. SPLOS/31, 4 June 1998. The Ninth Meeting of States Parties will be held in New York on 19-28 May 1999.

[8] Cf., e.g., contributions by President Thomas A. Mensah and Judge Tullio Treves in, 11 *Leiden Journal of International Law* (1998 in press); and *infra* n. 20. For comparative analysis of constituent instruments of the ICJ and the ITLOS, see S. Rosenne, 'Establishing the ITLOS', 89 *American Journal of International Law* (*AJIL*) (1995) pp. 806-814; S. Rosenne, 'The International Tribunal for the Law of the Sea and the International Court of Justice: Some Points of Difference', in R. Platzöder, ed., *The Baltic Sea: New Developments in National Policies and International Cooperation* (1996) pp. 200-215; and S. Rosenne, 'An Introduction to International Litigation', *IBRU Boundary and Security Bulletin* (Spring 1998) pp. 57-60.

Disputes, and a Chamber for Fisheries Disputes. Further organizational progress was marked by adoption in October 1997 of the ITLOS Rules of Procedure, Resolution on Internal Judicial Practice and Guidelines Concerning the Presentation of Cases Before the ITLOS. Preparation of drafts of the three instruments were chaired by Judges Tullio Treves, David Anderson and Chandrasekhara Rao respectively, whereas application of these instruments is being kept under review by the ITLOS Committee on Rules and Judicial Practice which is presided over by President Mensah. Observer status granted to the ITLOS by the United Nations General Assembly enables the Tribunal to participate in the Assembly's meetings which are of relevance to its work.

The important agreements adopted during organizational phase of the Tribunal include the Agreement on Privileges and Immunities of the ITLOS of 23 May 1997 and the Agreement on Cooperation and Relationships Between the United Nations and the ITLOS, which was signed by Secretary-General Kofi Annan and President Thomas A. Mensah on 18 December 1997 in New York. The latter Agreement, which has been applied provisionally by the United Nations and the Tribunal from the date of signature, had already been approved by the ITLOS and is awaiting the approval of the United Nations General Assembly. Upon that approval, the Agreement would enter into force.

As regards the Headquarters Agreement between the ITLOS and the Federal Republic of Germany, since the Tribunal was due to commence its functioning in the host country prior to the necessary formal arrangements, Dr. Hans Corell as the United Nations Legal Counsel requested the German authorities to take an early initiative, and pending the conclusion of a Headquarters Agreement, an interim ordinance was adopted by the host country. Among others, the interim arrangement applies, *mutatis mutandis*, the relevant provisions of the Convention on the Privileges and Immunities of the Specialized Agencies of the United Nations of 21 November 1947[9] to the Tribunal. Dr. Corell also participated – together with other dignitaries – in a ceremony to lay the foundation stone for the future premises of the Tribunal at the site on the Elbchaussee in Hamburg overlooking the river Elbe, which premises are scheduled to be ready at the end of 1999.

With respect to a critical issue of budget, the Meeting of States Parties decided provisionally to apply the scale of assessments of the United Nations. The States Parties approved a budget for 1998 totalling US $ 5.7 million, and for 1999 – totalling US $ 6.9 million. While this budget is reasonable, President Mensah noted a major problem of the non-payment by certain States Parties of their assessed contributions.[10] Pending the adoption of its own financial regulations, the Tribunal has been functioning in accordance with the Financial Regulations

[9] *Multilateral Treaties Deposited with the Secretary-General, Status as at 31 December 1997* (United Nations 1998) pp. 42-53.

[10] UN Doc. SPLOS/31, *supra* n. 7, at p. 6.

of the United Nations, and the draft pension scheme for the ITLOS Members (modelled on the ICJ's pension scheme) is to be adopted by the end of 1999. Publicity to its work has been given by the Tribunal by means of its *Press Releases* and information which you can find on the United Nations website.

The Tribunal has so far been no less successful in its judicial work, that is in its primary task to settle disputes concerning the interpretation or application of the Law of the Sea Convention and related treaties. Of the first two *Saint Vincent and the Grenadines* v. *Guinea M/V Saiga* cases:

– Case No.1 concerning prompt release of a vessel and its crew was decided by means of a 12:9 majority Judgment delivered by the ITLOS on 4 December 1997,[11]

– whereas Case No.2 involving phase of merits of the *Saiga* dispute is presently pending before the Tribunal and was a subject of its unanimous Order on Provisional Measures of 11 March 1998.

As the *SS Wimbledon*[12] and the *Corfu Channel*[13] cases, which inaugurated the contentious jurisprudence of the PCIJ and the ICJ respectively, the *M/V Saiga* cases resulted from an incident involving vessels, paving their way to a category of cases having far-reaching implications for the *jus communicationis*.

So far, the ITLOS should be commended for the inauguration of its practice by expeditious administration of international justice and by precedential contribution made to the application of both innovatory procedure of the prompt release of vessels and the incidental jurisdiction with respect to provisional measures, in pursuance of Articles 292 and 290 of the LOS Convention and the respective ITLOS Rules.[14] Significantly, it was the anticipated implementation of Article 292 which formed a subject of a special Workshop held in Hamburg in 1995,[15] with participation of Mr. Gritakumar Chitty of the United Nations Secretariat, who subsequently became the first Registrar of the Tribunal.[16]

Whereas the Tribunal proved that it can act with an impressive speed, we should keep in mind that in rendering its first two *M/V Saiga* decisions, the ITLOS exercised a residual jurisdiction applicable to two matters of considerable urgency, underlined by the humanitarian considerations for the detained crew –

[11] Apart from its availability on the United Nations website, see *supra* n. 1, the 1997 *M/V Saiga* Judgment was reprinted in, 37 *International Legal Materials* (1998) p. 360.

[12] *PCIJ Series A*, No.1, pp. 11, 15.

[13] *ICJ Rep.* (1947/1948) p.15, and (1949) pp. 1, 244.

[14] For legislative history, see S. Rosenne and L,B. Sohn, eds., *United Nations Convention on the Law of the Sea 1982 – A Commentary*, Vol. V (1989) pp. 52-59 [Article 290] and pp 66-71 [Article 292].

[15] R. Lagoni, ed., 'The International Tribunal for the Law of the Sea: Establishment and "Prompt Release" Procedures', 11 *International Journal of Marine and Coastal Law* (*IJMCL*) (1996 Special Issue) pp. 137-231.

[16] Election of Mr. Gritakumar Chitty as the First Registrar of the International Tribunal for the Law of the Sea, *ITLOS Press Release*, No.3, 23 October 1996.

prompt release of vessels and provisional measures. Urgency as the matter of procedure is likewise typical of the ICJ's treatment of requests for provisional measures, of which the latest instance was the *Paraguay* v. *USA Vienna Convention on Consular Relations* (*Provisional Measures*) Order of 9 April 1998,[17] and of other matters necessitating prompt action, such as was the case with the 1995 *New Zealand* v. *France Nuclear Tests* (*Request for an Examination of the Situation*) Order.[18] Since the ICJ may also be seised of applications based on Article 292 of the LOS Convention, it is important that the 1997 Agreement on Cooperation and Relationships Between the United Nations and the ITLOS envisages the prompt and regular exchange of information concerning such applications between the ICJ and the Tribunal (Article 3(2)).[19]

Practice inaugurated by the ITLOS gave moreover an appreciable expression to concern with preservation of the judicial consistency through reliance in the 1997 *M/V Saiga* Judgment on an approach adhered to by the ICJ in the 1953 *Ambatielos* Judgment.[20] And the 1998 *M/V Saiga (Provisional Measures)* Order confirmed practice of the ICJ noted by President Schwebel of giving the applicant the benefit of the doubt in deciding by the Court whether it has jurisdiction to indicate provisional measures.[21] The *M/V Saiga* Order also confirmed the binding nature of provisional measures which the ITLOS 'prescribes', and not – as does the ICJ – 'indicates'. Given urgency of both prompt release and provisional measures proceedings and the fact that, as

[17] *ICJ Rep.* (1998) including Declarations of President Schwebel and Judges Oda and Koroma (in press); *ICJ Communiqué*, No.98/13, 3 April, No.98/15, 7 April, No.98/16, 8 April, and Nos 98/17, 98/17bis and 98/18, 9 April 1998.

[18] *ICJ Rep.* (1995) p. 288. Cf., Luncheon Address of President Stephen M. Schwebel, in *Contemporary International Law Issues: New Forms, New Applications, Proceedings of the Fourth ASIL/NVIR Joint Conference, Kurhaus, 2-5 July 1997* (1998) pp. 260, 263, noting that in the *New Zealand* v. *France* case, the Court delivered its Order just five weeks after New Zealand filed its Request for an Examination of the Situation.

[19] See Rosenne, *The Law and Practice*, *op. cit.* n. 6, at p.161; Interim Report – Prepared by the Tribunal, UN Doc. SPLOS/21, 9 May 1997, at p. 12; and UN Doc. SPLOS/27, *supra* n. 7, at p. 16.

[20] 1997 *M/V Saiga* Judgment, para.51, relying on the *Greece* v. *UK Ambatielos* (Merits: Obligation to Arbitrate) Judgment, *ICJ Rep.* (1953) pp. 10, 18; Cf., B. Kwiatkowska, 'Introduction to Roundtable Discussion on The *M/V Saiga*', in B.H. Oxman, ed., *Building New Regimes and Institutions for the Sea, Proceedings of the 31st LSI Conference, Miami, 30-31 March 1998* (1999, in press); E. Laing, 'ITLOS' Approach to Article 292 of the UN Law of the Sea Convention – The *Saiga* #1', A paper presented at the 68th ILA Conference, Taipei, Taiwan, 24-30 May 1998; E. Lauterpacht, 'The First Decision of the ITLOS: The M/V *Saiga*', in G. Hafner, et al., eds., *Liber Amicorum Professor Seidl-Hohenveldern* (1998) pp. 395-418; B. Kwiatkowska, 'Inauguration of the ITLOS Jurisprudence: The *Saint Vincent and the Grenadines* v. *Guinea M/V Saiga* cases', 29 *Ocean Development and International Law* (1998 in press).

[21] *Nicaragua* v. *USA Military and Paramilitary Activities In and Against Nicaragua* (*Provisional Measures*) Dissenting Opinion of Judge Schwebel, *ICJ Rep.* (1984) pp.190, 206-207. See also Commentary and Answers to Questions by President Schwebel, in M.K. Bulterman and M. Kuijer, eds., *Compliance with Judgments of International Courts* (1996) pp. 39-42, 44, 46. Cf., Kwiatkowska, Introduction, loc. cit. n. 20; and Kwiatkowska, Inauguration, loc. cit. n. 20.

President Mensah and eight other dissenters showed, the 1997 *M/V Saiga* Judgment has indeed given the applicant the benefit of a great many doubts, the question could be posed whether the self-contained prompt release procedure will not develop itself towards the same tendency as that observed by President Schwebel with respect to provisional measures?

As regards the future judicial work, the Tribunal is scheduled to deliver its Judgment in the *M/V Saiga (Merits)* case by mid-1999, whereas its other work will depend on the cases which may yet be submitted to it. There seems to be nothing unusual in a newly established Tribunal having for the time being just one case on its docket, especially if we keep in mind that when President Schwebel was elected Member of the Court in 1981, the judicial activity of by then well established ICJ was no less limited; yet, it has developed to its present busiest docket in the Court's history.

In the remaining time at my disposal, I would like, Mr. Chairman, to say a few more words about the future of the ITLOS from the perspective of its relationship with the ICJ. Let me first recall that when I was asked about the prospects of that relationship on the occasion of my Guest Lecture on the ICJ and the Law of the Sea delivered at the Stockholm Faculty of Law, I said that, to start with, the longstanding friendship between President Schwebel and President Mensah seems to benefit constructive coexistence of the two courts.[22] This, however, as you may appreciate, cannot provide a full answer to all the questions raised by the issue of the ICJ/ITLOS relationship.

Whereas various opinions expressed on the matter for the past few years hold their respective merits,[23] I would like to reiterate my view, as shared by Ambassador Rosenne, that it still seems impossible to speculate with certainty on the practical effects of the overlapping of some of the ICJ and the ITLOS jurisdiction.[24] Most what could be anticipated at present is that, as President

[22] B. Kwiatkowska, 'The Contribution of the International Court of Justice to the Development of the Law of the Sea', Guest Lecture Delivered at the Faculty of Law, University of Stockholm, Sweden, on 3 March 1998 [available on the NILOS website, http://www.rgl.ruu.nl/english/isep/nilos-1a.asp].

[23] See, e.g., S. Oda, 'The International Court of Justice Viewed From the Bench (1976-1993)', 244 *Recueil des cours* (1993-VII) pp.12, 153-154; M. Bedjaoui, 'Mythes et realités d'une relance du règlement judiciaire des différends internationaux', in Yves Daudet, ed., *Actualités des conflits internationaux, Colloque des 4 et 5 décembre 1992* (1993) pp.125, 133; G. Guillaume, 'The Future of International Judicial Institutions', 44 *International and Comparative Law Quarterly* (1995) pp. 848, 854-855; A.G. Koroma, 'Interpretation of International Law', in *Contemporary International Law Issues, Proceedings of the Third ASIL/NVIR Joint Conference* (1996) pp. 154-157; J.I. Charney, 'The Implications of Expanding International Dispute Settlement Systems', 90 *AJIL* (1996) pp. 69-75 ; C.-A. Fleischhauer, 'The Relationship Between the International Court of Justice and the Newly Created International Tribunal for the Law of the Sea in Hamburg', in 1 *Max Planck Yearbook of United Nations Law* (1997) pp. 327-333.

[24] See Rosenne, *The Law and Practice*, op. cit. n. 6, at p. 1651, quoting B. Kwiatkowska, 'The International Court of Justice and the Law of the Sea – Some Reflections', 11 *IJMCL* (1996) pp. 491, 501 n.49. This author based herself, in turn, on S.M. Schwebel, *Justice in International Law* –

Stephen M. Schwebel remarked in the context of overlap in the jurisdiction of international judicial bodies:

> 'The World Court has dealt with the law of the sea for seventy-five years. The International Tribunal for the Law of the Sea will deal not only with the interpretation of the United Nations Convention on the Law of the Sea, and not only with claims of individuals, corporations and public authorities in that immense sphere, but with the law of the sea – essentially the inter-State law of the sea – as the World Court has contributed to shaping it. Inevitably it will also deal with subjects such as interpretation of treaties, another area of law much influenced by the judgments and opinions of the Court. Over time, there surely will be interplay and interaction between ITLOS and the Court.'[25]

The law of the sea related jurisprudence of the ICJ and its predecessor, PCIJ, provides indeed an outstanding evidence of what President Schwebel perceives as an 'intrinsic' authority of the Court's decisions and the coherence of its case-law in terms of fundamental factors which are characteristic to the unique role of the Court as the 'principal judicial organ' of the world community.[26] It also exemplifies the richness of the issues of general international law dealt with by the Court in the context of law of the sea related cases, including among them the prominent place of equity.[27] This raises some doubt whether in the areas of an overlap of contentious jurisdiction of the ITLOS and the ICJ, states would be able to find 'a sensible division of labour' by perhaps directing cases of 'a more specifically law of the sea nature' to the ITLOS and those with 'more ingredients of general international law' to the ICJ?[28] Such division might not be easily achieved in practice since, for instance, nothing is more both law of the sea related and involving issues of general international law than equitable maritime boundary delimitation. The same applies to at the first glance such 'a specifically law of the sea' issue as is prompt release of the vessel, settlement of which in the first *M/V Saiga* case was centered around the general rules of treaty interpretation.[29]

In conclusion, Mr. Chairman, let me voice my agreement with the view of President Mensah that there is no risk of a shift of emphasis in the future from constructive coexistence to possible conflict of jurisdiction between ITLOS and

Selected Writings of Judge Stephen M. Schwebel, chapter 2: Relations Between the International Court of Justice and the United Nations, p. 14, at p. 18.

[25] Plenary Address of President Stephen M. Schwebel on 'The Contribution of the International Court of Justice to the Development of International Law', elsewhere in the present publication.

[26] *Idem.*

[27] Cf., *idem*; and B. Kwiatkowska, 'The International Court of Justice and Equitable Maritime Boundary Delimitation', elsewhere in the present publication.

[28] See suggestion to this effect by Judge Fleischhauer, *supra* n. 23, at p. 333.

[29] See Judge Laing, loc. cit. n. 20, remarking on the first *M/V Saiga* case (*supra* n. 11) that: 'The differences between the Tribunal and the dissenters appear to have been clearly determined by their respective approaches to the interpretation of treaties.'

the ICJ.[30] We may expect, instead, what President Schwebel refers to as 'interplay and interaction' between ITLOS and the Court maintaining its unique role of the principal judicial organ of the United Nations.[31] International arbitration has for a long time and on more than one count coexisted successfully and to mutual benefit with the ICJ, and I see no reason why the same would not apply in the future to the ICJ/ITLOS relationship.

At the same time, we should not underestimate the difficulties which, in the view of Ambassador Shabtai Rosenne, might be caused to politicians and diplomats, and their legal advisers, when they have to take decisions on inter-state disputes regarding which there are overlapping competences between various courts and tribunals.[32] If residual jurisdiction was to be vested in any judicial organ to decide which court would be appropriate to settle the disputes in the areas of overlap between the ICJ and ITLOS, International Criminal Court or other tribunals, the ICJ seems to be uniquely available to fulfill this task.[33]

[30] Based on telephone conversation between this author and President Thomas A. Mensah on 25 June 1998.

[31] See President Schwebel's view quoted in the main text accompanying *supra* n. 25.

[32] Rosenne, An Introduction to International Litigation, loc. cit., n. 8, at p. 60.

[33] *Idem*;Cf., Report of the Secretary-General on the Work of the Organization, UN Doc. A/48/1, 10 September 1993, para.66, at p. 14, stating in the context of a tendency to proliferate the number of international tribunals: 'Accordingly, if specialized tribunals are to be created, it may be necessary to establish a common system for referrals of questions of law to the principal judicial organ of the United Nations.'

Note further that Article 119(2) of the Rome Statute of the International Criminal Court (ICC) confers a residual jurisdiction on the ICJ to settle disputes on the interpretation or application of the ICC Statute. See UN Doc. A/CONF.183/9, 17 July 1998 [available on the United Nations website http://www.un.org/icc/part1.htm].

ANNEX

THE COMPOSITION OF THE ITLOS

The composition of the ITLOS, in order of precedence, is as follows:

Thomas A. Mensah	Ghana	30 September 2005
Rüdiger Wolfrum	Germany	30 September 1999
Lihai Zhao	China	30 September 2002
Hugo Caminos	Argentina	30 September 2002
Vincent Marotta Rangel	Brazil	30 September 1999
Alexander Yankov	Bulgaria	30 September 2002
Soji Yamamoto	Japan	30 September 2005
Anatoly l. Kolodkin	Russia	30 September 1999
Choon-ho Park	Korea	30 September 2005
L. Dolliver Nelson	Grenada	30 September 2005
P. Chandrasekhara Rao	India	30 September 1999
Joseph Akl	Lebanon	30 September 1999
David Anderson	Britain	30 September 2005
Budislav Vukas	Croatia	30 September 2005
Joseph Sinde Warioba	Tanzania	30 September 1999
Edward Arthur Laing	Belize	30 September 2002
Tullio Treves	Italy	30 September 2002
Mohamed Mouldi Marsit	Tunisia	30 September 2005
Gudmundur Eiriksson	Iceland	30 September 2002
Tafsir Malick Ndiaye	Senegal	30 September 2002

* * *

REGIONAL COURTS

P.J.G. Kapteyn*

AN INTRODUCTION

The existence of regional courts is a fact. The extent to which they may contribute in their region to the enforcement of the rule of law should not be underestimated. But it is also a fact that the proliferation of regional courts may endanger the position of the International Court of Justice (ICJ) as a guardian of the universality of international law.[1] The role of the ICJ in contributing to the development of general international law in a deeply divided world is of considerable importance. It has a value which the international community should cherish. And I am not saying this only because I speak at The Hague, the city that is proud to host the ICJ.

The existence of regional courts, valuable as they may be, may on the long run undermine the universality of international law of which the ICJ is the guardian. It will thus be necessary to reduce the risk of such a development. This could, in my opinion, be done along two lines. Firstly, by developing criteria indicating when their establishment could be justified. And, secondly, by trying to develop a satisfactory relationship between the ICJ and such regional courts. In this short introduction I shall make a few observations on these two topics.

WHEN SHOULD THE ESTABLISHMENT OF A REGIONAL COURT BE JUSTIFIED?

To my mind at least two conditions have to be fulfilled:
– such a court should deal with the application and interpretation of a specific body of law closely linked to common cultural, social and economic values that exist in a region to an extent that is lacking on a world scale;

* Member of the Court of Justice of the European Communities.

[1] Cf., Gilbert Guillaume, 'The future of international judicial institutions', 44 *ICLQ* (1995) p. 848, at p. 861: '... the dangers for international law, resulting from the increasing number of judicial institutions in the modern world, should be stressed. These dangers may have been underestimated by lawyers'. See also the concern expressed by the former president of the ICJ, R.J. Jennings, 'The judiciary, international and national, and the development of international law', 45 *ICLQ* (1996) p. 1, at pp. 5-6.

W.P. Heere (Ed.), International Law and The Hague's 750th Anniversary

– such a court should be more than just a tribunal dealing with inter-state disputes. The ICJ is perfectly suited to dealing with such disputes. No, the regional court should have a jurisdiction in a broader sense, including the settlement of disputes between the regional organisation and its Member States and/or the administration of justice in cases affecting the rights and obligations of private persons or companies under such a regional body of law.

When the common values I have mentioned exist in a region, it is impossible to deny the states concerned the right to create a specific regional system of law and to charge a regional court with upholding it. This is so in particular where access to such a court is given to the regional organization itself or its organs and to private persons and companies, an access which is not given to them by the Statute of the ICJ.

WHAT KIND OF RELATIONSHIP SHOULD SUCH A COURT HAVE WITH THE ICJ?

Satisfactory relations with the ICJ could be established if certain conditions are fulfilled and certain guidelines observed by the courts concerned. In explaining some of them, I will use examples taken from the rules and practices of the Court of Justice of the European Communities (CJEC):

The regional court's jurisdiction should be limited to the application and interpretation of the regional body of law. This criterion is taken into account by Article 219 of the EC Treaty: 'Member States undertake not to submit a dispute concerning the interpretation or application of this Treaty to any other method of settlement other than those provided for therein'. This provision seems to be sufficiently clear to prevent the possibility of negative conflicts of jurisdiction involving the danger of denial of justice. The predecessor of the ICJ, the Permanent Court of International Justice, when defining its jurisdiction in relation to that of other tribunals, made this a requirement for allowing its own competence to give way.[2]

Limiting the regional court's jurisdiction to the application and interpretation of the regional body of law does not mean that it will never be called upon to apply principles or rules of general international law. The CJEC has to ensure that in the interpretation and application of the EC Treaty the law is observed. International law, according to the case-law of that Court, is part of the law to be observed. Most of the 25 or more cases in which the CJEC had to apply general international law were concerned with the rights and obligations of the European Community as a subject of international law, e.g. the limits of the Community's territorial or personal jurisdiction, and the interpretation of its rights and

[2] Judgment of 26 July 1927 in *Case concerning the Factory at Chorzów* (*Claim for Indemnity*) (Jurisdiction), *PCIJ Series A*, No. 9, p. 30.

obligations under multilateral treaties, general principles or customary rules of international law.[3]

In such a situation a regional court should take into account and respect the relevant case-law of the ICJ and its predecessor. In several cases decided by the CJEC and the EC Court of First Instance, and in a number of Opinions of Advocates General I found references to judgments of the ICJ and the Permanent Court of International Justice. The most recent case (*Racke*)[4] concerned the application of the *clausula rebus sic stantibus* by the CJEC in which it referred to the case-law of the ICJ concerning the customary-law nature of that clause, the importance of the principle *pacta sunt servanda* and the strict interpretation of the clause as an exception to that principle.

Demanding respect of the case-law of the ICJ and its predecessor by regional courts is not something special to them. It may also be required of domestic courts. In a way the CJEC functions as a domestic court common to the Members States of the Community. But 'noblesse oblige'. Its status as a court created by international law requires a special effort to adhere to this guideline.

Respect for the case-law of the ICJ does not solve all the problems raised by the coexistence of the ICJ and regional courts. One of these problems is the fact that, in the absence of relevant case-law, a regional court is bound to interpret international law autonomously. In such a situation there is a risk that a later judgment of the ICJ will prove it to be mistaken. It has been suggested therefore that the regional court should be enabled to request the ICJ to give a preliminary ruling on the interpretation of the relevant rule of international law.[5] The introduction of such a system of preliminary rulings would require a coordinated effort by all the states concerned to amend both the Statute of the ICJ and the rules concerning the competence of the regional courts. While one may be sceptical as to the willingness of governments to embark upon such amendment procedures, one cannot deny that, at least theoretically, such a system could solve many of the problems caused by the coexistence of several international courts. I doubt, however, whether such a proposal can be reconciled with the proper administration of justice. It is obvious that the introduction of such a procedure would considerably extend the already protracted proceedings before regional courts. For the CJEC it could even mean a cumulation of two preliminary procedures in a case referred to it by a national court.

[3] For a recent survey of the application of international law by the CJEC, see Jean-Pierre Puissochet, 'La place du droit international dans la jurisprudence de la Cour de justice des Communautés européennes', in *Scritti in onore di G.F. Mancini*, Vol. II, p. 779. See also, K.M. Meessen, 'The application of rules of public international law within Community law', 13 *CMLRev.* (1976) p. 485 and the surveys of principal decisions of the CJEC pertaining to international law, published in 1 *EJIL* (1990) p. 365, 4 *EJIL* (1993) p. 430 and 5 *EJIL* (1974) p. 448.

[4] Case C-162/96, Judgment of 16 June 1998, not yet published in *ECR*.

[5] E.g. Guillaume, loc. cit. n. 1, at p. 862.

Moreover, I wonder whether there is really a need for such procedures. As long as regional courts are willing to accept the normative value of the case-law of the ICJ as a leading authority on general international law, there is no serious problem. If international law – I quote Rosalyn Higgins[6] – is a 'continuing process of authoritative decisions', it has to be developed judicially in a permanent dialogue between all the international courts dealing with questions of general international law. Such a dialogue supposes, of course, that they are acquainted with each other's judgments and are ready to take them into account when deciding their cases. The first priority should therefore be to ensure an effective exchange of information between them about judgments they deliver on questions concerning the interpretation of general international law.

There is another problem that merits consideration. The application by regional courts of provisions of treaties concluded by the regional organization with third states or other international organizations may affect their rights and duties. It is therefore desirable that they should be given the right to intervene in cases before the regional court which affect their interests or to institute third-party proceedings to contest judgments rendered in such cases.

Under EC law, where such rights could be claimed,[7] I found, leaving aside the rather special case of Member States of the European Free Trade Association (EFTA),[8] only one case in which a third state, the Dominican Commonwealth, asked for and was granted leave to intervene.[9] It is not ignorance on the part of third states which could be the reason for which they do not avail them more frequently of the opportunity to intervene or institute third-party proceedings. It is rather their reluctance to submit themselves to a jurisdiction they consider to be foreign to them. Moreover, I suppose they prefer to keep their powder dry in case they should decide to hold the Community responsible for violating their rights and to start international proceedings to this end.

I would observe, in this context, that it is not surprising to find that the right of intervention expressly conferred on the EFTA States by EC law is frequently used by them. This may be explained by the fact that they are united with the Member States of the Community by the Agreement on a European Economic Area which establishes a very close cooperation with the European Community and contains a large number of provisions identical with provisions of EC law.

[6] 'Policy considerations and the international judicial process', 17 *ICLQ*, p.58, at pp. 58-59. See also, Rosalyn Higgins, *Problems and Process, International law and how we use it* (1994) pp. 2-12.

[7] See Art. 37 EC Statute and Art. 97 Rules of Procedure of the Court. It should be noted, however, that third parties are not allowed to intervene in cases between Community institutions or between Member States and Community institutions.

[8] See the special provisions, in the Statute of the CJEC, enabling them, as State Parties to the Agreement on a European Economic Area, to submit observations in preliminary proceedings (Art. 20) and to intervene in other proceedings (Art. 37) before the CJEC.

[9] Joined Cases 91 and 200/82, Order of the Court, *Chris International Foods* v. *Commission* [1983] *ECR*, p. 417.

In conclusion I would put forward the following propositions:

1. regional courts should only be established as organs of regional organizations, if certain objective conditions are satisfied;
2. their jurisdiction should be clearly confined to the interpretation and application of the regional body of law they have to administer;
3. having the task of ensuring that the law is observed, they may be called upon to apply general international law. In such cases they should take into account and respect the case-law of the ICJ;
4. third states and other international organizations that have concluded treaties with the regional organization should be given the right to intervene in cases before regional courts and to contest judgments of these courts whenever such cases or judgments affect their rights and duties under such treaties;
5. measures should be taken to ensure an effective exchange of information between the ICJ and the regional courts about judgments delivered on questions concerning the interpretation of general international law.

THE PROLIFERATION OF INTERNATIONAL JUDICIAL ORGANS AND THE FORMATION OF INTERNATIONAL LAW

Hugh Thirlway*

The term 'proliferation' in the title of this paper is, as has been observed elsewhere, somewhat tendentious, carrying the implication that the formation of international law may suffer rather than profit from the creation of numerous new tribunals. This was certainly the view expressed by Minister van Mierlo in his luncheon address on Thursday, and it has been advanced by certain much respected scholars[1], while doubted by others[2]. My own view is the more optimistic one; if what I have to say seems inconsistent with my pessimistic title, the explanation is that I was asked to stand in for a much more eminent speaker at the last moment, when the title had already been chosen.

What are the tribunals that we are talking about, that may have this upas-tree effect? I do not think that I need to list the institutions that have been created in recent years[3] – many examples will occur to you – or enquire into their jurisdictional or quasi-jurisdictional character, a question raised in this morning's panel discussion with regard to the WTO dispute settlement system. I propose to content myself with the definition of a category: since the problem, if problem there be, is that of the effect of their decisions on the formation of international law, the tribunals relevant to our enquiry are those whose decisions are capable of constituting a 'subsidiary means for the determination of rules of law' within the meaning of Article 38, paragraph 1 (d), of the Statute of the International Court of Justice. Now that clearly is a wide category, extending even beyond international tribunals to municipal courts, which suggests straight away that the problem is not a new one.

* Professor of International Law, Graduate Institute of International Studies, Geneva.

1 See Oda, 'The International Court of Justice viewed from the Bench', 244 Recueil des cours de l'Académie de droit international de la Haye, (1993-VII) pp. 139 ff., at p. 145, and 'Dispute Settlement Prospects in the Law of the Sea', 44 *ICLQ* (1995) p. 863; Jennings, 'The Proliferation of Adjudicatory Bodies: Dangers and Possible Answers', *American Society of International Law, Bulletin No. 9* (1995) p. 2; Guillaume, 'The Future of International Judicial Institutions', 44 *ICLQ* (1995), p. 848.

2 See Charney, 'The Implications of the International Dispute Settlement System of the 1982 Convention on the Law of the Sea on International Law', *American Society of International Law, Bulletin No. 9* (1995) pp. 33 ff., and 'Third Party Dispute Settlement and International Law', *Columbia Journal of Transnational Law* (1997); Boyle, 'Dispute Settlement and the Law of the Sea Convention', 45 *ICLQ* (1996) p. 37; Boisson de Chazournes, 'Multiplication des instances de règlement des différends: vers la promotion de la règle de droit', *Forum, Journal of the International Law Association*, introductory 'zero' issue (1998) pp. 14-15.

W.P. Heere (Ed.), International Law and The Hague's 750th Anniversary

That is in fact the first point that I should like to make. The threat which some perceive as posed by the proliferation of tribunals is a threat to the unity of international law; and I suggest that that unity can easily be exaggerated. While older arbitration awards may, if need be, be discounted, as not purporting to be based on or to declare general international law, certainly since around the beginning of this century arbitral *compromis* have generally directed arbitrators to apply general law, so that conflicts between arbitral decisions, or between such decisions and ICJ decisions, ought theoretically to be indefensible if international law is one and indivisible. Yet total harmony does not reign, and this has not until recently been found to be cause for concern. In the field of maritime delimitation, for example, it is only possible to reconcile all the ICJ and arbitral decisions between 1969 and 1995 if one refers them back to a 'fundamental norm' of delimitation so broad and vague as to be of no practical usefulness.[4]

Secondly, the International Court of Justice itself has never regarded itself, or been regarded by scholars, as bound by a rule of *stare decisis*. It does of course respect its own previous decisions; the determined and well-argued attempt of Nigeria in the recent case brought by Cameroon to induce the Court to reverse the ruling in the *Right of Passage* case on the effect of a non-notified optional-clause declaration, was unsuccessful; but nothing in the Court's decision on that point suggested any rigid rule of precedent. This of course is as well if international law is to develop, to move with the times; but there may be more than one opinion as to whether it should develop, and if so in what direction. Thus it is perfectly possible for there to be a *revirement de jurisprudence*, not because there has been a visible development of the law, but simply because the majority of the Court today do not hold the same view as the majority of the Court some years ago.[5] Something of the sort may be said to have occurred in the successive decisions, between 1950 and 1971, of the Court in relation to South West Africa (Namibia); and on a more minor point in the decisions of the Court and a Chamber on the conditions for intervention under Article 62 of the Statute.

Thirdly, the asserted unity of international law yet has room for the expression by individual ICJ judges, in separate and dissenting opinions, of views which may differ to a startling degree from the law as expounded in the majority decision. As between the parties to the case, it is that majority decision which

[3] For an excellent survey of the developments in this field up to 1991, see Elihu Lauterpacht, *Aspects of the Administration of International Justice*, chapter II *passim*, pp. 9 ff .

[4] For example, the decision of the Anglo-French arbitral tribunal in the 1977 *Western Approaches* maritime delimitation dispute did not entirely follow the 1969 ICJ decision in the *North Sea Continental Shelf* case, but rather was a precursor of later developments culminating in the *Jan Mayen* decision in 1994. The approach to delimitation in the *St. Pierre and Miquelon* arbitration also bore little relation to the jurisprudence of the ICJ.

[5] The creation of chambers increases this risk; note that the decision of the Chamber in the *Gulf of Maine* case bears very little relation to the dicta in earlier decisions on maritime delimitation, and seems, in its turn, to have been silently disregarded by the full Court in subsequent cases.

enjoys the authority of *res judicata*; but that is not the point here under discussion. The whole point of a dissenting opinion, and to a lesser extent a separate opinion, is that its author hopes that what he says will later be found to represent the better view, that is to say, that it will have a greater contribution to the formation of international law than the decision itself[6]. This is certainly theoretically possible; at the least, such opinions are 'teachings of the most highly qualified publicists of the various nations' for the purposes of Article 38, paragraph 1(d), of the Statute, already referred to. In one of the panels of this Conference attention has already been drawn to the abundance of very valuable and stimulating dissenting opinions in recent cases written by Vice-President Weeramantry, to whom we had the pleasure of listening on Thursday; I hope that he will not take it amiss if I observe that if we were serious about the unity of international law, if we really wanted a univocal jurisprudence, we should have to deny Vice-President Weeramantry access to a word-processor – and international law would be very much the poorer as a result! Furthermore, the Statute of the International Tribunal for the Law of the Sea, adopted in 1982, has preserved this right of judges to express their independent views in separate and dissenting opinions; and the experience of the recent Judgment in the *M/V Saiga* case suggests that they will not be slow to take advantage of it to the full.

These are however only signs and tokens of a more profound observation: while much of international law is unified, and generally accepted, there are still fields in which at least two differing views are advanced and maintained, and it is not possible to state *a priori* that the one does, and the other does not, represent international law. For example, in the recent proceedings leading to the Court's Advisory Opinion on the *Legality of the Threat or Use of Nuclear Weapons*, two sincerely and passionately held views were advanced as to the lawfulness of the retention of nuclear weapons and the system of deterrence; nor, as is well known, has the Court's opinion in that case wholly resolved the debate.[7] This is an extreme example, but for that very reason it demonstrates that the world, and the world of legal scholars (which is something different), can very well live with a non-unified international law, and does so.

Two views of the law may co-exist, at least until a judge has to decide between them; at that point, at least for the parties to the case, one view prevails. According to Heisenberg's uncertainty principle, insofar as I understand it, the position and velocity of a sub-atomic particle may be actually undetermined, so

[6] The classic statement of this is that of the US Chief Justice Charles Evans Hughes: 'A dissent in a court of last resort is an appeal to the brooding spirit of the law, to the intelligence of a future day, when a later decision may possibly correct the error into which the dissenting judge believes the court to have been betrayed', quoted by Sir Hersch Lauterpacht in *The Development of International Law by the International Court* (1958) p. 66, and by Judge Jessup in his Dissenting Opinion in the *South West Africa* case, *ICJ Rep.* (1966) pp. 325-326.

[7] Thereby raising another issue which remains controversial: the permissibility or otherwise of a *non liquet* declared by an international tribunal.

that no statement as to where it is, where it is going, and how fast, at any given moment can be either true or false, until an observer, by measuring the one property, causes both to become 'real'. That is one analogy to the effect of a judicial decision where the law is not a unity; but the 'collapse' of the uncertainty is only valid for the parties to the proceedings; whether the same point will be decided the same way in another court will depend on the relationship (if any) between them.[8]

There is another analogy, to be indicated in a moment, that seems to me more appropriate for the effect of a judicial decision on international law in general, as contemplated by Article 38, paragraph 1 (d), of the ICJ Statute. Various views have been expressed as to the distinction between the formal sources mentioned in the first three sub-paragraphs of that article, and the 'subsidiary' sources of the fourth. To my mind, the simplest demonstration of that distinction is the fact that neither the judge nor the scholar asserts that a given proposition is law 'because I say so'; he refers the proposition back, expressly or by implication, to one or other of the formal sources listed (treaty, custom, general principles of law). When one of those sources 'speaks', however, it speaks with its own authority. In a recent book[9], Judge Shahabuddeen has gone so far as to hold that in certain circumstances a judicial decision can constitute in itself a formal source of law[10], without relation back to treaty, custom or general principle, a view which I find impossible to harmonise with either the Statute or legal theory. It is of course a matter of controversy whether a judge 'makes' law, or whether he merely declares it. May I suggest that whether or not what he declares looks so new as to be equated with law-manufacture, it must be at least *deemed* to be the result of a process of application of existing norms.

Now here is my analogy: the judicial process, and particularly the judicial decision, may, I suggest, be compared to a lens, by which the principles and rules of international law are focussed, like rays of light, on to the specific dispute. An essential feature of the lens is that it is transparent; it adds nothing and takes nothing away, but it magnifies and emphasises the relevant part of the legal spectrum. But a lens may also be wrongly focussed; it may even contain defects.

[8] At one time in English legal history, there was a flat contradiction between the law as applied by the ecclesiastical courts and that applied by the King's courts on questions of legitimacy (bastardy); and the conflict was eventually resolved, not by legislation, but by procedural devices. Limitations of space (alas!) forbid fuller explanation here: see W.C.Bolland, *A Manual of Year Book Studies* (1925) pp. 89-90, and W.E.Megarry, *A Second Miscellany-at-Law* (1973) pp. 286-287.

[9] *Precedent in the World Court* (Cambridge, Grotius 1996).

[10] This occurs, in Shahabuddeen's view, when there are two successive judicial decisions on given point: '[A] new decision by which a rule of law has been determined on the basis of earlier decisions is not a subsidiary means; it is the source of a new rule of international law; it is made by the Court alone', see *supra* n. 9, p. 76.

In other words, a judge may be wrong, as Judge Lachs courageously admitted in his separate opinion in the *Nicaragua* case.[11]

If judicial error is admitted, if we do not apply to all judicial tribunals an irrebuttable presumption that *res judicata pro veritate habetur*, the danger to the formation of international law posed by the proliferation of international tribunals is at least brought down to reasonable proportions, if not exorcised. It is easier to live with the idea of fallible judges than with that of authoritative determinations of international law which conflict and yet are both right.[12] The problem of course remains of deciding which judicial decision is right and which is wrong, but that is, as we have seen, inherent in the non-unified character which has to be attributed to international law.

But in any event, how great is the risk of flatly contradictory decisions? It is instructive in this respect to examine the one decision known to me that has been represented as a clear example of such conflict: that of the European Court of Human Rights in the case of *Loizidou* v. *Turkey*.[13] The Court had to examine the validity of the Turkish Government's declaration accepting jurisdiction under Articles 25 and 46 of the Convention, and in particular the validity and effect of a reservation thereto purporting to limit its effect to 'acts or omissions of public authorities in Turkey performed within the boundaries of the territory to which the Constitution of the Republic of Turkey is applicable'[14], i.e. excluding acts performed in the 'Turkish Republic of Northern Cyprus', which was where the acts complained of had been performed. It was accepted that the wording of Article 36, paragraph 3, of the ICJ Statute was in all material respects identical to that of Articles 25 and 46 of the Convention, and that reservations to acceptances of jurisdiction under the ICJ (and PCIJ) Statute were generally accepted and regarded as valid. Nevertheless, the European Court held, first that the reservation of Turkey was invalid; and secondly, that its invalidity did not affect the validity of the acceptance, since the reservation was a severable part of the acceptance. On this latter point it therefore diverged from the view of the parallel situation under the ICJ Statute expressed by Judge Sir Hersch Lauterpacht in his separate opinion in the *Norwegian Loans* case[15], a view which, although it was

[11] *Military and Paramilitary Activities in and against Nicaragua (Nicaragua* v. *United States)*, *ICJ Rep.* (1986) pp. 170-171.

[12] The point was well taken by Judge Shahabuddeen in an article (which I have not traced) quoted by Sir Robert Jennings: the various international tribunals 'make decisions which can influence the development of international law. *If that influence can amount to law-making*, the absence of hierarchical authority to impose order is a prescription for conflicting precepts' (emphasis added), see Jennings, loc. cit. n. 13.

[13] 23 March 1995, Judgment 40/1993/435/514. See the discussion in Jennings, 'The Proliferation of Adjudicatory Bodies: Dangers and Possible Answers', *American Society of International Law, Bulletin No. 9* (1995) pp. 5-6.

[14] Reservation under Article 25, Judgment, p. 5, para. 15; for the similar reservation under Article 46, see ibid., p. 10 .

[15] *ICJ Rep.* (1957) pp. 55-59.

not adopted by the full Court (which based its decision on other grounds) is generally regarded as the ruling which the Court would have been likely to give had it dealt with the point.[16]

Any conflict between this decision and ICJ case-law was not at the level of the rules of interpretation of treaties; the European Court's approach was entirely orthodox, referring to the object and purpose of the Convention, the ordinary meaning to be given to its terms, other provisions of the Convention (including the Preamble) by way of context, and the subsequent practice of the contracting parties. By reference to these criteria, it nevertheless arrived at the conclusion that reservations other than temporal limitations were not compatible with the Convention, in marked contrast to the accepted position under the ICJ Statute. But to suppose that, because the Statute and the Convention used substantially identical wording, they must be interpreted as identical in effect, is to fall into the fallacy of supposing that the same words always carry the same meaning; what matters, however, is the intention of the parties[17]. Whether the ICJ, had it been seised of the question of interpretation of the European Convention, would have arrived at the same conclusion, is not the point; there is no conflict between the European Court's decision as to the interpretation of the Convention and the ICJ's interpretation of its Statute.

Similarly, the interpretation by which the reservation was held to be severable from the acceptance of jurisdiction itself was based on the finding of 'a willingness on [Turkey's] part to run the risk that the limitation clauses at issue would be declared invalid by the Convention institutions without affecting the validity of the declarations themselves'[18], i.e., an intention to accept the jurisdiction, conditionally if possible, but if not, then unconditionally. Similarly, for Judge Lauterpacht in the *Norwegian Loans* case, what mattered was the intention of Norway in making the reservation complained of: the reservation had 'been regarded by the declaring State as one of the crucial limitations – perhaps the crucial limitation – of the obligation undertaken by the acceptance of the Optional Clause.'[19] In the one case, the commitment to jurisdiction was held to be the overriding motive; in the other, the exclusion of a certain class of disputes. Again, the question is not whether an observer, or the ICJ, would have agreed that Turkey had intended to accept jurisdiction unconditionally; the European Court was perfectly correct in its application of the law in order to conclude that it had.

[16] Cf., Fitzmaurice, 'Hersch Lauterpacht: the Scholar as Judge', 39 *BYBIL* (1963) pp. 178-181.

[17] For a fuller exposition of this point, see the present writer in *British Year Book of International Law* (1991) pp. 66-71. The Court seems to have come very near making this mistake in the recent Judgment in the *Oil Platforms* case: Judgment of 12 December 1996, para. 20.

[18] Judgment, p. 28, para. 95.

[19] *ICJ Rep.* (1957) p. 57.

The prophets of doom see the greatest danger to the unity of international law as arising from the establishment of the International Tribunal for the Law of the Sea (ITLOS), and their doubts on this subject are often coupled with doubts as to whether there was any need for its establishment. It is true that the mistrust of the International Court of Justice that still reigned among many States at the time of the conclusion of the Montego Bay Convention has now to a large extent been dissipated. A more serious worry might be whether the ICJ as at present constituted and operating would be capable of dealing, with sufficient despatch[20], with the caseload it enjoys in its own right and that which may develop for the ITLOS. So far, indeed, the problem does not look grave: the only case brought so far, that of the *M/V Saiga,* could as well have been brought to The Hague as to Hamburg, without too much disruption of the ICJ's General List.

For good or ill, the ITLOS exists; and there is no doubt that its decisions and those of the ICJ are perfectly capable of diverging. An allusion to the jurisprudence of the ICJ is in fact to be found in the *M/V Saiga* case, though not in the Tribunal's Judgment: Vice-President Wolfrum and Judge Yamamoto in their Dissenting Opinion, referring to the majority decision to approach proceedings under Article 292 of the Convention on the basis of 'assessing whether the allegations made are arguable or of a sufficiently plausible character'[21], observe that 'A similar approach has been applied by the Judgment of the International Court of Justice in the *Ambatielos* case (*ICJ Rep*. (1953) p. 18)'[22], and go on to distinguish the circumstances of that case from those before the ITLOS. It is notable, however, that the Tribunal did not see fit to cite the *Ambatielos* decision in support of its findings[23], which suggests that the majority shared the views of Judges Wolfrum and Yamamoto as to its irrelevance! There is therefore here so far nothing to cause concern as to any future divergence of jurisprudence between the two tribunals.

It must be conceded that the fact that there are here two permanent tribunals, with no hierarchical relationship between them, having virtually identical spheres of competence under the Law of the Sea Convention – the choice of tribunal in any particular dispute depending entirely on the choice made in advance by the parties under Article 287 of the Convention, a choice which is likely to have been made before any assessment of their comparative jurisprudence was possible – means that it is in theory perfectly possible for two distinct lines of irreconcilable decisions to develop, on the same provision of the Convention or other legal

[20] On this, see 'The International Court of Justice: Process, Practice and Procedure', in Bowett, et al., ed., *British Institute of International and Comparative Law* (1997)

[21] Judgment, para. 51.

[22] Dissenting Opinion, para. 5. Judge Anderson takes the same point in his Dissenting Opinion, para. 4.

[23] Judge Anderson (loc. cit.) seems to think that, although no authority is cited in the Judgment, the use by the Tribunal of the same words as those used in the *Ambatielos* decision imply a reliance on it, which seems too far-reaching a conclusion.

point, each tribunal insisting stubbornly on its own view of the matter. But does this scenario not rest on an over-pessimistic view, both of the degree of respect of one set of judges for another, and for the ultimately greater weight of the more convincing view? As we have seen, legal truth may for a considerable period not be one and indivisible: yet *magna est veritas et praevalebit*.

In confirmation of this conclusion, I would like to refer to a system of judicial, or at least quasi-judicial, disputes settlement which exists somewhat outside the mainstream of international legal study, and is easy therefore to underrate: the system established in the World Trade Organization by the Disputes Settlement Understanding annexed to the WTO Agreement. That system is a closed one in the sense that it exists for settlement of disputes arising out of the WTO Agreement itself and the other instruments making up the body of GATT/WTO law listed in an annex to the Understanding (the 'covered agreements'), and only those instruments[24], and for settlement of such disputes recourse to other tribunals is excluded. Recourse is to a panel, established *ad hoc* for each dispute and therefore of varying composition[25], whose conclusions, to be effective, have to be (and invariably have been) adopted by the Disputes Settlement Body. Appeal lies to the standing Appellate Body, whose composition again varies from case to case.[26]

The need for unity of jurisprudence in the context of an elaborate and interlocking treaty system is evident, and is underlined by Article 3, paragraph 2, of the Disputes Settlement Understanding:

> 'The dispute settlement system of the WTO is a central element in providing security and predictability to the multilateral trading system. The Members recognize that it serves to preserve the rights and obligations of Members under the covered agreements, and to clarify the existing provisions of those agreements in accordance with customary rules of interpretation of public international law. Recommendations and rulings of the DSB [Disputes Settlement Body] cannot add to or diminish the rights and obligations provided in the covered agreements.'[27]

The practice of the dispute settlement panels and of the appeals body is already quite extensive: on this, may I refer to the paper presented by my friend and colleague Prof. Ernst-Ulrich Petersmann to this morning's panel meeting.[28] That practice has shown a respect for the rules of general international law, in particular those concerning the interpretation and effect of treaties, and for the

[24] Disputes Settlement Understanding, Art. 1 (1).

[25] *Idem*, Arts. 6, 7, 8.

[26] *Idem*, Art. 17.

[27] 'Understanding on Rules and Procedures Governing the Settlement of Disputes', Annex 2 of the WTO Agreement, in Petersmann, *The Gatt/WTO Dispute Settlement System* (Kluwer 1997) pp. 292-293.

[28] See E.-H. Petersmann's contribution: 'Dispute Settlement Procedures in the WTO – a View from The Hague', elsewhere in the present publication.

jurisprudence of the International Court of Justice. As for the internal jurisprudence, it has become clearly established that the decisions of one panel have no binding effect for another, seised of a different dispute[29]; nor have the decisions of the Appeals Body any binding effect on the hierarchically inferior panels, or subsequent Appeals Body decisions. Yet in practice panels and Appeals Body respect earlier jurisprudence, and apply it freely.

The WTO disputes settlement system, as Article 3, paragraph 2, makes clear, is one in which judges are expressly directed only to declare, and not to make law; and since the composition of the WTO panels and Disputes Appeals Body is not identical in all cases, these bodies may be regarded as so many independent tribunals, deciding according to international law, both general and peculiar to the WTO system. Each is free to disregard the legal findings of the others; but in practice does not do so, with the result that a solid body of coherent jurisprudence is in the process of being established. This structure seems to me to present a microcosm of how the international system of different tribunals with competences overlapping to a greater or less degree, in general can, and I confidently hope, will operate.

[29] An interesting detail in this respect is that the Disputes Settlement Understanding makes express provision (Art. 10) for the intervention of third parties, and other States have frequently made use of this possibility; the decisions given are however not regarded as binding on the intervening States. Cf., the ICJ Chamber decision in the *Land, Island and Maritime Frontier* Dispute, *ICJ Rep.* (1992), pp. 609-610, paras. 421-424.

ANNEX

THE FUTURE DEVELOPMENT OF BINDING DISPUTE SETTLEMENT MECHANISMS IN INTERNATIONAL LAW

H.A.F.M.O. van Mierlo*

Your Excellencies, ladies and gentlemen,

'All roads lead to Rome', as the saying goes. At present, that certainly seems to be true, at least as far as international lawyers are concerned. For ordinary mortals, of course, all roads lead to Paris at the moment. But that is another story, which perhaps we could discuss over dessert.

Only a few days ago I had the pleasure of attending the conference in Rome which is expected to establish a permanent International Criminal Court later this month. The creation of such a court undoubtedly represents a milestone in the development of international law. At this point, I should like to pay tribute to the role played by Adriaan Bos, the legal adviser to my Ministry, in the preparatory negotiations. Over the last three years, those preparing for the conference have been able to draw on the charters and the work of the Nuremberg and Tokyo Tribunals, set up to bring to justice those who committed crimes during the Second World War.

The two World Wars represented, in many ways, gross violations of international law. They interrupted the fragile development, since the end of the nineteenth century, of a system for the peaceful settlement of disputes. Mechanisms created by multilateral diplomacy were not proof against the venom of aggression. Here we may draw a parallel with the city in which we now find ourselves: even The Hague, after seven hundred years of growth and development, could not withstand the violence of war. Much damage was done, and despite reconstruction, the consequences could be seen and felt for decades afterwards. But anyone who visits the city centre today can see that The Hague is building for the future. It may be a process of trial and error but new tunnels and housing – the new side by side with the old – are indisputable evidence of progress. This brings us to another parallel: in the fragile structure of international dispute settlement, as in the city of The Hague, new foundations and new routes are finding a place within existing environments. I am sure you will soon see what I mean.

First I should like to touch on one aspect of the development of The Hague which is of great importance to myself as Minister for Foreign Affairs: the

* Minister of Foreign Affairs, the Netherlands.

location of international judicial institutions within our boundaries. On a visit to this city in 1992 Mr Boutros Ghali described it as 'the legal capital of the world'. Even then, it was nearly a hundred years since Tobias Asser, the eminent Dutch jurist, had laid the foundations for the Hague Conference on Private International Law, an institution that to this day plays a leading role in the development of that particular branch of international law. A little later, The Hague was the venue for the peace conferences which bear its name, and their centenary will be celebrated next year in The Hague and St Petersburg. Those conferences led to the establishment of the Permanent Court of Arbitration, which has been the focus of increasing interest in recent years, thanks in part to the efforts of its Secretary-General, former ambassador Hans Jonkman.

As you are all aware, for many years the Permanent Court of Arbitration has shared the Peace Palace with the International Court of Justice (ICJ), sometimes known as the World Court. This is probably the main source of the term 'judicial capital of the world'. The Netherlands is very proud that 1996, the year in which the ICJ celebrated its fiftieth anniversary, was also the year in which a Dutch judge – my predecessor Peter Kooijmans – was appointed to that august body for the first time in its history.

Other organisations, too, which have established their headquarters in The Hague in the twentieth century have helped it to acquire the title of world judicial capital. They include the Hague Academy of International Law, the Iran-US Claims Tribunal and the International Criminal Tribunal for the former Yugoslavia. What is more, it appears that we shall shortly be able to welcome the International Criminal Court to The Hague, if things go according to plan in Rome this month.

And so international law here in The Hague makes an almost imperceptible transition from the past to the future. I must admit that it is always less risky to evaluate the past than speculate about the future. However, I feel that certain unmistakable trends will influence the future of international law in general, and binding international dispute settlement in particular. I should like to look at three of these in detail.

Firstly, I expect to see more and more use being made of existing institutions. The workload of the International Court of Justice is increasing rather than decreasing, despite the advent of related judicial tribunals. Other institutions, too, such as the Court of Justice of the European Communities in Luxembourg and the European Court of Human Rights in Strasbourg are dealing with a rapid rise in the number of cases that come before them. The growing relevance of EU law to individuals and companies alike means that national courts increasingly avail themselves of the opportunity to submit questions to the European Court of Justice (ECJ) in Luxembourg for a preliminary ruling. As for Strasbourg, the Council of Europe has seen its membership double in less than ten years. The number of people claiming violations of their human rights has therefore risen accordingly. A new, full-time Court opens its doors in Strasbourg on 1 November this year, but that is no reason for the Council of Europe's members to take things easy. There is still too much uncertainty about the future case load for that.

Secondly, the development of international law, in terms of both depth and breadth, will also imply a need for differentiation and regionalisation in the dispensation of justice. The launching of the International Tribunal for the Law of the Sea and the World Trade Organisation's Dispute Settlement Body are striking examples of differentiation, while the OSCE's Court of Conciliation and Arbitration is evidence of greater regionalisation.

The third and last trend I would like to mention is perhaps the most spectacular: the unstoppable emergence of entities other than states as actors in international dispute settlement. While this trend is nothing new, and unlikely to come to an end soon, current developments are changing for ever what dispute settlement means: it is no longer a matter of a quiet get-together between a manageable number of states. Now it is a complicated interactive process involving the international community, a state, an organisation and the individual. The role of the individual in relation to the International Court of Justice is still that of a passive object, as shown by a recent case. After Paraguay had invoked the Vienna Convention on Consular Relations, the ICJ contemplated handing down a provisional measure imposing a moratorium on the execution of a Paraguayan national by the State of Virginia. In Strasbourg, on the other hand, the entry into force of the Eleventh Protocol to the ECHR will confer on the individual a *locus standi* equivalent to that of the State. For the last five years the Permanent Court of Arbitration has adhered to revised Optional Rules for arbitrating disputes between two parties of which only one is a State, thus opening its doors wide to non-state actors. The *Saiga* Judgment given by the International Tribunal for the Law of the Sea showed – especially in the Tribunal's order for the prompt release of the vessel and its crew – the extent to which the interests of shipping companies have permeated dispute settlement under the law of the sea, even though the flag state must still intervene.

I also regard the establishment of the *ad hoc* tribunals for the former Yugoslavia and Rwanda as symptomatic of the increasing importance of non-state actors in international law. This is particularly true of the great progress that has been made over the last few years in the preparations for an international criminal court. The reason is clear: when the international community confers more and more rights on individuals, it follows that those same individuals will be compelled to fulfil their obligations by the international community, represented by the public prosecutor. Let me add that after a hesitant start, the Yugoslavia Tribunal is now a fully operational judicial institution, which opened its second main courtroom only three weeks ago. Initial doubts about the value of this response by the international community to the most horrific crimes have gradually given way to a sense of satisfaction that the perpetrators are finally being brought to justice. This creates confidence in the prospects for a permanent, universal international criminal court. However, I believe that steps should be taken to ensure that the prosecutor's freedom to bring prosecutions is as independent as possible of political decisions taken by the Security Council. In my view, too great a dependence on the Security Council would jeopardise the autonomy of the International Criminal Court and subordinate the international legal order to *raison d'état*. It must be absolutely clear to those who commit crimes which outrage humanity that they cannot save themselves by negotiation.

Two conclusions can be drawn from what I have just said. The first is that international dispute settlement in the widest sense, that is dispute settlements involving states, the international community, national and international organisations and natural and legal persons as parties, is developing very rapidly. International law, sometimes regarded by legal experts in other fields as a hobby rather than a branch of the law, is increasingly being regarded as of equal status to national law.

The second conclusion is this. Uniformity in the decisions given by courts in the various branches of national law is guaranteed, as a rule, by a supreme and/or constitutional court. International law has no such institution, however. This was not a problem as long as the role of guardian of international law was entrusted to the International Court of Justice. However, the differentiation and regionalisation of international law and the advent of so many international tribunals carry with them the risk of fragmentation and hence endanger the consistency of international justice. For there are no official links between all these tribunals, far less a hierarchical structure.

I believe that this will generate a growing need for a mechanism for the uniform interpretation of international law. In other words, judicial institutions – whether national or international – could submit questions on the interpretation of the rules of international law to a single international tribunal. Given its role to date, the obvious course of action would be to entrust this task to the International Court of Justice. This would considerably extend the Court's work of giving advisory opinions on the basis of Article 65 of its Statute. If this scenario became a reality, jurists could say – with some truth – that all roads led to The Hague.

(Your Excellencies), ladies and gentlemen, may I wish you an enjoyable, productive conference. In conclusion, I would like to propose a toast to The Hague on its seven hundred and fiftieth anniversary and to the contribution of international law and international dispute settlement to a better, fairer world.

STATAL COOPERATION WITH A UNIVERSAL CRIMINAL COURT: RECOGNITION AND ENFORCEMENT OF SENTENCES

W. Sorgdrager*

Ladies and gentlemen,

As you know, negotiations are going on in Rome at the moment, which are devoted to the institution of a permanent international criminal court. The court will exercise penal jurisdiction over the individual directly responsible for serious violations of international law, such as in the case of war crimes. In case of conviction and sentencing, the States, having accepted the court's jurisdiction, will be under the obligation to recognize and enforce the sentences to be handed down by this judiciary. This judiciary will not have any penal enforcement-power of its own: it will be completely dependent on the preparedness and capacities of the contracting states to use their sovereign enforcement-power on behalf of the court.

In this context, I would like to make some initial and general remarks with regard to the recognition of judgments and the enforcement of sentences under the Statute of this court, the International Criminal Court, or ICC. At this very moment, a special session of the Rome conference is scheduled in order to solve this highly sensitive issue, a key issue in the ICC-framework.

The recognition of judgments of a foreign court is a typical form of legal cooperation at the international level, that is, the traditional framework in which the recognition of foreign judgments has been developed as an essential element in the international relations of states. The administering state, willing to accept the foreign judgment as an enforceable verdict within its territorial jurisdiction and its legal structure, has to assimilate to that end the final verdict of a foreign court to a judgment, rendered by its own judiciary. Therefore, in almost all national systems, a transformation procedure or exequatur procedure is provided in order to translate, so to speak, the foreign legal decision into a binding national one, substantially identical with the foreign judgment 'under its factual aspects as well as its legal aspects', but only rewritten in the legal terminology of the administering party.

However, in the ICC context we have to deal with enforcement obligations of states, parties under the Stature of an International Judiciary to be instituted. Those obligations are of an essentially different nature and character, compared

* Minister of Justice, the Netherlands.

with the traditional enforcement treaties. It has to do with the supranational legal status of the International Court that is not a state. As a supranational entity, it is unknown and has no legal existence whatsoever until the very moment of its institution. We are constructing legal frameworks *sui generis*. The court, when instituted, is indeed a supranational legal body, fit to function on its own in the framework of inter-statal relations in the area of international criminal law.

It is a material legal subject, notwithstanding its inability to act with its own penal enforcement power, like states do. Missing this ability to act with its own enforcement power, the ICC could be classified as an imperfect legal body. Nevertheless, in our view, that legal body has its own identity, its own competence. It is created by states. After this creative act, the body is by definition independent of the states, originally the founding fathers of the body, if I may use that antropomorph metaphor. One could state that the body has a certain irreducible sovereignty, if such a terminology would fit in this respect – I am not sure about this – because it reminds too much of the notion of the internal sovereignty of a territorial state. Such a state has the exclusive right to compose its internal legal order.

The court is not equal to a state. Its ambiguity is that there will be a permanent tie with its founding fathers, the states, because they are the only ones which are under strict obligations to grant the Court the penal enforcement power in order to secure its effectiveness as a supranational judiciary. It is because of that tie, that states parties are bound, from the moment of the entry-into-force of the statute, to assimilate the decisions and judgments of the Court as a substantial emanation of their own domestic judiciary. Therefore, the ICC Statute has – in our view – nothing to do with the recognition and enforcement of foreign judgments. The Statute does not offer a further elaboration of international judicial assistance and cooperation. The statute offers complete new rules concerning the obligatory extension of the domestic jurisdictions of the states parties from the moment of their respective ratifications.

The International Criminal Court has to be considered by those parties as a member of their own national judiciaries. As a consequence, the Statute itself has to stipulate that states parties have to recognize a judgment of the Court as a judgment of their own judiciaries. The total assimilation to nationally rendered judgements should be the decisive criterion for the obligations of the states. A national transformation procedure should be forbidden by the Statute itself.

The states parties, of course, are not used to submit the decisions of their national judiciary to an exequatur procedure. Assuming that the ICC is, by virtue of the mere ratification, a member of the judiciary of the contracting party, that implies that such an exequatur procedure is excluded. That exclusion has the same grounds valid for the already existing judiciary of the contracting party. In case the International Criminal Court renders a sentence, only a procedure of continued enforcement should be available. Therefore, there should be no room left to let it depend on the 'willingness' of states parties, whether or not they are prepared to execute sentences of the International Criminal Court, sentences, containing any condemnation whatsoever, rendered by that Court. What should be the decisive factor for determining the existence of the actual obligation to execute sentences of the ICC? The answer is: mere designation by the Court. The Statute has to provide for sufficient criteria in this respect. There should be a rule of equitable burden sharing. The Court should have the competence to elaborate this rule of burden sharing by virtue of a mandating clause. The court should be instructed to use mere criteria of a geographical nature in the elaboration of this rule of burden sharing. The obligation to execute should be an absolute one. The reasons are quite the same as the reasons justifying why states are under an absolute obligation to comply with ICC requests for cooperation and assistance.

Thank you very much.

THE HAGUE ACADEMY OF INTERNATIONAL LAW

Daniel Bardonnet*

When the Asser Institute asked me several months ago to come and speak to you about the Hague Academy of International Law, I was well aware of the honour of addressing these international lawyers who were together here to celebrate The Hague 750th anniversary. Because, more modestly, the Academy is celebrating its 75th anniversary this year, I seized the opportunity to present to you this evening several aspects of the history, structure and purpose of one of the fixtures of the international legal community of The Hague. The Hague that has kept developing throughout most of the 20th century. The Academy is responsible for education and research in the field of the law of nations at the international level. It is part of a cluster of prestigious institutions such as, in the sphere of judicial disputes settlement, the Permanent Court of Arbitration, the International Court of Justice, the Iran-United States Claims Tribunal and the International Criminal Tribunal for the Former Yugoslavia.[1] The Academy is also a companion to other equally prestigious international organizations such as the Conference on Private International Law, the Organization for the Prohibition of Chemical Weapons, and Europol. All of these institutions have, each in its own sphere, a common goal: the pursuit of peace and justice within the international community, which is the raison d'être of the Academy as well.

The idea at the origin of the Academy of International Law was conceived at the second Peace Conference, which took place in The Hague in 1907.[2] Otfried Nippold, then professor at Berne, suggested the establishment of an 'advanced school of international law,' headquartered with the Permanent Court of Arbitration and the suggestion was acted upon. There was indeed, at that time, great confidence in the belief that global peace would result from the rule of law, and that recourse to justice would be capable of eliminating war.

The Institute of International Law, established in 1873, had taken as its motto 'Justitia et Pace'. The International Law Association, established that same year was to expand the awareness of international law in the broadest range of legal circles. Universities were teaching that arbitration was the miracle cure that

* Professor D. Bardonnet is Secretary-General of the Hague Academy of International Law.

[1] The International Criminal Court, instituted by the Rome Treaty of 18 July 1998, will also have its seat at The Hague.

[2] See St. Verosta, 'L'histoire de l'académie de droit international de La Haye, établie avec le concours de la Dotation Carnegie pour la paix internationale', in *Jubilee Book 1923-1973* (Leyden, Sijthoff 1973) pp. 7-56.

W.P. Heere (Ed.), International Law and The Hague's 750th Anniversary

would alleviate all international tensions, and should therefore be made obligatory. Peace and security through law was the slogan of that era.

Two World Wars and the United Nations Charter itself have served to dispel these illusions, and today we know only too well that peace is a condition precedent to the rule of law and justice in international relations. This realistic approach is evidenced by Article 1, paragraph 1, of the Charter, which cites first among the goals of this global organization the maintenance of 'international peace and security', and only thereafter goes on to refer to respect for law as one of several means of achieving this ultimate goal.

This was not the case in 1907, and the statute of the Academy was drawn up in the idealistic climate of that era, at the impetus of the great Dutch jurist, Asser, winner of the Nobel Peace Prize in 1911, and with the help of the Institute of International Law, the Carnegie Foundation for International Peace, and the Government of the Netherlands. By January 1914, the Academy had legal personality and was ready to start operating, when the First World War broke out. This sudden intrusion of *Realpolitik* on the law did not serve to diminish the initiator's faith in international law, or the tenacity of the Netherlands Government, which once again proved faithful to its national motto 'Je Maintiendrai' The Academy was inaugurated on 14 July 1923, at the Peace Palace, in the Great Hall of the Permanent Court of International Justice. That same year of 1923 the Academy held its first session of courses, which was attended by 300 participants from 31 countries.

Three-quarters of a century later, from next Monday until the 15th of August, more than 600 participants from about 100 countries will be gathering in the building, with which many of you are familiar, next to the Peace Palace. Each year, the General Assembly of the United Nations can therefore commend the Academy's contribution to 'the teaching, study, and wider understanding of international law.'[3]

The structure of the Academy is simple. It is governed by two organs, the Curatorium and the Administrative Council. The Curatorium is the highest organ, responsible for the academic aspects of the institution. In this capacity, it determines the Academy's programmes, chooses the subjects of the courses, and selects lecturers from among the most eminent university professors and practitioners of the greatest international renown. The Curatorium is currently presided over by Mr. Nicolas Valticos, former Deputy Director-General of the International Labour Office and Judge of the European Court of Human Rights. The Curatorium counts among its 17 members, all of different nationalities, persons of great prestige in academic, judicial and diplomatic spheres. Many names come to mind, and I will mention just a few of those who are no longer

[3] See for example, the GA Resolution adopted on 24 January 1994, during the 48th session (A/Res.48/29, p. 4, par. 12). Already in 1925 Van Kleffens defined the Academy as 'An aid to the diffusion and to a clearer notion of the law of nations', see 'The Hague Academy of International Law', 6 *BYIL* (1925) pp. 172-184.

with us, such as James Brown Scott and Politis, Anzilotti and Max Huber, Gidel and McNair, Van Kleffens and Charles De Visscher, Verdross, Scelle and Fitzmaurice, Ago and Ruda, Paul De Visscher and René Jean Dupuy, the last two mentioned recently departed. Moreover, the Curatorium appoints the Secretary-General of the Academywho according to Article 7, par. 1 of the Statute, 'fulfills the functions of secretary of both institutions.'

In addition to the Curatorium, there is an Administrative Council that is currently chaired by Mr. Royer, former Chief Justice of the Supreme Court of the Netherlands. This Council consists of 7 members, all of Dutch nationality. With the assistance of the Treasurer, who is at the same time Director of the Dutch Carnegie Foundation, the Administrative Council manages the Academy's property and ensures the financing of its activities. The Council has always counted among its members persons at the highest level in the world of politics, diplomacy, economics and academia. As with the Curatorium, many names come to mind, and I will mention only a few of those among the departed: Prime Minister de Quay, Minister for Foreign Affairs Van Roijen, the president of the Bar, Bisdom, and Professor François The choice of such persons for the Administrative Council illustrates the importance attached to the Academy by the Dutch Government. I would like to stress that without the substantial financial assistance accorded to it by the Dutch Government the Academy would have been unable to accomplish all that it has.

I have just described the Academy's basic structure. As provided in Article 2 of its statute, the Academy constitutes 'a centre of advanced studies for international law (public and private) and connected sciences, and it aims at facilitating the thorough and impartial examination of questions concerning international juridical relations.'

Although a purely academic institution, the Academy is not a university. As indicated in a circular of its Curatorium, communicated to states in the spring of 1923 by the Dutch Ministry for Foreign Affairs, 'the Academy does not purport to substitute itself for the universities, and even less to compete with them. On the contrary, it aims also at enlightenment and progress, but not on the same grounds or in the same manner.'[4]

Indeed, the Academy is a centre of postgraduate teaching . It is a place of learning which remains truly international and pluralistic, as a result of the composition of both its Curatorium and its body of teachers and participants. As Mr. Boutros-Ghali said on 18 May 1993 (at a time when he was both Secretary-General of the United Nations and a Member of the Curatorium), during the ceremony at UNESCO in Paris at which the Academy of International Law was awarded the Houphouet-Boigny Peace Prize 'The teachings offered in the Academy form a veritable school of freedom. Freedom of the spirit, freedom of

[4] Quoted by St. Verosta, loc. cit. n. 2, at p. 41.

method, freedom of operation.' [5] This spirit of freedom is the backbone of the activities of the Academy, activities which have become increasingly diversified.

1) First of all, naturally, the summer courses, in July and August, each year, pronounced in English or French with simultaneous translation. They consist of two sessions, each of three weeks, one in private international law, the other in public international law, These courses lead to a high-level diploma, available to the best participants, which the Curatorium does not bestow generously. Both sessions are characterized by a diversity of topics and opinions. The Academy has no doctrine of its own, except as Professor Dupuy observed, 'that of being open to all doctrines that endeavor to explain and develop the law of nations.'[6] During the 75 years of the Academy's existence, the international community has been marked by very profound changes, and the Recueil des Cours, which has been published each year since 1923 (save for an interruption during the Second World War), bears true 'scholarly witness' to such transformations, The *Recueil*, which today runs up to 270 volumes, containing 1104 lectures, constitutes in itself a true 'library of international law.' In the future, it will be impossible to speak of international law in the 20th century without referring to the *Recueil*. The *Recueil* is tangible evidence of the work of the Academy, and it must be considered as part and parcel of the history of international law. Indeed Judge Philip Jessup observed, in 1960, 'Where else than in the *Recueil des Cours* will one find an equivalent record of the best thought of the scholars and statesmen of many nations on the actualities of international law, its nature, its history, its usefulness and its defects, its procedures and its organizational forms?'[7]

Furthermore, the Academy has never ceased to open itself up to the world. From session to session, thanks to a system of scholarships aimed in particular at lawyers from the third world, the youth of all nations come here, in ever increasing numbers. Undergraduate and graduate students, scholars, as well as diplomats, judges, lawyers and international civil servants all gather in The Hague. Here they discover the diversity of teaching methods and the diversity of points of view in the study of international legal relations. They sharpen their skills in the admirable Peace Palace library. In their eyes, the Academy is not only a place to perfect their legal knowledge, it is also a means of learning about others. Contacts and friendships are formed among young lawyers who later encounter one another at meetings of the AAA (Association of Attenders and Alumni of the Academy) or at other international meetings, where they never miss an opportunity to reminisce about the Academy.

[5] UNESCO, Ceremony for the Award of the 1992 Felix Houphouet-Boigny Peace Prize to The Hague Academy of International Law, Paris 18 May 1993, p.20.

[6] 'La contribution de l'Academie au developpement du droit international', *Recueil des Cours de l'Académie de droit international* (1973 -I) T. 138, p. 51.

[7] 'A Half-Century of Effort to Substitute Law for War', *Recueil des Cours de l'Académie de droit international* (1960-I) T. 99, p. 4.

2) Following the summer sessions – and constituting the Academy's second most important activity – the Centre for Studies and Research in International Law and International Relations[8] takes place each summer for one month. Established in 1957 at the initiative of Jessup, the Centre brings together 24 researchers – 12 French-speaking and 12 English-speaking – eminently qualified in the light of their intellectual maturity and knowledge of law, who prepare reports, under the guidance of two experts in the chosen topic. The best of such reports are published by the Academy. This stimulating scholarly activity reveals the Academy as an instrument of experimentation, as a means of discovery, and sometimes even prediction.[9] I need only mention the 1995 Centre, which explored 'the international law of natural and industrial disasters' a virtually uncharted territory, resulting in the imminent publication of an important work constituting the first in-depth study on the subject. One can only hope that the same will hold true for the 1998 Centre, which will address the 'Legal Implications of Global Telecommunications.'

3) The contribution of the Academy to the development of international law can also be found in its third activity, which was instituted in 1968. I mean the workshops that it organizes intermittently. The Curatorium always endeavours to give a forward-looking character to them. I will cite only two examples of this laboratory of ideas formed by the Academy's workshops: the particularly brilliant 1983 workshop which dealt with 'the future of international law in a multicultural world'[10] and that of 1994 on the OPCW, which shed particular light on the novel character of the 1993 Paris Convention for multilateral disarmament efforts, most notable for its implementation of international control over an entire field of industrial activity, which may serve as a model in other areas of disarmament.[11]

4) The same spirit of freedom and respect for others can be found in the Academy's fourth field of activity: the External Program. The External Programme was created in 1969 at the suggestion of a study group presided over by the much regretted Wolfgang Friedman and composed of professors Boutros-Ghali, Dupuy, Jennings, Oda and Van Panhuys.[12] In establishing the External Programme, the Academy left the Peace Palace in order to move into the outside world. Indeed, despite the scholarships that may benefit young, non-European international law scholars, it is clear that the Academy's location in The Hague is a serious obstacle to potential participants from other continents. Realizing that it

[8] See B. Boutros-Ghali, 'Le Centre d'étude et de recherche de droit international et de relations internationales', in *Jubilee Book 1932-1973* (Leyden, Sijthoff 1973) pp. 137-157.

[9] R.J. Dupuy, *Recueil des Cours de l'Académie de droit international* (1973-1) T. 138, pp. 55-63 and 64-72.

[10] M. Nijhoff 1984.

[11] M. Nijhoff 1995.

[12] Cf., St Verosta, loc. cit. n. 2, at pp. 50-51.

could no longer content itself with merely hosting its overseas participants, the Academy decided to go and seek out contact with them.[13]

Thus for nearly 30 years, alternating among Africa, Asia and Latin America, the Academy has each year organized an intensive two-week course in international law, with an emphasis on regional approaches and perspectives. In 1997, a session of this type took place in Hanoi, bringing together academics and practitioners from the Foreign Ministries of the region, i.e., the ASEAN countries and China.[14] Such a session will occur in October 1998 in Montevideo.

I should add, finally, that since 1991, the Academy has organized annual courses on human rights, aimed at judges and prosecutors, lawyers, and civil servants from Asia, Africa, Latin America, and Central and Eastern Europe who are, in one way or another, responsible for their Government's involvement in organizing the international protection of human rights.

The objective of the Academy is to provide an accurate analysis of international realities, to emphasize inadequacies in the international legal order – its normatives gaps and structural weaknesses – and to seek potential solutions. But, I repeat, the Academy is not a 'doctrinal school', it is not affiliated with any system. It merely attempts to remain faithful to the objectives of its founders, to continue to serve as a meeting place, a realm of friendship in which to work out any analysis, any suggestions, that might favour the development of international law, in the service of peace.

The Academy contributes to reinforcing the belief that the law is the keystone in the structure of the community of States. Progress in achieving this community must go hand in hand with the progress of the law that it formulates. The Academy also contributes to the understanding that international law is not a purely technical, dry and rigid discipline. Rather, as emphasized by Judge Ago, who was President of the Curatorium for many years, it is a 'living matter, which resides in the flesh of History. This means not only that it is in a constant state of evolution, it also means that it possesses a soul.'[15]

[13] On the philosophy behind this programme, see R.J. Dupuy, 'Le Programme exterieur', in *Jubilee Book 1932-1973* (Leyden, Sijthoff 1973) pp. 159-173.

[14] *Bulletin de l'Académie* 1998, p. 72.

[15] See *supra* n. 5, at p. 38.

ABBREVIATIONS

AAA	American Arbitration Association
ADR	Alternative Dispute Resolution
AJCL	American Journal of Comparative Law
AJIL	American Journal of International Law
All ER	All England Law Reports
ANP	Algemeen Nederlands Persbureau
ATF	Arrêts du Tribunal Fédéral Suisse
BB	Betriebs-Berater
BFHE	Entscheidungen des BundesFinanzhofes
BGBl	Bundesgesetzblatt
BGE	Entscheidungen des Schweizerischen Bundesgerichts
BGH	Bundesgerichtshof
BGHZ	Entscheidungen des Bundesgerichtshofes in Zivilsachen
BSE	Bovine Spongiform Encephalopathy
BVerfG	Bundesverfassungsgericht
BYBIL, BYIL	British Year Book of International Law
CAPH	Chambre d'Appel des Prud'hommes (Geneva)
CAS	Court of Arbitration for Sport
CCEE	Countries of Central and Eastern Europe
CEDR	Centre for Dispute Resolution (UK)
CEO	Chief Executive Officer
CITES	Convention on International Trade in Endangered Species
CJEC	Court of Justice of the European Communities (Luxembourg)
CMLR	Common Market Law Review
CSD	Claims Settlement Declaration (1981 Algiers)
CTE	Committee on Trade and Environment (WTO)
CWC	Chemical Weapons Convention
DS	Recueil Dalloz-Sirey
DSU	Dispute Settlement Understanding (WTO)
ECHR	European Court of Human Rights
ECJ	European Court of Justice (Luxembourg)
ECOWAS	Economic Community of West African States
ECR	European Court Reports
ECSI	European Convention on State Immunity
EDU	European Drugs Unit

EFG	Entscheidungen der Finanzgerichte
EJIL	European Journal of International Law
EPC	Convention on the Grant of European Patents
EPO	European Patent Office
EU	European Union
Europol	European Police Organization
EuZW	Europäische Zeitschrift für Wirtschaftsrecht
FAO	Food and Agricultural Organization (UN)
FT	Swiss Federal Tribunal
GA	General Assembly (UN)
GATS	General Agreement on Trade in Services (WTO)
GATT	General Agremeent on Tariffs and Trade
GD	General Declaration (1981 Algiers)
GDP	Gross Domestic Product
GRUR	Gewerblicher Rechtsschutz und Urheberrecht
ICAS	International Council for Arbitration of Sport (Lausanne)
ICC	International Criminal Court
ICJ	International Court of Justice
ICLQ	International and Comparative Law Quarterly
IF	International Federation (sports)
IHT	International Herald Tribune
ILA	International Law Association
ILC	International Law Commission
ILM	International Legal Materials
ILR	International Law Reports
IMO	International Maritime Organization
IPS	International Peace and Security
Iran-US CTR	Iran-United States Claims Tribunal Reports
ITLOS	International Tribunal for the Law of the Sea (Hamburg)
JAR	Jahrbuch für Schweizerisches Arbeitsrecht
JW	Juristische Wochenschrift
JWTL	Journal of World Trade Law
LJIL	Leiden Journal of International Law
MEA	Multilateral Environmental Agreement
NAI	Netherlands Arbitration Institute
NGO	Non-Governmental Organization

NILR	Netherlands International Law Review
NIPR	Nederlands Internationaal Privaatrecht
NJ	Nederlandse Jurisprudentie
NJB	Nederlands Juristenblad
NJW	Neue Juristische Wochenschrift
NYIL	Netherlands Yearbook of International Law
OECD	Organization for Economic Co-operation and Development
OGH	Oberster Gerichtshof
OJ	Official Journal of the European Communities
OLG	Oberlandesgericht
OPCW	Organization for the Prohibition of Chemical Weapons
OSCE	Organization for Co-operation and Security in Europe
PCA	Permanent Court of Arbitration
PCIJ	Permanent Court of International Justice
PIL	Private International Law
RabelsZ	Rabels Zeitschrift für ausländisches und internationales Privatrecht
RIAA	UN Reports of International Arbitral Awards
SCLR	Scottish Law Reports
SFRY	Socialist Federal Republic of Yugoslavia
SLT	Scots Law Times
SZIER	Schweizerisches Zeitschrift für internationales und europäisches Recht
TAS	Tribunal Arbitral du Sport (Lausanne)
TPH	Tribunal des Prud'hommes (Geneva)
UCLAF	Unité de coordination de lutte anti-fraudes (EU)
ULA	Uniform Laws Annotated (USA)
UNCITRAL	UN Commission for Trade Law
UNEP	UN Environmental Programme
UrhG	Gesetz über Urheberrecht und verwandte Schutzrechte
WLR	Weekly Law Reports
WM	Wertpapier Mitteilungen
ZfRVgl	Zeitschrift für Rechtsvergleichung

INDEX